United States
PATTERN COINS
EXPERIMENTAL AND TRIAL PIECES
Complete Source for History, Rarity, and Values

Original edition by
J. Hewitt Judd, M.D.

Edited by Q. David Bowers
Research Associate: Saul Teichman

Ninth Edition

3101 Clairmont Road, Suite C
Atlanta, Georgia 30329

The WCG™ pricing grid used throughout this publication is patent pending.

Copyright © 2005 Whitman Publishing, LLC, Atlanta, GA

ISBN: 0-7948-1823-4

Printed in Canada

About the coin on the cover: The 1792 silver-center cent (J-1 in the Judd numbering system) is a famous rarity from the earliest days of the United States Mint. It was designed as a coin with an intrinsic value of exactly one cent (attained by inserting a small silver plug into a copper planchet). Not many more than a dozen were struck, for examination. Today an example of this pattern is worth more than $500,000 in gem Uncirculated condition.

Table of Contents

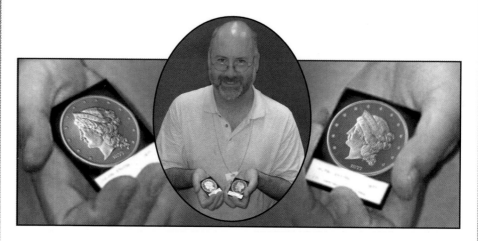

Acknowledgements

CREDITS AND ACKNOWLEDGMENTS

Sources are given in endnotes and in the text. In addition, the publisher expresses appreciation to the following:

CORE STAFF

Q. David Bowers wrote all of the introductory chapters, the "History and Overview" and "Collecting Perspective" sections for each year, and Appendix E. He coordinated many contributions by others. **Saul Teichman** added new listings, deleted spurious entries from earlier editions, and clarified many issues, often drawing upon his earlier established web site, www.uspatterns.com. He also wrote Appendix A and Appendix B. His help was essential and integral to this book.

Robert L. Hughes, Sr., gathered, coordinated, and reviewed the market price listings, with John Gervasoni, Julian Leidman, Andrew Lustig, and other numismatic professionals assisting.

INDIVIDUALS AND FIRMS

From the past:

John Babalis	Sol Kaplan
Robert Bashlow	Abe Kosoff
Harry W. Bass, Jr.	Abner Kreisberg
Willard Blaisdell	Russell Logan
Robert K. Botsford	Lester Merkin
Walter H. Breen	Earl C. Moore
Michael G. Brownlee	James P. Randall
Armand Champa	Wayte Raymond
Glenn Y. Davidson	Edmund A. Rice
John J. Ford, Jr.	William R. Sieck
Lee F. Hewitt	Dr. James O. Sloss
Dr. J. Hewitt Judd	Louis S. Werner
A.M. Kagin	Stewart P. Witham

Among living contributors, individuals as well as firms, the following have been very helpful over a long period of years, both in connection with the present text and in communications with the compilers. To this illustrious roster, several names are added for proofreaders and related consultants in recent times:

David W. Akers	James Gray	Casey Noxon
American Numismatic Rarities	Ron Guth	Dr. Joel J. Orosz
Dr. Richard A. Bagg	John Hamrick	John Pack
Mark Borckardt	Heritage Rare Coin Galleries	Vernon Padgett
Wynn Bowers	Dana Marie Hildebrand	Andrew W. Pollock III
Kenneth E. Bressett	Don Kagin	David Queller
C.E. Bullowa	Christine Karstedt	RARCOA
Roger W. Burdette	Myron Kliman	Ed Rector
David Calhoun	J.J. Teaparty Co.	Dr. Robert Schuman
David Cassel	R.W. Julian	Richard E. Snow
John Dannreuther	John Kraljevich, Jr.	Laura Sperber
Tom DeLorey	David W. Lange	Stack's Rare Coins
Bernard Edison	Lawrence Lee	Superior Galleries
Richard A. Eliasberg	Stuart Levine	Don Taxay
Dr. Michael Fey	Kevin Lipton	Anthony Terranova
Rogers M. Fred, Jr.	Denis Loring	David E. Tripp
Dr. George J. Fuld	Dwight Manley	Julius Turoff
Jeff Garrett	John McCloskey	Frank Van Valen
Ronald Gillio	Alan Meghrig	Malcolm Varner
Ira Goldberg	Raymond N. Merena	Fred Weinberg
Larry Goldberg	Rick Montgomery	
Kenneth Goldman	Eric P. Newman	

Acknowledgements

We also want to mention Kenneth E. Bressett, a friend of Q. David Bowers since the early 1950s, the editor of *A Guide Book of United States Coins* (and many other publications), and a highly respected author and researcher, a true great in the hobby. Over the years in connection with many projects, including the Judd book on patterns, Ken has been an important source for inspiration and information. Although he is not a member of the core team given above, his suggestions on the text were valuable.

INSTITUTIONS

The American Numismatic Association Museum, wherein portions of the Harry W. Bass, Jr., Collection are currently displayed, helped in various ways. • The American Numismatic Society has made items available for study. • The Harry W. Bass, Jr., Foundation has provided much information. • Independence National Historical Park provided images of the 1795 half dime. • The Library Company of Philadelphia and staff member Erika Piola rendered essential help. • The Smithsonian Institution, custodian of the National Coin Collection, has made many pieces available for study, including unique varieties. Dr. Richard Doty, present curator, and past curators Douglas Mudd, Vladimir Clain-Stefanelli, and Eliza Clain-Stefanelli, have been very helpful.

ILLUSTRATIONS

Illustrations are from the eighth edition of *United States Pattern Coins: Experimental and Trial Pieces, A Guide Book of United States Coins*, or private collections, or were composites—not actually specimens, but photographs that faithfully illustrate the die combinations described.

Most photos were graciously provided by grading services, auction houses, museums, and private foundations. First among these is the Numismatic Guaranty Corporation of America. We would especially like to thank Steve Eichenbaum and David Lange for their invaluable and expeditious assistance in supplying the majority of the new images for this publication. The teams at American Numismatic Rarities, Bowers and Merena Galleries, Ira and Larry Goldberg Coins and Collectibles, Inc., Heritage Numismatic Auctions, Kagin's, RARCOA, Stack's Rare Coins, Superior Galleries, Superior Stamp and Coin, Tangible Assets, and Teletrade Auctions were also extremely helpful to us. David Calhoun at the Harry W. Bass, Jr. Foundation and Charlene Peacock at the Library Company of Philadelphia were also instrumental in providing images. Photos also came from Mike Byers, J.E. Drew, Durham Western Heritage Museum, Early American History Auctions, Steve Ivy, Rick Kay, Tom Mulvaney, Jay Parrino's The Mint LLC, Princeton University Library, Rarities LLC, and Sarasota Rare Coin Galleries.

Foreword

It has been said many times that patterns tell the story of what "might have been." Although this is true, there is much more to America's pattern coinage. For the collector of coins, patterns represent the under-told story of where our regular-issue coinage comes from, and how it came to be where it is today. Whether they represent the birth of new denominations (such as the two-cent coin or trade dollar), or a new alloy (such as nickel or the clad coinage found in pocket change today), patterns are the physical remnants of this story over time.

Patterns also offer a history of the seamier practices of our Mint. Many of these coins were produced by various government personnel for their own benefit. (What better job for a coin collector than to be a Mint officer or employee in the period from 1859 to 1885!) Many of the greatest pattern coins trace their pedigrees directly to Mint officials—including the two magnificent $50 half unions, now part of the National Numismatic Collection of the Smithsonian Institution.

Because patterns are history, this book has been arranged chronologically to best illustrate the processes behind the pieces. The historical and numismatic text, built on the solid foundation laid by Dr. J. Hewitt Judd, has been masterfully rewritten by Q. David Bowers, whom I have had the pleasure to assist in his research.

Through these pages, you will learn about these rare collectible coins and their place alongside our more commonly known regular-issue pieces.

Let the journey begin.

Saul Teichman
Bayside, New York

Saul Teichman, research associate for *United States Pattern Coins*, is recognized as one of America's foremost numismatic scholars. For many years he has immersed himself in technical and historical aspects of coinage, specializing in patterns in particular, but with expertise in many other areas as well. He is a founding member of the Society of U.S. Pattern Collectors, editor of www.uspatterns.com, and a member of the Rittenhouse Society.

Preface

First of all, what is a pattern coin? The question has no single answer, as collectors have included many different things in their definitions over the years. By way of analogy, "What is a motor vehicle?" might be a similar question—the answer including various types of trucks, cars, motorcycles, farm tractors, and more.

A quick explanation might be: "A pattern coin is one that was struck at the Philadelphia Mint (with a few exceptions) for purposes of testing a design or concept, or perhaps from unusual die pairs, or in unusual metals, or to create delicacies for collectors, but which differs from normal circulating coins of standard design, date, and metal."

However, for every pattern rule there seem to be at least a few exceptions! An often quoted comment is that of Patterson DuBois, in "The Pattern Piece," published in the *American Journal of Numismatics*, January 1883:

> Open for me your cabinet of patterns, and I open for you a record, which, but for these half-forgotten witnesses, would have disappeared under the finger of Time. From the impracticable schemes of visionaries and hobbyists—a tale of national deliverance from minted evil.
>
> These are to be enjoyed as bygones, though there lingers a fear for the spark that still smolders under the ashes. Laws have been framed for them, words have warred over them. Now only these live to tell the tale of "what might have been"; only these remind us of what has been weighed, measured and set aside among the things that are not appropriate, not convenient, not artistic, in short, that are not wanted.

This description, somewhat poetic, is fine in part, but it overlooks the curious fact that Patterson DuBois was prominent at the Philadelphia Mint in the era in which many pieces that we now call patterns were not made to try out "impracticable schemes," but were produced at the Mint and secretly distributed to the numismatic community by its officials, who pocketed the profits, quite practical to the finances of those involved, it would seem! The abuses were so great that Don Taxay called the Mint "a workshop for their gain,"[1] referring to the unauthorized profits available to those who were employed there. It is probably true to say that for a long time, beginning in spring 1859 under the management of Director James Ross Snowden, the Mint was the largest coin dealer in the United States. W. Elliot Woodward related that in the 1860s a relative of a Mint insider traveled all the way to Boston to peddle dozens of pattern coins with the motto GOD OUR TRUST. The machinations of Dr. Henry Linderman, one-time Mint director, make fascinating reading today—he collected patterns avidly and made his own rarities.

Virtually no record at all was kept of the patterns made during the period roughly from 1859 to 1885! However, we can all be thankful that insiders at the Mint had a personal profit motive (ethics aside), for otherwise most pieces listed in this book would not have been created. Although the circumstances around the birth of such patterns may be questionable, the pieces do exist, and they are admired highly today. Indeed, in the panorama of pattern coinage of this era are to be found some beautiful pieces that far surpass standard issues used in circulation, at least in the opinion of many numismatists. Take for example an elegant pattern half dollars of 1877, combinations of classic portraits and differently styled eagles, or the ever charming "Schoolgirl" silver dollar of 1879, or the Coiled Hair $4 gold Stellas of 1879 and 1880, to mention just a few of the more that 1,500 varieties created. Rascals they may have been, but had it not been for Snowden, Linderman, and others, the field of pattern coins as we know it would be very sparse indeed. After the 36-year period of Mint secrecy ended in the summer of 1885, new patterns were few and far between, at least with respect to those known to us today. For the next 36 years fewer than 50 varieties have been recorded! That more may have been made is reflected by galvanos and plasters still at the Philadelphia Mint, but with no accompanying coins.

Pattern coins combine many elements—rarity, mystery (the story of many patterns has not yet been learned), beauty, and for the numismatist, the thrill of the chase and the pride of possession. The present text builds upon the seven editions of J. Hewitt Judd's *United States Pattern, Experimental, and Trial Pieces*, published 1959 through 1982, and the eighth edition, slightly modified in title to *United States Pattern Coins: Experimental and Trial Pieces*. This ninth edition includes modern contributions reflecting new studies and scholarship, and a simplified title.

The Judd book forms the foundation to which have been added many new features, including systematic pricing, revised (in many instances) rarity ratings, extensive historical and collecting commentary, and notes. All told, I hope that the present volume will at once inform, entertain, and delight you. If patterns are your specialty, I and the contributors hope you will value this volume highly. Beyond that, if you have a basic interest in American coinage, but do not know about patterns, the pages of this book will reveal to you the whys and wherefores of the various series—how they were conceived, designed, and eventually became standard issues.

In the pages that follow, the editor and contributors share with you what we have seen and learned, and hope that you will enjoy what you read. A knowledge of patterns is essential to the understanding of the entire panorama of American coinage. They are the foundation upon which the regular series have been built.

Q. David Bowers
Wolfeboro, New Hampshire

NUMISMATIC INTEREST IN PATTERNS

Historical Overview

In the Beginning

The Philadelphia Mint was established in 1792. In that year, the first pattern coins were struck—nearly a dozen different varieties—to illustrate ideas ranging from designs to metallic content. Patterns have been produced ever since. Although much is known about the patterns of 1792, the following years, through about 1835, are more of an enigma. In that early time, there were few if any numismatists interested in such things, and the Mint Cabinet itself would not be formed until June 1838.

Surely, patterns and test impressions were made of the new designs and denominations of 1795 and 1796, but, if so, no record has been found of them, save for a few stray pieces. Into the 19th century, the Mint continued to produce new motifs, designs, and style variations, but virtually nothing is known about patterns for them. We can only imagine that in 1807, when John Reich created his "Capped Bust" design, a few test pieces might have been made to pass around for comment, but nothing was recorded.

Numismatic Interest Increases

In 1835, Christian Gobrecht was hired at the Mint as second engraver, to work with Chief Engraver William Kneass. About this time, Kneass was incapacitated by a stroke, and it fell to the highly artistic and talented Gobrecht to create several new designs.

Many interesting patterns were made from 1836 through 1839. Some of them were saved by Adam Eckfeldt, an old-timer at the Mint, and later placed into the Mint Cabinet. Collectors took notice as well, and perhaps a dozen or two numismatists called at the Mint and obtained specimens. We can only conjecture.

Beginning in early 1857, when it was announced that the familiar large copper cent would be discontinued, and a small copper-nickel cent with a flying eagle design would take its place, a wave of nostalgia swept across the country. People looked in their purses, desk drawers, and elsewhere and endeavored to find one of each different date of the old coppers. Numismatics as we know it was born. In 1858, the American Numismatic Society was established, and by 1859 there were perhaps several thousand collectors across the country.

The Mint Cabinet and Beyond

In the late 1850s, there was great interest in the life and legends of George Washington. Famous orator Edward Everett capitalized on this popularity, in combination with a group of ladies who were raising money to preserve and maintain the derelict Mount Vernon homestead of the Father of Our Country. Everett traveled widely, gave more than 200 speeches, and contributed articles to newspapers and magazines. In the meantime, several books on the life of Washington became best sellers.

In 1859, Mint Director James Ross Snowden, apparently with a nascent numismatic interest, contemplated the Mint Cabinet and noticed that there were only a few tokens and medals of Washington—a poor showing, as dozens of different ones had been created, dating back to the 1780s.[2]

In the early part of 1859, it occurred to Snowden that it would be interesting, and no doubt gratifying to the public taste, to collect and place in the Cabinet of the National Mint one or more specimens of all the medallic memorials of Washington which could be obtained. At that time, he did not know of the existence of more than 20 such pieces. The Cabinet of the Mint contained only four or five specimens besides the pieces known as Washington cents.[3]

During an investigation subsequently made, it was determined that there were at least 60 different Washington medals. To obtain specimens of these medals and of others that had escaped notice, a circular was issued inviting the assistance of the public. Newspapers supported the effort by giving a general notice of the request, and many coin collectors rendered valuable and efficient assistance. Under these influences, and with these advantages, Snowden gathered a large and interesting collection of these medallic memorials, embracing 138 specimens.

Snowden also endeavored to expand the collection. He made it known that he would trade or strike rare coins and patterns in exchange for needed pieces. In January 1859, P. Clayton, who had purchased coins in the June 6, 1855, sale of the Peter Flandin Collection,[4] sent a letter to Snowden:

> Dear Sir,
>
> If you have specimens in copper of the new $20, also model half & quarter dollars & specimen cents struck last year before settling on the new device now used—& can spare them without

Introduction

detriment to the public interest, I would like to have them. My object is to give them to a friend who seems to have a passion for specimens of coins.

Snowden answered on January 24, cautiously marking his letter "unofficial":

Dear Sir,

I have rec'd your note of the 22nd inst. and learn from it that you are acquiring a personal knowledge of the "passion for specimens of coins" which possesses so many people in our country. On Saturday I had nine applications of a similar character—today (now 12 o'clock) I have had three.

It was in view of this increasing, as well as troublesome, taste that I made the request mentioned in my official letter of last Saturday (22nd inst.) which I hope will deserve the sanction of the department.

In reference to the specimens you ask for I have to state that the trial piece in copper of the double eagle of 1859 which I left at the Department is the only one I had: I have a few of the specimen cents but not all the varieties. I could send you two or three of these, but perhaps it will be best to defer sending them until the new arrangement is made, when your friend, and all other collectors of coins, AND THEIR NAME IS LEGION, can be supplied to their hearts' content.

The preceding reveals that Snowden had only a "few" of the 1858 specimen (pattern) cents, but that such demand for them by collectors would soon "'be supplied to their hearts' content."

The Mint had routinely restruck certain coins to supply collectors as early as the 1830s, including to the order of Baltimore numismatist Robert Gilmor, Jr. Now, in early 1859, with a widespread interest in rare coins, such requests had become "troublesome."

Although no specific records have been located, it seems that 1858 cents and other desiderata were struck from old as well as new dies and sold openly for a few months. Then they went "underground."[5]

Until the summer of 1885, making rarities and restrikes was a consuming "business" at the Mint. Sometimes entire series or panoramas of pattern coins were created, such as the almost endless Standard Silver issues of 1869 and the 1870s, and sold to collectors. Other times, striking was done secretly. The rare 1879 and 1880 Coiled Hair gold $4 pieces were not publicized until a generation after they were struck.

The scenario of producing more than 1,500 varieties of patterns from 1859 to 1885—in total tens of thousands of individual coins—necessarily involved many people. It seems that few records were kept. In 1887, when a new director of the Mint endeavored to look into the matter, all he could find was that in 1868 some aluminum strikings of Proof coins had been made. Since then, research in other Mint records, in the committee reports of Congress, and in other places has furnished documentation on a few additional varieties, but for well over a thousand varieties, there is no historical record.

Among the Mint directors, coiners, engravers, curators of the Mint Collection, and others who were involved in making and secretly selling patterns from 1859 to 1885, Dr. Henry R. Linderman is particularly fascinating. A medical doctor by training, his career path led elsewhere, including through the doors of the Philadelphia Mint. He clerked in the office of the director from 1853 to 1865, and served as director from April 1867 to April 1869 and again from April 1873 to December 1878. An avid numismatist, he made his own rarities—apparently including an example of the "King of American Coins," the 1804 silver dollar! Thanks to Linderman, numismatists today can admire a veritable panorama of 1877 pattern half dollars of exquisite beauty—pieces unknown to outside collectors of the era. In June 1878, a congressional subcommittee made charges of misconduct against him, but the allegations were never resolved. Linderman died on January 27, 1879. In his estate were many previously unpublicized patterns and rarities.

After the summer of 1885, the "workshop for their gain" closed down, and the secret production of pattern designs, rarities, and unusual die combinations was no more. Except for a few issues of 1896, later varieties, down to the present day, are essentially non-collectible. However, the vast landscape of pieces struck from 1859 to 1885 gave substance and character to the pattern series. Enough pieces were struck that, despite their general rarity, most pattern coins are available to meet demand today. Many are significantly less expensive than regular-issue pieces of a similarly elusive nature.

Categories of Pattern Coins

Although few people are particularly concerned with classifying patterns into categories today, in general these divisions, sometimes overlapping, are relevant and contribute to an understanding of the series:

Introduction

Pattern coins: True pattern coins in the basic sense represent pieces struck to test a design or some other aspect, with the intention of possibly adopting the style for circulating coinage.

Experimental pieces: Coins designated as experimental pieces are mostly with variations or are the result of explorations into such aspects as planchet diameter or format, shape, thickness, and composition—as opposed to any considerations of a new design.

Trial pieces struck from regular dies: These are strikings from regular design dies, but in a metal other than that used for circulating coinage, such as an 1870 $20 piece struck not in gold but in copper (J-1038), or an 1875 quarter dollar in aluminum instead of silver (J-1417). While a few of these may have been used to set up the dies or to test coining procedures, most of them seem to have been made surreptitiously for collectors. Included in this category are trial pieces actually used in the die set-up process or to create inexpensive samples of precious-metal denominations for study. One or more copper strikings of the 1799 $10 gold piece (J-26) were made to test the dies, and, afterward, the unique existing piece was defaced by cancellation marks. The use of actual gold would have required special security measures. • *Off-metal strikes* is another term for trial pieces. Sometimes confused with the off-metal strikes included among patterns are mint errors, not a main subject of this book but discussed in Appendix B.6

Trial pieces, die trials, paper-backed splashers: During the process of creating dies for a new design, test pieces or die trials were struck, sometimes on thin planchets and with just one die, instead of a pair. A die trial from one die is designated as uniface (with just one "face"). Sometimes uniface pieces were backed by paper; these are called paper-backed splashers by some (*chichés* in French). Many of these were made by pouring lead or a white metal alloy onto newsprint, and then pressing the die into the metal after it cooled slightly, but was still soft (see Appendix A for various splashers and other uniface issues).

Private Restrikes From Mint Dies

As many pieces listed among patterns are in fact so-called private restrikes (made from rusted dies at a date later than that appearing on the dies), it is appropriate to expand on them here.

Although it is likely that the Mint sold antedated and damaged dies as "old iron" or scrap for many years, little about the practice has appeared in print apart from information on the dies once owned by Joseph J. Mickley. He was a Philadelphia numismatist of long standing and impeccable reputation, said to have begun collecting coins about the year 1816, when he sought a copper cent struck in 1799, the year of his birth. Not being able to locate one, his interest was piqued, and he went on to explore the subject deeply. After his death on February 15, 1878, certain of his numismatic items were offered at auction, although the most important parts of his collection had been sold earlier (most notably in a transaction to dealer W. Elliot Woodward, who then showcased them at auction in 1867).

The following, written in December 1878 by Philadelphia pharmacist and pattern collector R. Coulton Davis, was published in the *American Journal of Numismatics*:

> The statement that the dies, hubs, &c., of U.S. coins, advertised for sale with the Mickley Collection, were seized by the United States authorities, has given rise to a great deal of comment. We have received from a gentleman in Philadelphia the following account of the affair.
>
> A few days previous to the sale, the United States authorities claimed the above, viz: Some 20 obverse and reverse dies of the U.S. coinage, mostly in a damaged and corroded condition, the same having been condemned by the Mint authorities above "half a century ago," and as tradition says was the custom in those days, "sold for old iron."
>
> Since then we have grown more artful, and it has been deemed politic under existing laws, that the whole multitude of dated dies should be annually destroyed in the presence of three designated officers of the Mint. In the above described lots in the catalogue, there was not a complete pair of obverse and reverse dies. Even the obverse die of the half-cent of 1811 was muled with the reverse die of a different year.
>
> We cannot conceive by what authority the government, after making sale of its "refuse material," could seize upon the same property without tendering some compensation. There is scarcely a numismatist in the United States, but who is aware of the existence and whereabouts of similar dies, and who is also aware of the many "re-strikes,"—known to be such,—being made from the dies, say of the 1804 cent, the 1811 half-cent, and of the 1823 cent, outside of the Mint.

Accounts such as the preceding, and others, resulted in many impressions from such dies being called "Mickley restrikes" or "restrikes by Mickley." It is highly unlikely that Mickley personally restruck any coins, but there were several medal and die shops in Philadelphia that could have made pieces on demand.

Introduction

Apart from the dies seized from the Mickley estate (some of which may have been part of a cache found in the basement of the old mint at an earlier time and given to Chief Coiner George K. Childs by John S. Warner in 1857), a handful of others survived into the 20th century, and some exist today, including those in the collections of the American Numismatic Society and the Smithsonian Institution. Other dies, canceled across the face, have appeared in auction sales in recent years, and thousands of modern dies have been partially defaced and sold as souvenirs by the United States Mint.

A few dozen varieties of "restrikes," some of which are plentiful today, have been made outside the Mint from discarded early 19th-century dies, nearly always by casually pairing an obverse die with a reverse die that was never mated with it for original coinage (although in some instances the design was similar). For generations, these pieces have been adopted as popular additions to the "pattern" series, although they are not patterns at all. In the present listings they are designated as private restrikes.

COLLECTING AND ENJOYING PATTERNS

Ever since the cradle days of American numismatics in the late 1850s, when the hobby became widely popular, patterns have been an integral part of the quest for interesting specimens. Indeed, in the 1860 book bearing the name of James Ross Snowden as author (but prepared by his staff), *A Description of Ancient and Modern Coins in the Cabinet Collection at the Mint of the United States*, extensive space is given to various patterns, comments concerning the design, and in some instances the quantities struck. During the same decade, numismatic auctions became very popular and were conducted by W. Elliot Woodward, Edward Cogan, and others, often featuring pattern coins for sale, always playing to enthusiastic audiences.

Now, early in the 21st century, patterns are more popular than ever. Numismatists eagerly pursue such pieces, using texts such as this work and other sources ranging from auction catalogs to scattered mentions in the *Guide Book of United States Coins*, to the Internet (most particularly the site coordinated by Saul Teichman, www.uspatterns.com.)

There is no single "right" way to collect pattern coins, and over the years, many numismatists have developed their own formulae.

Major Lenox R. Lohr formed what is probably the most extensive pattern collection of all time, comprising more than 1,400 different pieces, plus duplicates. Lohr had the advantage of being in the right place at the right time, tapping into patterns that appeared on the market from the estates of Virgil Brand, William H. Woodin, and Colonel E.H.R. Green, plus many important auction offerings including the 1954 Palace Collection sale of the holdings of King Farouk, the deposed monarch of Egypt.

No doubt the pattern collection formed at one time by William H. Woodin, author of the 1913 book *United States Pattern, Trial, and Experimental Pieces*, was very extensive—probably not exceeding that of Lohr, but no doubt including the majority of the pieces listed in his text (which remained the standard until the first edition of the Judd work, copyright 1959, appeared). Over a long period of years, many other important cabinets of patterns have been dispersed.

While a handful of numismatists have had the time, patience, and finances to collect one of each pattern they could find, the most popular discipline is to acquire pieces that are numismatic favorites, either by design or as part of related series.

Collecting With a Regular Series

Off-metal strikes furnish an interesting addition to a collection of regular-series coins. Thus, a specialist in Liberty Head or Coronet $10 gold coins of the late 19th century might well enjoy having a few strikings from Proof dies in aluminum or copper, rather than gold. Similarly, a collector of Indian Head cents might enjoy owning an 1868 cent struck in aluminum (J-612), certainly an item that would arouse great attention when shown to others.

For a long time, many specialists in Flying Eagle and Indian Head cents have found it a pleasant exercise to acquire related patterns, of which dozens of varieties exist. Indeed, sets of 12 different 1858 pattern die combinations became early stock-in-trade items for Mint officials. To these can be added the patterns cents of 1859, the issues of 1864, and others.

Similarly, specialists in nickel five-cent pieces can find a panorama of interesting and frequently available pattern coins produced from the general era of 1865 to 1896, sometimes incorporating dies used for the Shield series (struck for circulation from 1866 to 1883) and the Liberty Head series (of 1883 to 1912), but often in combination with strictly pattern reverses never used for circulating coinage. As a microcosm, the pattern nickels of 1881 through 1883 make a delightful study.

Collectors of Fractional Currency paper notes, issued by the Treasury Department in the 1860s and 1870s, may find the Postage Currency pattern coins of 1863 to be of interest (J-325 to J-330), as they are coins intended to be minted for the redemption of the early issues of Fractional Currency, the early issues of which were called Postage Currency. However, such coins were never adopted for general use.

Numismatists who enjoy regular-issue half dollars have often added a display of patterns to their cabinets, sometimes acquiring dozens of specimens. R.E. Cox, Jr., Texas numismatist and department store owner, did precisely that. Similarly, Morgan silver dollar specialists have a wide variety of 1878 and 1879 patterns to choose from. For aficionados of the Morgan head of Miss Liberty, there are also pattern Morgan dimes, quarter dollars, and half dollars with the same portrait. How interesting it is to display a "Morgan dime"!

Trade dollars, first called Commercial dollars, were made to the extent of dozens of patterns during the years 1871 through 1873, plus a few scattered later issues. These form a fascinating complement to a regular collection. Harry W. Bass, Jr., loved regular-issue $3 gold coins, and to go with them, he acquired every pattern coin he could find of the same denomination.

Collecting Transitional Patterns
Transitional patterns consist of pieces bearing obverse and reverse designs in the same combination as used for regular coinage, but struck and dated before regular coinage commenced. These pieces are pattern coins of which the designs were adopted.

One famous transitional pattern is the 1856 Flying Eagle cent (J-180), struck from the design adopted on February 21, 1857, but dated a year before. The 1859 Indian Head cent with the oak wreath and shield reverse (the type of 1860, J-228), is another transitional pattern, as is the 1863 bronze cent (J-299).

In the Shield nickel series, there are 1865-dated nickels with the Shield obverse and With Rays and Without Rays reverses, plus the 1866 Without Rays, a suite of three coins that makes a very nice addition to a regular set of the denomination. The 1882 Without CENTS Liberty Head nickel (J-1690) is similar in design to the famous 1883 issue made for circulation and is thus a transitional pattern. Quarter dollars, half dollars, and dollars of 1863, 1864, and 1865 exist with the motto IN GOD WE TRUST on the reverse, as regularly adopted in 1866.

Collecting Favorite Pattern Designs
Many patterns have been collected simply because they are beautiful and interesting to own, such as the 1872 "Amazonian" quarter dollar, half dollar, and dollar; the elegant series of 1877 half dollars; the 1879 "Schoolgirl" dollar; and the 1882 "Shield Earring" quarter dollar, half dollar, and dollar, among many others.

At the Eliasberg Collection sale, a bidder set his eye on just one pattern, as it had a story (yet another reason to acquire a favorite pattern)—the "ugly duckling" three-cent piece of 1849 (J-113 and J-114), depicting on one side simply an Arabic numeral 3 and on the other the Roman numeral III.

Collecting Other Sets and Specialties
Patterns themselves offer the opportunity to form sets and subsets of pieces of interest. Here are a few suggestions beyond those already mentioned:

Denomination type set: Collect one of each pattern denomination in the regular denominations from the half cent to the $20 or, if you are bold, include the pattern-only denominations of the $4 Stella and 1877 $50 piece. Metals of striking can be mixed or matched. A complete denomination set would include the half cent, cent, two-cent piece, nickel three-cent piece, silver trime, half dime, nickel five-cent piece, dime, twenty-cent piece, quarter dollar, half dollar, silver dollar, trade or Commercial dollar, gold dollar, $2.50, $3, $4, $5, $10, $20, and $50.

Year set: Pick a favorite year and endeavor to obtain as many different patterns as possible, either in terms of die combinations, or simpler, an example of each individual die.

Coins from an era: Patterns from the Civil War era (1861 through 1865) may form a specialty. Patterns from the era of the great "Silver Question" are of political importance, and when from the 1870s through the 1890s, silver (in particular) became a political issue. Or coins from a particular presidential administration might be a challenge.

Introduction

Favorite engraver: Concentrate on patterns from the hand of a favorite engraver—Christian Gobrecht, James B. Longacre, or George T. Morgan, for example—and collect examples of his work, adding to your enjoyment by learning of his life and background.

Standard Silver set: Review the Standard Silver listings of 1869 and 1870, with a few of 1871. Assembling an example of each die pair can be a fascinating challenge. Or you can focus on certain issues and obtain suites of six of the same pair (silver, copper, and aluminum, each with reeded or plain edge).

"Story" coins: Form an exhibit of patterns with emphasis on the odd and curious—e.g., design mistakes (as on the 1875 twenty-cent piece and the trade dollar with an illogical ship illustration), or two-headed coins. There are many possibilities.

Complete pattern set challenge: There are about 1,800 different patterns listed in this text, many of which are unique or are in institutions. If you are in a good financial position, obtaining one each of as many different patterns as possible is an interesting goal. You will be joining the ranks of William H. Woodin, Lenox H. Lohr, Dr. James O. Sloss, and probably Virgil M. Brand, who each crossed the 1,000 mark (Lohr had more than 1,400), with nods to Harry W. Bass, Jr., Armand Champa, King Farouk, Rogers M. Fred, Jr., T. Harrison Garrett, David Queller, William R. ("Rudy") Sieck, and dozens of others whose cabinets included wide panoramas below the 1,000 level.

Displaying Your Patterns

There are no rules regarding the best way to form a display. Most series of patterns contain pieces that are readily available, as well as others that are unique or will not likely be found during a collector's lifetime. Thus, there is the thrill of the chase for the latter. No one has ever completed a full set of 1877 pattern half dollars, although a number have tried; a good "score" is to get at least 10, with 15 or more being truly remarkable. Picking up a familiar analogy, it is like playing a round of golf—no one ever gets a perfect score of 18, but it is fun to try, and a score in the 80s or even the 90s can be a worthy accomplishment.

A comforting aspect of collecting patterns is their inherent value: all patterns are scarce, many are rare, and many others are exceedingly rare. However, as the majority of American numismatists do not know of the series, it is possible to obtain coins for which only a half dozen or a dozen pieces exist for prices that are but tiny fractions of the cost of varieties listed in the *Guide Book of United States Coins*. For example, among the most expensive of all pattern cents is the 1856 Flying Eagle, but it is also the most common. Because it is listed in the *Guide Book*, many people know about it, and the race is on to acquire one.

OTHER ASPECTS OF PATTERNS

Metals and Alloys

From 1792, many basic metals and alloys were used for federal coinage issued for circulation. In general, these included copper, copper-nickel, bronze, nickel alloy, silver, and gold.

As planchets or blank coinage discs of these metals were available at the Mint at any given time, it was natural that they were used to strike patterns as well, although from time to time special alloys were employed. Accordingly, when in 1865 some pattern nickel five-cent pieces were struck, standard coinage alloys of the time were used, these being bronze and nickel (what we call nickel actually was and is an alloy of 75% copper and 25% nickel, giving a silvery appearance to the coins). When pattern Commercial dollars were made in 1871, regular silver planchets (of an alloy of 90% silver and 10% copper) were used.

Basic metals used for patterns (outside of those used for the regular coinage) include aluminum, platinum, nickel (pure), and tin. Many alloys, familiar as well as experimental, were employed, among these being billon, white metal, goloid, oroide, Roulz's alloy, and German silver, among others.

The Challenge of Metal Composition

Much of what we know about certain pattern coins is derived from Mint records.

As an example, documents state that a special alloy of billon was created of 90% copper and 10% silver to strike certain pattern two-cent pieces in 1836 (the variety classified as J-53). In addition, we know that restrikes were made at the Mint at a later date, including those listed as copper and given numbers J-54 (plain edge) and J-55 (reeded edge).

As another example, 1853 pattern cents of J-149, J-150, and J-151 all have the same general appearance, but J-149 is of "German silver" (consisting of 40% nickel, 40% copper, and 20% zinc); J-150, also called "German silver," is of a different alloy (consisting of 30% nickel, 60% copper, and 10% zinc); and J-151 has traditionally been designated as "nickel" (but is 40% nickel and 60% copper).

In the curious case of certain nickel five-cent patterns of 1883, J-1704 through J-1706, the reverse die bears a forthright description within the center of the wreath: PURE NICKEL. However, only J-1704 is really pure nickel (and can be tested as such, as it is strongly attracted by a magnet); J-1705 is non-magnetic and, presumably, is some alloy of copper and nickel (perhaps the 75% copper and 25% nickel used for regular coinage, but who knows?); and J-1706 is aluminum.

Unless a coin is subjected to elemental analysis (a complicated procedure), it may be difficult if not impossible to determine its composition. In today's market, many patterns are encapsulated in certified "slabs," making even basic specific gravity tests impossible unless the coins are removed. Accordingly, there are many caveats regarding the metals listed or assigned to a given pattern variety, and the exact nature of the metal used.

This uncertainty is not particularly important to most collectors, who are satisfied with a basic example of the die combination. For more details on pattern coinage metals, see Appendix D.

Edges of Pattern Coins
Early Era
Pattern coins from 1792 through part of 1836 were struck on hand-operated presses in which a weighted lever arm was swung by two men, causing a screw to depress and one die to meet the other, impressing the planchet between them. Coins thus struck had one of three edge styles: plain edge (with no design; either caused by letting a planchet expand and giving a somewhat rounded curve to the edge [viewed edge-on]); reeded edge (with vertical ribs; caused by the metal being impressed into a retaining collar with corresponding indentations); and lettered edge (with an inscription provided separately by running the blank planchet through an edge-lettering Castaing machine).

Later Era
Patterns struck on steam-powered presses in 1836 and later had plain edges or reeded edges. A plain collar often imparted a mirrorlike surface to the edge, whereas a reeded collar imparted vertical reeds or *reeding*.[6]

Hydraulic presses were often used to produce Proof coins as well as patterns from the late 19th century onward. These presses operated at a slower speed and caused finer details to raise up on the finished coin. Generally, plain and reeded edge collars were used.

In a few scattered instances, other edge devices were imparted by collars, such as on the 1882 "blind man's nickel" (J-1683 and J-1697), with five raised bars on the edge; the curious 1885 Morgan design on the silver dollar from regular dies, but with edge lettered E PLURIBUS UNUM in raised letters (J-1747 to J-1749); and the Saint-Gaudens coinage of 1907 with raised stars and letters.

In general, most of 19th-century pattern coins have either plain edges or reeded edges, here abbreviated as PE or RE, respectively. Although there are exceptions, most pattern minor denominations (including the cent, two-cent piece, nickel three-cent piece, and nickel five-cent piece, struck in various metals) have plain edges, as do patterns for the silver three-cent piece. Higher denominations of silver, from the half dime through the trade dollar, generally have reeded edges, except for the twenty-cent piece. However, many plain-edge patterns of these silver denominations were made as well. Pattern gold dollars are usually found with plain edges, and higher denominations of gold with reeded edges.

From 1859 to 1885, many patterns of a given die combination and metal were made in both plain and reeded edge styles, yielding additional varieties for sale to numismatists.

Die Orientation of Pattern Coins
Coin-Turn Alignment
Nearly all regular-issue federal coins—circulating issues, as well as Proofs made for collectors, and also commemorative coins—were produced with the obverse and reverse dies aligned in opposite directions, or 180 degrees apart. In numismatic terminology, this is often referred to as *coin turn*. If a regular-issue coin is held with the obverse facing the viewer, and is rotated on its vertical axis so as to show the reverse, the reverse will appear upside down.

There are numerous exceptions, such as 1804 half cents with the reverse oriented in various alignments; certain Proof coins of 1868 with the dies oriented in the same direction (a neophyte must have set the dies in the press); and the error Proof 1903 nickel, also with the dies in the same direction.

Introduction

A general term for a regular-issue coin with an orientation other than the usual 180 degrees is *rotated die* or *misaligned reverse*. Of course, it was not necessarily the reverse die that was misaligned in the press—it could have been the obverse. However, as numismatists view coins from the perspective of the obverse being upright, it is the reverse that is used to describe die alignment variations.

Medal-Turn Alignment
Most medals, not a subject of discussion of the present text, were produced with the dies in the same direction, or *medal-turn*.

Pattern coins are usually seen in the coin-turn orientation, but many medal-turn varieties are known as well. These seem to have been produced deliberately, to differentiate varieties. A famous example is the 1836 Gobrecht silver dollar classified as J-60, a regular issue "adopted" into the pattern series; pieces struck in the calendar year 1836 are oriented coin-turn or 180 degrees apart, while those struck in early 1837 (from the same die pair, but with a different weight and composition of planchet) were struck medal-turn, so that they could be easily told apart.[7]

In other instances, it is likely that both originals and restrikes of patterns, usually made in the Medal Department of the Mint, were inadvertently made with medal-turn alignment. Little attention has been paid to die orientation of patterns over the years, except for a few selected issues.

GRADING AND RARITY OF PATTERNS

The Difference Between Mint State and Proof
As a prelude to grading, the distinction between circulation strike and Proof coins is important. These terms refer not to grades, but to methods of manufacture. Coins made for circulation were struck from dies that were dressed by filing and other preparation, but not polished. Certain coins struck for collectors were made from dies that were given a mirrorlike polish to the fields. Most patterns of 1836 and later were made in Proof format, but there were many exceptions.

Each of these two types of strike has its own grading nomenclature in the areas of higher preservation. A gem circulation strike is designated as gem Mint State or gem Uncirculated, or on the numerical scale, MS-65 or a similar number. A gem Proof is called such, or Proof-65.

Mint State Coins
A coin struck from regular or circulation-strike dies, when first minted, had brilliant frost or luster in the fields. Such coins, if remaining in high grades today, are designated as Uncirculated, or, in recent years, Mint State, by numismatists.

Among patterns, virtually all issues before 1836 were in Mint State when first coined, the 1792 half disme (J-7) being the most famous example. Among post-1836 patterns, there are occasional issues that were made with lustrous (rather than mirror Proof) surfaces, a well-known variety being the 1859 pattern Indian Head cent with oak wreath and shield reverse (J-228), of which probably more than a thousand Mint State coins are known today.

Certain other patterns were hastily struck to test a design or a die pairing, or for other reasons, and the dies were not polished. In still other instances, strikings in very hard alloys such as copper-nickel, brass, and nickel (75% copper and 25% nickel) sometimes did not acquire mirrorlike surfaces even when struck from Proof dies; such pieces, while resembling Mint State coins more than Proofs, fall between in nomenclature, but many such pieces are certified as "MS" today.[8]

Proof Coins
Proof coins of the 19th century were made from obverse and reverse dies that were usually (but not always) carefully polished to create a deep mirrorlike finish. Coins struck from these dies, usually at a slow speed on a hand-operated (rather than steam) press, are known as Proofs. These Proofs typically have deep mirror fields or flat surfaces and matte or lustrous designs and lettering.

There are many exceptions, such as most pieces in the extensive series of 1859 pattern half dollars. The dies were only partially polished, and many file marks and die preparation lines, called *striae*, remained in the fields. The resultant coins have countless raised striae in the fields, and to the uninitiated observer, they appear to have been cleaned with an abrasive.

Introduction

Condition and Value

Among the factors that determine a pattern coin's value is its condition, typically referred as its grade, this being an evaluation of the amount of handling or wear a given piece has experienced. In all instances, a pattern which has been carefully preserved over the years and is a gem Mint State or Proof example is worth more than one that has been mishandled or one that has spent years in circulation or has been carried as a pocket piece.

Among patterns, the issues of 1792 and many other early (pre-1836) varieties, exist today with indications of circulation or wear. In the present text, grades are given for these at such levels as Fine (F), Extremely Fine (EF), and Mint State (Unc). For patterns from 1836 onward, most are seen today in various high levels of Mint State or, usually, Proof, as made.

Grading guidelines have been formulated to aid numismatists in describing the condition of a coin. Accordingly, a buyer who is offered a Proof-60 specimen (basic Proof grade, with evidences of cleaning or mishandling) will want to pay less for it than if the variety were Proof-63 (choice) or Proof-65 (gem).

The Numerical Grading System

Background to the Sheldon Scale

The American Numismatic Association and a wide circle of numismatists have adopted the so-called Sheldon Grading Scale, in which grades are designated by numbers from 1 to 70, the latter indicating perfection. In earlier times, and sometimes today (particularly among old-timers in the hobby), adjectives were used, such as:

Poor: Extremely worn and scarcely identifiable. However, sometimes the motif can enable the coin to be recognized. As an example, a specimen of the 1792 half disme (J-7) could be identified even if the date, lettering, and most other features were worn away.

Fair: Extensively worn, with most lettering gone, though possibly part of the date is visible. Identifiable as to basic date and type.

About Good: Close to Good.

Good: With the date and most lettering readable.

Very Good: Better than Good, with more lettering readable, such as, perhaps, several (but not all) letters of LIBERTY in the headband of an Indian Head cent or on the shield of a Liberty Seated coin.

Fine: With all lettering readable, including LIBERTY on the headband or shield, although some letters may be weak.

Very Fine: With lettering and details sharper than the preceding.

Extremely Fine: With nearly all design details sharp (except in instances in which a coin was weakly struck).

About Uncirculated: Very sharp, with mint luster, and very close to Uncirculated (Mint State), but with limited evidences of wear and abrasion.

Uncirculated (Mint State): With no trace of wear. A coin that has probably never been in circulation, but which can show extensive abrasions at the lower levels, increasing in desirability with fewer such marks.

The above is but a sketch or outline, and for full details a grading book should be consulted, such as *The Official ANA Grading Standards for United States Coins*.

The Sheldon Grading System adds numbers to the preceding and divides the grade levels into specific categories. A basic abbreviation from the adjective is used as a prefix to each number (e.g., Good-4 is abbreviated G-4).

The Sheldon Grading Scale

Today, the Sheldon Grading Scale is used widely by many collectors and universally by coin certification services. It had its genesis in 1949 in Dr. William H. Sheldon's *Early American Cents*, and was intended for grading copper cents of 1793 to 1814. The original system was simpler than that now used, and in the Mint State range had just three divisions: MS-60, MS-65, and MS-70 (today, there are 11 different numbers used in the same span).

The modified Sheldon Grading Scale in use today is as follows:

Introduction

Poor-1
Fair-2
AG-3
G-4
VG-8
F-12 and -15
VF-20, -25, -30, and -35
EF-40 and -45
AU-50, -53, -55, and -58
MS-60, -61, -62, -63, -64, -65, -66, -67, -68, -69, and -70

For Proof coins, as is applicable to most issues of pattern coins 1836 and later, the above scale is used, except for the 50 to 70 span, which is:

Proof-50, -53, -55, and -58
Proof-60, -61, -62, -63, -64, -65, -66, -67, -68, -69, and -70

From a scientific viewpoint, the Sheldon formula, devised in 1949 as a marketing formula for copper cents, but later adopted because people "like numbers," is very flawed. Twenty numbers are allowed for the range from VF-20 to and including just below EF-40, whereas Mint State and Proof grades, very important in terms of market values, are shoehorned into just 11 spaces, from 60 to 70.

However, so long as all agree on what the abbreviations mean, most people are satisfied. In any event, if the same person grades a group of coins, the MS-65 is apt to be better than MS-63 or MS-60. In practice, not even the most expert of experts can consistently grade coins into minute divisions, such as Proof-62 and Proof-63. Also there is the problem that, while a number is intended to indicate the grade or amount of wear a coin has received, with regard to market value there are other important aspects as well—such as sharpness of strike, color of the surface, and aesthetic appeal. Thus, the advanced numismatist uses numbers only as a starting point, after which interpretation and subjectivity enter.

Grade Listings in This Book

In the present text, pattern coins from 1792 to 1834 are listed in various circulated grades plus MS-60. For coins of this era, Mint State specimens are seldom encountered. Any coin significantly finer than MS-60 (the highest listing) is worth much more money. However, various private restrikes from dies of these dates are exceptions and are usually found in Mint State, although typically with rough surfaces due to die rust.

For pattern coins of 1836 and later years, the present text employs three grading steps for the pricing of patterns: Proof-60, Proof-63, and Proof-65.

Aspects of Proof-60 to Proof-70 Grades

When first struck, if carefully taken from the presses, a Proof coin was perfect or nearly so, say Proof-68, Proof-69, or Proof-70. By all reasonable thinking, Proofs made for collectors should have been carefully preserved, and, except for normal toning or patination acquired over the years, should be in a condition essentially as struck. However, this is hardly the case.

In *The Numismatist*, August 1902, Farran Zerbe described his visit to the Mint Collection on display in Philadelphia (today it is part of the National Numismatic Collection in the Smithsonian Institution):

> I found many of the silver Proof coins of late years partially covered with a white coating. On inquiry I learned that an over zealous attendant during the last vacation months when the numismatic room was closed took it on himself to clean the tarnished coins, purchase some metal polish at a department store, and proceeded with his cleaning operation. Later a coating of white appeared on the coins, which was now slowly disappearing.

> I expressed my displeasure at this improper treatment of Proof coins, and the custodian explained, "That is nothing. I have been here eight years and they have been cleaned three or four times in my time."

Zerbe speculated that should this cleaning continue, in the future one would have nothing left except plain planchets and badly worn coins!

Over a long period of years, indeed generations, many if not most numismatists came to believe that "brightest is best," and many lotions, potions, and cleaning agents have been employed—some widely advertised in numismatic periodicals—to make "tarnished" coins brilliant, thus improving their value.

Sadly, King Farouk of Egypt, who collected coins avidly in the 1940s and early 1950s, and who enjoyed pattern coins, usually cleaned with polish his copper (in particular) and silver issues, making the copper pieces an unnatural bright orange, not to overlook removing much of the true mirror surface. Coins that could have been graded Proof-65 or finer when he bought them, now can be described as "Proof-60, polished." In recent years, some of these polished ex-Farouk patterns have been improved (really) by stripping down their surfaces and retoning or recoloring them to more pleasing hues.[9]

That the majority of Proof coins and patterns have been cleaned is implicit in the aforementioned grading scale. The only reason that 99% of patterns graded as Proof-60 to Proof-63 have hairlines or evidences of rubbing is that they have been cleaned; otherwise, these lines would not be present. However, as such cleaning is implicit, a pattern is properly described today as, for example, "Proof-60," not "Proof-60 with extensive hairlines from cleaning."

Similarly, any silver pattern that is fully brilliant and bright today stands a 99% chance of having been dipped, for silver is a chemically reactive metal and, without exception, silver coins preserved for a century or more (since their time of striking, such as in a family heirloom collection) exhibit some degree of toning. Most coins dipped or cleaned years ago have retoned since, either naturally or artificially. Accordingly, many are very pleasing to the eye.

As may be surmised, grading, cleaning, and toning are sometimes controversial subjects. However, an understanding of them is desirable. For many varieties of patterns, the point is moot—for if only a handful of specimens exist, and none is finer than Proof-63, even the most magnificent collection would be enhanced by such a coin.

In summary, Proof-65, or gem Proof, is an excellent quality for the connoisseur. Such a piece is apt to have very few hairlines and handling marks, even under high magnification. A Proof-63 pattern will have numerous hairlines, but those hairlines will be delicate and not particularly offending to the eye. A Proof-60 pattern may show nicks and extensive hairlines. The classification is subjective, and there are no precise rules as to how many hairlines or how many marks a coin should have to be in a particular grade. Often, numismatists say they "grade by instinct," although "by experience" would be more correct.

Certification Services

In 1986, the concept of hermetically sealing a coin in a hard plastic holder, with an insert imprinted as to variety and suggested grade, was popularized by the Professional Coin Grading Service (PCGS). In 1987, the Numismatic Guaranty Corporation of America (NGC) made its debut. ANACS, founded in 1972, began grading and encapsulating coins in 1989. Since that time, there have been other grading services as well, although ANACS, NGC, and PCGS are the most widely used.[10]

In any and all instances, it is advised to buy the coin, not to buy the holder. To paraphrase Abraham Lincoln's aphorism ("If you call a cow a horse, it is still a cow."), if someone takes a highly cleaned, ugly, and thoroughly undesirable coin and puts it in a holder and calls it Proof-65, this does not make it such.

Consult with established dealers who are specialists in patterns or who at least have a general familiarity with them, and talk with some old-time collectors of patterns. You will quickly learn which of the commercial services are considered to be useful and desirable. Afterward, if you are just beginning your adventure with patterns and are still seeking basic knowledge, ask for and consider for purchase only the coins certified by these services, assuming the coins meet your other expectations as well (eye appeal, price). In numismatics, many people prefer "raw" or uncertified coins, this being particularly true of specialists in regular-issue colonials, half cents, large cents, and tokens. Until you gain your own expertise, "raw" coins should be acquired only after consultation with a trusted advisor.

A bonus is that many (but not all) grading services guarantee that the coins they certify are genuine (not counterfeit or forgeries); however, it is often the case that the specific attribution to a given metal or striking is not guaranteed.[11] Grading itself is not guaranteed, as it is subject to interpretation, and often a grading service will assign a different grade to the same coin if it is resubmitted (although the differences are usually only within a point or two).

A Scale for Rarity
Historical Sheldon Scale (1949)
In his 1949 book, *Early American Cents*, the same text that featured a grading system, Dr. William H. Sheldon advised a numerical scale from 1 to 8, as shorthand for the approximate rarity of a coin. In its original form, the scale was given as follows:

Introduction

Rarity-1 (abbreviated R-1): more than 1,250 known
R-2: 501–1,250
R-3: 201–500
R-4: 76–200
R-5: 31–75
R-6: 14–30
R-7: 4–12
R-8: 2 or 3
Unique

While this scale is useful, its distinctions are less than ideal. For example, a rating of R-7 on the Sheldon scale indicates that four to twelve coins are known; the potential threefold difference in population can make a tremendous difference in market value, and therefore in your purchasing decision. Accordingly, intermediate levels are recommended for the R-6 and R-7 categories, creating the following scale:

Rarity Scale Used in this Book

Rarity-1: more than 1,250 known to exist today
R-2: 501–1,250
R-3: 201–500
R-4: 76–200
R-5: 31–75
Low R-6: 21–30
High R-6: 13–20
Low R-7: 7–12
High R-7: 4–6
R-8: 2 to 3
Unique: 1

Research into rarity (how many pieces are known today, not how many were struck) is ongoing. A coin listed today as L7, with 12 known, might be reclassified as H6 tomorrow if a 13th piece is found. Among issues classified as Low R-7 to Unique, it is useful to gain an idea of the frequency of market appearance and also how many may reside in museums. Coins held in the Smithsonian Institution, the Harry W. Bass, Jr. Foundation Collection, and the American Numismatic Society Collection, to name just three institutional repositories, are likely to be off the market for a long time, perhaps forever, and thus the pieces in those holdings cannot be factored into market availability. Among patterns of lesser rarity, R-6 to R-1, the distinction is not as important.

BUYING PATTERNS

Guidelines for "Smart" Buying

Now that various caveats have been given, an intelligent quest can be made for desirable specimens of pattern coins. A key to what quality should be accepted is provided by the rarity ratings and also by a degree of experience as to what type of grades exist among pieces preserved. The published reports by leading certification services provide excellent information in the latter regard. If the rarity rating suggests that several dozen or more examples are known of a given pattern, and a handful of pieces has crossed the auction block in the past decade, then it is quite probable that sooner or later a "nice" piece will come along to delight you.

On the other hand, if a pattern is sufficiently rare, you cannot be too particular if you ever want to own one. In such instances, it is highly desirable to obtain a piece that may be less than attractive. The remarkable, historical, and unique 1794 copper pattern dollar without obverse stars (J-18) is an excellent example of such a coin. The only known piece shows wear and has porous surfaces.

In today's market, many if not most buyers simply look at the number on a holder and make their purchases accordingly. This leaves ample opportunity for an aspiring *smart* buyer to use the holder as a starting point, as suggested, and beyond that, examine the piece for eye appeal.

A trustworthy professional dealer will always be a good friend, and it is worthwhile to get advice on matters concerning coin quality and market value, particularly in the period before you become personally

Introduction

acquainted with the ins and outs of pattern collecting. In patterns, as in any other numismatic discipline, there is a learning curve. Remember that at one time, even Edgar H. Adams, William H. Woodin, and Dr. J. Hewitt Judd did not know what a pattern is!

Importance of Eye Appeal

As a quick rule, if a pattern coin, no matter the numerical grade, looks attractive and pleasing to your eye, and if you find it delightful to view, then chances are that when the time comes for you to sell, others will find the piece to be desirable as well. However, if a coin is blotchy, stained, polished, or has other problems, then when the time comes to sell, many potential buyers will be turned away. Thus, some patience is recommended when acquiring patterns.

Beyond the numerical grade and eye appeal, it is desirable to consider other aspects that determine the value of a pattern coin. Gold denominations actually struck in gold metal—extremely rare except for the 1836 dollar (J-67, of which several dozen exist) and the 1879 $4 Stella of the Flowing Hair design (J-1635, of which several hundred are known)—tend to be basically brilliant and attractive, as the metal is inert and not susceptible to extensive toning or discoloration. Therefore, a gold pattern can be evaluated based on the hairlines and marks that it has, with toning not being a factor. Accordingly, if you want an 1879 Stella—and who doesn't?—you have the opportunity during the course of a year or two to review a couple dozen or more pieces and find one that is "just right." However, be aware that all have tiny parallel planchet lines on the hair.[12] (See "What to Expect" below for other illustrations.)

Silver coins tend to tone differently over a period of time, and, as noted, any silver pattern struck in the 19th century which has not been dipped or brightened will today have toning, from light to medium to dark. Fully bright coins, quite attractive to the eye, have been dipped or "conserved." There is nothing wrong with this, and if carefully done, the dipping of a coin can restore it to virtually as-struck appearance. However, if a silver coin naturally tones, then is dipped again, then tones, then is dipped again, it gradually becomes dull and cloudy. Try to not "improve" any pattern that you own. If a coin offered to you is not a rarity, and if it has problems, keep looking. If it is a rarity and might benefit from conservation, consult with specialists and dealer experts first.

Copper coins are the most delicate of all, as copper and its various alloys such as bronze are chemically reactive. Nineteenth-century patterns naturally tone to a light brown, then a darker brown. In addition, some patterns (such as 1862 $10 pieces struck in copper) were deliberately made with what was called a bronzed surface, color of chestnut brown, due to a special process. Many if not most copper patterns have problems, and a special degree of care is needed when purchasing them.

What to Expect

Patterns are remarkably different from each other, not only in basic designs, but also in the way they were struck, how the dies were prepared, the quality of the planchets used, and their general personalities.

Before determining if a coin is just right for you, it will pay to learn about it. The present text gives many guidelines in this respect, and beyond that, dealers, collectors, auction catalogs, and other sources can be tapped. Sometimes even obvious characteristics (such as planchet lines in the hair of the 1879 $4 Stella noted earlier) cannot be learned easily by reading catalogs.

To illustrate the significant differences that can be found among high-grade patterns, these examples might be useful:

1859 pattern half dollars, J-235 to J-255: Nearly all of these were struck from dies that were incompletely prepared and had many tiny lines and scratches from the die-making process. The finished coins display these lines in the form of raised die striae, going in many different directions, and in some instances almost suggesting that the coin had been rubbed with sandpaper!

1860 pattern half dime, silver, J-267: These were coined with lustrous, frosty surfaces (not Proof), with parts of the design weakly struck. They are nearly always found highly lustrous and of high quality, MS-63 or better.

1861 pattern $10 in copper, J-285: These were struck with bronzed surfaces, and display a matte-like chestnut color; very distinctive.

1879 and 1880 Goloid Metric dollars, Morgan design, goloid alloy, J-1631 and J-1654: Carefully struck from highly polished dies. Most are delightful deep-mirror gems.

Introduction

1896 pattern cents and five-cent pieces, J-1767 to J-1772: These were not struck with care, and although intended as brilliant Proofs, most had unsatisfactory surfaces. Certain dies had many striations.

Metal of Striking

The metal of striking can be important, and for denominations normally struck in silver or gold, patterns in those respective metals are generally more desired than are those in other metals such as copper, white metal, or aluminum. However, this rule does not hold for coins normally struck in bronze, as a pattern cent struck in visually dramatic aluminum would be more valuable. On the other hand, a Liberty Seated dime struck in aluminum rather than silver has little visual curiosity, as the coins can appear to be very similar. The value of a pattern in a variant metal must be determined on an issue-by-issue basis.

Market Conditions and Competition

Demand is another aspect of the value of a pattern, and this can be distinct from overall popularity. If, at a given time in the market, there are two or three specialists who lack a rare 1866 pattern nickel with the Lincoln portrait (J-486 to J-488), a classic of the era, and one comes up for auction, there is apt to be intense competition. On the other hand, if this factor is absent and there is just one bidder, then the price will not achieve the same level.

While the long-term trend of rare coin prices has been upward, sometimes intermediate values can be different. The editor had the pleasure of cataloging the Garrett Collection of coins for The Johns Hopkins University, sold in a series of four auctions from 1979 through 1981. The combination of superb quality, great rarity, and a strong coin market yielded record prices. However, in the seventh edition of the Judd book, Abe Kosoff commented: "When a Garrett figure is quoted, it is well to remember that those figures proved to be very high. The current market value of most of the Garrett patterns is only about one-third of the Garrett prices, as an average; some are even less, some are higher." [13]

In the field of patterns, time seems to correct all such aberrations, and today in the early 21st century, there are many Garrett patterns that would be bargains at the "very high" figures of yesteryear!

In the early 1990s, there were two pattern buyers who eagerly sought coins of the $3 denomination: Harry W. Bass, Jr., and Richard J. Salisbury. Each had ample financial resources. Time and again, when a rare pattern came up for auction, all bets would be off as these men competed—and shattered all past records. After both passed to their final rewards, competition lessened, and rare patterns of the $3 denomination returned to a normal market demand.

Often the dispersal of a fine cabinet of patterns will stimulate the market, as with the Garrett Collection. Many buyers of other coins, who had not thought of acquiring patterns, turned to them now that they were available, and used the auction catalog as a wish-list, often beginning what turned out to be a deep involvement.

To reiterate, the long-term trend of pattern prices has been upward, but at any given time other conditions such as demand, overall market conditions, and competition can have an effect.

Prices in This Book

The prices listed in this book have been compiled by Robert L. Hughes (coordinator), John Gervasoni, Julian Leidman, Saul Teichman, Andrew Lustig, John Hamrick, and other consultants. The figures, generally given in three different grades, are intended to represent the approximate market value—the estimated price an informed numismatist would pay an informed seller.

For frequently traded patterns such as the 1856 Flying Eagle cent (J-180) and 1879 $4 Flowing Hair gold Stella (J-1635), there are many auction and price records, and value can be determined with some degree of certainty. Many other varieties of patterns are apt to come on the market at widely spaced intervals, and thus their values are more theoretical.

The actual market value of a pattern in an auction or private transaction might be higher or lower than the figures given. Also, another group of people or consultants might arrive at different values. Accordingly, purchase decisions should be made with deliberation, perhaps in consultation with a trustworthy professional numismatist or fellow pattern specialist.

The rare coin market is dynamic, and prices of this year are apt to be higher or lower next year, and to be different from what they were five or 10 years ago. In general, over a long period of time, values have trended upward, perhaps best illustrated by the Major Lenox R. Lohr Collection of more than 1,400 different pattern coins, purchased by the editor and James F. Ruddy in 1961, for $100,000, said cabinet including seven different varieties of 1792 issues. Today, the same collection would probably be worth on the far side of $10,000,000. The coins were sold rapidly in 1961 and 1962, and today repose in hundreds of different collections.

IN CONCLUSION

Patterns have a lot to offer, and by subscribing to dealer catalogs, keeping an eye out for interesting articles in periodicals, and becoming acquainted with other enthusiasts, you will come to deeply love and enjoy these coins.

I became a numismatist as a young teenager in 1952, soon acquired a copy of the 1913 book by Edgar H. Adams and William H. Woodin, *United States Pattern, Trial, and Experimental Pieces*, read it avidly, memorized much, and have been excited about patterns ever since! My involvements have been many, including buying and selling nearly all of the varieties listed in this book, handling major collections, and working with Dr. J. Hewitt Judd and Abe Kosoff with the first edition of this book. It has been great fun! Of course, my latest involvement is the book you are holding in your hand.

Beyond the coins themselves, there are many elements of history that beckon. There are the biographies and adventures of others who have gone before us—such collectors and scholars as T. Harrison Garrett, R. Coulton Davis, Edgar H. Adams, William H. Woodin, John W. Haseltine, Stephen K. Nagy, and others, down to Abe Kosoff, Sol Kaplan, King Farouk, Dr. J. Hewitt Judd, and dozens more of the mid- and late 20th century, plus all of those lovable "Mint rascals" of the 19th century. Today, a new generation carries the torch. Many of the contributors to the first edition of the Judd book, 1959, have slipped into history, but the coins and their stories endure.

User's Guide

Whitman Coin Grid™
Whitman Publishing proudly presents a unique approach to understanding the pattern market. With our specially developed Whitman Coin Grid™, we offer valuable tools to begin or continue a pattern collection.

Specifications and Rarity
In addition to the Judd number, date, and denomination, the Whitman Coin Grid shows the type of metal used to strike the coin, and the type of edging (lettered, plain, reeded, or, when a coin is no longer traceable, UN for "unknown"). The Whitman Coin Grid also includes the coin's rarity listing, a designation of the number of coins believed to exist. Our rarity scale is an update of the traditional Sheldon scale, modified for greater precision.

Population Data
Many collectors have their coins graded by professional services, such as ANACS, the Numismatic Guaranty Corporation of America, and the Professional Coin Grading Service. While other grading services are available, we have limited our population figures to represent the number of times ANACS, NGC, and PCGS (the primary companies in the industry) have graded specific varieties. Note that if a specific coin is graded twice, its population number (or "pop") will be 2. Therefore, population number does not always equate with the number of coins actually in existence. Further, a pattern might have auction details and a rarity listing, but a population of 0; in that case, it simply means the piece has not been certified and encapsulated by a third-party grading service.

Times at Auction
The T/A column shows the number of times a coin has been at auction. In many cases, with coins that are not yet actively traded in today's market, this information is still being researched, especially for coins auctioned prior to 1990. The numbers in this column are derived from the research of professional numismatists. When there is no number in the column, but an auction is listed, the auction predates 1990.

Last Traded at Auction
The Whitman Coin Grid describes each pattern's most recent auction activity: the firm or auctioneer who sold the piece; the date and the amount of the sale; and its grade. The "Amount" is the hammer price plus a buyer's fee (typically 15%). Some patterns were sold in multiple-piece lots in Sotheby's February 1954 auction of King Farouk's collection; these are listed without individual grades and amounts.

Pricing and Grading
The editor and publisher have asked recognized pattern experts (Robert Hughes, John Gervasoni, Julian Leidman, Andrew Lustig, and others) to consider pricing in as many as three grades per coin. These prices are based on years of numismatic expertise; even so, we cannot guarantee that a particular coin, sold in a particular grade, will meet the price listed. Actual market transactions may take place at lower or higher figures. The future price of a pattern or any other coin cannot be predicted with certainty. Moreover, other experts in patterns and numismatics may have different thoughts and ideas as to the rarity, value, importance, and other aspects of a pattern coin. Grades of pattern coins are also a matter of opinion, and grades assigned by experts and certification services can and often do vary, sometimes widely.

Research and Attribution
Certain patterns described as "unconfirmed" or "unverified," and pieces that have been delisted, or relisted under other numbers, represent the collective opinions of the core contributors. The publisher invites feedback on these listings, which may be studied for possible change in a future edition.

In instances in which entries are based upon catalog listings of decades ago, it may be the case that certain pieces, if examined by modern scholars, would be attributed differently, or different conclusions might be drawn regarding authenticity, status, or origin. In many instances, pattern coins and related issues were struck at a period later than that indicated on the dies. Some pieces were struck outside of the Mint. While many such circumstances are described, there may be others that are not. Study and scholarship continues.

The assignment of certain metals has often been arbitrary in the past. Pieces described in various texts as "copper" might actually be an alloy such as bronze; pieces described as "nickel" are often actually an alloy (such as 75% copper and 25% nickel). In more than just a few instances, specimens listed in past catalogs as, for example, "silver," have been found to be silver-plated copper. This research is reflected in the text and Whitman Coin Grids following. Appendix D describes metals commonly used in pattern production. The book's glossary lists terms often used by numismatists in the study of patterns.

Whitman Coin Grid (WCG™)

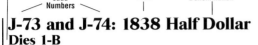

Obverse-Reverse Die Combination (if applicable)

Judd Numbers | Date | Denomination | Obverse | Judd Number of Piece Illustrated | Reverse

J-73 and J-74: 1838 Half Dollar
Dies 1-B

Silver pieces of 206-1/4 grains weight are believed to be originals; pieces of 192 grains, dies cracked, exhibit different states from light cracks to heavy cracks, the variety most often seen. • The copper striking is believed unique. From cracked reverse die.

Obverse: Liberty head.
Reverse: Flying eagle in plain field.

Historical Details

Description of Coin

J-73

Number	Metal	Edge	Rarity	Pop	T/A	Last Traded at Auction				60	63	65
						Firm	Date	Amount	Grade			
73	Silv	RE	5	55	40	Superior	5/2003	$9,775	NGCPF67	$3,100	$4,400	$8,000
74	C	RE	U	0	N/A	Macy's	6/1954	N/A	ChPF	N/A	N/A	N/A

Judd Numbers | Metal Used to Strike Coin | Coin's Edge | Rarity Listing (see below) | Number of Times Graded Professionally by ANACS, NGC, and PCGS | Number of Times at Significant Auctions Since 1990 | Auction House or Auctioneer (see below) | Last Date Coin Sold at Auction | Selling Price | Grade of Coin Sold (see below) | Prices You Might Expect To Pay For These Grade Levels

Reeded (RE); Plain (PE); Lettered (LE); Unknown (–)

Metal Listings (see Appendix D)

Alu: aluminum
Bil: billon
Brs: brass
Brz: bronze
C: copper
C-N: copper-nickel
Gold: gold
Golo: goloid
Lead: lead
Nick: nickel
Oro: oroide
Plat: platinum
Silv: silver
S-P: silver-plated
Tin: tin
WM: white metal
Zinc: zinc

Rarity Scale Abbreviations

1: more than 1,250 known to exist
2: 501–1,250
3: 201–500
4: 76–200
5: 31–75
L6: 21–30
H6: 13–20
L7: 7–12
H7: 4–6
8: 2–3
U: unique
–: existence unconfirmed

Auction Firm and Auctioneer Abbreviations

ANR: American Numismatic Rarities
MARCA: Mid-American Rare Coin Auctions
NASCA: Numismatic and Antiquarian Service Corporation
NERCG: New England Rare Coin Galleries
RARCOA: Rare Coin Company of America
SRCG: State Rare Coin Galleries

Grade Key

ANACS:	coin was graded by ANACS	**GemPF:**	gem Proof (PF-65)	**PlFl:**	planchet flaw
		ICG:	coin was graded by Independent Coin Grading	**PQ:**	premium quality
BN:	Brown (describes copper toning)			**RB:**	Red Brown (describes copper toning)
BrPF:	brilliant Proof	**ImpPF:**	impaired Proof	**RD:**	Red (describes copper toning)
BU:	brilliant Uncirculated	**MS:**	Mint State		
C, CA:	cameo	**NCS:**	coin was graded by Numismatic Conservation Service	**Scr:**	scratched
ChBU:	choice brilliant Uncirculated			**SEGS:**	coin was graded by Sovereign Entities Grading Service
ChPF:	choice Proof (PF-63)	**NGC:**	coin was graded by Numismatic Guaranty Corporation of America		
ChXF:	choice Extremely Fine			**S-P:**	silver-plated
Cld:	cleaned			**Unc:**	Uncirculated
Corr:	corroded	**PCGS:**	coin was graded by Professional Coin Grading Service	**VChPF:**	very choice Proof
DC, DCA:	deep cameo				
Dmg:	damaged	**PF:**	Proof		
EnvDmg:	environmental damage				

Patterns of 1792

History and Overview

In the summer of 1792, silver coins with the inscription denominated as HALF DISME were struck in Philadelphia. The style of the 1792 silver half disme is related to that of the famous copper Birch cent of the same year signed BIRCH, giving reason to attribute the authorship of the half disme to Birch as well.

Although the 1792 silver half disme has been called a pattern and is designated as J-7, it is most assuredly a coin made for general circulation. This is confirmed by the significant wear of such coins in existence today. However, there were a few copper impressions of the 1792 half disme, which can be called die trials, a category of patterns.

The other issues dated 1792 are indeed patterns in the typical sense inasmuch as they were made in very small quantities for examination and consideration, but not in large numbers for circulation. Included is the famous 1792 silver-center cent, J-1, which was an endeavor to create a coin with an intrinsic value of a cent, by using a small planchet of copper into which a silver plug was inserted at the center. Today, this is a famous and highly desired issue. This is the "cover coin" of this edition. Indeed, any and all 1792 coins are classics.

The 1792-dated eagle-on-globe pattern quarter dollar by Joseph Wright (J-12 and J-13) is especially elegant. Whether the dies for this were cut in 1792, or later in 1793, is not known. The breaking of the dies no doubt explains the extreme rarity of these pieces today. As the extant patterns are not from broken dies, the hardening likely occurred after these pieces were struck.

Collecting Perspective

The coinage of 1792 comprises slightly over a dozen different varieties, including the 1792 silver half disme. No patterns of 1792, nor any others through the first two decades of the Philadelphia Mint, were ever struck for numismatic or cabinet purposes, nor were any ever restruck from original dies.

J-1 and J-2: 1792 Silver-Center Cent

The dies possibly cut by Henry Voigt. One example of J-2 exists perforated at the center but lacking the silver plug, which was never inserted.

Obverse: Liberty head facing right, with hair flowing behind, and with the inscription LIBERTY PARENT OF SCIENCE & INDUSTRY: 1792, surrounding.
Reverse: A wreath, open at the top, tied with a ribbon at the bottom, enclosing the words ONE CENT, with UNITED STATES OF AMERICA surrounding and the fraction 1/100 below.

J-1

| Number | Metal | Edge | Rarity | Pop | T/A | Last Traded at Auction | | | | F/VF | EF | Unc |
						Firm	Date	Amount	Grade			
1	C/S-P	RE	H6	4	2	Stack's	1/2002	$414,000	BU	$110,000	$300,000	$525,000
2	C	RE	L7	2	2	Ira & Larry Goldberg	2/2005	$437,000	PCGSVF30PQ	$175,000	$600,000	N/A

J-3 to J-5: 1792 Birch Cent

Obverse: Liberty, facing right, bright-eyed and almost smiling, BIRCH lettered on neck truncation. Inscription LIBERTY PARENT OF SCIENCE & INDUSTRY around, and with the date 1792 just below the bust. On the truncation of the neck appears the word BIRCH, for the engraver of the dies. Today, no one has positively identified which Birch made the dies—perhaps William Birch or Thomas Birch.
Reverse: Wreath enclosing ONE CENT, UNITED STATES OF AMERICA around border. 1/100 below wreath.

J-4

| Number | Metal | Edge | Rarity | Pop | T/A | Last Traded at Auction | | | | F/VF | EF | Unc |
						Firm	Date	Amount	Grade			
3	C	PE	8	0	1	Stack's	5/1976	$42,000	Unc	N/A	N/A	$550,000
4	C	†	L7	2	1	Bowers & Merena	11/1988	$35,200	F15	$160,000	$300,000	$400,000
5	C	‡	8	0	1	Bowers & Merena	11/1988	$59,400	EF40	$175,000	$375,000	N/A

† Lettered edge reads TO BE ESTEEMED * BE USEFUL *
‡ Lettered edge reads TO BE ESTEEMED BE USEFUL*

J-6: 1792 Birch Cent

Dies seemingly from the same hand as the preceding.

Obverse: With curly hair and without the name BIRCH.
Reverse: In place of the fraction is the inscription: G.W. Pt, for "George Washington, President." One concept of the era, addressed in private coinage and tokens (but not in the federal series), was that of giving the name of the current president on coinage as it progressed, with a designation, such as PRESIDENT I, for Washington, the first.

J-6

Number	Metal	Edge	Rarity	Pop	T/A	Last Traded at Auction				F/VF	EF	Unc
						Firm	Date	Amount	Grade			
6	WM	PE	U	0	1	Bowers & Ruddy	1/1981	$90,000	Unc	N/A	N/A	$500,000

J-7 and J-8: 1792 Half Disme

This is the famous silver half disme of 1792. The quantity struck is not known, and a popular estimate seems to be about 1,500 to 2,000. These pieces circulated widely as regular issues and today most exhibit wear, often extensive, with more than just a few in such grades as AG-3, G-4, to VG-8, often with a few marks or dents. Higher-grade pieces are seen on occasion, in EF, AU, and, rarely, Mint State.

Obverse: Female head facing left, in the general style of the Birch cents and probably by the same engraver. Inscription LIB. PAR. Of SCIENCE & INDUSTRY around, 1792 below portrait.
Reverse: Eagle in flight with outstretched wings head toward top of coin, tail below. UNI. STATES OF AMERICA around, HALF DISME below.

J-7

Number	Metal	Edge	Rarity	Pop	T/A	Last Traded at Auction				F/VF	EF	Unc
						Firm	Date	Amount	Grade			
7	Silv	RE	4	109	22	ANR	7/2005	$138,000	PCGSAU55	$30,000	$85,000	$185,000
8	C	PE	U	0	1	Stack's	12/1983	$20,900	EF	N/A	N/A	N/A

J-9 to J-11: 1792 Disme

The 1792 disme occurs in one silver variety and two copper varieties, all of which are extremely rare, with J-10 more readily available than the others. Dies attributed to Henry Voigt.

Obverse: Liberty with flowing hair, quite similar style to J-1, but oriented in the opposite direction. The inscription surrounding is familiar: LIBERTY PARENT OF SCIENCE & INDUS, while the date 1792 is below the neck.
Reverse: Similar to the half disme, with eagle in flight, but with the denomination expressed as DISME.

J-10

Number	Metal	Edge	Rarity	Pop	T/A	Last Traded at Auction				F/VF	EF	Unc
						Firm	Date	Amount	Grade			
9	Silv	RE	8	0	1	Stack's	10/2000	$103,500	Net VG	$400,000	N/A	N/A
10	C	RE	H6	10	5	ANR	3/2004	$101,200	NGCEF40	$62,500	$150,000	$300,000
11	C	PE	8	1	2	Ira & Larry Goldberg	2/2005	$55,200	PCGSMS64BN	N/A	N/A	$300,000

J-12 and J-13: 1792 Eagle-on-Globe Quarter Dollar

Dies by Joseph Wright. In addition to the patterns of J-12 and J-13, uniface (single-sided) impressions exist of the obverse and reverse (see Appendix A).

Obverse: Liberty, her hair tied in a ribbon, facing right, small in size, permitting a large surrounding field, creating a cameo-like effect. The word LIBERTY is above and the date 1792 below.
Reverse: An American eagle perched on the top part of a globe, with the inscription UNITED STATES OF AMERICA surrounding, and a tiny circle near the border comprised of 87 little stars.

J-12

Number	Metal	Edge	Rarity	Pop	T/A	Last Traded at Auction				F/VF	EF	Unc
						Firm	Date	Amount	Grade			
12	C	RE	8	0	1	NY Coin & Stamp	6/1890	$210	Unc	N/A	N/A	N/A
13	WM	PE	H7	0	1	Bowers & Merena	11/1988	$28,600	EF	$65,000	$86,000	N/A

Patterns of 1794

History and Overview

The 1794 pattern half disme (J-14) and the pattern silver dollar (J-18) are similar in style to the later-issued circulation coins, but lack obverse stars. Concerning half dimes, although dies for regular coinage were prepared in 1794 and are so dated, these dies were first employed in calendar year 1795.

Collecting Perspective

All patterns of this year are exceedingly rare or even unique and are virtually non-collectible. Nearly all show evidence of wear and/or oxidation.

Although 1794-dated pattern coins have appeared on the market occasionally, they are sufficiently rare that it is not possible to collect them systematically. With patience and a measure of luck, perhaps a dedicated numismatist could acquire one or two examples during a collecting lifetime. These pieces have not, however, commanded high auction prices because the grades were less than the popular Mint State (or Proof) categories sought by investors, and, further, the market for such pieces was mainly with sophisticated buyers and not widespread.

J-14: 1794 Half Disme

The unique specimen of this highly important issue rests in the National Numismatic Collection in the Smithsonian Institution and certainly is one of the most significant of all early patterns.

Obverse: Liberty facing right, hair flowing in luxuriant tresses, LIBERTY above, and 1794 below. No stars (and thus differing in style from the half dimes made for circulation).

Reverse: Pattern die, style never used for general circulation, with perched eagle, low at the center, with UNITED STATES OF AMERICA / HALF DISME surrounding. This pattern continues the half disme nomenclature of 1792 (J-7).

J-14

Number	Metal	Edge	Rarity	Pop	T/A	Last Traded at Auction				F/VF	EF	Unc
						Firm	Date	Amount	Grade			
14	C	RE	U	0	0	N/A	N/A	N/A	N/A	N/A	N/A	N/A

J-15 and J-16: 1794 Half Dime

Struck from regular dies. There are three different varieties of this: Valentine-2, Logan McCloskey-2. Unique specimen once owned by Virgil M. Brand (1861–1926), the most acquisitive American numismatist of all time. • V-3, LM-3 (ex Stickney and Woodin collections). • V-4, LM-4 (ex Parsons Collection). • J-15 (V-3 and -4). • J-16 (V-2).

J-15

Number	Metal	Edge	Rarity	Pop	T/A	Last Traded at Auction				F/VF	EF	Unc
						Firm	Date	Amount	Grade			
15	C	RE	8	2	1	Stack's	7/1985	$7,370	AU	N/A	$65,000	$125,000
16	C	PE	U	1	1	Stack's	1/1987	$3,190	VF	$155,000	N/A	N/A

J-17: 1794 Half Dollar

Struck from regular dies. Four known pieces are in the form of undertypes on 1795 half cents (the half cents being the Cohen-6a variety, the undertype half dollars being the Overton-101, -104, -105, and -105a die combinations). These half dollars were struck as die trials, and afterward planchets to strike half cents were cut from them. However, certain features of the half dollar inscriptions can still be discerned. In addition, there are two intact specimens (not cut down for use as a half cent) in the Smithsonian Institution and in a Vienna museum, dies of Overton-109 with lettered edges.

J-17

Number	Metal	Edge	Rarity	Pop	T/A	Last Traded at Auction				F/VF	EF	Unc
						Firm	Date	Amount	Grade			
17	C	LE	H7	0	2	ANR	6/2004	$13,800	VG10	$15,000	N/A	N/A

Patterns of 1794

J-18: 1794 Silver Dollar

The edge is lettered HUNDRED CENTS ONE DOLLAR OR UNIT, with decorations between the words.

Obverse: Without stars, its distinguishing feature. Otherwise similar to the die cut for the regular-issue 1794 silver dollar. Head of Liberty, with flowing hair, facing right, the inscription LIBERTY above and the date 1794 below. This die is not the same die (later with stars added) known to strike regular 1794 dollars.

Reverse: The regular die used to strike silver dollars of 1794, perched eagle within wreath, UNITED STATES OF AMERICA around border.

J-18

Number	Metal	Edge	Rarity	Pop	T/A	Last Traded at Auction				F/VF	EF	Unc
						Firm	Date	Amount	Grade			
18	C	LE	U	1	1	Ira & Larry Goldberg	2/2001	$92,000	PCGSVF20	$170,000	N/A	N/A

J-19: 1794 Silver Dollar

Struck from regular dies, with standard edge lettering, as above. This unique pattern appeared in a series of sales from the 19th to the mid-20th century (Stack's Davis-Graves sale, 1954), and now reposes in the National Numismatic Collection at the Smithsonian Institution.

J-19

Number	Metal	Edge	Rarity	Pop	T/A	Last Traded at Auction				F/VF	EF	Unc
						Firm	Date	Amount	Grade			
19	C	LE	U	0	1	Stack's	4/1954	$1,400	PF	N/A	N/A	N/A

Patterns of 1795

History and Overview

The pattern coins of 1795 are primarily copper strikings of silver denominations, except that the dies used were also employed for regular circulating coinage.

Collecting Perspective

Patterns of this year are for all practical purposes uncollectible, although occasional pieces appear on the market at widely spaced intervals. A possible exception is J-20, very rare and in great demand by collectors of regular copper cents, but not in the rarity league of the others. As patterns of this year were not made for numismatic purposes, most show handling or other evidence of wear.

J-20: 1795 Cent

Copper cent from the regular dies used to coin Sheldon-79 (Breen-1677, dies 6-G), flowing hair style, but with reeded edge. These seem to have been struck on 168-grain planchets. The edge has vertical raised ridges or reeds. About a half dozen pieces are known, the demand for which is exceedingly strong as these are listed among regular-issue copper cents.

J-20

Number	Metal	Edge	Rarity	Pop	T/A	Last Traded at Auction				F/VF	EF	Unc
						Firm	Date	Amount	Grade			
20	C	RE	H7	0	1	Superior	1/1989	$63,800	G6	$160,000	N/A	N/A

Patterns of 1795

J-21: 1795 Half Dime

Struck from regular dies. Only two known: one in the
Congress Hall Collection in Philadelphia, defaced, V-6;
the other pierced and plugged.

J-21

Number	Metal	Edge	Rarity	Pop	T/A	Last Traded at Auction				F/VF	EF	Unc
						Firm	Date	Amount	Grade			
21	C	RE	8	0	1	Mason & Co.	6/1870	$19	PF	N/A	N/A	N/A

J-22: 1795 Half Dollar

Struck in copper from regular dies (Overton-117), made
as a pattern to test the dies, then run through compres-
sion rollers and used as a planchet strip; a disk for a half
cent was cut from it. This pattern half dollar is actually
known to us only through traces visible on a half cent.
Believed to be unique.

J-22

Number	Metal	Edge	Rarity	Pop	T/A	Last Traded at Auction				F/VF	EF	Unc
						Firm	Date	Amount	Grade			
22	C	LE	U	0	1	Superior	2/1974	$1,550	VG	N/A	N/A	N/A

J-23: 1795 $5

Struck from regular dies. Two confirmed to exist:
Breen-1A (defaced); and Breen-3D (not defaced;
weakly struck).

J-23

Number	Metal	Edge	Rarity	Pop	T/A	Last Traded at Auction				F/VF	EF	Unc
						Firm	Date	Amount	Grade			
23	C	RE	8	5	1	Ira & Larry Goldberg	2/2001	$13,800	PCGSVG10	$35,000	N/A	N/A

Patterns of 1796

History and Overview

There are no known patterns dated 1796, although this was a pivotal year for the introduction of new denominations—
the dime, quarter dollar, and quarter eagle. Without doubt, different trial pieces must have been made for the new
denominations. No records of any exist today. The piece described below is a later restrike that bears the date 1796,
but has no connection with true patterns of that year.

Collecting Perspective

While no patterns made in 1796 exist today, listed under this date is a white metal impression, probably made generations later from dies discarded as scrap by the Mint.

J-23a: 1796 $2.50

Struck from regular dies, no stars, private restrike.
Made decades after the date on the dies. Rusted dies,
partially reeded edge. Believed to be unique.

J-23a

Number	Metal	Edge	Rarity	Pop	T/A	Last Traded at Auction				F/VF	EF	Unc
						Firm	Date	Amount	Grade			
23a	WM	RE	U	0	1	Heritage	3/1998	$5,520	Unc	N/A	N/A	$15,000

History and Overview

Two pattern die varieties from 1797 are known, both being trial impressions from regular dies used to strike gold coins. As is true of other patterns of the era, these were made strictly for utilitarian purposes, to test the appearance of the dies, with no numismatic considerations.

Collecting Perspective

Of the two pattern varieties of this year, only one example of each has been traced, making them essentially non-collectible, although they are each held in the private sector.

Both were defaced after they were struck, to prevent them from being gilt and passed into circulation. One can envision that such copper patterns were made for many other denominations and dies in this era, and then destroyed, probably by recycling through the melting and rolling process to create strips from which half cent and cent planchets were cut.

In the present instance, the defacing marks are part of the history and personality of the patterns and are not considered to be a negative aspect.

J-24: 1797 $5

Trial striking from regular dies for the half eagle, 16-Star obverse, Small Eagle reverse, possibly the dies known as Breen-12. This piece, defaced by blows from the edge of a tool, was preserved, remarkably, for later generations of numismatists, although undoubtedly at the time of issue it was meant to have been discarded. Today, a gold impression of this die pair is known to exist, residing in the Harry W. Bass, Jr. Foundation Collection.

J--24

Number	Metal	Edge	Rarity	Pop	T/A	Last Traded at Auction				F/VF	EF	Unc
						Firm	Date	Amount	Grade			
24	C	RE	U	0	1	Bowers & Merena	6/1988	$2,310	Net VG	$15,000	N/A	N/A

J-25: 1797 $10

Struck from regular dies. Breen-2B variety, Heraldic Eagle reverse. The single known piece is well-worn and once bent, perhaps carried as a pocket piece or souvenir. A highly significant example representing the earliest known pattern coin of this, the largest gold denomination at the time.

J-25

Number	Metal	Edge	Rarity	Pop	T/A	Last Traded at Auction				F/VF	EF	Unc
						Firm	Date	Amount	Grade			
25	C	RE	U	1	1	Bowers & Ruddy	11/1974	$550	F15	N/A	N/A	N/A

Patterns of 1799

History and Overview

By 1799 the Philadelphia Mint had been in operation for the better part of the decade, routinely turning out coins from the half cent to the $10 gold piece. Numismatically, the year is best remembered in the regular series for the large copper cent, the rarest regular date of the 1793–1857 years.

The pattern listing for the year 1799 is a unique piece. Our knowledge of pattern coins of this era comes from a few copper strikings of silver and gold denominations, pieces intended as patterns and probably intended to be destroyed, but kept as souvenirs or otherwise preserved. No doubt at the time there were unadopted ideas of other pieces that would be interesting to contemplate now, but no record of them has been located.

Collecting Perspective

Just one 1799 pattern is known, a $10 piece from regular dies struck in copper. It has appeared at auction several times, never attracting much attention as it was deliberately damaged soon after it was made.

J-26: 1799 $10

Struck from regular dies. Defaced on the reverse by two impressions of a chisel, crosswise, intended to mark the piece as having been used for pattern purposes, and therefore no longer of relevance or value. This piece appeared in the Lorin G. Parmelee sale (June 1890, Lot 15), with a notation, "purchased in the Mint."[1]

J-26

Number	Metal	Edge	Rarity	Pop	T/A	Last Traded at Auction				F/VF	EF	Unc
						Firm	Date	Amount	Grade			
26	C	RE	U	0	2	Bowers & Merena	9/1994	$5,775	MS60BN	N/A	N/A	$13,500

Patterns of 1803

History and Overview

In 1803 the Philadelphia Mint continued to be the only federal coinage facility. Recent years had not been easy for the Mint, as there had been disruptions due to yellow fever epidemics, shortages of metal, and other problems, not to overlook occasional resistance from members of Congress who sought to abolish the Mint, in favor of having coinage performed by private contract.

Although pattern coins and trial strikings may have been made in 1803, no record of them survives today.[2] The piece listed below is of a different nature—made outside of the Mint at a later date, although from an 1803 die.

Collecting Perspective

The unique "pattern" of this year is a restrike from dies not necessarily correctly matched, although the variety has not been examined to confirm this. It is in the category of a private restrike, among many such pieces listed in the present text.

J-27 and J-27a: 1803 $5

Private restrikes. Copper striking of a half eagle, a restrike privately produced probably circa the late 1850s from rusted dies, not necessarily matching a pair actually used for coinage. Information concerning this issue is elusive.

Number	Metal	Edge	Rarity	Pop	T/A	Last Traded at Auction				F/VF	EF	Unc
						Firm	Date	Amount	Grade			
27	C	PE	8	0	0	N/A	N/A	N/A	N/A	N/A	N/A	N/A
27a	Brs	PE	U	0	0	N/A	N/A	N/A	N/A	N/A	N/A	N/A

History and Overview

True pattern coins and trial strikes of 1804 may or may not have been struck. No record of them exists today. In the regular series, the year 1804 achieved its own measure of fame from two factors: the copper cent (being the scarcest 19th-century date of the denomination), and the 1804-dated silver dollar, now popularly known as "The King of American Coins" (made in several varieties, first struck in 1834 but from new dies dated 1804).

In the early 1800s, there was little or no numismatic interest in the United States coinage series, and not even the Mint preserved specimens of its own products. Thus, the various pieces regularly struck during this era slipped into circulation, these being the denominations of the half cent, cent, dime, quarter dollar, $2.50, $5, and $10.

Any die trials that were made were probably of copper and were defaced or melted after examination.

In 1834, the Mint desired to present as diplomatic gifts a number of sets reflecting current (1834) coinage as well as two other denominations no longer being struck in 1834, but believed to have last been struck in 1804, these being the silver dollar and gold $10. Appropriate dies were not on hand, and new dies were created for the $1 and $10, differing from the originals in several stylistic aspects including more modern numerals and plain (rather than crosslet) style 4, a beaded border, and certain other more modern characteristics. The quantity struck is not recorded, but was probably very small. Today eight related 1804 silver dollars are known, and four 1804 gold $10 pieces are known (J-33), suggesting that at least a few other 1804 $10 pieces may have existed at one time. These $10 coins have a brilliant Proof finish quite unlike originals. Examples are highly priced and are cherished for what they are, novodels made not for numismatic purposes, but for diplomatic presentation purposes and thus of great historical importance.

The so-called "restrike," sometimes incorrectly called the "Mint restrike," of the 1804 cent is a private production utilizing rusted dies discarded as old iron by the Mint. The obverse was originally used to coin 1803 cents, but was altered in the 1860s to read 1804. The reverse is a cent die of a later date and type.[3]

Collecting Perspective

The several pieces listed as patterns for this year all have special stories and fall into the category of private restrikes from mismatched dies or, in the case of the $10, a later striking from dies bearing an earlier date.

The 1804 $10 strikings have a market demand from specialists in gold coins as well as from pattern enthusiasts.

J-28: 1804 Cent

Private restrike. Believed to have been struck in Philadelphia by an unknown person, circa 1860s, to create a "filler" for collectors who had not been able to locate this rare date. Copper strikings (not listed here) are plentiful. Traditionally listed as tin (here as white metal). Two specimens known.

Obverse: Die originally used to strike 1803-dated cents, Sheldon-261, crudely altered so that the last digit would represent a 4.
Reverse: Die of an incorrect style for 1804, a later type (originally used to strike 1820 copper cents of the variety Newcomb-12).

J-28

Number	Metal	Edge	Rarity	Pop	T/A	Last Traded at Auction				F/VF	EF	Unc
						Firm	Date	Amount	Grade			
28	WM	PE	8	1	1	Superior	5/2003	$17,250	MS60	N/A	N/A	$25,000

J-29 to J-32: 1804 $5

Private restrikes. Rough surfaces due to die finish.[4]

Obverse: 1804-dated half eagle die, either an original 1804 die or one altered to 1804 from a circa-1807 die of the same type.[5]
Reverse: Die of the 1804 era "strengthened to near unrecognizability."[6]

J-30

Number	Metal	Edge	Rarity	Pop	T/A	Last Traded at Auction				F/VF	EF	Unc
						Firm	Date	Amount	Grade			
29	Silv	RE	8	0	1	Kosoff	8/1958	$250	PF	N/A	N/A	N/A
30	Silv	PE	8	0	1	Bowers & Merena	5/1999	$13,800	MS65	N/A	N/A	$22,500
31	C	RE	8	0	1	Kagin's	1/1975	$2,550	Unc	N/A	N/A	N/A
31a	C	PE	8	1	0	N/A	N/A	N/A	N/A	N/A	N/A	N/A
32	WM	PE	8	1	1	Superior	9/1998	withdrawn	NGC63	N/A	N/A	$26,000

Patterns of 1804

J-33 to J-34a: 1804 $10

Struck from regular dies. Mint novodel for diplomatic presentation.

Obverse: New or novodel die created at the Mint in 1834, but bearing the date 1804, and of the design of original 1804 $10 coins.
Reverse: Novodel die created in 1834, of the 1804 design type.

J-33

Number	Metal	Edge	Rarity	Pop	T/A	Last Traded at Auction				F/VF	EF	Unc
						Firm	Date	Amount	Grade			
33	Gold	RE	8	0	1	Stack's	10/1988	$290,000	GemPF	N/A	N/A	$675,000
34	Silv	RE	H7	1	1	Bowers & Merena	5/1992	$13,200	PF58	N/A	N/A	$90,000
34a	Silv	PE	U	0	0	N/A	N/A	N/A	N/A	N/A	N/A	N/A

Patterns of 1805

History and Overview

As with the previous year, no relevant pattern records have come to the attention of the numismatic community. However, there are certain private restrikes from discarded dies that have been classified under the year 1805.

In 1805 at the Mint, production of regular denominations for circulation included the half cent, cent, half dime, dime, quarter dollar, half dollar, $2.50, and $5. Silver dollars had not been coined since 1804, and those few that were struck in the year 1804 were from dies dated earlier, possibly 1803. The $10 denomination was discontinued in 1804 and would not be struck again until 1838.

Collecting Perspective

The private restrikes listed below are not patterns, but have been adopted into the series by many early catalogers and compilers of texts including Adams, Woodin, and Judd. These pieces provide interesting alternatives for numismatists to acquire off-metal strikes of these dates, an era from which contemporary patterns are not available.

J-35: 1805 Quarter Dollar

Private restrike. Regular dies, possibly mismatched.
Listed tentatively, pending further investigation.

Obverse: Regular 1805 die.
Reverse: Regular die of the 1804 through 1807 style.

Number	Metal	Edge	Rarity	Pop	T/A	Last Traded at Auction				F/VF	EF	Unc
						Firm	Date	Amount	Grade			
35	C	RE	U	0	1	Haseltine	4/1882	$0.30	G	N/A	N/A	N/A

J-36 to J-38: 1805 $5

Private restrikes. Regular dies, possibly mismatched.

Obverse: 1805 half eagle die of the regular design.
Reverse: Regular Heraldic Eagle $5 die of the era.

J-38

Number	Metal	Edge	Rarity	Pop	T/A	Last Traded at Auction				F/VF	EF	Unc
						Firm	Date	Amount	Grade			
36	Silv	PE	8	0	1	Kagin's	5/1972	$3,100	Unc	N/A	N/A	$25,000
37	C	PE	8	1	2	Bowers & Merena	4/2005	$16,388	NGCPF64BN	N/A	N/A	$22,500
38	WM	PE	8	1	2	Bowers & Merena	4/2005	$16,675	NGCMS63	N/A	N/A	$22,500

Patterns of 1806

History and Overview

Continuing the preceding theme, no patterns are known to have actually been produced in the calendar year 1806, although some may have been made. At the time there was no numismatic interest in patterns, and none were saved for cabinet purposes, nor has anyone ever located records of their production. The piece listed under this date is a curious die combination of unknown origin and purpose.

The year 1806 was a busy one at the Mint, with substantial quantities of coinage made of different denominations, including the half cent, cent, quarter dollar, half dollar, $2.50, and $5.

A half dollar obverse die survives from this year and is presently owned by the American Numismatic Society. In the early 20th century it was used to make a series of uniface impressions and other items for collectors (see Appendix A).

Collecting Perspective

The copper quarter dollar/cent is unique.

J-38a: 1806 Quarter Dollar/Cent

Private restrike, cent mule. A very curious piece struck over a Matron Head large copper cent of the style first made in 1816.

Obverse: Regular quarter dollar die of 1806.
Reverse: Die used to coin the 1807 cent, variety not known to have been used for regular coinage.[7]

J-38a

Number	Metal	Edge	Rarity	Pop	T/A	Last Traded at Auction				F/VF	EF	Unc
						Firm	Date	Amount	Grade			
38a	C	PE	U	0	1	Superior	6/2002	$4,600	G2	N/A	N/A	N/A

Patterns of 1808

History and Overview

Patterns of 1808 are private restrikes made in the 1860s or later from dies discarded by the Mint as scrap metal. These dies existed into the 20th century, and may exist now, but information concerning their restriking is not known.

Collecting Perspective

These private restrikes come on the market at widely spaced intervals and are desirable for what they are. The surfaces of the coins are rough due to rust on the dies.

J-39 and J-40: 1808 $5

Private restrikes. J-39 (reeded-edge) pieces are unconfirmed, as all the listings from the 1800s do not note the edge. About a half dozen examples of J-40 are believed to exist, including one in the Durham Western Heritage Museum.

Obverse: 1808 half eagle die of the regular design by John Reich.
Reverse: Regular Heraldic Eagle $5 die of an earlier era (last regularly used for coinage in 1807).

J-40

Number	Metal	Edge	Rarity	Pop	T/A	Last Traded at Auction				F/VF	EF	Unc
						Firm	Date	Amount	Grade			
39	Silv	RE	8	0	0	N/A	N/A	N/A	N/A	N/A	N/A	$25,000
40	Silv	PE	H7	0	1	Superior	8/1979	$2,100	Unc	N/A	N/A	$25,000

29

Patterns of 1810

History and Overview

The listed variety of this year is a private restrike from mismatched dies. This year continues the long stretch after 1799 for which no contemporary pattern or trial pieces are known to exist.

J-41, a private restrike from mismatched dies, combines an 1810 cent obverse (Sheldon-285) with a reverse used in 1820 to strike cents of the Newcomb-12 variety. This identical reverse was used to make the so-called "restrike" 1804 cents in copper and tin (here listed as white metal).

Collecting Perspective

Examples of the 1810 cent in white metal are very rare. Demand for them comes not from only pattern specialists, but also from cent enthusiasts.

J-41: 1810 Cent

Private restrike.

Obverse: 1810 cent die used to strike Sheldon-285.
Reverse: Cent die used to strike 1820 cents of the Newcomb-12 variety, a different style from that originally used in 1810. This reverse die was also used to make a private restrike.

J-41

Number	Metal	Edge	Rarity	Pop	T/A	Last Traded at Auction				F/VF	EF	Unc
						Firm	Date	Amount	Grade			
41	WM	PE	8	0	1	Bowers & Merena	3/1997	$8,250	AU	N/A	N/A	$45,000

Patterns of 1813

History and Overview

The listings for 1813 are limited to private restrikes of the half dollar denomination. No contemporary patterns have been recorded, and almost nothing is known about experiments and ideas tried at the Mint during this era.

Collecting Perspective

The so-called restrikes of this year were made generations later from dies discarded as scrap iron by the Mint. The obverse die was originally used to strike 1813 half dollars of the Overton-107 variety, while the reverse was originally employed to strike 1810 Overton-104 coins. The varieties known as J-42 and J-43 are highly collectible and highly desired in their own right today, specialists recognizing them for what they are. Examples are very rare.

J-42 and J-43: 1813 Half Dollar

Private restrikes. Rusted and mismatched dies.

Obverse: Regular-issue die originally used to strike the Overton-107 variety.
Reverse: Regular-issue die originally used to strike Overton-104.

J-43

Number	Metal	Edge	Rarity	Pop	T/A	Last Traded at Auction				F/VF	EF	Unc
						Firm	Date	Amount	Grade			
42	C	PE	8	0	1	Kagin's	11/1974	$4,625	Unc	N/A	N/A	$32,500
43	Brs	PE	8	0	1	Bowers & Merena	11/2002	$12,650	MS63	N/A	N/A	$30,000

Patterns of 1814

History and Overview

In existence today are three examples struck in platinum of the 1814 half dollar, obverse and reverse in regular combination, dies unrusted, normally used to strike Overton-107 in silver. These pieces were struck in 1814, or perhaps in 1815.[1] Platinum was considered to be a precious metal at the time, but was not widely used in the Western Hemisphere for wrought items or coinage.

The circumstances of the production of the platinum 1814 half dollars are not known. One example bears the letter P counterstamped many times on the obverse, and with the word "Platina" engraved on the reverse by the eagle's head, this referring to platinum.

Collecting Perspective

J-44 is of special importance as the only known 19th-century pattern coin to have been made in platinum, and, further, as an object of desire by collectors of Capped Bust half dollars of the 1807–1836 design. Moreover, it is one of only a few original early 19th-century United States pattern coin varieties in existence today.

J-44: 1814 Half Dollar

Just three examples are known today, one of which is in the National Numismatic Collection of the Smithsonian Institution. Another piece has 33 P's punched on the obverse, and the word PLATINA engraved on the reverse in cursive.

Obverse: Regular die used to strike variety Overton-107.
Reverse: Regular reverse die used to strike variety Overton-107.

J-44

| Number | Metal | Edge | Rarity | Pop | T/A | Last Traded at Auction | | | | F/VF | EF | Unc |
						Firm	Date	Amount	Grade			
44	Plat	LE	8	0	1	Bowers & Merena	11/2002	$50,600	AU50	N/A	$50,000	$75,000

Patterns of 1818

History and Overview

The listing for 1818 is a private restrike from mismatched dies of 1818, restruck no earlier than the 1850s, from dies discarded from the Mint as scrap metal. No contemporary patterns are known to exist for any year after 1814 through the early 1830s.

Collecting Perspective

The sole variety listed for this year combines the obverse originally used to make 1818 quarter dollars of the Browning-2 variety with an incongruous reverse die used to make 1818 copper cents of the Newcomb-8 variety.

J-45: 1818 Quarter Dollar/Cent

Restrike. Struck over a reeded-edge quarter dollar. Probably struck circa 1860s.

Obverse: 1818 quarter dollar obverse die, Browning-2.
Reverse: Cent die used to coin 1818 cents of the Newcomb-8 variety.

J-45

| Number | Metal | Edge | Rarity | Pop | T/A | Last Traded at Auction | | | | F/VF | EF | Unc |
						Firm	Date	Amount	Grade			
45	Silv	RE	U	0	1	Stack's	3/1985	$8,800	Unc	N/A	N/A	$22,500

Patterns of 1823

History and Overview
Although no record exists of patterns being struck in 1823, there are impressions in silver of the so-called 1823 cent private restrike from mismatched dies.

Collecting Perspective
The cent restrikes from this year were made outside of the Mint circa 1860, by mismatching two dies. Dr. Judd noted that 12 pieces were restruck by dealer John W. Haseltine in 1878 and 1879. This may be the case, but information provided by Haseltine is notoriously unreliable. Probably more than 1,000 copper restrikes were made over a period of time. These are highly collectible and readily located today (copper impressions are not listed here). Several die states exist. The dies exist today.

Demand for this variety, especially the silver impressions, comes not only from pattern enthusiasts, but also from cent specialists.

J-46: 1823 Cent
Private restrike. J-46a, the regular restrike in copper, has been delisted.

Obverse: Die used originally to strike 1823 Newcomb-2 cents, rusted, cracked, and relapped.
Reverse: Die used originally to strike copper cents of 1813, Sheldon-293.

J-46

| Number | Metal | Edge | Rarity | Pop | T/A | Last Traded at Auction | | | | F/VF | EF | Unc |
						Firm	Date	Amount	Grade			
46	Silv	PE	L7	0	1	Bowers & Merena	3/1997	$6,600	MS63	N/A	N/A	$20,000

J-47: 1823 Half Dollar
Examples seen to date have not been verified as genuine.

| Number | Metal | Edge | Rarity | Pop | T/A | Last Traded at Auction | | | | F/VF | EF | Unc |
						Firm	Date	Amount	Grade			
47	C	N/A	–	0	0	N/A	N/A	N/A	N/A	Unconf	Unconf	Unconf

Patterns of 1827

History and Overview
If any patterns were produced at the Philadelphia Mint in 1827, no record of them exists today. However, there is a copper version of the 1827 restrike quarter dollar from mismatched dies. Silver restrikes have been added as J-48a, these being very early restrikes from polished dies, with an appearance quite unlike the rusted-die restrikes normally seen.

Collecting Perspective
The restrike quarter dollars of 1827 were made at an unknown location, perhaps at the Mint itself, from mismatched dies, probably in the 1850s. The obverse is the regular die for the 1827/3 quarter dollar (a great rarity in original form),[2] while the reverse is from another variety, used in 1819. Two silver restrikes are known from unrusted dies, indicating a separate coinage at an earlier time. These are from highly polished dies showing striae from the polishing process.

J-48 and J-48a: 1827 Quarter Dollar
Restrikes. Silver restrikes include two from unrusted dies and apparently struck in a modified "close" collar; struck over quarter dollars of the 1804 through 1807 Draped Bust obverse, Heraldic Eagle reverse type. All copper restrikes are from rusted dies.

Obverse: Die used to strike 1827/3 quarter dollars.
Reverse: Die used to strike 1819 quarters of the Browning-2 variety (with square-base 2 in 25C, unlike the curl-base 2 on original strikings of 1827 quarters).[3]

J-48

| Number | Metal | Edge | Rarity | Pop | T/A | Last Traded at Auction | | | | F/VF | EF | Unc |
						Firm	Date	Amount	Grade			
48	C	RE	H7	5	4	Stack's	1/2004	$37,375	PCGSPF65RB	N/A	N/A	$45,000
48a	Silv	RE	8	0	1	Bowers & Merena	4/1997	$77,000	PF65	N/A	N/A	$130,000

History and Overview

Listed as a pattern for this date is an 1831 striking from regular quarter eagle dies, but in silver rather than gold. Apparently, one or more of these were struck in the same date as on the coin. It has been suggested that this may be a "mint error," struck on a silver dime planchet. If so, it is unlikely to have escaped from the Mint as a ten-cent piece.

Collecting Perspective

The silver quarter eagle of 1831, J-49, is unique.

J-49: 1831 $2.50

This is possibly a mint error, struck on a dime planchet (see Taxay, *Comprehensive Catalogue and Encyclopedia*).

Obverse: Regular 1831 die used to coin circulation strikes as well as Proof quarter eagles.
Reverse: Regular die used to coin circulation strikes as well as Proof quarter eagles.

J-49

Number	Metal	Edge	Rarity	Pop	T/A	Last Traded at Auction				F/VF	EF	Unc
						Firm	Date	Amount	Grade			
49	Silv	RE	U	0	0	N/A	N/A	N/A	N/A	N/A	N/A	N/A

History and Overview

During the years from circa 1820 leading up to 1834, federal gold coins were worth more in bullion or melt-down value than in face value. Such pieces were coined on demand for depositors who placed gold bullion or foreign coins with the Mint and asked for returns in the largest denomination of the time, the half eagle, plus some smaller requests for quarter eagles. Such coins were largely used in the export trade where they were valued as bullion, not at face value, and were useful in international transactions. Today, the majority of regular gold coins of the 1820s and early 1830s no longer exist, as they were melted down in foreign lands and converted to other coins.

Collecting Perspective

No examples are known of the quarter eagle patterns, although they are something to look for among offerings of regular 1833 $2.50 pieces of this year.

J-49a to J-49f: 1833 $2.50

All are unconfirmed. According to Taxay, these should have periods punched over the eagle's heads. J-49a: No. 1 in the Moore list given above. Pure gold. 61-7/8 grains. • J-49b: No. 2 in the Moore list. Gold with silver as an alloy. 67-1/2 grains. • J-49c: No. 3 in the Moore list. Gold alloyed with silver and copper, the last two metals in equal proportions. 67-1/2 grains. • J-49d: No. 4 in the Moore list. Gold alloyed with copper, the standard composition for regular issues. Not a pattern, but listed here as part of the suite of other pieces, for reference. 67-1/2 grains. • J-49e: No. 5 in the Moore list. Gold alloyed with silver and copper, the last two metals in equal proportions. 66 grains. • J-49f: No. 6 in the Moore list. Gold alloyed with silver and copper, with one part silver and two parts copper. 66 grains.

Obverse: Regular die used to strike 1834 quarter eagles of the old style (1821–1834 design).
Reverse: Regular die with motto (E PLURIBUS UNUM) used to strike 1834 quarter eagles of the old style (1821–1834 design).

J-49a

Number	Metal	Edge	Rarity	Pop	T/A	Last Traded at Auction				F/VF	EF	Unc
						Firm	Date	Amount	Grade			
49a	Gold	RE	–	0	0	N/A	N/A	N/A	N/A	Unconf	Unconf	Unconf
49b	Gold	RE	–	0	0	N/A	N/A	N/A	N/A	Unconf	Unconf	Unconf
49c	Gold	RE	–	0	0	N/A	N/A	N/A	N/A	Unconf	Unconf	Unconf
49d	Gold	RE	–	0	0	N/A	N/A	N/A	N/A	Unconf	Unconf	Unconf
49e	Gold	RE	–	0	0	N/A	N/A	N/A	N/A	Unconf	Unconf	Unconf
49f	Gold	RE	–	0	0	N/A	N/A	N/A	N/A	Unconf	Unconf	Unconf

Patterns of 1834

History and Overview
There is but one pattern listed this year, again a private restrike, in this instance a quarter dollar. Half eagle die impressions in copper of the new Classic Head design (J-51 and J-51a) are listed tentatively until examples are studied.

Collecting Perspective
One or two restrikes in copper exist of an 1834-dated quarter dollar struck from rusted dies, the obverse used to originally strike Browning-3 and -5, the reverse identity not known. Little is known about the copper $5 pieces. At least one well-known piece (the Byron Reed example) has been found to be a counterfeit.

J-50: 1834 Quarter Dollar
Private restrike. Rusted dies.

Obverse: Die originally used to strike 1834 quarter dollars of the Browning-3 and -5 varieties. 1 in date and some dentils now strengthened.
Reverse: Quarter dollar die of contemporary style, but not known to have been used to strike quarter dollars in 1834.

J-50

Number	Metal	Edge	Rarity	Pop	T/A	Last Traded at Auction				F/VF	EF	Unc
						Firm	Date	Amount	Grade			
50	C	PE	U	0	1	Bowers & Merena	11/1989	$154	F15	N/A	N/A	N/A

J-51a and J-51: 1834 $5
Regular Classic Head type dies. No positively authentic specimen of either edge variety has been seen by the contributors to this text. The piece illustrated is a fake.

J-51a (fake)

Number	Metal	Edge	Rarity	Pop	T/A	Last Traded at Auction				F/VF	EF	Unc
						Firm	Date	Amount	Grade			
51a	C	RE	–	0	1	Superior	2/1991	$550	PF30	Unconf	Unconf	Unconf
51	C	PE	–	0	1	RLH Enterprises	7/1980	$2,500	EF45	Unconf	Unconf	Unconf

Patterns of 1836

History and Overview
On March 23, 1836, the first steam-powered coining press at the U.S. Mint was inaugurated. Cents were struck by steam power in that month, and on November 10, the first silver coins were struck on steam presses. Many processes were improved and mechanized, including the making of dies.

In 1836, patterns came to the forefront, creating the first truly grand year after 1792 in the series. We see the emergence of Christian Gobrecht's Liberty Seated design and, in strictly pattern form, the production of coins of the two-cent and gold dollar denominations. The Liberty Seated issues in particular set the stage for later coinage.

The Liberty Seated/Flying Eagle Design of 1836
In 1835, well-known local artists Titian Peale and Thomas Sully had received commissions to prepare sketches for new coin designs, to be used by the engraver in making models. Patterson felt that the traditional figure of a goddess, seated, would be ideal, this having been used on coinage of other lands for generations, including Great Britain and ancient Rome. A sketch of this concept was created by Chief Engraver William Kneass shortly before he suffered a stroke. Sully and Peale made revisions, gave them to Gobrecht, and on October 15, 1836, an impression on or from a copper plate was sent to Treasury Secretary Levi Woodbury for review.

Work progressed, and on January 28, 1836, impressions or strikings or splashings from an obverse die were sent to Woodbury and to President Andrew Jackson for their approval, which was granted. Some further discussion concerning the treatment of the seated figure took place at the Mint, and a few revisions were made, including to the position of the pole supporting the liberty cap. By April 9, 1836, a revised obverse die was created.

Patterns of 1836

Die Alignments of Gobrecht Dollars (1836–1839)

The die alignment of a Gobrecht dollar can be a guide to the time it was struck.

To test for die alignments I and III hold the coin, obverse up, by the edges at 9 o'clock and 3 o'clock; rotate along this horizontal axis and notice the position of the eagle. If the eagle is belly up, test for die alignment II and IV by holding the coin (obverse up) at the 12 o'clock and 6 o'clock edges between thumb and forefinger, rotate along this vertical axis, and note the position of the eagle. These procedures will yield one of the four alignments below:

Alignment I, coin turn: The eagle flies slightly upward ("onward and upward"); the two circular dots or pellets (one each side of ONE DOLLAR) are level after rotation along the horizontal axis. The head of Miss Liberty on the obverse is opposite the O in DOLLAR on the reverse. This is also called "coin turn" and is used on most United States coins.

Alignment II, medal turn: The reverse die is oriented 180 degrees differently from the preceding. This alignment is also called "medal turn" and is used on many medals (but only few circulating U.S. coins). The eagle flies "onward and upward" to the left, and the two ornaments flanking ONE DOLLAR are level after rotating along the vertical axis. The head of Liberty is opposite the E in STATES on the reverse.

Alignment III: The eagle flies horizontally, thus the two pellets on each side of ONE DOLLAR are not level (the one on the left is lower) after rotating the coin along the horizontal axis. The head of Liberty is opposite the N in ONE on the reverse.

Alignment IV: The eagle flies horizontally as preceding, after rotation along the vertical axis. The head of Liberty is opposite the space between F in OF and first A in AMERICA on the reverse.

Pattern Two-Cent Pieces of 1836

Although the Gobrecht silver coinage of 1836 has captured the most attention of numismatists and is the most important historically, in the same year, two new denominations were made in pattern form: the two-cent piece and the gold dollar.

Pattern Gold Dollars of 1836

Early in 1836, while work was being done on dies for the silver dollar, pattern gold dollars were struck, these employing the Liberty Cap and Rays motif used by Gobrecht on his February 22, 1836 medal (overdated to March 23) for the inauguration of the steam press. Patterns of the new gold dollar were ready by March 14, 1836. The gold dollar denomination may have attracted slight interest at the time.

Collecting Perspective

The year 1836 offers the earliest dated patterns of which several different true patterns (not private restrikes) are available to collectors today. Today, restrikes exist of the 1836 two-cent piece, the Gobrecht silver dollar with the name below the base (and also the variety with the name on the base), and the gold dollar. In addition, some novodel (or combination of dies that were never used originally) silver dollar patterns exist combining the two different Gobrecht obverse dies with a reverse die without stars—in effect creating a completely starless issue.

A representative example of the 1836 two-cent piece can be obtained without difficulty, although examples are scarce. The market makes little differentiation between originals and restrikes.

The regular-issue 1836 Capped Bust half dollar with reeded edge has been "adopted" into the pattern series and listed as such for generations, although it has no pattern status.[1] Gobrecht silver dollars of the regular issue (J-60), fondly adopted into the pattern series and for a long time considered to be patterns, exist by the hundreds, and are in great demand due to their distinctive design. The majority of specimens of J-60 are in grades from VF through Proof-55 or so. At least four different die alignments and variations occur for the J-60 1836 Gobrecht dollar with the name on the base and with stars on the reverse, and it is a challenge to determine when they might have been struck.

The true patterns are those with the legend C. GOBRECHT. F below the base and above the date. This legend is an abbreviation of "C. Gobrecht Fecit," Latin for "C. Gobrecht Made It." Restrikes, quite rare, are encountered from time to time. The various restrikes of 1836, some from die pairs never originally used in 1836, are all extreme rarities.[1]

Gold dollars of 1836, actually struck in gold, exist to the extent of perhaps as many as 50 to 75 pieces, some original and others restrikes made circa 1859. Restrikes exist in other metals as well. Gold strikings with silver alloy were made in January 1844 to review the concept of the gold dollar denomination. These are restrikes, but were made from the original dies in the course of normal Mint activities, not to create pieces for collectors.

Interestingly, the only two readily available collectible "patterns" dated 1836 are J-57 and J-60, described below, each of which is really a regular issue that has been adopted by pattern collectors.

Patterns of 1836

J-52 to J-56a: 1836 Two-Cent Piece

These dies were used in a combination of metals and edge treatments. J-52, buckled die (but not perfect die) examples of J-54, and varieties J-54, and J-55 to J-56a are restrikes. J-53 coins are original, and perfect die (weight about 60 grains) specimens of J-54 are not original. Originals are from circulation type (non-Proof) die finish; all others are with Proof finish. Some of J-53 were pickled at the Mint to simulate their appearance after a degree of circulation; such coins quickly turned dull gray or black.[2] • J-52: restrike, medal turn. • J-53: original, coin turn, non-Proof dies (as struck, reeding coarse). • J-54: cracked obverse die, medal turn. • J-55: restrike, medal turn.[3] • J-55a: restrike, medal turn. • J-55b: restrike, medal turn, struck as PE, but later given RE (reeded after striking, delicate reeding[4]). • J-56 and J-56a: exact nature and existence are uncertain.

Obverse: Perched "small eagle" similar to that used for the reverse of Draped Bust silver coinage of the late 1790s. The inscription UNITED STATES OF AMERICA / 1836 surrounds.
Reverse: Heavy wreath close to the border, enclosing TWO CENTS.

J-52

Number	Metal	Edge	Rarity	Pop	T/A	Last Traded at Auction			60	63	65
						Firm	Date	Amount	Grade			
52	Bil	PE	L6	19	9	Stack's	3/2004	$6,900	ChPF	$2,400	$4,250	$7,750
53	Bil	RE	L6	21	11	Heritage	1/2004	$3,680	PCGSMS63	$2,500	$4,750	$9,000
54	C	PE	L6	13	12	Heritage	7/2005	$5,463	NGCPF65RB	$2,350	$5,200	$7,250
55	C	RE	H7	3	2	Superior	5/1999	$1,840	NGCPF63BN	$4,200	$8,000	$14,000
55a	C-N	PE	8	1	1	Bowers & Merena	8/1995	$2,970	PCGSPF55	$4,200	$8,000	$14,000
55b	C-N	RE	8	0	1	Bowers & Merena	5/1996	$3,740	AU55	$4,200	$8,000	$14,000
56	WM	PE	8	1	1	Mid-American	5/1987	$1,400	PF64	$11,500	$22,000	$35,000
56a	WM	RE	8	3	4	Heritage	6/2005	$7,763	NGCMS63	$5,850	$10,500	$16,500

J-57: 1836 Half Dollar

Regular issue. Not a pattern but by tradition often collected along with the pattern series.[5] At least a dozen or two were struck from mirror Proof dies, some for presentation. Circulation strikes were made from unpolished dies. Examples exist today in all circulated grades, Mint State, and Proof.

Obverse: Modified Capped Bust design, stars to left and right, date below.
Reverse: Perched eagle, UNITED STATES OF AMERICA and denomination as 50 CENTS around border.

J-57

Number	Metal	Edge	Rarity	Pop	T/A	Last Traded at Auction			60	63	65
						Firm	Date	Amount	Grade			
57	Silv	RE	2	363	151	Bowers & Merena	12/2003	$12,650	NGCMS63	$10,000	$25,000	$40,000

J-58 and J-59: 1836 Silver Dollar

Eighteen originals are said to have been struck in 1836, these from a perfect (no cracks) die pair, dies aligned coin-turn. All seen have been restrikes with lightly cracked reverse die (alignments IV and III). The absence of originals is a first-class numismatic mystery; not even the Mint Cabinet (coins now in the Smithsonian Institution) has one! J-59: restrike (alignment III).

Obverse: Liberty Seated design, no stars in field. C GOBRECHT. F. in raised letters below base and above date.
Reverse: Eagle flying to the left in a starry field of 13 small and 13 large stars, a total of 26, representing the number of states in the Union at the time. UNITED STATES OF AMERICA / ONE DOLLAR around border.

J-59

Number	Metal	Edge	Rarity	Pop	T/A	Last Traded at Auction			60	63	65
						Firm	Date	Amount	Grade			
58	Silv	PE	L6	20	10	Ira & Larry Goldberg	2/2005	$48,875	PCGSPF45PQ	$55,000	$72,500	$110,000
59	C	PE	8	3	2	Bowers & Merena	7/2002	$62,100	PCGS64RB	$32,500	$52,500	$110,000

J-60: 1836 Silver Dollar

Regular issue. 1,000 struck by December 31, 1836, coin-turn die alignment; 600 more struck from same dies in early 1837, medal-turn alignment. In addition, restrikes were made with alignment III, 1860s to 1870s. Grades range from well worn to Proof. Not a pattern, but a regular issue that has been listed in the pattern series and until recent decades generally regarded as a pattern—until the history of the piece was carefully studied.

Obverse: Liberty Seated design, no stars in field. C GOBRECHT. F. in recessed letters on base. Date in field below.
Reverse: Eagle flying amid 26 stars.

J-60

Number	Metal	Edge	Rarity	Pop	T/A	Last Traded at Auction				60	63	65
						Firm	Date	Amount	Grade			
60	Silv	PE	1	574	146	Ira & Larry Goldberg	2/2005	$17,250	PCGSPF55PQ	$18,000	$25,000	$80,000

J-61 and J-62: 1836 Silver Dollar

Dies as preceding. Restrikes. • J-61: die alignment IV; status is uncertain. • J-62: die alignment III, circa 1876, often with rust in field left of Liberty's face.

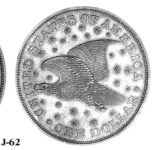

J-62

Number	Metal	Edge	Rarity	Pop	T/A	Last Traded at Auction				60	63	65
						Firm	Date	Amount	Grade			
61	Silv	RE	8	1	1	Stack's	5/2003	$195,500	PCGSPF63	$110,000	$200,000	$300,000
62	C	PE	8	2	1	RLH Enterprises	7/1980	$12,250	ChPF	$90,000	$175,000	$260,000

J-63 and J-64: 1836 Silver Dollar

Restrikes with die alignment III, struck circa 1876.

Obverse: Liberty Seated design, no stars in field. C GOBRECHT. F. in raised letters below base and above date; obverse of J-58.
Reverse: Eagle flying to the left in a plain field (die first regularly used in 1838).

J-64

Number	Metal	Edge	Rarity	Pop	T/A	Last Traded at Auction				60	63	65
						Firm	Date	Amount	Grade			
63	Silv	PE	8	2	1	Stack's	5/2003	$149,500	PCGS63	$110,000	$160,000	$225,000
64	C	PE	8	2	3	ANR	3/2004	$132,250	PCGSPF65RD	$45,000	$85,000	$150,000

Patterns of 1836

J-65 and J-66: 1836 Silver Dollar

Restrikes with die alignment III, circa 1876, with rust in field left of Liberty's face.

Obverse: Liberty Seated design, no stars in field. C. GOBRECHT. F. in recessed letters on base. Date in field below; obverse of J-60.
Reverse: As preceding.

J-65

Number	Metal	Edge	Rarity	Pop	T/A	Last Traded at Auction				F/VF	EF	Unc
						Firm	Date	Amount	Grade			
65	Silv	PE	8	2	2	Ira & Larry Goldberg	5/2004	$184,000	PCGSPF65PQ	$65,000	$110,000	$200,000
66	C	PE	–	0	0	N/A	N/A	N/A	N/A	Unconf	Unconf	Unconf

J-67 to J-71: 1836 Gold Dollar

Originals struck with coin-turn die alignment, a situation complicated by some restrikes also having the same alignment. An example plainly struck over an 1859 dated regular-issue gold dollar confirms that restrikes were made (J-67a). J-69 to J-71 are restrikes made circa 1859 and later. • J-67: dies aligned coin-turn. • J-68: dies aligned medal-turn; struck for pattern purposes in January 1844.

Obverse: Liberty cap inscribed LIBERTY, surrounded by a glory of rays; motif also used in the 1836 Mint medal inaugurating steam coinage.
Reverse: Palm branch arranged in a circle enclosing 1 D. Around the border, UNITED STATES OF AMERICA / 1836.

J-67

Number	Metal	Edge	Rarity	Pop	T/A	Last Traded at Auction				60	63	65
						Firm	Date	Amount	Grade			
67	Gold	PE	5	41	24	Heritage	5/2005	$14,950	NGCPF63	$9,000	$15,000	$22,500
67a	Gold	PE	8	1	0	N/A	N/A	N/A	N/A	N/A	$35,000	$50,000
68	*	PE	H7	2	1	NERCG	7/1979	$4,600	PF63	$13,000	$18,000	$26,000
69	Silv	PE	H7	7	7	Heritage	6/2004	$9,775	PCGSPF64	$5,000	$7,500	$14,000
70	C	PE	L7	6	5	Superior	10/2001	$6,613	NGCPF66RB	$3,500	$5,500	$9,000
71	Oro	PE	8	0	1	NERCG	7/1979	$1,650	PF	$12,000	$20,000	$30,000

* J-68: gold alloyed with silver

Patterns of 1838

History and Overview

No patterns are known bearing the date 1837, although certain 1836-dated Gobrecht silver dollars (of a variety with the name on the base, and medal-turn alignment) were struck early in 1837. In June 1838, the Mint Cabinet, or reference collection of coins, was inaugurated, and thenceforth served as a repository for selected impressions of regular coinage as well as patterns. At the time, Mint officials regularly exchanged coins with numismatists.

In 1838, new half dollar and silver dollar patterns were produced. Most of the dies were by Christian Gobrecht (except for the reverse die used to coin J-75a and J-75b, a die of 1859 by Paquet).

It is likely the half dollar was selected as the primary denomination for patterns of this year, as the design of the dollar, struck for circulation in 1836, may have been considered as having been completed. Now it was time to turn attention to the second highest-value silver coin.

Basically, the obverse dies for the 1838 half dollar pattern coinage are three, numbered here for convenience, probably in the order that the dies were made:

Half Dollar Obverse Dies of 1838

Obverse 1: "Liberty head." Gobrecht's head of Liberty facing left, luxuriant tresses falling to her shoulder, with the word LIBERTY on the ribbon in her hair, seven stars to the right, six stars to the left, and the date 1838 below. This is the die that Snowden attributed to Kneass. • Used with J-72 to J-75b.

Obverse 2: "Liberty seated, raised letters." Liberty Seated motif as employed on the 1836 Gobrecht silver dollar, with the word LIBERTY in raised rather than incuse letters, and with 13 stars to the left and right, the date 1838 below. Date in a gentle curve. All strikings from this die have been original issues. • Used with J-76b, J-79, J-82, J-83.

Obverse 3: "Liberty seated, incuse letters." Liberty Seated motif and details as foregoing, except with the word LIBERTY in incuse letters. Date straight (not gently curved). • Used with J-76 to J-78 (restrikes), J-79a (original), and J-80, J-81 (restrikes).

The reverse motifs employed for the 1838 pattern half dollar coinage are several, including one (on J-82) from 1836 and another possibly created in 1858 (J-222 of 1858, used extensively in 1859).

Half Dollar Reverse Dies of 1838

Reverse A: "Perched eagle holding four arrows." Perched eagle holding olive branch and four arrows, head turned towards viewer's right. UNITED STATES OF AMERICA above, HALF DOLLAR below. • Used with J-72, J-76 to J-78.

Reverse B: "Flying eagle in plain field." Eagle flying to the left, mouth open, neck feathers somewhat ruffled. UNITED STATES OF AMERICA above, HALF DOLLAR below. • Used with J-73, J-74, J-79, J-79a.

Reverse C: "Regular reverse of 1838." Perched upright eagle holding olive branch and three arrows, UNITED STATES OF AMERICA above, denomination as HALF DOL. below. • Used with J-75, J-83.

Reverse D: "Paquet's perched eagle, broken ribbon." Perched eagle with a ribbon across the shield, continuing to the eagle's beak, eagle's head facing to viewer's left, olive branch and arrows below. Legends in tall letters, UNITED STATES OF AMERICA / HALF DOLLAR. Broken ribbon; groups of three vertical lines in the shield; six tail feathers; split wingtip at right; stem or half-leaf above A (in HALF). By engraver Anthony C. Paquet. Listed in the present text as J-75a and J-75b (listed out of order in Judd, seventh edition, under 1859, as J-254 and J-255). Same as Reverse B of 1859, in the 1838-dated die combination extensively relapped with some details ground off the die. • Used with J-75a, J-75b.

Reverse E: "Perched eagle, side view, facing left, holding arrows and branch." Eagle perched, view from side, facing left in the manner of a flying eagle, but with tail downward and with an olive branch and arrows below. Inscription UNITED STATES OF AMERICA / HALF DOL around. • Used with J-80, J-81.

Reverse F: "Regular reverse of 1836." Perched eagle facing viewer, shield on breast, head turned to observer's left, talons holding olive branch and three arrows. UNITED STATES OF AMERICA above, 50 CENTS below. The style used on regular-issue reeded-edge Capped Bust half dollars of 1836 and 1837. • Used with J-82.

The preceding dies occur in several combinations in both original (contemporary with 1838) and restrike (1859 and later) productions.

Pattern silver dollars are known from a single 1838 obverse die, with Liberty seated, LIBERTY raised on the shield, and with 13 stars to the left and right, date 1838 below. Two reverse dies were employed, one with 26 stars (as used in 1836 for J-60) and the other without stars. It is believed that the use of the 26-star die was limited only to restrikes, as the stars were redundant with those on the obverse. No silver dollars were struck for circulation in 1838, and thus all are patterns.[6] See "Die Alignment of Gobrecht Dollars" under Patterns of 1836, above.

Collecting Perspective

The half dollar patterns of 1838 provide a fertile field for the specialist, as many different varieties exist. It is impossible to collect them all, and therein lies the challenge to acquire as many different varieties as possible. However, if an effort is made to collect at least one impression from each obverse and reverse die, success may be nearer to reality.

Collectors have paid little attention to the status of originals vis-à-vis restrikes. Today most certified coin holders do not list the weight, and sometimes make it impossible to tell the difference without removing them from their plastic holders. All 1838 pattern half dollars are scarce, and most are quite rare.

The pattern silver dollars of 1838 are in special demand as they are listed in *A Guide Book of United States Coins* and thus play to a wider audience. Of the three dates of Gobrecht dollars (without regard to die combinations), 1836, 1838, and 1839, the 1838 is regarded as the rarest. The usually seen 1838 variety has an obverse with stars and a starless reverse, was struck in silver, and has a reeded edge.

J-72: 1838 Half Dollar
Dies 1-A

Silver examples exist of approximately 206 grains weight (originals) and 192 grains (restrikes), the last coined 1859 and later. Anomalous-weight silver pieces exist.[7]

Obverse: Liberty head.
Reverse: Perched eagle holding four feathers.

J-72

Number	Metal	Edge	Rarity	Pop	T/A	Last Traded at Auction				60	63	65
						Firm	Date	Amount	Grade			
72	Silv	RE	5	43	31	ANR	1/2005	$6,900	PCGSPF63	$4,000	$7,000	$12,000

Patterns of 1838

J-73 and J-74: 1838 Half Dollar
Dies 1-B

Silver pieces of 206-1/4 grains weight are believed to be originals; pieces of 192 grains, dies cracked, exhibit different states from light cracks to heavy cracks, the variety most often seen. • The copper striking is believed unique. From cracked reverse die.

Obverse: Liberty head.
Reverse: Flying eagle in plain field.

J-73

Number	Metal	Edge	Rarity	Pop	T/A	Last Traded at Auction				60	63	65
						Firm	Date	Amount	Grade			
73	Silv	RE	5	59	42	Heritage	5/2005	$3,738	PCGSPF64	$3,100	$4,400	$8,000
74	C	RE	U	0	1	Macy's	6/1954	N/A	ChPF	N/A	N/A	N/A

J-75: 1838 Half Dollar
Dies 1-C

Original. An example is in the Smithsonian Institution.[8]

Obverse: Liberty head.
Reverse: Regular reverse of 1838.

J-75

Number	Metal	Edge	Rarity	Pop	T/A	Last Traded at Auction				60	63	65
						Firm	Date	Amount	Grade			
75	Silv	RE	U	0	0	N/A	N/A	N/A	N/A	N/A	N/A	N/A

J-75a and J-75b: 1838 Half Dollar
Dies 1-D

Restrikes believed to have been struck in the 1870s. J-75a is unconfirmed.

Obverse: Liberty head.
Reverse: Paquet's perched eagle, broken ribbon.

J-75b

Number	Metal	Edge	Rarity	Pop	T/A	Last Traded at Auction				60	63	65
						Firm	Date	Amount	Grade			
75a	Silv	RE	–	0	0	N/A	N/A	N/A	N/A	Unconf	Unconf	Unconf
75b	C	RE	8	1	1	Ira & Larry Goldberg	5/2001	$4,945	NGCPF62BN	$8,500	$13,000	$22,500

J-76b: 1838 Half Dollar
Dies 2-A

Original only. Two are known. One is the Eliasberg coin. The other is in the Smithsonian Institution.

Obverse: Liberty seated, raised letters.
Reverse: Perched eagle holding four arrows.

J-76b

Number	Metal	Edge	Rarity	Pop	T/A	Last Traded at Auction				60	63	65
						Firm	Date	Amount	Grade			
76b	Silv	RE	8	1	3	Superior	1/2004	$29,900	PCGSPF63	N/A	$35,000	N/A

J-76 to J-78: 1838 Half Dollar
Dies 3-A

Restrikes made at later dates, possibly to the mid-1870s.

Obverse: Liberty seated, incuse letters.
Reverse: Perched eagle holding four arrows.

J-77

Number	Metal	Edge	Rarity	Pop	T/A	Firm	Date	Amount	Grade	60	63	65
							Last Traded at Auction					
76	Silv	PE	8	1	1	Heritage	7/2003	$11,213	ANACSPF55	$14,000	$25,000	$42,500
76a	Silv	RE	8	1	3	Superior	4/2003	$26,450	NGCPF64	$18,000	$26,000	$37,500
77	C	PE	H7	3	5	Superior	7/2003	$24,150	NGCPF66RB	$8,000	$14,000	$22,500
78	C	RE	H7	2	2	Superior	4/2003	$25,300	NGCPF66RB	$18,000	$25,000	$35,000

J-79: 1838 Half Dollar
Dies 2-B

Original.

Obverse: Liberty seated, raised letters.
Reverse: Flying eagle in plain field.

J-79

Number	Metal	Edge	Rarity	Pop	T/A	Firm	Date	Amount	Grade	60	63	65
							Last Traded at Auction					
79	Silv	RE	8	0	1	Stack's	3/1986	$8,250	ChPF	$13,000	$24,000	$40,000

J-79a: 1838 Half Dollar
Dies 3-B

Original.

Obverse: Liberty seated, incuse letters.
Reverse: Flying eagle in plain field.

J-79a

Number	Metal	Edge	Rarity	Pop	T/A	Firm	Date	Amount	Grade	60	63	65
							Last Traded at Auction					
79a	Silv	RE	L7	5	4	Heritage	5/2003	$12,650	NGCPF63	$10,000	$20,000	$29,000

J-80 and J-81: 1838 Half Dollar
Dies 3-E

Restrikes.

Obverse: Liberty seated, incuse letters.
Reverse: Perched eagle, side view, facing left, holding arrows and branch.

J-80

Number	Metal	Edge	Rarity	Pop	T/A	Firm	Date	Amount	Grade	60	63	65
							Last Traded at Auction					
80	Silv	RE	H7	4	5	Stack's	9/1999	$11,788	ChPF	$12,500	$25,000	$37,500
81	C	RE	H7	2	4	Stack's/ANR	6/2005	$17,250	NGCPF66BN	$6,500	$11,500	$20,000

Patterns of 1838

J-82: 1838 Half Dollar
Dies 2-F

Original.

Obverse: Liberty seated, raised letters.
Reverse: Regular reverse of 1836.

J-82

Number	Metal	Edge	Rarity	Pop	T/A	Firm	Date	Amount	Grade	60	63	65
						Last Traded at Auction						
82	Silv	RE	8	1	1	Bowers & Merena	5/1999	$17,250	PCGSPF63	$19,000	$27,500	$47,500

J-83: 1838 Half Dollar
Dies 2-C

Original.

Obverse: Liberty seated, raised letters.
Reverse: Regular reverse of 1838.

J-83

Number	Metal	Edge	Rarity	Pop	T/A	Firm	Date	Amount	Grade	60	63	65
83	Silv	RE	8	0	1	B. Max Mehl	10/1923	$125	BrPF	N/A	N/A	N/A

J-83a: 1838 Half Dollar

Struck from regular dies. Possibly a trial piece. The only known piece is worn, and was double struck on a 1798 large cent.

J-83a

Number	Metal	Edge	Rarity	Pop	T/A	Firm	Date	Amount	Grade	60	63	65
83a	C	PE	U	0		Coin Galleries	8/1987	$2,228	EF	N/A	N/A	N/A

J-84, J-85, and J-87: 1838 Silver Dollar

Silver issues with some originals (some J-84), others restrikes. One is struck over an 1859 Liberty Seated dollar, with the 1859 date still visible.[9] Copper issues are restrikes.
• J-84: Originals are alignment IV, struck from perfect dies.[10] Restrikes are alignment III[11] and IV with reverse die cracks. • J-85: restrikes, alignment III.[12] • J-87: restrikes, alignment III.[13]

Obverse: Liberty seated with stars.
Reverse: Flying eagle in plain field.

J-84

Number	Metal	Edge	Rarity	Pop	T/A	Firm	Date	Amount	Grade	60	63	65
84	Silv	RE	5	51	19	Heritage	5/2005	$34,500	PCGSPF62	$30,000	$57,500	$90,000
85	Silv	PE	H7	6	1	Stack's	5/2003	$80,500	PF64	$45,000	$90,000	$150,000
87	C	PE	8	1	3	Bowers & Merena	1/1997	$14,300	NGCPF63BN	$50,000	$125,000	$185,000

The piece listed prior to the 8th edition as J-86 is no longer believed to exist.

J-88 and J-89: 1838 Silver Dollar

Restrikes, alignment III.

Obverse: Liberty seated with stars, die as preceding.
Reverse: Flying eagle in field of 26 stars (style of 1836).

J-88

Number	Metal	Edge	Rarity	Pop	T/A	Last Traded at Auction				60	63	65
						Firm	Date	Amount	Grade			
88	Silv	PE	8	2	2	Stack's	5/2003	$201,250	NGCPF64	$70,000	$135,000	$250,000
89	C	PE	U	1	1	Bowers & Merena	1/1999	$27,600	NGCPF63BN	$70,000	$135,000	$200,000

The piece listed prior to the 8th edition as J-90 is not believed to exist.

Patterns of 1839

History and Overview

Patterns for the year 1839 parallel those of 1838. They are comprised of half dollars and silver dollars, each in different die combinations. Originals and restrikes both exist, with a general rule of thumb that half dollars weighing approximately 206 grains are original and those weighing approximately 192 grains, consistent with the Act of February 21, 1853, reducing the weight, are restrikes. The latter are believed to have been first made in 1859, a scenario similar to that for pattern halves of 1838. Often, actual specimens do not neatly fit into either weight category but are close to them.

One distinctly new half dollar die was introduced: its design featured Liberty facing right, with LIBERTY on the coronet, similar to the portrait used on contemporary $10 gold coins, except facing in the other direction. It is unusual to see the word LIBERTY begin near the back of the head, a departure from standard procedure. Neither this die nor any like it were ever used for coinage.

Similar to the situation for 1838-dated pattern half dollars, those of the same denomination in 1839 consist of combinations of several different obverses and reverses, the reverses including some that had been used for 1838-dated pieces.

Half Dollar Obverse Dies of 1839

Obverse 1: "Coronet Head facing right." Gobrecht's Coronet or Braided Hair head, facing right, with the word LIBERTY beginning above the ear and ending with the Y above the forehead, an arrangement much different from any Liberty Head ever used on any coinage. 13 stars around, date below. • Used with J-91 to J-98.
Obverse 2: "Regular Capped Bust die." Regular Capped Bust die of the year as employed on circulating coinage. • Used with J-99 and J-100.
Obverse 3: "Regular Liberty Seated, With Drapery die." Regular Liberty Seated half dollar die as used later in the year for circulating coinage, of the style with drapery at the elbow. • Used with J-101 to J-103.

The reverse motifs employed for the 1839 pattern half dollar coinage are several, a mixture of those used in 1838 with certain regular-issue dies. Those dies used in 1838 are listed first, Reverse A and B, with the same letter designations as employed in 1838.

Half Dollar Reverse Dies of 1839

Reverse A: "Perched eagle holding four arrows." Perched eagle holding olive branch and four arrows, head turned toward viewer's right. UNITED STATES OF AMERICA above, HALF DOLLAR below. • Same as Reverse A of 1838. • Used for restrikes J-99, J-101.
Reverse B: "Flying eagle in plain field." Eagle flying to the left, mouth open, neck feathers somewhat ruffled. UNITED STATES OF AMERICA above, HALF DOLLAR below. • Same as Reverse B of 1838. • Used for restrikes J-91, J-92, J-100, J-102.
Reverse C: "Regular reverse die, Small Letters." Regular reverse die used on Liberty Seated half dollars made for circulation, Small Letters. • Used for originals J-93, J-94.
Reverse D: "Regular reverse die, Medium Letters." Regular reverse die used in this era, Medium Letters. • Used for restrikes J-95, J-96, J-103.
Reverse E: "Regular reverse die, Large Letters." Regular reverse die used 1842 and later, Large Letters. • Used for restrikes J-97, J-98.

Patterns of 1839

The preceding dies occur in several combinations in both original productions (contemporary with 1838, these limited to J-93 and J-94) and restrikes (1859 or later, most likely in the 1870s[14]). Likely, the originals are of approximately 206 grains weight, this being the standard for a half dollar planchet prior to the Act of February 21, 1853, at which time the weight was reduced to 192 grains. When restrikes were made at the Mint, current planchets were used, these being of the lighter weight.

The silver dollars essentially parallel the die combinations of 1838. The obverse die, with stars, is dated 1839. Varieties exist with the eagle in a plain field as well as a starry field. Coinage records state that 300 examples were made with a plain reverse, these being struck for circulation (J-104), now known to have been in alignment IV from perfect dies.

In 1839 a dollar of the same type as the pattern dollar of the previous year was struck. The Director's Report of that time states that 300 of these were coined, but we have been unable to find any memorandum to that effect in any of the Mint records, where it should properly appear if such were the case. They are not as rare as the dollars of 1838, and the coinage was probably more extensive.

Collecting Perspective

Similar to the pattern half dollar and dollars of 1838, those dated 1839 range from rare to extremely rare. Likewise, those of 1839 can never be collected in their entirety, but the goal of obtaining an example of each die is a reasonable challenge.

In addition to the pattern half dollar dies, a regular 1839 Capped Bust obverse was used this year and also employed was a regular 1839 Liberty Seated half dollar (of the second Liberty Seated style of 1839, with drapery at the elbow).[15]

The 1839 Gobrecht dollars are in demand by pattern collectors and even more so by those who are not pattern specialists, but who are attracted to the listings in *A Guide Book of United States Coins*. The variety usually seen is that with the reverse in a plain field, reeded edge, certain examples of which are regular issues. As such, they are of extraordinary importance. See "Die Alignments of Gobrecht Dollars" under the 1836 listing above.

J-91 and J-92: 1839 Half Dollar
Dies 1-B

Restrikes. At least two silver strikings are confirmed, one in the Durham Western Heritage Museum.

Obverse: Coronet Head facing right.
Reverse: Flying eagle in plain field.

J-91

Number	Metal	Edge	Rarity	Pop	T/A	Last Traded at Auction				60	63	65
						Firm	Date	Amount	Grade			
91	Silv	RE	8	0	1	RARCOA	7/1981	$3,100	PF	$18,000	$27,500	$50,000
92	C	RE	–	0	0	N/A	N/A	N/A	N/A	Unconf	Unconf	Unconf

J-93 and J-94: 1839 Half Dollar
Dies 1-C

Originals.

Obverse: Coronet Head facing right.
Reverse: Regular reverse die, Small Letters.

J-93

Number	Metal	Edge	Rarity	Pop	T/A	Last Traded at Auction				60	63	65
						Firm	Date	Amount	Grade			
93	Silv	RE	L7	6	4	Superior	5/2004	$21,850	NGCPF64	$14,000	$27,500	$45,000
94	C	RE	8	0	1	Stack's	5/1970	$320	ChPF	$17,500	$27,500	$60,000

J-95 and J-96: 1839 Half Dollar
Dies 1-D

Restrikes. Two are known in silver and three in copper.

Obverse: Coronet Head facing right.
Reverse: Regular reverse die, Medium Letters.

J-95

Number	Metal	Edge	Rarity	Pop	T/A	Last Traded at Auction				60	63	65
						Firm	Date	Amount	Grade			
95	Silv	RE	8	2	3	Bowers & Merena	5/2005	$27,600	NGCPF66	$18,000	$27,000	$45,000
96	C	RE	8	1	1	Bowers & Merena	5/1999	$12,650	PCGSPF64BN	$10,500	$18,000	$27,500

J-97 and J-98: 1839 Half Dollar
Dies 1-E

Restrikes.

Obverse: Coronet Head facing right.
Reverse: Regular reverse die, Large Letters.

J-97

Number	Metal	Edge	Rarity	Pop	T/A	Last Traded at Auction				60	63	65
						Firm	Date	Amount	Grade			
97	Silv	RE	H7	2	3	Superior	5/2003	$32,200	PCGSPF64	$20,000	$32,500	$47,500
98	C	RE	H7	2	2	Bowers & Merena	5/1999	$7,475	PCGSPF64BN	$16,000	$25,000	$40,000

J-99: 1839 Half Dollar
Dies 2-A

Restrike. Two examples are known, including the former Bass Foundation and Witham piece, now in the Queller collection.

Obverse: Regular Capped Bust die.
Reverse: Perched eagle holding four arrows.

J-99

Number	Metal	Edge	Rarity	Pop	T/A	Last Traded at Auction				60	63	65
						Firm	Date	Amount	Grade			
99	Silv	RE	8	2	1	Bowers & Merena	5/1999	$16,100	PCGSPF63	$17,500	$30,000	$50,000

J-100: 1839 Half Dollar
Dies 2-B

Restrike.[16] Two are known.

Obverse: Regular Capped Bust die.
Reverse: Flying eagle in plain field.

J-100

Number	Metal	Edge	Rarity	Pop	T/A	Last Traded at Auction				60	63	65
						Firm	Date	Amount	Grade			
100	Silv	RE	8	0	1	RARCOA	7/1981	$4,500	ChPF	N/A	$35,000	$65,000

Patterns of 1839

J-101: 1839 Half Dollar
Dies 3-A

Restrike. Two pieces are confirmed.

Obverse: Regular Liberty Seated, With Drapery die.
Reverse: Perched eagle holding four arrows.

J-101

Number	Metal	Edge	Rarity	Pop	T/A	Last Traded at Auction				60	63	65
						Firm	Date	Amount	Grade			
101	Silv	RE	8	3	4	Superior	1/2004	$36,800	NGCPF67	$17,500	$30,000	$55,000

J-102 and J-102a: 1839 Half Dollar
Dies 3-B

Restrikes. Struck from rusty dies.

Obverse: Regular Liberty Seated, With Drapery die.
Reverse: Flying eagle in plain field.

J-102

Number	Metal	Edge	Rarity	Pop	T/A	Last Traded at Auction				60	63	65
						Firm	Date	Amount	Grade			
102	Silv	RE	H7	2	2	Heritage	1/2004	$14,950	PCGSPF63	$12,000	$18,000	$30,000
102a	Silv	PE	U	0	1	Sotheby's	2/1954	$75	VF	N/A	N/A	N/A

J-103: 1839 Half Dollar
Dies 3-D

Restrike. Two examples are known.

Obverse: Regular Liberty Seated, With Drapery die.
Reverse: Regular reverse die, Medium Letters.

J-103

Number	Metal	Edge	Rarity	Pop	T/A	Last Traded at Auction				60	63	65
						Firm	Date	Amount	Grade			
103	C	RE	8	0	2	Stack's	11/2001	$13,800	PF60	$14,000	$22,500	$39,000

J-104, J-105, and J-107: 1839 Silver Dollar

J-104 is a regular issue, with originals in alignment IV,[17] and restrikes in alignment III or IV.[18] J-105 and J-107 are restrikes, in alignment III.

Obverse: Liberty seated with stars.
Reverse: Flying eagle in plain (starless) field (style of 1838).

J-104

Number	Metal	Edge	Rarity	Pop	T/A	Last Traded at Auction				60	63	65
						Firm	Date	Amount	Grade			
104	Silv	RE	3	96	44	Heritage	6/2005	$34,500	NGCPF63	$25,000	$36,500	$67,500
105	Silv	PE	L7	7	1	Bowers & Merena	5/1992	$17,600	NGCPF62	$30,000	$50,000	$110,000
107	C	PE	U	0	1	Kagin's	10/1966	$4,750	PF	N/A	N/A	N/A

J-108 and J-109: 1839 Silver Dollar

Restrikes made with the die used to coin J-60 of 1836. The use of stars on both obverse and reverse is illogical. Die alignment III.

Obverse: Liberty seated with stars, die as preceding.
Reverse: Flying eagle in field of 26 stars (style of 1836).

J-108

Number	Metal	Edge	Rarity	Pop	T/A	Last Traded at Auction				60	63	65
						Firm	Date	Amount	Grade			
108	Silv	PE	8	3	1	ANR	1/2004	$184,000	PCGSPF64	$70,000	$120,000	$200,000
109	C	PE	U	0	1	Kagin's	9/1972	$4,250	PF	N/A	N/A	N/A

History and Overview

No pattern coins are known of 1840, but one or more impressions exist from incomplete dies, struck on a wide brass planchet. Certain other uniface impressions of pattern coins are known and are preserved in the Ridgway Library in Philadelphia.[19]

Although no patterns survive, if indeed any were made, the year 1840 saw the Liberty Seated silver dollar struck in quantity for the first time for circulation. The design was modified from that made by Gobrecht, with Liberty now appearing less delicate, and with drapery from her left elbow. The reverse of the circulating coins featured a perched eagle holding an olive branch and three arrows, with the denomination ONE DOL. below, an adaptation of that used to coin half dollars for circulation beginning in 1838 (with Capped Bust obverse).

The modifications were made by Robert Ball Hughes, who was employed by the Mint to finesse the earlier Liberty Seated motif by Gobrecht.

Collecting Perspective

The unique brass impression from incomplete hubs (not working dies or master dies) was at one time owned by the Empire Coin Co., and at that time considered by their cataloger to be a test piece rather than a pattern coin.[20]

J-110: (Circa) 1840 Hub or Related Impressions

Struck on a broad, thick brass disc (not a coin planchet).

Obverse: Impression in relief of an unfinished hub or related die, an early stage, not a working die, lacking stars, but with a scribe line to position such. No date (as expected; dates were added sequentially later on working dies).
Reverse: Impression in relief of a hub or related early-process die.

J-110

Number	Metal	Edge	Rarity	Pop	T/A	Last Traded at Auction				60	63	65
						Firm	Date	Amount	Grade			
110	Brs	PE	U	1	1	Pine Tree	9/1974	$35,000	Unc	$50,000	N/A	N/A

Patterns of 1846

History and Overview

No patterns are known bearing dates 1841 through 1845. Examples described as patterns in certain earlier texts and catalogs have proven to be early counterfeits of circulating coins, sometimes from crude dies, made for deception in the channels of commerce (not for numismatic purposes).

Collecting Perspective

With the date 1846, a curious piece exists about the diameter of a quarter eagle, with the obverse and reverse of an 1846 die pair, but then with the reverse additionally overstruck with an 1846 half eagle die.

J-110a: 1846 $2.50

Reverse overstruck with the obverse of an 1846 half eagle, for a purpose unknown.

J-110a

Number	Metal	Edge	Rarity	Pop	T/A	Last Traded at Auction				60	63	65
						Firm	Date	Amount	Grade			
110a	C	RE	U	1	1	Bowers & Merena	5/1993	$3,630	PF55	N/A	$32,500	N/A

Patterns of 1849

History and Overview

In 1849, James B. Longacre, chief engraver since 1844, produced a variety of interesting and numismatically important patterns, today the most remembered being the famous double eagle of that year.

Consideration was given to making a three-cent piece in silver, a new addition to the coinage lineup, representing a value above the cent and below the half dime. The coinage of pattern cents of a new format would wait until 1850, but pattern three-cent coins were made posthaste in 1849, with examples ready by January 18.

In the rush to test a silver three-cent piece, or trime (as it was later referred to in Treasury documents), in 1849, a regular half dime obverse die was combined with two hastily created reverses: one simply with the numeral 3 and the other with the same value expressed as III.

Impressions of the three-cent piece were made in different alloys, one with 50% silver and 50% copper and another with 60% silver and 40% copper. Restrikes were produced at a later date, probably beginning in 1859, from normal silver planchet stock used for circulating coinage at that time (90% silver and 10% copper). Today, elemental analysis would be needed to differentiate the coinage metals to assure proper attribution.

In 1849, large quantities of gold from the California fields reached the East. Gold became "common" in comparison to silver, and the historic ratio of value between the two metals changed. The price of silver bullion rose on the international market, and by 1850, it took more silver to produce a half dime, dime, quarter dollar, half dollar, or silver dollar, than the face value of such coins. Eventually, a silver three-cent piece of reduced silver content was made for general circulation in 1851, by which time almost all regular silver coins had been removed from circulation by hoarders and speculators. The regular-issue silver three-cent piece was of a different alloy, 25% copper and 75% silver (instead of 90% silver), thus making them unprofitable to melt down. However, the pattern silver three-cent pieces of 1849 are of a different status, and the rising value of silver was not considered during their preparation, nor had hoarding of silver coins become widespread.

The influx of vast quantities of gold in 1849 prompted consideration for two new denominations, the $1 and $20. The gold dollar, made in pattern form at the Mint in 1836 and, of a different design, privately by Christopher Bechtler in North Carolina earlier, again became important. The prospect of coining a federal gold dollar had arisen again in 1844, and some patterns were restruck from 1836-dated dies, but no production for circulation materialized.

In 1849, Chief Engraver Longacre produced several examples of hand-engraved gold dollars. These had a square opening at the center, in the manner of Oriental coins, so that an appropriate weight of gold could be used in a coin larger in diameter than would otherwise be the case. These pieces, not struck from dies, can be considered numismatic folk art in a way, as they are directly from the hand of Longacre. Examples exist in gold and also gold-plated silver.[21] However, numismatists enumerate them as coins, again proving that among patterns, most rules have exceptions.

The centerpiece pattern of 1849 is the double eagle, the largest regular denomination in American coinage. Authorized by the Act of March 3, 1849, as was the gold dollar, the double eagle was twice the size of the eagle or $10 piece, thus giving rise to its name. Longacre set to work on this and the gold dollar, both of which would be the first entries of a specific new design created by his hand. The same motif was used for both, a distinctive head of Liberty, facing left, with LIBERTY on a coronet, stars around, no date on the gold dollar but the date 1849 on the double eagle. No struck gold-dollar patterns are known; no doubt some were made.

Longacre began first on the reverse of the double eagle, creating a distinct motif with a heraldic eagle loosely adapted from the Great Seal, but with the sides of the shield on the eagle's breast being parallel, and the wings treated differently. The left and right were ornamental bands, giving an overall bulbous shape to the center motif. Above the eagle's head was an ellipse of 13 stars and resplendent rays. The inscription UNITED STATES OF AMERICA / 20D was around the border.

The obverse of the double eagle presented problems, as the relief was too high to fully strike up the details in a regular coining press. However, the proper relief was finally accomplished, and double eagles, first struck for circulation in 1850, were a resounding success. In the meantime, several patterns were struck in gold with an 1849 date. Just one is known to exist today, perhaps the most famous of all rarities held in the National Numismatic Collection in the Smithsonian Institution.[22]

Collecting Perspective

Today the pattern three-cent pieces of 1849 are highly collectible, and the three different die combinations can be acquired without great difficulty, although they are hardly common.

Engraved patterns for the gold dollar, in gold and in gold-plated silver, are very rare and appear on the market at only widely spaced intervals. Regarding the 1849 pattern double eagle, the unique piece rests in the Smithsonian Institution. There is a gilt brass example, believed to be a restrike, which made its debut in the 1870s[23] but it has not been located today.

J-111 and J-111a: 1849 Three-Cent Piece

Originals struck in an alloy supposedly of 50% silver and 50% copper, average weight 22 grains. Restrikes may be in 90% silver. Elemental analysis is required to tell the difference.

Obverse: The die of the regular Liberty Seated half dime.
Reverse: The numeral 3, with no further inscriptions.

J-111

| Number | Metal | Edge | Rarity | Pop | T/A | Last Traded at Auction | | | | 60 | 63 | 65 |
						Firm	Date	Amount	Grade			
111	Bil	RE	L7	5	5	ANR	3/2005	$19,950	PCGSPF65	$5,000	$9,000	$16,000
111a	Silv	RE	H7	0	0	N/A	N/A	N/A	N/A	$4,750	$7,500	$12,500

J-112 and J-112a: 1849 Three-Cent Piece

Obverse: Liberty seated half dime die as preceding.
Reverse: The Roman numeral III, with no further inscriptions.

J-112

| Number | Metal | Edge | Rarity | Pop | T/A | Last Traded at Auction | | | | 60 | 63 | 65 |
						Firm	Date	Amount	Grade			
112	*	RE	L7	11	6	Heritage	6/2005	$5,175	PCGSPF64	$3,500	$5,500	$8,250
112a	Silv	RE	L7	0	0	N/A	N/A	N/A	N/A	$3,500	$5,500	$8,250

* J-112: 60% silver, 40% copper

J-113 to J-114a: 1849 Three-Cent Piece

Combination of the 3 and III dies, the "Ugly Duckling" pattern. Either side could be called the obverse or reverse. Silver and copper alloy, unknown proportions, plain edge. Originals and restrikes, the last probably in 90% silver. The copper-nickel issues are restrikes.

Obverse: The numeral 3, with no further inscriptions.
Reverse: The Roman numeral III, with no further inscriptions.

J-113

| Number | Metal | Edge | Rarity | Pop | T/A | Last Traded at Auction | | | | 60 | 63 | 65 |
						Firm	Date	Amount	Grade			
113	*	PE	H7	4	1	MARCA	1/1986	$1,700	ChPF	$5,000	$7,500	$13,000
114	C-N	PE	L7	11	8	Heritage	6/2005	$8,913	PCGSPF65	$3,750	$6,250	$9,000
114a	C	PE	U	0	0	Sotheby's	2/1954	N/A	N/A	N/A	N/A	N/A

* J-113: silver-copper alloy of unknown proportions

Patterns of 1849

J-115 and J-116: 1849 Gold Dollar

Hand-engraved (not struck) piece with incuse lettering and inscriptions, made by Longacre to test the diameter and concept. Not a coin in the regular sense. Square hole at center. • Analysis of certain of the gold issues reveals them to range widely, from 50% to 100% fine.

Obverse: Hand-engraved with 1. DOLLAR. 1849, and stars.
Reverse: Hand engraved with U. STATES OF AMERICA and wreath.

J-115

Number	Metal	Edge	Rarity	Pop	T/A	Last Traded at Auction				60	63	65
						Firm	Date	Amount	Grade			
115	Gold	PE	H7	3	2	Bowers & Merena	11/2002	$10,350	MS60	$16,000	$23,000	$45,000
116	*	PE	H7	5	2	Ira & Larry Goldberg	5/2003	$17,825	PCGSPF62	$9,500	$15,000	$25,000

* J-116: gold-plated silver

J-117 and J-118: 1849 $20

Said to be in "minutely higher relief" than the later circulating coins (of 1850). The gold impression is unique and in the National Numismatic Collections of the Smithsonian Institution. The existence of a second gold example has been rumored for a long time, but no evidence of it has ever surfaced. A brass piece is stated to have been "restruck for R.C. Davis," but its location is now unknown.[24]

Obverse: Liberty Head or Coronet Head, facing left, 13 stars surrounding, date 1849 below. Initials JBL, for Longacre, on neck truncation.
Reverse: Heraldic eagle, ornate bands to left and right, stars and rays above. UNITED STATES OF AMERICA / TWENTY D. around border.

J-117

Number	Metal	Edge	Rarity	Pop	T/A	Last Traded at Auction				60	63	65
						Firm	Date	Amount	Grade			
117	Gold	RE	U	0	0	N/A	N/A	N/A	N/A	N/A	N/A	N/A
118	Brs	PE	U	0	1	NY Coin & Stamp	4/1892	$55	Unc	N/A	N/A	N/A

Patterns of 1850

History and Overview

In 1850, patterns were struck for a new version of the cent. This was the first in an extensive series of patterns for a small-diameter cent to replace the copper "large cent" so familiar in circulation. A smaller, lighter coin would be less expensive to produce and would also result in increased profits for the Mint. At the time, the Mint had its own profit account for half cents and cents, while the larger silver and gold denominations returned only the expenses of coining, not an operating profit.[1]

The pattern cents of 1850 were made of billon, an alloy of 90% copper and 10% silver, to bring the intrinsic value of the coin up to an acceptable level, creating a piece that was lighter than the pure copper cent then in use. A perforation at the center, in the style of Oriental coins, enabled the pieces to be of larger diameter than would otherwise be the case, and helped distinguish them from dimes.[2]

Also highly important among the patterns of 1850 is J-125, a silver three-cent piece, featuring on the obverse a liberty cap with rays, with the date 1850 below—the same general motif having been used elsewhere earlier (such as on the March 23, 1836 Mint medal and the pattern gold dollar of the same date). The reverse of the trime features a circular palm branch (in the style of the reverse of the 1836 pattern gold dollar) with UNITED STATES OF AMERICA surrounding, and III within. Rather than being a hastily made combination of dies such as the J-111 to J-114 trimes of 1849, J-125 of 1850 is a pattern with distinctive designs made especially for what was anticipated to be a new denomination.

The final piece attributed to 1850 is J-126, a striking of the $20 gold design in silver, from an obverse working die for which the date had not been punched in. Whether this was struck in 1850 or some other year of the era is not known.

Collecting Perspective

Among the patterns of 1850, the cents from J-119 to J-124 exist in sufficient numbers that perforated as well as unperforated examples can be acquired.[3] Some of the original billon pieces have a dull surface, possibly from pickling at the Mint, or possibly from effects of metal instability combined with age. Generally, little distinction is made in the market between originals and restrikes. Later, beginning circa 1859, extensive restrikes were made, generating most of the pieces that are available for acquisition today, these being J-120 through J-124. Some of these restrikes were not perforated in the center. Another variety, known in white metal (J-124a), combines an 1850 obverse die with rosettes (like that used to strike J-119 through J-124), with a reverse of a die known to have been employed in 1853 (J-149).

The 1850 trime or silver three-cent pattern with liberty cap and rays marks a prize acquisition for any collector, representing the first distinctively different die pairing of what would become a regular coinage denomination in the following year, 1851.

J-119 to J-124: 1850 Cent

These patterns have a central perforation. The perforations on various specimens are not completely circular, but are irregular. It is likely that the planchet itself was perforated with a circular hole prior to striking, then during the striking process, the metal movement caused the edges of the perforation to become irregular in shape. • J-119, J-121, and J-123 are perforated. • J-120, J-122, and J-124 are unperforated.

Obverse: CENT above, 1850 below, with an ornamental rosette to left and right.
Reverse: USA above, ONE TENTH SILVER to the sides and below.

J-120

Number	Metal	Edge	Rarity	Pop	T/A	Last Traded at Auction				60	63	65
						Firm	Date	Amount	Grade			
119	Bil	PE	L6	36	22	Heritage	6/2005	$1,610	PCGSPF63	$1,200	$1,750	$3,000
120	Bil	PE	H7	5	4	ANR	3/2004	$2,760	ICGPF63	$3,000	$5,500	$10,000
121	C	PE	H6	17	38	Heritage	5/2003	$719	ANACSAU50	$1,750	$2,500	$4,200
122	C	PE	H7	4	1	Superior	5/2003	$9,775	NGCPF66RB	$3,000	$5,500	$10,000
123	C-N	PE	L7	6	2	Bowers & Merena	3/1999	$2,300	PCGSPF64	$1,450	$2,400	$4,500
124	C-N	PE	L7	8	9	Heritage	3/2005	$1,955	ANACSAU55 reverse tooled	$1,700	$2,600	$4,500

J-124a to J-124e: 1850 Cent

J-124b through 124d were earlier listed under 1853 as J-152, J-152a, and J-152c. J-124a, J-124b, and J-124d are perforated.

Obverse: Die as preceding.
Reverse: Wreath enclosing ONE CENT as used in 1853 to strike other patterns, the denomination on some varieties being mostly obliterated by a perforation.

J-124e

Number	Metal	Edge	Rarity	Pop	T/A	Last Traded at Auction				60	63	65
						Firm	Date	Amount	Grade			
124a	WM	PE	8	1	5	Heritage	4/2001	$2,070	NGCPF64	$7,800	$13,000	$19,500
124b	*	PE	8	0	0	N/A	N/A	N/A	N/A	$3,000	$5,200	$9,750
124c	Nick	PE	8	1	2	Heritage	5/2005	$4,600	NGCPF65	$3,000	$5,200	$9,750
124d	Nick	PE	8	0	0	N/A	N/A	N/A	N/A	$3,000	$5,200	$9,750
124e	C	PE	U	1	1	ANR	8/2004	$6,900	NGCPF64BN	N/A	$6,250	N/A

* J-124b: German silver

J-124f: 1850 Cent

Unique. In the Smithsonian Institution.[4]

Obverse: Die as preceding.
Reverse: Open wreath with ribbon at the bottom, enclosing a space for the perforation. UNITED STATES OF AMERICA surrounding (die used for J-127 of 1851).

J-124f

Number	Metal	Edge	Rarity	Pop	T/A	Last Traded at Auction				60	63	65
						Firm	Date	Amount	Grade			
124f	*	PE	U	0	0	N/A	N/A	N/A	N/A	N/A	N/A	N/A

* copper or copper-nickel

Patterns of 1850

J-124g and J-124h: 1850 Cent

Obverse: Die as preceding.
Reverse: Unfinished die with dentils around border but no lettering or motifs.[5]

J-124g

Number	Metal	Edge	Rarity	Pop	T/A	Last Traded at Auction				60	63	65
						Firm	Date	Amount	Grade			
124g	Nick	PE	H7	1	1	ANR	1/2004	$4,140	NGCPF64	$2,500	$3,750	$6,500
124h	C	PE	H7	2	1	Bowers & Merena	11/1985	$358	MS63	$2,500	$3,750	$6,500

J-125: 1850 Trime

Original. 12-3/8 grains weight. Restrikes exist.

Obverse: Liberty cap with resplendent rays surrounding, LIBERTY on bottom of cap, date 1850 below.
Reverse: Palm branch arranged in a continuous circle to make a wreath, enclosing III. UNITED STATES OF AMERICA around border.

J-125

Number	Metal	Edge	Rarity	Pop	T/A	Last Traded at Auction				60	63	65
						Firm	Date	Amount	Grade			
125	Silv	PE	4	71	44	Heritage	6/2005	$3,450	NGCPF65	$1,500	$2,400	$4,500

J-126 and J-126a: 1850 $20

Year of striking not known, but attributed to 1850. Two silver strikes known. A gilt copper piece is in the Harry W. Bass, Jr. Collection.

Obverse: Regular double eagle die by Longacre, but without a date.
Reverse: Regular-issue die.

J-126

Number	Metal	Edge	Rarity	Pop	T/A	Last Traded at Auction				60	63	65
						Firm	Date	Amount	Grade			
126	Silv	RE	8	1	1	Superior	7/1989	$14,300	ChPF	$30,000	$50,000	$75,000
126a	C	RE	U	0	0	N/A	N/A	N/A	N/A	N/A	N/A	N/A

Patterns of 1851

History and Overview

The patterns of 1851 reflect the efforts of 1850—the endeavor to create a more useful one-cent piece of smaller diameter than the large copper version that had been in use since 1793. Billon was again the metal of choice.

In 1850 and later, certain ring-form or annular patterns were struck. Original 1851 pattern cents were struck in billon. Restrikes were made in copper and various alloys, including billon.

As part of James Ross Snowden's restriking activities in 1859, Proof examples of certain rare silver dollars of earlier dates were made, including the 1851 and 1852. For the 1851 dollar, the original die (with four-date digit logotype slanting slightly upward and the date close to the base of Liberty) probably could not be located in 1859. In any event, a different die, not originally used in 1851, with the date horizontal and centered, was employed. Whether this die was created new in 1859 and given an 1851 date, or whether it was made in 1851 and not used at that time, is not known. Restrikes in silver are well known on the numismatic market today and are highly prized, for original strikings are extremely rare and in any event are not known to have been made in Proof format. Listed in the present text are off-metal impressions in copper and nickel.

Collecting Perspective

One or more examples of the pattern cents of this year, J-127 through J-131, can be obtained relatively easily, either in perforated or unperforated form, most being restrikes. Collectors desiring just a single coin might opt for a billon original.

The off-metal strikes of the 1851 silver dollar occasionally come on the market. More often seen are regular silver impressions (not listed here). The nickel—possibly copper-nickel—impression is unique.

J-127 to J-131a: 1851 Cent

Apart from perforated billon examples (J-127, J-127a, and J-129a), all are restrikes. • J-127a supposedly has a larger-diameter perforation.

Obverse: CENT above, ONE TENTH SILVER to the sides and below, raised rim at center, within which is a perforation.[6]
Reverse: Open wreath with ribbon at the bottom, enclosing a space for the perforation. UNITED STATES OF AMERICA surrounding.

J-127

Number	Metal	Edge	Rarity	Pop	T/A	Firm	Date	Amount	Grade	60	63	65
127	Bil	PE	L6	29	20	Heritage	6/2005	$2,703	PCGSMS65	$1,200	$1,750	$3,000
127a	Bil	PE	8	0	0	N/A	N/A	N/A	N/A	$1,400	$2,000	$3,000
128	Bil	PE	8	0	1	Kagin's	5/1968	$110	PF	$4,250	$7,150	$11,000
128a	Bil	RE	8	5	3	ANR	5/2004	$5,175	PCGSPF65	$2,000	$3,750	$6,500
128b	Silv	RE	8	1	1	Bowers & Merena	8/1955	$5,500	PF64	N/A	N/A	N/A
129	C	PE	L7	7	9	ANR	11/2004	$2,990	PCGSPF65RB	$1,500	$2,250	$4,000
130	C	PE	H7	4	4	Stack's/ANR	6/2004	$8,338	PCGSPF64RB	$2,600	$5,000	$8,750
131	C-N	RE	H7	3	3	ANR	8/2004	$10,350	PCGSPF65	$4,250	$7,150	$12,000
131a	Nick	RE	H7	5	5	ANR	3/2005	$4,600	PCGSPF66	$2,000	$3,550	$6,750

J-131b and J-131c: 1851 Cent

Obverse: Die as preceding.
Reverse: Unfinished die with dentils around border but no lettering or motifs.

J-131b

Number	Metal	Edge	Rarity	Pop	T/A	Firm	Date	Amount	Grade	60	63	65
131b	Bil	PE	8	0	0	N/A	N/A	N/A	N/A	$2,400	$3,750	$6,500
131c	C	PE	8	0	0	N/A	N/A	N/A	N/A	$2,500	$3,750	$6,500

J-132 and J-133: 1851 Silver Dollar

Struck from regular dies. Centered date. Restrikes, possibly from a newly created obverse die, after the spring of 1859.

J-132

Number	Metal	Edge	Rarity	Pop	T/A	Firm	Date	Amount	Grade	60	63	65
132	C	RE	L7	8	3	Ira & Larry Goldberg	5/2004	$18,975	PCGSPF64BN	$11,500	$23,000	$32,000
133	Nick	RE	U	0	1	Sotheby's	2/1954	$155	EF	N/A	N/A	N/A

Patterns of 1852

History and Overview

Beginning in 1849, large quantities of gold bullion from the Californian gold fields reached the East, and many coins were struck from this metal. On the international market, silver became "rare" in relation to gold, and the historic ratio of values was disrupted. In 1851, 1852, and early 1853, federal silver coins disappeared from circulation and went into the hands of speculators, hoarders, and melters, as they were worth more in bullion value than the face value stamped on them. In 1851, the silver three-cent piece or trime reached circulation and was successful, using a new alloy of 75% silver and 25% copper (instead of the regular standard of 90% silver 10% copper), with a metal value insufficient to attract hoarders. Accordingly, silver three-cent pieces minted during this time remained in circulation.

In 1852, thoughts were given to producing a half dollar in gold, as the gold dollar was very popular and as silver half dollars were not to be found in commerce. A few patterns were produced at the Mint, from combining a blank half dime die with a reverse die of the half dime, striking pieces containing 50 cents' worth of gold, but with a large perforation in the center to enable the pieces to be of a diameter that would be comfortable to handle. The concept proved unfeasible and was dropped.

Gold dollars were produced in the ring or annular format, also with perforated centers, in an effort to make this coin more easy to use in circulation. An extensive listing of pattern coins exists today from these experiments: rare originals plus elusive restrikes.

In addition, Proof dies of the 1852 Liberty Seated silver dollar were employed to produce restrikes for sale to collectors. Most were made in silver (not listed here), but a few were struck in copper, the latter being J-134.

Collecting Perspective

Collectors focus on 1852 pattern gold dollars of this year, existing in several designs. Gold impressions are known for four different die combinations and are exceedingly rare today. Quite collectible are others, mostly restrikes, in metals and alloys such as copper and copper-nickel. Certain restrikes are from dies that show cracks.

The copper impressions of the 1852 silver dollar are exceedingly rare today and in the same league as the copper impressions of the 1851 Liberty Seated dollar (J-132). These are of primary interest to silver dollar specialists who enjoy having these curious and rare pieces to accompany their silver issues.

J-134: 1852 Silver Dollar

Struck from regular dies. Restrikes were produced circa 1859 and later for sale to collectors. Silver and copper impressions were made, the copper being listed here and believed to have been made circa the early 1870s.

J-134

Number	Metal	Edge	Rarity	Pop	T/A	Last Traded at Auction			60	63	65
						Firm	Date	Amount	Grade		
134	C	RE	H7	1	2	ANR	9/2003	$21,850	NGCPF62BN	$14,000	$26,000	N/A

J-135: 1852 Gold Half Dollar

Experimental or concept piece. Impressions were struck in gold from a die pair hastily combined. The pieces have large perforation at the center to enable a half dollar's worth of gold to be coined in a diameter larger than otherwise would be possible. Two perforated blank planchets also exist.

Obverse: Impression from a plain die, half dime size, with dentils surrounding the border.
Reverse: The regular half dime die of the year.

J-135

Number	Metal	Edge	Rarity	Pop	T/A	Last Traded at Auction			60	63	65
						Firm	Date	Amount	Grade		
135	Gold	RE	H7	5	1	Bowers & Merena	9/1993	$13,750	PCGSPF66	$9,000	$16,000	$25,000

J-136: 1852 Gold Dollar

Related to the experimental half dollar, this gold dollar was made from dies combined to illustrate the concept of a large-diameter piece to facilitate handling, with perforation.

Obverse: A blank planchet of dime size without inscription, but with edge dentils.
Reverse: Regular dime die of the era.

J-136

Number	Metal	Edge	Rarity	Pop	T/A	Last Traded at Auction				60	63	65
						Firm	Date	Amount	Grade			
136	Gold	RE	H7	3	1	Heritage	7/1997	$9,430	PCGSPF65	$11,000	$17,500	$27,500

J-137 to J-140a: 1852 Gold Dollar

This pair of dies was never intended for regular coinage, but was made to test the concept. Used to strike gold impressions of a diameter larger than currently in use, perforated so that the value of gold could be maintained in a larger-format coin. Two examples of J-137 are known, one using an already struck 1846 quarter eagle as the planchet, and the other an 1859 quarter eagle as the planchet. All varieties are restrikes, including gold impressions.

Obverse: USA above, 1852 below. Otherwise blank. A simple, hastily made die to test the concept.
Reverse: Circular laurel wreath.

J-137

Number	Metal	Edge	Rarity	Pop	T/A	Last Traded at Auction				60	63	65
						Firm	Date	Amount	Grade			
137	Gold	PE	8	1	1	Superior	10/1991	$2,530	PF65	$15,500	$22,500	$39,000
138	Silv	PE	L7	9	7	Heritage	5/2003	$5,175	NGCPF64	$2,600	$3,850	$7,250
139	C	PE	H7	2	1	Superior	10/1992	$2,310	NGCPF63BN	$4,800	$8,000	$15,000
140	C-N	PE	L7	11	6	Heritage	5/2004	$4,600	PCGSPF64	$2,500	$3,500	$5,500
140a	Nick	PE	8	1	1	NERCG	4/1980	$2,000	PF	$7,150	$14,000	$24,000

J-141 to J-144: 1852 Gold Dollar

Large-diameter pattern with perforation at the center to enable the same value of gold to be used. All varieties are restrikes, including gold impressions.

Obverse: USA above perforation. 1852 below. Otherwise blank. A simple, hastily made die to test the concept.
Reverse: DOLLAR at top border, open wreath below. A distinctive reverse made especially for this pattern, giving the denomination.

J-141

Number	Metal	Edge	Rarity	Pop	T/A	Last Traded at Auction				60	63	65
						Firm	Date	Amount	Grade			
141	Gold	PE	L7	9	1	Bowers & Merena	3/1980	$20,000	ChPF	$11,000	$16,500	$25,000
142	Silv	PE	8	0	1	W.E. Woodward	11/1862	$2	PF	$8,500	$15,500	$26,000
143	C	PE	8	1	1	Heritage	8/2004	$12,650	NGCPF67RB	$7,250	$14,000	$24,000
144	Nick	PE	U	0	1	Stack's	3/1973	$400	PF	N/A	N/A	N/A

J-145 to J-148b: 1852 Gold Dollar

Perforated at the center to permit a larger diameter coin than would otherwise be possible. Most of these are restrikes.

Obverse: UNITED STATES OF AMERICA around, date 1852 below, with raised ring and ornaments within.
Reverse: DOLLAR above, open wreath below; same die as used for J-141.

J-145

Number	Metal	Edge	Rarity	Pop	T/A	Last Traded at Auction				60	63	65
						Firm	Date	Amount	Grade			
145	Gold	PE	L6	22	16	Heritage	3/2005	$18,400	PCGSPF65	$9,000	$15,000	$22,000
146	Silv	PE	L7*	1	1	NERCG	7/1979	$1,600	MS63	$8,500	$15,000	$26,000
147	C	PE	L7	10	7	ANR	1/2004	$6,670	PCGSPF66RB	$2,750	$4,500	$6,500
148	C-N	PE	L7	9	9	ANR	11/2004	$6,325	NGCPF65	$2,750	$4,000	$6,500
148a	Nick	PE	8	0	1	NERCG	7/1979	$800	MS60	$8,500	$15,500	$26,000
148b	Brs	PE	8	1	1	Superior	5/1994	$3,300	PCGSPF65	$2,600	$5,200	$10,000

* Five are in museums.

Patterns of 1853

History and Overview

The Mint continued producing a new format of one-cent piece to replace the cumbersome copper "large" cents that had been the standard for many years. To test various metal concepts, an existing quarter eagle die of 1853 was employed in combination with a possibly newly created reverse die, the latter featuring an open wreath enclosing the words ONE CENT, spaced too widely apart with an open space at the center, and obviously made in haste.7 Pieces were struck in various alloys, generally known as "German silver," this being a term for an alloy of silvery color, with nickel, copper, and other metals, but lacking precious silver. J-149 was struck with a content of 40% nickel, 40% copper, and 20% zinc; J-150 was made of 30% nickel, 60% copper, and 10% zinc; and J-151 was struck in 40% nickel, 60% copper. Apparently, some were made in "60% nickel, the remainder copper."8 Elemental analysis of the cent patterns of this year suggests that at best the stated metal percentages were approximate.

For collectors, novodels were created by combining the obverse of the 1850 perforated cent die (J-119) with the reverse of the 1853 (J-149).9

A curious pattern trime or three-cent piece was described by W. Elliot Woodward in his catalog of the Joseph J. Mickley Collection (sold from October 28 to November 2, 1867). The location of this piece is not known today.

Also listed under patterns of 1853 are copper impressions from Proof dies of the Liberty Seated dollar dated 1853. These have an interesting background inasmuch as years later it seems to have been realized by collectors that no original Proof impressions were struck in 1853. To fill sets, the Mint produced restrikes from Proof dies, 12 said to have been made in silver and an unknown number in copper. The copper pieces are listed here as J-154.

Collecting Perspective

The German-silver-pattern cents of 1853 seem to have been made in fairly large quantities and can be obtained readily today. The surfaces, not mirrorlike, are properly described as being Mint State. Although J-149 through J-153 were made in different metal compositions, in the absence of elemental analysis, these are impossible to determine today. Accordingly, certain attributions in past market offerings have been speculative.

The varieties under J-152 in the seventh edition of Judd, made from an 1850-dated die, were produced for collectors and might best be collected along with other pieces bearing the 1850 date. They have been reassigned to that year's section under the numbers J-124a to J-124e.

J-149 to J-151: 1853 Cent

The alloys used in this pattern are not confirmed.

Obverse: Regular production die for the 1853 quarter eagle.
Reverse: Wreath, open at the top, enclosing the inscription ONE CENT.

J-149

Number	Metal	Edge	Rarity	Pop	T/A	Last Traded at Auction				60	63	65
						Firm	Date	Amount	Grade			
149	*	RE	H6	16	17	Heritage	8/2004	$2,070	PCGSPF64	$1,550	$2,300	$4,150
150	**	RE	L7	9	2	Heritage	3/2004	$3,450	NGCPF63	$2,750	$5,000	$8,500
151	***	RE	L6	44	29	ANR	3/2005	$1,955	NGCPF62	$1,750	$2,750	$4,500

  * J-149: German silver (40% nickel, 40% copper, 20% zinc)
  ** J-150: German silver (30% nickel, 60% copper, 10% zinc)
  *** J-151: 40% nickel, 60% copper

J-151b to J-151d: 1853 Cent

Obverse: Unfinished die with dentils around border, but no lettering or motifs.
Reverse: Die as preceding, wreath enclosing ONE CENT.

J-151c

Number	Metal	Edge	Rarity	Pop	T/A	Last Traded at Auction				60	63	65
						Firm	Date	Amount	Grade			
151b	C	PE	H7	0	1	Bowers & Merena	11/1985	$308	MS63	$2,500	$3,750	$6,500
151c	C-N	PE	H7	2	2	ANR	3/2004	$3,450	ICGPF64	$2,500	$3,750	$6,500
151d	Bil	PE	H7	3	2	Heritage	3/2005	$4,025	PCGSPF65	$2,500	$3,500	$5,500

J-153: 1853 Trime

Transitional pattern coined on April 10, 1853.

Obverse: Shield mounted on a six-pointed star but with a triple border around the star, this being different from the regular issue; the so-called Type II style regularly adopted in 1854.
Reverse: The regular dies used to strike 1854 trimes, known as the Type II design, with olive sprig above III and three arrows below, within the ornamental letter C.

J-153

Number	Metal	Edge	Rarity	Pop	T/A	Last Traded at Auction				60	63	65
						Firm	Date	Amount	Grade			
153	Silv	PE	U	0	1	W.E. Woodward	10/1867	$0.25	PF	N/A	N/A	N/A

J-154: 1853 Silver Dollar

Struck from regular dies. Restrike made for collectors from Proof dies, in silver and in copper, circa the early 1870s, the copper being listed here.

J-154

Number	Metal	Edge	Rarity	Pop	T/A	Last Traded at Auction				60	63	65
						Firm	Date	Amount	Grade			
154	C	RE	H7	5	6	Ira & Larry Goldberg	5/2004	$8,338	PF60BN	$8,500	$13,000	$27,500

History and Overview

In 1854, pattern activity continued to emphasize the modification of the large copper cent, a process that had been ongoing since 1850. In 1853, several distinctive designs were created, including one reduced from an 1854 silver dollar die and another with Gobrecht's Flying Eagle design as used on certain pattern half dollars of 1838 (for example, J-73). In addition, regular dies for the 1854 silver half dime were used to strike impressions in German silver.

The first cent in the listing (J-156) is one of the most interesting in the series. The obverse features stars surrounding the seated figure of Liberty, with the date below. This die was made by the transfer process using a lathe, in which a stylus was impressed in a slow spiral on the obverse of a regularly struck 1854 silver dollar, in the process showing many transfer lines and irregularities, but reducing the motif to a much smaller size. The crossbar of the 4 is not evident, making the date appear as "1851."

A larger suite of pattern cents comprises the head of Liberty taken from the hub or punch used to create the motif for contemporary Braided Hair large copper cents, with the date 1854 below, without stars, and on a reduced-diameter planchet. The reverse of these pieces is similar in concept to those made for circulation, but with smaller letters and smaller diameter. Then follow the Flying Eagle cents of 1854, for which James B. Longacre copied Gobrecht's motif, in this instance an eagle first known to have been used on half dollars of 1838 (differing slightly in execution from that on the Gobrecht silver dollars of 1836). The reverse is similar to the foregoing.

Collecting Perspective

A trial piece of the regular half-cent dies in a special copper alloy (J-155) is sufficiently rare as to be unobtainable.

Among the pattern cents of 1854, the Liberty Seated variety turns up with some frequency. All of these have very rough and irregular obverse surfaces due to the way the die was prepared. Liberty Head and Flying Eagle pattern cents exist in fair numbers and are readily collectible, although some varieties are elusive. Many were restruck, although the difference between restrikes and originals is not well delineated in the literature nor is it often mentioned in sale descriptions. For varieties J-160 to J-165, pieces listed in bronze are probably all restrikes, if, indeed, they were made in bronze, as this metal was not standard at the Mint in the 1850s.

Among the issues J-160 through J-165, there are two different obverse dies (Liberty Head and Flying Eagle), and three different styles of reverse wreaths, as delineated in the descriptions below. Most numismatists aspire to collect simply one example of each obverse type. Thus far, the wreath differences have not attracted much attention.

The final piece in the listing is a striking from regular half dime dies but in German silver, which is exceedingly rare.

Patterns of 1854

J-155: 1854 Half Cent

Struck from regular dies. • Bronze or oroide alloy (80% copper, 16% tin, 4% silver).[10]

J-155

Number	Metal	Edge	Rarity	Pop	T/A	Last Traded at Auction				60	63	65
						Firm	Date	Amount	Grade			
155	Oro	PE	U	0	1	Bowers & Merena	10/1987	$1,980	Unc	N/A	N/A	N/A

J-156 to J-159a: 1854 Cent

Experimental cent produced to test the concept of diameter and thickness, not to illustrate a proposed design. The alloys are not confirmed.

Obverse: Struck from a die created by reducing design elements of an 1854 silver dollar, but with the crossbar of the 4 not evident, thus appearing as "1851." Certain other features are irregular and in some instances indistinct.
Reverse: New die with a heavy wreath, open at the top, enclosing 1 CENT.

J-159a

Number	Metal	Edge	Rarity	Pop	T/A	Last Traded at Auction				60	63	65
						Firm	Date	Amount	Grade			
156	*	RE	H7	2	5	Superior	5/1992	$3,410	NGCPF64	$3,200	$6,000	$11,500
157	**	RE	H7	4	1	ANR	11/2004	$6,325	PCGSPF65	$2,400	$4,500	$6,750
157a	***	RE	U	2	0	Ira & Larry Goldberg	5/2005	–	NGCPF64	N/A	N/A	N/A
158	†	RE	H6	12	7	Superior	5/2004	$2,760	PCGSPF63	$2,250	$3,200	$4,500
158a	‡	RE	U	0	1	Heritage	8/1998	$1,668	MS63	N/A	N/A	N/A
159	C	PE	L7	18	15	Heritage	11/2003	$2,185	NGCMS61RB	N/A	N/A	N/A
159a	‡‡	PE	H6	2	3	ANR	3/2005	$3,450	NGCPF65RB	$2,200	$3,000	$4,500

* J-156: German silver (40% nickel, 40% copper, 20% zinc)
** J-157: German silver (30% nickel, 60% copper, 10% zinc)
*** J-157a: German silver (20% nickel, 71% copper, 9% zinc)
† J-158: 40% nickel, 60% copper
‡ J-158a: alloy of 78% silver, 5.6% nickel, 13.7% copper, 2.7% zinc
‡‡ J-159a: copper electrotype

J-160 to J-162: 1854 Cent

Struck in a diameter smaller than that of the current circulating cents.

Obverse: Head of Liberty with braided hair and coronet, facing left, same style as used on circulating cents. No stars. Date 1854 below.
Reverse: Continuous laurel wreath, ribbon at bottom, enclosing ONE CENT. Around the border is UNITED STATES OF AMERICA.

J-160

Number	Metal	Edge	Rarity	Pop	T/A	Last Traded at Auction				60	63	65
						Firm	Date	Amount	Grade			
160	C	PE	4	87	84	Heritage	6/2005	$1,725	PCGSPF65BN	$1,100	$1,400	$2,000
161	Brz	PE	4	175	81	Heritage	5/2005	$1,380	PCGSPF64BN	$1,050	$1,300	$1,900
162	Oro	PE	8	0	1	NERCG	4/1980	$2,500	PF63	$5,200	$7,800	$13,000

J-163 and J-164: 1854 Cent

Struck in a diameter smaller than that of the current circulating cents.

Obverse: Eagle flying left, adapted from Gobrecht's 1838 half dollar motif, stars around, date 1854 below.

Reverse: Continuous wreath with ribbon at bottom, enclosing ONE CENT, with inscription UNITED STATES OF AMERICA surrounding. Two leaves in wreath under E (in STATES)

J-164

Number	Metal	Edge	Rarity	Pop	T/A	Last Traded at Auction				60	63	65
						Firm	Date	Amount	Grade			
163	C	PE	H6	20	19	Heritage	1/2005	$4,313	NGCPF65BN	$1,750	$3,000	$5,000
164	Brz	PE	5	30	15	ANR	3/2005	$16,100	NGCPF67BN	$1,500	$2,150	$4,000

J-165: 1854 Cent

Obverse: 1854 Flying Eagle die as preceding.
Reverse: Similar to the preceding, but wreath slightly larger. Four leaves in wreath under E (in STATES).

J-165

Number	Metal	Edge	Rarity	Pop	T/A	Last Traded at Auction				60	63	65
						Firm	Date	Amount	Grade			
165	C	PE	8	0	1	Bolender	3/1955	$31	PFRD	N/A	N/A	N/A

J-165b: 1854 Cent

Obverse: 1854 Flying Eagle die as preceding.
Reverse: Similar to J-163 and J-165 in concept, but slightly different in size. Three leaves under E (in STATES).

J-165b

Number	Metal	Edge	Rarity	Pop	T/A	Last Traded at Auction				60	63	65
						Firm	Date	Amount	Grade			
165b	Brz	PE	8	3	0	N/A	N/A	N/A	N/A	$4,250	$7,800	$13,000

J-166: 1854 Half Dime

Struck from regular dies. All are struck off center. All are on extremely thick planchets. About a half dozen are believed to exist.

J-166

Number	Metal	Edge	Rarity	Pop	T/A	Last Traded at Auction				60	63	65
						Firm	Date	Amount	Grade			
166	*	PE	H7	3	2	RARCOA/Akers	8/1991	$1,500	PF63	$2,150	$4,200	$7,700

* J-166: German silver

Patterns of 1855

History and Overview

This year saw continuing experiments for a reduced-diameter copper cent, employing an 1855 dated Flying Eagle obverse similar to that used in 1854 in combination with two different styles of reverse wreath (both of which had been used in 1854). Various alloys including French bronze were tested. Mint records indicated three metal compositions:[11] bronze (95% copper, 4% tin, 1% zinc); 90% copper, 10% nickel; and 80% copper, 20% nickel.

At least one half dollar was struck of this date, from regular dies but in aluminum. It is not known whether it is indeed a contemporary (not restrike) impression, or whether it is part of the numerous later aluminum restrikes. (In 1855, aluminum was considered a very expensive metal, hard to obtain and refine.) The only piece traced resides at Princeton University, where it has been since the 1880s.

Collecting Perspective

Numismatic interest for patterns of this year is focused on the Flying Eagle cents, of which most numismatists aspire to have one example, although two different wreath variations and several metal variations can be obtained. The metal variations, delineated below, are virtually impossible to distinguish from each other in the absence of elemental analysis. Again, although originals may have been struck in bronze (as believed by Dr. Judd), it may be that any and all bronze pieces are restrikes.

J-167 to J-171a: 1855 Cent

The alloys used in this pattern are not confirmed.

Obverse: Eagle flying to the left, stars around, motif as used in 1854, but date 1855 below.
Reverse: Wreath as used on J-165 of 1854 with four leaves under E (in STATES).

J-168

Number	Metal	Edge	Rarity	Pop	T/A	Firm	Date	Amount	Grade	60	63	65
							Last Traded at Auction					
167	C	PE	5	78	67	Heritage	5/2005	$2,530	PCGSPF64BN	$1,850	$2,250	$3,250
167a	Nick	PE	8	1	0	N/A	N/A	N/A	N/A	N/A	N/A	$3,250
168	Brz	PE	4	202	63	Heritage	3/2005	$4,025	NGCPF65RB	$1,850	$2,250	$4,000
169	Oro	PE	L7	10	5	ANR	3/2005	$2,185	NGCPF62	$2,000	$3,250	$6,200
170	*	PE	L7	7	6	Heritage	7/1997	$2,415	PCGSPF64	$2,500	$4,000	$6,750
170a	**	PE	8	N/A	N/A	N/A	N/A	N/A	N/A	N/A	N/A	N/A
171	†	PE	L7	11	4	Superior	5/1995	$1,760	PCGSPF60	$2,500	$4,000	$6,750
171a	‡	PE	8	1	1	ANR	1/2004	$5,450	NGCPF62	$3,500	$5,500	$8,000

    * J-170: 80% copper, 20% nickel
   ** J-170a: 90% copper, 10% nickel
   † J-171: 60% copper, 40% nickel
   ‡ J-171a: German silver (75% copper, 12% nickel, 13% zinc);
           German silver (66% copper, 20% nickel, 14% zinc);
           German silver (64% copper, 19% nickel, 17% zinc)

J-172 to J-174b: 1855 Cent

Obverse: Die as preceding.
Reverse: As used on J-163, smaller wreath than preceding, with two leaves under E (in STATES).

J-173

Number	Metal	Edge	Rarity	Pop	T/A	Firm	Date	Amount	Grade	60	63	65
							Last Traded at Auction					
172	C	PE	L6	19	13	ANR	8/2004	$4,830	NGCPF66BN	$1,900	$3,100	$5,000
173	Brz	PE	L7	8	9	ANR	3/2004	$3,220	NGCPF64BN	$2,250	$3,750	$6,250
174	Oro	PE	8	0	1	SRCG	10/1981	$600	AU55	N/A	N/A	N/A
174a	C-N	PE	U	0	0	N/A	N/A	N/A	N/A	N/A	N/A	N/A

J-175: 1855 Half Dollar

Trial piece struck from regular dies. This was the first piece struck by the U.S. Mint in aluminum. Currently in the Princeton University collection (Numismatic Collection, Department of Rare Books and Special Collections, Princeton University Library).

J-175

Number	Metal	Edge	Rarity	Pop	T/A	Last Traded at Auction				60	63	65
						Firm	Date	Amount	Grade			
175	Alu	RE	U	0	0	N/A	N/A	N/A	N/A	N/A	N/A	N/A

J-175a: 1855 Gold Dollar

Struck from regular dies. Irregular planchet. The genuineness of this piece has been questioned. (The illustration is of an authentic regular-strike coin in gold.)

see text

Number	Metal	Edge	Rarity	Pop	T/A	Last Traded at Auction				60	63	65
						Firm	Date	Amount	Grade			
175a	WM	RE	U	0	1	Lester Merkin	10/1972	$600	Unc	N/A	N/A	N/A

J-176: 1855 $10

Restrike struck from rusty regular dies. Silver or silver-plated pieces may exist. The genuineness of all has been questioned. (The illustration is of an authentic regular-strike coin in gold.)

see text

Number	Metal	Edge	Rarity	Pop	T/A	Last Traded at Auction				60	63	65
						Firm	Date	Amount	Grade			
176	C	RE	8	0	1	Kagin's	10/1966	$395	No Grade	N/A	$15,000	N/A

Patterns of 1856

History and Overview

The 1856 Flying Eagle cent is a very well-known popular rarity, as these cents have formed the focus of attention since the time they were struck. Experiments that had been conducted at the Mint since 1850 for a smaller diameter cent came to a conclusion, and a new alloy, today known as copper-nickel (consisting of 88% copper and 12% nickel), was found to be superior to other tested alloys.

The 1856 Flying Eagle cent has the distinction that both sides are copies of something else—the obverse derived from Gobrecht's silver dollar and the reverse from Longacre's own earlier work. The diameter of the cent was reduced to three-quarters of an inch, so that four pieces, arranged side by side, would span three inches—perhaps a handy guide for measuring.

Many strikings of the 1856 Flying Eagle cent were in fact restrikes, although this makes no market difference today. Original pieces struck in 1856 were sent to congressmen, newspaper editors, and others of influence to acquaint them with the new design. The total number of these originals struck is not known, but the figure is estimated at nearly 1,000 pieces.

Probably beginning in spring 1859, the highly prized 1856 Flying Eagle cent became one of the most important items for sale as part of the vast production of restrikes under the aegis of Director Snowden, there being an insatiable demand for them. On the market, pieces sold for $1 or more, not a remarkable figure today in the early 21st century, but in 1859 equal to a day's pay for many people. New dies were made with the date of 1856, and to make them especially attractive to numismatists, were given highly polished Proof surfaces. These were produced in large quantities, perhaps 1,500 to 2,000 over a period of time, but again no records were kept; the distribution was secret. Beyond the standard 1856 pattern Flying Eagle cent (J-180), a few other pattern cents were made, mostly restrikes. Theses are delineated below. No patterns of higher denominations are known to have been struck.

Patterns of 1856

Collecting Perspective

The 1856 Flying Eagle cent is far and away the most plentiful of all pattern coins today, and at least a couple thousand exist. No matter, it is also one of the most expensive—a paradox to be sure, but such things are part of the allure of the pattern series.

Since the late 1850s, the 1856 Flying Eagle cent has been the Holy Grail, a "must have" for generations of numismatists. While made as a pattern, this piece was soon adopted by collectors of the regular series, and today it is considered to be the first date in the Flying Eagle set, which includes the more numerous regular issues of 1857 and 1858. It is likely that pieces offered today in grades showing wear, up to and including, say, AU-58, are originals made in 1856 or early 1857. Proofs are nearly all restrikes. The marketplace does not differentiate originals from restrikes, and the point is moot, except that the subject is of interest to specialists. Collectors of Flying Eagle and Indian Head cents have forum in the pages of *Longacre's Ledger*, published by a society of enthusiasts. Richard Snow, for one, has studied the die differences of 1856 Flying Eagle cents in detail, and today "Snow numbers" are used by specialists to differentiate them.

Beyond the J-180 1856 Flying Eagle cent, other patterns dated this year are very elusive.

J-177: 1856 Half Cent

Struck from regular dies. Trial pieces made to the extent of at least 50 pieces, apparently in two slightly differing copper-nickel alloys: one with 88% copper, 12% nickel alloy; the other 90% copper, 10% nickel alloy. These are impossible to distinguish today except by elemental analysis. Some auction listings may represent misattributed examples.

J-177

Number	Metal	Edge	Rarity	Pop	T/A	Last Traded at Auction				60	63	65
						Firm	Date	Amount	Grade			
177	C-N	PE	5	15	N/A	Superior	2/2005	$2,875	PF60	$2,400	$3,500	$6,500

J-178 and J-179: Undated Cent

Obverse: Flying Eagle motif, but in plain field, without inscription or date.
Reverse: "Agricultural wreath" enclosing ONE CENT, the design used for regular-issue Flying Eagle cents in 1857 and 1858.

J-179

Number	Metal	Edge	Rarity	Pop	T/A	Last Traded at Auction				60	63	65
						Firm	Date	Amount	Grade			
178	C-N	PE	H7	3	1	Superior	2/1999	$3,680	PCGSPF45	$12,000	$22,000	$37,500
179	C	PE	L7	7	4	Heritage	5/2004	$16,100	PCGSPF64BN	$10,000	$16,000	$25,000
179a	Nick	PE	–	0	0	N/A	N/A	N/A	N/A	Unconf	Unconf	Unconf

J-180 to J-183: 1856 Cent

J-180 is the famous and popular "1856 Flying Eagle cent" widely collected transitional pattern, listed in *A Guide Book of United States Coins*, and of commanding importance to generations of numismatists. Examples exist in all grades. Die varieties exist and have been described by Richard Snow in his text on Flying Eagle cents.

Obverse: Eagle flying left, UNITED STATES OF AMERICA above, 1856 below.
Reverse: Agricultural wreath as foregoing.

J-180

Number	Metal	Edge	Rarity	Pop	T/A	Last Traded at Auction				60	63	65
						Firm	Date	Amount	Grade			
180	C-N	PE	1	1,253	280	Heritage	11/2003	$21,275	PCGSMS64	$12,000	$17,000	$28,000
181	C	PE	H6	15	5	Heritage	9/2003	$19,550	PCGSPF64RB	$10,500	$18,000	$32,500
182	Brz	PE	L7	7	0	N/A	N/A	N/A	N/A	$13,000	$22,000	$37,500
183	Nick	PE	H7	4	3	Heritage	5/2004	$16,100	PCGSPF62	$18,000	$27,000	$46,000

J-184 and J-185: 1856 Cent

Obverse: Similar to preceding, but with open E's, light date, thin letters.
Reverse: Pattern die made in 1858, oak wreath with arrows at bottom, tied by ribbon, ornamented shield above, ONE CENT within wreath.

J-184

Number	Metal	Edge	Rarity	Pop	T/A	Last Traded at Auction				60	63	65
						Firm	Date	Amount	Grade			
184	C-N	PE	L7	12	10	ANR	3/2005	$17,250	NGCPF64CA	$9,000	$16,000	$24,000
185	C	PE	H7	2	1	Bowers & Merena	1/1996	$6,050	PCGSPF64BN	$13,000	$23,000	$42,000

History and Overview

The year 1857 was the launching pad for American numismatics as a widespread hobby. The Act of February 12 mandated the discontinuation of the copper half cent and cent, effective two years thence (but later given a six-month extension). Soon, all such pieces, including the familiar large "pennies" of childhood, would be gone from circulation. Nostalgia swept America, and countless citizens looked through loose coins and elsewhere to see how many different dates they could acquire.

The new Flying Eagle cents were struck in quantity from 1857-dated dies, and on May 25, the first pieces were released to the general public.

Other patterns listed under 1857 are those actually dated in that year, including J-186 (featuring the head of Liberty essentially as used years later on the 1865 nickel three-cent piece), an interesting quarter dollar (J-188) from an incomplete reverse die, and a $2.50 gold coin with the same Liberty Head as used on J-186 (J-189).

Collecting Perspective

All patterns dated from 1857 range from rare to unobtainable, although with some patience a few representative pieces may be obtained.

J-186: 1857 Cent

Obverse: Head of Liberty facing left, coronet inscribed LIBERTY, essentially the same style as later used on the regular nickel three-cent pieces of 1865: 13 stars around, date 1857 below. Die also used to strike the J-189 $2.50 and later muled with an 1860 die to create a numismatic fantasy (J-270).
Reverse: Open wreath enclosing ONE CENT widely spaced, die used in 1853 to coin J-149 and other issues.

J-186

Number	Metal	Edge	Rarity	Pop	T/A	Last Traded at Auction				60	63	65
						Firm	Date	Amount	Grade			
186	C-N	PE	H7	4	2	ANR	3/2004	$12,075	PCGSPF65	$3,550	$6,000	$12,000

J-187 and J-187a: 1857 Cent

Trial piece struck from regular dies. Two or three examples of each metal are believed to exist, including one copper piece in the National Numismatic Collection, Smithsonian Institution.

J-187

Number	Metal	Edge	Rarity	Pop	T/A	Last Traded at Auction				60	63	65
						Firm	Date	Amount	Grade			
187	C	PE	8	1	1	Superior	1/1990	$5,280	PCGSPF63BN	$10,000	$16,000	$27,000
187a	Nick	PE	8	1	1	Stack's	1/1987	$1,100	Unc	$10,000	$16,000	$27,000

Patterns of 1857

J-188: 1857 Quarter Dollar

Obverse: Regular Liberty Seated die of the year.
Reverse: Incomplete die with letters around the border, smaller font than on the regular issue: UNITED STATES OF AMER-ICA / QUAR. DOL. Blank at the center.

J-188

Number	Metal	Edge	Rarity	Pop	T/A	Last Traded at Auction				60	63	65
						Firm	Date	Amount	Grade			
188	C	PE	L7	4	3	Stack's	10/2003	$5,750	PCGSPF62RB	$2,500	$5,500	$10,000

J-189: 1857 $2.50

Obverse die varieties exist. One reverse die trial known (see Appendix A).

Obverse: Head of Liberty facing left, coronet inscribed LIB-ERTY, essentially the same style as later used on the regular nickel three-cent pieces of 1865. 13 stars around, date 1857 below (same die used to strike J-186 with a cent reverse).
Reverse: Eagle at the center, wings outstretched, shield on breast, holding olive branch and three arrows. UNITED STATES OF AMERICA / 2 1/2 D around border.

J-189

Number	Metal	Edge	Rarity	Pop	T/A	Last Traded at Auction				60	63	65
						Firm	Date	Amount	Grade			
189	C	RE	L7	4	6	ANR	12/2003	$4,600	PF60Gilt	$4,500	$7,500	$12,500

J-190: 1857 $20

Experimental piece. The regular reverse, uniface, was made very concave by passing it through the upsetting machine before and after striking.

Obverse: Blank.
Reverse: From the regular die of the period.

J-190

Number	Metal	Edge	Rarity	Pop	T/A	Last Traded at Auction				60	63	65
						Firm	Date	Amount	Grade			
190	C	PE	U	1	2	Heritage	7/2003	$28,750	PCGSPF63BN	N/A	$30,000	N/A

Patterns of 1858

History and Overview

1858 was a "very good year" in terms of patterns, as by this time the numismatic community was dynamic, societies had been formed, and there was an eager market for interesting specimens. At the same time, the Mint was displeased with the Flying Eagle cent design used in circulation since 1857, as deep parts of the obverse die, particularly the head and tail of the eagle, were opposite in the coining press from deep parts of the reverse die, specifically the wreath, with the result that the features of the eagle were often lightly struck up.

A new pattern combining an Indian Head obverse with a laurel wreath reverse (J-208) was the one to be used for circulation. The design went into official use the next year.

Several different obverse and reverse dies were prepared, apparently mostly in the autumn. In addition, regular dies of the 1858 year were used to create patterns. The various dies involved can be described as follows:

Cent Obverse Dies of 1858
Obverse 1: "Flying Eagle in plain field." Flying eagle die, but without inscription or date. • Used with J-219.
Obverse 2: "Flying Eagle, Large Letters, no date." Regular Flying Eagle cent die, Large Letters, UNITED STATES OF AMERICA above, but no date. • Used with J-201, J-219.
Obverse 3: "Flying Eagle, Small Letters, no date." Regular Flying Eagle cent die, Small Letters, UNITED STATES OF AMERICA above, but no date. • Used with J-200.

Obverse 4: "Flying Eagle, Large Letters, regular die." Regular Flying Eagle cent die, Large Letters, UNITED STATES OF AMERICA above, date 1858 below. • Used with J-196 to J-199, J-218, J-218a.

Obverse 5: "Flying Eagle, Small Letters, regular die." Regular Flying Eagle cent die, Small Letters, UNITED STATES OF AMERICA above, date 1858 below. • Used with J-191 to J-195, J-217, J-217a. Also J-362 of 1864.

Obverse 6: "Small Flying Eagle." Small or "skinny" flying eagle, UNITED STATES OF AMERICA above, date 1858 below. • Director Snowden called this "a small eagle, volant, presented in a different position from that on the legal cent."[12] • Used with J-202 to J-207a, J-220.

Obverse 7: "Indian Head, no date." Indian Head, but no date. UNITED STATES to the left, OF AMERICA, to the right. • Used with J-214 to J- 216.

Obverse 8: "Indian Head." Indian Head cent as adopted in 1859 (two portrait varieties: style with narrow bust point as adopted in 1859, and style with rounded bust point as mostly used on patterns of 1858), UNITED STATES to the left, OF AMERICA, to the right, date 1858 below. • Several die varieties exist. • The rounded bust style was the most popular for use on 1858 patterns; in 1860 it reappeared on regular issue cents. The pointed bust was less often used on 1858 patterns and was the standard style for regular 1859 cents. • Used with J-208 to J-213, J-220.

Cent Reverse Dies of 1858

Reverse A: "Regular die with agricultural wreath." "Agricultural wreath" as used on regular issue Flying Eagle cents of the year. • There are two main styles of reverse:[13] the "High Leaves" and the "Low Leaves." • Used with J-201, J-206 to J-207a, J-213, J-217 to J-218a.

Reverse B: "Oak wreath." Oak wreath with arrows below, tied with ribbon, open at top ONE CENT at the center. • Used with J-192, J-197, J-200, J-203, J-211.

Reverse C: "Oak wreath with ornamented shield." Oak wreath with arrows below, tied with ribbon, ornamented shield at wreath apex, ONE CENT at the center. "The objection to this was that the shield had the appearance of a harp."[14] Sometimes called ornamental shield. • Used with J-193 to J-195, J-198, J-199, J-204, J-205, J-212, J-216.

Reverse D: "Laurel wreath." Laurel wreath with ONE CENT at the center, variously described in Mint correspondence as "laurel" or "olive," tied with ribbon below. This die was later used on the regular issue cent of 1859. Variations in wreath details exist, the most notable being either five or six leaves in each cluster. Most 1858 patterns had five leaves (and with the wreath slightly off center); a few had six leaves (with the wreath centered) as did all regular issue 1859 cents.[15] • Used with J-191, J-196, J-202, J-208 to J-210, J-214, J-215.

The preceding designations are useful in listing the various combinations made in 1858. Examples existing in larger numbers today, Rarity-4 or Rarity-5, are those that were included in 12-piece sets made up at the Mint and sold to numismatists. These sets included three obverse dies (Obverses 5, 6, and 8[16]) combined in each instance with Reverses A through D[17]. Of these 12 coins, the combination of Obverse 5 with Reverse A yielded a regular issue (1858 Small Letters Proof striking) and thus is not listed among patterns today.

In addition, many other pattern cents, probably most of them, were sold individually here and there to collectors and dealers. As can be seen from the die combinations, most of these were probably conceived for use to sell to the numismatic trade. Not only were pieces struck in 1858, but also these became a stock in trade item for years thereafter. J-208, the well-known 1858 transitional Indian Head cent with reverse of 1859, seems to have been a particularly popular variety, and several die varieties exist. How late such restrikes were made is anyone's guess, but it is likely that production continued for years afterward.

A quarter dollar pattern was made this year, employing the regular Liberty Seated die for the obverse and, on the reverse, a new version of a perched eagle, attributed to Anthony C. Paquet. Pattern half dollars dated 1858 were also made from a regular obverse die and a reverse die by Paquet, the last featuring an eagle with a shield on its breast and a ribbon across the shield. Paquet also tried his hand at making a pattern gold dollar, similar to that in current use, but with the lettering in a taller font.

Collecting Perspective

Pattern cents of the year 1858 form a playground for numismatists, and in time, most of them can be collected, this being particularly true of those designated as R-4, R-5, and even R-6. Specialists with a technical turn of mind can investigate certain die variations and states, most notably with Obverse 8 and Reverse D described above.

Generally, pattern cents of this year were struck from dies with at least a partial prooflike surface, although some dies were made in haste and had numerous striae. Deep full-mirror Proofs are in the minority, and when found, are most likely to be the Flying Eagle obverses, either the regular-issue style (after Gobrecht) or the Small Flying Eagle. Additional strikings of certain combinations and metals were produced in very small numbers, designated as R-7 and R-8 today, and were not widely sold to collectors at the time.

The pattern quarter dollars and half dollars of 1858 with the Paquet reverse are scarce, and pieces appear on the market only occasionally. Whether these were actually struck in 1858 or, more likely, struck a year or two later but using an 1858 obverse die, is not known. The Paquet gold dollar is likewise elusive.

Patterns of 1858

J-191: 1858 Cent
Dies 5-D

Transitional issue, obverse of 1858, reverse as adopted in 1859. Reverse die varieties exist.

Obverse: Flying Eagle, Small Letters, regular die.
Reverse: Laurel wreath.

J-191

Number	Metal	Edge	Rarity	Pop	T/A	Firm	Date	Amount	Grade	60	63	65
						Last Traded at Auction						
191	C-N	PE	5	49	37	Heritage	1/2005	$3,738	NGCPF65	$1,650	$3,100	$6,250

J-192: 1858 Cent
Dies 5-B

Obverse: Flying Eagle, Small Letters, regular die.
Reverse: Oak wreath.

J-192

Number	Metal	Edge	Rarity	Pop	T/A	Firm	Date	Amount	Grade	60	63	65
						Last Traded at Auction						
192	C-N	PE	5	41	20	Heritage	3/2005	$2,760	PCGSPF64	$1,650	$3,000	$5,000

J-193 to J-195: 1858 Cent
Dies 5-C

J-194 was struck on a broad planchet.

Obverse: Flying Eagle, Small Letters, regular die.
Reverse: Oak wreath with ornamented shield.

J-193

Number	Metal	Edge	Rarity	Pop	T/A	Firm	Date	Amount	Grade	60	63	65
						Last Traded at Auction						
193	C-N	PE	5	46	34	ANR	8/2004	$3,105	NGCPF63	$1,650	$3,150	$6,250
194	C-N	PE	–	0	0	N/A	N/A	N/A	N/A	Unconf	Unconf	Unconf
195	C	PE	U	0	1	Kosoff	8/1966	$1,200	No Grade	N/A	N/A	N/A

J-196: 1858 Cent
Dies 4-D

Transitional issue, obverse of 1858, reverse as adopted in 1859. Reverse with 5-leaf clusters.

Obverse: Flying Eagle, Large Letters, regular die.
Reverse: Laurel wreath.

J-196

Number	Metal	Edge	Rarity	Pop	T/A	Firm	Date	Amount	Grade	60	63	65
						Last Traded at Auction						
196	C-N	PE	U	0	1	Heritage	2/1989	$975	PF65	$7,800	$13,000	$20,000

J-197: 1858 Cent
Dies 4-B

Obverse: Flying Eagle, Large Letters, regular die.
Reverse: Oak wreath.

J-197

Number	Metal	Edge	Rarity	Pop	T/A	Firm	Date	Amount	Grade	60	63	65
						Last Traded at Auction						
197	C-N	PE	H7	1	1	Superior	1/2005	$4,255	PCGSPF64	$6,000	$9,000	$15,000

J-198 and J-199: 1858 Cent
Dies 4-C

J-199 was struck on a broad planchet.

Obverse: Flying Eagle, Large Letters, regular die.
Reverse: Oak wreath with ornamented shield.

J-198

Number	Metal	Edge	Rarity	Pop	T/A	Last Traded at Auction				60	63	65
						Firm	Date	Amount	Grade			
198	C-N	PE	L6	23	15	Heritage	6/2004	$3,105	PCGSPF64	$2,250	$3,850	$7,500
199	C-N	PE	H7	1	1	Superior	10/1992	$4,400	PCGSPF64	$7,500	$16,000	$30,000

J-200: Undated Cent
Dies 3-B

Obverse: Flying Eagle, Small Letters, no date.
Reverse: Oak wreath.

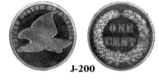

J-200

Number	Metal	Edge	Rarity	Pop	T/A	Last Traded at Auction				60	63	65
						Firm	Date	Amount	Grade			
200	C-N	PE	–	0	0	N/A	N/A	N/A	N/A	Unconf	Unconf	Unconf

J-201: 1858 Cent
Dies 2-A

Obverse: Flying Eagle, Large Letters, no date.
Reverse: Regular die with agricultural wreath.

J-201

Number	Metal	Edge	Rarity	Pop	T/A	Last Traded at Auction				60	63	65
						Firm	Date	Amount	Grade			
201	C-N	PE	U	0	1	Bebee's	8/1955	$365	BrPF	$8,500	$15,000	$25,000

J-202: 1858 Cent
Dies 6-D

Reverse die varieties exist.

Obverse: Small Flying Eagle.
Reverse: Laurel wreath.

J-202

Number	Metal	Edge	Rarity	Pop	T/A	Last Traded at Auction				60	63	65
						Firm	Date	Amount	Grade			
202	C-N	PE	5	67	49	Heritage	6/2005	$1,610	NGCPF55	$1,900	$3,000	$5,500

J-203: 1858 Cent
Dies 6-B

Obverse: Small Flying Eagle.
Reverse: Oak wreath.

J-203

Number	Metal	Edge	Rarity	Pop	T/A	Last Traded at Auction				60	63	65
						Firm	Date	Amount	Grade			
203	C-N	PE	3	44	27	Heritage	6/2005	$5,175	NGCPF65	$1,900	$3,000	$5,750

Patterns of 1858

J-204 and J-205: 1858 Cent
Dies 6-C

Obverse: Small Flying Eagle.
Reverse: Oak wreath with ornamented shield.

J-204

Number	Metal	Edge	Rarity	Pop	T/A	Firm	Date	Amount	Grade	60	63	65
							Last Traded at Auction					
204	C-N	PE	5	82	53	Bowers & Merena	3/2005	$2,645	PCGSPF64	$1,600	$2,400	$4,000
205	C	PE	8	4	2	Stack's	3/1992	$3,300	PFBN	$4,250	$7,500	$13,000

J-206 to J-207a: 1858 Cent
Dies 6-A

Obverse: Small Flying Eagle.
Reverse: Regular die with agricultural wreath.

J-207a

Number	Metal	Edge	Rarity	Pop	T/A	Firm	Date	Amount	Grade	60	63	65
							Last Traded at Auction					
206	C-N	PE	5	52	25	ANR	3/2005	$2,415	NGCPF63CA	$1,750	$2,900	$5,750
207	C	PE	8	3	1	Superior	1/1996	$528	PF60BN	$3,750	$7,500	$14,000
207a	Nick	PE	8	3	3	ANR	3/2005	$10,925	NGCPF64CA	$4,000	$9,500	$16,000

J-208 to J-210: 1858 Cent
Dies 8-D

Transitional issue, same obverse and reverse as adopted in 1859. Obverse and reverse die varieties exist for J-208, including different date positions on the obverse and different wreath details on the reverse.[18] The most notable differences are wreaths with five leaves per cluster and wreaths with six leaves per cluster. These seem to have been struck over a long period of time.

Obverse: Indian Head (two styles: pointed bust and rounded bust).
Reverse: Laurel wreath.

J-208

Number	Metal	Edge	Rarity	Pop	T/A	Firm	Date	Amount	Grade	60	63	65
							Last Traded at Auction					
208	C-N	PE	1	232	104	Stack's	6/2005	$1,380	NGCPF64	$1,000	$1,350	$2,500
209	C	PE	8	3	2	Ira & Larry Goldberg	5/2005	$8,050	PCGSPF64RB	$4,000	$8,000	$13,500
210	Brz	PE	U	1	1	Heritage	7/1997	$4,082	PCGSPF64	N/A	$15,000	N/A

J-211: 1858 Cent
Dies 8-B

Obverse die varieties exist.

Obverse: Indian Head.
Reverse: Oak wreath.

J-211

Number	Metal	Edge	Rarity	Pop	T/A	Firm	Date	Amount	Grade	60	63	65
							Last Traded at Auction					
211	C-N	PE	4	82	46	Heritage	6/2005	$1,438	NGCPF62	$1,250	$1,650	$2,750

J-212: 1858 Cent
Dies 8-C

Obverse die varieties exist.

Obverse: Indian Head.
Reverse: Oak wreath with ornamented shield.

J-212

Number	Metal	Edge	Rarity	Pop	T/A	Firm	Date	Amount	Grade	60	63	65
							Last Traded at Auction					
212	C-N	PE	4	142	79	Heritage	11/2004	$4,320	NGCPF65	$1,100	$1,500	$2,500

J-213: 1858 Cent
Dies 8-A

Transitional issue, obverse as adopted in 1859, reverse as used in 1858. Obverse die varieties exist. Reverse varieties include high leaves (rare) and low leaves.[19]

Obverse: Indian Head.
Reverse: Regular die with agricultural wreath.

J-213

Number	Metal	Edge	Rarity	Pop	T/A	Last Traded at Auction				60	63	65
						Firm	Date	Amount	Grade			
213	C-N	PE	5	55	35	ANR	3/2005	$1,380	NGCPF62	$1,300	$2,000	$3,200

J-214 and J-215: Cent
Dies 7-D

Obverse: Indian Head, no date.
Reverse: Laurel wreath.

J-214

Number	Metal	Edge	Rarity	Pop	T/A	Last Traded at Auction				60	63	65
						Firm	Date	Amount	Grade			
214	C-N	PE	8	1	1	Stack's	10/1997	$8,250	ChPF	$10,000	$17,500	$28,500
215	C	PE	8	0	0	N/A	N/A	N/A	N/A	$13,000	$24,000	$35,000

J-216: 1858 Cent
Dies 7-C

Obverse: Indian Head, no date.
Reverse: Oak wreath with ornamented shield.

J-216

Number	Metal	Edge	Rarity	Pop	T/A	Last Traded at Auction				60	63	65
						Firm	Date	Amount	Grade			
216	C-N	PE	8	1	1	Bowers & Ruddy	6/1982	$1,500	PF	$10,000	$17,500	$28,500

J-217 and J-217a: 1858 Cent
Dies 5-A

Obverse: Flying Eagle, Small Letters, regular die.
Reverse: Regular die with agricultural wreath.

J-217a

Number	Metal	Edge	Rarity	Pop	T/A	Last Traded at Auction				60	63	65
						Firm	Date	Amount	Grade			
217	C	PE	8	1	2	Superior	8/2002	$5,750	PCGSAU58	$12,000	$20,000	$35,000
217a	Nick	PE	H7	3	3	ANR	3/2005	$16,100	PCGSPF64	$7,500	$12,000	$20,000

J-218 and J-218a: 1858 Cent
Dies 4-A

Obverse: Flying Eagle, Large Letters, regular die.
Reverse: Regular die with agricultural wreath.

J-218

Number	Metal	Edge	Rarity	Pop	T/A	Last Traded at Auction				60	63	65
						Firm	Date	Amount	Grade			
218	C	PE	8	0	1	Bolender	6/1944	$7	EF	$8,000	$13,500	$22,000
218a	Nick	PE	8	0	0	N/A	N/A	N/A	N/A	N/A	N/A	N/A

Patterns of 1858

J-219: Undated Flying Eagle Cent/Undated Flying Eagle Cent
Dies 1-2

A true fantasy piece—no doubt a delight to those who have owned this unique coin over the years.

Obverse: Flying Eagle in plain field.
Reverse: Actually an obverse die: Flying Eagle, Large Letters, no date.

J-219

Number	Metal	Edge	Rarity	Pop	T/A	Last Traded at Auction				60	63	65
						Firm	Date	Amount	Grade			
219	C-N	PE	U	1	2	Stack's	5/1997	$11,550	PCGSPF62	N/A	$32,500	N/A

J-220: 1858 Flying Eagle Cent/1858 Indian Head Cent
Dies 6-8

One of the great numismatic curiosities of the era. This unique piece was once part of the Judd collection.

Obverse: Small Flying Eagle.
Reverse: Actually an obverse die: Indian Head.

J-220

Number	Metal	Edge	Rarity	Pop	T/A	Last Traded at Auction				60	63	65
						Firm	Date	Amount	Grade			
220	C-N	PE	U	1	0	Doyle Galleries	12/1983	$1,700	PF	N/A	$32,500	N/A

J-221: 1858 Quarter Dollar

Obverse: Regular Liberty Seated die of the year.
Reverse: Perched Eagle motif by Anthony Paquet, variation on the standard design. UNITED STATES OF AMERICA / QUARTER DOLLAR in tall letters around border.

J-221

Number	Metal	Edge	Rarity	Pop	T/A	Last Traded at Auction				60	63	65
						Firm	Date	Amount	Grade			
221	Silv	RE	H7	6	2	Heritage	7/2003	$16,100	NGCPF66	$5,000	$10,000	$17,500

J-222 and J-223: 1858 Half Dollar

Obverse: Regular Liberty Seated die of the year.
Reverse: Paquet's Perched Eagle. Perfect ribbon (as opposed to "broken ribbon"); groups of four vertical lines in the shield; seven tail feathers; pointed wingtip at right; full leaf above A (in HALF). Perched eagle with a ribbon across the shield, continuing to the eagle's beak, eagle's head facing to viewer's left, olive branch and arrows below. Legends in tall letters, UNITED STATES OF AMERICA / HALF DOLLAR. By engraver Anthony C. Paquet. This is Reverse A of 1859.

J-222

Number	Metal	Edge	Rarity	Pop	T/A	Last Traded at Auction				60	63	65
						Firm	Date	Amount	Grade			
222	Silv	RE	H7	2	2	ANR	11/2004	$9,603	PCGSPF61	$10,000	$17,500	$30,000
223	C	RE	U	0	0	N/A	N/A	N/A	N/A	N/A	N/A	N/A

J-223a: 1858 Half Dollar Reverse

Listed prior to the 8th edition in Appendix A.

Obverse: Impression of the reverse die as described above, Reverse A of 1859.
Reverse: Incomplete impression of the same reverse die design (but necessarily from a different die); die extensively lapped so as to remove all but a few details; possibly Reverse B of 1859, but this has not been confirmed.

J-223a

Number	Metal	Edge	Rarity	Pop	T/A	Last Traded at Auction				60	63	65
						Firm	Date	Amount	Grade			
223a	C	RE	8	0	1	Bowers & Merena	9/1988	$2,420	PF60	$4,250	$8,000	$15,000

J-224 and J-225: 1858 Gold Dollar

J-224 is in the collection of the American Numismatic Society.

Obverse: Indian Princess design similar to regular issue, but with lettering in a taller font; attributed to Anthony C. Paquet.
Reverse: Similar to regular issue but with lettering in a taller font; attributed to Anthony C. Paquet.

J-224

Number	Metal	Edge	Rarity	Pop	T/A	Last Traded at Auction				60	63	65
						Firm	Date	Amount	Grade			
224	Gold	RE	U	0	0	N/A	N/A	N/A	N/A	N/A	N/A	N/A
225	C	RE	H7	0	1	Bowers & Ruddy	6/1979	$500	EF	$10,000	$16,000	$26,000

Patterns of 1859

History and Overview

After 1858, the Flying Eagle cent was discontinued for regular circulation use, and in 1859, the Indian Head motif was adopted, descending from the pattern issues of 1858, specifically J-208. The Indian Head style would be used through 1909, modified slightly along the way. The reverse for the 1859 cent illustrates the "laurel" or "olive" (Mint correspondence used both terms) wreath earlier used on 1858 patterns. The motif proved to be excellent for striking the coins up properly as the high-relief Indian Head at the center was opposite the dies from the laurel wreath on the reverse.

Several interesting varieties of pattern Indian Head cents were made in 1859, the most famous being J-228, a transitional issue, probably struck to the extent of over a thousand pieces, nearly all in circulation format, creating pieces seen today in Mint State (not Proof). The reverse featured a new design, an oak wreath with a narrow shield at the top, which was subsequently used for regular coinage beginning in 1860, continuing until 1909. These pieces may have been struck for circulation, but in small quantities.[1]

In the silver half dime series, a few transitional pieces were struck combining the regular Liberty Seated die of 1859, with stars, with a reverse die of 1860 with the inscription HALF DIME within an agricultural wreath.[2] This particular coin did not include the inscription UNITED STATES OF AMERICA, and therefore a "stateless" coin was created, one of many in the pattern series.[3] A related pattern was struck in 1860 (J-267). Transitional 1859 dimes were also made in the same "stateless" format.

Pattern quarter dollars combined a regular 1859 die with the Paquet reverse die used in 1858 to strike J-221.

Most activity in the pattern series in 1859 was concentrated on the half dollar denomination, mostly from new dies distinctive in their appearance. Two obverse dies were made, one by Longacre and the other by Paquet. Three reverse dies employed what Mint Director James Ross Snowden called Harold P. Newlin's "'Wreath of Cereals,' composed of cotton, tobacco, sugar cane, corn, wheat, and oak leaves, which was deliberately designed to admit perfect striking of the head on the obverse." Another reverse was cut by Paquet and was described as having "the American eagle, with its wings expanded in flight, grasping an olive branch in a scroll, inscribed E PLURIBUS UNUM. Upon its breast is suspended the United States shield. Legend, UNITED STATES OF AMERICA…. HALF DOLLAR."[4]

Half Dollar Obverse Dies of 1859
Obverse 1: "Paquet's Seated Liberty with fasces." • Used with J-235, J-236, J-247 to J-253.
Obverse 2: "Longacre's French Liberty Head." • Used with J-237 to J-246, J-253.

Half Dollar Reverse Dies of 1859
Reverse A: "Paquet's perched eagle, perfect ribbon." • Employed in 1858 with J-222. Used with 1859-dated dies with J-235, J-236, J-245, J-246.

Patterns of 1859

Reverse B: "Paquet's perched eagle, broken ribbon." • Used with a rusted 1838 die to strike J-75a and J-75b. Used with 1859-dated dies to restrike J-235, J-236, J-245, J-246.
Reverse C: "'Cereal wreath' enclosing inscription HALF DOLLAR." • Used with J-237, J-238, J-247, J-248.
Reverse D: "'Cereal wreath' enclosing inscription 1/2 DOLLAR." • Used with J-239 to J-240b, J-249, J-250.
Reverse E: "'Cereal wreath' enclosing 50 CENTS." • Used with J-241, J-242, J-251, J-252.
Reverse F: "Regular half dollar reverse of this year." • Used with J-243, J-244.

Somewhat similar to the pattern cents of 1858, the pattern half dollars of 1859 provided a rich opportunity for Mint officials to make interesting combinations, restrikes, and other pieces for collectors. In general, the dies for half dollars of this year were not highly polished, and most of them show significant parallel raised marks or striae. In time, certain of the dies, particularly Reverse B, deteriorated and were heavily relapped. Curiously, certain 1838 pattern half dollars (J-75a and J-75b) were struck from this deteriorated die. The actual time of manufacture was likely in the 1870s.

Of special historic and numismatic importance is the $20 known as J-260, employing a new die by Anthony C. Paquet, appropriately called the "Paquet Reverse," similar to the regular issue, but with UNITED STATES OF AMERICA / TWENTY D in very tall letters. From 1859 to 1861 several die varieties of the Paquet Reverse were made and used in 1860 to coin J-272a and J-273 and later to coin the regular-issue 1861 Paquet Reverse and 1861-S Paquet Reverse double eagles, the first being an extreme rarity (just two are known) and the last being a well-known scarce variety (several hundred are known).

Collecting Perspective

Among the pattern coins of 1859, the transitional Indian Head cent (J-228) is a collector's favorite. Most known examples are in gem Mint State. Hundreds exist, but it is still several times rarer than an 1856 Flying Eagle cent, another transitional pattern. The good news is that, unlike the latter, the 1859 is not listed in *A Guide Book of United States Coins*. Otherwise, it would become so popular that it would cost tens of thousands of dollars!

Half dollars of 1859 furnish a veritable playground for study and collecting, somewhat similar in this respect to the pattern cents of 1858. In general, most numismatists aspire to obtain the four most readily available varieties, these being J-235 and J-236 (silver and copper), J-237 and J-238, J-239 and J-240, and J-241 and J-242. Accomplishing this is easy enough. The die surfaces are often incompletely polished and irregular. Copper strikings are apt to be dull, cleaned, and otherwise unsatisfactory, and to find choice pieces requires extensive searching, perhaps viewing a half dozen to find one with at least a small degree of eye appeal.

Paquet's ungainly pattern double eagle, J-257, appears with some frequency, usually with unsatisfactory fields, somewhat porous or granular. This is true of regular copper pieces as well as those that are gilt.

J-226: 1859 Cent

Obverse: Regular Indian Head cent die of the year.
Reverse: Pattern die with oak wreath enclosing ONE CENT (same as Reverse B of 1858).

J-226

Number	Metal	Edge	Rarity	Pop	T/A	Last Traded at Auction				60	63	65
						Firm	Date	Amount	Grade			
226	C-N	PE	H6	251	N/A	Superior	1/2004	$2,185	PCGSPF63	$1,400	$2,250	$4,500

J-227: 1859 Cent

Obverse: Die as preceding.
Reverse: Oak wreath with ornamented shield (same as Reverse C of 1858).

J-227

Number	Metal	Edge	Rarity	Pop	T/A	Last Traded at Auction				60	63	65
						Firm	Date	Amount	Grade			
227	C-N	RE	L6	31	14	Stack's	9/2003	$1,035	PF	$1,000	$1,550	$2,500

J-228 and J-229: 1859 Cent

The famous transitional issue. Generally seen in Mint State, not Proof.[5] Proofs of J-228 are valued at four times their Mint State counterparts.

Obverse: Die as preceding.
Reverse: Oak wreath and narrow shield, the reverse regularly adopted in 1859 for general use.

J-228

Number	Metal	Edge	Rarity	Pop	T/A	Last Traded at Auction				60	63	65
						Firm	Date	Amount	Grade			
228	C-N	PE	1	103	N/A	Heritage	6/2005	$2,760	NGCMS65	$700	$1,000	$1,500
229	C	PE	H7	2	2	Ira & Larry Goldberg	5/2005	$8,050	NGCMS64RB	$3,850	$7,500	$15,000

J-229a: 1859 Cent

Purpose unknown, probably a mint error (wrong die in press) struck early in the year.[6]

Obverse: Regular Indian Head cent die of the year.
Reverse: Also an obverse, from another regular Indian Head cent die of the year.

J-229a

Number	Metal	Edge	Rarity	Pop	T/A	Last Traded at Auction				60	63	65
						Firm	Date	Amount	Grade			
229a	C-N	PE	U	0	1	Superior	10/2000	$33,350	ANACSMS60	N/A	N/A	N/A

J-230 to J-231a: 1859 Cent

Struck from regular dies. The differentiation of J-230, designated as copper, and J-231, designated as bronze, would require elemental analysis. Copper and bronze pieces are typically encountered on thick planchets with the dies aligned medal-turn.[7]

J-230

Number	Metal	Edge	Rarity	Pop	T/A	Last Traded at Auction				60	63	65
						Firm	Date	Amount	Grade			
230	C	PE	H7	3	4	Ira & Larry Goldberg	5/2005	$4,600	NGCPF64RD	$1,600	$2,900	$5,800
231	Brz	PE	H7	5	8	ANR	3/2005	$2,530	NGCPF62BN	$3,000	$6,250	$9,500
231a	Lead	PE	U	0	0	N/A	N/A	N/A	N/A	N/A	N/A	N/A

J-232: 1859 Half Dime

"Stateless" issue not giving the country of origin.

Obverse: Regular die of the 1859 year, Liberty Seated with stars, date 1859 below.
Reverse: Agricultural wreath as adopted in 1860, enclosing HALF DIME.

J-232

Number	Metal	Edge	Rarity	Pop	T/A	Last Traded at Auction				60	63	65
						Firm	Date	Amount	Grade			
232	Silv	RE	L7	3	2	Bowers & Merena	4/2005	$66,700	PCGSPF65	$16,000	$25,000	$45,000

J-233: 1859 Dime

"Stateless" issue not giving the country of origin.

Obverse: Regular die of the 1859 year, Liberty Seated with stars, date 1859 below.
Reverse: Cereal wreath as adopted in 1860, enclosing DIME.

J-233

Number	Metal	Edge	Rarity	Pop	T/A	Last Traded at Auction				60	63	65
						Firm	Date	Amount	Grade			
233	Silv	RE	H6	12	N/A	Bowers & Merena	4/2005	$41,400	PCGSPF66	$9,500	$15,500	$25,000

Patterns of 1859

J-234: 1859 Quarter Dollar

Obverse: Regular Liberty Seated die of the year.
Reverse: Pattern die of Anthony C. Paquet, perched eagle. UNITED STATES OF AMERICA / QUARTER DOLLAR surrounding.

J-234

| Number | Metal | Edge | Rarity | Pop | T/A | Last Traded at Auction | | | | 60 | 63 | 65 |
						Firm	Date	Amount	Grade			
234	Silv	RE	L7	7	10	Heritage	11/2004	$4,888	PCGSPF65	$2,500	$4,500	$7,000

J-235 and J-236: 1859 Half Dollar
Dies 1-A and 1-B

Obverse: Paquet's Liberty Seated with fasces.
Reverse: Paquet's Perched Eagle; perfect ribbon and broken ribbon varieties.

J-235

| Number | Metal | Edge | Rarity | Pop | T/A | Last Traded at Auction | | | | 60 | 63 | 65 |
						Firm	Date	Amount	Grade			
235	Silv	RE	5	73	48	Heritage	6/2005	$2,990	NGCPF62	$1,750	$2,500	$4,500
236	C	RE	5	46	30	Heritage	5/2004	$2,300	PCGSPF63BN	$1,650	$2,500	$4,500

J-237 and J-238: 1859 Half Dollar
Dies 2-C

Obverse: Longacre's French Liberty Head.
Reverse: "Cereal wreath" enclosing inscription HALF DOLLAR.

J-238

| Number | Metal | Edge | Rarity | Pop | T/A | Last Traded at Auction | | | | 60 | 63 | 65 |
						Firm	Date	Amount	Grade			
237	Silv	RE	4	73	41	Heritage	8/2004	$1,955	PCGSPF63	$1,500	$2,250	$4,000
238	C	RE	5	35	19	ANR	1/2004	$2,070	PCGSPF64BN	$1,650	$2,250	$4,000

J-239 to J-240b: 1859 Half Dollar
Dies 2-D

J-240a and J-240b, each with the letter H in relief counterstamped 16 times, irregularly spaced, may represent some experiment the nature of which is not known today.

Obverse: Longacre's French Liberty Head.
Reverse: "Cereal wreath" enclosing inscription 1/2 DOLLAR.

J-240

| Number | Metal | Edge | Rarity | Pop | T/A | Last Traded at Auction | | | | 60 | 63 | 65 |
						Firm	Date	Amount	Grade			
239	Silv	RE	4	71	41	Heritage	3/2005	$1,610	PCGSPF60	$1,500	$2,250	$4,000
240	C	RE	5	35	38	Stack's	6/2005	$2,530	NGCPF64BN	$1,650	$2,500	$4,500
240a	C	RE	U	0	1	Bowers & Merena	11/1985	$1,650	PF63	$3,750	$6,250	$12,500
240b	C	PE	U	1	1	Bowers & Merena	5/1999	$4,140	PCGSPF64BN	$3,750	$6,250	$12,500

J-241 and J-242: 1859 Half Dollar
Dies 2-E
Obverse: Longacre's French Liberty Head.
Reverse: "Cereal wreath" enclosing 50 CENTS.

J-241

Number	Metal	Edge	Rarity	Pop	T/A	Last Traded at Auction				60	63	65
						Firm	Date	Amount	Grade			
241	Silv	RE	4	79	36	Heritage	1/2005	$1,380	NGCPF62	$1,500	$2,250	$4,000
242	C	RE	5	32	21	Heritage	12/2004	$1,450	ANACSPF63RB	$1,650	N/A	$4,500

J-243 and J-244: 1859 Half Dollar
Dies 2-F
Obverse: Longacre's French Liberty Head.
Reverse: Regular reverse of this year used to strike Liberty Seated half dollars.

J-243

Number	Metal	Edge	Rarity	Pop	T/A	Last Traded at Auction				60	63	65
						Firm	Date	Amount	Grade			
243	Silv	RE	H7	4	2	Bowers & Merena	5/1999	$2,875	PCGSPF63	$2,350	$4,500	$8,250
244	C	RE	H7	1	1	Bowers & Merena	8/1998	$6,613	PF65RB	$5,150	$9,500	$16,000

J-245 and J-246: 1859 Half Dollar
Dies 2-A and 2-B
Obverse: Longacre's French Liberty Head.
Reverse: Paquet's Perched Eagle; perfect ribbon and broken ribbon varieties.

J-245

Number	Metal	Edge	Rarity	Pop	T/A	Last Traded at Auction				60	63	65
						Firm	Date	Amount	Grade			
245	Silv	RE	H6	9	9	Heritage	11/2003	$3,450	PCGSPF64	$2,000	$3,850	$6,250
246	C	RE	L7	12	11	Heritage	5/2004	$5,750	NGCPF66BN	$2,000	$3,850	$6,250

J-247 and J-248: 1859 Half Dollar
Dies 1-C
Obverse: Paquet's Liberty Seated with fasces.
Reverse: "Cereal wreath" enclosing inscription HALF DOLLAR.

J-247

Number	Metal	Edge	Rarity	Pop	T/A	Last Traded at Auction				60	63	65
						Firm	Date	Amount	Grade			
247	Silv	RE	H7	4	7	Stack's/ANR	6/2004	$8,165	PCGSPF63	$2,600	$4,500	$8,250
248	C	RE	H7	1	1	Heritage	8/1995	$6,270	PCGSPF65BN	$4,800	$9,500	$16,000

Patterns of 1859

J-249 and J-250: 1859 Half Dollar
Dies 1-D

Obverse: Paquet's Liberty Seated with fasces.
Reverse: "Cereal wreath" enclosing inscription
HALF DOLLAR.

J-249

Number	Metal	Edge	Rarity	Pop	T/A	Last Traded at Auction				60	63	65
						Firm	Date	Amount	Grade			
249	Silv	RE	H7	1	2	Superior	1/2003	$6,900	NGCPF64	$4,750	$9,500	$16,000
250	C	RE	H7	2	2	Superior	2/1999	$2,185	PCGSPF64RB	$4,500	$7,500	$12,500

J-251 and J-252: 1859 Half Dollar
Dies 1-E

Obverse: Paquet's Liberty Seated with fasces.
Reverse: "Cereal wreath" enclosing 50 CENTS.

J-251

Number	Metal	Edge	Rarity	Pop	T/A	Last Traded at Auction				60	63	65
						Firm	Date	Amount	Grade			
251	Silv	RE	H7	5	4	Ira & Larry Goldberg	5/2003	$4,945	PCGSPF62	$2,600	$4,500	$8,250
252	C	RE	8	1	1	Stack's	10/1986	$3,520	ChPF	$4,750	$9,500	$16,000

J-253: 1859 Half Dollar
Dies 1-2

Curious muling, of which about a half dozen
are known.

Obverse: Paquet's Liberty Seated with fasces.
Reverse: Actually an obverse: Longacre's
French Liberty Head.

J-253

Number	Metal	Edge	Rarity	Pop	T/A	Last Traded at Auction				60	63	65
						Firm	Date	Amount	Grade			
253	Silv	RE	H7	5	1	Bowers & Merena	5/1996	$10,780	PF65	$11,000	$19,000	$33,000

J-254 and J-255: 1859 Half Dollar

Now designated as J-75a and J-75b, listed under
1838. • Restrikes from rusted dies exist for
many 1859 half dollar die varieties.

J-256: 1859 Gold Dollar

Similar in concept to J-224 and J-225 of 1858. Often seen gilt. The jury is still out as to whether this is a Mint issue or a private production.[8]

Obverse: Indian Princess design similar to regular issue, but with lettering in a taller font, attributed to Anthony C. Paquet.
Reverse: Similar to regular issue but with lettering in a taller font, attributed to Anthony C. Paquet.

J-256

Number	Metal	Edge	Rarity	Pop	T/A	Last Traded at Auction			60	63	65
						Firm	Date	Amount	Grade			
256	C	RE	L7	3	4	Superior	1/1993	$3,520	PCGSPF64BN	$4,500	$7,500	$12,500

J-257 and J-257a: 1859 $20

Pieces are often seen gilt, and some are bronzed.

Obverse: Paquet Liberty Seated design with fasces, shield, and eagle; 13 stars around, date 1859 in very small numerals below.
Reverse: Heavy wreath enclosing UNITED STATES OF AMERICA around inside of wreath and with 20 DOLLARS 1859 at the center.

J-257

Number	Metal	Edge	Rarity	Pop	T/A	Last Traded at Auction			60	63	65
						Firm	Date	Amount	Grade			
257	C	RE	H6	17	19	Bowers & Merena	8/2001	$6,210	PF63RB	$7,500	$11,000	$16,500
257a	C	PE	U	0	0	N/A	N/A	N/A	N/A	N/A	N/A	N/A

J-258: 1859 $20

Obverse: Regular double eagle die by Longacre, but without date. Die described by Judd: "The third Longacre die in which the 6th star points to the left side of a denticle, the shape of the truncation differs from the first two dies and the initials JBL on the truncation are much farther to the left. The Y in LIBERTY is perfect with no signs of recutting. This master die was used to make the regular issue dies."
Reverse: Paquet's die with heavy wreath, as preceding.

J-258

Number	Metal	Edge	Rarity	Pop	T/A	Last Traded at Auction			60	63	65
						Firm	Date	Amount	Grade			
258	C	RE	H7	1	1	Bowers & Ruddy	7/1981	$1,600	PF	N/A	$25,000	N/A

J-259: 1859 $20

Only two examples are believed to exist. One, gilt, was part of the Woodin collection, and was part of the 1914 American Numismatic Society exhibit. Another was sold in 1922. Neither has been seen in recent years.

Obverse: Undated Longacre die, as preceding.
Reverse: Regular die used to strike double eagles this year.

J-259

Number	Metal	Edge	Rarity	Pop	T/A	Last Traded at Auction			60	63	65
						Firm	Date	Amount	Grade			
259	C	RE	8	0	1	Kosoff	8/1966	$800	No Grade	$12,500	$25,000	$50,000

J-260: 1859 $20

Obverse: Regular issue die of the year, Coronet or Liberty Head, with stars and date 1859.
Reverse: Paquet's design with distinctive tall letters around border, UNITED STATES OF AMERICA / TWENTY D.

J-260

Number	Metal	Edge	Rarity	Pop	T/A	Last Traded at Auction				60	63	65
						Firm	Date	Amount	Grade			
260	C	RE	8	1	2	ANR	1/2005	$31,050	NGCPF61	N/A	$40,000	N/A

J-261: 1859 $20

Two examples of this muling are believed to exist.

Obverse: Regular issue die as preceding.
Reverse: Paquet's pattern die with heavy wreath, as used on J-257.

J-261

Number	Metal	Edge	Rarity	Pop	T/A	Last Traded at Auction				60	63	65
						Firm	Date	Amount	Grade			
261	C	RE	8	1	2	Bowers & Merena	11/2001	$14,375	NGCPF61BN	$32,000	N/A	N/A

J-262: 1859 $20

Obverse: Paquet's Liberty Seated design, as used on J-257.
Reverse: Regular die of the year.

J-262

Number	Metal	Edge	Rarity	Pop	T/A	Last Traded at Auction				60	63	65
						Firm	Date	Amount	Grade			
262	C	RE	L7	4	3	ANR	1/2005	$25,300	PCGSPF64BN	$10,000	$16,000	$32,500

J-263: 1859 $20

Struck from regular dies. It is unknown if this is a true die trial piece, or a rarity deliberately struck for sale to collectors. The Byron Reed specimen has been described as Uncirculated (rather than Proof).

J-263

Number	Metal	Edge	Rarity	Pop	T/A	Last Traded at Auction				60	63	65
						Firm	Date	Amount	Grade			
263	C	RE	8	3	1	Bowers & Merena	5/1999	$6,325	PCGSPF58	$13,000	$22,500	$35,000

History and Overview

A number of interesting patterns were produced in 1860, perhaps the most featured today being the J-267 transitional half dime; these pieces were made with frosty, lustrous surfaces (Mint State), not Proof, and were not sharply detailed. These pieces are "stateless" and the obverse depicts a distinctive 1860 die with stars (the old style of 1859, rather than the new style of 1860 with UNITED STATES OF AMERICA), with the regular reverse of 1860 reading HALF DIME within a cereal wreath. As there was no particular reason to strike these for pattern purposes, they can be considered numismatic delicacies. As is true for more than 1,000 other varieties of patterns made during the era 1859 to 1885, today we can all be grateful that they were made, as they are popular and interesting to collect.

The innovative and distinctive pattern half eagles of 1860 (J-271 and J-272) were struck in a large-diameter format, on thin planchets. Pattern eagles were made that featured the head of Liberty facing right, wearing a cap (a motif that was used years later on the Standard Silver patterns of 1869). Unfortunately, today the only remnants of these experiments are pieces with normal reeded edges struck on large diameter planchets from the J-271 and J-272 die combinations, and we know little about any pieces with lettered edges other than what can be surmised from examining the several specimens of the pattern half dollars (J-269).

Among the patterns of 1860 is an anomalous quarter eagle (J-186 and J-189) combining an obverse die dated and used in 1857 for a cent and quarter eagle, with a new reverse with wreath around the border enclosing the inscription 2 1/2 DOLLARS / 1860, creating a most curious item of numismatica—one with a date on each side and with the dates being different!

Rounding out the selection of patterns of 1860 is a double eagle employing a regular obverse die with the Paquet Reverse, tall letters, as adopted for regular use in 1861. The illustrated copper version is from a highly repolished die. The gold impression in the Smithsonian Institution is a Proof.

Collecting Perspective

The most readily available and popular pattern of 1860 is J-267, the "stateless" transitional silver half dime in Mint State. These pieces appear with some regularity today, with probably at least a dozen different pieces showing up on the market in any given year.

The broad-diameter 1860 $5 gold exists in gold and copper, but is generally collectible only in copper. Curiously, this comes with plain or convex fields, indicating two different dies, a point for specialists to consider—although Saul Teichman, who has carefully studied the technical aspects of patterns, questions the existence of two styles of field surfaces. Most other patterns of the year range from extremely rare to unique.

J-264: Undated Cent

Obverse: Recessed or incuse impression from a master die, without date, features reversed, of the obverse of the Indian Head cent.
Reverse: Incuse impression of the reverse master die for the 1859 regular-issue cent with laurel wreath.

J-264

Number	Metal	Edge	Rarity	Pop	T/A	Last Traded at Auction				60	63	65
						Firm	Date	Amount	Grade			
264	C-N	PE	8	0	1	Doyle Galleries	12/1983	$1,000	Unc65	N/A	$39,000	N/A

J-265: 1860 Cent

Trial piece struck from regular dies. Two or three are believed to exist, including one in the Smithsonian Institution.

J-265

Number	Metal	Edge	Rarity	Pop	T/A	Last Traded at Auction				60	63	65
						Firm	Date	Amount	Grade			
265	C	PE	8	1	1	Bowers & Merena	11/1992	$990	PF63BN	$3,850	$8,000	$16,000

Patterns of 1860

J-266: 1860 Cent

Obverse: Regular die of the year.
Reverse: Similar to the regular die but lacking the denomination ONE CENT.

J-266

Number	Metal	Edge	Rarity	Pop	T/A	Last Traded at Auction				60	63	65
						Firm	Date	Amount	Grade			
266	C-N	PE	U	0	1	Kosoff	3/1961	$175	PF	N/A	N/A	N/A

J-267: 1860 Half Dime

Transitional issue made as a numismatic delicacy, in circulation strike format (Mint State rather than Proof).

Obverse: New Liberty Seated die made in the old style of 1859, but with 1860 date.
Reverse: Regular die of 1860 with HALF DIME within an agricultural wreath.

J-267

Number	Metal	Edge	Rarity	Pop	T/A	Last Traded at Auction				60	63	65
						Firm	Date	Amount	Grade			
267	Silv	RE	4	63	N/A	Heritage	6/2005	$2,875	ANACSMS60	$2,500	$3,750	$7,500

J-268: 1860 Quarter Dollar

Struck from regular dies. The only confirmed specimen is on an undersized planchet and may be some kind of mint error rather than a pattern.[9]

J-268

Number	Metal	Edge	Rarity	Pop	T/A	Last Traded at Auction				60	63	65
						Firm	Date	Amount	Grade			
268	C-N	RE	8	0	1	Stack's	9/1986	$1,100	Unc	$7,500	$13,000	$22,500

J-269: 1860 Half Dollar

Struck from regular dies. Lettered edge, probably part of the Barclay experiments. Three are known, all defaced, each displaying the edge lettered E PLURIBUS UNUM, but with the letters not strongly impressed.[10]

J-269

Number	Metal	Edge	Rarity	Pop	T/A	Last Traded at Auction				60	63	65
						Firm	Date	Amount	Grade			
269	C	LE	8	0	1	Steve Ivy Rare Coin	2/1983	$6,000	Unc	N/A	N/A	N/A

J-270: 1860 $2.50

Fantasy muling with two different dates, an unusual situation even among numismatic delicacies.

Obverse: From Liberty Head die dated 1857 (used in 1857 to strike the J-186 cent and the J-189 $2.50).
Reverse: Pattern die with wreath enclosing 2 1/2 DOLLARS / 1860.

J-270

Number	Metal	Edge	Rarity	Pop	T/A	Last Traded at Auction				60	63	65
						Firm	Date	Amount	Grade			
270	C	RE	L7	3	8	Ira & Larry Goldberg	5/2005	$6,613	PCGSPF64BN	$4,000	$6,500	$12,000

J-271 and J-272: 1860 $5

Broad-diameter planchet pattern intended to eliminate the deception of slicing a gold coin in half and
scooping out the gold in the center, replacing it with
a lesser-value metal.

Obverse: Liberty Head by Longacre, facing right,
wearing Phrygian cap, three stars above forehead,
ribbon with LIBERTY at neck, stars surrounding,
date 1860 below.
Reverse: Perched eagle with undulating ribbon above
head, UNITED STATES OF AMERICA / FIVE
DOLLARS around border.

J-271

| Number | Metal | Edge | Rarity | Pop | T/A | Last Traded at Auction | | | | 60 | 63 | 65 |
						Firm	Date	Amount	Grade			
271	Gold	RE	8	2	0	N/A	N/A	N/A	N/A	$120,000	$200,000	$300,000
272	C	RE	L6	21	21	Stack's	3/2005	$6,325	ChPF64BN	$3,500	$6,000	$10,500

J-272a and J-273: 1860 $20

The gold and copper examples are each from different reverse dies. • J-273 was possibly struck at
a date later than on the die.[11] J-272a is in the Smithsonian Institution.

Obverse: Regular double eagle die of the year.
Reverse: Paquet Reverse die with tall letters.

J-272a

| Number | Metal | Edge | Rarity | Pop | T/A | Last Traded at Auction | | | | 60 | 63 | 65 |
						Firm	Date	Amount	Grade			
272a	Gold	RE	U	0	0	N/A	N/A	N/A	N/A	N/A	N/A	N/A
273	C	RE	8	1	2	Auction '90	8/1990	$23,000	NGCPF64RB	N/A	$27,500	$55,000

History and Overview

By November 13, 1861, the Civil War had been in progress for seven months. A day after the fall of Fort Sumter on April 14, 1861, President Abraham Lincoln had declared war on the Confederate States of America. Northerners thought this would be an easy win, considering that most industrial might was in the North, as were most banks and sources of finance, factories turning out equipment and machines, and other foundations of commerce. The South was viewed as a land of plantations, with rice, corn, tobacco, and cotton growing in endless fields tended by slaves, while plantation owners sat on the verandas of mansions and enjoyed the good life.

Reality proved to be far different, and by November 1861, the North had suffered many bloody losses, the South had similarly sustained much damage, and there was no clear prospect of which side would win. The scenario changed, and the outlook became grim. Citizens were frightened, and beginning in December, gold coins were hoarded, then silver. By the second week in July 1862, Indian Head cents had disappeared from circulation as well, as in times of uncertainty "hard money" was always preferred to paper.

On November 13, 1861, Reverend M.R. Watkinson of Ridleyville, Pennsylvania, sent a letter to Secretary of the Treasury Salmon P. Chase, suggesting that coins should bear a reference to God, to whom many citizens looked for help in that uncertain time. Chase was warm to the idea and wrote to Mint Director James Pollock, stating that no nation could be strong except in the strength of God, or safe except in His defense, and that "The trust of our people in God should be declared on our national coins. You will cause a device to be prepared without unnecessary delay with a motto expressing in the fewest tersest terms possible this national recognition."

Pattern coins were made with various mottos, an early suggestion being OUR TRUST IS IN GOD, which may have been too lengthy for use. In any event, no patterns are known with this inscription.

Patterns of the half dollar and $10 denominations soon became popular with collectors, and many of them were struck in both the "scroll" style and with GOD OUR TRUST directly in the field. These copper issues were produced with a bronzed surface caused by pickling the finished coins to achieve a minutely etched surface of rich brown color.[12]

Patterns of 1861

Although there was no real pattern purpose for them, related GOD OUR TRUST half dollars and eagles were produced in 1862 and 1863 as well, apparently in significantly larger quantities than in 1861.[13] In some instances, additional dies for certain varieties had to be prepared to service the numismatic demand!

Patterns produced in 1861 also included the half eagle on a thin broad planchet. Beyond that, cents, quarter dollars, and double eagles were struck in copper rather than their intended metals.

Collecting Perspective

The greatest interest in the patterns of 1861 focuses upon the half dollar and $10 with GOD OUR TRUST, two styles, on scroll and in plain letters. The half dollars and $10 coins in copper appear with some regularity on the market and are highly collectible.

Other 1861 patterns are seldom seen. The two gold varieties, J-284 and J-286, have not been confirmed in modern times and may be misdescriptions of J-349 and J-351 of 1863.

J-274: 1861 Cent

Struck from regular dies. Elemental analysis is required to tell copper from bronze. Examples have not been available for study to determine whether struck from Proof or circulation-strike dies. Only two or three are believed to exist and are probably masquerading as toned copper-nickel pieces in error.

J-274

Number	Metal	Edge	Rarity	Pop	T/A	Last Traded at Auction				60	63	65
						Firm	Date	Amount	Grade			
274	C	PE	8	0	1	Kagin's	2/1974	$1,250	AU	$11,000	$20,000	$32,500

J-275 and J-276: 1861 Quarter Dollar

Some if not most copper issues were produced with bronzed surfaces.

J-275

Number	Metal	Edge	Rarity	Pop	T/A	Last Traded at Auction				60	63	65
						Firm	Date	Amount	Grade			
275	C	RE	8	0	1	NASCA	11/1977	$200	EF	$5,850	$11,000	$20,000
276	C-N	RE	8	0	0	N/A	N/A	N/A	N/A	N/A	N/A	N/A

J-277 and J-278: 1861 Half Dollar

Patterns originally issued in December 1861 to test the concept of a motto on coinage. Copper impressions usually with bronzed surfaces. Obverse die varieties exist.

Obverse: Regular Liberty Seated die of the year.
Reverse: Design similar to the regular issue except with GOD OUR TRUST on scroll above the eagle.

J-277

Number	Metal	Edge	Rarity	Pop	T/A	Last Traded at Auction				60	63	65
						Firm	Date	Amount	Grade			
277	Silv	RE	L7	4	3	Heritage	1/2004	$7,475	PCGSPF63	$4,500	$8,000	$12,000
278	C	RE	L7	12	6	Bowers & Merena	9/2003	$5,290	PCGSPF65BN	$2,000	$3,200	$5,800

J-279 and J-280: 1861 Half Dollar

The second pattern issued to test the concept of a motto on coinage. Copper impressions usually with bronzed surfaces.

Obverse: Regular Liberty Seated die of the year.
Reverse: Design similar to the regular issue except with GOD OUR TRUST in small letters in field above the eagle (no scroll).

J-280

Number	Metal	Edge	Rarity	Pop	T/A	Last Traded at Auction				60	63	65
						Firm	Date	Amount	Grade			
279	Silv	RE	L7	8	6	Heritage	7/2003	$3,105	PCGSPF64	$2,250	$3,850	$6,750
280	C	RE	L7	9	5	Heritage	7/2003	$1,495	ANACSPF55Cld	$2,250	$3,850	$6,750

J-281 and J-282: 1861 $2.50

Trial piece struck from regular dies. Silver examples might be mint errors struck on dime planchets.

J-281

Number	Metal	Edge	Rarity	Pop	T/A	Last Traded at Auction				60	63	65
						Firm	Date	Amount	Grade			
281	Silv	RE	H7	2	2	Heritage	4/2002	$8,912	PCGSMS63	$7,500	$14,000	$22,000
282	C	RE	H7	3	1	Superior	5/1995	$1,760	PCGSPF50	$4,250	$8,250	$17,500

J-283: 1861 $5

Pattern proposal for a large-diameter coin intended to eliminate the fraud of hollowing out the center of a gold coin and filling it with lower-value metal, a continuation of Dr. Barclay's ideas. None are known in gold.

Obverse: Design used in 1860 for J-271, by Longacre, Miss Liberty facing right, wearing Phrygian cap, three stars above forehead, ribbon with LIBERTY at neck, stars surrounding, date 1861 below.
Reverse: Die by Longacre, letter font probably by Anthony C. Paquet. Die used to strike J-271 of 1860, perched eagle holding undulating ribbon in beak inscribed E PLURIBUS UNUM, UNITED STATES OF AMERICA / FIVE DOLLARS around.

J-283

Number	Metal	Edge	Rarity	Pop	T/A	Last Traded at Auction				60	63	65
						Firm	Date	Amount	Grade			
283	C	RE	L7	6	4	Bowers & Merena	3/2004	$4,025	NGCPF62BN	$4,500	$8,000	$13,500

J-284 and J-285: 1861 $10

Pattern produced to illustrate the use of the motto on coinage. Copper impressions usually with bronzed surfaces. Obverse die varieties exist.

Obverse: Regular $10 gold eagle die of the year.
Reverse: Style of the regular $10 gold eagle but with motto GOD OUR TRUST on scroll.

J-285

Number	Metal	Edge	Rarity	Pop	T/A	Last Traded at Auction				60	63	65
						Firm	Date	Amount	Grade			
284	Gold	RE	–	0	0	N/A	N/A	N/A	N/A	Unconf	Unconf	Unconf
285	C	RE	H6	13	14	Heritage	5/2005	$4,370	PCGSPF62BN	$3,000	$5,000	$8,000

Patterns of 1861

J-286 and J-287: 1861 $10

Pattern produced to illustrate the use of the motto on coinage. Copper impressions usually with bronzed surfaces. Obverse die varieties exist.

Obverse: Regular $10 gold eagle die of the year.
Reverse: Style of the regular $10 gold eagle but with motto GOD OUR TRUST in small letters in field above eagle.

J-287

Number	Metal	Edge	Rarity	Pop	T/A	Last Traded at Auction				60	63	65
						Firm	Date	Amount	Grade			
286	Gold	RE	–	0	0	N/A	N/A	N/A	N/A	Unconf	Unconf	Unconf
287	C	RE	H6	13	7	ANR	7/2003	$7,130	PCGSPF63BN	$3,000	$5,000	$8,000

J-288: 1861 $20

Struck from regular dies. Perhaps an experimental striking with beveled edge, copper planchet (but without a collar). Details of manufacture not known, as it is broad diameter, but does have edge reeding (indicating it was struck in a collar).

J-288

Number	Metal	Edge	Rarity	Pop	T/A	Last Traded at Auction				60	63	65
						Firm	Date	Amount	Grade			
288	C	RE	8	1	1	Bowers & Merena	3/2000	$1,265	NGCPF64BN	$17,000	$32,500	N/A

J-289: 1861 $20

Struck from regular dies. Copper striking struck normally, and of regular diameter, in collar.

J-289

Number	Metal	Edge	Rarity	Pop	T/A	Last Traded at Auction				60	63	65
						Firm	Date	Amount	Grade			
289	C	RE	U	1	2	Heritage	8/2001	$28,750	PCGSPF63BN	N/A	$45,000	N/A

Patterns of 1862

History and Overview

Patterns for the year 1862 echo those of 1861 and consist of reprise issues of the half dollar and $10 denominations with the motto GOD OUR TRUST. The same reverse dies were used, one with the motto on a scroll and one with the letters plain in the field. Copper issues were nearly all produced with bronzed surfaces. Beyond these, several varieties of pattern cents were made.

Collecting Perspective

Paralleling the situation of 1861, pattern strikings of the 1862 half dollar in silver and copper as well as the 1862 $10 in copper are readily available. In fact, in comparison to the varieties of 1861, they are even more plentiful. Apparently, sales by Mint officials reached new high levels! These were revenue producers, and it is likely that as many were struck as homes could be found for them. Today, this translates into the opportunity to obtain pieces that might not be available otherwise.

J-290 to J-292: 1862 Cent

Trial piece struck from regular dies.

J-290

Number	Metal	Edge	Rarity	Pop	T/A	Last Traded at Auction				60	63	65
						Firm	Date	Amount	Grade			
290	C	PE	L7	4	7	Heritage	2/2005	$2,530	PCGSPF58	$4,000	$6,000	$10,000
291	C-N	RE	–	0	0	N/A	N/A	N/A	N/A	Unconf	Unconf	Unconf
292	Oro	PE	8	0	0	N/A	N/A	N/A	N/A	N/A	N/A	N/A

J-293 and J-294: 1862 Half Dollar

Copper impressions usually with bronzed surfaces.

Obverse: Regular Liberty Seated die of the year.
Reverse: The same die used to strike patterns in
1861 with motto GOD OUR TRUST on scroll.

J-293

Number	Metal	Edge	Rarity	Pop	T/A	Last Traded at Auction				60	63	65
						Firm	Date	Amount	Grade			
293	Silv	RE	5	31	28	Heritage	3/2005	$2,185	NGCPF64	$1,600	$2,850	$4,500
294	C	RE	L7	12	9	Heritage	2/2005	$3,450	PCGSPF64BN	$2,000	$2,900	$5,200

J-295 and J-296: 1862 Half Dollar

Copper impressions usually with bronzed surfaces.

Obverse: Regular Liberty Seated die of the year.
Reverse: The same die used to strike patterns in
1861, with GOD OUR TRUST in small letters in
field above the eagle (no scroll).

J-295

Number	Metal	Edge	Rarity	Pop	T/A	Last Traded at Auction				60	63	65
						Firm	Date	Amount	Grade			
295	Silv	RE	5	27	20	Superior	5/2004	$3,600	PCGSPF64	$1,750	$2,850	$4,500
296	C	RE	H6	16	13	Stack's/ANR	6/2004	$2,185	PCGSPF64BN	$1,750	$2,800	$4,500

J-297: 1862 $10

Usually with bronzed surfaces. Obverse die varieties exist.

Obverse: Regular $10 gold eagle die of the year.
Reverse: The same die used to strike patterns in
1861, with motto GOD OUR TRUST on scroll.

J-297

Number	Metal	Edge	Rarity	Pop	T/A	Last Traded at Auction				60	63	65
						Firm	Date	Amount	Grade			
297	C	RE	L6	36	24	Heritage	11/2004	$3,565	PCGSPF65BN	$2,600	$3,500	$5,100

Patterns of 1862

J-298: 1862 $10

Usually with bronzed surfaces. Obverse die varieties exist.

Obverse: Regular $10 gold eagle die of the year.
Reverse: The same die used to strike patterns in 1861, with GOD OUR TRUST in small letters in field above the eagle (no scroll).

J-298

Number	Metal	Edge	Rarity	Pop	T/A	Last Traded at Auction			60	63	65
						Firm	Date	Amount	Grade			
298	C	RE	L6	25	21	Heritage	8/2004	$3,680	PCGSPF65BN	$2,000	$3,000	$5,000

Patterns of 1863

History and Overview

By early 1863, the American monetary system was in turmoil. Gold coins had not circulated at par since late December 1861; silver coins had been trading at a premium since spring 1862; and even copper-nickel Flying Eagle and Indian Head cents were scarcely seen. Coin substitutes included paper Postage Currency notes, Legal Tender bills, private scrip, and more. Encased postage stamps bore denominations from 1¢ to 90¢. Soon, a vast flood of privately issued tokens appeared, some bearing patriotic motifs and others the advertisements of merchants. These were struck by private shops in various places, most particularly New York City and Cincinnati, but also in other locations. Struck on thin bronze planchets, these pieces circulated widely and were readily accepted in commerce.

At the Mint, the production of gold and silver coins was sharply reduced as they were made only on the request of depositors of bullion who desired such pieces for use in international commerce. By the summer of 1863, it required $140 to $150 in federal "greenback" dollars to buy $100 worth of gold or silver coins. By the end of the year, it took $200 to $220 in paper to buy $100 in gold or silver! Accordingly, pieces hoarded earlier remained tightly held, as no one would dream of spending them for face value. Exchange offices and bullion dealers did a lively business in the purchase and sale of silver and gold coins at current market levels.

The Mint sought to restore at least the one-cent coin to circulation. Not lost on officials was the acceptance of millions of privately issued bronze Civil War tokens (as collectors designate them today). At the same time, the copper-nickel alloy (88% copper and 12% nickel), first used for circulating coins with the 1857 Flying Eagle cent, had been difficult to strike, as dies wore rapidly and often cracked.

The most famous pattern this year is the J-299 Indian Head cent struck from regular dies, but on a thin bronze planchet, in the style of the ubiquitous, privately-minted Civil War tokens. Nearly always the dies for J-299 are oriented medal-wise.

Pattern two-cent pieces were made in several varieties, including a die with the portrait of Washington, facing right, and the motto GOD AND OUR COUNTRY above, this being a variation on the GOD OUR TRUST theme.[14] Although the image of Washington had been proposed for federal coins for a long time, this represents the first actual striking of such a piece. Still other two-cent pieces have GOD OUR TRUST and also the motto IN GOD WE TRUST, the last being that adopted for regular coinage the year afterward (and listed as J-316 to J-318). However, these transitional patterns were not made in 1863 or any time close. None were known to exist until the 1870s and, further, they employ a reverse die thought to have been first used on a regular basis a few years after the date on the coins. In the early 1870s, a number of minor-denomination regular issue Proofs and patterns with dates of the mid-1860s were restruck, often from tell-tale later reverse dies.

In 1863, there was also some interest in creating a new variety of three-cent piece to complement the small silver three-cent piece introduced in 1851 and to go along with the proposed new two-cent denomination. Such pieces were struck at the Mint in the summer of 1863.[15]

Postage Currency redemption ten-cent pieces (called dimes now, but called tokens then) were made in multiple varieties. Certain pieces dated 1868 were actually struck in 1863 (but are listed in the present text under 1868; see J-644 and related).[16]

The year 1863 included additional coinage of half dollars and $10 pieces with the two varieties of GOD OUR TRUST motto, one on a scroll and one in plain letters. Copper pieces were issued with bronzed surfaces made by a pickling process.

A series of pattern quarter dollars, half dollars, and silver dollars with motto IN GOD WE TRUST above the eagle on the reverse began this year and continued through 1865. At a later date, possibly 1865, patterns for the silver coins were made with IN GOD WE TRUST. It was a natural marketing idea to resurrect some older Proof dies dated 1863 and 1864 and thus produce patterns for these dates.[17] Accordingly, for the year 1863, we have quarter dollars, half dollars, and dollars, in silver, copper, and aluminum—nice sets for the numismatic trade. Off-metal strikings, as in aluminum, from regular Proof dies are mostly restrikes made years later.

Collecting Perspective

The year 1863 offers a fascinating field for the pattern enthusiast. Most of the truly historical and popular issues are available on the market, including J-299 (the piece that led to the adoption of the thin bronze cent a year later in 1864); both the Washington and the shield designs of the two-cent piece, with motto variations; and even the cumbersome bronze three-cent that resembles an older large copper cent.

The Postage Currency redemption issues exist in a wide variety of metals and alloys, not all of which have been sorted out. Actual elemental testing has revealed further variations. The GOD OUR TRUST half dollar and $10 pieces were made in fairly large quantities, resulting in them being highly collectible today. As a general rule, the bronzed copper patterns of 1861 to 1863 are available in higher average grades than are copper or bronze patterns with mirror Proof surfaces, as many of the latter have been cleaned.

The antedated 1863 IN GOD WE TRUST silver denominations in silver, copper, and aluminum are also available, but quite scarce, and much patience is required to acquire them. Those struck in silver are popular with specialists in the related regular-issue silver series.

J-299 and J-300: 1863 Cent

Struck from regular dies. J-299 is a transitional issue usually seen with dies oriented medal-turn. Some thick planchet pieces exist and were struck for an unknown reason. Most examples of J-299 were issued with a bronzed finish of chocolate brown hue; all but one known piece are aligned medal-turn.[18] Both circulation strikes and Proofs exist of J-300. Die varieties exist for J-299.

J-299

Number	Metal	Edge	Rarity	Pop	T/A	Last Traded at Auction				60	63	65
						Firm	Date	Amount	Grade			
299	Brz	PE	3	115	93	ANR	3/2005	$1,380	NGCPF65BN	$875	$1,100	$1,750
300	C-N	RE	H6	20	24	ANR	3/2005	$2,185	NGCMS64	$1,500	$2,250	$4,500

J-301 to J-304: 1863 Cent

Struck for purposes unknown and at a later time using a Proof reverse die used to strike regular Proof 1869 and 1870 cents.[19]

Obverse: Die of later 1864 type with L on ribbon.
Reverse: Regular die of the year.

J-304

Number	Metal	Edge	Rarity	Pop	T/A	Last Traded at Auction				60	63	65
						Firm	Date	Amount	Grade			
301	Brz	PE	8	2	1	Bowers & Merena	9/1993	$10,450	PF62BN	$13,000	$26,000	$45,000
302	C-N	PE	H7	3	3	Bowers & Merena	1/1994	$20,900	PCGSPF65	$6,500	$12,500	$25,000
303	Oro	PE	8	0	1	Lyman Low	6/1903	$0.55	Unc	$13,500	$25,000	$40,000
304	Alu	PE	8	4	2	Heritage	7/2003	$16,100	NGCPF63	$10,500	$20,000	$32,500

J-305 to J-308: 1863 Two-Cent Piece

Earliest dated Mint pattern featuring Washington's portrait. Thick and thin varieties exist of J-305.

Obverse: Washington head facing right, GOD AND OUR COUNTRY above, date and two stars below.
Reverse: Similar to adopted 1864 issue but with CENTS more curved.

J-305

Number	Metal	Edge	Rarity	Pop	T/A	Last Traded at Auction				60	63	65
						Firm	Date	Amount	Grade			
305	C	PE	4	81	64	Heritage	6/2005	$3,910	PCGSPF66RB	$1,550	$2,150	$3,100
306	C-N	PE	H7	4	1	Bowers & Merena	11/1992	$3,520	PF62	$3,200	$5,800	$11,000
307	Oro	PE	U	0	0	N/A	N/A	N/A	N/A	N/A	$15,000	$22,500
308	Alu	PE	8	2	4	ANR	11/2004	$11,213	PCGSPF62	$6,500	$10,500	$17,500

Patterns of 1863

J-309 to J-311: 1863 Two-Cent Piece

Electrotypes exist of J-309.

Obverse: Washington die as preceding.
Reverse: As regularly adopted in 1864, wreath enclosing 2 CENTS (only slightly curved), UNITED STATES OF AMERICA around.

J-309

Number	Metal	Edge	Rarity	Pop	T/A	Last Traded at Auction				60	63	65
						Firm	Date	Amount	Grade			
309	Brz	PE	8	1	2	Stack's	9/1999	$4,025	PF	$7,500	$12,500	$25,000
310	C-N	PE	L7	10	6	Heritage	1/2004	$2,530	PCGSPF61	$2,000	$4,200	$7,000
311	Alu	PE	8	3	2	Superior	2/1997	$4,950	PCGSPF62	$6,500	$10,500	$17,500

J-312 to J-314: 1863 Two-Cent Piece

Obverse: Wide shield with arrows behind it, heavy wreath to left and right, GOD OUR TRUST on scroll above.
Reverse: Similar to the preceding except with CENTS more curved.

J-312

Number	Metal	Edge	Rarity	Pop	T/A	Last Traded at Auction				60	63	65
						Firm	Date	Amount	Grade			
312	Brz	PE	4	134	91	Heritage	6/2005	$2,300	PCGSPF65RB	$1,650	$1,750	$2,750
312a	C	PE	L6	14	7	Heritage	1/2004	$2,185	PCGSPF65BN	$2,000	$3,000	$5,500
313	C-N	PE	H7	3	1	Stack's	5/1991	$2,860	BrPF	$3,200	$5,500	$10,500
314	Alu	PE	8	1	0	N/A	N/A	N/A	N/A	$8,000	$15,000	$26,000

J-315: 1863 Two-Cent Piece

Obverse: Shield die as preceding, GOD OUR TRUST motto.
Reverse: The regular die adopted in 1864.

J-315

Number	Metal	Edge	Rarity	Pop	T/A	Last Traded at Auction				60	63	65
						Firm	Date	Amount	Grade			
315	Brz	PE	H7	4	3	Heritage	1/2004	$8,625	PCGSPF64BN	$3,200	$5,150	$9,500

J-316 to J-318: 1863 Two-Cent Piece

A numismatic delicacy; a novodel created in the 1870s. Of interest to two-cent piece specialists as well as pattern collectors.

Obverse: The regular Shield design dated 1863, with motto IN GOD WE TRUST in large letters as used in 1864 and 1873.
Reverse: The regular reverse design used from 1864 to 1873; this die with broken serif on the D in UNITED.

J-316

Number	Metal	Edge	Rarity	Pop	T/A	Last Traded at Auction				60	63	65
						Firm	Date	Amount	Grade			
316	C & Brz	PE	H6	13	10	Bowers & Merena	8/2001	$7,475	PCGSPF65RD	$3,200	$5,500	$10,000
317	C-N	PE	8	0	1	Stack's	5/1998	$3,520	ChPF	$5,000	$10,000	$20,000
318	Alu	PE	H7	4	2	Heritage	8/1995	$9,075	PCGSPF64	$3,850	$7,500	$13,500

J-319 and J-320: 1863 Three-Cent Piece

Pattern produced to determine the feasibility of issuing a large bronze three-cent piece for circulation, this in addition to the small silver trime. Originals (about 144 grains) and restrikes (about 119 grains) exist of J-319.[20]

Obverse: Braided Hair cent with 13 stars surrounding, as used on large copper cents 1843–1857, but with date 1863 below.
Reverse: Small wreath enclosing 3 CENTS. UNITED STATES OF AMERICA around border.

J-319

Number	Metal	Edge	Rarity	Pop	T/A	Last Traded at Auction				60	63	65
						Firm	Date	Amount	Grade			
319	Brz	PE	5	42	40	Heritage	6/2005	$3,220	NGCPF66RB	$2,050	$2,800	$4,000
320	Alu	PE	H7	3	1	Bowers & Merena	1/1997	$5,775	PCGSPF64	$4,000	$7,500	$13,500

J-321 and J-322: 1863 Trime

Struck from regular dies. Believed to be restrikes.

J-321

Number	Metal	Edge	Rarity	Pop	T/A	Last Traded at Auction				60	63	65
						Firm	Date	Amount	Grade			
321	C	PE	L7	6	5	Stack's/ANR	6/2004	$11,213	PCGSPF64RB	$4,000	$6,500	$11,000
322	Alu	PE	H7	7	4	Heritage	6/2005	$9,775	PCGSPF66DC	$3,500	$5,250	$9,000

J-323 and J-324: 1863 Half Dime

Struck from regular dies. Believed to be restrikes.

J-323

Number	Metal	Edge	Rarity	Pop	T/A	Last Traded at Auction				60	63	65
						Firm	Date	Amount	Grade			
323	C	RE	H7	5	3	Ira & Larry Goldberg	5/2003	$6,613	PCGSPF64RD	$2,900	$4,900	$8,500
324	Alu	RE	H7	2	2	Ira & Larry Goldberg	5/2003	$8,338	NGCPF64	$3,250	$7,500	$13,000

J-325 to J-330a: 1863 Dime

Produced to study the feasibility of a special coin to take the place of Postage Currency bills. Many alloys and variations including as listed, plus others. The obverse die was also used in 1868 to strike J-644 and related issues.[21]

Obverse: Small shield at center with crossed arrows behind, wreath around most of perimeter. EXCHANGED FOR U.S. NOTES at border.
Reverse: Composed entirely of lettering with: POSTAGE CURRENCY above, ACT JULY 1862 below, with 10 CENTS 1863 at center.

J-330

Number	Metal	Edge	Rarity	Pop	T/A	Last Traded at Auction				60	63	65
						Firm	Date	Amount	Grade			
325	Silv	PE	L6	33	22	Heritage	7/2003	$2,300	PCGSPF64	$1,400	$2,250	$3,850
325a	Silv	–	–	0	0	N/A	N/A	N/A	N/A	Unconf	Unconf	Unconf
326a	Bil	PE	H6	15	11	Heritage	7/2003	$2,185	PCGSPF63	$1,800	$3,200	$4,800
326b	C	PE	8	3		Superior	1/2005	$12,650	PCGSPF64RB	$4,000	$8,000	$15,000
326	C	RE	U	2	1	Superior	5/1994	$3,520	PCGSPF64	N/A	N/A	N/A
327	Alu	PE	H6	15	7	Heritage	11/2004	$2,300	PCGSPF64	$1,800	$3,200	$4,800
328	Alu	RE	H7	5	2	Superior	4/2003	$6,038	NGCPF65CA	$2,600	$5,000	$9,500
329	Tin	PE	L6	16	12	ANR	12/2003	$1,495	PCGSPF62	$1,750	$3,150	$4,750
330	*	PE	L6	10	8	Heritage	8/2004	$2,530	PCGSPF64	$1,300	$3,150	$4,750
330a	Nick	RE	H7	1	2	Ira & Larry Goldberg	10/2000	$3,910	PCGSPF65	$2,850	$5,500	$11,500

* J-330: 97% tin, 3% copper

Patterns of 1863

J-331 and J-331a: 1863 Dime

Obverse: Regular Liberty Seated die but without date.
Reverse: POSTAGE CURRENCY text, as preceding.

J-331

Number	Metal	Edge	Rarity	Pop	T/A	Last Traded at Auction				60	63	65
						Firm	Date	Amount	Grade			
331	Nick	RE	H7	1	3	Superior	1/2003	$8,050	PCGSPF64	$3,500	$7,500	$15,500
331a	C	RE	U	0	1	Heritage	8/1997	$5,250	PCGSPF64BN	N/A	$13,000	N/A

J-332: 1863 Dime

Obverse: Postage Currency die as J-325.[22]
Reverse: Regular die used to coin dimes of this year.

J-332

Number	Metal	Edge	Rarity	Pop	T/A	Last Traded at Auction				60	63	65
						Firm	Date	Amount	Grade			
332	Alu	PE	U	1	1	Superior	9/1998	$3,220	NGCPF62	$8,000	$15,000	N/A

J-333 and J-334: 1863 Dime

Struck from regular dies. Believed to be restrikes.

J-333

Number	Metal	Edge	Rarity	Pop	T/A	Last Traded at Auction				60	63	65
						Firm	Date	Amount	Grade			
333	C	RE	L7	8	2	Bowers & Merena	6/1991	$3,190	PF63BN	$2,050	$4,200	$8,250
334	Alu	RE	H7	3	3	Heritage	5/2004	$4,945	PCGSPF63	$2,750	$5,500	$14,000

J-335 to J-337: 1863 Quarter Dollar

Transitional pattern produced at the Mint at a later date.

Obverse: Regular Liberty Seated die of the year.
Reverse: Similar to regular die of the year but with motto IN GOD WE TRUST in ribbon above eagle; type adopted in 1866.

J-336

Number	Metal	Edge	Rarity	Pop	T/A	Last Traded at Auction				60	63	65
						Firm	Date	Amount	Grade			
335	Silv	RE	L7	4	3	Heritage	9/2003	$7,935	PCGSPF64	$3,250	$6,000	$11,000
336	C	RE	L7	8	5	Superior	5/2003	$5,463	NGCPF66RB	$1,950	$3,200	$5,750
337	Alu	RE	H7	3	1	Kagin's	8/1977	$1,550	ChPF	$4,200	$9,500	$16,000

J-338 and J-339: 1863 Half Dollar

A continuation of the experimental model series begun in 1861. Seven sets of originals said to have been struck, and restrikes exist. Copper impressions usually with bronzed surfaces.

Obverse: Regular Liberty Seated die of the year.
Reverse: Similar to regular die of the year but with GOD OUR TRUST on scroll; die first used in 1861 for J-277.

J-338

Number	Metal	Edge	Rarity	Pop	T/A	Last Traded at Auction				60	63	65
						Firm	Date	Amount	Grade			
338	Silv	RE	5	27	24	Bowers & Merena	7/2004	$3,163	PCGSPF64CA	$1,600	$2,800	$4,600
339	C	RE	L6	19	13	Heritage	6/2005	$2,185	PCGSPF64BN	$1,500	$2,250	$3,500

J-340 and J-341: 1863 Half Dollar

A continuation of the experimental model began the series of 1861. Copper impressions usually with bronzed surfaces.

Obverse: Regular Liberty Seated die of the year.

Reverse: Similar to regular die of the year but with motto GOD OUR TRUST in plain letters in the field above eagle.

J-340

| Number | Metal | Edge | Rarity | Pop | T/A | Last Traded at Auction | | | | 60 | 63 | 65 |
						Firm	Date	Amount	Grade			
340	Silv	RE	L6	23	20	Heritage	1/2005	$1,840	PCGSPF62	$2,000	$3,200	$5,000
341	C	RE	5	25	29	Stack's	11/2004	$1,955	NGCPF62BN	$1,450	$2,250	$3,500

J-342 to J-344: 1863 Half Dollar

Transitional pattern produced at the Mint at a later date.

Obverse: Regular Liberty Seated die of the year.

Reverse: Similar to regular die of the year but with motto IN GOD WE TRUST in ribbon above eagle; type adopted in 1866.

J-342

| Number | Metal | Edge | Rarity | Pop | T/A | Last Traded at Auction | | | | 60 | 63 | 65 |
						Firm	Date	Amount	Grade			
342	Silv	RE	L7	9	4	Heritage	11/2003	$14,950	PCGSPF65CA	$5,250	$9,500	$16,000
343	C	RE	L7	5	2	Heritage	11/2003	$8,625	PCGSPF64RB	$3,000	$6,000	$10,500
344	Alu	RE	H7	2	1	Heritage	1/2004	$8,625	PCGSPF64	$6,400	$10,500	$19,000

J-345 to J-347: 1863 Silver Dollar

Transitional pattern produced at the Mint at a later date.

Obverse: Regular Liberty Seated die of the year.

Reverse: Similar to regular die of the year but with motto IN GOD WE TRUST in ribbon above eagle; type adopted in 1866.

J-346

| Number | Metal | Edge | Rarity | Pop | T/A | Last Traded at Auction | | | | 60 | 63 | 65 |
						Firm	Date	Amount	Grade			
345	Silv	RE	L7	5	5	ANR	9/2003	$50,600	NGCPF66	$12,000	$26,000	$42,000
346	C	RE	L7	7	4	Heritage	11/2003	$16,100	PCGSPF64RB	$5,800	$12,500	$26,500
347	Alu	RE	H7	3	4	Heritage	11/2003	$19,550	PCGSPF64	$10,000	$18,500	$32,500

Patterns of 1863

J-348: 1863 Silver Dollar

Struck from regular dies.

J-348

Number	Metal	Edge	Rarity	Pop	T/A	Last Traded at Auction				60	63	65
						Firm	Date	Amount	Grade			
348	C	RE	8	0	1	Kagin's	8/1977	$1,000	PF	$6,500	$11,500	$21,500

J-349 and J-350: 1863 $10

Gold striking believed unique; copper pieces made in quantity, mostly with bronzed surfaces.

Obverse: Regular Liberty die of the year.
Reverse: Similar to regular die of the year but with GOD OUR TRUST on scroll; die first used in 1861 for J-277.

J-349

Number	Metal	Edge	Rarity	Pop	T/A	Last Traded at Auction				60	63	65
						Firm	Date	Amount	Grade			
349	Gold	RE	U	1	1	Superior	1/1988	$64,900	PF	N/A	$275,000	N/A
350	C	RE	L6	23	12	Heritage	11/2003	$4,600	PCGSPF66BN	$3,000	$5,000	$8,000

J-351 and J-352: 1863 $10

Gold striking believed unique; copper pieces made in quantity, mostly with bronzed surfaces.

Obverse: Regular Liberty die of the year.
Reverse: Similar to regular die of the year but with GOD OUR TRUST in field; die first used in 1861 for J-277.

J-352

Number	Metal	Edge	Rarity	Pop	T/A	Last Traded at Auction				60	63	65
						Firm	Date	Amount	Grade			
351	Gold	RE	U	1	1	Bowers & Ruddy	1/1988	$50,000	PF	N/A	$300,000	N/A
352	C	RE	H6	21	16	Superior	8/2004	$2,875	PCGSPF64RB	$2,500	$4,500	$7,000

Patterns of 1864

History and Overview

Early in the year, experiments were conducted in variations of copper alloy, mixing silver and aluminum to create different colors and appearances.[23] These experimental examples are virtually indistinguishable today except by elemental analysis. Later, in 1864, the obverse die of the Indian Head cent was modified and the tiny letter L, for the engraver Longacre, was added to the ribbon.

Several varieties of two-cent patterns were produced in various metals. The transitional series with motto on reverse was continued for the quarter dollar, half dollar, and silver dollar, again in different metals. Several other patterns were struck, as noted in detail below. Most off-metal strikings from regular Proof dies are likely restrikes made in the 1870s.[24]

Collecting Perspective

Patterns of this year range from scarce to rare. The types are not as distinctive as in 1863, but there are many interesting varieties among Indian Head cents, two-cent pieces, and transitional coins.

Patterns of 1864

J-353 to J-356b: 1864 Cent

Struck from regular dies without L on ribbon. Various strikings in experimental alloys. Obverse die varieties exist.

J-356

Number	Metal	Edge	Rarity	Pop	T/A	Firm	Date	Amount	Grade	60	63	65
							Last Traded at Auction					
353	*	PE	L6	20	20	Heritage	6/2005	$2,875	PCGSMS65	$1,400	$2,200	$4,200
354	**	PE	8	2	4	Superior	10/2001	$6,153	PCGSMS67	$3,000	$6,000	$10,000
355	†	PE	H7	3	3	Heritage	11/2003	$4,600	PCGSMS64	$2,500	$5,500	$11,000
356	‡	PE	L6	16	13	ANR	12/2003	$3,450	NGCMS66	$1,200	$1,800	$3,500
356a	C	PE	L6	18	22	ANR	5/2005	$1,495	PCGSPF64BN	$1,200	$2,000	$4,000
356b	C-N	PE	8	8	3	Heritage	3/2005	$4,543	NGCMS65	$1,800	$3,400	$5,250

* J-353: 93% copper, 7% aluminum   † J-355: 90% copper, 10% aluminum
** J-354: 95% copper, 5% aluminum   ‡ J-356: 90% copper, 10% tin

J-357 to J-361: 1864 Cent

Struck from regular dies with L on ribbon. Obverse die varieties exist.

J-358

Number	Metal	Edge	Rarity	Pop	T/A	Firm	Date	Amount	Grade	60	63	65
							Last Traded at Auction					
357	C	PE	8	4	0	N/A	N/A	N/A	N/A	N/A	N/A	N/A
358	C-N	PE	H7	3	1	Ira & Larry Goldberg	2/2001	$17,250	PCGSPF64	$6,500	$12,500	$22,500
359	Nick	PE	8	1	1	Stack's	9/1989	$1,210	PF	$11,000	$19,000	$32,500
360	Oro	PE	8	0	1	Stack's	9/1989	$935	PF	N/A	N/A	N/A
361	Alu	PE	8	4	1	Superior	7/2003	$31,050	NGCPF66CA	$8,500	$15,000	$30,000

J-362: 1864 Indian Head Cent/1858 Flying Eagle Cent

Obverse: Regular Indian Head cent die of 1864 without L on ribbon.
Reverse: Actually an obverse die. 1858 Flying Eagle, Small Letters, regular die.

J-362

Number	Metal	Edge	Rarity	Pop	T/A	Firm	Date	Amount	Grade	60	63	65
							Last Traded at Auction					
362	C-N	PE	8	0	1	Stack's	12/1980	$4,600	ChPF	$20,000	$28,500	$40,000

J-363 and J-365: 1864 Two-Cent Piece

J-364 is now listed as J-371a.

Obverse: Regular die with large motto IN GOD WE TRUST.
Reverse: Similar to regular die but with CENTS very curved.

J-363

Number	Metal	Edge	Rarity	Pop	T/A	Firm	Date	Amount	Grade	60	63	65
							Last Traded at Auction					
363	C	PE	8	0	1	MARCA	8/1991	$1,150	PF63BN	$3,000	$4,500	$9,000
365	Alu	PE	U	0	1	B. Max Mehl	11/1944	$19	PF	N/A	N/A	N/A

Patterns of 1864

J-366 to J-369: 1864 Two-Cent Piece

Obverse: Regular die with small motto IN GOD
WE TRUST.
Reverse: Same as preceding but with CENTS
very curved.

J-367

Number	Metal	Edge	Rarity	Pop	T/A	Last Traded at Auction				60	63	65
						Firm	Date	Amount	Grade			
366	Brz	PE	H7	3	3	Heritage	1/2004	$7,475	PCGSPF62	$3,000	$5,000	$10,000
367	C	PE	8	1	2	ANR	3/2004	$10,925	NGCPF64BN	$3,400	$5,500	$12,000
368	C-N	PE	8	0	0	N/A	N/A	N/A	N/A	$8,500	$16,000	$30,000
369	Alu	PE	U	0	1	Bowers & Merena	6/1996	$2,310	PF60	$19,500	N/A	N/A

J-370 to J-372a: 1864 Two-Cent Piece

Struck from regular dies with large motto. Die
varieties exist among the various strikings. J-371a
was struck on a broad planchet.

J-371

Number	Metal	Edge	Rarity	Pop	T/A	Last Traded at Auction				60	63	65
						Firm	Date	Amount	Grade			
370	C	PE	L7	8	2	Heritage	8/1995	$5,170	PCGSPF65RD	$1,200	$2,500	$5,000
371	C-N	PE	L6	45	24	Heritage	6/2005	$2,990	NGCPF65	$1,700	$2,350	$3,850
371a	C-N	PE	U	0	1	Pine Tree	9/1974	$2,000	PF	N/A	N/A	N/A
372	Alu	PE	8	2	1	Doyle Galleries	12/1983	$1,600	MS63	$6,500	$11,000	$20,000
372a	Nick	PE	U	1	1	Bowers & Ruddy	1/1975	$950	PF	N/A	N/A	N/A

J-373 and J-374: 1864 Two-Cent Piece

Struck from regular dies with small motto. J-373
is indistinguishable from a regular-strike bronze
Proof, except by elemental analysis.

J-373

Number	Metal	Edge	Rarity	Pop	T/A	Last Traded at Auction				60	63	65
						Firm	Date	Amount	Grade			
373	C	PE	8	3	0	N/A	N/A	N/A	N/A	$7,500	$16,000	$35,000
374	C-N	PE	8	0	0	N/A	N/A	N/A	N/A	$7,150	$13,000	$23,000

J-375 to J-377: 1864 Trime

Struck from regular dies. Believed to be restrikes.

J-377

Number	Metal	Edge	Rarity	Pop	T/A	Last Traded at Auction				60	63	65
						Firm	Date	Amount	Grade			
375	C	PE	L7	5	2	Heritage	8/1995	$3,410	PCGSPF64RB	$4,500	$7,500	$12,000
376	Alu	PE	8	2	1	Superior	7/1984	$1,375	PF	$10,000	$16,000	$28,000
377	Nick	PE	8	1	1	Heritage	9/2002	$20,700	PCGSPF64	$11,500	$22,500	$35,000

J-378 to J-380: 1864 Half Dime
Struck from regular dies. Believed to be restrikes.

J-378

Number	Metal	Edge	Rarity	Pop	T/A	Last Traded at Auction				60	63	65
						Firm	Date	Amount	Grade			
378	C	RE	L7	11	9	Heritage	8/2004	$3,910	NGCPF66RB	$1,800	$3,200	$5,150
379	Alu	RE	8	2	1	NASCA	11/1977	$525	PF	$5,200	$10,500	$20,000
380	Nick	RE	8	3	1	ANR	7/2003	$13,800	NGCPF66RB	$4,250	$7,800	$13,000

J-381 to J-383: 1864 Dime
Struck from regular dies. Believed to be restrikes.

J-381

Number	Metal	Edge	Rarity	Pop	T/A	Last Traded at Auction				60	63	65
						Firm	Date	Amount	Grade			
381	C	RE	L7	13	11	Heritage	8/2004	$3,220	PCGSPF65RB	$1,300	$2,000	$4,200
382	Alu	RE	8	1	1	B. Max Mehl	6/1941	$15	PF	$5,850	$10,500	$18,500
383	Nick	RE	H7	2	1	Superior	5/1990	$2,640	PCGSPF63	$3,850	$7,500	$12,500

J-384 and J-385: 1864 Quarter Dollar
Believed to be restrikes.

Obverse: Regular Liberty Seated die of the year.
Reverse: Paquet's die of 1858 (J-221), variant of Perched Eagle with tall letters surrounding.

J-384

Number	Metal	Edge	Rarity	Pop	T/A	Last Traded at Auction				60	63	65
						Firm	Date	Amount	Grade			
384	Silv	RE	L7	11	15	Superior	1/2004	$3,335	PCGSPF63	$2,250	$4,200	$8,250
385	C	RE	H7	1	1	Superior	10/2000	$2,760	PCGSPF63RB	$4,200	$9,500	$20,000

J-386 to J-389: 1864 Quarter Dollar
Transitional pattern produced at the Mint at a later date.

Obverse: Regular Liberty Seated die of the year.
Reverse: Similar to regular die of the year, but with motto IN GOD WE TRUST in ribbon above eagle; type adopted in 1866.

J-387

Number	Metal	Edge	Rarity	Pop	T/A	Last Traded at Auction				60	63	65
						Firm	Date	Amount	Grade			
386	Silv	RE	L7	6	6	Heritage	10/2003	$9,085	PCGSPF66DC	$3,200	$7,000	$12,500
387	C	RE	H6	17	12	Scotsman	5/2005	$2,789	NGCPF64BN	$2,000	$4,200	$7,750
388	Alu	RE	8	3	1	Ira & Larry Goldberg	2/2000	$10,350	PCGSPF67	$4,250	$8,750	$17,500
389	Nick	RE	8	2	2	Ira & Larry Goldberg	2/2000	$9,200	PCGSPF65	N/A	N/A	$21,500

Patterns of 1864

J-390: 1864 Quarter Dollar

Trial piece struck from regular dies.

J-390

Number	Metal	Edge	Rarity	Pop	T/A	Firm	Date	Amount	Grade	60	63	65
						Last Traded at Auction						
390	C	RE	–	0	0	N/A	N/A	N/A	N/A	Unconf	Unconf	Unconf

J-391 to J-394: 1864 Half Dollar

Transitional pattern produced at the Mint at a later date.

Obverse: Regular Liberty Seated die of the year.

Reverse: Similar to regular die of the year but with motto IN GOD WE TRUST in ribbon above eagle; type adopted in 1866.

J-394

Number	Metal	Edge	Rarity	Pop	T/A	Firm	Date	Amount	Grade	60	63	65
						Last Traded at Auction						
391	Silv	RE	L7	8	5	Superior	5/2003	$12,650	NGCPF66	$5,150	$9,500	$16,000
392	C	RE	L7	11	6	Bowers & Merena	5/2004	$3,565	PCGSPF66BN	$2,000	$3,500	$6,400
393	Alu	RE	8	2	4	Heritage	11/2003	$21,850	PCGSPF67	$5,500	$10,500	$16,500
394	Nick	RE	8	2	2	ANR	1/2005	$18,400	PCGSPF65	N/A	N/A	$25,000

J-395: 1864 Half Dollar

Trial piece struck from regular dies. This was originally in the William Idler collection—he being a middleman between Mint personnel and collectors.

J-395

Number	Metal	Edge	Rarity	Pop	T/A	Firm	Date	Amount	Grade	60	63	65
						Last Traded at Auction						
395	Alu	RE	U	1	1	Superior	8/1991	$3,520	NGCPF64	N/A	$10,500	$20,000

J-396 to J-399: 1864 Silver Dollar

Transitional pattern produced at the Mint at a later date.

Obverse: Regular Liberty Seated die of the year.

Reverse: Similar to regular die of the year but with motto IN GOD WE TRUST in ribbon above eagle; type adopted in 1866.

J-396

Number	Metal	Edge	Rarity	Pop	T/A	Firm	Date	Amount	Grade	60	63	65
						Last Traded at Auction						
396	Silv	RE	L7	6	5	ANR	9/2003	$34,500	NGCPF66	$9,500	$23,000	$38,500
397	C	RE	L7	7	3	ANR	9/2003	$36,800	NGCPF66RD	$9,500	$17,000	$27,500
398	Alu	RE	H7	3	2	Superior	9/1998	$15,525	PCGSPF67	$11,000	$11,000	$19,000
399	Nick	RE	8	1	1	Bowers & Merena	3/1999	$8,050	PF63	$10,000	$17,500	$25,000

Patterns of 1864

J-400 to J-402: 1864 $3

Struck from regular dies. J-400 is unconfirmed. J-401 and J-402 may be hard to differentiate and may be one and the same composition; at least one example may be a mint error.

J-400

Number	Metal	Edge	Rarity	Pop	T/A	Last Traded at Auction				60	63	65
						Firm	Date	Amount	Grade			
400	C	RE	–	0	0	N/A	N/A	N/A	N/A	Unconf	Unconf	Unconf
401	C-N	RE	8	0	1	Bowers & Ruddy	5/1972	$600	Unc	$17,000	$25,000	$35,000
402	Nick	RE	U	0	0	N/A	N/A	N/A	N/A	$17,000	$25,000	$35,000

Patterns of 1865

History and Overview

The year 1865 saw the creation of a pattern nickel three-cent piece, quite like the regular die adopted under the Act of March 3, 1865, but with minor differences. The nickel three-cent piece was intended to be a convenience to trade, offering a larger denomination. Some patterns of nickel five-cent pieces were also produced.

The transitional IN GOD WE TRUST silver patterns were first produced in this year. In addition, transitional patterns with IN GOD WE TRUST were produced of the $5, $10, and $20 denominations.

To the preceding can be added several other varieties of patterns, including a curious two-cent piece (J-407) struck on a planchet made of compressed or bonded silver metal against copper metal, said to have been struck from native Michigan ore. The same silver/copper planchet style was used to coin certain other patterns in the decade.

Collecting Perspective

The majority of 1865-dated patterns are collectible with some patience, although many numismatists opt to acquire but a single die pair, and not the variations in different metals that exist.

Of particular interest are the pattern nickel five-cent pieces. The 1865 Shield nickel with rays on the reverse is later production reflecting the design actually adopted in 1866. Another numismatic delicacy is the Shield nickel without rays, as adopted in 1867, and probably not struck before early 1867. The transitional silver and gold denominations with IN GOD WE TRUST have always been popular.[25] To these can be added selected off-metal strikes of various denominations

J-403 to J-406a: 1865 Cent

Struck from regular dies. Obverse varieties include Plain 5 and Fancy 5 in date. Thick and thin planchet variations exist for J-403a, J-404 (also known with three obverse die varieties), and J-405, indicating that such pieces were struck on multiple occasions over a period of time, no doubt as numismatic delicacies. Certain alloys are difficult to distinguish from others except by elemental analysis. J-406 and J-406a are probably the same. J-404 and J-406 may be mint errors.

J-406

Number	Metal	Edge	Rarity	Pop	T/A	Last Traded at Auction				60	63	65
						Firm	Date	Amount	Grade			
403	C	PE	H7	2	1	Mid-American	8/1987	$475	PF63	$1,500	$2,750	$5,000
403a	C	RE	8	0	1	Stack's	6/1986	$1,100	PF	$1,950	$5,200	$10,000
404	C-N	PE	L7	14	6	ANR	1/2004	$5,060	NGCPF65	$1,500	$2,750	$5,000
405	C-N	RE	H7	2	2	Stack's	10/2000	$633	PF	$2,250	$4,200	$8,250
406	Nick	PE	L6	30	22	ANR	3/2005	$5,060	NGCPF66CA	$1,200	$2,000	$4,250
406a	Nick-Silv	PE	H7	6	4	Heritage	1/2005	$2,473	PCGSPF64	$1,500	$3,250	$6,500

Patterns of 1865

J-407 to J-409: 1865 Two-Cent Piece

Trial piece struck from regular dies.

J-409

Number	Metal	Edge	Rarity	Pop	T/A	Last Traded at Auction				60	63	65
						Firm	Date	Amount	Grade			
407	*	PE	H7	3	4	Stack's	10/2003	$8,050	PCGSPF62	$5,500	$10,000	$18,000
408	**	PE	H7	6	2	Heritage	8/1995	$3,300	PCGSPF65RD	$1,000	$2,500	$4,000
409	C-N	PE	H6	17	8	Stack's	3/2004	$4,600	ChPF	$1,700	$3,000	$5,500
409a	Nick	PE	H7	3	2	Heritage	8/1996	$6,600	PCGSMS65	$2,700	$5,000	$9,000

* J-407: silver and copper rolled   ** J-408: copper, usually silver plated

J-410 to J-412: 1865 Three-Cent Piece

Produced early in 1865 and quite similar to type adopted.

Obverse: Liberty Head similar to that regularly adopted, but with date closer to bust.
Reverse: Similar to adopted type, but with ribbon ends larger and extending into the dentils.

J-411

Number	Metal	Edge	Rarity	Pop	T/A	Last Traded at Auction				60	63	65
						Firm	Date	Amount	Grade			
410	Nick	PE	L6	23	12	Heritage	6/2005	$9,200	PCGSPF67CA	$1,400	$2,750	$5,250
411	C	PE	H6	20	11	Heritage	1/2005	$3,163	PCGSPF65RB	$1,400	$2,500	$4,500
412	Alu	PE	U	0	0	N/A	N/A	N/A	N/A	N/A	$15,000	$28,500

J-413 to J-414a: 1865 Three-Cent Piece

Trial piece struck from regular dies.

J-413

Number	Metal	Edge	Rarity	Pop	T/A	Last Traded at Auction				60	63	65
						Firm	Date	Amount	Grade			
413	C	PE	5	33	23	Heritage	6/2005	$2,875	NGCPF66RB	$1,300	$1,900	$2,650
414	Oro	PE	H7	7	1	Heritage	1/2003	$5,980	PCGSPF64	$2,600	$5,150	$10,500
414a	Alu	PE	8	1	1	Steve Ivy	8/1980	$3,600	Unc65	$4,900	$9,000	$16,500

J-415: 1865 Trime

Trial piece struck from regular dies.

J-415

Number	Metal	Edge	Rarity	Pop	T/A	Last Traded at Auction				60	63	65
						Firm	Date	Amount	Grade			
415	C	PE	H7	5	1	Heritage	8/1998	$1,840	NGCPF64	$4,200	$7,000	$12,500

J-416 and J-417: 1865 Five-Cent Piece[26]

Transitional pattern believed to have been made in the 1870s.

Obverse: Shield design as adopted in 1865.
Reverse: Design with rays between the stars, as adopted in 1866.

J-417

Number	Metal	Edge	Rarity	Pop	T/A	Last Traded at Auction				60	63	65
						Firm	Date	Amount	Grade			
416	Nick	PE	H6	16	17	Heritage	6/2005	$9,775	NGCPF65	$3,200	$7,250	$14,000
417	C	PE	L7	12	11	Superior	7/2003	$8,050	NGCPF65RB	$2,600	$5,800	$10,500

J-418 and J-419: 1865 Five-Cent Piece

Transitional pattern believed to have been made in the 1870s.

Obverse: As preceding; Shield design adopted in 1866.
Reverse: Design without rays, as adopted in 1867.

J-418

Number	Metal	Edge	Rarity	Pop	T/A	Last Traded at Auction				60	63	65
						Firm	Date	Amount	Grade			
418	Nick	PE	H6	14	12	Heritage	6/2005	$10,925	PCGSPF66CA	$2,200	$4,500	$8,500
419	C	PE	–	0	0	N/A	N/A	N/A	N/A	Unconf	Unconf	Unconf

J-420: 1865 Half Dime

Trial piece struck from regular dies.

J-420

Number	Metal	Edge	Rarity	Pop	T/A	Last Traded at Auction				60	63	65
						Firm	Date	Amount	Grade			
420	C	RE	H7	3	1	Bowers & Ruddy	7/1981	$900	PF	$4,200	$7,750	$12,500

J-421 and J-422: 1865 Dime

Trial piece struck from regular dies.

J-421

Number	Metal	Edge	Rarity	Pop	T/A	Last Traded at Auction				60	63	65
						Firm	Date	Amount	Grade			
421	C	RE	H7	4	1	Superior	1/1996	$506	PF60BN	$3,500	$7,500	$12,500
422	Nick	RE	U	1	0	N/A	N/A	N/A	N/A	$8,500	$15,500	$26,000

J-423 and J-424: 1865 Quarter Dollar

Believed to be restrikes.

Obverse: Regular Liberty Seated die of the year.
Reverse: Die by Paquet, variant of Perched Eagle, first used on J-221 of 1858.

J-424

Number	Metal	Edge	Rarity	Pop	T/A	Last Traded at Auction				60	63	65
						Firm	Date	Amount	Grade			
423	Silv	RE	L7	12	9	Heritage	2/2005	$12,650	NGCPF67DCA	$2,700	$5,250	$10,000
424	C	RE	H7	4	3	Superior	1/2003	$7,475	PCGS65BN	$2,600	$5,150	$9,500

J-425 to J-427: 1865 Quarter Dollar

Transitional pattern.

Obverse: Regular Liberty Seated die of the year.
Reverse: Similar to regular die of the year but with IN GOD WE TRUST on scroll above eagle as adopted in 1866.

J-425

Number	Metal	Edge	Rarity	Pop	T/A	Last Traded at Auction				60	63	65
						Firm	Date	Amount	Grade			
425	Silv	RE	H6	13	5	Stack's	10/2003	$5,750	ChPF	$2,900	$5,750	$11,000
426	C	RE	L7	9	12	Heritage	3/2005	$6,900	NGCPF66BN	$2,250	$3,850	$7,000
427	Alu	RE	U	0	1	Empire	1/1960	$250	PF	N/A	N/A	N/A

Patterns of 1865

J-428 and J-428a:
1865 Quarter Dollar

Trial piece struck from regular dies. J-428a was listed as J-424a prior to the eighth edition.

J-428

Number	Metal	Edge	Rarity	Pop	T/A	Last Traded at Auction				60	63	65
						Firm	Date	Amount	Grade			
428	C	RE	–	0	0	N/A	N/A	N/A	N/A	Unconf	Unconf	Unconf
428a	*	RE	U	0	1	Stack's	7/1986	$1,980	AU	N/A	N/A	N/A

* J-428a: silver and copper rolled

J-429 to J-431:
1865 Half Dollar

Transitional pattern.

Obverse: Regular Liberty Seated die of the year.
Reverse: Similar to regular die of the year but with IN GOD WE TRUST on scroll above eagle, as adopted in 1866.

J-429

Number	Metal	Edge	Rarity	Pop	T/A	Last Traded at Auction				60	63	65
						Firm	Date	Amount	Grade			
429	Silv	RE	L7	9	6	Heritage	1/2004	$10,925	PCGSPF65	$5,150	$9,500	$16,000
430	C	RE	H6	14	13	Heritage	7/2004	$10,925	NGCPF67BNCA	$1,950	$3,500	$6,350
431	Alu	RE	U	0	1	Stack's	6/1984	$2,310	PF	$12,500	$22,500	$40,000

J-432 and J-433:
1865 Half Dollar

Trial piece struck from regular dies.

J-432

Number	Metal	Edge	Rarity	Pop	T/A	Last Traded at Auction				60	63	65
						Firm	Date	Amount	Grade			
432	C	RE	L7	10	5	ANR	1/2004	$2,990	PCGSPF64BN	$2,250	$3,850	$7,050
433	Alu	RE	8	0	0	Stack's	4/1962	N/A	N/A	$14,000	$22,500	$37,500

J-434 to J-436:
1865 Dollar

Transitional pattern. A specimen owned by Harry W. Bass, Jr., was struck over an 1853 Liberty Seated silver dollar.

Obverse: Regular Liberty Seated die of the year.
Reverse: Similar to regular die of the year but with IN GOD WE TRUST on scroll above eagle, as adopted in 1866.

J-435

Number	Metal	Edge	Rarity	Pop	T/A	Last Traded at Auction				60	63	65
						Firm	Date	Amount	Grade			
434	Silv	RE	L7	11	6	ANR	9/2003	$16,100	NGCPF62	$15,000	$30,000	$52,000
435	C	RE	L7	10	17	Heritage	8/2004	$6,900	PCGSPF64RB	$5,250	$11,000	$23,000
436	Alu	RE	U	0	0	N/A	N/A	N/A	N/A	$22,500	$39,000	$65,000

J-437: 1865 Dollar

Trial piece struck from regular dies. Four are known.

J-437

Number	Metal	Edge	Rarity	Pop	T/A	Last Traded at Auction				60	63	65
						Firm	Date	Amount	Grade			
437	C	RE	H7	2	1	Heritage	11/2003	$18,400	PCGSPF64RB	$6,500	$11,500	$30,000

J-438: 1865 Dollar

Trial piece struck from regular dies.

J-438

Number	Metal	Edge	Rarity	Pop	T/A	Last Traded at Auction				60	63	65
						Firm	Date	Amount	Grade			
438	C	RE	L7	5	8	Heritage	5/2005	$10,925	PCGSPF65RB	$3,500	$5,500	$10,000

J-439: 1865 $2.50

Trial piece struck from regular dies. Made for sale to collectors, similar to other off-metal strikes of this year.

J-439

Number	Metal	Edge	Rarity	Pop	T/A	Last Traded at Auction				60	63	65
						Firm	Date	Amount	Grade			
439	C	RE	L7	7	6	ANR	7/2003	$8,050	PCGSPF65RB	$3,500	$5,750	$10,500

J-441: 1865 $3

Restrike made circa 1872. J-440, listed in earlier editions, is actually not a pattern, and so has been removed.

Obverse: Regular design (but identifiable as a particular die first used in 1872, due to certain characteristics).
Reverse: Similar to regular design except with date slanting up to the right.

J-441

Number	Metal	Edge	Rarity	Pop	T/A	Last Traded at Auction				60	63	65
						Firm	Date	Amount	Grade			
441	C	RE	L7	10	5	Heritage	3/2003	$3,795	PCGSPF62	$4,000	$6,000	$12,000

Patterns of 1865

J-442 to J-444: 1865 $3

Obverse: Regular design (but die used to strike Proofs beginning in 1867).
Reverse: Similar to regular issue, but date placed low and well to the right.

J-442

Number	Metal	Edge	Rarity	Pop	T/A	Last Traded at Auction				60	63	65
						Firm	Date	Amount	Grade			
442	C	RE	8	0	1	NERCG	7/1979	$2,400	Unc	$9,000	$15,500	$26,000
443	C-N	RE	8	0	1	Stack's	8/1976	$525	PF	$9,000	$16,500	$30,000
444	Nick	RE	8	1	1	Heritage	8/1996	$4,510	PCGSPF60	$8,500	$15,500	$24,000

J-445 and J-446: 1865 $5

Transitional pattern.

Obverse: Regular die of the year.
Reverse: Type adopted in 1866 with motto IN GOD WE TRUST on scroll above eagle.

J-445

Number	Metal	Edge	Rarity	Pop	T/A	Last Traded at Auction				60	63	65
						Firm	Date	Amount	Grade			
445	Gold	RE	8	0	1	Sotheby's	2/1954	$170	PF	N/A	$175,000	$275,000
446	C	RE	H6	11	10	Stack's	10/2003	$7,188	NGCPF66BN	$3,500	$6,250	$10,500

J-447 and J-448: 1865 $5

Trial piece struck from regular dies. J-447 is unconfirmed, and might be a misdescription of J-446. The single example of J-448, once owned by King Farouk of Egypt, might be a restrike.

J-447

Number	Metal	Edge	Rarity	Pop	T/A	Last Traded at Auction				60	63	65
						Firm	Date	Amount	Grade			
447	C	RE	–	0	0	N/A	N/A	N/A	N/A	Unconf	Unconf	Unconf
448	Alu	RE	U	0	0	Sotheby's	2/1954	N/A	N/A	N/A	N/A	N/A

J-449 and J-450: 1865 $10

Transitional pattern. Two examples of J-449 are known. One was owned by King Farouk. The other currently resides in the Smithsonian Institution.

Obverse: Regular eagle die of the year.
Reverse: Type adopted in 1866 with motto IN GOD WE TRUST on scroll above eagle.

J-449

Number	Metal	Edge	Rarity	Pop	T/A	Last Traded at Auction				60	63	65
						Firm	Date	Amount	Grade			
449	Gold	RE	8	0	1	Sotheby's	2/1954	$265	No Grade	N/A	$300,000	$475,000
450	C	RE	H6	15	17	ANR	1/2004	$4,140	PF64Gilt	$3,500	$5,500	$9,000

Patterns of 1865

J-451: 1865 $10

Struck from regular dies with no motto.

J-451

Number	Metal	Edge	Rarity	Pop	T/A	Last Traded at Auction				60	63	65
						Firm	Date	Amount	Grade			
451	C	RE	–	0	0	N/A	N/A	N/A	N/A	Unconf	Unconf	Unconf

J-452 to J-453b: 1865 $20

Transitional pattern. J-453a might be silver-plated copper. J-453b might be a misdescription of J-453a.

Obverse: Regular double eagle die of the year.
Reverse: Type adopted in 1866, with motto IN GOD WE TRUST inside arrangement of 13 stars above eagle.

J-452

Number	Metal	Edge	Rarity	Pop	T/A	Last Traded at Auction				60	63	65
						Firm	Date	Amount	Grade			
452	Gold	RE	8	2	1	Auction '90	8/1990	$400,000	PCGSPF64	N/A	N/A	$750,000
453	C	RE	H6	16	10	Heritage	11/2003	$10,925	PCGSPF64BN	$7,000	$11,000	$22,500
453a	Silv	RE	U	1	0	N/A	N/A	N/A	N/A	N/A	N/A	N/A
453b	Alu	RE	–	0	0	N/A	N/A	N/A	N/A	Unconf	Unconf	Unconf

J-454: 1865 $20

Trial piece struck from regular dies. Possibly struck deliberately for sale to collectors. Fewer than three are believed to exist.

J-454

Number	Metal	Edge	Rarity	Pop	T/A	Last Traded at Auction				60	63	65
						Firm	Date	Amount	Grade			
454	C	RE	8	2	1	Bowers & Merena	6/1988	$990	VF	$10,000	$17,500	$32,500

Patterns of 1866

History and Overview

The Act of May 17, 1866 authorized a new format for the five-cent piece. The new Shield type nickel reached circulation during the summer. Many interesting patterns exist for the new nickel five-cent piece, some employing Washington's portrait with the motto GOD AND OUR COUNTRY, for reasons not known today, but perhaps to create numismatic delicacies (IN GOD WE TRUST had already been selected, and it seems unlikely that a different motto would have been considered for the five-cent piece). Outstanding among the nickel patterns of this year are several with the portrait of Abraham Lincoln (J-486 to J-488a), this being the first appearance of the martyred president on federal coinage (he would not appear on regular circulating coinage until the Lincoln cent of 1909). Among other patterns of the five-cent denomination are mules and other curiosities. In all instances, pieces described as copper cannot be differentiated from those described as bronze except by elemental analysis.

Patterns of 1866

Five-Cent Piece Obverse Dies of 1866

Obverse 1: "Washington portrait, UNITED STATES OF AMERICA." Low-relief portrait facing right, inscription around border, date 1866 below. • At least two die varieties exist, "A" and "B" per Dr. George J. Fuld, "A Group of Restruck Patterns," *The Numismatist*, May 1998. On die A the O (in OF) is more nearly round than on die B; die A was most popular for restrikes. • Used with J-461 to J-463, J-513 to J-528, J-545. Also used on J-579 of 1867.

Obverse 2: "Washington portrait, IN GOD WE TRUST." Low-relief portrait facing right, inscription around border, date 1866 below. • Used with J-464 to J-479. Also used on J-580, J-581 of 1867.

Obverse 3: "High-relief portrait of Washington, GOD AND OUR COUNTRY." High-relief portrait facing right, inscription around border, date 1866 below. • Used with J-480 to J-485.

Obverse 4: "Lincoln portrait." Head of Lincoln facing right, UNITED STATES OF AMERICA around, date 1866 below. • Used with J-486 to J-488a.

Obverse 5: "Shield design, but ball divides date." Shield nickel similar to regular die except the date divided by the ball at the bottom of the shield. • Used with J-489 to J-500.

Obverse 6: Regular Shield nickel die of the year. • Used with J-501 to J-512, J-531, J-531a.

Five-Cent Piece Reverse Dies of 1866

Reverse A: "Large wreath, IN GOD WE TRUST above." Large bushy wreath, open at top, 5 CENTS. Above is IN GOD WE TRUST in small letters. • Used with J-461 to J-463, J-466a, J-486 to J-488, J-531, J-533.

Reverse B: "Dutch 5 die." Popularly designated "Dutch 5" variety. Small wreath enclosing 5 with large knob at upper right of numeral. UNITED STATES OF AMERICA around border. • Used with J-464 to J-466a, J-480, J-489 to J-491.

Reverse C: "Tall 5 die." Small wreath enclosing tall 5 with pointed top of numeral. UNITED STATES OF AMER-ICA around border. • Used with J-467 to J-469, J-481, J-482, J-492, J-493, J-501 to J-503, J-527.

Reverse D: "Short 5 die." Short 5 with large bushy open wreath enclosing 5 CENTS. Leaves at the bottom of the wreath are especially prominent and bushy. UNITED STATES OF AMERICA in tall letters at border. • Used with J-470 to J-472, J-483 to J-485, J-494 to J-496, J-504 to J-506, J-528.

Reverse E: Regular with-rays die of the year. • Used with J-473 to J-475, J-497 to J-499, J-510 to J-515.

Reverse F: Regular die without rays, as adopted in 1867.[27] • Used with J-476 to J-479, J-507 to J-509a, J-516 to J-520, J-532 (variation).

Reverse G: "Large 5, CENTS in straight line." Large open wreath enclosing 5 CENTS, with CENTS in a straight line. IN GOD WE TRUST in small letters at top border. • Used with J-529, J-530.

Off-metal strikings produced in 1866 include minor denominations in different alloys, and the silver and gold denominations in copper, these being from regular Proof dies of the year.

Of great interest among 1866-dated coins are three varieties: the quarter dollar, half dollar, and silver dollar (J-536, J-538, J-540) using the old-style reverse without motto IN GOD WE TRUST. These are not patterns, but are postdated rarities made for the numismatic trade, in the same context as the 1868 large copper cent, the 1913 Liberty Head nickel, and the 1884 and 1885 trade dollar.

Collecting Perspective

First and foremost among patterns of 1866 are nickel five-cent pieces in fascinating variety. Houdon's 1785 bust of Washington, first seen in the pattern series among two-cent pieces of 1863 (e.g., J-205), appears on several varieties of 1866 nickels. An entirely different version of Washington's head, loosely adapted from Houdon, larger in size and in higher relief (Obverse 3), is seen on J-480 through J-485, all examples of which are very rare.

There may be 20 pieces of the Lincoln portrait five-cent pieces across four different metals (J-487 in copper and J-488 in bronze being virtually impossible to distinguish), but the demand for them is so widespread that they cannot be easily obtained. It is said that only five were struck in nickel.[28] Still other pattern nickels employ the regular Shield obverse of the year with different reverses (including J-507 to J-509a, incorporating the without-rays adopted the following year). Certain double-obverse mules appear beginning with J-521; they were struck in small numbers, and were no doubt highly prized by the unknown coiners who created them outside of the walls of the Mint, perhaps at the shop of William H. Key. While no one will ever acquire a complete set of five-cent varieties of this year, obtaining at least one impression from each of the dies is a practical goal. Certain reverse dies were also used in later years.

The off-metal strikings from Proof dies of regular denominations all range from rare to very rare. White-metal impressions of nickel five-cent dies were probably struck privately.

The 1866 quarter dollar, half dollar, and silver dollar without motto described above have exceptional numismatic interest as they are listed among regular issues in *A Guide Book of United States Coins*. The quarter dollar and half dollar are believed to be unique, and two examples are known of the dollar.

J-455 to J-457: 1866 Cent

Trial piece struck from regular dies.

J-455

Number	Metal	Edge	Rarity	Pop	T/A	Last Traded at Auction				60	63	65
						Firm	Date	Amount	Grade			
455	C	PE	8	2	1	Heritage	8/2004	$6,325	NGCPF65BN	N/A	N/A	$20,000
456	C-N	PE	L7	10	10	Heritage	6/2005	$3,738	PCGSPF65	$1,500	$2,750	$5,000
457	Nick	PE	H7	2	1	Bowers & Merena	3/2003	$3,450	NGCMS65	$9,500	$15,000	$22,500

J-458 and J-459: 1866 Two-Cent Piece

Trial piece struck from regular dies.

J-458

Number	Metal	Edge	Rarity	Pop	T/A	Last Traded at Auction				60	63	65
						Firm	Date	Amount	Grade			
458	C-N	PE	H7	3	1	Stack's	1/1987	$1,650	Unc	$2,600	$4,750	$8,250
459	Nick	PE	8	1	1	Superior	1/1990	$3,080	PCGSMS65	$7,000	$12,500	$22,500

J-460: 1866 Three-Cent Piece

Struck from regular dies. Struck from a cracked reverse die.

J-460

Number	Metal	Edge	Rarity	Pop	T/A	Last Traded at Auction				60	63	65
						Firm	Date	Amount	Grade			
460	C	PE	8	1	1	Heritage	1/2002	$7,475	PCGSPF55	$6,000	$10,000	$17,500

J-461 to J-463: 1866 Five-Cent Piece
Dies 1-A

First die combination in an extensive series made primarily for the numismatic trade.

Obverse: Washington portrait, UNITED STATES OF AMERICA.
Reverse: Large wreath, IN GOD WE TRUST above.

J-461

Number	Metal	Edge	Rarity	Pop	T/A	Last Traded at Auction				60	63	65
						Firm	Date	Amount	Grade			
461	Nick	PE	5	37	33	Heritage	6/2005	$2,645	PCGSPF65CA	$1,300	$1,900	$3,300
462	C	PE	L7	6	10	Heritage	1/2005	$3,738	PCGSPF64RB	$2,200	$4,000	$8,250
463	C-N	PE	8	0	1	NERCG	4/1980	$3,750	PF	$5,850	$10,500	$20,000

J-464 to J-466: 1866 Five-Cent Piece
Dies 2-B

Obverse: Washington portrait, IN GOD WE TRUST.
Reverse: Dutch 5 die.

J-464

Number	Metal	Edge	Rarity	Pop	T/A	Last Traded at Auction				60	63	65
						Firm	Date	Amount	Grade			
464	Nick	PE	H7	2	1	Heritage	2/1984	$1,000	PF63/65	$2,900	$5,750	$11,000
465	C	PE	8	0	1	Stack's	1/1992	$8,500	GemPFBN	$5,850	$10,500	$20,000
466	Brz	PE	H7	2	3	Bowers & Merena	3/1997	$7,150	PCGSPF65BN	$2,600	$5,500	$10,500

Patterns of 1866

J-466a: 1866 Five-Cent Piece
Dies 2-A

A rarity, known only in silver. Listing tentative; perhaps
a misdescription of another variety.[29]

Obverse: Washington portrait, IN GOD WE TRUST.
Reverse: Large wreath, IN GOD WE TRUST above.

J-466a

Number	Metal	Edge	Rarity	Pop	T/A	Last Traded at Auction				60	63	65
						Firm	Date	Amount	Grade			
466a	Silv	PE	–	0	0	N/A	N/A	N/A	N/A	Unconf	Unconf	Unconf

J-467 to J-469: 1866 Five-Cent Piece
Dies 2-C

Obverse: Washington portrait, IN GOD WE TRUST.
Reverse: Tall 5 die.

J-468

Number	Metal	Edge	Rarity	Pop	T/A	Last Traded at Auction				60	63	65
						Firm	Date	Amount	Grade			
467	Nick	PE	H7	2	1	Stack's	6/1987	$1,650	PF	$2,900	$5,750	$11,000
468	C	PE	8	4	4	ANR	3/2005	$6,900	PCGSPF64BN	$5,500	$10,500	$20,000
469	Brz	PE	L7	6	6	Heritage	8/2004	$3,565	PCGSPF62RB	$2,600	$5,150	$7,250

J-470 to J-472: 1866 Five-Cent Piece
Dies 2-D

Obverse: Washington portrait, IN GOD WE TRUST.
Reverse: Short 5 die.

J-470

Number	Metal	Edge	Rarity	Pop	T/A	Last Traded at Auction				60	63	65
						Firm	Date	Amount	Grade			
470	Nick	PE	L6	25	18	Heritage	1/2005	$2,530	PCGSPF64CA	$1,400	$2,000	$3,250
471	C	PE	8	2	3	Bowers & Merena	3/1996	$2,970	PF63RB	$5,850	$10,000	$18,000
472	Brz	PE	L7	4	3	Bowers & Merena	1/2003	$7,820	PCGS65RB	$2,850	$5,750	$10,500

J-473 to J-475: 1866 Five-Cent Piece
Dies 2-E

Obverse: Washington portrait, IN GOD WE TRUST.
Reverse: Regular with-rays die of the year.

J-473

Number	Metal	Edge	Rarity	Pop	T/A	Last Traded at Auction				60	63	65
						Firm	Date	Amount	Grade			
473	Nick	PE	L6	27	18	Heritage	8/2004	$4,945	PCGSPF66	$1,500	$2,100	$3,500
474	C	PE	8	0	0	N/A	N/A	N/A	N/A	$5,850	$10,500	$20,000
475	Brz	PE	8	0	0	N/A	N/A	N/A	N/A	$5,850	$10,500	$20,000

J-476 to J-479: 1866 Five-Cent Piece
Dies 2-F
Believed to have been struck privately.

Obverse: Washington portrait, IN GOD WE TRUST.
Reverse: Regular die without rays, as adopted in 1867.[30]

J-476

Number	Metal	Edge	Rarity	Pop	T/A	Last Traded at Auction				60	63	65
						Firm	Date	Amount	Grade			
476	Nick	PE	8	1	1	Bowers & Ruddy	3/1980	$13,500	PF	N/A	$20,000	N/A
477	C	PE	8	0	1	Superior	10/1992	$6,325	NGCPF62BN	N/A	$13,000	N/A
478	Brs	PE	–	0	0	N/A	N/A	N/A	N/A	Unconf	Unconf	Unconf
479	WM	PE	8	1	1	Heritage	8/1996	$8,800	PCGSPF64	$5,200	$11,000	$20,000

J-480: 1866 Five-Cent Piece
Dies 3-B
This begins the short series of die combinations with this very rare obverse, made for reasons not known today.

Obverse: High-relief portrait of Washington, GOD AND OUR COUNTRY.
Reverse: Dutch 5 die.

J-480

Number	Metal	Edge	Rarity	Pop	T/A	Last Traded at Auction				60	63	65
						Firm	Date	Amount	Grade			
480	Nick	PE	U	0	0	N/A	N/A	N/A	N/A	N/A	N/A	N/A

J-481 and J-482: 1866 Five-Cent Piece
Dies 3-C
Obverse: High-relief portrait of Washington, GOD AND OUR COUNTRY.
Reverse: Tall 5 die.

J-481

Number	Metal	Edge	Rarity	Pop	T/A	Last Traded at Auction				60	63	65
						Firm	Date	Amount	Grade			
481	Nick	PE	L7	11	11	Heritage	6/2005	$4,888	PCGSPF65	$2,000	$4,000	$5,800
482	C	PE	8	0	1	Stack's	6/1994	$4,400	PFBN	$8,500	$15,500	$26,000

J-483 to J-485: 1866 Five-Cent Piece
Dies 3-D
Obverse: High-relief portrait of Washington, GOD AND OUR COUNTRY.
Reverse: Short 5 die.

J-483

Number	Metal	Edge	Rarity	Pop	T/A	Last Traded at Auction				60	63	65
						Firm	Date	Amount	Grade			
483	Nick	PE	8	0	1	Elder	6/1908	$8	PF	N/A	N/A	N/A
484	C	PE	8	1	1	Bowers & Merena	6/1991	$2,310	PF65BN	$4,250	$8,450	$16,300
485	Brz	PE	H7	3	2	Heritage	6/2005	$12,650	PCGSPF66BN	$2,900	$5,800	$10,900

J-486 to J-488a: 1866 Five-Cent Piece
Dies 4-A
These pieces are of intense interest to numismatists as they represent the only Lincoln portrait pattern coin of the 19th century.

Obverse: Lincoln portrait.
Reverse: Large wreath, IN GOD WE TRUST above.

J-486

Number	Metal	Edge	Rarity	Pop	T/A	Last Traded at Auction				60	63	65
						Firm	Date	Amount	Grade			
486	Nick	PE	L7	7	4	Stack's	10/2003	$8,740	ChPF	$4,000	$8,000	$13,500
487	C	PE	L7	7	8	Heritage	3/2004	$23,000	PCGSPF65RB	$4,000	$9,000	$15,000
488	Brz	PE	H7	3	5	ANR	3/2005	$36,800	PCGSPF64BN	$10,000	$17,500	$37,500
488a	Brs	PE	U	0	0	N/A	N/A	N/A	N/A	$15,000	$25,000	$40,000

Patterns of 1866

J-489 to J-491: 1866 Five-Cent Piece
Dies 5-B

Obverse: Shield design, but ball divides date.
Reverse: Dutch 5 die.

J-489

Number	Metal	Edge	Rarity	Pop	T/A	Firm	Date	Amount	Grade	60	63	65
						Last Traded at Auction						
489	Nick	PE	L6	21	16	Heritage	6/2005	$3,163	NGCPF66	$1,400	$2,050	$4,500
490	C	PE	L7	9	17	Stack's	6/2005	$3,450	NGCPF64RB	$1,800	$3,200	$5,750
491	Brz	PE	L7	7	6	ANR	3/2005	$3,680	NGCPF64BN	$2,150	$4,500	$7,000

J-492 and J-493: 1866 Five-Cent Piece
Dies 5-C

Obverse: Shield design, but ball divides date.
Reverse: Tall 5 die.

J-492

Number	Metal	Edge	Rarity	Pop	T/A	Firm	Date	Amount	Grade	60	63	65
						Last Traded at Auction						
492	Nick	PE	U	0	1	Kreisberg-Schulman	2/1958	$68	PF	N/A	N/A	N/A
493	C	PE	U	0	0	Kosoff	3/1961	N/A	N/A	N/A	N/A	N/A

J-494 to J-496: 1866 Five-Cent Piece
Dies 5-D

Obverse: Shield design, but ball divides date.
Reverse: Short 5 die.

J-494

Number	Metal	Edge	Rarity	Pop	T/A	Firm	Date	Amount	Grade	60	63	65
						Last Traded at Auction						
494	Nick	PE	8	0	1	S.H. Chapman	6/1916	$6	PF	N/A	N/A	N/A
495	C	PE	H7	4	3	Bowers & Merena	5/1996	$4,620	PF64BN	$3,550	$7,000	$12,500
496	Brz	PE	H7	2	1	Bowers & Merena	1/2003	$10,350	PCGSPF64BN	$4,500	$9,500	$16,500

J-497 to J-499: 1866 Five-Cent Piece
Dies 5-E

Obverse: Shield design, but ball divides date.
Reverse: Regular with-rays die of the year.

J-497

Number	Metal	Edge	Rarity	Pop	T/A	Firm	Date	Amount	Grade	60	63	65
						Last Traded at Auction						
497	Nick	PE	H7	4	2	Bowers & Merena	1/2003	$8,913	PCGSPF64	$4,500	$9,500	$16,500
498	C	PE	H7	5	9	ANR	7/2003	$8,625	PCGSPF65RB	$2,250	$4,500	$9,500
499	Brz	PE	H7	3	2	Bowers & Merena	1/2003	$8,913	PCGSPF64BN	$3,850	$7,500	$14,500

J-500: 1866 Five-Cent Piece
Dies 5-F

Obverse: Shield design, but ball divides date.
Reverse: Regular die without rays, as adopted in 1867.

J-500

Number	Metal	Edge	Rarity	Pop	T/A	Firm	Date	Amount	Grade	60	63	65
						Last Traded at Auction						
500	Nick	PE	U	1	0	N/A	N/A	N/A	N/A	N/A	N/A	N/A

J-501 to J-503: 1866 Five-Cent Piece
Dies 6-C

Obverse: Regular Shield nickel die of the year.
Reverse: Tall 5 die.

J-501

| Number | Metal | Edge | Rarity | Pop | T/A | Last Traded at Auction | | | | 60 | 63 | 65 |
						Firm	Date	Amount	Grade			
501	Nick	PE	8	0	1	Stack's	6/1994	$4,600	PF	$5,850	$10,500	$20,000
502	C	PE	8	1	2	Superior	5/2004	$20,700	PCGSPF65RB	$6,500	$12,500	$22,500
503	Brz	PE	8	0	1	McIntire	7/1981	$1,000	PF60	$5,850	$10,500	$20,000

J-504 to J-506: 1866 Five-Cent Piece
Dies 6-D

Obverse: Regular Shield nickel die of the year.
Reverse: Short 5 die.

J-504

| Number | Metal | Edge | Rarity | Pop | T/A | Last Traded at Auction | | | | 60 | 63 | 65 |
						Firm	Date	Amount	Grade			
504	Nick	PE	L7	8	5	Heritage	6/2005	$5,175	PCGSPF66CA	$2,250	$4,100	$8,000
505	C	PE	8	0	0	N/A	N/A	N/A	N/A	$5,850	$10,500	$20,000
506	Brz	PE	8	0	0	N/A	N/A	N/A	N/A	$5,850	$10,500	$20,000

J-507 to J-509a: 1866 Five-Cent Piece
Dies 6-F

Highly important transitional pattern, struck at a later date.

Obverse: Regular Shield nickel die of the year.
Reverse: Regular die without rays, as adopted in 1867.[31]

J-507

| Number | Metal | Edge | Rarity | Pop | T/A | Last Traded at Auction | | | | 60 | 63 | 65 |
						Firm	Date	Amount	Grade			
507	Nick	PE	5	43	34	Heritage	6/2005	$4,313	PCGSPF65CA	$1,550	$2,550	$4,500
508	C	PE	H6	18	18	Superior	1/2004	$2,990	NGCPF64BN	$1,300	$2,800	$4,750
509	Brz	PE	H6	13	15	Heritage	6/2005	$4,313	PCGSPF66RB	$1,300	$2,500	$5,000
509a	WM	PE	U	0	0	Pine Tree	9/1974	N/A	N/A	N/A	N/A	N/A

J-510 to J-512: 1866 Five-Cent Piece
Dies 6-E

Struck from regular dies.

Obverse: Regular Shield nickel die of the year.
Reverse: Regular with-rays die of the year.

J-510

| Number | Metal | Edge | Rarity | Pop | T/A | Last Traded at Auction | | | | 60 | 63 | 65 |
						Firm	Date	Amount	Grade			
510	C	PE	8	1	1	Superior	1/1990	$3,520	PCGSPF63BN	N/A	$8,500	$16,500
511	Brz	PE	8	0	0	N/A	N/A	N/A	N/A	N/A	$15,500	$26,000
512	*	PE	U	0	1	Bowers & Merena	3/1996	$4,400	PF65	N/A	N/A	$26,000

* J-512: steel or pure nickel

J-513 to J-515: 1866 Five-Cent Piece
Dies 1-E

All impressions are elusive, and modern scholars have not been able to locate any for detailed examination. An illogical die combination, as both sides have the inscription UNITED STATES OF AMERICA. J-515 is said to be struck on a broad planchet.[32]

Obverse: Washington portrait, UNITED STATES OF AMERICA.
Reverse: Regular with-rays die of the year.

J-513

Number	Metal	Edge	Rarity	Pop	T/A	Last Traded at Auction				60	63	65
						Firm	Date	Amount	Grade			
513	Nick	PE	–	0	0	N/A	N/A	N/A	N/A	Unconf	Unconf	Unconf
514	C	PE	–	0	0	N/A	N/A	N/A	N/A	Unconf	Unconf	Unconf
515	Brs	PE	–	0	0	N/A	N/A	N/A	N/A	Unconf	Unconf	Unconf

J-516 to J-520: 1866 Five-Cent Piece
Dies 1-F

An illogical die combination, as both sides have the inscription UNITED STATES OF AMERICA; probably struck privately. One example of J-516 is clearly struck over an 1867 regular-issue Shield nickel.[33]

Obverse: Washington portrait, UNITED STATES OF AMERICA.
Reverse: Regular die without rays, as adopted in 1867.[34]

J-516

Number	Metal	Edge	Rarity	Pop	T/A	Last Traded at Auction				60	63	65
						Firm	Date	Amount	Grade			
516	Nick	PE	–	0	1	Bowers & Ruddy	8/1978	$800	MS60	Unconf	Unconf	Unconf
517	C	PE	H7	3	2	Heritage	11/2003	$11,500	NGCPF63BN	$4,500	$12,500	$22,500
518	Silv	PE	–	0	0	N/A	N/A	N/A	N/A	Unconf	Unconf	Unconf
519	Brs	PE	8	0	1	Stack's	10/2000	$3,910	PF	$8,500	$15,500	$26,000
520	Lead	PE	8	1	3	Heritage	8/1996	$3,520	PCGSPF60	$12,500	N/A	N/A

J-521a to J-524: 1866 Five-Cent Piece/1866 Five-Cent Piece
Dies 1-2

A curious mule made for the numismatic trade, probably outside of the Mint.

Obverse: Washington portrait, UNITED STATES OF AMERICA around; date 1866 below.
Reverse: Actually an obverse die: Washington portrait, IN GOD WE TRUST.

J-521

Number	Metal	Edge	Rarity	Pop	T/A	Last Traded at Auction				60	63	65
						Firm	Date	Amount	Grade			
521a	Nick	PE	8	0	1	Bowers & Merena	3/1997	$7,700	PCGSPF63	N/A	$15,000	N/A
521	Silv	PE	8	1	1	RARCOA	8/1989	$2,310	ChPF	$4,250	$8,500	$16,500
522	C	PE	8	1	1	Heritage	3/1996	$9,075	PCGSPF64RB	$4,250	$8,500	$16,500
523	Brs	PE	8	0	1	RARCOA	8/1989	$3,190	ChPF	$8,500	$15,500	$26,000
524	WM	PE	8	0	1	Bowers & Ruddy	10/1978	$750	PF63	$8,500	$15,500	$26,000

J-525 and J-526: 1866 Five-Cent Piece/1866 Five-Cent Piece
Dies 1-1

The existence of this piece proves that at least two obverse dies were made of this general design, differences being observable but slight. Struck outside the Mint.

Obverse: Washington portrait, UNITED STATES OF AMERICA.
Reverse: Actually an obverse die: same as the obverse, but from different die.

J-526

Number	Metal	Edge	Rarity	Pop	T/A	Last Traded at Auction				60	63	65
						Firm	Date	Amount	Grade			
525	C	PE	8	1	1	Bowers & Ruddy	3/1980	$6,000	PF60	$4,250	$8,500	$16,500
526	WM	PE	8	3	3	Bowers & Merena	3/1997	$3,960	PF63	$4,250	$8,500	$16,500

J-527: 1866 Five-Cent Piece
Dies 1-C

No specimen verified in recent generations.

Obverse: Washington portrait, UNITED STATES OF AMERICA.
Reverse: Tall 5 die.

J-527

Number	Metal	Edge	Rarity	Pop	T/A	Last Traded at Auction				60	63	65
						Firm	Date	Amount	Grade			
527	Nick	PE	–	0	0	N/A	N/A	N/A	N/A	Unconf	Unconf	Unconf

J-528: 1866 Five-Cent Piece
Dies 1-D

No specimen verified in recent generations.

Obverse: Washington portrait, UNITED STATES OF AMERICA.
Reverse: Short 5 die.

J-528

Number	Metal	Edge	Rarity	Pop	T/A	Last Traded at Auction				60	63	65
						Firm	Date	Amount	Grade			
528	Nick	PE	–	0	0	N/A	N/A	N/A	N/A	Unconf	Unconf	Unconf

J-529 and J-530: 1866 Five-Cent Piece
Dies 2-G

No examples have been studied by modern scholars.[35]

Obverse: Washington portrait, IN GOD WE TRUST.
Reverse: Large 5, CENTS in straight line.

J-529

Number	Metal	Edge	Rarity	Pop	T/A	Last Traded at Auction				60	63	65
						Firm	Date	Amount	Grade			
529	Nick	RE	–	0	0	N/A	N/A	N/A	N/A	Unconf	Unconf	Unconf
530	WM	PE	–	0	0	N/A	N/A	N/A	N/A	Unconf	Unconf	Unconf

J-531: 1866 Five-Cent Piece
Dies 6-A

Obverse: Regular Shield nickel die of the year.
Reverse: Large 5, CENTS in curved line.

J-531

Number	Metal	Edge	Rarity	Pop	T/A	Last Traded at Auction				60	63	65
						Firm	Date	Amount	Grade			
531	Nick	PE	H7	3	2	Bowers & Merena	3/2001	$4,140	PCGSPF64	$3,500	$7,000	$12,500

J-531a: 1866 Five-Cent Piece/Undated $3

A fantasy produced for the numismatic market, probably outside the Mint.

Obverse: Regular Shield nickel die of the year.
Reverse: Actually an obverse die for the $3 gold of this era.

J-531a

Number	Metal	Edge	Rarity	Pop	T/A	Last Traded at Auction				60	63	65
						Firm	Date	Amount	Grade			
531a	Nick	PE	U	0	0	S.H. & H. Chapman	6/1905	N/A	N/A	N/A	N/A	N/A

Patterns of 1866

J-532: Undated Five-Cent Piece
Dies F-F

This piece was probably struck outside the Mint. One die is cracked.

Obverse: Actually a reverse die: regular die without rays, as adopted in 1867, but slightly differing in some particulars.
Reverse: Regular die without rays, as adopted in 1867.[36]

J-532

Number	Metal	Edge	Rarity	Pop	T/A	Firm	Date	Amount	Grade	60	63	65
						Last Traded at Auction						
532	WM	PE	U	0	1	Superior	6/1977	$900	Unc	$8,500	$15,500	$26,000

J-533: Undated Five-Cent Piece
Dies F-A

No specimens have been verified in recent generations.

Obverse: Actually a reverse die: regular die without rays, as adopted in 1867.
Reverse: Large 5, CENTS in curved line.

J-533

Number	Metal	Edge	Rarity	Pop	T/A	Firm	Date	Amount	Grade	60	63	65
						Last Traded at Auction						
533	C	PE	–	0	0	N/A	N/A	N/A	N/A	Unconf	Unconf	Unconf

J-534 and J-535: 1866 Dime

Struck from regular dies. Both of these varieties are likely the same; analysis is needed.

J-535

Number	Metal	Edge	Rarity	Pop	T/A	Firm	Date	Amount	Grade	60	63	65
						Last Traded at Auction						
534	Nick	RE	H7	3	3	Superior	9/1998	$3,105	PCGSPF64	$3,850	$7,500	$12,500
535	Nick-Silv	RE	8	1	1	Ira & Larry Goldberg	10/2000	$2,990	NGCPF66	$5,850	$10,500	$18,000

J-536: 1866 Quarter Dollar

Believed to be unique. Not a pattern, but a muling created at a later date as a numismatic rarity.[37]

Obverse: Regular Liberty Seated die of the year.
Reverse: Regular Liberty Seated die of the type before 1866, without motto.

J-536

Number	Metal	Edge	Rarity	Pop	T/A	Firm	Date	Amount	Grade	60	63	65
						Last Traded at Auction						
536	Silv	RE	U	0	1	Kosoff	3/1961	$24,500	BrPF	N/A	N/A	N/A

J-537: 1866 Quarter Dollar

Trial piece struck from regular dies.

J-537

Number	Metal	Edge	Rarity	Pop	T/A	Firm	Date	Amount	Grade	60	63	65
						Last Traded at Auction						
537	C	RE	H7	4	2	Stack's/ANR	6/2004	$8,338	PCGSPF63BN	$3,500	$8,000	$13,500

J-538: 1866 Half Dollar

Believed to be unique. Not a pattern, but a mule created at a later date as a numismatic rarity.

Obverse: Regular Liberty Seated die of the year.
Reverse: Regular Liberty Seated die of the type before 1866, without motto.

J-538

Number	Metal	Edge	Rarity	Pop	T/A	Last Traded at Auction				60	63	65
						Firm	Date	Amount	Grade			
538	S	RE	U	0	1	Kosoff	3/1961	$15,500	PF	N/A	N/A	N/A

J-539: 1866 Half Dollar

Trial piece struck from regular dies.

J-539

Number	Metal	Edge	Rarity	Pop	T/A	Last Traded at Auction				60	63	65
						Firm	Date	Amount	Grade			
539	C	RE	H7	6	6	Bowers & Merena	3/2003	$7,360	PF64RB	$2,750	$5,250	$9,500

J-540: 1866 Silver Dollar

Two known. Not a pattern, but a mule created at a later date as a numismatic rarity.

Obverse: Regular Liberty Seated die of the year.
Reverse: Regular Liberty Seated die of the type before 1866, without motto.

J-540

Number	Metal	Edge	Rarity	Pop	T/A	Last Traded at Auction				60	63	65
						Firm	Date	Amount	Grade			
540	Silv	RE	8	0	2	ANR	1/2005	$1,207,500	ChPF	N/A	$1,200,000	N/A

J-541: 1866 Silver Dollar

Trial piece struck from regular dies.

J-541

Number	Metal	Edge	Rarity	Pop	T/A	Last Traded at Auction				60	63	65
						Firm	Date	Amount	Grade			
541	C	RE	L6	28	19	Heritage	5/2005	$7,188	PCGSPF65RB	$2,500	$4,000	$7,000

Patterns of 1866

J-542: 1866 $2.50

Struck from regular dies. Might be a mint error.

J-542

Number	Metal	Edge	Rarity	Pop	T/A	Last Traded at Auction				60	63	65
						Firm	Date	Amount	Grade			
542	Nick	RE	H7	4	1	Stack's	8/1976	$900	PF	$4,100	$7,700	$14,000

J-543 to J-544: 1866 $3

Trial piece struck from regular dies.

J-543

Number	Metal	Edge	Rarity	Pop	T/A	Last Traded at Auction				60	63	65
						Firm	Date	Amount	Grade			
543	Nick	RE	H7	5	5	Heritage	6/2004	$7,188	PCGSPF64	$5,150	$10,000	$14,000
543a	C	RE	U	0	1	E. Cogan	9/1869	$4	PF	N/A	N/A	N/A
544	Alu	RE	–	0	0	N/A	N/A	N/A	N/A	Unconf	Unconf	Unconf

J-545: 1866 $5

Privately struck. Broadstruck (without the use of a collar). Believed to be unique.

Obverse: Washington portrait, IN GOD WE TRUST; Obverse 2 die for the five-cent piece.
Reverse: Regular half eagle die of the pre-1866 type, without motto.

J-545

Number	Metal	Edge	Rarity	Pop	T/A	Last Traded at Auction				60	63	65
						Firm	Date	Amount	Grade			
545	WM	PE	U	0		Bowers & Ruddy	5/1974	$2,400	PF	N/A	N/A	N/A

J-546: 1866 $5

Trial piece struck from regular dies.

J-546

Number	Metal	Edge	Rarity	Pop	T/A	Last Traded at Auction				60	63	65
						Firm	Date	Amount	Grade			
546	C	RE	H7	2	3	ANR	8/2004	$14,174	PCGSPF64RB	$6,500	$10,000	$19,000

J-547: 1866 $5

Broadstruck (without the use of a collar). Believed to be unique. Privately struck.

Obverse: Washington portrait, UNITED STATES OF AMERICA; Obverse 1 die for the five-cent piece.
Reverse: Regular half eagle die of the pre-1866 type, without motto.[38]

J-547

Number	Metal	Edge	Rarity	Pop	T/A	Last Traded at Auction				60	63	65
						Firm	Date	Amount	Grade			
547	WM	PE	U	0	1	Kagin's	10/1983	$1,250	AU	$10,000	N/A	N/A

J-548: 1866 $10

Trial piece struck from regular dies.

J-548

Number	Metal	Edge	Rarity	Pop	T/A	Last Traded at Auction				60	63	65
						Firm	Date	Amount	Grade			
548	C	RE	8	1	1	Superior	5/1999	$4,830	PF64BN	$7,000	$14,000	$26,000

J-549: 1866 $20

Trial piece struck from regular dies.

J-549

Number	Metal	Edge	Rarity	Pop	T/A	Last Traded at Auction				60	63	65
						Firm	Date	Amount	Grade			
549	C	RE	H7	1	1	Superior	1/2003	$35,650	NGCPF63Gilt	$25,000	$36,000	$47,000

History and Overview

The patterns for 1867 are distinguished by a variety of different die combinations and metals in the nickel five-cent series. Several new portraits are introduced, including one with Liberty wearing feathers and with the engraver's name spelled out in full below, LONGACRE F., the F being for "fecit" or "made it," perhaps inspired by the C. GOB-RECHT. F. signature on the 1836 Gobrecht dollars. Reverse styles include two new designs as well as two used on pattern coinage in 1866, and the two regular dies of the year (with rays and without rays).

Special historical significance is attached to J-561, the Longacre die with a feathered headdress, as this was struck in aluminum, at that time a valuable metal. Longacre, whose interest in aluminum as a coinage metal dated back at least to 1859, designed a piece the same size as the nickel five-cent piece and the same weight as the silver half dime, because, at that time, aluminum was worth exactly as much as silver, weight for weight. For the obverse, Longacre used an unusual head of Liberty wearing a headdress of four large feathers from which hangs a ribbon inscribed UNION & LIBERTY. For the reverse, he designed a large V on a shield in an oval ornamented frame. Had this aluminum piece been adopted, it would have eliminated not only the die breakage caused by the hard nickel planchets, but also the necessity of having two coins of the same face value in different metals.

The second obverse design for the five-cent piece this year, Liberty with a coronet, is an adaptation of that used on the three-cent piece, and was part of an interest in adopting uniform designs for the different minor denominations. In the next year, 1868, the idea bore more extensive fruit, but still only in pattern form.

Other patterns of the year include off-metal strikings from regular Proof dies made in the Medal Department of the Mint, and curious mules made outside of the Mint.[39]

Five-Cent Piece Obverse Dies of 1867

Obverse 1: "Indian Princess head." Head of Liberty with feathered headdress, facing left, ribbon inscribed UNION & LIBERTY on hair, four stars to right, signature LONGACRE F. below portrait, UNITED STATES OF AMERICA around, 1867, below. • Used with J-561 to J-565.

Obverse 2: "Coronet Head, no star." Head of Liberty facing right, no star on coronet. Coronet inscribed LIBERTY. Around border, UNITED STATES OF AMERICA, 1867 below. • Used with J-566, J-567, J-569, J-574 to J-581.

Obverse 3: "Coronet Head, with star." Head of Liberty facing right, with star on coronet below the word LIBERTY. Around border, UNITED STATES OF AMERICA, 1867 below. • At least two date position varieties exist, 7 distant from curl and 7 close to curl.[40] • Used with J-568, J-579, J-571, J-582, J-583.

Patterns of 1867

Obverse 4: Regular Shield nickel die of the year. • Used with J-572 to J-573a.

Five-Cent Piece Reverse Dies of 1867
Reverses B, E, F, and G are the same as the 1866 dies with the same letters. Dies C and D are new for 1867. The designation A is not used.

Reverse B: "Dutch 5 die." Popularly designated "Dutch 5" variety. Small wreath enclosing 5 with large knob at upper right of numeral. UNITED STATES OF AMERICA around border. Die first used in 1866. • Used with J-576.

Reverse C: "V on shield die." Large V on shield with ornamented frame surrounding, IN GOD WE TRUST in small letters above. • Used with J-561 to J-564.

Reverse D: "V within wreath die." Large V within heavy wreath of oak and olive, connected at the top by scrolls and ornamented with a six-pointed star. • Used with J-565.

Reverse E: "Regular with-rays die." With-rays die regularly used early in the year. • Used with J-572, J-574.

Reverse F: "Regular without-rays die." Regular die without rays as adopted early in the year. • Used with J-573, J-575, J-583, J-583.

Reverse G: "Large 5, CENTS in straight line." Large open wreath enclosing 5 CENTS, with CENTS in a straight line. IN GOD WE TRUST in small letters at top border. • Die first used in 1866. • Used with J-566 to J-568, J-573a.

Reverse H: "Large 5, CENTS in curved line." Large open wreath enclosing 5 CENTS, with CENTS in a curved line. IN GOD WE TRUST in small letters at top border. • Die first used in 1866. • Used with J-569 to J-571, J-577.

Collecting Perspective

The nickel five-cent pieces of this year are highly collectible, and while only J-561 (aluminum, plain edge) and J-562 (aluminum, reeded edge) appear on the market with any frequency, examples of many other dies can be obtained over a period of time.

The other patterns range from rare to extremely rare and are usually obtainable only in widely spaced intervals. Curious and illogical mules are all rare, and most if not all were made outside of the Mint from "borrowed" dies.

J-550 to J-553: 1867 Cent

Trial piece struck from regular dies.

J-550

Number	Metal	Edge	Rarity	Pop	T/A	Last Traded at Auction				60	63	65
						Firm	Date	Amount	Grade			
550	C	PE	8	0	0	N/A	N/A	N/A	N/A	$1,500	$2,500	$4,000
551	C-N	PE	8	1	1	Kagin's	1/1967	$810	PF	$10,000	$15,500	$26,000
552	Nick	PE	8	1	1	Bowers & Merena	1/1997	$2,365	PF50	$14,000	$21,000	$35,000
553	Oro	PE	8	0	0	N/A	N/A	N/A	N/A	N/A	$11,000	$20,000

J-554 to J-557: 1867 Two-Cent Piece

Struck from regular dies. Two different obverse die varieties were used for these off-metal strikes.

J-557

Number	Metal	Edge	Rarity	Pop	T/A	Last Traded at Auction				60	63	65
						Firm	Date	Amount	Grade			
554	C	PE	8	0	1	NERCG	12/1976	$280	PF	$1,500	$2,500	$4,000
555	C-N	PE	8	0	0	N/A	N/A	N/A	N/A	$7,150	$13,000	$22,500
556	Nick	PE	H7	2	1	Heritage	8/1990	$5,720	PCGSMS65	$6,100	$10,500	$16,500
557	Oro	PE	8	0	1	B. Max Mehl	11/1944	$25	Unc	$7,750	$14,000	$26,000

J-558 and J-559: 1867 Three-Cent Piece

Trial piece struck from regular nickel three-cent piece dies.

J-558

Number	Metal	Edge	Rarity	Pop	T/A	Firm	Date	Amount	Grade	60	63	65
							Last Traded at Auction					
558	C	PE	L7	7	3	Heritage	1/1997	$2,645	NGCPF64RB	$1,800	$3,200	$5,150
559	Oro	PE	8	1	1	Superior	8/1982	$750	Unc	$4,900	$9,100	$16,500

J-560: 1867 Trime

Trial piece struck from regular dies.

J-560

Number	Metal	Edge	Rarity	Pop	T/A	Firm	Date	Amount	Grade	60	63	65
							Last Traded at Auction					
560	C	PE	H7	3	3	Bowers & Merena	7/2004	$10,063	PCGSPF63BN	$6,000	$10,500	$13,500

J-561 to J-564: 1867 Five-Cent Piece
Dies 1-C

Obverse: Indian Princess head.
Reverse: V on shield die.

J-561

Number	Metal	Edge	Rarity	Pop	T/A	Firm	Date	Amount	Grade	60	63	65
							Last Traded at Auction					
561	Alu	PE	5	37	27	Heritage	6/2005	$3,450	PCGSPF63CA	$1,750	$3,300	$5,500
562	Alu	RE	L7	7	3	Heritage	6/2005	$8,338	NGCPF66	$3,850	$7,000	$12,500
563	C	PE	H7	2	2	Heritage	7/2004	$17,250	PCGSPF64BN	$6,500	$12,500	$22,500
564	C	RE	H7	4	2	Bowers & Merena	1/2003	$14,375	PCGS64RD	$4,500	$9,500	$16,000

J-565: 1867 Five-Cent Piece
Dies 1-D

Obverse: Indian Princess head.
Reverse: V within wreath die.

J-565

Number	Metal	Edge	Rarity	Pop	T/A	Firm	Date	Amount	Grade	60	63	65
							Last Traded at Auction					
565	Nick	PE	8	1	1	Bowers & Merena	6/1984	$4,950	PF65	$4,250	$8,500	$17,500

J-566 and J-567: 1867 Five-Cent Piece
Dies 2-G

This same combination was listed by Dr. Judd as J-566 and
J-567 and also as J-578 and J-578a; the last two are deleted
from the present study.

Obverse: Coronet Head, no star.
Reverse: Large 5, CENTS in straight line.

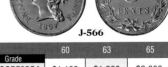

J-566

Number	Metal	Edge	Rarity	Pop	T/A	Firm	Date	Amount	Grade	60	63	65
							Last Traded at Auction					
566	Nick	PE	L6	31	28	Heritage	6/2005	$2,300	PCGSPF65CA	$1,100	$1,800	$2,800
567	C	PE	L7	5	5	ANR	11/2004	$2,760	ANACSPF64BN	$1,700	$3,200	$5,800

Patterns of 1867

J-568: 1867 Five-Cent Piece
Dies 3-G

This piece is unconfirmed.

Obverse: Coronet Head, with star.
Reverse: Large 5, CENTS in straight line.

J-568

Number	Metal	Edge	Rarity	Pop	T/A	Last Traded at Auction				60	63	65
						Firm	Date	Amount	Grade			
568	Nick	PE	–	0	N/A	N/A	N/A	N/A	N/A	Unconf	Unconf	Unconf

J-569: 1867 Five-Cent Piece
Dies 2-H

This piece is unconfirmed.

Obverse: Coronet Head, no star.
Reverse: Large 5, CENTS in curved line.

J-569

Number	Metal	Edge	Rarity	Pop	T/A	Last Traded at Auction				60	63	65
						Firm	Date	Amount	Grade			
569	Nick	PE	–	0	N/A	N/A	N/A	N/A	N/A	Unconf	Unconf	Unconf

J-570 and J-571: 1867 Five-Cent Piece
Dies 3-H

Obverse die varieties exist.

Obverse: Coronet Head, with star.
Reverse: Large 5, CENTS in curved line.

J-570

Number	Metal	Edge	Rarity	Pop	T/A	Last Traded at Auction				60	63	65
						Firm	Date	Amount	Grade			
570	Nick	PE	5	43	33	Heritage	2/2005	$1,265	NGCPF62	$1,150	$1,800	$3,150
571	C	PE	L7	5	5	Bowers & Merena	1/2003	$5,980	PCGSPF64RB	$2,250	$4,500	$7,700

J-572: 1867 Five-Cent Piece
Dies 4-E

Struck from regular dies, with rays.

J-572

Number	Metal	Edge	Rarity	Pop	T/A	Last Traded at Auction				60	63	65
						Firm	Date	Amount	Grade			
572	C	PE	L7	8	10	Heritage	11/2003	$7,475	PCGSPF63	$2,600	$5,000	$9,000

J-573: 1867 Five-Cent Piece
Dies 4-F

Struck from regular dies, without rays. Two reverse varieties exist, each differing from the other slightly.[41]

J-573

Number	Metal	Edge	Rarity	Pop	T/A	Last Traded at Auction				60	63	65
						Firm	Date	Amount	Grade			
573	C	PE	L6	24	21	Stack's/ANR	6/2004	$2,300	PCGSPF64RB	$1,750	$2,550	$5,200

J-573a: 1867 Five-Cent Piece
Dies 4-G

Obverse: Regular Shield nickel die of the year.
Reverse: Large 5, CENTS in straight line.

J-573a

Number	Metal	Edge	Rarity	Pop	T/A	Last Traded at Auction				60	63	65
						Firm	Date	Amount	Grade			
573a	C	PE	8	1	4	Stack's	10/2003	$8,050	PF	$2,600	$4,800	$8,000

J-574: 1867 Five-Cent Piece
Dies 2-E

This piece is unconfirmed.

Obverse: Coronet Head, no star.
Reverse: Regular with-rays die.

J-574

Number	Metal	Edge	Rarity	Pop	T/A	Last Traded at Auction				60	63	65
						Firm	Date	Amount	Grade			
574	WM	PE	–	0	0	N/A	N/A	N/A	N/A	N/A	N/A	N/A

J-575: 1867 Five-Cent Piece
Dies 2-F

This piece has not been examined by Bowers or Teichman, but one example has been encapsulated by PCGS.

Obverse: Coronet Head, no star.
Reverse: Regular without-rays die.

J-575

Number	Metal	Edge	Rarity	Pop	T/A	Last Traded at Auction				60	63	65
						Firm	Date	Amount	Grade			
575	Nick	PE	U	1	0	N/A	N/A	N/A	N/A	N/A	N/A	N/A

J-576: 1867 Five-Cent Piece
Dies 2-B or 2-1866C

This piece might actually employ Reverse C of 1866; if so, that would be the only use of that die on an 1867 pattern.

Obverse: Coronet Head, no star.
Reverse: Dutch 5 die or Tall 5 die (Reverse C of 1866).[42]

J-576

Number	Metal	Edge	Rarity	Pop	T/A	Last Traded at Auction				60	63	65
						Firm	Date	Amount	Grade			
576	Nick	PE	U	0	0	N/A	N/A	N/A	N/A	N/A	N/A	N/A

J-577: 1867 Five-Cent Piece
Dies 2-A

Obverse: Coronet Head, no star.
Reverse: Large wreath, IN GOD WE TRUST above (Reverse A of 1866).

J-577

Number	Metal	Edge	Rarity	Pop	T/A	Last Traded at Auction				60	63	65
						Firm	Date	Amount	Grade			
577	Nick	PE	–	0	0	N/A	N/A	N/A	N/A	Unconf	Unconf	Unconf

Patterns of 1867

J-579: 1867 Five-Cent Piece/ 1866 Five-Cent Piece

Unconfirmed. A mule for the numismatic trade, combining two different dates. Privately struck, as were most related productions.

Obverse: Coronet Head, no star (Obverse 2 of 1867).
Reverse: Actually an obverse die: Washington portrait, UNITED STATES OF AMERICA (Obverse 1 of 1866).

J-579

Number	Metal	Edge	Rarity	Pop	T/A	Last Traded at Auction				60	63	65
						Firm	Date	Amount	Grade			
579	Silv	PE	–	0	0	N/A	N/A	N/A	N/A	Unconf	Unconf	Unconf

J-580 and J-581: 1867 Five-Cent Piece/1866 Five-Cent Piece

A mule for the numismatic trade, believed to have been privately struck, combining two different dates.

Obverse: Coronet Head, no star (Obverse 2 of 1867).
Reverse: Actually an obverse die: Washington portrait, IN GOD WE TRUST (Obverse 2 of 1866).

J-580

Number	Metal	Edge	Rarity	Pop	T/A	Last Traded at Auction				60	63	65
						Firm	Date	Amount	Grade			
580	Nick	PE	–	0	0	N/A	N/A	N/A	N/A	Unconf	Unconf	Unconf
581	WM	PE	U	0	1	Heritage	5/1991	$2,310	PF60	$15,500	$26,000	N/A

J-582 and J-583: 1867 Five-Cent Piece
Dies 3-F

Believed to have been privately struck.

Obverse: Coronet Head, with star.
Reverse: Regular without-rays die.

J-583

Number	Metal	Edge	Rarity	Pop	T/A	Last Traded at Auction				60	63	65
						Firm	Date	Amount	Grade			
582	Nick	PE	8	1	1	Heritage	3/1988	$495	PF45	$4,250	$8,500	$16,500
583	Silv	PE	8	1	1	Heritage	8/2001	$4,140	PCGSPF55	$4,250	$8,500	$16,500

J-584 to J-584b: 1867 Five-Cent Piece/1866 Five-Cent Piece

Privately struck.

Obverse: Coronet Head, with star (Obverse 3 of 1867).
Reverse: Actually an obverse die: Washington portrait, UNITED STATES OF AMERICA (Obverse 1 of 1866).

J-584a

Number	Metal	Edge	Rarity	Pop	T/A	Last Traded at Auction				60	63	65
						Firm	Date	Amount	Grade			
584	WM	PE	–	0	0	N/A	N/A	N/A	N/A	Unconf	Unconf	Unconf
584a	Nick	PE	U	2	2	Bowers & Merena	1/2003	$19,550	PCGSPF62	$18,000	$30,000	$45,000
584b	Silv	PE	U	0	1	Bowers & Merena	1/1996	$3,740	VF20	N/A	N/A	N/A

J-585: 1867 Five-Cent Piece/ 1866 Five-Cent Piece

Privately struck.

Obverse: Coronet Head, with star (Obverse 3 of 1867).
Reverse: Actually an obverse die: Washington portrait, IN GOD WE TRUST (Obverse 2 of 1866).

J-585

Number	Metal	Edge	Rarity	Pop	T/A	Last Traded at Auction				60	63	65
						Firm	Date	Amount	Grade			
585	WM	PE	8	0	1	Kagin's	10/1983	$900	MS60	$8,500	$16,000	$26,000

J-586: 1867 Half Dime

Trial piece struck from regular dies. These are part of the complete copper sets struck in 1867. Andrew Pollock mentions two in the Iowa State Historical Department. A third set was in the famous Garrett collection, sold in 1976.

J-586

Number	Metal	Edge	Rarity	Pop	T/A	Firm	Date	Amount	Grade	60	63	65
							Last Traded at Auction					
586	C	RE	H7	2	3	Ira & Larry Goldberg	5/2005	$6,210	PCGSPF65RB	$2,600	$4,500	$9,000

J-587 to J-589: 1867 Dime

Trial piece struck from regular dies. Pollock mentions two complete sets of copper sets in the Iowa State Historical Department.

J-587

Number	Metal	Edge	Rarity	Pop	T/A	Firm	Date	Amount	Grade	60	63	65
							Last Traded at Auction					
587	C	RE	L7	4	7	Heritage	3/2004	$3,910	NGCPF64RB	$1,800	$3,200	$6,400
588	Nick	RE	8	1	2	Superior	10/2000	$3,910	PCGSPF62	$5,850	$10,500	$18,500
589	Nick-Silv	PE	8	0	0	N/A	N/A	N/A	N/A	$2,600	$3,250	$7,150

J-590: 1867 Quarter Dollar

Trial piece struck from regular dies. T. Harrison Garrett owned one example, and two are in the Iowa State Historical Department.

J-590

Number	Metal	Edge	Rarity	Pop	T/A	Firm	Date	Amount	Grade	60	63	65
							Last Traded at Auction					
590	C	RE	H7	4	3	Heritage	7/2003	$5,750	NGCPF65RB	$2,250	$3,500	$6,250

J-591: 1867 Half Dollar

Trial piece struck from regular dies. T. Harrison Garrett owned one example, and two are in the Iowa State Historical Department.

J-591

Number	Metal	Edge	Rarity	Pop	T/A	Firm	Date	Amount	Grade	60	63	65
							Last Traded at Auction					
591	C	RE	H7	3	7	Heritage	3/2005	$8,050	PCGSPF65RB	$7,500	$11,000	$17,500

Patterns of 1867

J-592 and J-593: 1867 Silver Dollar

Trial piece struck from regular dies. J-592 pieces were among the complete copper sets struck this year, which also included the other trial pieces on this page.

J-592

Number	Metal	Edge	Rarity	Pop	T/A	Last Traded at Auction				60	63	65
						Firm	Date	Amount	Grade			
592	C	RE	L7	14	7	Stack's	1/2005	$4,888	VChPFBN	$2,750	$5,500	$11,500
593	Brs	RE	H7	3	4	ANR	9/2003	$18,975	NGCPF64	$6,000	$13,000	$27,500

J-594: 1867 Gold Dollar

Trial piece struck from regular dies.

J-594

Number	Metal	Edge	Rarity	Pop	T/A	Last Traded at Auction				60	63	65
						Firm	Date	Amount	Grade			
594	C	RE	H7	1	1	Superior	10/1990	$3,960	NGCPF65BN	$7,150	$13,000	$22,500

J-595: 1867 $2.50

Trial piece struck from regular dies.

J-595

Number	Metal	Edge	Rarity	Pop	T/A	Last Traded at Auction				60	63	65
						Firm	Date	Amount	Grade			
595	C	RE	H7	5	5	Heritage	1/2004	$6,613	PCGSPF63BN	$3,250	$6,000	$11,000

J-596 to J-598: 1867 $3

Trial piece struck from regular dies.

J-596

Number	Metal	Edge	Rarity	Pop	T/A	Last Traded at Auction				60	63	65
						Firm	Date	Amount	Grade			
596	C	RE	H7	6	1	Superior	10/1989	$6,325	NGCPF64RB	$4,500	$8,000	$18,000
597	Nick	RE	H7	2	3	Heritage	3/1999	$18,400	NGCPF68	$8,250	$15,000	$26,000
598	Silv	RE	8	0	1	Bowers & Ruddy	7/1981	$5,250	PF	$13,000	N/A	N/A

J-599 and J-600: 1867 $5

Struck from regular dies.

J-599

Number	Metal	Edge	Rarity	Pop	T/A	Last Traded at Auction				60	63	65
						Firm	Date	Amount	Grade			
599	C	RE	H7	1	1	Superior	10/1990	$3,740	NGCPF63RB	$6,000	$9,500	$17,500
600	Nick	RE	8	0	0	N/A	N/A	N/A	N/A	$15,000	$22,500	$27,500

J-601a and J-601: 1867 $5

Privately struck from regular dies.

Obverse: Five-cent pattern die with Liberty head and diadem, star, first seen under J-568 (Obverse 3).
Reverse: Regular half eagle die of the pre-1866 type without motto.

J-601

Number	Metal	Edge	Rarity	Pop	T/A	Last Traded at Auction				60	63	65
						Firm	Date	Amount	Grade			
601a	Silv	PE	8	0	1	Stack's	10/1997	$7,150	NGCPF63	$7,800	$13,000	$22,500
601	Nick	PE	U	1	4	Bowers & Merena	1/1997	$3,960	NGCMS63	$21,000	$32,500	N/A

J-602 and J-603: 1867 $10

Trial piece struck from regular dies.

J-602

Number	Metal	Edge	Rarity	Pop	T/A	Last Traded at Auction				60	63	65
						Firm	Date	Amount	Grade			
602	C	RE	H7	6	4	Superior	5/2003	$13,225	PCGSPF64RB	$5,150	$10,000	$18,500
603	Nick	RE	–	0	0	N/A	N/A	N/A	N/A	Unconf	Unconf	Unconf

J-604: 1867 $20

Trial piece struck from regular dies.

J-604

Number	Metal	Edge	Rarity	Pop	T/A	Last Traded at Auction				60	63	65
						Firm	Date	Amount	Grade			
604	C	RE	H7	6	9	Stack's	1/2005	$8,625	ChPFBN	$10,000	$17,500	$32,500

Patterns of 1868

History and Overview

The pattern coins of this year feature the uniform designs for the cent, nickel three-cent piece, and nickel five-cent denominations, with an obverse portrait of Liberty wearing a coronet, similar to that used on the regular-issue three-cent piece. The reverses were made in two styles, each with the denomination in Roman numerals, one being a copy of Longacre's "agricultural wreath" (later used on the 1856 Flying Eagle cent); and the second was a laurel wreath similar to that used on certain pattern 1858 cents and the regular-issue Indian Head cents of 1859.

These uniform one-cent, three-cent, and five-cent coins were never adopted for circulation.

In 1868, silver and gold coins still sold at a sharp premium in terms of federal paper money. It was desired to return America to the use of silver dimes, half dollars, gold quarter eagles, and other denominations familiar from the days before the Civil War but not seen since. However, as long as the premium existed, the Mint realized it would be an exercise in futility to produce new coins with standard gold and silver content.

Patterns of 1868

Among other patterns of 1868 is the intriguing "1868 large cent" (J-610 and J-611) incorporating an obverse die identical in its concept to a Braided Hair large copper cent of the 1843 to 1857 era, but dated 1868. The reverse die is identical to that used from 1843 to 1857 on the cents. Impressions were made in nickel and copper. Many collectors have been startled to learn of the existence of a genuine 1868 large cent. The history of this strange anachronism, 11 years after the regular series had ended, is at once complete and incomplete. It is known, for instance, that a ten-cent coin of similar design had previously been struck as part of an experimental coinage. The obverse die was prepared from a large cent hub, the current date then being punched in. What happened next was, perhaps, inevitable. By some inscrutable means, the regular reverse die of the large cent that had been stored away suddenly appeared together with—of all things—a dozen or so large cent planchets of exact size and weight and perfectly proofed! After these wondrous events—which we can only construe as being providential—there was nothing left to do but strike the coins!

Among other patterns bearing the date of this year, the EXCHANGED FOR U.S. NOTES die, used in 1863 to produce J-325 and related pieces, was combined with a new reverse dated 1868 in error, and denominated as ONE DIME.[1] The date should have been 1863, and these pieces are properly issues of 1863, not 1868.

A bill in Congress proposed to adjust the weight of the $5 gold piece (which had not circulated at par since late December 1861) from 129 grains to 124.9 grains, to make it compatible with 25 French francs. Anthony C. Paquet, who had worked as an engraver for the Mint for more than a decade, created a pattern piece with the inscription 5 DOLLARS / 25 FRANCS. The Paris Mint produced a complementary piece, designed by Barre, depicting Napoleon III on the obverse, and inscriptions including the same denominations as on the American coin. Moreover, for use in Austria, a related piece was made with the denomination as 10 FLORINS / 25 FRANCS. Congress did not pass the bill, and the design faded into oblivion. Later, such pattern issues as the 1874 Bickford $10 (J-1373) and the metric coinages of 1878 to 1880 would revisit the concept.

Further included among the other patterns of 1868 is a $10 piece with the Liberty head with coronet motif similar to that used on the minor coins, again part of a proposal to have the same design across a range of denominations.

Off-metal strikes were produced from the Proof dies of various denominations, with special attention being paid to aluminum. This seems to be the only time that the Mint actually kept a record of special off-metal Proof sets being made; this set was the only one that could be verified when a new Mint director investigated patterns in 1887.

Collecting Perspective

The cent, three-cent, and nickel five-cent patterns of 1868 with Liberty wearing a coronet are highly collectible in both reverse wreath styles, although, as they were not produced in quantity, patience will be required to obtain them. The 1868 large copper cent plays to an audience of pattern collectors as well as to specialists in regular-issue large cents of the 1793 to 1857 span. Among patterns of the five-cent denominations are several interesting reverse dies, reprising some used earlier plus a new style (as first listed under J-631).

Paquet's international $5 pattern exists in copper and aluminum and appears on the market with some frequency.[2]

J-605 to J-607: 1868 Cent

Obverse: Liberty Head with coronet. UNITED STATES OF AMERICA surrounding, small date numerals below, high date, touching curl.
Reverse: Roman numeral I within agricultural wreath.

J-605

Number	Metal	Edge	Rarity	Pop	T/A	Firm	Date	Amount	Grade	60	63	65
						Last Traded at Auction						
605	Nick	PE	5	34	20	Heritage	6/2005	$2,243	PCGSPF66	$1,000	$1,400	$2,000
606	C	PE	L7	9	4	Heritage	6/2005	$2,473	PCGSPF63RB	$1,950	$3,200	$5,800
607	Alu	PE	U	0	1	Sotheby's	2/1954	N/A	N/A	N/A	N/A	N/A

J-608 and J-609: 1868 Cent

Obverse: Liberty Head with coronet. UNITED STATES OF AMERICA surrounding, small date numerals below.
Reverse: Laurel wreath enclosing Roman numeral I. Die varieties exist.

J-608

Number	Metal	Edge	Rarity	Pop	T/A	Firm	Date	Amount	Grade	60	63	65
						Last Traded at Auction						
608	Nick	PE	4	74	54	Heritage	6/2005	$1,783	PCGSPF66	$1,000	$1,400	$1,900
609	C	PE	H7	4	7	ANR	10/2004	$5,233	PCGSPF64RB	$2,100	$4,000	$7,500

J-610 and J-611:
1868 Large Copper Cent

The copper striking is one of America's great postdated rarities, made after the regular series ended.[3]

Obverse: Die of the design of a large copper cent (1853 to 1857) but dated 1868.
Reverse: Regular large cent die of the 1843 to 1857 type.

J-610

Number	Metal	Edge	Rarity	Pop	T/A	Last Traded at Auction				60	63	65
						Firm	Date	Amount	Grade			
610	Nick	PE	L7	7	8	Heritage	1/2004	$23,575	PCGSPF64	$11,500	$19,000	$32,500
611	C	PE	L7	7	3	ANR	3/2005	$36,800	NGCPF66BN	$20,000	$27,500	$37,500

J-612:
1868 Cent

Struck from regular dies. Two pairs of Proof dies were used for J-612.[4]

J-612

Number	Metal	Edge	Rarity	Pop	T/A	Last Traded at Auction				60	63	65
						Firm	Date	Amount	Grade			
612	Alu	PE	L7	8	3	Heritage	8/2001	$1,380	PCGSPF62	$2,250	$4,000	$7,500

J-613 and J-614:
1868 Two-Cent Piece

Trial piece struck from regular dies.

J-614

Number	Metal	Edge	Rarity	Pop	T/A	Last Traded at Auction				60	63	65
						Firm	Date	Amount	Grade			
613	Nick	PE	8	1	1	Mid-American	9/1989	$2,200	MS64	$7,800	$14,000	$26,000
614	Alu	PE	L7	9	3	Stack's	3/2004	$13,800	GemPF	$2,500	$4,750	$8,250

J-615 to J-617:
1868 Three-Cent Piece

Obverse: Liberty Head with coronet. UNITED STATES OF AMERICA surrounding, small date numerals below.
Reverse: Roman numeral III within agricultural wreath.

J-615

Number	Metal	Edge	Rarity	Pop	T/A	Last Traded at Auction				60	63	65
						Firm	Date	Amount	Grade			
615	Nick	PE	5	38	20	Heritage	6/2005	$2,875	PCGSPF66	$1,150	$1,750	$2,500
615a	C-N	PE	H7	3	4	Superior	8/2002	$2,645	PCGSPF64	$2,600	$5,150	$9,500
616	C	PE	H6	12	6	Ira & Larry Goldberg	1/2004	$3,450	NGCPF66 BNStar	$1,400	$2,500	$4,500
617	Alu	PE	H7	0	1	NERCG	7/1979	In Set	No Grade	$6,250	$11,500	$21,000

J-617a to J-617c:
1868 Three-Cent Piece

Obverse: Liberty Head with coronet. UNITED STATES OF AMERICA surrounding, small date numerals below.
Reverse: Laurel wreath enclosing Roman numeral III.

J-617a

Number	Metal	Edge	Rarity	Pop	T/A	Last Traded at Auction				60	63	65
						Firm	Date	Amount	Grade			
617a	Alu	PE	H7	2	1	Bowers & Ruddy	9/1975	In Set	N/A	$2,850	$6,500	$11,500
617b	C	PE	8	1	1	Bowers & Merena	5/1992	$7,700	PCGSPF64RB	$3,900	$7,500	$14,000
617c	C-N	PE	8	0	0	N/A	N/A	N/A	N/A	$5,850	$10,000	$18,500

Patterns of 1868

J-618 to J-620: 1868 Three-Cent Piece

Obverse: Liberty Head with coronet. UNITED STATES OF AMERICA surrounding, large date numerals below.
Reverse: Laurel wreath enclosing Roman numeral III.

J-618

Number	Metal	Edge	Rarity	Pop	T/A	Last Traded at Auction				60	63	65
						Firm	Date	Amount	Grade			
618	Nick	PE	4	84	52	Heritage	6/2005	$1,783	NGCPF65	$950	$1,350	$2,000
619	C	PE	L7	7	1	Superior	6/1998	$3,850	PCGSPF63BN	$1,550	$2,850	$5,500
620	Alu	PE	8	0	1	Kelly	4/1941	$13	PF	$6,200	$11,500	$20,000

J-621: 1868 Three-Cent Piece

Trial piece struck from regular dies.

J-621

Number	Metal	Edge	Rarity	Pop	T/A	Last Traded at Auction				60	63	65
						Firm	Date	Amount	Grade			
621	Alu	PE	L7	10	2	Heritage	8/2001	$1,725	PCGSPF62	$1,500	$2,700	$5,150

J-622: 1868 Trime

Trial piece struck from regular dies.

J-622

Number	Metal	Edge	Rarity	Pop	T/A	Last Traded at Auction				60	63	65
						Firm	Date	Amount	Grade			
622	Alu	PE	L7	7	2	Heritage	8/2001	$1,265	PCGSPF62	$3,550	$5,150	$8,250

J-623 to J-629a: 1868 Five-Cent Piece

J-624, J-625, J-627, J-628, and J-629a were struck on broad planchets.

Obverse: Liberty Head with coronet on which LIBERTY is in raised letters, no star. UNITED STATES OF AMERICA surrounding, date below.
Reverse: Large open wreath enclosing 5 CENTS, with CENTS in a curved line. IN GOD WE TRUST in small letters at top border (Reverse H of 1866).

J-624

Number	Metal	Edge	Rarity	Pop	T/A	Last Traded at Auction				60	63	65
						Firm	Date	Amount	Grade			
623	Nick	PE	L6	27	18	Heritage	2/2005	$1,495	NGCPF64CA	$1,150	$1,800	$3,000
624	Nick	PE	L6	24	22	Superior	2/2005	$1,265	PCGSPF63	$1,400	$2,250	$4,100
625	Nick	RE	–	0	0	N/A	N/A	N/A	N/A	Unconf	Unconf	Unconf
626	C	PE	H7	3	1	Superior	4/2003	$6,900	NGCPF64RB	$4,000	$8,000	$14,000
627	C	PE	L7	7	5	Bowers & Merena	1/2003	$5,520	PCGS65BN	$2,050	$4,200	$8,000
628	C	RE	H7	5	6	Heritage	8/2004	$8,050	PCGS65RB	$3,500	$3,500	$11,000
629	Alu	PE	8	1	1	Stack's	1/1999	$1,495	PF	$4,250	$8,500	$16,500
629a	Alu	PE	–	0	0	N/A	N/A	N/A	N/A	Unconf	Unconf	Unconf

J-630: 1868 Five-Cent Piece

Obverse: Liberty Head with coronet, as preceding.
Reverse: Large Roman numeral V on shield with ornamented frame surrounding, IN GOD WE TRUST in small letters above (Reverse C of 1867).

J-630

Number	Metal	Edge	Rarity	Pop	T/A	Last Traded at Auction				60	63	65
						Firm	Date	Amount	Grade			
630	Nick	PE	H7	5	3	Stack's	10/2003	$6,440	PCGSPF64	$2,250	$4,500	$8,000

J-631: 1868 Five-Cent Piece

This represents the first listing of this reverse die.

Obverse: Liberty Head with coronet, as preceding.
Reverse: Thin laurel wreath enclosing Roman numeral V, ribbon at top inscribed IN GOD WE TRUST, with small Maltese cross near top.

J-631

Number	Metal	Edge	Rarity	Pop	T/A	Last Traded at Auction				60	63	65
						Firm	Date	Amount	Grade			
631	C	PE	8	1	1	Bowers & Merena	5/1999	$5,750	PCGSPF64BN	$4,250	$8,500	$16,500

J-632 and J-632a: 1868 Five-Cent Piece

Obverse: Liberty Head with coronet. UNITED STATES OF AMERICA surrounding, large date numerals below.
Reverse: Large Roman numeral V within heavy wreath of oak and olive, connected at the top by scrolls and ornamented with a six-pointed star (Reverse D of 1867).

J-632

Number	Metal	Edge	Rarity	Pop	T/A	Last Traded at Auction				60	63	65
						Firm	Date	Amount	Grade			
632	C	PE	H7	6	5	Heritage	6/2005	$9,200	NGCPF65RB	$3,550	$6,500	$11,000
632a	Alu	PE	U	0	1	Sotheby's	2/1954	N/A	N/A	N/A	N/A	N/A

J-633 and J-634: 1868 Five-Cent Piece

Obverse die varieties exist.

Obverse: Liberty Head with coronet on which LIBERTY is in raised letters, with star. UNITED STATES OF AMERICA surrounding, date below.
Reverse: Thin laurel wreath enclosing Roman numeral V, ribbon at top inscribed IN GOD WE TRUST, with small Maltese cross near top (as die of J-631).

J-633

Number	Metal	Edge	Rarity	Pop	T/A	Last Traded at Auction				60	63	65
						Firm	Date	Amount	Grade			
633	Nick	PE	4	77	44	Heritage	5/2005	$1,265	NGCPF63	$1,150	$1,800	$2,550
634	C	PE	H7	3	3	Bowers & Merena	1/2003	$7,590	PCGSPF65BN	$2,900	$5,800	$11,000

J-635 and J-636: 1868 Five-Cent Piece

Trial piece struck from regular dies.

J-636

Number	Metal	Edge	Rarity	Pop	T/A	Last Traded at Auction				60	63	65
						Firm	Date	Amount	Grade			
635	C	PE	–	0	0	N/A	N/A	N/A	N/A	Unconf	Unconf	Unconf
636	Alu	PE	L7	7	6	Heritage	2/2005	$1,495	NGCAU55	$3,000	$6,500	$9,500

J-637 to J-639: 1868 Half Dime

Struck from regular dies. Die varieties exist.

J-638

Number	Metal	Edge	Rarity	Pop	T/A	Last Traded at Auction				60	63	65
						Firm	Date	Amount	Grade			
637	C	PE	8	1	2	Superior	1/2004	$6,325	PCGSPF63RB	$4,200	$7,500	$12,500
638	Nick	PE	L6	26	18	Heritage	2/2005	$2,243	NGCPF65	$1,750	$2,900	$4,500
639	Alu	RE	L7	7	5	Bowers & Merena	7/2004	$1,696	PCGSPF61	$2,250	$3,500	$5,800

Patterns of 1868

J-640 to J-642: 1868 Dime

Research by David Cassel has revealed that these coins were struck in 1863 from a die erroneously dated 1868. The obverse without date is same as that used in 1863 to strike J-331.[5]

Obverse: Liberty Seated die, but without date.
Reverse: Agricultural wreath enclosing a six pointed star, ONE DIME / 1868.

J-641

Number	Metal	Edge	Rarity	Pop	T/A	Last Traded at Auction				60	63	65
						Firm	Date	Amount	Grade			
640	Silv	RE	–	0	0	N/A	N/A	N/A	N/A	Unconf	Unconf	Unconf
641	Nick	RE	L7	6	9	Heritage	4/2002	$2,875	PCGSPF64	$2,150	$3,250	$5,500
642	C	RE	8	1	2	Stack's	12/2003	$9,775	PF	$3,000	$5,000	$10,000

J-643 to J-646: "1868" Dime

Obverse first used in 1863 for J-325 and related pieces.[6] Research by David Cassel has revealed that these coins were struck in 1863 from a die erroneously dated 1868.

Obverse: Small shield at center with crossed arrows behind, wreath around most of perimeter. EXCHANGED FOR U.S. NOTES at border.
Reverse: Die as used on J-641 and related.

J-645

Number	Metal	Edge	Rarity	Pop	T/A	Last Traded at Auction				60	63	65
						Firm	Date	Amount	Grade			
643	Silv	RE	–	0	1	Bowers & Merena	5/1999	$3,680	PCGSPF65	Unconf	Unconf	Unconf
644	Nick	RE	H7	6	3	Superior	5/2003	$7,935	NGCPF66	$2,250	$4,200	$8,000
645	C	PE	H7	5	2	Heritage	3/2003	$6,038	PCGSPF64	$2,250	$4,200	$8,250
646	Alu	PE	L7	5	5	Stack's/ANR	6/2004	$4,600	PCGSPF64	$2,250	$4,200	$8,250

J-647 and J-648: 1868 Ten-Cent Piece

Denominated as TEN CENTS, not necessarily intended to be known as a dime.

Obverse: Die of the design of a large copper cent of 1853–1857, but dated 1868.
Reverse: Wreath similar to that on the old copper cent, but enclosing the denomination TEN CENTS.

J-647

Number	Metal	Edge	Rarity	Pop	T/A	Last Traded at Auction				60	63	65
						Firm	Date	Amount	Grade			
647	Nick	PE	L6	17	17	Heritage	6/2005	$4,313	PCGSPF65	$1,750	$2,800	$4,500
648	C	PE	H6	18	13	Heritage	1/2003	$3,680	PCGSPF65RB	$1,950	$3,050	$5,000

J-649: 1868 Dime

Trial piece struck from regular dies.

J-649

Number	Metal	Edge	Rarity	Pop	T/A	Last Traded at Auction				60	63	65
						Firm	Date	Amount	Grade			
649	Alu	RE	L7	8	3	Superior	2/2003	$1,840	PCGSPF62	$2,250	$4,500	$8,250

J-650: 1868 Quarter Dollar

Trial piece struck from regular dies.

J-650

Number	Metal	Edge	Rarity	Pop	T/A	Last Traded at Auction				60	63	65
						Firm	Date	Amount	Grade			
650	Alu	RE	L7	8	2	Heritage	8/2001	$1,380	PCGSPF61	$1,800	$2,850	$5,500

J-651: 1868 Half Dollar

Trial piece struck from regular dies.

J-651

Number	Metal	Edge	Rarity	Pop	T/A	Last Traded at Auction				60	63	65
						Firm	Date	Amount	Grade			
651	Alu	RE	L7	9	4	Bowers & Merena	11/2002	$5,060	PCGSPF65	$2,600	$4,500	$8,250

J-652: 1868 Silver Dollar

Trial piece struck from regular dies.

J-652

Number	Metal	Edge	Rarity	Pop	T/A	Last Traded at Auction				60	63	65
						Firm	Date	Amount	Grade			
652	Alu	RE	L7	7	2	ANR	9/2003	$13,800	NGCPF66	$4,000	$7,000	$13,000

J-653: 1868 Gold Dollar

Trial piece struck from regular dies.

J-653

Number	Metal	Edge	Rarity	Pop	T/A	Last Traded at Auction				60	63	65
						Firm	Date	Amount	Grade			
653	Alu	RE	L7	7	2	Akers	10/1997	$3,575	PF	$3,000	$5,000	$8,750

J-654: 1868 $2.50

Trial piece struck from regular dies.

J-654

Number	Metal	Edge	Rarity	Pop	T/A	Last Traded at Auction				60	63	65
						Firm	Date	Amount	Grade			
654	Alu	RE	L7	6	3	Superior	9/1998	$3,910	PCGSPF64	$3,250	$5,500	$10,500

J-655: 1868 $3

Trial piece struck from regular dies.

J-655

Number	Metal	Edge	Rarity	Pop	T/A	Last Traded at Auction				60	63	65
						Firm	Date	Amount	Grade			
655	Alu	RE	L7	7	2	Bowers & Merena	5/1999	$3,910	PCGSPF64	$5,500	$9,000	$15,500

Patterns of 1868

J-656 to J-659: 1868 $5

Proposal for an international coinage discussed at the monetary conference in Paris in 1867 (see "History and Overview"). Dies by Anthony Paquet.

Obverse: Liberty head facing left, LIBERTY on ribbon, star at top of ribbon, hair tied behind. UNITED STATES OF AMERICA surrounding, 1868 below.
Reverse: Wreath of laurel and oak leaves enclosing 5 DOLLARS / 25 FRANCS.

J-656

Number	Metal	Edge	Rarity	Pop	T/A	Firm	Date	Amount	Grade	60	63	65
						Last Traded at Auction						
656	C	RE	L7	7	11	ANR	3/2005	$20,700	PCGSPF65BN	$6,000	$12,000	$20,000
657	C	PE	H7	1	1	Bowers & Merena	6/2002	$7,475	NGCPF63	$8,000	$14,000	$25,000
658	Alu	RE	L7	3	7	Stack's	12/2003	$2,875	PF	$6,000	$10,500	$19,000
659	Alu	PE	L7	8	7	Superior	9/2003	$7,763	PCGSPF64	$4,000	$7,000	$11,500

J-660: 1868 $5

Trial piece struck from regular dies.

J-660

Number	Metal	Edge	Rarity	Pop	T/A	Firm	Date	Amount	Grade	60	63	65
						Last Traded at Auction						
660	Alu	RE	L7	7	3	Akers	10/1997	$4,950	PF	$4,500	$7,500	$12,500

J-661 to J-663: 1868 $10

Obverse: Liberty Head with coronet inscribed LIBERTY in raised letters, stars surrounding, date 1868 below. Die varieties exist.
Reverse: Perched eagle but different from the regular design. IN GOD WE TRUST in ribbon above, UNITED STATES OF AMERICA / TEN D. around border.

J-661

Number	Metal	Edge	Rarity	Pop	T/A	Firm	Date	Amount	Grade	60	63	65
						Last Traded at Auction						
661	Gold	RE	H7	8	1	Auction '90	8/1990	$100,000	PCGSPF63	$100,000	$175,000	$275,000
662	C	RE	L7	11	10	Heritage	6/2005	$5,750	NGCPF64BN	$4,000	$7,500	$12,500
663	Alu	RE	L6	21	12	Stack's	10/2003	$9,200	GemPF	$3,000	$5,000	$9,000

J-664: 1868 $10

Trial piece struck from regular dies.

J-664

Number	Metal	Edge	Rarity	Pop	T/A	Firm	Date	Amount	Grade	60	63	65
						Last Traded at Auction						
664	Alu	RE	L7	7	3	Stack's	10/2003	$1,955	ANACSPF20 Dmg	$4,500	$7,500	$12,500

J-665: 1868 $20

Trial piece struck from regular dies.

J-665

| Number | Metal | Edge | Rarity | Pop | T/A | Last Traded at Auction | | | | 60 | 63 | 65 |
						Firm	Date	Amount	Grade			
665	Alu	RE	L7	10	6	Superior	4/2003	$13,800	NGCPF64CA	$10,000	$17,500	$30,000

Patterns of 1869

History and Overview

The year 1869 inaugurated certain pattern designs that would continue for the next several years. Well over 100 different varieties were produced in 1869, more than 200 in 1870, and more than 100 in 1871, followed by dozens more for most succeeding years through 1885. All bets were off; the numismatic world was up for grabs, and the Mint officers eagerly created legitimate patterns and (more often) pieces that differed from each other by metal and edge, creating for many the Standard Silver set issues (sets of six coins in order to be complete). Occasionally, even more secretly, a nickel, brass, or other unusual impression would be made. As no records were kept, there is no way to ascertain original mintages today.

The intent was to make coins of regular alloy (90% silver and 10% copper) of certain silver denominations, but of a lighter weight and slightly smaller diameter, the lower intrinsic value to make the hoarding of such coins not worthwhile. They would replace the flood of Fractional Currency paper then in circulation.

Chief Engraver James B. Longacre died on January 1, 1869, ending a career at the Mint that had commenced with his appointment on September 16, 1844. However, certain of Longacre's sketches, models, and hubs were employed posthumously in 1869 (and several following years) to create varieties of patterns, some motifs of which had not been struck during the engraver's lifetime.[7]

Patterns in the so-called Standard Silver series, inscribed on each coin STANDARD SILVER, relate not to the standard or regular series half dime, dime, quarter dollar, half dollar, and silver dollar denominations then being made per earlier legislation, but to a new series specifically called Standard Silver. The denominations produced were the dime, quarter dollar, and half dollar, some with dies by Barber after motifs by Longacre (see J-271 of 1860). In the next year, 1870, other denominations were added.

The suite of Standard Silver patterns was basically a simple one, appealing then and now to a numismatist's sense of order. For each of the three denominations, there were four different obverse dies in combination with a common reverse. In 1869, just one reverse die was made for each denomination, featuring a wreath encircling the value, with STANDARD SILVER 1869 around the border. Sets of nine pieces—three dimes, three quarter dollars, and three half dollars—were made in silver with reeded edge, silver with plain edge, copper with reeded edge, copper with plain edge, aluminum with reeded edge, and aluminum with plain edge—six per obverse die, or 18 coins per denomination, 54 coins in all.

Although the Standard Silver patterns dominate the year, other interesting varieties were made as well. These latter coins include 1869 versions of the Liberty Head with coronet and star, and with UNITED STATES OF AMERICA around the border, resembling the nickel three-cent piece design. These were made with denominations I, III, and V, in a continuing attempt to standardize the minor coinage.

Among other patterns of the year are J-716 and J-717, existing in metallic varieties including Ruolz's alloy.

The panorama of patterns dated 1868 also includes some curious mules, a $10 piece of the same Liberty Head motif as used on the matched set of I, III, and V minor coins, and, as expected, off-metal strikings of regular denominations. Regarding the latter, a notation in the George D. Woodside Collection, April 23, 1892, under Lot 235, suggested that 15 full Proof sets were struck in aluminum from regular Proof dies. This may have been the case, but any and all mintage figures quoted anywhere regarding patterns struck from the general era 1859 to 1885 are considered today to be unreliable.

Patterns of 1869

Standard Silver Dime Obverse Dies of 1869 and 1870
Obverse 1: "Liberty Head with cap and three stars." Head of Liberty facing right, wearing a Phrygian cap decorated at the front with three stars, plain ribbon from base of cap across hair on neck. UNITED STATES OF AMERICA and, on a curved ribbon, IN GOD WE TRUST around border below. • Used with J-696 to J-701 (1869).

Obverse 2: "Liberty Head, no star on tiara." Head of Liberty facing right, wearing a tiara, no stars, plain band around her head behind the tiara. UNITED STATES OF AMERICA and, on a curved ribbon, IN GOD WE TRUST around border below. • Used with J-702 to J-707 (1869).

Obverse 3: "Liberty Head with star on band." Head of Liberty facing right, wearing a band decorated at the front with one star. UNITED STATES OF AMERICA and, on a curved ribbon, IN GOD WE TRUST around border below. • Used with J-708 to J-713 (1869).

Standard Silver Quarter Dollar Obverse Dies of 1869 and 1870
Obverse 1: "Liberty Head with cap and three stars." Head of Liberty facing right, wearing a Phrygian cap decorated at the front with three stars, plain ribbon from base of cap across hair on neck. Ribbon with LIBERTY in raised letters extends from the base of the cap across the hair. UNITED STATES OF AMERICA and, on a curved ribbon, IN GOD WE TRUST around border below. • Used with J-675, J-721 to J-726 (1869).

Obverse 2: "Liberty Head, no star on tiara." Head of Liberty facing right, wearing a tiara, no stars, LIBERTY in raised letters on band around her head behind the tiara. UNITED STATES OF AMERICA and, on a curved ribbon, IN GOD WE TRUST around border below. • Used with J-727 to J-732 (1869).

Obverse 3: "Liberty Head with star on band." Head of Liberty facing right, wearing a band inscribed LIBERTY in raised letters and decorated at the front with one star. UNITED STATES OF AMERICA and, on a curved ribbon, IN GOD WE TRUST around border below. • Used with J-733 to J-738 (1869).

Standard Silver Half Dollar Obverse Dies of 1869 and 1870
Obverse 1: "Liberty Head with cap and two stars, LIBERTY in raised letters, B on ribbon." Head of Liberty facing right, wearing a Phrygian cap decorated at the front with two stars. Ribbon with LIBERTY in raised letters extends from the base of the cap across the hair, with initial B (for Barber) in fold of ribbon below bottom of cap. UNITED STATES OF AMERICA and, on a curved ribbon, IN GOD WE TRUST (the letters of which are double punched) around border below. • In later use, the die cracked from the border through the ribbon at 8 o'clock. • Used with J-742, J-743 to J-747 (1869); J-975 to J-980 (1870).

Obverse 2: "Liberty Head with cap and two stars, LIBERTY in raised letters, without B on ribbon." Head of Liberty facing right, wearing a Phrygian cap decorated at the front with two stars. Ribbon with LIBERTY in raised letters extends from the base of the cap across the hair, without initial B in fold of ribbon below bottom of cap. UNITED STATES OF AMERICA and, on a curved ribbon, IN GOD WE TRUST around border below. • Used with J-742a, J-747a (1869); J-969 to J-974 (1870).

Obverse 3a and b: "Liberty Head with cap and two stars, LIBERTY in incuse letters, without B on ribbon." Head of Liberty facing right, wearing a Phrygian cap decorated at the front with two stars. Ribbon with LIBERTY in incuse letters extends from the base of the cap across the hair, without initial B in fold of ribbon below bottom of cap. UNITED STATES OF AMERICA and, on a curved ribbon, IN GOD WE TRUST around border below. • Two die varieties (first described by Andrew W. Pollock III: Obverse 3a: Second S (in STATES) is over top of cap, tip of neck truncation over TR (in TRUST). Obverse 3b: Second S (in STATES) is mostly to the right of cap, tip of neck truncation over RU (in TRUST). • This style with incuse LIBERTY is not known to have been used in 1869. • Obverse 3a used with J-939 to J-944 (1869). Obverse 3b used with J-939 to J-944, J-963 to J-968 (1870).

Obverse 4: "Liberty Head, no stars on tiara." Head of Liberty facing right, wearing a tiara, no stars, LIBERTY in raised letters on band around her head behind the tiara. UNITED STATES OF AMERICA and, on a curved ribbon, IN GOD WE TRUST around border below. • Used with J-748 to J-753a (1869); J-951 to J-956, J-981 to J-986 (1870).

Obverse 5: "Liberty Head with star on band." Head of Liberty facing right, wearing a band inscribed LIBERTY in raised letters and decorated at the front with one star. UNITED STATES OF AMERICA and, on a curved ribbon, IN GOD WE TRUST around border below. • Used with J-754 to J-759a (1869); J-957 to J-962, J-987 to J-992 (1870).

Standard Silver Reverse Dies of 1869
Dime: "Standard Silver reverse die." Open oak and laurel wreath enclosing 10 CENTS. STANDARD SILVER / 1869 around the border.

Quarter dollar: "Standard Silver reverse die." Open oak and laurel wreath enclosing 25 CENTS. STANDARD SILVER / 1869 around the border.

Half dollar: "Standard Silver reverse die." Open oak and laurel wreath enclosing 50 CENTS. STANDARD SILVER / 1869 and two six-pointed stars around the border.

Collecting Perspective

Assembling a set of the 54 basic different Standard Silver patterns is a pursuit that can be accomplished with some effort. The copper coins in particular are difficult to find in choice preservation as many have been polished or retoned, or are spotted. The silver pieces require some searching, but many choice and gem pieces exist, including some with exquisite toning. Aluminum pieces are usually no problem and have light gray surfaces from normal oxidation. Similarly, the uniform I, III, and V set of minor denominations with the coronet head of Liberty can be acquired without much difficulty. Off-metal strikings are found now and then, and the dime die made to strike the experimental Ruolz's alloy was also employed to strike other mixtures.

Several mulings, a combination 1869 Indian Head cent and Shield nickel (J-691) being but one example, were made in this or in other years, but with 1869-dated dies. Some of these were no doubt made in the Mint, but others were likely done outside, possibly in the medal shop of William H. Key.

There are enough specimens of 1869 patterns around that a handsome showing of them typically characterizes the cabinet of a pattern specialist who has been active for several years.

J-666 and J-667: 1869 Cent

This is an 1869 version of J-608 and J-609 of 1868. At least three obverse and at least two reverse die varieties exist.

Obverse: Liberty Head with coronet. UNITED STATES OF AMERICA surrounding, date low.
Reverse: Laurel wreath enclosing Roman numeral I.

J-666

Number	Metal	Edge	Rarity	Pop	T/A	Last Traded at Auction				60	63	65
						Firm	Date	Amount	Grade			
666	Nick	PE	4	56	34	Bowers & Merena	8/2004	$1,495	NGCPF65	$900	$1,200	$1,750
667	C	PE	H7	5	3	Heritage	1/2004	$4,888	PCGSPF64RB	$2,050	$3,850	$7,000

J-668 to J-671: 1869 Cent

Struck from regular dies. J-669 is known in both Proof and circulation strike format; the latter may be a mint error.[8]

J-668

Number	Metal	Edge	Rarity	Pop	T/A	Last Traded at Auction				60	63	65
						Firm	Date	Amount	Grade			
668	C	PE	H7	0	0	N/A	N/A	N/A	N/A	$2,000	$4,250	$6,500
669	C-N	PE	H7	3	2	Heritage	7/1997	$3,220	PCGSMS63	$2,050	$3,850	$7,000
670	Nick	PE	H7	1	1	Superior	8/1991	$2,310	PF63	$9,600	$15,400	$25,000
671	Alu	PE	H7	1	2	Heritage	7/2003	$19,550	PCGSPF64	$7,000	$15,000	$25,000

J-672 to J-674a: 1869 Two-Cent Piece

Struck from regular dies. These are off-metal strikings of the year, with J-674a being the curious bonded bi-metallic strip combining copper and aluminum, similar in concept to the copper and silver strips used for the 1865-dated J-407.

J-674

Number	Metal	Edge	Rarity	Pop	T/A	Last Traded at Auction				60	63	65
						Firm	Date	Amount	Grade			
672	C	PE	H7	2	1	Heritage	8/1995	$2,805	PCGSPF65BN	$600	$1,100	$2,400
673	Nick	PE	8	2	1	Heritage	8/1995	$4,620	PCGSPF63	$6,500	$11,500	$18,500
674	Alu	PE	L7	7	3	Bowers & Merena	5/1992	$3,960	PCGSPF65	$2,000	$4,000	$6,500
674a	*	PE	U	0	1	Kagin's	7/1978	$610	PF	N/A	N/A	N/A

* J-674a: silver and copper rolled

Patterns of 1869

J-675: 1869 Two-Cent Piece

Produced with bonded or clad silver and copper strip, silver on one side and copper on the other, similar in concept to that used to coin J-407 dated 1865.

Obverse: Regular two-cent die of the year.
Reverse: Actually an obverse die: Liberty Head with cap and three stars (Obverse 1 of the Standard Silver quarter dollar).

J-675

Number	Metal	Edge	Rarity	Pop	T/A	Last Traded at Auction				60	63	65
						Firm	Date	Amount	Grade			
675	*	PE	U	0	1	Paramount	4/1965	$750	PF	$13,000	$24,000	$35,000

* J-675: silver and copper rolled

J-676 and J-677: 1869 Three-Cent Piece

This is an 1869 version of J-618. Two reverse varieties are known of the nickel striking, one having larger border dentils than the other.

Obverse: Liberty Head with coronet. UNITED STATES OF AMERICA surrounding, large date numerals below.
Reverse: Laurel wreath enclosing Roman numeral III.

J-676

Number	Metal	Edge	Rarity	Pop	T/A	Last Traded at Auction				60	63	65
						Firm	Date	Amount	Grade			
676	Nick	PE	4	71	33	Heritage	2/2005	$2,760	PCGSPF65	$1,250	$1,750	$2,800
677	C	PE	8	0	1	Kagin's	5/1957	$56	PF	$5,850	$10,500	$18,500

J-678 and J-679: 1869 Three-Cent Piece

Trial piece struck from regular dies.

J-678

Number	Metal	Edge	Rarity	Pop	T/A	Last Traded at Auction				60	63	65
						Firm	Date	Amount	Grade			
678	C	PE	L7	5	3	Heritage	11/2003	$8,050	PCGSPF64RB	$3,600	$6,000	$10,000
679	Alu	PE	H7	4	1	NERCG	7/1979	In Set	PF	$1,950	$3,850	$7,000

J-680 to J-682: 1869 Trime

Trial piece struck from regular dies.

J-680

Number	Metal	Edge	Rarity	Pop	T/A	Last Traded at Auction				60	63	65
						Firm	Date	Amount	Grade			
680	C	PE	H7	4	2	Heritage	3/2003	$6,325	PCGSPF64	$3,600	$5,500	$9,500
681	Nick	PE	8	0	0	N/A	N/A	N/A	N/A	$10,000	$15,000	$27,500
682	Alu	PE	H7	4	1	Kreisberg	10/1978	$500	Unc	$4,000	$5,800	$11,000

J-683: 1869 Five-Cent Piece

Obverse: Liberty Head facing left, coronet inscribed LIBERTY and with star. UNITED STATES OF AMERICA around border, 1869 below.
Reverse: Large Roman numeral V on shield with ornamented frame surrounding, IN GOD WE TRUST in small letters above (Reverse C of 1867) .

J-683

Number	Metal	Edge	Rarity	Pop	T/A	Last Traded at Auction				60	63	65
						Firm	Date	Amount	Grade			
683	Nick	PE	L7	4	7	Heritage	6/2005	$4,313	PCGSPF65	$2,100	$3,500	$6,900

J-684 and J-685: 1869 Five-Cent Piece

Obverse: Liberty Head, as preceding.
Reverse: Thin laurel wreath enclosing Roman numeral V, ribbon inscribed IN GOD WE TRUST, with small Maltese cross near the top (as earlier used on J-631 of 1868).

J-684

Number	Metal	Edge	Rarity	Pop	T/A	Last Traded at Auction				60	63	65
						Firm	Date	Amount	Grade			
684	Nick	PE	5	81	46	ANR	3/2005	$1,955	PCGSPF65	$1,150	$1,750	$2,800
685	C	PE	8	0	1	Superior	2/2000	$633	PF40	$5,850	$11,000	$20,000

J-686: 1869 Five-Cent Piece

Obverse: Liberty Head, as preceding.
Reverse: Large open wreath enclosing 5 CENTS, with CENTS in a straight line. IN GOD WE TRUST in small letters at top border (Reverse G of 1866 and 1867).

J-686

Number	Metal	Edge	Rarity	Pop	T/A	Last Traded at Auction				60	63	65
						Firm	Date	Amount	Grade			
686	Nick	PE	8	0	1	B. Max Mehl	11/1938	$13	PF	N/A	$25,000	N/A

J-687 to J-689: 1869 Five-Cent Piece

Trial piece struck from regular dies.

J-689

Number	Metal	Edge	Rarity	Pop	T/A	Last Traded at Auction				60	63	65
						Firm	Date	Amount	Grade			
687	C	PE	8	0	1	Heritage	1/1999	$1,438	ANACSPF60BN	$5,850	$11,000	$20,000
688	Alu	PE	H7	3	6	Ira & Larry Goldberg	5/2005	$6,900	PCGSPF63	$3,750	$10,000	$17,500
689	*	PE	U	1	1	Bowers & Merena	11/2001	$7,820	PCGSPF61	$15,500	N/A	N/A

* J-689: steel or pure nickel

J-690: 1869 Five-Cent Piece

This piece is unconfirmed.

Obverse: Liberty Head facing left, coronet inscribed LIBERTY and with star. UNITED STATES OF AMERICA around border, 1869 below.
Reverse: Small wreath enclosing tall 5 with pointed top of numeral. UNITED STATES OF AMERICA around border (Reverse C of 1866).

J-690

Number	Metal	Edge	Rarity	Pop	T/A	Last Traded at Auction				60	63	65
						Firm	Date	Amount	Grade			
690	Nick	PE	–	0	0	N/A	N/A	N/A	N/A	Unconf	Unconf	Unconf

J-690a: 1869 Five-Cent Piece/1866 Five-Cent Piece

Unusual two-headed, two-dated mule made outside of the Mint as a numismatic delicacy. Ex Garrett Collection, March 1980, Lot 1229, earlier from S.S. Crosby.[9]

Obverse: 1869 Liberty Head, as preceding.
Reverse: Actually an obverse die: Washington portrait, IN GOD WE TRUST (Obverse 2 of 1866).

J-690a

Number	Metal	Edge	Rarity	Pop	T/A	Last Traded at Auction				60	63	65
						Firm	Date	Amount	Grade			
690a	Nick	PE	U	0	1	Bowers & Merena	3/1997	$10,450	PCGSPF63	N/A	$25,000	N/A

Patterns of 1869

J-691: 1869 Five-Cent Piece/1869 Cent

A nonsensical mule for the numismatic trade. This piece could be listed earlier under a cent, taking the lower of the two denominations, but here the Judd sequence is preserved.[10] Moreover, it is struck on a nickel planchet.

Obverse: Regular Shield nickel die of the year.
Reverse: Actually an obverse die, the 1869 Indian Head cent.

J-691

Number	Metal	Edge	Rarity	Pop	T/A	Last Traded at Auction				60	63	65
						Firm	Date	Amount	Grade			
691	Nick	PE	U	0	1	B. Max Mehl	11/1944	$178	Unc	N/A	N/A	N/A

J-692 to J-695: 1869 Half Dime

Trial piece struck from regular dies.

J-692

Number	Metal	Edge	Rarity	Pop	T/A	Last Traded at Auction				60	63	65
						Firm	Date	Amount	Grade			
692	C	RE	H7	2	1	Bowers & Merena	6/1991	$2,970	PF63BN	$3,200	$5,800	$9,500
693	Alu	RE	H7	3	3	Superior	1/2004	$4,313	PCGSPF63CA	$2,600	$4,750	$8,000
694	Nick	RE	8	1	2	Superior	1/2004	$12,650	PCGSPF63	$5,000	$10,000	$17,500
695	Nick	PE	U	0	1	S.H. Chapman	6/1907	$2	PF	$18,500	$27,500	$45,000

J-696 to J-701: 1869 Standard Silver Dime

The beginning of the extensive Standard Silver issues.

Obverse: Liberty Head with cap and three stars.
Reverse: Standard Silver reverse die.

J-696

Number	Metal	Edge	Rarity	Pop	T/A	Last Traded at Auction				60	63	65
						Firm	Date	Amount	Grade			
696	Silv	RE	5	70	43	ANR	5/2005	$1,380	PCGSPF64	$1,400	$1,750	$2,250
697	Silv	PE	H6	21	11	Scotsman	10/2004	$2,128	NGCMS65	$1,300	$1,800	$2,700
698	C	RE	L7	6	2	Heritage	7/2003	$3,565	NGCPF65RB	$1,500	$2,200	$3,500
699	C	PE	H7	4	2	Bowers & Merena	5/1992	$3,860	PF64BN	$1,800	$2,850	$5,150
700	Alu	RE	L7	6	3	Bowers & Merena	3/2001	$1,150	NGCPF64	$1,600	$2,200	$3,600
701	Alu	PE	L7	8	3	Superior	8/2002	$1,840	PCGSPF65	$1,500	$2,000	$3,100

J-702 to J-707: 1869 Standard Silver Dime

Obverse: Liberty Head, no stars on tiara.
Reverse: Standard Silver reverse die.

J-702

Number	Metal	Edge	Rarity	Pop	T/A	Last Traded at Auction				60	63	65
						Firm	Date	Amount	Grade			
702	Silv	RE	5	57	30	Bowers & Merena	3/2005	$1,323	NGCPF64	$1,400	$1,750	$2,250
703	Silv	PE	H6	18	9	Heritage	3/2004	$1,955	NGCPF65	$1,300	$1,800	$2,700
704	C	RE	L7	11	7	Heritage	8/2004	$3,220	PCGSPF65BN	$1,500	$1,900	$3,250
705	C	PE	L7	9	7	Bowers & Merena	3/2003	$1,840	PCGSPF64BN	$1,450	$1,900	$3,000
706	Alu	RE	L7	9	3	Heritage	1/2005	$3,335	PCGSPF65DC	$1,500	$2,000	$3,250
707	Alu	PE	L7	6	2	Heritage	1/2000	$1,840	PCGSPF65	$1,600	$2,200	$3,600

J-708 to J-713: 1869 Standard Silver Dime

Obverse: Liberty Head with star on band.
Reverse: Standard Silver reverse die.

J-708

Number	Metal	Edge	Rarity	Pop	T/A	Last Traded at Auction				60	63	65
						Firm	Date	Amount	Grade			
708	Silv	RE	5	48	28	Heritage	3/2005	$1,380	NGCPF64	$1,000	$1,400	$1,900
709	Silv	PE	H6	14	11	Ira & Larry Goldberg	2/2003	$2,300	PCGSPF66	$1,300	$1,800	$2,700
710	C	RE	L7	6	1	Heritage	1/2002	$1,840	PCGSPF65BN	$1,500	$2,000	$3,200
711	C	PE	H7	3	2	Heritage	9/2002	$1,380	ANACSPF63RB	$1,950	$2,900	$5,500
712	Alu	RE	H7	2	3	Heritage	7/2003	$6,210	NGCPF65	$2,250	$4,500	$8,000
713	Alu	PE	L7	7	2	Ira & Larry Goldberg	6/2000	$1,380	PF61	$1,300	$1,700	$2,600

J-714 and J-715: 1869 Dime

Experimental piece intended to test a silver alloy substituting one part nickel, for the one part copper used in regular coinage of the era. Composition of "silver-nickel" pieces may vary, not yet studied by modern numismatists; elemental analysis is required; only standard nickel alloy (75% copper, 25% nickel) pieces are known of light color.[11]

Obverse: Regular Liberty Seated die without date (as also used for J-331 of 1863 and elsewhere).
Reverse: Inscription SIL. 9 / NIC. 1 / 1869.

J-715

Number	Metal	Edge	Rarity	Pop	T/A	Last Traded at Auction				60	63	65
						Firm	Date	Amount	Grade			
714	Nick	RE	L7	9	8	Heritage	7/2003	$3,680	PCGSPF64	$1,600	$3,750	$7,500
715	C	RE	L7	4	3	Heritage	9/2003	$4,025	PCGSPF64RD	$2,250	$3,750	$7,000

J-716 to J-717a: 1869 Dime

The composition noted on the reverse die is Ruolz's alloy, although no specimen has been found struck in this specific alloy. Strikings in other metals are known. • J-716: "Ruolz's alloy" per conventional wisdom, but actually of varying compositions.[12]

Obverse: Regular Liberty Seated die without date as preceding.
Reverse: Inscription SIL. / NIC. / COP. / 1869.

J-716

Number	Metal	Edge	Rarity	Pop	T/A	Last Traded at Auction				60	63	65
						Firm	Date	Amount	Grade			
716	Silv-Nick-C	RE	H6	7	6	Heritage	7/2003	$3,450	PCGSPF64	$2,100	$3,350	$5,500
716a	Silv	RE	H7	5	4	Heritage	7/2003	$8,625	PCGSPF64	$2,600	$5,500	$12,000
717	C	RE	L7	5	3	Heritage	9/2003	$5,635	PCGSPF64RD	$2,250	$3,750	$7,000
717a	Nick	RE	H7	4	2	Heritage	7/2003	$9,200	PCGSPF65	$2,600	$5,000	$10,000

J-718 to J-720: 1869 Dime

Trial piece struck from regular dies.

J-718

Number	Metal	Edge	Rarity	Pop	T/A	Last Traded at Auction				60	63	65
						Firm	Date	Amount	Grade			
718	C	RE	H7	2	6	Ira & Larry Goldberg	1/2004	$8,050	NGCPF65BN	$2,600	$5,000	$9,500
719	Alu	RE	H7	3	4	Ira & Larry Goldberg	5/2005	$4,255	PCGSPF64	$2,600	$5,000	$9,500
720	Nick	RE	H7	5	7	ANR	3/2005	$1,840	NGCPF65	$2,350	$4,200	$7,700

Patterns of 1869

J-721 to J-726:
1869 Standard Silver Quarter Dollar

Obverse: Liberty Head with cap and three stars.
Reverse: Standard Silver reverse die.

J-723

Number	Metal	Edge	Rarity	Pop	T/A	Firm	Date	Amount	Grade	60	63	65
721	Silv	RE	5	49	33	ANR	3/2005	$1,840	NGCPF65	$1,350	$1,850	$2,500
722	Silv	PE	H6	14	12	Bowers & Merena	12/2003	$1,783	ICGPF63	$1,500	$2,000	$3,000
723	C	RE	L7	12	12	ANR	3/2005	$3,450	NGCPF65RD	$1,700	$2,600	$4,750
724	C	PE	H7	2	2	Ira & Larry Goldberg	5/2005	$5,750	PCGSPF63RD	$3,250	$6,000	$12,500
725	Alu	RE	H7	3	1	Heritage	1/2004	$5,405	PCGSPF64	$2,200	$4,100	$8,000
726	Alu	PE	H7	4	4	ANR	12/2003	$3,220	NGCPF63	$2,250	$3,850	$6,750

J-727 to J-732:
1869 Standard Silver Quarter Dollar

Obverse: Liberty Head, no stars on tiara.
Reverse: Standard Silver reverse die.

J-727

Number	Metal	Edge	Rarity	Pop	T/A	Firm	Date	Amount	Grade	60	63	65
727	Silv	RE	5	59	40	Stack's	6/2005	$5,750	NGCPF67	$1,250	$1,750	$2,400
728	Silv	PE	H6	18	15	ANR	3/2005	$2,760	PF64	$1,600	$2,250	$3,200
729	C	RE	L7	10	9	Heritage	11/2003	$2,990	NGCPF66BN	$1,600	$2,250	$3,350
730	C	PE	L7	6	6	Heritage	3/2004	$3,220	PCGSPF64RD	$1,700	$2,600	$4,800
731	Alu	RE	H7	6	2	Superior	1/1996	$2,860	PF60	$2,250	$3,850	$6,750
732	Alu	PE	L7	8	7	ANR	7/2003	$3,680	PCGSPF66CA	$1,700	$2,400	$3,750

J-733 to J-738:
1869 Standard Silver Quarter Dollar

Obverse: Liberty Head with star on band.
Reverse: Standard Silver reverse die.

J-733

Number	Metal	Edge	Rarity	Pop	T/A	Firm	Date	Amount	Grade	60	63	65
733	Silv	RE	5	53	35	Stack's	9/2004	$1,265	PF	$1,300	$1,800	$2,400
734	Silv	PE	H6	18	6	Superior	3/2001	$2,300	NGCPF66	$1,400	$1,950	$2,700
735	C	RE	L7	11	7	Heritage	8/2004	$1,610	PCGSPF64BN	$1,600	$2,250	$3,350
736	C	PE	L7	6	5	Heritage	9/2002	$3,220	PCGSPF64RD	$1,700	$2,600	$4,800
737	Alu	RE	H7	4	4	Heritage	7/2003	$4,830	NGCPF64	$2,250	$4,200	$7,700
738	Alu	PE	L7	6	1	Superior	5/2003	$3,220	NGCPF64	$1,800	$2,900	$5,150

J-739 to J-741:
1869 Quarter Dollar

Trial piece struck from regular dies.

J-739

Number	Metal	Edge	Rarity	Pop	T/A	Firm	Date	Amount	Grade	60	63	65
739	C	RE	H7	4	2	Stack's/ANR	6/2004	$8,740	PCGSPF64RB	$3,250	$6,000	$12,000
740	Alu	RE	L7	5	2	Heritage	1/2003	$5,750	PCGSPF64	$2,250	$3,850	$6,750
741	Nick	RE	U	0	1	Empire	1/1960	$125	PF	N/A	N/A	N/A

J-742 to J-747:
1869 Standard Silver
Half Dollar

Obverse: Liberty Head with cap and two stars,
LIBERTY in raised letters, B on ribbon.
Reverse: Standard Silver reverse die.

J-744

Number	Metal	Edge	Rarity	Pop	T/A	Last Traded at Auction				60	63	65
						Firm	Date	Amount	Grade			
742	Silv	RE	5	49	25	Heritage	5/2005	$3,220	PCGSPF64	$1,550	$2,300	$3,500
743	Silv	PE	H6	17	9	ANR	8/2004	$4,025	PCGSPF65	$1,750	$2,550	$4,400
744	C	RE	L7	10	10	ANR	3/2005	$2,185	PCGSPF64BN	$1,600	$2,500	$4,200
745	C	PE	L7	8	6	Superior	5/1999	$2,703	NGCPF65BN	$1,600	$2,500	$4,200
745a	Brs	RE	8	0	0	N/A	N/A	N/A	N/A	N/A	N/A	N/A
746	Alu	RE	L7	8	10	Heritage	2/2005	$6,900	PCGSPF65CA	$2,300	$4,500	$6,900
747	Alu	PE	H7	4	7	Heritage	5/2005	$5,175	NGCPF66	$3,200	$5,400	$9,000

J-742a:
1869 Standard Silver
Half Dollar

Rare use of this obverse die.

Obverse: Liberty Head with cap and two stars,
LIBERTY in raised letters, without B on ribbon.
Reverse: Standard Silver reverse die.

J-742a

Number	Metal	Edge	Rarity	Pop	T/A	Last Traded at Auction				60	63	65
						Firm	Date	Amount	Grade			
742a	Silv	RE	U	0	1	Bowers & Merena	8/1998	$1,495	PF58	$6,500	$11,500	$16,500

J-748 to J-753a:
1869 Standard Silver
Half Dollar

Obverse: Liberty Head, no stars on tiara.
Reverse: Standard Silver reverse die.

J-748

Number	Metal	Edge	Rarity	Pop	T/A	Last Traded at Auction				60	63	65
						Firm	Date	Amount	Grade			
748	Silv	RE	5	61	40	Heritage	2/2005	$1,926	PCGSPF63	$1,400	$2,000	$3,150
749	Silv	PE	H6	17	7	Bowers & Merena	3/2005	$1,495	PCGSPF61	$1,750	$2,550	$4,150
750	C	RE	L7	9	11	Stack's	6/2005	$3,680	PCGSPF65BN	$1,600	$2,450	$4,200
751	C	PE	L7	6	5	Heritage	11/2001	$1,840	PCGSPF64BN	$1,700	$2,600	$4,500
752	Alu	RE	L7	8	8	Heritage	1/2004	$5,405	PCGSPF65CA	$2,250	$3,850	$6,400
753	Alu	PE	H7	6	5	Heritage	5/2004	$5,520	PCGSPF65CA	$3,100	$4,800	$8,250
753a	Brs	RE	U	0	1	Empire	1/1960	$150	EF	N/A	N/A	N/A

Patterns of 1869

J-754 to J-759a: 1869 Standard Silver Half Dollar

Obverse: Liberty Head with star on band.
Reverse: Standard Silver reverse die.

J-754

Number	Metal	Edge	Rarity	Pop	T/A	Last Traded at Auction				60	63	65
						Firm	Date	Amount	Grade			
754	Silv	RE	5	56	36	ANR	3/2005	$2,760	NGCPF65	$1,550	$2,150	$3,150
755	Silv	PE	H6	13	12	Bowers & Merena	3/2002	$2,760	NGCPF65	$1,750	$2,550	$4,150
756	C	RE	L7	9	4	Heritage	11/2003	$3,450	PCGSPF64RB	$1,600	$2,500	$4,200
757	C	PE	L7	7	7	ANR	12/2003	$4,370	PCGSPF65RB	$1,650	$2,500	$4,200
758	Alu	RE	L7	6	5	Heritage	8/2004	$3,853	PCGSPF65CA	$2,050	$3,400	$5,800
759	Alu	PE	L7	7	4	Heritage	1/2004	$4,025	PCGSPF65CA	$2,250	$3,850	$6,400
759a	Brs	RE	U	1	1	Bowers & Merena	8/1998	$5,520	PF63	N/A	$22,500	N/A

J-760 to J-762: 1869 Half Dollar

Trial piece struck from regular dies.

J-761

Number	Metal	Edge	Rarity	Pop	T/A	Last Traded at Auction				60	63	65
						Firm	Date	Amount	Grade			
760	C	RE	H7	4	4	Stack's	10/1997	$3,520	NGCPF64RD	$2,050	$3,000	$5,800
761	Alu	RE	L7	4	5	Heritage	6/2004	$9,488	NGCPF67	$2,250	$3,850	$6,750
762	Nick	RE	8	2	1	Bowers & Merena	11/2001	$6,325	NGCPF64	$4,550	$7,800	$12,500

J-763 to J-765: 1869 Silver Dollar

Trial piece struck from regular dies.

J-764

Number	Metal	Edge	Rarity	Pop	T/A	Last Traded at Auction				60	63	65
						Firm	Date	Amount	Grade			
763	C	RE	H7	6	3	Heritage	11/2003	$12,650	PCGSPF64RD	$2,600	$5,150	$9,500
764	Alu	RE	L7	4	6	Stack's	1/2005	$9,200	NGCPF65	$4,200	$7,000	$12,500
765	Nick	RE	8	1	2	ANR	9/2003	$36,800	PCGSPF65CA	$12,500	$22,500	$40,000

J-766 to J-768: 1869 Gold Dollar

Trial piece struck from regular dies.

J-766

Number	Metal	Edge	Rarity	Pop	T/A	Last Traded at Auction				60	63	65
						Firm	Date	Amount	Grade			
766	C	RE	H7	1	1	Heritage	6/1995	$4,180	PF60BN	$6,500	$11,500	$20,500
767	Alu	RE	H7	4	1	Superior	1/1990	$5,280	PCGSPF64	$4,800	$8,350	$15,500
768	Nick	RE	8	0	1	Stack's	8/1976	$900	PF	$8,450	$15,500	$26,000

J-769 to J-771: 1869 $2.50

Trial piece struck from regular dies.

J-770

| Number | Metal | Edge | Rarity | Pop | T/A | Last Traded at Auction | | | | 60 | 63 | 65 |
						Firm	Date	Amount	Grade			
769	C	RE	H7	2	1	NERCG	7/1979	$800	PF60	$4,500	$9,000	$18,000
770	Alu	RE	L7	11	6	Stack's	10/2003	$12,650	GemPF	$3,000	$6,250	$11,500
771	Nick	RE	8	1	1	Heritage	8/1996	$5,720	PCGSPF63	$6,000	$11,000	$20,000

J-772 to J-774: 1869 $3

Trial piece struck from regular dies.

J-773

| Number | Metal | Edge | Rarity | Pop | T/A | Last Traded at Auction | | | | 60 | 63 | 65 |
						Firm	Date	Amount	Grade			
772	C	RE	H7	1	1	Auction '90	8/1990	$4,400	PCGSPF64RB	$6,000	$12,000	$22,000
773	Alu	RE	L7	7	4	Bowers & Merena	5/1999	$3,910	PF64	$6,000	$9,000	$15,500
774	Nick	RE	8	1	1	Steve Ivy Rare Coin	4/1977	$1,950	PF60	$8,500	$15,500	$24,000

J-775 to J-777: 1869 $5

Struck from regular dies.

Obverse: Regular half eagle die of the year.
Reverse: Regular die of the year.

J-776

| Number | Metal | Edge | Rarity | Pop | T/A | Last Traded at Auction | | | | 60 | 63 | 65 |
						Firm	Date	Amount	Grade			
775	C	RE	H7	1	1	Superior	1/1989	$2,860	PF63	$6,000	$11,000	$21,000
776	Alu	RE	H7	2	1	Bowers & Ruddy	7/1981	$2,000	PF65	$6,000	$10,500	$20,000
777	Nick	RE	8	1	1	Bowers & Ruddy	8/1978	$875	PF60	$7,000	$14,000	$26,000

J-778: 1869 $5

Privately struck.

Obverse: Five-cent pattern die. Liberty Head facing left, coronet inscribed LIBERTY and with star. UNITED STATES OF AMERICA around border, 1869 below, as used on J-683 and others.
Reverse: Regular half eagle die of the pre-1866 type without motto.

J-778

| Number | Metal | Edge | Rarity | Pop | T/A | Last Traded at Auction | | | | 60 | 63 | 65 |
						Firm	Date	Amount	Grade			
778	Brs	RE	U	1	1	Bowers & Ruddy	3/1980	$8,000	PF	N/A	N/A	N/A

J-779 and J-780: 1869 $10

Obverse: Longacre's head of Liberty with tiara inscribed LIBERTY.[13]
Reverse: Regular $10 die of the year.

J-779

| Number | Metal | Edge | Rarity | Pop | T/A | Last Traded at Auction | | | | 60 | 63 | 65 |
						Firm	Date	Amount	Grade			
779	C	RE	H7	3	2	ANR	7/2003	$12,650	PCGSPF65BN	$6,000	$9,000	$16,500
780	Alu	RE	–	0	0	N/A	N/A	N/A	N/A	Unconf	Unconf	Unconf

Patterns of 1869

J-781 to J-783: 1869 $10

Trial piece struck from regular dies.

J-781

Number	Metal	Edge	Rarity	Pop	T/A	Last Traded at Auction				60	63	65
						Firm	Date	Amount	Grade			
781	C	RE	H7	3	2	Superior	9/1993	$5,060	PCGSPF65BN	$6,000	$10,000	$17,500
782	Alu	RE	H7	9	6	ANR	12/2003	$3,680	PF63Gilt	$5,000	$7,500	$12,500
783	Nick	RE	8	0	0	N/A	N/A	N/A	N/A	$8,500	$16,500	$32,500

J-784 to J-786: 1869 $20

Trial piece struck from regular dies.

J-785

Number	Metal	Edge	Rarity	Pop	T/A	Last Traded at Auction				60	63	65
						Firm	Date	Amount	Grade			
784	C	RE	H7	0	1	Kagin's	1/1981	$3,500	PF	$7,500	$12,500	$27,500
785	Alu	RE	H7	3	3	Heritage	6/1998	$10,465	PCGSPF64	$7,050	$12,500	$32,000
786	Nick	RE	8	1	1	Kreisberg-Schulman	2/1960	$290	ChPF	N/A	N/A	$32,500

Patterns of 1870

History and Overview

The year 1870 represented the crest of the flood tide of issuing patterns at the Philadelphia Mint, this being an era of great enthusiasm in the coin collecting hobby and, at the same time, a milieu in which certain coiners within the Mint had more liberties than before.

After the death of James B. Longacre on January 1, 1869, William Barber was appointed as Chief Engraver. While in 1869 many of the patterns bore motifs created earlier by Longacre, in the 1870s, many new works by Barber took precedence. The various styles of Liberty Head dies designed by Longacre and engraved by Barber for the Standard Silver series in 1869 were continued in 1870 (see listing under 1869 for various obverse dies of both 1869 and 1870). Sets of nine coins, each with a different obverse mated with a common reverse for the dime, quarter dollar, and half dollar, were said to have been offered for $15 each, following the procedure in 1869.

Certain new Standard Silver dies by Barber were introduced, these featuring his version of Liberty, seated, facing to the left. In this year, the illogical combinations and rarities outdid those of the 1869, and now Standard Silver issues extended downward to include the trime and half dime denominations. Never mind that these had been rendered obsolete in circulation by the nickel three-cent piece and five-cent piece, and there was no thought of issuing new designs of these pieces for use in commerce. Some denominations were made with two reverse styles: date within wreath and date below wreath. In addition, a Standard Silver dollar was added to the lineup and, further, regular-issue dies were combined with Standard Silver dies—with the result that the Philadelphia Mint, the largest "coin dealer" in the United States, albeit unofficially, now had more than 250 different pattern varieties for its officers and insiders to sell.

Among dollar coins, the Indian Princess design, the work of the late Longacre, was used to create several patterns with Standard Silver as well as regular die reverses (J-1008 to J-1019), these bearing the full signature, LONGACRE, in the field, no doubt a tribute to the departed artist.[14] Off-metal strikings from regular Proof dies added to the repertoire of patterns produced this year.

Collecting Perspective

The pattern enthusiast will find issues of this year quite straightforward, largely uninterrupted, with few one-of-a-kind double denomination mules and the like (which, in the 1860s, at once tantalized numismatists and frustrated anyone trying to find them!), save for a curious combination quarter dollar/two-cent piece (J-793a). Accordingly, it is possible to assemble complete or nearly complete sets of the various die pairings, including the Standard Silver issues, repeating the scenario of 1869 in that a given pair was typically struck in silver, copper, and aluminum, each metal with plain-edge as well as reeded-edge varieties. As is always the case with patterns of this era, copper strikings are very difficult to find in a combination of high grade and pleasing eye appeal.

Barber's version of the Liberty Seated design has always been popular and is available across the various silver denominations. The Indian Princess dollar is beautiful and highly desired. The off-metal strikings from regular Proof dies of the different denominations are all rare, nickel impressions being particularly so.

Welcome to the greatest pattern zoo of all time—the hundreds of varieties of 1870!

J-787 to J-789: 1870 Cent

Trial piece struck from regular dies.

J-787

| Number | Metal | Edge | Rarity | Pop | T/A | Last Traded at Auction | | | | 60 | 63 | 65 |
						Firm	Date	Amount	Grade			
787	C	PE	8	0	1	Kreisberg-Schulman	6/1956	$31	PF	$3,500	$6,000	$10,000
788	Alu	PE	8	1	1	Doyle Galleries	12/1983	$800	MS65	$11,000	$20,000	$32,500
789	Nick	PE	8	0	0	N/A	N/A	N/A	N/A	N/A	N/A	N/A

J-790 to J-793: 1870 Two-Cent Piece

Struck from regular dies. J-793 represents another cabinet coin created from a planchet and made of compressed or bonded silver on one side and copper on the other.

J-792

| Number | Metal | Edge | Rarity | Pop | T/A | Last Traded at Auction | | | | 60 | 63 | 65 |
						Firm	Date	Amount	Grade			
790	C	PE	8	0	1	Kosoff	8/1966	$150	PF	$1,850	$3,750	$6,250
791	Alu	PE	H7	1	1	Doyle Galleries	12/1983	$2,000	MS63	$7,000	$12,500	$22,500
792	Nick	PE	8	2	0	N/A	N/A	N/A	N/A	$7,500	$14,000	$26,000
793	*	PE	H7	0	2	Stack's	3/2004	$13,800	BU (PF)	$7,000	$13,000	$22,500

* J-793: silver and copper rolled

J-793a: 1870 Two-Cent Piece/ 1870 Standard Silver Quarter Dollar

Bimetallic numismatic delicacy from unrelated dies; two curiosities in one.[15]

Obverse: Regular two-cent die of the year.
Reverse: Open agricultural wreath enclosing 25 CENTS / 1870. STANDARD at top border.

J-793a

| Number | Metal | Edge | Rarity | Pop | T/A | Last Traded at Auction | | | | 60 | 63 | 65 |
						Firm	Date	Amount	Grade			
793a	*	PE	U	0	1	Federal Brand	10/1961	$188	No Grade	N/A	N/A	N/A

* J-793a: silver and copper rolled

Patterns of 1870

J-794 and J-795: 1870 Three-Cent Piece

Trial piece struck from regular dies.

J-794

Number	Metal	Edge	Rarity	Pop	T/A	Firm	Date	Amount	Grade	60	63	65
						Last Traded at Auction						
794	C	PE	H7	4	1	Bowers & Merena	9/1994	$2,970	PCGSPF64RB	$1,750	$3,500	$6,500
795	Alu	PE	8	2	1	Superior	5/1989	$1,540	PF63	$2,600	$5,150	$9,500

J-796 to J-801: 1870 Trime

Made in quantity as a numismatic curiosity, the obverse apparently being intended for the Standard Silver five-cent piece of this year, and the reverse being a slightly mismatched (in terms of diameter) trime die.

Obverse: Barber's Liberty Seated design, with figure seated, facing left, with her right hand supporting a shield, liberty cap on pole behind, and with an olive branch in her left hand. UNITED STATES to left, OF AMERICA to right, date 1870 below.
Reverse: Regular die used to coin silver three-cent pieces.

J-797

Number	Metal	Edge	Rarity	Pop	T/A	Firm	Date	Amount	Grade	60	63	65
						Last Traded at Auction						
796	Silv	PE	H7	1	1	Bowers & Merena	3/1989	$2,750	PF63	$7,000	$11,500	$20,000
797	Silv	RE	L7	8	3	Heritage	2/2005	$7,475	PCGSPF65	$3,500	$6,250	$9,500
798	C	PE	L7	14	10	Heritage	6/2005	$3,594	NGCPF65RB	$2,850	$3,850	$6,500
799	C	RE	L7	8	3	ANR	1/2004	$5,865	NGCPF64BN	$3,500	$4,800	$7,750
800	Alu	PE	8	1	1	Superior	6/1977	$450	ChPF	$8,500	$14,000	$22,500
801	Alu	RE	H7	2	1	Superior	5/1989	$3,960	PF63	$7,000	$11,500	$19,000

J-802 to J-804a: 1870 Trime

Trial piece struck from regular dies.

J-802

Number	Metal	Edge	Rarity	Pop	T/A	Firm	Date	Amount	Grade	60	63	65
						Last Traded at Auction						
802	C	PE	H7	3	1	Stack's	6/1990	$3,300	ChPFBN	$4,000	$6,000	$11,500
803	Alu	PE	8	2	1	Superior	6/1977	$325	PF	$4,200	$6,000	$11,500
804	Nick	PE	8	0	0	N/A	N/A	N/A	N/A	$10,000	$15,500	$27,500
804a	Brs	PE	U	1	1	Bowers & Ruddy	7/1981	$1,000	PF	N/A	N/A	N/A

J-805 to J-808: 1870 Five-Cent Piece

Trial piece struck from regular dies. J-807 was struck on a thin planchet.

J-805

Number	Metal	Edge	Rarity	Pop	T/A	Firm	Date	Amount	Grade	60	63	65
						Last Traded at Auction						
805	C	PE	H7	3	2	ANR	9/2003	$8,050	NGCPF65BN	$3,550	$7,000	$12,500
806	Alu	PE	8	0	1	MARCA	9/1985	$850	PF	$5,850	$11,000	$20,000
807	Nick	PE	L7	6	2	Heritage	3/2004	$3,738	NGCPF63	$2,700	$5,400	$9,000
808	*	PE	U	0	0	N/A	N/A	N/A	N/A	N/A	N/A	N/A

* J-808: steel or pure nickel

J-809 to J-814: 1870 Standard Silver Half Dime

A numismatic production, as no new designs for silver half dimes were ever seriously contemplated. This represents the first appearance of this denomination in the Standard Silver pattern series.

Obverse: Barber's Liberty Seated design. UNITED STATES to left, OF AMERICA to right, 1870 below.
Reverse: Open agricultural wreath enclosing 5 CENTS. STANDARD at border above.

J-811

Number	Metal	Edge	Rarity	Pop	T/A	Last Traded at Auction				60	63	65
						Firm	Date	Amount	Grade			
809	Silv	RE	L7	8	5	Heritage	6/2004	$3,623	PCGSPF65	$2,600	$3,650	$6,100
810	Silv	PE	H7	4	6	ANR	3/2005	$4,600	PCGSPF62	$3,250	$6,000	$10,000
811	C	RE	L7	7	3	Superior	1/2004	$3,795	PCGSPF64RB	$2,450	$3,850	$5,500
812	C	PE	L7	10	3	Bowers & Merena	3/2001	$4,370	NGCPF67RB	$2,250	$3,200	$5,250
813	Alu	RE	H7	2	1	Superior	1/2004	$9,775	NGCPF65	$3,200	$5,800	$11,000
814	Alu	PE	8	0	1	Heritage	12/1984	$950	PF	$10,500	$20,000	$32,500

J-815 to J-820: 1870 Half Dime

Obverse: Barber's Liberty Seated design. UNITED STATES to left, OF AMERICA to right, 1870 below.
Reverse: Regular half dime die of the year.

J-817

Number	Metal	Edge	Rarity	Pop	T/A	Last Traded at Auction				60	63	65
						Firm	Date	Amount	Grade			
815	Silv	RE	L7	10	9	Heritage	6/2005	$4,600	NGCPF66	$2,250	$3,600	$5,150
816	Silv	PE	L7	10	10	Superior	1/2004	$3,163	NGCPF64	$2,250	$3,600	$5,150
817	C	RE	H6	22	12	Heritage	6/2005	$2,990	NGCPF66BN	$2,000	$3,200	$4,500
818	C	PE	L7	10	9	Bowers & Merena	7/2004	$3,680	NGCPF65RB	$2,000	$3,200	$5,150
819	Alu	RE	H7	1	1	Christie's	9/1988	$1,430	PF	$4,800	$9,600	$17,000
820	Alu	PE	H7	3	1	Heritage	2/1999	$2,415	PCGSPF65	$2,600	$4,200	$8,250

J-821 to J-824: 1870 Half Dime

Trial piece struck from regular dies.

J-821

Number	Metal	Edge	Rarity	Pop	T/A	Last Traded at Auction				60	63	65
						Firm	Date	Amount	Grade			
821	C	RE	H7	3	1	ANR	9/2003	$4,830	PF62BN	$2,600	$4,800	$9,500
822	C	PE	–	0	0	N/A	N/A	N/A	N/A	Unconf	Unconf	Unconf
823	Alu	RE	8	2	1	Superior	1/2004	$9,775	PCGSPF65	$3,200	$6,000	$11,000
824	Nick	RE	8	0	0	N/A	N/A	N/A	N/A	$9,000	$16,000	$34,000

J-825 to J-830: 1870 Standard Silver Dime

Obverse: Barber's Liberty Seated design. UNITED STATES to left, OF AMERICA to right, 1870 below.
Reverse: Open agricultural wreath enclosing 10 CENTS. STANDARD at border above.

J-828

Number	Metal	Edge	Rarity	Pop	T/A	Last Traded at Auction				60	63	65
						Firm	Date	Amount	Grade			
825	Silv	RE	L7	5	5	Heritage	2/2005	$5,175	NGCPF67	$2,400	$4,250	$6,250
826	Silv	PE	H6	10	4	Heritage	11/2004	$3,450	PCGSPF65	$2,250	$3,600	$5,500
827	C	RE	L7	7	5	Superior	5/2003	$3,910	NGCPF65BN	$2,000	$2,900	$4,750
828	C	PE	H6	12	10	Superior	5/2003	$3,565	NGCPF65BN	$2,000	$2,900	$4,350
829	Alu	RE	H7	3	1	Stack's	10/2003	$10,350	VChPF	$3,200	$6,000	$11,500
830	Alu	PE	H7	1	1	RLH Enterprises	1/1980	$1,400	PF65	$5,150	$9,500	$16,500

J-831 to J-836: 1870 Dime

Obverse: Barber's Liberty Seated design. UNITED STATES to left, OF AMERICA to right, 1870 below.
Reverse: Regular dime die of the year.

J-833

Number	Metal	Edge	Rarity	Pop	T/A	Firm	Date	Amount	Grade	60	63	65
							Last Traded at Auction					
831	Silv	RE	H6	13	12	Heritage	5/2005	$3,680	NGCPF65	$2,000	$2,900	$4,250
832	Silv	PE	L7	8	5	Heritage	7/2003	$2,990	PCGSPF64	$2,200	$2,900	$4,500
833	C	RE	H6	18	12	Heritage	5/2005	$2,760	NGCPF64BN	$1,800	$2,800	$4,150
834	C	PE	H6	14	15	Superior	5/2005	$2,587	NGCPF65RB	$1,800	$2,800	$4,150
835	Alu	RE	H7	2	4	Heritage	8/2001	$2,300	PCGSPF64	$3,200	$6,000	$11,500
836	Alu	PE	H7	3	1	Heritage	6/1998	$3,105	PCGSPF65	$2,600	$5,000	$9,500

J-837 to J-842: 1870 Standard Silver Dime

Obverse: Liberty Head with cap and three stars.
Reverse: Open agricultural wreath enclosing 10 CENTS / 1870. STANDARD at border above.

J-838

Number	Metal	Edge	Rarity	Pop	T/A	Firm	Date	Amount	Grade	60	63	65
							Last Traded at Auction					
837	Silv	RE	5	55	30	Scotsman	7/2004	$5,060	NGCPF66Star	$1,250	$1,800	$3,000
838	Silv	PE	H6	9	11	ANR	10/2004	$1,530	PCGSPF61	$1,300	$1,800	$2,700
839	C	RE	H7	3	5	Stack's/ANR	6/2004	$7,188	PCGSPF63BN	$4,200	$7,200	$12,000
840	C	PE	H7	5	2	Superior	9/2004	$2,680	PF64BN	$2,000	$2,750	$5,250
841	Alu	RE	H7	3	4	Stack's/ANR	6/2004	$5,750	PCGSPF62	$3,600	$6,000	$9,000
842	Alu	PE	H7	5	5	Heritage	7/1997	$2,760	PCGSPF65	$1,700	$2,350	$4,100

J-843 to J-848: 1870 Standard Silver Dime

Obverse: Liberty Head, no stars on tiara.
Reverse: Open agricultural wreath enclosing 10 CENTS / 1870. STANDARD at border above.

J-846

Number	Metal	Edge	Rarity	Pop	T/A	Firm	Date	Amount	Grade	60	63	65
							Last Traded at Auction					
843	Silv	RE	L6	41	22	Heritage	8/2004	$1,380	PCGSPF64	$1,000	$1,400	$2,000
844	Silv	PE	L6	19	12	Ira & Larry Goldberg	2/2005	$1,265	PF60+	$1,300	$1,700	$2,600
845	C	RE	L7	9	3	Heritage	1/2002	$1,955	PCGSPF66BN	$1,300	$1,700	$2,600
846	C	PE	L7	7	4	ANR	8/2004	$1,725	PCGSPF63BN	$1,500	$2,000	$3,200
847	Alu	RE	H7	5	1	Stack's	10/2003	$7,590	GemPF	$2,050	$4,250	$8,000
848	Alu	PE	H7	1	1	Bowers & Ruddy	1/1983	$688	PF	$4,200	$7,750	$12,500

J-849 to J-854: 1870 Standard Silver Dime

Obverse: Liberty Head with star on band.
Reverse: Open agricultural wreath enclosing 10 CENTS / 1870. STANDARD at border above.

J-849

Number	Metal	Edge	Rarity	Pop	T/A	Firm	Date	Amount	Grade	60	63	65
							Last Traded at Auction					
849	Silv	RE	5	38	22	Heritage	5/2005	$1,380	PCGSPF62	$1,000	$1,400	$1,900
850	Silv	PE	H6	13	5	Heritage	11/2004	$1,380	NGCPF67	$1,300	$1,800	$2,700
851	C	RE	L7	8	4	Superior	2/2003	$2,530	PCGSPF64BN	$1,500	$2,000	$3,200
852	C	PE	H7	2	3	ANR	11/2004	$6,785	PCGSPF65RB	$3,500	$6,400	$11,000
853	Alu	RE	H7	3	1	Heritage	3/2003	$5,750	PCGSPF63	$3,200	$6,000	$10,000
854	Alu	PE	H7	5	1	Superior	5/1990	$1,650	PCGSPF64	$1,700	$2,350	$4,100

J-855 to J-860: 1870 Standard Silver Dime

The reverse die is the same used for J-696 (1869).

Obverse: Liberty Head with cap and three stars.
Reverse: Oak and laurel wreath enclosing 10 CENTS.
STANDARD SILVER / 1870 around border.

J-860

Number	Metal	Edge	Rarity	Pop	T/A	Last Traded at Auction				60	63	65
						Firm	Date	Amount	Grade			
855	Silv	RE	H6	10	4	Heritage	11/2003	$2,040	NGCPF65	$1,300	$1,800	$2,700
856	Silv	PE	H6	10	5	Stack's	10/2003	$2,760	GemPF	$1,300	$1,800	$2,700
857	C	RE	H7	6	3	Heritage	1/2000	$2,760	PCGSPF65RD	$1,700	$2,250	$3,850
858	C	PE	H7	3	1	Superior	5/1990	$2,420	NGCPF65RB	$2,000	$2,900	$5,500
859	Alu	RE	H7	3	4	Heritage	9/2002	$4,370	PCGSPF65	$2,000	$3,200	$5,800
860	Alu	PE	L7	1	2	ANR	3/2004	$17,825	PCGSPF65CA	$6,500	$11,000	$20,000

J-861 to J-866: 1870 Standard Silver Dime

Same obverse die used for J-702 (1869).

Obverse: Liberty Head, no stars on tiara.
Reverse: Oak and laurel wreath enclosing 10 CENTS.
STANDARD SILVER / 1870 around border.

J-862

Number	Metal	Edge	Rarity	Pop	T/A	Last Traded at Auction				60	63	65
						Firm	Date	Amount	Grade			
861	Silv	RE	H6	14	9	Heritage	11/2004	$4,313	NGCPF67	$1,300	$1,800	$2,700
862	Silv	PE	H7	5	6	Stack's/ANR	6/2004	$1,380	PCGSPF62	$1,800	$2,850	$5,150
863	C	RE	L7	6	3	Heritage	7/1997	$1,840	PCGSPF64RB	$1,500	$2,000	$3,200
864	C	PE	H7	4	4	Stack's/ANR	6/2004	$4,255	PCGSPF63RB	$2,250	$4,500	$8,000
865	Alu	RE	H7	2	1	Superior	6/1977	$275	PF	$2,250	$4,200	$7,700
866	Alu	PE	H7	6	6	Heritage	5/2005	$6,900	NGCPF67Star	$1,700	$2,350	$4,000

J-867 to J-872: 1870 Standard Silver Dime

Same obverse die used for J-708 (1869).

Obverse: Liberty Head with star on band.
Reverse: Oak and laurel wreath enclosing 10 CENTS.
STANDARD SILVER / 1870 around border.

J-869

Number	Metal	Edge	Rarity	Pop	T/A	Last Traded at Auction				60	63	65
						Firm	Date	Amount	Grade			
867	Silv	RE	H6	11	10	Superior	1/2004	$5,463	NGCPF67	$1,300	$1,800	$2,700
868	Silv	PE	L7	7	3	Bowers & Merena	5/1996	$4,180	PF65	$1,600	$2,250	$3,350
869	C	PE	H7	4	3	Stack's	3/1992	$5,250	PFBN	$1,800	$2,600	$4,700
870	C	PE	H7	2	1	Superior	6/1977	$250	PF	$3,500	$6,400	$11,000
871	Alu	RE	H7	3	1	Bowers & Ruddy	7/1981	$600	PF	$2,250	$4,200	$7,750
872	Alu	PE	H7	2	1	Superior	10/1989	$2,090	PCGSPF64	$2,250	$4,200	$7,750

J-873 to J-875: 1870 Dime

Trial piece struck from regular dies.

J-873

Number	Metal	Edge	Rarity	Pop	T/A	Last Traded at Auction				60	63	65
						Firm	Date	Amount	Grade			
873	C	RE	H7	3	3	Stack's	1/2005	$6,038	PCGSPF64BN	$2,250	$4,500	$7,500
874	Alu	RE	8	1	1	Heritage	8/1995	$5,060	PCGSPF64	$4,200	$7,500	$12,500
875	Nick	RE	8	0	1	B. Max Mehl	6/1941	$20	PF	$6,500	$11,000	$20,000

Patterns of 1870

J-876 to J-881: 1870 Standard Silver Quarter Dollar

There is no mention of the United States of America on this illogical combination, this also being true of related higher denominations with this combination of motifs.

Obverse: Barber's Liberty Seated design. Thirteen stars around border, 1870 below.
Reverse: Open agricultural wreath enclosing 25 CENTS. STANDARD at border above.

J-880

Number	Metal	Edge	Rarity	Pop	T/A	Last Traded at Auction				60	63	65
						Firm	Date	Amount	Grade			
876	Silv	RE	L7	5	4	Heritage	11/2004	$3,680	PCGSPF64CA	$2,250	$4,250	$7,500
877	Silv	PE	L7	6	3	David Lawrence RC	7/2004	$9,200	NGCPF67	$2,250	$4,000	$7,500
878	C	RE	L7	8	4	Heritage	3/2004	$4,485	PCGSPF65RB	$2,150	$3,200	$5,750
879	C	PE	H6	16	16	Heritage	9/2004	$4,313	NGCPF65RB	$2,000	$3,200	$6,000
880	Alu	RE	H7	4	3	Ira & Larry Goldberg	5/2005	$5,750	PCGSPF65	$2,250	$4,200	$8,000
881	Alu	PE	H7	1	1	Herbert L. Melnick	7/1982	$825	PF	$4,000	$8,750	$16,000

J-882 to J-887: 1870 Quarter Dollar

Obverse: Barber's Liberty Seated design with stars.
Reverse: Regular die of the year.

J-887

Number	Metal	Edge	Rarity	Pop	T/A	Last Traded at Auction				60	63	65
						Firm	Date	Amount	Grade			
882	Silv	RE	H7	8	1	Bowers & Merena	5/1996	$4,620	PF65	$2,250	$4,200	$7,700
883	Silv	PE	L7	8	4	Bowers & Merena	5/1996	$5,280	PF63/65	$2,250	$3,850	$7,000
884	C	RE	H6	17	16	ANR	3/2005	$3,220	NGCPF64BN	$1,750	$2,550	$4,600
885	C	PE	L7	13	7	Heritage	8/2004	$3,105	NGCPF65BN	$1,750	$2,500	$4,000
886	Alu	RE	H7	2	3	Ira & Larry Goldberg	5/2005	$9,200	PCGSPF65	$2,600	$4,800	$9,000
887	Alu	PE	H7	3	3	Heritage	7/2004	$9,890	PCGSPF66	$4,200	$7,700	$12,500

J-888 to J-893a: 1870 Standard Silver Quarter Dollar

Obverse: Liberty Head with cap and three stars.
Reverse: Open agricultural wreath enclosing 25 CENTS / 1870. STANDARD at border above.

J-891

Number	Metal	Edge	Rarity	Pop	T/A	Last Traded at Auction				60	63	65
						Firm	Date	Amount	Grade			
888	Silv	RE	5	44	29	Heritage	5/2005	$2,530	NGCPF66	$1,350	$1,850	$2,500
889	Silv	PE	L7	11	6	Heritage	2/2005	$6,325	NGCPF67	$1,300	$2,250	$4,000
890	C	RE	H7	3	1	Heritage	6/1989	$3,000	PCGSPF65RB	$2,250	$4,100	$8,000
891	C	PE	H7	4	1	Heritage	7/1988	$700	PF63BN	$2,250	$4,200	$7,500
892	Alu	RE	H7	3	1	Heritage	12/1983	$1,000	PF	$2,250	$4,200	$8,000
893	Alu	PE	H7	4	2	Bowers & Merena	3/2001	$1,380	NGCPF63	$2,600	$4,100	$7,400
893a	Nick	RE	U	1	0	N/A	N/A	N/A	N/A	N/A	$13,000	N/A

J-894 to J-899: 1870 Standard Silver Quarter Dollar

Obverse: Liberty Head, no star on tiara.
Reverse: Open agricultural wreath enclosing 25 CENTS / 1870.
STANDARD at border above.

J-894

Number	Metal	Edge	Rarity	Pop	T/A	Last Traded at Auction Firm	Date	Amount	Grade	60	63	65
894	Silv	RE	5	56	28	Heritage	8/2004	$1,610	PCGSPF64	$1,300	$1,800	$2,400
895	Silv	PE	L7	14	7	Ira & Larry Goldberg	6/2002	$4,600	NGCPF67	$1,750	$2,400	$3,500
896	C	RE	L7	6	3	Bowers & Merena	1/1997	$1,540	PF60BN	$1,700	$2,600	$4,800
897	C	PE	H7	3	3	Heritage	5/2005	$5,175	NGCPF64RB	$2,600	$4,500	$9,000
898	Alu	RE	H7	2	2	Bowers & Merena	3/2002	$2,875	PCGSPF65	$2,250	$4,100	$8,000
899	Alu	PE	L7	7	2	R.M. Smythe	10/2001	$2,310	PF66	$1,700	$2,600	$4,500

J-900 to J-905: 1870 Standard Silver Quarter Dollar

Obverse: Liberty Head with star on band.
Reverse: Open agricultural wreath enclosing 25 CENTS / 1870.
STANDARD at border above.

J-900

Number	Metal	Edge	Rarity	Pop	T/A	Last Traded at Auction Firm	Date	Amount	Grade	60	63	65
900	Silv	RE	5	39	32	Stack's	10/2004	$1,265	PF	$1,350	$1,850	$2,600
901	Silv	PE	H6	15	13	Scotsman	5/2005	$2,099	PCGSPF62	$1,400	$1,950	$2,800
902	C	RE	L7	5	5	Stack's/ANR	6/2004	$3,680	NGCPF64BN	$1,700	$2,600	$4,500
903	C	PE	H7	4	3	Heritage	7/2002	$2,185	PCGSPF64RB	$2,050	$3,350	$6,100
904	Alu	RE	H7	2	2	Stack's	10/2003	$12,650	GemPF	$4,000	$7,500	$15,000
905	Alu	PE	H7	3	1	Mid American	5/1985	$650	PF	$2,250	$4,100	$8,000

J-906 to J-911: 1870 Standard Silver Quarter Dollar

Obverse: Liberty Head with cap and three stars.
Reverse: Open oak and laurel wreath enclosing 25 CENTS.
STANDARD SILVER / 1870 around border.

J-906

Number	Metal	Edge	Rarity	Pop	T/A	Last Traded at Auction Firm	Date	Amount	Grade	60	63	65
906	Silv	RE	L7	8	8	Heritage	8/2004	$3,795	NGCPF66	$1,700	$2,400	$3,750
907	Silv	PE	L7	6	2	Bowers & Merena	5/1996	$4,840	PF64/65	$1,750	$2,700	$5,000
908	C	RE	L7	7	1	Superior	2/2003	$4,025	NGCMS65BN	$1,700	$2,600	$4,800
909	C	PE	H7	4	6	Bowers & Merena	7/1997	$2,420	PCGSPF63RB	$2,250	$3,850	$6,750
910	Alu	RE	H7	2	2	Ira & Larry Goldberg	6/2000	$2,760	PCGSPF65	$2,250	$4,100	$8,000
911	Alu	PE	H7	2	2	Heritage	7/1997	$3,795	PCGSPF65	$2,250	$4,100	$8,000

Patterns of 1870

J-912 to J-917:
1870 Standard Silver
Quarter Dollar

Obverse: Liberty Head, no stars on tiara.
Reverse: Open oak and laurel wreath enclosing 25 CENTS.
STANDARD SILVER / 1870 around border.

J-913

Number	Metal	Edge	Rarity	Pop	T/A	Last Traded at Auction				60	63	65
						Firm	Date	Amount	Grade			
912	Silv	RE	H6	13	9	Heritage	9/2003	$3,220	NGCPF66	$1,500	$2,000	$3,000
913	Silv	PE	L7	10	4	Ira & Larry Goldberg	5/2001	$1,552	PCGSPF64	$1,700	$2,400	$3,750
914	C	RE	L7	9	4	Scotsman	7/2004	$1,668	PCGSMS61BN	$1,600	$2,250	$3,350
915	C	PE	L7	6	2	Ira & Larry Goldberg	2/2000	$4,600	PCGSPF65RB	$1,700	$2,600	$4,800
916	Alu	RE	H7	4	1	Ira & Larry Goldberg	6/2000	$2,645	PCGSPF65	$2,250	$4,200	$8,000
917	Alu	PE	H7	4	2	Superior	8/2002	$3,910	PCGSPF66	$2,250	$4,200	$8,000

J-918 to J-923:
1870 Standard Silver
Quarter Dollar

Obverse: Liberty Head with star on band.
Reverse: Open oak and laurel wreath enclosing 25 CENTS.
STANDARD SILVER / 1870 around border.

J-918

Number	Metal	Edge	Rarity	Pop	T/A	Last Traded at Auction				60	63	65
						Firm	Date	Amount	Grade			
918	Silv	RE	L7	9	7	Superior	8/2002	$2,300	PCGSPF65	$1,950	$2,850	$4,500
919	Silv	PE	H7	3	2	Heritage	11/2003	$3,795	PCGSPF63	$2,250	$4,200	$8,000
920	C	RE	H7	4	3	Heritage	11/2003	$3,565	PCGSPF64BN	$2,250	$3,850	$6,750
921	C	PE	L7	11	8	ANR	3/2005	$1,725	PCGSPF64BN	$1,600	$2,250	$3,350
922	Alu	RE	H7	3	2	Stack's	10/2003	$9,775	GemPF	$3,200	$6,000	$10,000
923	Alu	PE	H7	2	2	Superior	5/2003	$10,925	PCGSPF66	$3,500	$6,500	$11,000

J-924 to J-926:
1870 Quarter Dollar

Trial piece struck from regular dies.

J-924

Number	Metal	Edge	Rarity	Pop	T/A	Last Traded at Auction				60	63	65
						Firm	Date	Amount	Grade			
924	C	RE	H7	4	3	Heritage	5/2004	$2,760	PCGSPF60BN	$2,000	$3,200	$5,500
925	Alu	RE	8	1	1	Stack's	5/1997	$3,300	PCGSPF64	$4,200	$8,350	$15,500
926	Nick	RE	8	1	1	RARCOA	7/1989	In Set	ChPF	$7,150	$13,000	$22,500

J-927 to J-932:
1870 Standard Silver
Half Dollar

Illogical die combination with no mention of the United States of America.

Obverse: Barber's Liberty Seated design with stars.
Reverse: Open agricultural wreath enclosing 50 CENTS. STANDARD at border above.

J-928

Number	Metal	Edge	Rarity	Pop	T/A	Last Traded at Auction				60	63	65
						Firm	Date	Amount	Grade			
927	Silv	RE	8	1	1	Bowers & Ruddy	6/1976	$850	PF63	$7,800	$13,000	$22,500
928	Silv	PE	H7	3	1	Bowers & Merena	1/2001	$5,060	PF64	$4,200	$7,500	$13,000
929	C	RE	H7	1	1	Superior	1/1996	$1,760	PF58	$4,500	$8,500	$16,000
930	C	PE	H7	6	3	ANR	9/2003	$4,140	NGCPF64BN	$3,000	$4,650	$8,250
931	Alu	RE	H7	3	2	Heritage	11/2003	$10,925	PCGSPF64	$4,250	$8,250	$15,000
932	Alu	PE	H7	0	1	Stack's	3/1985	$1,375	PF	$7,800	$13,000	$22,500

J-933 to J-938:
1870 Half Dollar

Obverse: Barber's Liberty Seated design, with 13 stars around border, 1870 below.
Reverse: Regular die of the year.

J-934

Number	Metal	Edge	Rarity	Pop	T/A	Last Traded at Auction				60	63	65
						Firm	Date	Amount	Grade			
933	Silv	RE	L7	9	6	Bowers & Merena	3/2001	$2,300	PF63	$2,850	$4,500	$7,500
934	Silv	PE	L7	9	12	Superior	11/2004	$5,750	NGCPF65	$2,850	$4,500	$7,500
935	C	RE	H6	16	21	ANR	3/2005	$5,980	NGCPF65BN	$2,300	$3,850	$7,000
936	C	PE	H6	9	10	Heritage	6/2005	$4,830	PCGSPF65BN	$2,300	$3,850	$7,000
937	Alu	RE	H7	3	1	Heritage	1/2004	$9,775	PCGSPF65CA	$4,500	$8,500	$14,000
938	Alu	PE	H7	4	1	Superior	10/1989	$3,960	PCGSPF64	$4,100	$7,500	$12,500

J-939 to J-944:
1870 Standard Silver Half Dollar

Obverse die varieties exist.

Obverse: Liberty Head with cap and two stars, LIBERTY in incuse letters, without B on ribbon. Die varieties Obverse-3a and 3b (see listing under 1869[16]).
Reverse: Open agricultural wreath enclosing 50 CENTS / 1870. STANDARD at border above.

J-939

Number	Metal	Edge	Rarity	Pop	T/A	Last Traded at Auction				60	63	65
						Firm	Date	Amount	Grade			
939	Silv	RE	5	30	20	Heritage	5/2005	$1,380	PCGSPF58	$1,550	$2,150	$3,150
940	Silv	PE	H6	14	6	Heritage	7/2003	$1,265	ANACSPF55	$1,750	$2,550	$4,150
941	C	RE	L7	7	6	Heritage	2/2005	$3,738	PCGSPF64RB	$1,700	$2,600	$4,500
942	C	PE	H7	2	1	Heritage	1/2003	$7,015	PCGSPF64RD	$2,900	$4,550	$8,250
943	Alu	RE	H7	3	2	Superior	5/2003	$11,500	NGCPF66CA	$3,750	$6,250	$11,000
944	Alu	PE	H7	8	4	ANR	8/2004	$5,060	PCGSPF64CA	$2,250	$3,850	$6,500

Patterns of 1870

J-945 to J-950: 1870 Standard Silver Half Dollar

The obverse die is similar to Obverse 2 of 1869, but without initial.

Obverse: Liberty Head with cap and two stars, LIBERTY in raised letters, without B on ribbon.
Reverse: Open agricultural wreath enclosing 50 CENTS / 1870. STANDARD at border above.

J-945

Number	Metal	Edge	Rarity	Pop	T/A	Firm	Date	Amount	Grade	60	63	65
						\multicolumn{4}{Last Traded at Auction}				
945	Silv	RE	L7	9	7	Heritage	7/2003	$1,265	ANACSPF55Cld	$2,000	$3,200	$5,150
946	Silv	PE	H7	4	2	Superior	2/2005	$4,255	PCGSPF64CA	$3,100	$4,800	$8,250
947	C	RE	H7	2	2	Bowers & Merena	5/1999	$2,645	PCGSPF66BN	$2,850	$4,500	$8,000
948	C	PE	H7	3	1	Heritage	7/2003	$3,335	ANACSPF50Cld	$2,850	$4,500	$8,000
949	Alu	RE	8	1	2	Heritage	7/1997	$4,945	PCGSPF63	$4,550	$7,800	$12,500
950	Alu	PE	8	2	1	Bowers & Ruddy	9/1975	$380	ChPF	$3,300	$5,850	$10,500

J-951 to J-956: 1870 Standard Silver Half Dollar

The obverse die is the same used in J-748 (1869).

Obverse: Liberty Head, no stars on tiara.
Reverse: Open agricultural wreath enclosing 50 CENTS / 1870. STANDARD at border above.

J-952

Number	Metal	Edge	Rarity	Pop	T/A	Firm	Date	Amount	Grade	60	63	65
951	Silv	RE	5	36	18	Heritage	3/2005	$3,220	NGCPF66CA	$1,550	$2,150	$3,150
952	Silv	PE	L7	10	8	Heritage	6/2004	$5,060	NGCPF66	$1,950	$3,200	$5,150
953	C	RE	L7	5	1	Auction '90	8/1990	$3,400	PCGSPF65RB	$1,950	$3,200	$5,150
954	C	PE	H7	3	5	Heritage	1/2004	$5,463	PCGSPF64BN	$2,850	$4,500	$8,000
955	Alu	RE	H7	3	5	Bowers & Merena	3/2001	$2,760	PCGSPF65	$3,100	$4,800	$8,250
956	Alu	PE	H7	3	2	Heritage	1/2004	$6,325	PCGSPF65	$3,550	$5,800	$10,500

J-957 to J-962: 1870 Standard Silver Half Dollar

The obverse die is the same used in J-754 (1869).

Obverse: Liberty Head with star on band.
Reverse: Open agricultural wreath enclosing 50 CENTS / 1870. STANDARD at border above.

J-959

Number	Metal	Edge	Rarity	Pop	T/A	Firm	Date	Amount	Grade	60	63	65
957	Silv	RE	5	40	21	Bowers & Merena	4/2005	$2,415	NGCPF65	$1,550	$2,050	$3,150
958	Silv	PE	H6	13	6	Heritage	11/2003	$2,645	PCGSPF64	$1,700	$2,300	$3,850
959	C	RE	H7	5	5	Heritage	8/2004	$3,680	PCGSPF65RB	$2,000	$3,000	$5,800
960	C	PE	L7	6	7	Heritage	5/2005	$2,990	NGCPF63BN	$2,000	$3,400	$5,800
961	Alu	RE	H7	2	2	Heritage	11/2003	$6,325	PCGSPF63CA	$4,200	$7,000	$11,500
962	Alu	PE	H7	5	1	Bowers & Merena	5/1992	$4,400	PCGSPF64	$2,250	$3,850	$6,400

J-963 to J-968: 1870 Standard Silver Half Dollar

Obverse: Liberty Head with cap and two stars, LIBERTY in incuse letters, without B on ribbon (Obverse 3a of 1869).
Reverse: Open oak and laurel wreath enclosing 50 CENTS. STANDARD SILVER / 1870 and two stars around border.

J-963

Number	Metal	Edge	Rarity	Pop	T/A	Last Traded at Auction				60	63	65
						Firm	Date	Amount	Grade			
963	Silv	RE	L7	8	1	Heritage	7/2003	$4,255	PCGSPF64	$1,950	$3,200	$5,500
964	Silv	PE	L7	7	7	ANR	12/2003	$3,220	PCGSPF64	$1,950	$3,200	$5,750
965	C	RE	H7	2	0	N/A	N/A	N/A	N/A	$3,200	$5,800	$9,300
966	C	PE	8	0	1	Heritage	7/1988	$908	PF65BN	$5,200	$9,000	$14,500
967	Alu	RE	8	0	0	N/A	N/A	N/A	N/A	$6,500	$11,000	$16,500
968	Alu	PE	8	0	1	Bolender	3/1955	$21	PF	$6,500	$11,000	$16,500

J-969 to J-974: 1870 Standard Silver Half Dollar

Obverse: Liberty Head with cap and two stars, LIBERTY in raised letters, without B on ribbon (Obverse 2 of 1869).
Reverse: Open oak and laurel wreath enclosing 50 CENTS. STANDARD SILVER / 1870 and two stars around border.

J-973

Number	Metal	Edge	Rarity	Pop	T/A	Last Traded at Auction				60	63	65
						Firm	Date	Amount	Grade			
969	Silv	RE	H7	2	2	David Lawrence RC	7/2005	$7,762	NGCPF65	$3,200	$5,400	$9,000
970	Silv	PE	8	0	1	McIntire	4/1984	$908	PF63	$6,500	$11,000	$16,500
971	C	RE	H7	2	0	Bowers & Merena	5/1992	$4,620	PCGSPF63RB	$2,850	$4,500	$8,000
972	C	PE	H7	3	1	Superior	10/1989	$2,970	NGCPF64RB	$2,250	$3,850	$6,400
973	Alu	RE	8	1	1	Bowers & Merena	5/1999	$5,750	PCGSPF63	$4,500	$7,800	$12,500
974	Alu	PE	8	1	0	N/A	N/A	N/A	N/A	$4,500	$7,800	$12,500

J-975 to J-980: 1870 Standard Silver Half Dollar

Obverse: Liberty Head with cap and two stars, LIBERTY in raised letters, B on ribbon (Obverse 1 of 1869).
Reverse: Open oak and laurel wreath enclosing 50 CENTS. STANDARD SILVER / 1870 and two stars around border.

J-979

Number	Metal	Edge	Rarity	Pop	T/A	Last Traded at Auction				60	63	65
						Firm	Date	Amount	Grade			
975	Silv	RE	8	0	0	N/A	N/A	N/A	N/A	$6,500	$11,100	$16,500
976	Silv	PE	8	0	0	N/A	N/A	N/A	N/A	$6,500	$11,100	$16,500
977	C	RE	L7	6	2	Bowers & Merena	5/1999	$1,093	PCGSPF62RD	$1,950	$3,200	$5,150
978	C	PE	H7	2	4	Ira & Larry Goldberg	10/2000	$3,450	NGCPF66RB	$2,850	$4,500	$8,000
979	Alu	RE	H7	4	1	Superior	5/1990	$6,600	PCGSPF65	$3,100	$4,800	$8,250
980	Alu	PE	H7	1	1	Bowers & Merena	5/1999	$7,475	PCGSPF65	$4,550	$7,800	$12,500

Patterns of 1870

J-981 to J-986: 1870 Standard Silver Half Dollar

Obverse: Liberty Head, no stars on tiara.
Reverse: Open oak and laurel wreath enclosing 50 CENTS.
STANDARD SILVER / 1870 and two stars around border.

J-984

Number	Metal	Edge	Rarity	Pop	T/A	Last Traded at Auction				60	63	65
						Firm	Date	Amount	Grade			
981	Silv	RE	H6	11	1	Ira & Larry Goldberg	5/2001	$2,530	PCGSPF65	$1,750	$2,550	$4,150
982	Silv	PE	L7	10	7	Heritage	1/2004	$2,530	PCGSPF64CA	$1,950	$3,200	$5,150
983	C	RE	H7	3	4	Superior	9/1999	$1,898	NGCPF64RB	$2,600	$4,200	$7,000
984	C	PE	L7	7	5	Heritage	8/2004	$3,278	PCGSPF65RB	$1,950	$3,200	$5,150
985	Alu	RE	H7	1	1	Heritage	11/2003	$13,800	PCGSPF64CA	$6,500	$11,500	$20,000
986	Alu	PE	H7	4	1	Heritage	1/2004	$6,900	PCGSPF66CA	$3,100	$4,800	$8,250

J-987 to J-992: 1870 Standard Silver Half Dollar

Obverse: Liberty Head with star on band.
Reverse: Open oak and laurel wreath enclosing 50 CENTS.
STANDARD SILVER / 1870 and two stars around border.

J-992

Number	Metal	Edge	Rarity	Pop	T/A	Last Traded at Auction				60	63	65
						Firm	Date	Amount	Grade			
987	Silv	RE	H6	11	6	ANR	12/2003	$4,600	PCGSPF66	$2,000	$2,700	$4,500
988	Silv	PE	H7	4	3	Heritage	1/2004	$4,140	PCGSPF63	$2,600	$4,400	$7,000
989	C	RE	L7	11	11	Bowers & Merena	1/2005	$2,703	PCGSPF64RB	$1,600	$2,450	$4,200
990	C	PE	H7	4	3	ANR	9/2003	$7,590	NGCPF64RB	$2,000	$3,000	$5,800
991	Alu	RE	H7	2	2	Bowers & Merena	8/1998	$4,025	PF64	$3,500	$5,850	$10,500
992	Alu	PE	L7	5	6	ANR	3/2004	$10,925	NGCPF67CA	$2,600	$4,750	$8,500

J-993 to J-995a: 1870 Half Dollar

Trial piece struck from regular dies.

J-993

Number	Metal	Edge	Rarity	Pop	T/A	Last Traded at Auction				60	63	65
						Firm	Date	Amount	Grade			
993	C	RE	8	2	2	Heritage	1/2005	$11,213	PCGSPF64RB	$7,500	$12,000	$20,000
994	Alu	RE	H7	3	2	Scotsman	10/2004	$9,775	NGCPF65	$6,000	$10,000	$16,000
995	Nick	RE	8	1	1	Heritage	12/1990	$4,000	PF64	$9,100	$14,300	$22,800
995a	C-N	RE	U	0	0	N/A	N/A	N/A	N/A	$10,000	$16,000	$25,000

J-996 to J-1001: 1870 Standard Silver Dollar

First appearance of the dollar denomination in the Standard Silver series. There is no mention of the United States of America on this illogical die combination.

Obverse: Barber's Liberty Seated design. Thirteen stars around border, 1870 below.
Reverse: Open agricultural wreath enclosing 1 DOLLAR. STANDARD at border above.

J-996

Number	Metal	Edge	Rarity	Pop	T/A	Last Traded at Auction			60	63	65
						Firm	Date	Amount	Grade			
996	Silv	RE	L7	6	5	Stack's	10/2003	$13,800	VChPF	$6,000	$9,000	$16,000
997	Silv	PE	L7	5	3	Bowers & Merena	3/1994	$4,400	PCGSPF61	$4,800	$8,000	$15,000
998	C	RE	L7	13	5	Superior	5/2003	$7,475	NGCPF64BN	$3,100	$6,000	$11,000
999	C	PE	L7	8	7	Heritage	11/2003	$9,488	PCGSPF64RB	$2,850	$6,250	$12,000
1000	Alu	RE	8	3	1	Bowers & Merena	11/1995	$10,175	PCGSPF66	$7,800	$13,000	$22,000
1001	Alu	PE	8	1	1	Bowers & Merena	6/1991	$3,520	PF65	$8,450	$16,000	$32,500

J-1002 to J-1007: 1870 Silver Dollar

Obverse: Barber's Liberty Seated design with stars.
Reverse: Regular die of the year.

J-1002

Number	Metal	Edge	Rarity	Pop	T/A	Last Traded at Auction			60	63	65
						Firm	Date	Amount	Grade			
1002	Silv	RE	L6	16	14	Superior	1/2004	$7,475	NGCPF65	$2,550	$5,600	$10,000
1003	Silv	PE	L7	11	6	Stack's	6/2005	$3,910	PCGSPF62	$4,200	$7,500	$12,500
1004	C	RE	L7	20	14	Heritage	8/2004	$4,945	PCGSPF64RB	$2,900	$5,150	$11,000
1005	C	PE	L6	24	16	Stack's	6/2005	$6,440	NGCPF65RD	$3,050	$4,800	$8,900
1006	Alu	RE	H7	3	1	Heritage	3/1998	$2,185	PF62	$5,800	$9,000	$16,000
1007	Alu	PE	H7	4	3	ANR	3/2005	$16,100	PCGSPF64CA	$4,000	$10,000	$19,000

Patterns of 1870

J-1008 to J-1013: 1870 Standard Silver Dollar

There is no mention of the United States of America on this illogical die combination.

Obverse: Longacre's Indian Princess design. Liberty facing left, wearing an Indian head-dress, holding in her right hand a spear on top of which is a liberty cap, her left hand rests on a globe inscribed LIBERTY. Behind her are two flags, one with 22 stars. The signature LONGACRE is in the field below the base at the right.
Reverse: Open agricultural wreath enclosing 1 DOLLAR. STANDARD at border above.

J-1010

Number	Metal	Edge	Rarity	Pop	T/A	Firm	Date	Amount	Grade	60	63	65
						Last Traded at Auction						
1008	Silv	RE	H7	2	1	Ira & Larry Goldberg	6/2000	$5,290	PCGSPF62	$12,500	$21,000	$38,500
1009	Silv	PE	L7	5	2	ANR	9/2003	$12,650	NGCPF65	$5,500	$10,000	$18,000
1010	C	RE	H7	2	2	ANR	9/2003	$19,550	NGCPF64RB	$11,000	$19,000	$31,000
1011	C	PE	L7	7	2	Heritage	11/2003	$10,925	PCGSPF64RB	$4,200	$9,000	$16,000
1012	Alu	RE	8	2	3	Superior	2/2003	$18,975	PCGSPF65	$8,500	$16,000	$29,000
1013	Alu	PE	8	1	1	Scotsman	10/2004	$39,100	PCGSPF65	$13,000	$21,500	$39,000

J-1014 to J-1019: 1870 Silver Dollar

Obverse: Longacre's Indian Princess design, as preceding.
Reverse: Regular die of the year.

J-1017

Number	Metal	Edge	Rarity	Pop	T/A	Firm	Date	Amount	Grade	60	63	65
						Last Traded at Auction						
1014	Silv	RE	L7	8	5	Bowers & Merena	5/1999	$14,950	PCGSPF65	$7,700	$11,500	$22,500
1015	Silv	PE	L7	7	10	Stack's/ANR	6/2004	$1,438	Fine	$7,700	$11,500	$22,500
1016	C	RE	L7	11	4	Stack's	5/1998	$4,180	ChPFBN	$2,850	$5,150	$11,000
1017	C	PE	L7	13	14	Heritage	8/2004	$5,405	NGCPF65BN	$2,850	$5,150	$9,000
1018	Alu	RE	H7	2	1	Heritage	5/2003	$29,900	NGCPF64	$15,000	$28,000	$50,000
1019	Alu	PE	H7	4	1	Bowers & Merena	9/1993	$8,250	PCGSPF64	$3,850	$5,800	$11,500

J-1020 to J-1022: 1870 Silver Dollar

Trial piece struck from regular dies.

J-1020

Number	Metal	Edge	Rarity	Pop	T/A	Firm	Date	Amount	Grade	60	63	65
1020	C	RE	L7	6	3	ANR	9/2003	$32,200	NGCPF67RB	$6,000	$10,500	$18,000
1021	Alu	RE	8	1	1	Superior	10/1990	$8,800	PCGSPF65	$9,500	$15,000	$27,500
1022	Nick	RE	L7	5	3	Heritage	7/1994	$17,050	PF66	$6,400	$11,500	$19,000

J-1023 to J-1025: 1870 Gold Dollar

Trial piece struck from regular dies.

J-1023

Number	Metal	Edge	Rarity	Pop	T/A	Firm	Date	Amount	Grade	60	63	65
1023	C	RE	H7	3	2	Stack's	10/2003	$8,338	PCGSPF62RB	$4,000	$7,000	$12,500
1024	Alu	RE	8	0	1	NERCG	7/1979	$1,000	PF63	$7,150	$13,000	$22,500
1025	Nick	RE	8	1	1	NERCG	7/1979	$750	PF60	$7,500	$13,000	$22,500

J-1026 to J-1028: 1870 $2.50

Trial piece struck from regular dies.

J-1026

Number	Metal	Edge	Rarity	Pop	T/A	Firm	Date	Amount	Grade	60	63	65
1026	C	RE	H7	2	1	NERCG	7/1979	$950	PF63	$4,500	$9,000	$18,000
1027	Alu	RE	8	0	1	Bowers & Merena	5/1992	$3,520	PF61	$8,500	$16,000	$26,000
1028	Nick	RE	8	1	1	Superior	5/1990	$8,800	PCGSPF64	$7,250	$13,000	$22,500

J-1029 to J-1031: 1870 $3

Trial piece struck from regular dies.

J-1029

Number	Metal	Edge	Rarity	Pop	T/A	Firm	Date	Amount	Grade	60	63	65
1029	C	RE	H7	3	1	Bowers & Merena	6/1988	$2,800	PF60	$5,000	$9,000	$18,000
1030	Alu	RE	8	2	1	ANR	8/2004	$24,150	PCGSPF65	$7,000	$12,500	$24,000
1031	Nick	RE	8	1	1	Stack's	2/1977	$625	PF	$8,500	$15,500	$24,000

Patterns of 1870

J-1032 to J-1034: 1870 $5

Trial piece struck from regular dies.

J-1032

Number	Metal	Edge	Rarity	Pop	T/A	Firm	Date	Amount	Grade	60	63	65
						Last Traded at Auction						
1032	C	RE	H7	2	1	Bowers & Merena	5/1999	$6,900	PCGSPF65BN	$5,500	$10,500	$19,000
1033	Alu	RE	8	1	1	Stack's	2/1977	$775	PF	$6,000	$11,000	$20,500
1034	Nick	RE	8	0	1	Stack's	8/1976	$1,000	PF	$10,000	$18,000	$30,000

J-1035 to J-1037: 1870 $10

Trial piece struck from regular dies.

J-1036

Number	Metal	Edge	Rarity	Pop	T/A	Firm	Date	Amount	Grade	60	63	65
						Last Traded at Auction						
1035	C	RE	8	2	2	Heritage	7/1997	$3,220	PF60BN	$7,000	$14,500	$26,000
1036	Alu	RE	8	2	1	Akers	7/1988	$4,840	PF65	$7,000	$14,500	$26,000
1037	Nick	RE	8	0	1	Bowers & Ruddy	11/1979	$6,000	PF63	$8,500	$16,000	$32,500

J-1038 to J-1040: 1870 $20

Trial piece struck from regular dies.

J-1039

Number	Metal	Edge	Rarity	Pop	T/A	Firm	Date	Amount	Grade	60	63	65
						Last Traded at Auction						
1038	C	RE	H7	3	4	Bowers & Merena	11/1993	$16,500	NGCPF64BN	$10,000	$17,500	$35,000
1039	Alu	RE	8	3	2	Heritage	3/2005	$35,075	PCGSPF66DC	$10,000	$17,500	$35,000
1040	Nick	RE	8	0	1	Pine Tree	9/1978	$3,500	PFGilt	N/A	N/A	N/A

Patterns of 1871

History and Overview

Pattern issues were again numerous in 1871, surpassing 100 pieces. Certain Standard Silver pieces were produced, seemingly as numismatic delicacies rather than in sets as earlier. Longacre's Indian Princess design was again employed, with variations including a starless obverse field. Off-metal strikings were produced from regular Proof dies.

Especially important among patterns of this year are those for a new denomination designated as the commercial dollar, made of silver, and intended to be a heavier weight than a regular silver dollar. These were designed for trade in the Orient and were officially designated as COMMERCIAL DOLLAR on the reverse, with the weight given as 420 grains and fineness of .900, of use to merchants in China who valued silver coins by their metal value, not by country of origin or anything else. Soon thereafter, the designation *trade dollar* was adopted instead.

The idea of an American export dollar was hardly new, as in 1859, merchants in San Francisco suggested that the mint in that city produce silver dollars for the China trade, this denomination not having been struck there before. Some 20,000 1859-S Liberty Seated dollars were produced and sent to the Orient, and were very successful for their intended purpose. However, California was distant from the seat of government in Washington, DC, and the needs of merchants in San Francisco were not particularly important to politicians. Later, in the 1870s, the California legislature requested that the federal government produce a new coin of 420 grains and .900 fineness, which would about equal the Spanish-American dollar, and thus be competitive with it.

This set the scene for an extensive series of commercial dollar and trade dollar patterns produced from 1871 through 1873, in which latter year the denomination became official. After that time, additional patterns and die combinations were made, but mostly for the numismatic trade, not with the intention of modifying the design.

Collecting Perspective

Pattern coins of 1871 are highly collectible today. In particular, variations of Longacre's Indian Princess design have been in great numismatic demand, the style without obverse stars having a cameo-like appearance and being particularly attractive.

The year 1871 also saw many different Standard Silver designs produced in combination with different versions of Longacre's Indian Princess design, which had made its debut in 1870. Most of these patterns are "stateless," with UNITED STATES OF AMERICA omitted, reflecting their illogical creation. Several patterns of the nickel five-cent piece and the usual off-metal strikes from regular Proof dies complete the scenario.

The commercial dollar patterns of the year, commencing with J-1154, are of exceptional interest and play to an audience not only of pattern enthusiasts but also to those who specialize in trade dollars. Three different obverse dies (one being the regular Liberty Seated issue of the year) were mated with a common COMMERCIAL DOLLAR reverse, and it is pleasurable to acquire one coin from each die pair. The off-metal strikes from regular Proof dies for this year are all rare.

J-1041 to J-1042a: 1871 Cent
Trial piece struck from regular dies.

J-1042

Number	Metal	Edge	Rarity	Pop	T/A	Last Traded at Auction				60	63	65
						Firm	Date	Amount	Grade			
1041	C	PE	8	0	1	NERCG	7/1979	In Set	PF	$1,850	$3,750	$6,250
1042	Alu	PE	8	1	1	Heritage	6/2002	$7,130	PCGSPF64	$9,600	$15,000	$25,000
1042a	Nick	PE	U	0	1	Stack's	6/1986	$880	F15	N/A	N/A	N/A

J-1043 and J-1044: 1871 Two-Cent Piece
Trial piece struck from regular dies.

J-1044

Number	Metal	Edge	Rarity	Pop	T/A	Last Traded at Auction				60	63	65
						Firm	Date	Amount	Grade			
1043	C	PE	U	1	1	Heritage	1/1997	$1,207	PF66RB	N/A	N/A	N/A
1044	Alu	PE	8	2	1	ANR	8/2004	$14,950	PCGSPF64	$6,000	$11,500	$19,000

J-1045 and J-1046: 1871 Three-Cent Piece
Trial piece struck from regular dies.

J-1045

Number	Metal	Edge	Rarity	Pop	T/A	Last Traded at Auction				60	63	65
						Firm	Date	Amount	Grade			
1045	C	PE	H7	3	1	SRCG	1/1981	$1,350	PF	$1,750	$3,550	$6,400
1046	Alu	PE	8	1	1	Superior	6/1977	$400	PF	$4,800	$9,000	$16,000

Patterns of 1871

J-1047 to J-1049: 1871 Trime

Trial piece struck from regular dies.

J-1047

Number	Metal	Edge	Rarity	Pop	T/A	Firm	Date	Amount	Grade	60	63	65
1047	C	PE	H7	4	3	Heritage	11/2003	$10,925	NGCPF65RB	$4,000	$5,800	$13,000
1048	Nick	PE	U	1	1	Bowers & Ruddy	9/1975	$600	ChPF	N/A	N/A	N/A
1049	Alu	PE	8	1	1	Bowers & Ruddy	9/1975	$390	ChPF	$8,500	$14,000	$22,500

J-1050 to J-1052a: 1871 Five-Cent Piece

J-1052a is struck on a broad planchet.

Obverse: Liberty Head with coronet, small portrait, facing left, similar to that used on the nickel three-cent piece as well as earlier patterns.
Reverse: Wreath enclosing V CENTS, the V being erroneously shaded on the right, rather than on the left, and presenting a curious appearance.[17]

J-1050

Number	Metal	Edge	Rarity	Pop	T/A	Firm	Date	Amount	Grade	60	63	65
1050	Nick	PE	L6	26	27	Heritage	6/2005	$2,530	PCGSPF65CA	$1,300	$1,950	$3,500
1051	C	PE	L6	30	29	Heritage	6/2005	$4,313	PCGSPF65RD	$1,300	$1,950	$4,400
1052	Alu	PE	L7	6	6	Heritage	2/2005	$4,543	PCGSPF66 reverse laminated	$2,250	$4,500	$9,000
1052a	Alu	PE	U	0	0	N/A	N/A	N/A	N/A	N/A	N/A	N/A

J-1053 to J-1055: 1871 Five-Cent Piece

Obverse: Die as preceding.
Reverse: Laurel wreath enclosing 5 CENTS (curved). Closely related to the preceding die, with essentially the same wreath features.

J-1053

Number	Metal	Edge	Rarity	Pop	T/A	Firm	Date	Amount	Grade	60	63	65
1053	Nick	PE	H6	15	11	Heritage	6/2005	$1,438	NGCPF63	$1,400	$2,350	$4,500
1054	C	PE	H6	20	13	ANR	3/2005	$1,840	NGCPF64BN	$1,300	$2,300	$3,850
1055	Alu	PE	L7	7	3	Bowers & Merena	1/2003	$3,680	PCGSPF63	$1,950	$2,600	$6,750

J-1056 to J-1058: 1871 Five-Cent Piece

Trial piece struck from regular dies.

J-1056

Number	Metal	Edge	Rarity	Pop	T/A	Firm	Date	Amount	Grade	60	63	65
1056	C	PE	8	2	1	Scotsman	10/2004	$16,963	NGCPF67RB	$7,500	$12,500	$20,000
1057	Alu	PE	8	1	1	Heritage	8/2001	$3,335	PCGSPF62	$4,250	$8,500	$16,500
1058	*	PE	U	0	0	N/A	N/A	N/A	N/A	N/A	N/A	N/A

* J-1058: steel or pure nickel

J-1059 to J-1061: 1871 Standard Silver Half Dime

Obverse: Longacre's Indian Princess design, plain (starless) field.
Reverse: Open agricultural wreath enclosing 5 CENTS. STANDARD at border above (reuse of 1870 die).

J-1060

Number	Metal	Edge	Rarity	Pop	T/A	Firm	Date	Amount	Grade	60	63	65
						Last Traded at Auction						
1059	Silv	RE	H7	4	4	Heritage	7/2003	$6,900	PCGSPF64	$2,500	$5,000	$8,500
1060	C	RE	L7	10	6	Superior	1/2004	$5,175	NGCPF66RB	$2,000	$3,500	$5,150
1061	Alu	RE	8	1	2	Superior	1/2004	$9,775	PCGSPF64CA	$4,900	$10,000	$17,000

J-1062 to J-1064: 1871 Half Dime

Obverse: Longacre's Indian Princess design, plain (starless) field.
Reverse: Regular die of the year.

J-1062

Number	Metal	Edge	Rarity	Pop	T/A	Firm	Date	Amount	Grade	60	63	65
						Last Traded at Auction						
1062	Silv	RE	L7	6	4	Heritage	11/2004	$4,025	NGCPF65	$2,400	$3,850	$6,500
1063	C	RE	H7	4	4	Heritage	6/2005	$3,795	PCGSPF64RB	$2,000	$4,200	$6,750
1064	Alu	RE	8	3	4	Stack's/ANR	6/2004	$13,513	PCGSPF64	$3,500	$8,500	$16,000

J-1065 to J-1067a: 1871 Standard Silver Half Dime

Obverse: Longacre's Indian Princess design, 13 stars around, date below.
Reverse: Open agricultural wreath enclosing 5 CENTS. STANDARD at border above (reuse of 1870 die).

J-1066

Number	Metal	Edge	Rarity	Pop	T/A	Firm	Date	Amount	Grade	60	63	65
						Last Traded at Auction						
1065	Silv	RE	L7	7	10	Heritage	6/2005	$4,313	PCGSPF66	$2,250	$3,350	$6,000
1066	C	RE	L7	6	9	Heritage	1/2005	$2,933	PCGSPF64RB	$2,250	$3,500	$5,500
1067	Alu	RE	8	1	2	Bowers & Merena	11/1992	$7,425	PCGSPF65	$4,900	$10,000	$17,500
1067a	Nick	RE	U	0	0	N/A	N/A	N/A	N/A	N/A	N/A	$32,500

J-1068 to J-1070: 1871 Half Dime

Obverse: Longacre's Indian Princess design, 13 stars around.
Reverse: Regular die of the year.

J-1069

Number	Metal	Edge	Rarity	Pop	T/A	Firm	Date	Amount	Grade	60	63	65
						Last Traded at Auction						
1068	Silv	RE	H7	5	3	Superior	1/2004	$5,750	PCGSPF65	$2,200	$3,200	$6,750
1069	C	RE	L7	11	15	Heritage	3/2005	$2,990	PCGSPF64BN	$2,000	$2,900	$5,150
1070	Alu	RE	8	2	1	Heritage	7/2003	$14,950	PCGSPF65	$4,100	$9,000	$17,000

J-1071 to J-1073: 1871 Half Dime

Trial piece struck from regular dies.

J-1071

Number	Metal	Edge	Rarity	Pop	T/A	Firm	Date	Amount	Grade	60	63	65
						Last Traded at Auction						
1071	C	RE	H7	4	3	Stack's	1/2005	$3,450	PCGSPF62BN	$3,500	$6,500	$12,500
1072	Alu	RE	8	1	1	Superior	10/1989	$3,300	NGCPF64	$4,500	$8,500	$14,000
1073	Nick	RE	U	1	2	Superior	1/2004	$16,100	NGCPF65	$7,800	$13,000	$20,000

Patterns of 1871

J-1074 to J-1076:
1871 Standard Silver Dime

Obverse: Longacre's Indian Princess design, plain (starless) field.
Reverse: Open agricultural wreath enclosing 10 CENTS.
STANDARD at border above (reuse of 1870 die).

J-1075

Number	Metal	Edge	Rarity	Pop	T/A	Firm	Date	Amount	Grade	60	63	65
							Last Traded at Auction					
1074	Silv	RE	H7	3	2	Bowers & Merena	5/1999	$4,600	PCGSPF65	$3,500	$6,000	$11,500
1075	C	RE	L7	8	9	Superior	7/2003	$9,200	NGCPF67RB	$2,700	$4,200	$7,700
1076	Alu	RE	8	0	1	Superior	2/1987	$1,100	PF65	$2,600	$4,500	$8,500

J-1077 to J-1079:
1871 Dime

Obverse: Longacre's Indian Princess design, plain (starless) field.
Reverse: Regular die of the year.

J-1077

Number	Metal	Edge	Rarity	Pop	T/A	Firm	Date	Amount	Grade	60	63	65
							Last Traded at Auction					
1077	Silv	RE	H7	4	4	Superior	2/2003	$10,350	PCGSPF66	$3,200	$6,250	$12,000
1078	C	RE	H7	3	1	Heritage	7/2003	$6,900	PCGSPF63RB	$3,500	$6,500	$12,000
1079	Alu	RE	H7	4	3	Heritage	7/2003	$10,638	PCGSPF65	$3,200	$5,800	$11,000

J-1080 to J-1082:
1871 Standard Silver Dime

J-1083 has been delisted.

Obverse: Longacre's Indian Princess design, 13 stars around.
Reverse: Open agricultural wreath enclosing 10 CENTS. STAN-
DARD at border above (reuse of 1870 die).

J-1080

Number	Metal	Edge	Rarity	Pop	T/A	Firm	Date	Amount	Grade	60	63	65
							Last Traded at Auction					
1080	Silv	RE	H6	15	8	Heritage	1/2005	$2,818	NGCPF63	$2,500	$3,500	$6,000
1081	C	RE	L7	7	7	Heritage	11/2003	$6,728	NGC65PFRD	$2,600	$4,200	$7,500
1082	Alu	RE	8	1	3	Superior	1/1994	$2,255	PCGSPF62	$2,300	$3,900	$7,500

J-1084 to J-1086:
1871 Dime

Obverse: Longacre's Indian Princess design, 13 stars around.
Reverse: Regular die of the year.

J-1085

Number	Metal	Edge	Rarity	Pop	T/A	Firm	Date	Amount	Grade	60	63	65
							Last Traded at Auction					
1084	Silv	RE	L7	6	8	Heritage	8/2004	$3,795	NGCPF64	$2,900	$5,500	$10,500
1085	C	RE	H6	15	6	Heritage	7/2003	$3,565	PCGSPF64RB	$1,950	$2,800	$4,800
1086	Alu	RE	8	2	1	Heritage	3/2003	$12,650	PCGSPF64	$4,250	$8,700	$16,500

J-1087 to J-1089:
1871 Dime

Trial piece struck from regular dies.

J-1089

Number	Metal	Edge	Rarity	Pop	T/A	Firm	Date	Amount	Grade	60	63	65
							Last Traded at Auction					
1087	C	RE	H7	6	1	Heritage	1/2003	$2,300	ANACSPF60RB	$2,250	$4,500	$9,000
1088	Alu	RE	8	1	1	Spink	3/1983	$600	PF	$4,800	$9,000	$15,500
1089	Nick	RE	U	2	2	Superior	5/1993	$3,520	NGCPF64	$7,800	$13,000	$20,000

J-1090 to J-1092:
1871 Standard Silver
Quarter Dollar

Obverse: Longacre's Indian Princess design, plain (starless) field.
Reverse: Open agricultural wreath enclosing 25 CENTS. STANDARD at border above.

J-1090

Number	Metal	Edge	Rarity	Pop	T/A	Last Traded at Auction				60	63	65
						Firm	Date	Amount	Grade			
1090	Silv	RE	H7	2	1	Bowers & Ruddy	7/1981	$3,000	PF63	$3,850	$7,400	$14,000
1091	C	RE	L7	10	3	Bowers & Merena	11/2002	$6,613	PCGSPF65RB	$2,250	$4,000	$7,750
1092	Alu	RE	8	0	1	Paramount	7/1986	$1,705	PF65	$7,800	$13,000	$22,500

J-1093 to J-1095:
1871 Quarter Dollar

Obverse: Longacre's Indian Princess design, plain (starless) field.
Reverse: Regular die of the year.

J-1093

Number	Metal	Edge	Rarity	Pop	T/A	Last Traded at Auction				60	63	65
						Firm	Date	Amount	Grade			
1093	Silv	RE	H7	3	2	Bowers & Merena	7/2004	$11,500	PCGSPF63	$5,000	$11,000	$18,500
1094	C	RE	H7	6	3	Heritage	11/2003	$6,613	ANACSPF64RB	$2,250	$4,100	$7,700
1095	Alu	RE	8	3	1	Bowers & Merena	5/1999	$4,140	PCGSPF66	$4,500	$7,800	$13,000

J-1096 to J-1098:
1871 Standard Silver
Quarter Dollar

Obverse: Longacre's Indian Princess design, 13 stars around.
Reverse: Open agricultural wreath enclosing 25 CENTS. STANDARD at border above.

J-1096

Number	Metal	Edge	Rarity	Pop	T/A	Last Traded at Auction				60	63	65
						Firm	Date	Amount	Grade			
1096	Silv	RE	L7	6	6	Heritage	11/2004	$6,038	NGCPF66	$3,200	$4,750	$8,000
1097	C	RE	H6	14	12	Heritage	8/2004	$2,875	NGCPF64BN	$2,250	$3,850	$6,350
1098	Alu	RE	8	3	1	Auction '90	8/1990	$7,250	PCGSPF66	$3,900	$7,150	$11,500

J-1099 to J-1101:
1871 Quarter Dollar

Obverse: Longacre's Indian Princess design, 13 stars around.
Reverse: Regular die of the year.

J-1100

Number	Metal	Edge	Rarity	Pop	T/A	Last Traded at Auction				60	63	65
						Firm	Date	Amount	Grade			
1099	Silv	RE	H7	4	4	Stack's	1/2005	$3,335	PCGSPF60	$3,200	$5,150	$9,000
1100	C	RE	L7	10	13	ANR	3/2005	$5,290	PCGSPF65RD	$2,600	$4,000	$6,750
1101	Alu	RE	8	1	1	Heritage	2/1991	$4,300	PF65	$4,250	$8,500	$16,500

Patterns of 1871

J-1102 to J-1104:
1871 Quarter Dollar

Trial piece struck from regular dies.

J-1102

Number	Metal	Edge	Rarity	Pop	T/A	Last Traded at Auction				60	63	65
						Firm	Date	Amount	Grade			
1102	C	RE	H7	5	4	Heritage	1/2005	$3,738	NGCPF65BN	$2,250	$3,750	$6,500
1103	Alu	RE	8	1	1	Kingswood	11/2004	$10,072	PCGSPF65	$4,200	$7,500	$14,000
1104	Nick	RE	U	1	1	ANR	8/2004	$25,300	PCGSPF64	N/A	$20,000	$30,000

J-1105 to J-1107:
1871 Standard Silver
Half Dollar

Obverse: Longacre's Indian Princess design, plain (starless) field.
Reverse: Open agricultural wreath enclosing 50 CENTS. STANDARD at border above.

J-1105

Number	Metal	Edge	Rarity	Pop	T/A	Last Traded at Auction				60	63	65
						Firm	Date	Amount	Grade			
1105	Silv	RE	H7	3	3	Superior	2/2003	$11,500	NGCPF64	$5,150	$9,500	$15,500
1106	C	RE	L7	8	2	Bowers & Merena	3/1994	$6,875	PCGSPF65BN	$3,850	$6,400	$9,500
1107	Alu	RE	8	2	2	Heritage	1/2004	$31,050	PCGSPF66CA	$11,000	$17,500	$28,000

J-1108 to J-1110:
1871 Half Dollar

Obverse: Longacre's Indian Princess design, plain (starless) field.
Reverse: Regular reverse die.

J-1109

Number	Metal	Edge	Rarity	Pop	T/A	Last Traded at Auction				60	63	65
						Firm	Date	Amount	Grade			
1108	Silv	RE	H7	5	2	Heritage	7/2003	$3,220	ANACSPF55 Scr	$4,500	$7,700	$12,500
1109	C	RE	L7	5	7	Heritage	11/2003	$8,800	PCGSPF65RB	$4,100	$8,000	$11,000
1110	Alu	RE	8	3	2	Heritage	8/2004	$16,100	PCGSPF65CA	$6,500	$12,000	$21,000

J-1111 to J-1113:
1871 Standard Silver
Half Dollar

Obverse: Longacre's Indian Princess design, 13 stars around.
Reverse: Open agricultural wreath enclosing 50 CENTS. STANDARD at border above.

J-1111

Number	Metal	Edge	Rarity	Pop	T/A	Last Traded at Auction				60	63	65
						Firm	Date	Amount	Grade			
1111	Silv	RE	L7	6	4	Superior	8/2004	$8,050	NGCPF65	$4,800	$7,700	$11,500
1112	C	RE	L7	9	4	ANR	3/2004	$6,900	NGCPF65BN	$3,850	$6,400	$9,500
1113	Alu	RE	8	2	5	Ira & Larry Goldberg	5/2005	$23,000	NGCPF66	$6,500	$11,500	$20,500

J-1114 to J-1116:
1871 Half Dollar

Obverse: Longacre's Indian Princess design, 13 stars around.
Reverse: Regular reverse die.

J-1114

Number	Metal	Edge	Rarity	Pop	T/A	Firm	Date	Amount	Grade	60	63	65
						Last Traded at Auction						
1114	Silv	RE	H7	4	3	Heritage	6/2005	$4,888	PCGSPF63	$5,150	$9,500	$15,500
1115	C	RE	L7	11	8	Heritage	8/2004	$5,980	NGCPF64RB	$3,850	$6,250	$9,500
1116	Alu	RE	8	1	1	Heritage	1/2004	$29,325	PF65	$10,000	$16,500	$28,000

J-1117 to J-1119:
1871 Half Dollar

Trial piece struck from regular dies.

J-1117

Number	Metal	Edge	Rarity	Pop	T/A	Firm	Date	Amount	Grade	60	63	65
						Last Traded at Auction						
1117	C	RE	H7	3	2	Superior	5/2003	$13,513	NGCPF65BN	$6,500	$10,500	$20,000
1118	Alu	RE	8	0	0	N/A	N/A	N/A	N/A	$9,750	$16,500	$26,000
1119	Nick	RE	U	1	1	Heritage	1/2004	$37,375	PF	N/A	N/A	$60,000

J-1120 to J-1125:
1871 Standard Silver Dollar

Obverse: Longacre's Indian Princess design, plain (starless) field, with initials J.B.L. below base at lower right (for James B. Longacre).
Reverse: Open agricultural wreath enclosing 1 DOLLAR. STANDARD at border above.

J-1124

Number	Metal	Edge	Rarity	Pop	T/A	Firm	Date	Amount	Grade	60	63	65
						Last Traded at Auction						
1120	Silv	RE	H7	2	3	ANR	9/2003	$41,400	NGCPF65	$10,000	$20,000	$45,000
1121	Silv	PE	H7	7	2	Bowers & Merena	7/2002	$13,800	PCGSPF64	$5,150	$10,000	$20,000
1122	C	RE	H7	4	2	Bowers & Merena	5/1999	$6,325	PCGSPF62RB	$7,000	$12,500	$22,500
1123	C	PE	H7	6	3	Superior	5/2003	$15,525	NGCPF66BN	$5,150	$9,500	$18,000
1124	Alu	RE	8	3	3	Superior	11/2004	$28,750	NGCPF66	$11,000	$21,500	$32,500
1125	Alu	PE	8	1	1	Bowers & Ruddy	10/1977	$3,600	PF65	$13,000	$21,500	$39,000

Patterns of 1871

J-1126 to J-1131: 1871 Silver Dollar

Obverse: Longacre's Indian Princess design, plain (starless) field, with initials J.B.L. below base at lower right.
Reverse: Regular die of the year.

J-1126

| Number | Metal | Edge | Rarity | Pop | T/A | Last Traded at Auction | | | | 60 | 63 | 65 |
						Firm	Date	Amount	Grade			
1126	Silv	RE	8	1	3	Stack's	10/2003	$21,850	VChPF	$15,000	$26,000	$45,000
1127	Silv	PE	8	0	1	Bowers & Ruddy	7/1981	$3,800	PF63	$15,000	$45,000	$45,000
1128	C	RE	H7	0	1	Bowers & Merena	6/1991	$10,175	PF60BN	$15,000	$26,000	$45,000
1129	C	PE	H7	4	2	Heritage	11/2003	$21,850	PCGSPF64CA	$7,000	$18,000	$25,000
1130	Alu	RE	8	1	1	Bowers & Merena	5/1999	$8,625	PCGSPF64	$13,000	$21,500	$39,000
1131	Alu	PE	8	6	2	ANR	9/2003	$25,300	NGCPF66	$5,150	$12,000	$23,500

J-1132 and J-1132a: 1871 Silver Dollar

Obverse: Longacre's Indian Princess design, as preceding.
Reverse: Regular reverse die of the 1840 to 1865 type without motto, here an anachronism.

J-1132

| Number | Metal | Edge | Rarity | Pop | T/A | Last Traded at Auction | | | | 60 | 63 | 65 |
						Firm	Date	Amount	Grade			
1132	C	RE	8	2	2	ANR	9/2003	$46,000	PCGSPF65BN	$18,000	$28,000	$48,000
1132a	C	PE	U	1	1	Bowers & Merena	5/1999	$6,210	PCGSPF61RB	$13,000	$19,500	N/A

J-1133 to J-1138: 1871 Standard Silver Dollar

Obverse: Longacre's Indian Princess design, 13 stars around, 13 stars on the flag.
Reverse: Open agricultural wreath enclosing 1 DOLLAR. STANDARD at border above.

J-1133

| Number | Metal | Edge | Rarity | Pop | T/A | Last Traded at Auction | | | | 60 | 63 | 65 |
						Firm	Date	Amount	Grade			
1133	Silv	RE	H6	17	11	Heritage	6/2005	$13,225	NGCPF66	$6,350	$9,500	$19,000
1134	Silv	PE	8	0	0	Kagin's	5/1969	$560	GemBrPF	$15,000	$26,000	$45,000
1135	C	RE	L7	7	3	Bowers & Merena	1/1997	$4,620	PCGSPF64RB	$4,200	$8,250	$16,000
1136	C	PE	8	0	0	Bowers & Ruddy	7/1981	$3,000	PF65	$15,000	$26,000	$45,000
1137	Alu	RE	8	2	1	Superior	5/1999	$1,553	PCGSPF65	$13,000	$21,500	$39,000
1138	Alu	PE	8	0	0	N/A	N/A	N/A	N/A	$15,000	$26,000	$45,000

J-1138a to J-1138f:
1871 Silver Dollar

J-1138e was listed as J-1138b prior to the 8th edition.[18]

Obverse: Longacre's Indian Princess design, 13 stars around, 13 stars on the flag.
Reverse: Regular reverse die.

J-1138a

Number	Metal	Edge	Rarity	Pop	T/A	Last Traded at Auction				60	63	65
						Firm	Date	Amount	Grade			
1138a	Silv	RE	8	2	0	N/A	N/A	N/A	N/A	$18,000	$30,000	$50,000
1138b	Silv	RE	–	0	0	N/A	N/A	N/A	N/A	Unconf	N/A	N/A
1138c	C	RE	8	1	1	Bowers & Merena	11/2002	$28,700	PCGSPF65RB	N/A	N/A	$42,500
1138d	C	PE	–	0	0	N/A	N/A	N/A	N/A	Unconf	N/A	N/A
1138e	Alu	RE	8	0	1	Stack's	3/1965	$500	PF	N/A	N/A	N/A
1138f	Alu	PE	–	0	0	N/A	N/A	N/A	N/A	Unconf	N/A	N/A

J-1139 to J-1144:
1871 Standard
Silver Dollar

Obverse: Longacre's Indian Princess design, 13 stars around, 22 stars on the flag.
Reverse: Open agricultural wreath enclosing 1 DOLLAR. STANDARD at border above.

J-1144

Number	Metal	Edge	Rarity	Pop	T/A	Last Traded at Auction				60	63	65
						Firm	Date	Amount	Grade			
1139	Silv	RE	H7	2	2	ANR	9/2003	$27,600	NGCPF66	$9,500	$14,000	$28,000
1140	Silv	PE	8	0	1	Kagin's	11/1973	$2,100	PF	$10,000	$20,000	$36,000
1141	C	RE	H7	5	5	Heritage	8/2001	$8,683	NGCPF66BN	$4,200	$7,750	$14,000
1142	C	PE	H7	7	6	ANR	3/2005	$18,400	PCGSPF64RD	$6,250	$12,000	$22,000
1143	Alu	RE	8	1	1	Bowers & Merena	8/2001	$9,200	PF64	$13,000	$21,500	$39,000
1144	Alu	PE	8	1	0	N/A	N/A	N/A	N/A	$17,500	$30,000	$55,000

J-1145 to J-1150:
1871 Silver Dollar

Obverse: Longacre's Indian Princess design, 13 stars around, 22 stars on the flag.
Reverse: Regular die of the year.

J-1147

Number	Metal	Edge	Rarity	Pop	T/A	Last Traded at Auction				60	63	65
						Firm	Date	Amount	Grade			
1145	Silv	RE	L7	6	2	Bowers & Merena	7/2004	$5,750	NGCPF60	$9,000	$15,000	$25,000
1146	Silv	PE	L7	6	3	ANR	9/2003	$10,350	NGCPF64	$6,400	$11,500	$22,500
1147	C	RE	H6	19	15	Heritage	8/2004	$10,350	PCGSPF66BN	$3,000	$6,000	$10,000
1148	C	PE	L7	14	13	Scotsman	5/2005	$4,025	PCGSPF62RB	$2,850	$5,150	$10,500
1149	Alu	RE	L7	7	5	Superior	5/2003	$17,250	NGCPF66	$5,150	$10,000	$19,000
1150	Alu	PE	H7	6	9	Heritage	3/2005	$21,275	NGCPF66	$9,500	$19,000	$29,000

Patterns of 1871

J-1151 to J-1153:
1871 Silver Dollar

Trial piece struck from regular dies.

J-1151

Number	Metal	Edge	Rarity	Pop	T/A	Last Traded at Auction				60	63	65
						Firm	Date	Amount	Grade			
1151	C	RE	8	2	1	SRCG	1/1981	$3,300	PF	$9,500	$15,500	$28,000
1152	Alu	RE	8	0	1	Superior	10/1989	$16,500	PCGSPF65	$9,000	$15,000	$29,000
1153	Nick	RE	U	2	3	ANR	9/2003	$34,500	NGCPF65	N/A	N/A	$40,000

J-1154 to J-1157:
1871 Commercial Dollar

The first appearance of the Commercial dollar die, predecessor of the trade dollar.

Obverse: Longacre's Indian Princess design, 13 stars around, 22 stars on the flag.
Reverse: Commercial dollar die. Large wreath enclosing COMMERCIAL DOLLAR / 420 GRS. 900 FINE. On wreath ribbon is GOD OUR TRUST.[19] At the top border is UNITED STATES OF AMERICA.

J-1154

Number	Metal	Edge	Rarity	Pop	T/A	Last Traded at Auction				60	63	65
						Firm	Date	Amount	Grade			
1154	Silv	RE	H7	3	3	ANR	9/2003	$23,000	NGCPF65	$9,500	$19,000	$29,000
1155	Silv	PE	8	2	2	Superior	5/2004	$36,800	NGCPF65	$15,000	$26,000	$45,000
1156	C	RE	H7	1	2	Heritage	8/2004	$23,000	PCGSPF63BN	$12,500	$25,000	$39,000
1157	C	PE	8	2	2	ANR	9/2003	$16,100	NGCPF64BN	$12,500	$24,000	$36,000

J-1158 and J-1159:
1871 Commercial Dollar

Obverse: Longacre's Indian Princess design, 13 stars around, 13 stars on the flag.
Reverse: Commercial dollar die, as preceding.

J-1158

Number	Metal	Edge	Rarity	Pop	T/A	Last Traded at Auction				60	63	65
						Firm	Date	Amount	Grade			
1158	Silv	RE	–	0	0	N/A	N/A	N/A	N/A	Unconf	Unconf	Unconf
1159	C	RE	–	0	0	N/A	N/A	N/A	N/A	Unconf	Unconf	Unconf

J-1160: 1871 Commercial Dollar

Obverse: Regular Liberty Seated die of the year.
Reverse: Commercial dollar die, as preceding.

J-1160

Number	Metal	Edge	Rarity	Pop	T/A	Last Traded at Auction				60	63	65
						Firm	Date	Amount	Grade			
1160	Silv	RE	–	0	0	N/A	N/A	N/A	N/A	Unconf	Unconf	Unconf

J-1161 to J-1163: 1871 Gold Dollar

Trial piece struck from regular dies.

J-1161

Number	Metal	Edge	Rarity	Pop	T/A	Last Traded at Auction				60	63	65
						Firm	Date	Amount	Grade			
1161	C	RE	8	1	1	Heritage	7/1994	$3,410	PF64BN	$7,000	$15,000	$25,000
1162	Alu	RE	8	0	1	Bowers & Ruddy	6/1979	$1,000	PF65	$8,500	$17,500	$30,000
1163	Nick	RE	8	0	1	Bowers & Ruddy	6/1979	$1,000	PF60	$8,500	$17,500	$30,000

J-1164 to J-1166: 1871 $2.50

Trial piece struck from regular dies.

J-1164

Number	Metal	Edge	Rarity	Pop	T/A	Last Traded at Auction				60	63	65
						Firm	Date	Amount	Grade			
1164	C	RE	H7	5	5	Bowers & Merena	11/2001	$4,600	PCGSPF63RB	$3,500	$7,000	$12,500
1165	Alu	RE	8	1	1	Superior	5/1999	$3,910	PCGSPF64	$7,250	$13,000	$22,500
1166	Nick	RE	8	0	1	Paramount	4/1977	$650	PF65	$8,500	$15,500	$26,000

J-1167 to J-1169: 1871 $3

Trial piece struck from regular dies.

J-1167

Number	Metal	Edge	Rarity	Pop	T/A	Last Traded at Auction				60	63	65
						Firm	Date	Amount	Grade			
1167	C	RE	H7	4	1	Superior	5/2003	$13,225	NGCPF64RB	$5,250	$10,500	$20,000
1168	Alu	RE	8	1	1	Bowers & Ruddy	6/1979	$3,500/Set	PF63	$8,500	$15,000	$25,000
1169	Nick	RE	U	0	1	Bowers & Ruddy	6/1979	$3,500/Set	PF63	$10,000	$18,000	$27,500

Patterns of 1871

J-1170 to J-1172: 1871 $5

Trial piece struck from regular dies.

J-1171

Number	Metal	Edge	Rarity	Pop	T/A	Last Traded at Auction				60	63	65
						Firm	Date	Amount	Grade			
1170	C	RE	H7	1	1	Bowers & Merena	5/1999	$4,600	PCGSPF65RB	$6,000	$10,000	$19,000
1171	Alu	RE	8	1	1	Superior	7/1993	$5,720	NGCPF64	$5,000	$9,000	$17,000
1172	Nick	RE	8	1	1	Heritage	8/2001	$3,220	PCGSPF53	$9,750	N/A	N/A

J-1173 to J-1175: 1871 $10

Trial piece struck from regular dies.

J-1173

Number	Metal	Edge	Rarity	Pop	T/A	Last Traded at Auction				60	63	65
						Firm	Date	Amount	Grade			
1173	C	RE	H7	4	5	Heritage	2/2005	$6,900	NGCPF63BN	$6,000	$10,000	$17,500
1174	Alu	RE	8	0	1	Paramount	4/1977	$1,200	PF65	$8,500	$16,500	$32,500
1175	Nick	RE	U	0	1	Paramount	4/1977	$560	PF65	$8,500	$16,500	$32,500

J-1176 to J-1178: 1871 $20

Trial piece struck from regular dies.

J-1177

Number	Metal	Edge	Rarity	Pop	T/A	Last Traded at Auction				60	63	65
						Firm	Date	Amount	Grade			
1176	C	RE	H7	4	3	Heritage	7/2003	$17,250	PCGSPF64RD	$10,000	$18,000	$28,500
1177	Alu	RE	8	2	1	Paramount	4/1977	$1,700	PF65	$10,000	$18,000	$30,000
1178	Nick	RE	U	0	1	Paramount	4/1977	$2,300	PF65	N/A	N/A	N/A

Patterns of 1872

History and Overview

Pattern varieties diminished sharply in 1872, but they were still quite extensive. Highlighting the issues of this year are the so-called Amazonian designs by Chief Engraver William Barber, certainly among his finest productions from the standpoint of art and classicism. The silver issues depicted Liberty seated, facing left, with her right hand touching the head of a perched eagle, her left arm resting on a shield and her hand holding a sword. Perhaps Thorvaldsen's early 19th-century sculpture, *Ganymede and the Eagle*, with its quiescent eagle and figure (in that case a man) with Phrygian cap, was an inspiration. Similarly, a goddess feeding a perched eagle was a popular motif on certain currency notes of the 1850s. The reverse illustrated a bold standing eagle, with a shield to the right, with a ribbon across inscribed IN GOD WE TRUST, held by the eagle's talons.

Patterns were made from the Commercial dollar reverse die cut in 1871, plus the introduction of new dies bearing the name TRADE DOLLAR, which became the official term. These were produced in various combinations, some no doubt as patterns, mostly for numismatists.

William Barber produced a new portrait of Liberty, facing left, for the pattern gold coinage, with examples struck across the full spectrum of denominations in use at the time: $1, $2.50, $3, $5, $10, and $20, the first and last time such a suite of new-design patterns had been so extensive. The reverse of these pieces employed an eagle holding the shield, similar to that on Amazonian silver issues.

In addition, off-metal strikes were produced from regular Proof dies of denominations from the cent through the double eagle.

Collecting Perspective

Numismatic interest in the patterns of 1872 is focused primarily upon the Amazonian silver denominations, the quarter, half dollar, and dollar, which are at once beautiful and rare. However, given a few years of effort, one may put together at least a set of die combinations, perhaps even a full trio in a given metal. As is always the case, copper strikings of this or any other pattern are exceedingly difficult to find in a combination of truly high grade and excellent eye appeal (not having been polished, or recolored). Often, copper patterns are the connoisseur's nemesis. The Barber pattern gold denominations are unique in gold metal, but are collectible in copper, although not easily found. In addition, aluminum pieces were made and are apt to be encountered only at scattered intervals.

The commercial dollar and trade dollar patterns of the year are of great importance and have always been popular. The issues are a combination of obverses with the COMMERCIAL DOLLAR reverse employed in 1870 (with variant GOD OUR TRUST motto), plus two new reverses each inscribed TRADE DOLLAR.

J-1179 to J-1182: 1872 Cent

Trial piece struck from regular dies.

J-1179

Number	Metal	Edge	Rarity	Pop	T/A	Last Traded at Auction				60	63	65
						Firm	Date	Amount	Grade			
1179	C	PE	8	0	0	N/A	N/A	N/A	N/A	$1,800	$3,750	$6,500
1180	C-N	PE	8	0	1	B. Max Mehl	11/1944	$78	Unc	N/A	N/A	N/A
1181	Alu	PE	8	1	2	ANR	3/2005	$32,200	NGCPF67CA	N/A	N/A	$32,000
1182	Nick	PE	8	0	1	Bolender	9/1958	$130	BU	N/A	N/A	N/A

J-1183 and J-1184: 1872 Two-Cent Piece

Trial piece struck from regular dies.

J-1184

Number	Metal	Edge	Rarity	Pop	T/A	Last Traded at Auction				60	63	65
						Firm	Date	Amount	Grade			
1183	C	PE	8	0	1	Bolender	3/1955	$40	PFRD	$1,800	$3,750	$6,500
1184	Alu	PE	H7	2	1	Doyle Galleries	12/1983	$1,700	MS63	$5,750	$10,000	$16,000

J-1185 and J-1186: 1872 Three-Cent Piece

Trial piece struck from regular dies.

J-1186

Number	Metal	Edge	Rarity	Pop	T/A	Last Traded at Auction				60	63	65
						Firm	Date	Amount	Grade			
1185	C	PE	H7	3	2	Ira & Larry Goldberg	2/2000	$3,450	PCGSPF65RB	$1,750	$3,400	$6,500
1186	Alu	PE	8	2	1	Superior	11/2004	$12,075	PCGSPF66	$3,250	$6,500	$11,500

Patterns of 1872

J-1187 and J-1188: 1872 Trime

Trial piece struck from regular dies.

J-1188

Number	Metal	Edge	Rarity	Pop	T/A	Last Traded at Auction				60	63	65
						Firm	Date	Amount	Grade			
1187	C	PE	H7	1	1	Superior	2/1987	$750	PF	$8,500	$14,000	$22,500
1188	Alu	PE	8	3	3	Heritage	6/2005	$7,763	PCGSPF65CA	$6,000	$10,000	$16,000

J-1189 and J-1190: 1872 Five-Cent Piece

Trial piece struck from regular dies.

J-1189

Number	Metal	Edge	Rarity	Pop	T/A	Last Traded at Auction				60	63	65
						Firm	Date	Amount	Grade			
1189	C	PE	H7	2	3	Ira & Larry Goldberg	5/2005	$11,500	NGCPF66RB	$3,500	$7,000	$12,000
1190	Alu	PE	8	1	1	Paramount	2/1970	$160	PF	$4,250	$8,500	$16,500

J-1191 and J-1192: 1872 Half Dime

Trial piece struck from regular dies.

J-1191

Number	Metal	Edge	Rarity	Pop	T/A	Last Traded at Auction				60	63	65
						Firm	Date	Amount	Grade			
1191	C	RE	8	2	1	Bowers & Ruddy	7/1981	$650	PF	$4,200	$7,500	$12,500
1192	Alu	RE	8	1	1	Stack's	3/1977	$400	PF	$4,500	$8,500	$14,000

J-1193 and J-1194: 1872 Dime

Trial piece struck from regular dies.

J-1193

Number	Metal	Edge	Rarity	Pop	T/A	Last Traded at Auction				60	63	65
						Firm	Date	Amount	Grade			
1193	C	RE	8	1	2	Heritage	3/2003	$9,775	PCGSPF64	$4,800	$9,000	$15,500
1194	Alu	RE	8	2	1	Herbert L. Melnick	11/1982	$875	PF	$3,850	$6,400	$11,500

J-1195 to J-1197: 1872 Quarter Dollar

The first in a series of three denomination depicting this classic obverse motif, a high point in Barber's repertoire.

Obverse: William Barber's Amazonian design: Liberty seated, facing left, with her right hand touching the head of a perched eagle, her left arm resting on a shield and her hand holding a sword.
Reverse: Barber's standing eagle with talons holding shield inscribed IN GOD WE TRUST. UNITED STATES OF AMERICA / QUAR. DOL. around border.

J-1195

Number	Metal	Edge	Rarity	Pop	T/A	Last Traded at Auction				60	63	65
						Firm	Date	Amount	Grade			
1195	Silv	RE	L7	7	2	Stack's	10/2003	$36,800	ChPF	$22,500	$35,000	$60,000
1196	C	RE	L7	5	1	Stack's	3/2002	$24,150	PCGSPF65RB	$11,500	$19,000	$31,000
1197	Alu	RE	8	2	1	RLH Enterprises	1/1980	$7,750	PF65	$30,000	$45,000	$85,000

J-1198 and J-1199: 1872 Quarter Dollar

Trial piece struck from regular dies.

J-1198

Number	Metal	Edge	Rarity	Pop	T/A	Last Traded at Auction				60	63	65
						Firm	Date	Amount	Grade			
1198	C	RE	8	3	2	Heritage	8/1992	$3,905	PF64BN	$4,500	$7,500	$12,000
1199	Alu	RE	H7	1	1	Bolender	3/1955	$40	PF	$6,200	$12,000	$20,000

J-1200 to J-1202: 1872 Half Dollar

Obverse: William Barber's Amazonian design.
Reverse: Barber's Standing Eagle with talons holding shield. UNITED STATES OF AMERICA / HALF DOL. around border.

J-1201

Number	Metal	Edge	Rarity	Pop	T/A	Last Traded at Auction				60	63	65
						Firm	Date	Amount	Grade			
1200	Silv	RE	L7	7	5	Heritage	6/2004	$40,250	NGCPF66	$20,500	$33,000	$54,000
1201	C	RE	L7	8	7	Stack's	3/2002	$27,600	PCGSPF64BN	$12,500	$19,000	$32,000
1202	Alu	RE	8	2	1	Bowers & Merena	11/1995	$17,600	PCGSPF64	$23,000	$39,000	$65,000

J-1203 and J-1204: 1872 Half Dollar

Trial piece struck from regular dies.

J-1203

Number	Metal	Edge	Rarity	Pop	T/A	Last Traded at Auction				60	63	65
						Firm	Date	Amount	Grade			
1203	C	RE	H7	2	1	Stack's	4/1962	$145	PF	$4,200	$8,000	$12,500
1204	Alu	RE	8	2	2	Superior	6/1998	$6,050	PCGSPF65	$4,500	$8,250	$14,000

J-1205 to J-1207: 1872 Silver Dollar

Obverse: William Barber's Amazonian design.
Reverse: Barber's Standing Eagle with talons holding shield, one feather in eagle's right wing unfinished. UNITED STATES OF AMERICA / ONE DOL. around border.

J-1205

Number	Metal	Edge	Rarity	Pop	T/A	Last Traded at Auction				60	63	65
						Firm	Date	Amount	Grade			
1205	Silv	RE	L7	3	2	Stack's	10/2003	$34,500	PF	$37,500	$70,000	$125,000
1206	C	RE	L7	8	4	ANR	9/2003	$39,100	NGCPF66RB	$17,500	$32,000	$55,000
1207	Alu	RE	8	3	3	Bowers & Merena	11/1995	$22,550	PCGSPF65	$24,000	$42,000	$75,000

Patterns of 1872

J-1208 and J-1209: 1872 Silver Dollar

Obverse: William Barber's adaptation of James B. Longacre's Indian Princess design, facing left, 13 stars around, 13 stars on the flag, date below.
Reverse: Regular die of the year.

J-1208

Number	Metal	Edge	Rarity	Pop	T/A	Last Traded at Auction				60	63	65
						Firm	Date	Amount	Grade			
1208	Silv	RE	8	1	1	Bowers & Merena	5/1999	$16,100	PCGSPF65	$15,000	$25,000	$45,000
1209	Silv	PE	U	1	1	ANR	9/2003	$41,400	NGCPF66	$15,000	$25,000	$45,000

J-1210 and J-1211: 1872 Silver Dollar

Trial piece struck from regular dies.

J-1210

Number	Metal	Edge	Rarity	Pop	T/A	Last Traded at Auction				60	63	65
						Firm	Date	Amount	Grade			
1210	C	RE	8	1	1	Stack's	9/1992	$7,700	ChPFBN	$8,000	$16,000	$31,000
1211	Alu	RE	8	0	0	N/A	N/A	N/A	N/A	$9,000	$15,500	$30,000

J-1212 to J-1213a: 1872 Commercial Dollar

Obverse: Longacre's Indian Princess design, 13 stars around, 22 stars on the flag, without name below base, as first used posthumously in 1870 (cf. J-1008).
Reverse: Commercial dollar die as first used in 1871.

J-1212

Number	Metal	Edge	Rarity	Pop	T/A	Last Traded at Auction				60	63	65
						Firm	Date	Amount	Grade			
1212	Silv	RE	L6	18	12	Heritage	6/2005	$5,463	PCGSPF62	$5,000	$9,500	$17,500
1213	Silv	PE	–	0	0	N/A	N/A	N/A	N/A	Unconf	Unconf	Unconf
1213a	C	RE	U	0	0	N/A	N/A	N/A	N/A	N/A	N/A	N/A

* J-1213a: only known example was silver-plated

J-1214 to J-1218: 1872 Commercial Dollar

Obverse: William Barber's adaptation of James B. Longacre's Indian Princess design, facing left, 13 stars around, 13 stars on the flag, date below.
Reverse: Commercial dollar die.

J-1216

| Number | Metal | Edge | Rarity | Pop | T/A | Last Traded at Auction | | | | 60 | 63 | 65 |
						Firm	Date	Amount	Grade			
1214	Silv	RE	H7	4	3	Heritage	5/2005	$12,650	PCGSPF62	$11,000	$21,000	$32,000
1215	Silv	PE	H7	5	4	ANR	9/2003	$18,400	NGCPF65	$5,500	$11,000	$20,000
1216	C	RE	L7	7	11	Heritage	1/2005	$7,418	PCGSPF64RB	$4,200	$8,350	$16,000
1217	C	PE	8	0	1	Superior	6/1977	$850	PF	$11,500	$21,500	$42,500
1218	Alu	RE	8	0	1	Paramount	8/1972	$450	PF	$15,500	$26,000	$45,500

J-1219 and J-1219a: 1872 Commercial Dollar

About a dozen examples are known in silver (J-1219), including pieces in the Smithsonian Institution, the ANS collection, the Connecticut State Library, and the Harry J. Bass, Jr. Research Foundation.

The unique copper piece (J-1219a) is in the Connecticut State Library collection.

Obverse: Regular Liberty Seated die.
Reverse: Commercial dollar die.

J-1219

| Number | Metal | Edge | Rarity | Pop | T/A | Last Traded at Auction | | | | 60 | 63 | 65 |
						Firm	Date	Amount	Grade			
1219	Silv	RE	L7	5	14	Stack's	1/2005	$4,600	PF	$4,500	$8,350	$18,000
1219a	C	RE	U	0	0	N/A	N/A	N/A	N/A	N/A	N/A	N/A

J-1220 to J-1222: 1872 Trade Dollar

The reverse is the first trade dollar die, inspired by the Commercial dollar die.

Obverse: William Barber's adaptation of James B. Longacre's Indian Princess design, facing left, 13 stars around, 13 stars on the flag, date below.
Reverse: Large open laurel wreath enclosing TRADE DOLLAR / 420 GRAINS 900 FINE. On ribbon below, IN GOD WE TRUST. At the top border, UNITED STATES OF AMERICA.

J-1220

| Number | Metal | Edge | Rarity | Pop | T/A | Last Traded at Auction | | | | 60 | 63 | 65 |
						Firm	Date	Amount	Grade			
1220	Silv	RE	H7	4	3	Stack's	1/2005	$6,613	ChPF	$5,800	$12,000	$23,500
1221	C	RE	H7	2	3	ANR	9/2003	$13,800	NGCPF63RD	$7,000	$15,000	$22,500
1222	Alu	RE	8	0	1	Paramount	8/1972	$525	PF	$15,500	$26,000	$45,000

J-1223: 1872 Trade Dollar

Obverse: William Barber's adaptation of James B. Longacre's Indian Princess design, as preceding.

Reverse: Barber's Standing Eagle, with shield on which there is a ribbon lettered IN GOD WE TRUST, scroll in beak inscribed E PLURIBUS UNUM. In the field below the eagle, 420 GRAINS, 900 FINE. UNITED STATES OF AMERICA / TRADE DOLLAR around border.

J-1223

Number	Metal	Edge	Rarity	Pop	T/A	Last Traded at Auction				60	63	65
						Firm	Date	Amount	Grade			
1223	Silv	RE	8	1	2	Stack's	5/2003	$32,200	PCGSPF64	$16,000	$27,500	$45,000

J-1224 to J-1226: 1872 Gold Dollar

J-1224 is part of the unique Amazonian gold set.

Obverse: Barber's Liberty Head facing left, headband inscribed LIBERTY, tresses flowing down to right.
Reverse: Barber's Standing Eagle with talons holding shield. Similar to the silver Amazonian issues. UNITED STATES OF AMERICA / ONE DOL. around border.

J-1224

Number	Metal	Edge	Rarity	Pop	T/A	Last Traded at Auction				60	63	65
						Firm	Date	Amount	Grade			
1224	Gold	RE	U	1	1	Superior	10/1990	In Set	No Grade	N/A	N/A	$400,000
1225	C	RE	L7	5	3	Akers	10/1997	$9,900	PFBN	$5,000	$8,000	$12,500
1226	Alu	RE	8	3	1	Akers	10/1997	$20,900	ChPF	$7,500	$13,000	$22,500

J-1227 to J-1229: 1872 Gold Dollar

Trial piece struck from regular dies.

J-1229

Number	Metal	Edge	Rarity	Pop	T/A	Last Traded at Auction				60	63	65
						Firm	Date	Amount	Grade			
1227	C	RE	8	1	1	Bowers & Merena	5/1999	$6,900	PCGSPF64BN	$7,000	$13,000	$22,500
1228	Alu	RE	8	0	1	Stack's	8/1976	$850	PF	$7,000	$11,500	$21,000
1229	Silv	RE	U	0	1	RARCOA	4/1972	$550	PF	N/A	N/A	N/A

J-1230 to J-1232: 1872 $2.50

J-1230 is part of the unique Amazonian gold set.

Obverse: Barber's Liberty Head facing left, headband inscribed LIBERTY, tresses flowing down to right.
Reverse: Barber's Standing Eagle with talons holding shield. Similar to the silver Amazonian issues. UNITED STATES OF AMERICA / 2 1/2 DOL. around border.

J-1230

Number	Metal	Edge	Rarity	Pop	T/A	Last Traded at Auction				60	63	65
						Firm	Date	Amount	Grade			
1230	Gold	RE	U	1	1	Superior	10/1990	In Set	No Grade	N/A	N/A	$425,000
1231	C	RE	L7	8	3	Stack's	6/2003	$9,200	PFGilt	$4,800	$10,500	$22,500
1232	Alu	RE	8	3	2	Bowers & Merena	8/2004	$29,900	PCGSPF66	$7,000	$11,500	$24,000

Patterns of 1872

J-1233 and J-1234: 1872 $2.50

Trial piece struck from regular dies.

J-1234

Number	Metal	Edge	Rarity	Pop	T/A	Firm	Date	Amount	Grade	60	63	65
1233	C	RE	8	0	1	Bowers & Ruddy	10/1977	$650	ChPF	$8,500	$15,500	$26,000
1234	Alu	RE	8	1	1	NERCG	7/1979	$1,150	PF63	$7,500	$13,000	$22,500

J-1235 to J-1237: 1872 $3

J-1235 is part of the unique Amazonian gold set.

Obverse: Barber's Liberty Head facing left, headband inscribed LIB-ERTY, tresses flowing down to right.
Reverse: Barber's Standing Eagle with talons holding shield. Similar to the silver Amazonian issues. UNITED STATES OF AMERICA / THREE DOL. around border.

J-1237

Number	Metal	Edge	Rarity	Pop	T/A	Firm	Date	Amount	Grade	60	63	65
1235	Gold	RE	U	1	1	Superior	10/1990	In Set	No Grade	N/A	N/A	$900,000
1236	C	RE	H6	8	3	Heritage	7/2003	$17,250	NGCPF64Gilt	$8,500	$15,000	$22,500
1237	Alu	RE	8	3	4	Bowers & Merena	7/2004	$46,000	PCGSPF67	$10,000	$17,500	$30,000

J-1238 and J-1239: 1872 $3

Trial piece struck from regular dies.

J-1238

Number	Metal	Edge	Rarity	Pop	T/A	Firm	Date	Amount	Grade	60	63	65
1238	C	RE	H7	2	1	Bowers & Merena	5/1999	$4,140	PCGSPF62RB	$6,500	$11,500	$20,500
1239	Alu	RE	8	3	1	Stack's	10/1997	$6,050	NGCPF64	$6,000	$10,000	$20,000

J-1240 to J-1242: 1872 $5

J-1240 is part of the unique Amazonian gold set.

Obverse: Barber's Liberty Head facing left, headband inscribed LIB-ERTY, tresses flowing down to right.
Reverse: Barber's Standing Eagle with talons holding shield. Similar to the silver Amazonian issues. UNITED STATES OF AMERICA / FIVE DOL. around border.

J-1240

Number	Metal	Edge	Rarity	Pop	T/A	Firm	Date	Amount	Grade	60	63	65
1240	Gold	RE	U	1	1	Superior	10/1990	In Set	No Grade	N/A	N/A	$450,000
1241	C	RE	L7	8	6	Ira & Larry Goldberg	5/2004	$16,100	PCGSPF65BN	$5,500	$10,000	$17,500
1242	Alu	RE	8	3	2	Akers	10/1997	$14,850	GemPF	$7,500	$13,500	$25,000

J-1243 and J-1244: 1872 $5

Trial piece struck from regular dies.

J-1244

Number	Metal	Edge	Rarity	Pop	T/A	Firm	Date	Amount	Grade	60	63	65
1243	C	RE	H7	2	1	Bowers & Merena	5/1999	$3,220	PCGSPF62BN	$6,000	$10,000	$20,000
1244	Alu	RE	8	1	1	Herbert L. Melnick	11/1982	$2,000	PF	$6,000	$11,000	$22,500

Patterns of 1872

J-1245 to J-1247: 1872 $10

J-1245 is part of the unique Amazonian gold set.

Obverse: Barber's Liberty Head facing left, headband inscribed LIBERTY, tresses flowing down to right.
Reverse: Barber's Standing Eagle with talons holding shield. Similar to the silver Amazonian issues. UNITED STATES OF AMERICA / TEN DOL. around border

J-1245

Number	Metal	Edge	Rarity	Pop	T/A	Last Traded at Auction				60	63	65
						Firm	Date	Amount	Grade			
1245	Gold	RE	U	1	1	Superior	10/1990	In Set	No Grade	N/A	N/A	$750,000
1246	C	RE	L7	5	3	Heritage	2/2005	$40,250	PCGSPF65RD	$12,000	$24,000	$41,000
1247	Alu	RE	8	2	1	Akers	10/1997	$16,500	ChPF	$10,000	$18,000	$32,500

J-1248 and J-1249: 1872 $10

Trial piece struck from regular dies.

J-1249

Number	Metal	Edge	Rarity	Pop	T/A	Last Traded at Auction				60	63	65
						Firm	Date	Amount	Grade			
1248	C	RE	8	2	3	Stack's	10/1997	$4,620	ChPFBN	$6,000	$10,000	$17,500
1249	Alu	RE	8	1	1	Bowers & Merena	3/1996	$4,620	PF62/65	$7,000	$20,000	$35,000

J-1250 to J-1252: 1872 $20

J-1250 is part of the unique Amazonian gold set.

Obverse: Barber's Liberty Head facing left, headband inscribed LIBERTY, tresses flowing down to right.
Reverse: Barber's Standing Eagle with talons holding shield. Similar to the silver Amazonian issues. UNITED STATES OF AMERICA / TWENTY DOL. around border.

J-1250

Number	Metal	Edge	Rarity	Pop	T/A	Last Traded at Auction				60	63	65
						Firm	Date	Amount	Grade			
1250	Gold	RE	U	2	1	Superior	10/1990	In Set	No Grade	N/A	N/A	$1,500,000
1251	C	RE	L7	6	8	Heritage	11/2003	$9,775	PCGSPF58	$10,000	$20,000	$35,000
1252	Alu	RE	8	1	1	Akers	10/1997	$49,500	ChPF	$13,500	$24,000	$60,000

J-1253 and J-1254: 1872 $20

Trial piece struck from regular dies.

J-1253

Number	Metal	Edge	Rarity	Pop	T/A	Last Traded at Auction				60	63	65
						Firm	Date	Amount	Grade			
1253	C	RE	H7	2	2	Superior	7/2003	$16,100	NGCPF63Gilt	$10,000	$18,000	$30,000
1254	Alu	RE	H7	2	1	Paramount	7/1979	$2,200	PF65	$10,000	$17,500	$35,000

History and Overview

The year 1873 is a rich one for patterns, although production was below 100 different varieties. All but a few were secretly struck and privately distributed.

Among the patterns of this year are many trade dollars, some of which were sold in sets of six consisting of J-1276, J-1281, J-1293, J-1310, J-1315, and J-1322. It is estimated that 50 such sets found buyers at the time.

The Coinage Act of February 12, 1873, provided sweeping changes. The silver three-cent piece (trime) and half dime were abolished, and the new trade dollar denomination was authorized. The weights of the silver dime, quarter dollar, and half dollar were adjusted. The silver dollar was discontinued, it having been a *de facto* trade coin from the 1850s onward, with none seen in domestic circulation.

The trade dollar became a reality and large amounts of silver bullion were deposited at the Philadelphia, Carson City, and San Francisco mints, particularly the latter as it was closest to the Orient. Such pieces were intended for the China trade, but were legal tender in the United States (until July 22, 1876, when this provision was repealed). Trade dollars were coined to order by commercial interests that deposited bullion and asked for trade dollars in return. The trade dollar denomination, which continued through 1878, was a tremendous success, and millions were coined. However, political interests in the West influenced Congress to pass the Bland-Allison Act (February 28, 1878), providing for the government to purchase millions of ounces of silver for its own account, to be coined into lighter-weight (412.5 grains as opposed to 420 grains for the trade dollar) Morgan silver dollars. The trade dollar was discontinued, except for Proofs made for collectors through 1885.

Trade Dollar Obverse Dies of 1873

Obverse 1: "Coronet Head facing left." Head of Liberty facing left, wearing a coronet with LIBERTY in raised letters. Her hair is tied behind with a strand of pearls. 13 stars around border, 1873 below. • Used with J-1276 to J-1280.
Obverse 2: "Bailly Head facing left." Head of Liberty, crowned with leaves, hair braided and coiled behind, all compactly arranged. Thirteen stars around border, 1873 below. • Die by Joseph Alexis Bailly (1825–1883), who worked as an occasional assistant to Charles E. Barber, son of the chief engraver, who was on the Mint staff. • Used with J-1281 to J-1286.
Obverse 3: "Coronet Head facing right." William Barber's head of Liberty facing right, LIBERTY on coronet with Y at front.[3] Thirteen stars around border, 1873 below. • Used with J-1287.
Obverse 4: "Double Eagle Head." A close copy of the 1873 $20 gold die, here made as a trade dollar die, Longacre's Coronet Head facing left, 13 stars around border, 1873 below. • Used with J-1288 and J-1289.
Obverse 5: "Liberty seated on globe, short plow handles." Liberty seated, facing left, her right hand holding a pole atop which is a liberty cap, her left hand resting on a globe. Behind her is a plow (with short handles) and a small sheaf of wheat. To the lower left are two bales of cotton. The sea is in the distance at the left, 13 stars around border, 1873 below. • Used with J-1290 to J-1298.
Obverse 6: "Liberty seated on globe, long plow handles." Liberty seated, facing left, her right hand holding a pole atop which is a liberty cap, her left hand resting on a larger globe than on Obverse 5. Behind her is a plow (with long handles) and a larger sheaf of wheat than on Obverse 5. To the lower left are two bales of cotton, smaller than on Obverse 5. The sea is in the distance at the left. 13 stars around border, 1873 below. • Used with J-1299 to J-1306.
Obverse 7: "Barber's Indian Princess." Barber's Indian Princess design, inspired by James B. Longacre. Indian Princess seated, facing left, her right hand holding a pole atop which is a liberty cap, her left hand resting on a globe. Two small flags are behind, one with 13 stars. The sea is in the distance at the left, 13 stars around border, 1873 below. • Used with J-1307 to J-1314.
Obverse 8: "Bailly's Liberty Seated." J.A. Bailly's depiction of Liberty, seated, facing left. Her right hand holding a pole atop which is a liberty cap, her left hand resting on a globe inscribed LIBERTY, behind which is a wheat sheaf. In the front are two bales of cotton and a cotton plant. The design is such that to the viewer the figure of Liberty is overwhelmed by the items which are near her. 13 stars around border, 1873 below. • Used with J-1315 to J-1319.
Obverse 9: "Similar to regular trade dollar die, but with wider sea." Similar to the regular trade dollar die, but sea extends farther to the left and nearly touches dentils. Liberty seated on bales, sheaf of wheat to right. Her left hand holding a branch extended to the left (toward China), while her right hand is holding the top of a ribbon inscribed LIBERTY. Horizontally on base, IN GOD WE TRUST. Sea to left extends nearly to dentils, 13 stars around border, 1873 below. • Used with J-1322 to J-1326.
Obverse 10: "Regular trade dollar die." Liberty seated on bales, sheaf of wheat to right. Her left hand is holding a branch extended to the left (toward China), while her right hand is holding the top of a ribbon inscribed LIBERTY. Horizontally on base, IN GOD WE TRUST. Sea to left is distant from dentils, 13 stars around border, 1873 below.

Trade Dollar Reverse Dies of 1873

Reverse A: "TRADE DOLLAR inscription in laurel wreath." Large open laurel wreath enclosing TRADE DOLLAR / 420 GRAINS. 900 FINE. On ribbon below, IN GOD WE TRUST. At the top border, UNITED STATES OF AMERICA. First used in 1872 on J-1220. • Used with J-1276 to J-1280, J-1287, J-1304a to J-1306.
Reverse B: "Barber's Standing Eagle holding shield, motto in field above eagle." Barber's Standing Eagle with shield on which is a ribbon lettered IN GOD WE TRUST. In the field above the eagle's head is E PLURIBUS UNUM. In the field below the eagle, 420 GRAINS, 900 FINE. UNITED STATES OF AMERICA / TRADE DOLLAR around border. • Used with J-1281 to J-1284, J-1293 to J-1298, J-1299, J-1307.

Patterns of 1873

Reverse C: "Barber's Standing Eagle holding shield, motto on ribbon in eagle's beak." Barber's Standing Eagle with shield on which is a ribbon lettered IN GOD WE TRUST; scroll in beak inscribed E PLURIBUS UNUM. In the field below the eagle, 420 GRAINS, 900 FINE. UNITED STATES OF AMERICA / TRADE DOLLAR around border. First used in 1872 on J-1223. • Used with J-1285, J-1286, J-1293 to J-1298, J-1300 to J-1303, J-1308, J-1309.

Reverse D: "Small stocky eagle perched on shield, facing right." Small stocky eagle standing on a shield, wings raised and with beak extending to the right. Three arrows in the left talon and an olive branch in the right. E PLURIBUS UNUM above eagle. IN GOD WE TRUST on scroll below shield, below which is 420 GRAINS. 900 FINE. Around the border, UNITED STATES OF AMERICA / TRADE DOLLAR. • Used with J-1288, J-1315 to J-1319.

Reverse E: "Small eagle with raised wings, very wide ribbon above head and both wings." Small stocky eagle holding three arrows and an olive branch. Above on a very wide ribbon, E PLURIBUS UNUM. In the field below the eagle, 420 GRAINS 900 FINE and (on a ribbon) IN GOD WE TRUST. Around border, UNITED STATES OF AMERICA / TRADE DOLLAR. • Used with J-1304, J-1310 to J-1314.

Reverse F: "Small perched eagle with ribbon in beak; ribbon in nearly a closed loop." Small perched eagle holding in its beak a ribbon inscribed E PLURIBUS UNUM, three arrows and olive branch in talons. Below in field, 420 GRAINS, 900 FINE. Around border, UNITED STATES OF AMERICA / TRADE DOLLAR. • Used with J-1322 to J-1326.

Reverse G: "Regular trade dollar die." Eagle perched, holding three arrows and olive branch. E PLURIBUS on ribbon above. In field below, 420 GRAINS, 900 FINE. Around border, UNITED STATES OF AMERICA / TRADE DOLLAR. • Used on J-1327 to J-1330.

Beyond the fascinating series of trade dollar patterns are off-metal strikes from regular Proof dies and other varieties of interest, including a $5 pattern by Barber.

Collecting Perspective

Patterns of 1873 have formed the core of several fine collections in the past, most notably that of Harry X Boosel. Today, among the patterns of 1873, the trade dollars form the greatest interest to numismatists, especially in view of the interesting die variations. The authorship of all of the dies is not known. Examples from most dies are readily available. Quite a few have been cleaned, this being true not only of copper strikings (as expected), but also of silver impressions. In addition to collectible issues, there are some delicacies created for unknown numismatists, perhaps Mint Director Linderman himself, J-1288 and J-1289 being examples. Both feature a version of the double eagle obverse design, certainly not a consideration of the time for actual use on a trade dollar!

The off-metal die strikings from Proof dies range from the Indian Head cent to the double eagle and all have the Closed 3 numeral—more appropriately called Close 3—in which the knobs on the last digit are fairly close together (but not touching), at quick glance resembling an 8. Later in 1873, the "Open 3" was created (past the time when most pattern dies were made); this became the standard for new dies.

J-1255 to J-1257: 1873 Cent, Close 3

Struck from regular dies.

J-1256

Number	Metal	Edge	Rarity	Pop	T/A	Last Traded at Auction				60	63	65
						Firm	Date	Amount	Grade			
1255	C	PE	8	0	1	Stack's	6/1986	$1,100	PF63RD	$1,850	$3,750	$6,250
1256	Alu	PE	8	1	1	Superior	5/1992	$3,410	PF64	$3,250	$7,000	$12,000
1257	Nick	PE	8	1	1	Bolender	10/1955	$71	Unc	$10,000	$15,500	$26,000

J-1258 and J-1259: 1873 Two-Cent Piece, Close 3

Struck from regular dies.

J-1258

Number	Metal	Edge	Rarity	Pop	T/A	Last Traded at Auction				60	63	65
						Firm	Date	Amount	Grade			
1258	C	PE	8	0	1	Bolender	3/1955	$76	PF	N/A	N/A	N/A
1259	Alu	PE	H7	2	1	Doyle Galleries	12/1983	$1,200	MS63	$5,800	$10,000	$16,000

J-1260 to J-1261: 1873 Three-Cent Piece, Close 3

Struck from regular dies. J-1260a is struck on a broad planchet.

J-1261

Number	Metal	Edge	Rarity	Pop	T/A	Last Traded at Auction				60	63	65
						Firm	Date	Amount	Grade			
1260	C	PE	H7	3	1	ANR	7/2003	$10,925	PCGSPF65RD	$3,250	$7,000	$12,000
1260a	Nick	PE	8	1	0	N/A	N/A	N/A	N/A	N/A	N/A	N/A
1261	Alu	PE	H7	2	1	Bowers & Ruddy	3/1981	$1,600	GemPF	$2,250	$4,500	$8,250

J-1262 and J-1263: 1873 Trime, Close 3

Struck from regular dies.

J-1262

Number	Metal	Edge	Rarity	Pop	T/A	Last Traded at Auction				60	63	65
						Firm	Date	Amount	Grade			
1262	C	PE	H7	3	2	Heritage	7/2002	$3,910	NGCPF62RB	$4,200	$6,000	$11,500
1263	Alu	PE	H7	4	2	ANR	7/2003	$14,950	PCGSPF66	$5,000	$8,500	$14,000

J-1264 and J-1265: 1873 Five-Cent Piece, Close 3

Struck from regular dies.

J-1264

Number	Metal	Edge	Rarity	Pop	T/A	Last Traded at Auction				60	63	65
						Firm	Date	Amount	Grade			
1264	C	PE	H7	3	3	Bowers & Merena	1/2003	$7,130	PCGSPF64RB	$3,550	$7,000	$12,500
1265	Alu	PE	8	1	1	Bowers & Merena	3/1996	$4,400	PCGSPF64	$3,850	$8,000	$14,000

J-1266 and J-1267: 1873 Half Dime, Close 3

Struck from regular dies. This is the last year that half dimes were coined for circulation.[4]

J-1266

Number	Metal	Edge	Rarity	Pop	T/A	Last Traded at Auction				60	63	65
						Firm	Date	Amount	Grade			
1266	C	RE	H7	2	1	Bowers & Merena	4/1986	$632	PF	$2,900	$5,150	$9,500
1267	Alu	RE	8	2	1	Bowers & Merena	4/1986	$797	PF	$3,200	$5,800	$11,000

J-1268 and J-1269: 1873 Dime, Close 3, No Arrows at Date

Struck from regular dies.

J-1269

Number	Metal	Edge	Rarity	Pop	T/A	Last Traded at Auction				60	63	65
						Firm	Date	Amount	Grade			
1268	C	RE	H7	2	3	Superior	9/1998	$4,140	PCGSPF65RD	$2,900	$5,800	$11,000
1269	Alu	RE	8	2	1	Bowers & Merena	3/1996	$3,520	PF64	$3,850	$6,400	$11,500

Patterns of 1873

J-1270 and J-1271:
1873 Quarter Dollar, Close 3,
No Arrows at Date

Struck from regular dies.

J-1270

Number	Metal	Edge	Rarity	Pop	T/A	Last Traded at Auction				60	63	65
						Firm	Date	Amount	Grade			
1270	C	RE	H7	3	6	Heritage	11/2003	$8,050	NGCPF64BN	$3,000	$5,400	$9,000
1271	Alu	RE	8	2	1	Early American History Auctions	4/2003	$5,750	PF64	$4,500	$8,500	$15,000

J-1272 and J-1273:
1873 Half Dollar, Close 3,
No Arrows at Date

Struck from regular dies.

J-1272

Number	Metal	Edge	Rarity	Pop	T/A	Last Traded at Auction				60	63	65
						Firm	Date	Amount	Grade			
1272	C	RE	H7	3	4	Superior	10/2001	$6,325	NGCPF66RB	$4,500	$6,250	$11,000
1273	Alu	RE	H7	6	2	Superior	1/2003	$9,775	PCGS65	$4,500	$6,250	$11,000

J-1274 and J-1275:
1873 Silver Dollar,
Close 3

Struck from regular dies. This is the last year that Liberty Seated silver dollars were struck.

J-1274

Number	Metal	Edge	Rarity	Pop	T/A	Last Traded at Auction				60	63	65
						Firm	Date	Amount	Grade			
1274	C	RE	L7	6	4	Ira & Larry Goldberg	2/2000	$12,650	PCGSPF65RB	$4,200	$7,000	$12,500
1275	Alu	RE	8	1	1	Superior	6/1977	$1,250	PF	$10,000	$15,000	$26,000

J-1276 to J-1280:
1873 Trade Dollar
Dies 1-A

Both dies by William Barber.

Obverse: Coronet Head facing left.
Reverse: TRADE DOLLAR inscription in laurel wreath.

J-1276

Number	Metal	Edge	Rarity	Pop	T/A	Last Traded at Auction				60	63	65
						Firm	Date	Amount	Grade			
1276	Silv	RE	4	53	45	Heritage	6/2005	$2,760	NGCPF60	$2,850	$5,000	$9,500
1277	Silv	PE	L7	9	5	Superior	8/2002	$2,070	NGCPF60	$3,500	$6,400	$11,500
1278	C	RE	L7	6	6	Heritage	11/2004	$7,188	PCGSPF64BN	$4,200	$8,000	$15,500
1279	Alu	RE	8	0	1	Bowers & Ruddy	3/1981	$3,600	PF65	$12,000	$21,000	$42,500
1280	WM	PE	8	0	1	Bowers & Ruddy	7/1981	$1,400	PF65	$11,000	$19,500	$39,000

J-1281 to J-1284:
1873 Trade Dollar
Dies 2-B

Obverse: Bailly Head facing left.
Reverse: Barber's Standing Eagle holding shield, motto in field above eagle.

J-1281

Number	Metal	Edge	Rarity	Pop	T/A	Last Traded at Auction				60	63	65
						Firm	Date	Amount	Grade			
1281	Silv	RE	4	62	43	Heritage	6/2005	$4,888	PCGSPF62	$2,500	$4,750	$9,000
1282	Silv	PE	H7	2	4	Heritage	5/2003	$4,140	NGCPFImpCld	$4,200	$8,000	$15,500
1283	C	RE	L7	7	5	Superior	5/2003	$13,225	NGCPF66RB	$4,200	$8,000	$15,500
1284	Alu	RE	8	0	1	Kagin's	1/1975	$900	PF	$11,500	$21,500	$42,500

J-1285 and J-1286:
1873 Trade Dollar
Dies 2-C

The aluminum piece (J-1286) might actually be unique.

Obverse: Bailly Head facing left.
Reverse: Barber's Standing Eagle holding shield, motto on ribbon in eagle's beak.

J-1285

Number	Metal	Edge	Rarity	Pop	T/A	Last Traded at Auction				60	63	65
						Firm	Date	Amount	Grade			
1285	C	RE	8	2	3	Bowers & Merena	5/1999	$6,325	PCGSPF62BN	$7,150	$13,000	$22,500
1286	Alu	RE	8	0	1	Kreisberg-Schulman	2/1960	$110	PF	$11,500	$21,500	$42,500

J-1287:
1873 Trade Dollar
Dies 3-A

Obverse: Coronet Head facing right.
Reverse: TRADE DOLLAR inscription in laurel wreath.

J-1287

Number	Metal	Edge	Rarity	Pop	T/A	Last Traded at Auction				60	63	65
						Firm	Date	Amount	Grade			
1287	WM	PE	8	1	2	Bowers & Merena	11/1995	$9,625	PCGSPF64	N/A	$26,000	$39,000

J-1288:
1873 Trade Dollar
Dies 4-D

Obverse: Double Eagle Head.
Reverse: Small stocky eagle perched on shield, facing right.

J-1288

Number	Metal	Edge	Rarity	Pop	T/A	Last Traded at Auction				60	63	65
						Firm	Date	Amount	Grade			
1288	C	RE	8	0	1	Paramount	8/1972	$700	PF	$11,500	$21,500	$42,500

J-1289:
1873 Trade Dollar
Dies 4-B

Obverse: Double Eagle Head.
Reverse: Barber's Standing Eagle holding shield, motto in field above eagle.

J-1289

Number	Metal	Edge	Rarity	Pop	T/A	Last Traded at Auction				60	63	65
						Firm	Date	Amount	Grade			
1289	C	RE	8	1	1	Bowers & Merena	5/1999	$9,775	PCGSPF60RB	$20,000	N/A	N/A

J-1290 to J-1292:
1873 Trade Dollar
Dies 5-B

Obverse: Liberty seated on globe, short plow handles.
Reverse: Barber's Standing Eagle holding shield, motto in field above eagle.

J-1290

Number	Metal	Edge	Rarity	Pop	T/A	Last Traded at Auction				60	63	65
						Firm	Date	Amount	Grade			
1290	Silv	RE	U	0	0	N/A	N/A	N/A	N/A	$12,000	$22,500	$45,000
1291	Silv	PE	U	0	0	N/A	N/A	N/A	N/A	$12,000	$22,500	$45,000
1292	WM	PE	8	0	1	Bowers & Ruddy	3/1981	$1,800	PF	$10,000	$20,000	$39,000

J-1293 to J-1298:
1873 Trade Dollar
Dies 5-C

Obverse: Liberty seated on globe, short plow handles.
Reverse: Barber's Standing Eagle holding shield, motto on ribbon in eagle's beak.

J-1293

Number	Metal	Edge	Rarity	Pop	T/A	Last Traded at Auction				60	63	65
						Firm	Date	Amount	Grade			
1293	Silv	RE	4	52	45	Heritage	5/2005	$4,600	NGCPF64	$2,800	$4,650	$9,500
1294	Silv	PE	H7	4	1	Heritage	2/1999	$4,600	NGCPF62	$5,800	$11,000	$19,000
1295	C	RE	L7	2	2	ANR	10/2004	$20,700	PCGSPF65RB	$6,250	$12,500	$22,500
1296	C	PE	–	0	0	N/A	N/A	N/A	N/A	Unconf	Unconf	Unconf
1297	Alu	RE	8	0	0	N/A	N/A	N/A	N/A	$11,500	$21,500	$42,500
1298	WM	PE	8	1	1	Heritage	1/2002	$9,488	PCGSPF63	$11,000	$20,000	N/A

J-1299: 1873 Trade Dollar
Dies 6-B

Obverse: Liberty seated on globe, long plow handles.
Reverse: Barber's Standing Eagle holding shield, motto in field above eagle.

J-1299

Number	Metal	Edge	Rarity	Pop	T/A	Last Traded at Auction				60	63	65
						Firm	Date	Amount	Grade			
1299	WM	PE	H7	2	1	Bowers & Merena	5/1999	$5,520	PCGSPF64	$7,000	$15,000	$22,500

Patterns of 1873

J-1300 to J-1303:
1873 Trade Dollar
Dies 6-C

Obverse: Liberty seated on globe, long plow handles.
Reverse: Barber's Standing Eagle holding shield, motto on ribbon in eagle's beak.

J-1303

Number	Metal	Edge	Rarity	Pop	T/A	Last Traded at Auction				60	63	65
						Firm	Date	Amount	Grade			
1300	Silv	RE	H7	5	6	ANR	9/2003	$19,550	NGCPF66	$5,500	$11,000	$19,000
1301	C	RE	8	1	2	Heritage	9/2002	$16,675	PCGSPF64RB	$12,000	$21,000	$36,000
1302	C	PE	–	0	0	N/A	N/A	N/A	N/A	Unconf	Unconf	Unconf
1303	Alu	RE	8	3	1	Heritage	5/2003	$27,600	PCGSPF64	$18,000	$32,000	$50,000

J-1304:
1873 Trade Dollar
Dies 6-E

Obverse: Liberty seated on globe, long plow handles.
Reverse: Small eagle with raised wings, very wide ribbon above head and both wings.

J-1304

Number	Metal	Edge	Rarity	Pop	T/A	Last Traded at Auction				60	63	65
						Firm	Date	Amount	Grade			
1304	WM	PE	8	2	2	ANR	9/2003	$25,300	NGCPF64	$11,000	$22,000	$32,000

J-1304a to J-1306:
1873 Trade Dollar
Dies 6-A

Obverse: Liberty seated on globe, long plow handles.
Reverse: TRADE DOLLAR inscription in laurel wreath.

J-1304a

Number	Metal	Edge	Rarity	Pop	T/A	Last Traded at Auction				60	63	65
						Firm	Date	Amount	Grade			
1304a	Silv	RE	U	0	0	N/A	N/A	N/A	N/A	N/A	N/A	N/A
1305	C	RE	8	0	0	N/A	N/A	N/A	N/A	$10,000	$20,000	$39,000
1306	WM	PE	8	0	1	Bowers & Ruddy	3/1981	$2,100	PF	$12,000	$22,500	$45,000

J-1307:
1873 Trade Dollar
Dies 7-B

Obverse: Barber's Indian Princess.
Reverse: Barber's Standing Eagle holding shield, motto in field above eagle.

J-1307

Number	Metal	Edge	Rarity	Pop	T/A	Last Traded at Auction				60	63	65
						Firm	Date	Amount	Grade			
1307	WM	PE	U	0	1	Bowers & Ruddy	3/1981	$1,300	EF	$12,000	$22,500	$45,000

J-1308 and J-1309:
1873 Trade Dollar
Dies 7-C

Earlier listings of J-1326a and J-1326b were incorrect descriptions of J-1308 and J-1309.

Obverse: Barber's Indian Princess.
Reverse: Barber's Standing Eagle holding shield, motto on ribbon in eagle's beak.

J-1308

Number	Metal	Edge	Rarity	Pop	T/A	Last Traded at Auction				60	63	65
						Firm	Date	Amount	Grade			
1308	Silv	RE	U	1	0	N/A	N/A	N/A	N/A	N/A	$32,500	$52,000
1309	WM	PE	8	1	1	Bowers & Merena	5/1999	$2,415	PCGSPF62	$13,000	$20,000	N/A

J-1310 to J-1314:
1873 Trade Dollar
Dies 7-E

Obverse: Barber's Indian Princess.
Reverse: Small eagle with raised wings, very wide ribbon above head and both wings.

J-1310

Number	Metal	Edge	Rarity	Pop	T/A	Last Traded at Auction				60	63	65
						Firm	Date	Amount	Grade			
1310	Silv	RE	4	62	43	Heritage	6/2005	$4,888	NGCPF62	$3,300	$5,500	$10,500
1311	Silv	PE	H7	2	1	Superior	2/2003	$24,150	NGCPF65	$9,000	$16,000	$30,000
1312	C	RE	L7	3	3	ANR	8/2004	$15,396	PCGSPF64RD	$6,000	$12,500	$24,000
1313	Alu	RE	8	0	0	N/A	N/A	N/A	N/A	$12,000	$21,500	$42,500
1314	WM	PE	8	1	1	Heritage	11/2003	$25,300	PCGSPF63	$11,000	$28,000	$45,000

Patterns of 1873

J-1315 to J-1319:
1873 Trade Dollar
Dies 8-D

Obverse: Bailly's Liberty Seated.
Reverse: Small stocky eagle perched on shield, facing right.

J-1315

Number	Metal	Edge	Rarity	Pop	T/A	Firm	Date	Amount	Grade	60	63	65
						Last Traded at Auction						
1315	Silv	RE	4	63	45	Stack's	1/2005	$3,565	ChPF	$2,500	$4,500	$9,000
1316	Silv	PE	H7	3	2	Superior	5/1994	$4,620	PF63	$6,000	$11,000	$19,000
1317	C	RE	L7	8	3	Heritage	11/2003	$13,225	NGCPF65BN	$4,800	$8,000	$13,500
1318	Alu	RE	8	0	1	Kagin's	1/1975	$975	PF	$11,700	$21,500	$42,500
1319	WM	PE	8	1	1	Superior	2/1991	$3,300	NGCPF63	$10,000	$20,000	$39,000

J-1320 and J-1321:
Undated Trade Dollar

Now listed under 1876 J-1475a and J-1475b.

J-1322 to J-1326:
1873 Trade Dollar
Dies 9-F

Obverse: Similar to regular trade dollar die, but with wider sea.
Reverse: Small perched eagle with ribbon in beak; ribbon in nearly a closed loop.

J-1322

Number	Metal	Edge	Rarity	Pop	T/A	Firm	Date	Amount	Grade	60	63	65
						Last Traded at Auction						
1322	Silv	RE	4	63	35	Heritage	5/2005	$2,588	PCGSPF60	$2,500	$4,250	$9,000
1323	Silv	PE	H7	2	1	Heritage	1/2000	$2,990	PCGSPF65	$8,000	$13,500	$22,000
1324	C	RE	L7	8	5	ANR	9/2003	$23,000	NGCPF65RD	$6,250	$12,500	$25,000
1325	Alu	RE	8	0	1	Bowers & Ruddy	3/1981	$5,500	GemPF	$11,500	$21,500	$42,500
1326	WM	PE	8	0	1	Bowers & Ruddy	10/1977	$800	PF	$10,000	$20,000	$39,000

J-1327 to J-1330: 1873
Trade Dollar, Close 3
Dies 10-G

Struck from regular dies. Two of the copper examples (J-1327) are in a Wyoming collection. About a half dozen of the white metal (J-1329) and tin (J-1330) pieces are known, including one in the Connecticut State Library and two in the aforementioned Wyoming collection.

J-1327

Number	Metal	Edge	Rarity	Pop	T/A	Firm	Date	Amount	Grade	60	63	65
						Last Traded at Auction						
1327	C	RE	H7	0	1	Bowers & Merena	5/1993	$4,290	PF60BN	$8,500	$15,500	$26,000
1328	Alu	RE	8	0	1	Bolender	3/1955	$105	PF	$11,500	$21,500	$32,500
1329	WM	RE	H7	2	2	Bowers & Merena	9/1994	$1,210	PF55	$9,500	$16,000	$25,000
1330	Tin	RE	8	0	0	N/A	N/A	N/A	N/A	$9,000	$17,500	$32,500

J-1331 and J-1332: 1873
Gold Dollar, Close 3

Struck from regular dies.

J-1332

Number	Metal	Edge	Rarity	Pop	T/A	Firm	Date	Amount	Grade	60	63	65
						Last Traded at Auction						
1331	C	RE	H7	3	5	ANR	7/2003	$9,085	PCGSPF64BN	$4,000	$7,000	$12,500
1332	Alu	RE	8	1	2	Bowers & Merena	11/2001	$11,500	PCGSPF65	$6,500	$13,000	$22,500

J-1333 and J-1334: 1873
$2.50, Close 3

Struck from regular dies.

J-1334

Number	Metal	Edge	Rarity	Pop	T/A	Firm	Date	Amount	Grade	60	63	65
						Last Traded at Auction						
1333	C	RE	H7	2	2	Superior	1/2003	$6,038	PCGSPF64BN	$4,500	$8,000	$15,000
1334	Alu	RE	8	2	1	Bowers & Merena	5/1999	$3,335	PCGSPF65	$4,500	$9,000	$18,000

J-1335 and J-1336: 1873
$3, Close 3

Struck from regular dies.

J-1335

Number	Metal	Edge	Rarity	Pop	T/A	Firm	Date	Amount	Grade	60	63	65
						Last Traded at Auction						
1335	C	RE	H7	2	2	Bowers & Merena	11/2001	$5,750	PCGSPF63BN	$6,500	$11,500	$21,000
1336	Alu	RE	8	2	2	Bowers & Merena	5/1999	$5,530	PCGSPF64	$7,000	$12,500	$22,500

Patterns of 1873

J-1337 to J-1339:
1873 $5

Obverse: Design by William Barber. Liberty Head facing right. LIBERTY on coronet with Y at the front of the coronet (similar in general concept but differently done than J-1287 trade dollar).
Reverse: Barber's Standing Eagle and shield die used in 1872 J-1240.

J-1338

| Number | Metal | Edge | Rarity | Pop | T/A | Last Traded at Auction | | | | 60 | 63 | 65 |
						Firm	Date	Amount	Grade			
1337	Gold	RE	8	0	1	Sotheby's	2/1954	$200	EF	N/A	N/A	$375,000
1338	C	RE	H7	4	4	ANR	7/2003	$16,100	NGCPF64	$8,000	$15,000	$25,000
1339	Alu	RE	8	1	1	Stack's	6/1983	$3,750	ChPF	$11,000	$20,000	$35,000

J-1340 and J-1341:
1873 $5, Close 3

Struck from regular dies.

J-1340

| Number | Metal | Edge | Rarity | Pop | T/A | Last Traded at Auction | | | | 60 | 63 | 65 |
						Firm	Date	Amount	Grade			
1340	C	RE	H7	1	2	Bowers & Merena	11/2001	$5,290	NGCPF63BN	$6,000	$11,000	$22,000
1341	Alu	RE	8	2	2	Bowers & Merena	5/1999	$4,600	PCGSPF64	$7,000	$15,000	$26,000

J-1342 and J-1343:
1873 $10, Close 3

Struck from regular dies.

J-1343

| Number | Metal | Edge | Rarity | Pop | T/A | Last Traded at Auction | | | | 60 | 63 | 65 |
						Firm	Date	Amount	Grade			
1342	C	RE	8	2	2	Bowers & Merena	11/2001	$7,188	PCGSPF64RB	$7,000	$15,000	$26,000
1343	Alu	RE	8	2	2	Ira & Larry Goldberg	2/2000	$7,187	PCGSPF65	$7,000	$15,000	$26,000

J-1344 and J-1345:
1873 $20, Close 3

Struck from regular dies.

J-1345

| Number | Metal | Edge | Rarity | Pop | T/A | Last Traded at Auction | | | | 60 | 63 | 65 |
						Firm	Date	Amount	Grade			
1344	C	RE	H7	2	2	Bowers & Merena	11/2001	$13,225	NGCPF65RB	$10,000	$17,500	$35,000
1345	Alu	RE	8	1	1	Bowers & Merena	5/1999	$8,625	PCGSPF66	$10,000	$17,500	$35,000

History and Overview

Patterns of the year 1874 are limited to a few dozen varieties. The most important are those associated with a new denomination, the twenty-cent piece. For these J.A. Bailly's obverse design was borrowed from his motif created for certain trade dollars of 1873 (J-1315 to J-1319). Whether there was serious consideration for this motif for regular circulation is not known today. There were two reverse dies made—one with a standing eagle somewhat similar to that used on the regular-issue trade dollar, and the other with the denomination 20 CENTS at the center. As to the utility of the twenty-cent denomination, the proposal was hardly new and had been proposed to the Senate as early as 1803, when Mr. Tracey proposed "double dismes of standard silver."

Dana Bickford, a world traveler and indefatigable entrepreneur, proposed to the Mint that an international $10 gold coin be created that could be spent easily in different countries. He thought the value in metal should be given on the back so that such pieces could be evaluated as to intrinsic worth by any foreign bank, and, at the same time, the exchange rate in dollars, British sterling, German marks, Swedish kronen, Dutch gulden, and French francs would be plainly stated. Unfortunately, exchange rates seldom remained constant for very long, often changing within a matter of weeks or months, and such a coin would be obsolete from virtually the time it was issued.

Beyond various patterns for the twenty-cent coin and the Bickford $10, off-metal strikes from regular Proof dies were produced, these in very limited quantities and apparently distributed to friends and associates of Mint insiders.

Collecting Perspective

The dedicated pattern specialist will surely want to obtain examples of the two die combinations made for twenty-cent pieces, those for J-1354 to J-1356 and J-1357 and J-1358. These are quite elusive, but in time there is a good chance of obtaining them. The Bickford $10 piece is virtually impossible to obtain in gold, as just two are known, but copper pieces appear on the market with some regularity, always playing to enthusiastic demand. Impressions in other metals are significantly more rare.[1]

The off-metal strikings from the Indian cent to the double eagle are of everlasting popularity due to their novelty—what a surprise it would be for an Indian cent specialist to display an 1874 in silver-colored aluminum! Such pieces can be located only at widely spaced intervals, and while it would be virtually impossible to form a full set, scattered examples can be acquired with a bit of luck.

J-1346 to J-1347: 1874 Cent

Trial piece struck from regular dies. J-1346a might be a Mint error.

J-1347

Number	Metal	Edge	Rarity	Pop	T/A	Last Traded at Auction				60	63	65
						Firm	Date	Amount	Grade			
1346	C	PE	8	0	0	N/A	N/A	N/A	N/A	$1,850	$3,750	$6,250
1346a	Nick	PE	8	0	1	Stack's	1/1987	$963	AU	N/A	N/A	N/A
1347	Alu	PE	H7	1	1	Heritage	3/2003	$16,100	PCGSPF64	$9,500	$15,000	$25,000

J-1348 and J-1349: 1874 Three-Cent Piece

Trial piece struck from regular dies.

J-1348

Number	Metal	Edge	Rarity	Pop	T/A	Last Traded at Auction				60	63	65
						Firm	Date	Amount	Grade			
1348	C	PE	8	1	1	Bowers & Merena	6/1991	$2,310	PF65BN	$3,850	$7,500	$14,000
1349	Alu	PE	8	2	1	B. Max Mehl	2/1944	$16	PF	$2,600	$5,150	$9,500

J-1350 and J-1351: 1874 Five-Cent Piece

Trial piece struck from regular dies.

J-1350

Number	Metal	Edge	Rarity	Pop	T/A	Last Traded at Auction				60	63	65
						Firm	Date	Amount	Grade			
1350	C	PE	8	1	1	Stack's	10/1997	$4,620	PFBN	$4,250	$8,500	$16,500
1351	Alu	PE	8	2	1	B. Max Mehl	2/1944	$23	PF	$4,250	$8,250	$15,500

Patterns of 1874

J-1352 and J-1353:
1874 Dime

Trial piece struck from regular dies.

J-1353

| Number | Metal | Edge | Rarity | Pop | T/A | Last Traded at Auction | | | | 60 | 63 | 65 |
						Firm	Date	Amount	Grade			
1352	C	RE	H7	2	2	Ira & Larry Goldberg	1/2004	$4,715	PCGSPF62RD	$2,900	$5,800	$11,000
1353	Alu	RE	8	4	1	Superior	5/2003	$9,775	PCGSPF65	$3,200	$5,800	$12,500

J-1354 to J-1356a:
1874 Twenty-Cent Piece

Obverse: J.A. Bailly's design adopted from the 1873 pattern trade dollar, J-1315. Liberty seated, facing left, stars around, date below.
Reverse: Similar to the die adopted in 1875, but with minor differences (the terminal leaves of the olive branch overlap).

J-1355

| Number | Metal | Edge | Rarity | Pop | T/A | Last Traded at Auction | | | | 60 | 63 | 65 |
						Firm	Date	Amount	Grade			
1354	Silv	PE	L7	7	7	Stack's	10/2003	$5,463	VChPF	$2,900	$5,150	$10,500
1355	C	PE	L6	17	16	ANR	3/2005	$6,900	NGCPF64BN	$2,550	$5,000	$9,000
1355a	Nick	PE	U	0	0	N/A	N/A	N/A	N/A	$9,000	$16,000	$26,000
1356	Alu	PE	H7	3	5	Heritage	11/2003	$10,925	PCGSPF64	$4,200	$7,500	$14,000

J-1357 and J-1358:
1874 Twenty-Cent Piece

Obverse: Bailly's design, same as preceding.
Reverse: Open wreath enclosing 20 CENTS with UNITED STATES OF AMERICA at border.

J-1358

| Number | Metal | Edge | Rarity | Pop | T/A | Last Traded at Auction | | | | 60 | 63 | 65 |
						Firm	Date	Amount	Grade			
1357	Silv	PE	U	1	0	N/A	N/A	N/A	N/A	N/A	N/A	N/A
1358	Nick	PE	H7	4	2	Bowers & Merena	5/1999	$6,900	PCGSPF66	$3,500	$6,000	$12,500

J-1359 and J-1360:
1874 Quarter Dollar

Trial piece struck from regular dies.

J-1359

| Number | Metal | Edge | Rarity | Pop | T/A | Last Traded at Auction | | | | 60 | 63 | 65 |
						Firm	Date	Amount	Grade			
1359	C	RE	8	0	1	Heritage	12/1988	$1,500	PF	$7,800	$13,000	$22,500
1360	Alu	RE	8	3	1	Bowers & Ruddy	2/1978	$575	ChPF	$3,250	$5,200	$10,000

J-1361 and J-1362:
1874 Half Dollar

Trial piece struck from regular dies.

J-1361

Number	Metal	Edge	Rarity	Pop	T/A	Last Traded at Auction				60	63	65
						Firm	Date	Amount	Grade			
1361	C	RE	8	2	2	Heritage	9/1997	$3,795	PCGSPF63RB	$4,250	$8,000	$13,000
1362	Alu	RE	8	1	1	Bowers & Merena	6/1996	$4,400	PF64	$10,000	$16,000	$24,000

J-1363 and J-1364:
1874 Trade Dollar

Trial piece struck from regular dies. At least four examples are known of the copper pattern (J-1363), including an example in the Connecticut State Library and one in a Wyoming collection. Only two aluminum examples (J-1364) are confirmed.

J-1363

Number	Metal	Edge	Rarity	Pop	T/A	Last Traded at Auction				60	63	65
						Firm	Date	Amount	Grade			
1363	C	RE	H7	2	2	ANR	12/2003	$25,300	PCGSPF64RB	$10,000	$18,000	$30,000
1364	Alu	RE	8	2	1	Bowers & Merena	5/1992	$4,290	PF63	$8,450	$15,000	$26,000

J-1365 and J-1366:
1874 Gold Dollar

Trial piece struck from regular dies.

J-1366

Number	Metal	Edge	Rarity	Pop	T/A	Last Traded at Auction				60	63	65
						Firm	Date	Amount	Grade			
1365	C	RE	8	1	1	Bowers & Merena	5/1999	$7,475	PCGSPF65BN	$6,500	$13,000	$22,500
1366	Alu	RE	8	0	1	NERCG	7/1979	$1,050	PF63	$8,500	$15,000	$26,000

J-1367 and J-1368:
1874 $2.50

Trial piece struck from regular dies.

J-1368

Number	Metal	Edge	Rarity	Pop	T/A	Last Traded at Auction				60	63	65
						Firm	Date	Amount	Grade			
1367	C	RE	8	1	1	MARCA	1/1987	$1,300	PF	$7,500	$13,000	$22,500
1368	Alu	RE	8	2	1	Bowers & Ruddy	10/1977	$525	ChPF	$4,500	$9,000	$18,000

Patterns of 1874

J-1369 and J-1370: 1874 $3

Trial piece struck from regular dies.

J-1369

Number	Metal	Edge	Rarity	Pop	T/A	Last Traded at Auction				60	63	65
						Firm	Date	Amount	Grade			
1369	C	RE	8	1	1	Bowers & Ruddy	9/1975	$1,050	ChPF	$6,400	$12,000	$20,500
1370	Alu	RE	H7	4	1	Bowers & Merena	5/1999	$6,325	PCGSPF64	$5,150	$9,000	$18,000

J-1371 and J-1372: 1874 $5

Trial piece struck from regular dies.

J-1372

Number	Metal	Edge	Rarity	Pop	T/A	Last Traded at Auction				60	63	65
						Firm	Date	Amount	Grade			
1371	C	RE	8	2	2	Bowers & Merena	5/1999	$4,830	PCGSPF64RB	$5,550	$10,000	$20,000
1372	Alu	RE	8	3	1	Stack's	1/2003	$14,663	ChPF	$5,550	$10,800	$20,000

J-1373 to J-1378: 1874 Bickford International $10

Obverse: Liberty head facing left, tiara inscribed LIBERTY and with six stars above. Across the neck is an olive branch with a ribbon at the back. UNITED STATES OF AMERICA / 1874 around border

Reverse: Inscription giving at the center the details of the coin: 16.72 / GRAMS / 900 FINE / UBIQUE, the last word meaning ubiquitous, or existing everywhere. Around, seven cartouches or areas framed with a cord design, enclosing inscriptions (from top, clockwise) DOLLARS 10; STERLING £2.1.1; MARKEN 41.99; KRONEN 37.31; GULDEN 20.73; FRANCS 51.81.

J-1373

Number	Metal	Edge	Rarity	Pop	T/A	Last Traded at Auction				60	63	65
						Firm	Date	Amount	Grade			
1373	Gold	RE	8	3	2	Stack's	10/2003	$276,000	GemPF	N/A	$275,000	$425,000
1374	C	RE	L6	9	8	Stack's	3/1999	$10,925	PFBN	$5,000	$9,000	$15,000
1375	C	PE	L7	4	4	Stack's	7/2003	$7,763	PFBN	$8,000	$13,500	$25,000
1376	Alu	RE	8	1	1	Akers	10/1997	$30,800	ChPF	$15,000	$26,000	$45,500
1377	Nick	RE	H7	3	3	Heritage	11/2003	$14,950	PCGSPF64	$7,000	$11,500	$20,000
1378	Nick	PE	8	0	1	Kreisberg-Schulman	2/1960	$450	PF	$11,000	$20,000	$35,000

J-1379 and J-1380: 1874 $10

Trial piece struck from regular dies.

J-1379

Number	Metal	Edge	Rarity	Pop	T/A	Last Traded at Auction				60	63	65
						Firm	Date	Amount	Grade			
1379	C	RE	8	2	1	Bowers & Merena	5/1999	$5,520	PCGSPF65BN	$7,000	$14,000	$25,000
1380	Alu	RE	8	2	1	RARCOA/Akers	8/1991	$4,250	PF64	$8,000	$15,000	$26,000

J-1381 and J-1382: 1874 $20

Trial piece struck from regular dies.

J-1381

Number	Metal	Edge	Rarity	Pop	T/A	Last Traded at Auction				60	63	65
						Firm	Date	Amount	Grade			
1381	C	RE	8	1	1	Heritage	8/2001	$6,613	PCGSPF60RB	$10,000	$17,500	$35,000
1382	Alu	RE	8	1	1	Stack's	8/1976	$1,700	PF	$10,000	$17,500	$35,000

Patterns of 1875

History and Overview

The year 1875 hosts a potpourri of pattern issues, some with true pattern intent (certain of the twenty-cent pieces may be in this category) and others created as numismatic delicacies, the latter including illogical varieties and mulings. No doubt, Mint Director Henry R. Linderman was among the recipients of these delicacies. All of the illogical combinations as well as off-metal strikings from regular Proof dies were made in secrecy, and the existence of most was not known until years later.

Some twenty-cent pieces and trade dollar patterns show a ship at sea in the distance, its auxiliary sails billowing forward, while smoke from its stack drifts to the rear—in defiance of the laws of physics, creating one of the most egregious gaffes in American coinage.

William Barber designed $5 and $10 pieces this year, with the head of Liberty facing right, essentially the same motif used elsewhere with modifications (such as on the twenty-cent piece, J-1392), combined in each instance with a reverse die featuring an eagle similar to that on the trade dollar.

Collecting Perspective

Most of the twenty-cent patterns of this year were made in quantities sufficient to be obtained today with some patience. The demand for the twenty-cent denominations is intense, not only from serious pattern collectors but also from others attracted to the regular (circulation strike) coins that were minted in quantity only in this year.[2]

The patterns of the trade dollar obverse range from rare to virtually impossible to collect, although it is in the realm of feasibility to acquire at least one example showing the obverse die. Beyond that, luck is required.

The 1875 pattern $5 and $10 pieces by Barber are virtually unobtainable in gold, but appear occasionally in copper and aluminum and are very rare. Off-metal strikings of different denominations, from the cent to the double eagle, are rare and seldom encountered.

J-1383 and J-1384: 1875 Cent

Trial piece struck from regular dies.

J-1384

Number	Metal	Edge	Rarity	Pop	T/A	Last Traded at Auction				60	63	65
						Firm	Date	Amount	Grade			
1383	C	PE	8	0	1	NERCG	3/1983	$350	PF63	$1,850	$3,750	$6,250
1384	Alu	PE	8	0	1	Doyle Galleries	12/1983	$950	MS63	$11,100	$19,500	$32,500

J-1385 and J-1386: 1875 Three-Cent Piece

Trial piece struck from regular dies.

J-1385

Number	Metal	Edge	Rarity	Pop	T/A	Last Traded at Auction				60	63	65
						Firm	Date	Amount	Grade			
1385	C	PE	H7	2	1	Superior	6/1977	$575	PF	$2,250	$4,500	$8,350
1386	Alu	PE	8	2	1	Superior	6/1977	$325	BrPF	$2,600	$5,150	$9,600

Patterns of 1875

J-1387 and J-1388: 1875 Five-Cent Piece

Trial piece struck from regular dies.

J-1387

Number	Metal	Edge	Rarity	Pop	T/A	Last Traded at Auction				60	63	65
						Firm	Date	Amount	Grade			
1387	C	PE	8	2	4	Bowers & Merena	7/2004	$13,800	PCGSPF65RD	$4,500	$8,250	$15,000
1388	Alu	PE	8	2	1	Bowers & Merena	1/1997	$6,875	PCGSPF65	$4,200	$7,050	$12,800

J-1390 and J-1391: 1875 Dime

Trial piece struck from regular dies.

J-1391

Number	Metal	Edge	Rarity	Pop	T/A	Last Traded at Auction				60	63	65
						Firm	Date	Amount	Grade			
1390	C	RE	8	2	1	Superior	6/1977	$290	PF	$2,900	$5,800	$10,900
1391	Alu	RE	8	2	1	Heritage	1/2000	$2,415	PCGSPF64	$3,850	$6,400	$11,600

J-1392 to J-1395: 1875 Twenty-Cent Piece

Obverse: Liberty head by William Barber, sometimes nick-named the Sailor Head, facing left, with coronet inscribed LIB-ERTY, hair tied back with ribbon.
Reverse: Spade-type shield with 20 incuse, rays above shield, two arrows and olive branch at lower border of shield. Around border, UNITED STATES OF AMERICA / CENTS.

J-1392

Number	Metal	Edge	Rarity	Pop	T/A	Last Traded at Auction				60	63	65
						Firm	Date	Amount	Grade			
1392	Silv	PE	L6	19	18	ANR	3/2004	$3,220	NGCPF62	$2,500	$4,750	$8,250
1393	C	PE	L7	7	8	Superior	7/2003	$6,210	PCGSPF64RB	$2,900	$5,900	$10,500
1394	Alu	PE	H7	2	3	Bowers & Merena	1/2005	$17,250	PCGSPF66	$4,900	$9,100	$16,500
1395	Nick	PE	H7	4	1	Bowers & Merena	8/1998	$5,060	PCGSPF65	$3,500	$6,100	$12,500

J-1396 to J-1398: 1875 Twenty-Cent Piece

Obverse: Liberty seated at the seashore, olive branch in right hand, left hand resting on globe inscribed LIBERTY. Two flags and a wheat sheaf behind her. A steamship in the distance with sails and smoke going in opposite directions.
Reverse: Open wreath enclosing 1/5 OF A DOLLAR. Around border, UNITED STATES OF AMERICA / TWENTY CENTS.

J-1396

Number	Metal	Edge	Rarity	Pop	T/A	Last Traded at Auction				60	63	65
						Firm	Date	Amount	Grade			
1396	Silv	PE	H7	5	4	David Lawrence RC	3/2005	$6,038	NGCPF65	$3,500	$6,000	$11,000
1397	C	PE	H7	4	6	ANR	7/2003	$9,200	PCGSPF64RB	$3,500	$7,250	$14,000
1398	Alu	PE	H7	2	4	ANR	8/2004	$12,219	PCGSPF64	$5,250	$10,000	$18,000

J-1399 to J-1402: 1875 Twenty-Cent Piece

Reverse die earlier used to strike J-1354 in 1874.

Obverse: Liberty seated at the seashore, as preceding, with illogical ship depiction.
Reverse: Similar to the die adopted 1875, but with minor differences (terminal leaves of the olive branch overlap).

J-1402

Number	Metal	Edge	Rarity	Pop	T/A	Last Traded at Auction				60	63	65
						Firm	Date	Amount	Grade			
1399	Silv	PE	L6	18	9	David Lawrence RC	3/2005	$10,063	NGCPF66CA	$2,550	$5,200	$10,000
1400	C	PE	L7	6	10	Heritage	1/2004	$12,650	PCGSPF66RB	$3,100	$5,500	$11,000
1401	Alu	PE	U	0	1	Krueger	2/1982	$900	AU	$9,000	$19,000	$35,000
1402	Nick	PE	8	3	2	Stack's	10/2003	$17,250	GemPF	$4,900	$9,000	$16,500

J-1403 to J-1406: 1875 Twenty-Cent Piece

Reverse die first used on J-1357 in 1874.

Obverse: Liberty seated at the seashore, as preceding, with illogical ship depiction.
Reverse: Open wreath enclosing 20 CENTS with UNITED STATES OF AMERICA around the border.

J-1406

Number	Metal	Edge	Rarity	Pop	T/A	Last Traded at Auction				60	63	65
						Firm	Date	Amount	Grade			
1403	Silv	PE	H6	10	9	ANR	12/2003	$5,060	NGCPF64	$2,700	$5,000	$9,250
1404	C	PE	H6	13	14	Heritage	9/2004	$6,038	PCGSPF66BN	$2,700	$4,750	$8,000
1405	Alu	PE	L7	5	6	Heritage	7/2003	$10,925	PCGSPF66	$3,100	$5,500	$11,000
1406	WM	PE	8	0	1	Stack's	2/1977	$850	PF	$6,200	$12,000	$21,000

J-1407 to J-1410: 1875 Twenty-Cent Piece

Obverse: Liberty seated, similar in appearance to the regular die, but with the date in smaller numerals, and with LIBERTY incuse in the shield, instead of raised as on circulation strikes.
Reverse: Open wreath enclosing 1/5 OF A DOLLAR. Around border, UNITED STATES OF AMERICA / TWENTY CENTS; die of J-1396.

J-1408

Number	Metal	Edge	Rarity	Pop	T/A	Last Traded at Auction				60	63	65
						Firm	Date	Amount	Grade			
1407	Silv	PE	L6	24	17	Heritage	11/2004	$4,370	PCGSPF64	$2,000	$3,850	$6,350
1408	C	PE	L7	10	11	Heritage	6/2004	$6,325	PCGSPF65BN	$2,900	$5,150	$9,000
1409	Alu	PE	U	0	0	N/A	N/A	N/A	N/A	$9,000	$19,000	$35,000
1410	Nick	PE	8	1	2	Stack's	10/2003	$25,300	GemPF	$7,000	$15,000	$26,000

J-1411 to J-1413: 1875 Twenty-Cent Piece

Obverse: Liberty seated, as preceding.
Reverse: Similar to the design adopted in 1875, but with minor differences (terminal leaves of the olive branch overlap).

J-1411

Number	Metal	Edge	Rarity	Pop	T/A	Last Traded at Auction				60	63	65
						Firm	Date	Amount	Grade			
1411	Silv	PE	L7	6	4	Bowers & Merena	9/1994	$2,860	PF63	$3,100	$5,500	$11,000
1412	C	PE	H6	10	10	Heritage	9/2002	$5,750	NGCPF65RB	$2,700	$5,000	$9,500
1413	Alu	PE	H7	3	1	Superior	2/1997	$4,620	PCGSPF63	$4,200	$7,600	$14,000

Patterns of 1875

J-1414 and J-1415:
1875 Twenty-Cent Piece

Struck from regular dies. On the regular die, the word LIBERTY is raised, rather than incuse, the only circulating Liberty Seated issue to have the word raised except for the 1836 Gobrecht dollar (J-60).

J-1414

Number	Metal	Edge	Rarity	Pop	T/A	Last Traded at Auction				60	63	65
						Firm	Date	Amount	Grade			
1414	C	RE	H7	5	7	Heritage	1/2004	$9,200	PCGSPF64RB	$3,500	$6,000	$12,500
1415	Alu	RE	8	0	1	Superior	6/1977	$950	PF	$6,000	$12,000	$21,000

J-1416 and J-1417:
1875 Quarter Dollar

Trial piece struck from regular dies.

J-1416

Number	Metal	Edge	Rarity	Pop	T/A	Last Traded at Auction				60	63	65
						Firm	Date	Amount	Grade			
1416	C	RE	H7	1	1	RARCOA	7/1988	$2,860	PF	$6,200	$12,000	$20,000
1417	Alu	RE	8	0	1	Bowers & Ruddy	9/1975	$450	BrPF	$7,500	$13,000	$22,500

J-1418 and J-1419:
1875 Half Dollar

Trial piece struck from regular dies.

J-1419

Number	Metal	Edge	Rarity	Pop	T/A	Last Traded at Auction				60	63	65
						Firm	Date	Amount	Grade			
1418	C	RE	H7	2	1	ANR	7/2003	$23,000	PCGSPF65RD	$5,000	$15,000	$25,000
1419	Alu	RE	8	0	1	Bowers & Ruddy	8/1978	$210	VF30	$9,000	$14,000	$22,500

J-1420 to J-1422:
1875 Silver Dollar

Obverse: Actually a trade dollar pattern die, with Liberty seated at the seashore, similar to J-1396 twenty-cent piece (complete with illogical depiction of ship), but here with a ribbon below the base inscribed IN GOD WE TRUST.
Reverse: Regular silver dollar die, Without Motto style, of 1840 to 1865.[3]

J-1420

Number	Metal	Edge	Rarity	Pop	T/A	Last Traded at Auction				60	63	65
						Firm	Date	Amount	Grade			
1420	Silv	RE	H7	2	2	Stack's	10/2003	$40,250	GemPF	$13,500	$27,000	$45,000
1421	C	RE	H7	4	4	Heritage	5/2004	$12,075	PCGSPF64RB	$7,000	$12,500	$22,500
1422	Alu	RE	8	0	1	Heritage	6/1987	$6,500	PF65	$11,500	$21,500	$42,500

J-1423 to J-1425:
1875 Commercial Dollar

Reverse die first seen with 1871 J-1154. By 1875, the Commercial dollar die was obsolete. The piece is a numismatic delicacy.

Obverse: Die as preceding, with illogical ship.
Reverse: Commercial dollar die. Large wreath enclosing COMMERCIAL DOLLAR / 420 GRS. / 900 FINE. On wreath ribbon is GOD OUR TRUST. At the top border is UNITED STATES OF AMERICA.

J-1423

Number	Metal	Edge	Rarity	Pop	T/A	Last Traded at Auction				60	63	65
						Firm	Date	Amount	Grade			
1423	Silv	RE	H7	4	4	ANR	9/2003	$39,100	NGCPF65	$12,000	$24,000	$40,000
1424	C	RE	L7	8	3	ANR	9/2003	$27,600	NGCPF65RD	$7,000	$12,000	$20,000
1425	Alu	RE	8	0	1	Heritage	6/1987	$6,500	PF65	$11,500	$21,500	$42,500

J-1426 to J-1429:
1875 Trade Dollar

Obverse: Die as preceding, with illogical ship.
Reverse: Regular trade dollar of the 1873 to 1875 design with berry below claw (Type I, the reverse style of 1873 to 1876).

J-1426

Number	Metal	Edge	Rarity	Pop	T/A	Last Traded at Auction				60	63	65
						Firm	Date	Amount	Grade			
1426	Silv	RE	H7	1	2	ANR	9/2003	$43,700	NGCPF66	$13,000	$23,000	$38,000
1427	C	RE	H7	5	2	ANR	12/2003	$25,300	NGCPF67RB	$5,800	$11,000	$20,000
1428	Alu	RE	H7	2	2	ANR	9/2003	$25,300	NGCPF64	$11,500	$22,000	$40,000
1429	WM	RE	U	0	1	RARCOA	4/1972	$320	PF	$13,000	$26,000	$47,500

J-1430 and J-1431:
1875 Trade Dollar

Trial piece struck from regular dies.

Reverse: Type I, as preceding.

J-1430

Number	Metal	Edge	Rarity	Pop	T/A	Last Traded at Auction				60	63	65
						Firm	Date	Amount	Grade			
1430	C	RE	8	2	3	Heritage	11/2003	$27,600	PCGSPF65RB	$8,150	$14,000	$30,000
1431	Alu	RE	8	0	1	Kagin's	7/1975	$925	PF	$9,000	$17,500	$32,500

Patterns of 1875

J-1432 and J-1433: 1875 Gold Dollar
Trial piece struck from regular dies.

J-1432

Number	Metal	Edge	Rarity	Pop	T/A	Last Traded at Auction				60	63	65
						Firm	Date	Amount	Grade			
1432	C	RE	H7	3	2	Superior	2/2000	$2,990	PF62BN	$5,000	$8,500	$15,500
1433	Alu	RE	8	1	1	Superior	10/1989	$4,620	PF63	$6,500	$13,000	$22,500

J-1434 and J-1435: 1875 $2.50
Trial piece struck from regular dies.

J-1434

Number	Metal	Edge	Rarity	Pop	T/A	Last Traded at Auction				60	63	65
						Firm	Date	Amount	Grade			
1434	C	RE	H7	3	3	Superior	2/2003	$10,925	NGCPF65RB	$4,500	$9,000	$18,000
1435	Alu	RE	8	2	3	Ira & Larry Goldberg	2/2000	$10,350	PCGSPF65	$4,500	$9,000	$18,000

J-1436 and J-1437: 1875 $3
Trial piece struck from regular dies.

J-1436

Number	Metal	Edge	Rarity	Pop	T/A	Last Traded at Auction				60	63	65
						Firm	Date	Amount	Grade			
1436	C	RE	H7	3	1	Bowers & Merena	6/1990	$9,680	PF60BN	$10,000	$18,000	$35,000
1437	Alu	RE	8	3	4	Heritage	11/2004	$7,188	ANACSPF50Cld	$12,500	$21,000	$42,000

J-1438 to J-1440a: 1875 $5
The purpose of this and the similar $10 pattern is not known, for no record has been encountered of any interest in changing the current Liberty Head or Coronet design for the $5.

Obverse: Barber's Liberty Head ("Sailor Head") facing left, wearing a coronet inscribed LIBERTY, hair tied back with a ribbon; similar to the motif used on the J-1392 twenty-cent piece.
Reverse: Eagle similar to that used on the trade dollar and twenty-cent piece, perched, holding three arrows and an olive branch, E PLURIBUS UNUM in field above eagle, IN GOD WE TRUST on ribbon below. Around border, UNITED STATES OF AMERICA / FIVE DOLLARS.

J-1439

Number	Metal	Edge	Rarity	Pop	T/A	Last Traded at Auction				60	63	65
						Firm	Date	Amount	Grade			
1438	Gold	RE	8	2	1	Bowers & Ruddy	7/1981	$45,000	GemPF	N/A	N/A	$300,000
1439	C	RE	L7	10	11	ANR	1/2005	$27,600	PCGSPF67RB	$6,400	$11,000	$22,500
1440	Alu	RE	U	0	0	N/A	N/A	N/A	N/A	N/A	N/A	N/A
1440a	WM	RE	U	0	1	Bowers & Merena	11/1985	$1,320	AU	N/A	N/A	N/A

J-1441 and J-1442: 1875 $5
Trial piece struck from regular dies.

J-1442

Number	Metal	Edge	Rarity	Pop	T/A	Last Traded at Auction				60	63	65
						Firm	Date	Amount	Grade			
1441	C	RE	H7	3	7	ANR	7/2003	$13,800	PCGSPF64RB	$6,500	$11,000	$17,000
1442	Alu	RE	H7	1	1	Heritage	5/2003	$20,700	PCGSPF66	$6,500	$11,500	$22,500

J-1443 to J-1445a: 1875 $10

Obverse: Barber's Liberty Head ("Sailor Head") facing left, wearing a coronet inscribed LIBERTY, hair tied back with a ribbon; similar to the motif used on the J-1392 twenty-cent piece.

Reverse: Eagle similar to that used on the trade dollar and twenty-cent piece, perched, holding three arrows and an olive branch, E PLURIBUS UNUM in field above eagle, IN GOD WE TRUST on ribbon below. Around border, UNITED STATES OF AMERICA / FIVE DOLLARS.

J-1444

Number	Metal	Edge	Rarity	Pop	T/A	Last Traded at Auction				60	63	65
						Firm	Date	Amount	Grade			
1443	Gold	RE	8	1	1	Paramount	7/1984	In Set	No Grade	N/A	N/A	$300,000
1444	C	RE	L7	12	7	Heritage	1/2003	$13,800	PCGSPF65RB	$5,000	$9,500	$16,000
1445	Alu	RE	U	1	1	Bowers & Merena	11/1995	$15,125	PCGSPF65	N/A	N/A	$30,000
1445a	WM	RE	U	0	1	Scott Stamp & Coin	2/1888	In Set	No Grade	N/A	N/A	N/A

J-1446 and J-1447: 1875 $10

Trial piece struck from regular dies.

J-1446

Number	Metal	Edge	Rarity	Pop	T/A	Last Traded at Auction				60	63	65
						Firm	Date	Amount	Grade			
1446	C	RE	H7	4	4	Heritage	8/2001	$13,225	PCGSPF66RB	$6,000	$9,250	$17,000
1447	Alu	RE	8	1	2	Superior	1/2003	$18,400	NGC65	$8,000	$15,000	$28,000

J-1448 to J-1449: 1875 $20

Trial piece struck from regular dies.

J-1449

Number	Metal	Edge	Rarity	Pop	T/A	Last Traded at Auction				60	63	65
						Firm	Date	Amount	Grade			
1448	C	RE	H7	1	3	Heritage	2/2002	$8,683	PCGSPF63	$10,000	$17,500	$35,000
1448a	Brs	RE	U	0	0	Sotheby's	2/1954	N/A	N/A	N/A	N/A	N/A
1449	Alu	RE	H7	2	3	Heritage	8/2001	$14,950	NGCPF65	$10,000	$17,500	$35,000

Patterns of 1876

History and Overview

In 1876, the Centennial Exhibition was held in Philadelphia to observe the 100th anniversary of American independence. This was a year of celebration across the land. Pattern production was primarily of numismatic delicacies for privileged insiders, likely including Henry Linderman. In particular, several varieties of dollar-sized pieces were issued, with just two specimens each said to have been made of certain silver strikings, and few if any more in copper. In the same category, the Mint struck in aluminum and copper most if not all of the regular denominations, using Proof dies, although aluminum impressions have not been located for certain of these values and therefore are not listed.

In 1876, Mint Director Linderman proposed a special commemorative reverse design for the trade dollar, to observe the centennial of independence. No pattern coin was developed, but certain of his motif suggestions were employed on the 1876 Assay Commission medal.

Dana Bickford, who in 1874 influenced the Mint to strike pattern $10 pieces for use in international trade, submitted additional designs in 1876. His sketches were not transformed into pattern coins.

Collecting Perspective

For all practical purposes, patterns of 1876 are unobtainable. That said, across the spectrum of the several dozen different varieties produced, occasional pieces come on the market now and then, so with some patience, the truly dedicated collector is apt to be able to acquire a few scattered examples. The dollar coins in particular are highly prized, and even the most extensive collections in the past were apt to lack representatives of the different die pairs.

It is likely that full sets from regular Proof dies were struck, but certain denominations are not recorded in the pattern literature (i.e., five-cent pieces).

J-1450 and J-1451: 1876 Cent

Struck from regular dies. The nickel impressions are mint errors on Venezuelan 1-centavo planchets.

J-1451

Number	Metal	Edge	Rarity	Pop	T/A	Last Traded at Auction				60	63	65
						Firm	Date	Amount	Grade			
1450	Alu	PE	–	0	0	N/A	N/A	N/A	N/A	Unconf	Unconf	Unconf
1451	Nick	PE	8	2	2	Superior	1/2003	$4,600	PCGSAU50	$6,500	$11,500	$22,500

J-1451a: 1876 Three-Cent Piece

Trial piece struck from regular dies.

J-1451a

Number	Metal	Edge	Rarity	Pop	T/A	Last Traded at Auction				60	63	65
						Firm	Date	Amount	Grade			
1451a	C	PE	8	0	1	NASCA	7/1980	$3,600	PF63	N/A	N/A	N/A

J-1452 and J-1453: 1876 Dime

Trial piece struck from regular dies.

J-1452

Number	Metal	Edge	Rarity	Pop	T/A	Last Traded at Auction				60	63	65
						Firm	Date	Amount	Grade			
1452	C	RE	8	0	1	Stack's	6/1986	$1,045	PF	$2,250	$3,600	$5,850
1453	Nick	RE	–	0	0	N/A	N/A	N/A	N/A	Unconf	Unconf	Unconf

J-1453a and J-1453b: 1876-CC Dime

Struck from regular dies. Of extraordinary importance as they are from dies made for a branch mint (Carson City). All dies were made in Philadelphia, and it is likely that these trial pieces were struck there.[4]

J-1453a

Number	Metal	Edge	Rarity	Pop	T/A	Last Traded at Auction				60	63	65
						Firm	Date	Amount	Grade			
1453a	C	PE	8	3	1	Heritage	1/2000	$16,100	PF63BN	N/A	$45,000	N/A
1453b	Nick	PE	U	1	1	Superior	7/2003	*	NGCMS64	N/A	N/A	N/A

* Hammered at $24,000, but failed to meet reserve.

J-1454: 1876 Twenty-Cent Piece

Trial piece struck from regular dies.

J-1454

Number	Metal	Edge	Rarity	Pop	T/A	Last Traded at Auction				60	63	65
						Firm	Date	Amount	Grade			
1454	C	PE	8	2	2	Bowers & Merena	9/1994	$5,775	PCGSPF64BN	$4,900	$9,000	$16,500

J-1455: 1876 Quarter Dollar

Trial piece struck from regular dies.

J-1455

Number	Metal	Edge	Rarity	Pop	T/A	Last Traded at Auction				60	63	65
						Firm	Date	Amount	Grade			
1455	C	RE	8	0	1	Stack's	6/1986	$1,320	ChPF	$7,500	$13,000	$22,500

J-1456: 1876 Half Dollar

Trial piece struck from regular dies.

J-1456

Number	Metal	Edge	Rarity	Pop	T/A	Last Traded at Auction				60	63	65
						Firm	Date	Amount	Grade			
1456	C	RE	8	2	4	ANR	8/2004	$15,151	NGCPF67RB	$3,900	$6,500	$12,000

Patterns of 1876

J-1457 to J-1458a: 1876 Silver Dollar

Obverse: Barber's Liberty Head ("Sailor Head") facing left, wearing a coronet inscribed LIBERTY, hair tied back with a ribbon, 1876 below. Starless field.

Reverse: Open laurel wreath enclosing ONE DOLLAR. Inscription UNITED STATES OF AMERICA at top border; E PLURIBUS UNUM at bottom border.

J-1457

Number	Metal	Edge	Rarity	Pop	T/A	Firm	Date	Amount	Grade	60	63	65
						\multicolumn{4}{l}{Last Traded at Auction}				
1457	Silv	RE	8	2	1	Bowers & Merena	11/1995	$12,650	PCGSPF62	$26,000	$45,000	$80,000
1458a	C	RE	H7	4	2	Bowers & Merena	5/1999	$16,100	PCGSPF66RB	$14,000	$28,000	$45,000
1458	C	PE	U	0	1	Bowers & Ruddy	7/1981	$5,100	GemPF	$22,500	$50,000	$95,000

J-1459 to J-1461: 1876 Silver Dollar

Obverse: Barber's Liberty Head, similar to preceding but with inscription IN GOD WE TRUST between head and date, 1876 below. Starless field.

Reverse: Same die as preceding.

J-1459

Number	Metal	Edge	Rarity	Pop	T/A	Firm	Date	Amount	Grade	60	63	65
						\multicolumn{4}{l}{Last Traded at Auction}				
1459	Silv	RE	8	2	1	Bowers & Merena	5/1999	$29,900	PCGSPF64	$26,000	$45,000	$80,000
1460	C	RE	H7	4	1	Bowers & Merena	8/2000	$6,440	NGCPF62BN	$14,000	$28,000	$45,000
1461	C	PE	U	1	2	Bowers & Merena	10/2000	$9,775	PCGSPF62BN	$39,000	$65,000	N/A

J-1462 to J-1463a: 1876 Silver Dollar

Obverse: Barber's Liberty Head, similar to preceding but with inscription IN GOD WE TRUST at top border in small letters, seven stars left, six stars right, 1876 below.

Reverse: Same die as preceding.

J-1462

Number	Metal	Edge	Rarity	Pop	T/A	Firm	Date	Amount	Grade	60	63	65
						\multicolumn{4}{l}{Last Traded at Auction}				
1462	Silv	RE	8	1	1	Superior	7/1986	$4,620	PF60	$30,000	$50,000	$95,000
1463	C	RE	L7	6	2	Bowers & Merena	3/1994	$9,625	PCGSPF64RB	$10,000	$17,500	$30,000
1463a	C	PE	U	0	1	Bowers & Merena	5/1999	$8,050	PCGSPF62	N/A	N/A	N/A

J-1464 to J-1466:
1876 Silver Dollar

Obverse: Barber's Liberty Head, similar to preceding but with pearls added to top of coronet.
Reverse: Same die as preceding.

J-1464

Number	Metal	Edge	Rarity	Pop	T/A	Firm	Date	Amount	Grade	60	63	65
						Last Traded at Auction						
1464	Silv	RE	8	1	1	Bowers & Merena	11/1985	In Set	GemPF	$30,000	$50,000	$95,000
1465	C	RE	H7	3	2	Superior	10/2001	$12,075	NGCPF65RB	$8,000	$15,000	$40,000
1466	C	PE	U	0	0	N/A	N/A	N/A	N/A	N/A	N/A	N/A

J-1467 to J-1469:
1876 Silver Dollar

Obverse: Liberty seated at the seashore, holding an olive branch in her right hand, her left resting on a globe marked LIB-ERTY in relief. Behind her are two flags and a wheat sheaf. A ship is in the distance. Below the base is IN GOD WE TRUST in a cartouche, below which is the date 1876.
Reverse: Same die as preceding.

J-1467

Number	Metal	Edge	Rarity	Pop	T/A	Firm	Date	Amount	Grade	60	63	65
						Last Traded at Auction						
1467	Silv	RE	H7	4	5	Stack's/ANR	6/2004	$34,500	PCGSPF64CA	$14,000	$28,000	$45,000
1468	C	RE	H7	3	5	ANR	1/2005	$28,750	NGCPF66RB	$11,000	$19,000	$32,500
1469	C	PE	8	1	2	ANR	9/2003	$48,300	NGCPF65BN	$17,000	$32,000	$60,000

J-1470 and J-1471:
1876 Silver Dollar

Reverse die also used on J-1420 to J-1422 of 1875.[5]

Obverse: Liberty seated at the seashore; same die as preceding.
Reverse: Regular silver dollar die, Without Motto style, of 1840 to 1865.

J-1470

Number	Metal	Edge	Rarity	Pop	T/A	Firm	Date	Amount	Grade	60	63	65
						Last Traded at Auction						
1470	Silv	RE	8	2	1	Bowers & Merena	5/1999	$19,550	PCGSPF63	$25,000	$45,000	$80,000
1471	C	RE	8	2	1	Superior	5/2004	$43,700	NGCPF65RD	$17,500	$33,000	$55,000

Patterns of 1876

J-1472 and J-1473: 1876 Commercial Dollar

Obverse: Liberty seated at the seashore; die as preceding
Reverse: Commercial dollar die first used in 1871.

J-1472

Number	Metal	Edge	Rarity	Pop	T/A	Last Traded at Auction				60	63	65
						Firm	Date	Amount	Grade			
1472	Silv	RE	8	4	2	Stack's/ANR	6/2004	$62,252	PCGSPF64	$23,000	$45,000	$80,000
1473	C	RE	H7	4	2	Bowers & Merena	5/1999	$16,100	PCGSPF64RD	$14,000	$28,000	$45,000

J-1474 and J-1475: 1876 Trade Dollar

Obverse: Liberty seated at the seashore; die as preceding.
Reverse: The regular die of the Type II design, used 1875 to 1885, without the berry below the eagle's claw.

J-1474

Number	Metal	Edge	Rarity	Pop	T/A	Last Traded at Auction				60	63	65
						Firm	Date	Amount	Grade			
1474	Silv	RE	8	3	1	ANR	9/2003	$64,400	NGCPF64	$20,000	$45,000	$70,000
1475	C	RE	8	2	2	Bowers & Merena	5/1999	$21,850	PCGSPF65RB	$14,000	$28,000	$45,000

J-1475a and J-1475b: Undated Trade Dollar
Dies 9-F

J-1475a and J-1475b were listed prior to the 8th edition as J-1320 and J-1321 of 1873, respectively. This undated pattern is believed to have been made in 1876, at which time modifications were being considered.

Obverse: Liberty seated, facing left, somewhat similar to the regular design, but with differences. She is seated on two cotton bales, wears a diadem, and holds an olive branch in her right hand and a ribbon inscribed LIBERTY in her left, with wheat sheaf behind. Sea in distance with rounded edges of the sea to the left. IN GOD WE TRUST on base. Thirteen stars around border; no date.
Reverse: Large perched eagle with detailed wing feathers, holding three arrows and an olive branch. Above, E PLURIBUS UNUM on ribbon. Below, 420 GRAINS, 900 FINE. Around border, UNITED STATES OF AMERICA / TRADE DOLLAR.

J-1475a

Number	Metal	Edge	Rarity	Pop	T/A	Last Traded at Auction				60	63	65
						Firm	Date	Amount	Grade			
1475a	Silv	RE	H7	1	1	Bowers & Merena	11/1995	$15,400	PF65	$8,250	$16,000	$31,000
1475b	C	RE	H7	2	1	Bowers & Merena	5/1999	$5,290	PCGSPF64RB	$5,800	$11,000	$19,000

J-1476 and J-1477:
1876 Trade Dollar

Struck from regular dies. Specific obverse and reverse varieties (Type I or II) are not noted in the literature.

J-1476

Number	Metal	Edge	Rarity	Pop	T/A	Last Traded at Auction				60	63	65
						Firm	Date	Amount	Grade			
1476	C	RE	8	0	1	Paramount	8/1972	$550	GemPF	$20,000	$35,000	$60,000
1477	Alu	RE	–	0	0	N/A	N/A	N/A	N/A	Unconf	Unconf	Unconf

J-1478 and J-1479:
1876 Gold Dollar

Trial piece struck from regular dies.

J-1478

Number	Metal	Edge	Rarity	Pop	T/A	Last Traded at Auction				60	63	65
						Firm	Date	Amount	Grade			
1478	C	RE	8	1	2	Heritage	1/2003	$11,500	PCGSPF64BN	$6,500	$13,000	$22,500
1479	Alu	RE	–	0	0	N/A	N/A	N/A	N/A	Unconf	Unconf	Unconf

J-1480 and J-1481:
1876 $2.50

Trial piece struck from regular dies.

J-1480

Number	Metal	Edge	Rarity	Pop	T/A	Last Traded at Auction				60	63	65
						Firm	Date	Amount	Grade			
1480	C	RE	8	2	2	Heritage	6/1998	$5,750	NGCPF65RB	$4,200	$8,500	$17,000
1481	Alu	RE	–	0	0	N/A	N/A	N/A	N/A	Unconf	Unconf	Unconf

J-1482 and J-1483:
1876 $3

Trial piece struck from regular dies.

J-1482

Number	Metal	Edge	Rarity	Pop	T/A	Last Traded at Auction				60	63	65
						Firm	Date	Amount	Grade			
1482	C	RE	8	1	1	Superior	10/1992	$5,775	NGCPF64BN	$9,000	$15,000	$25,000
1483	Alu	RE	8	0	1	Superior	2/1976	$2,500	PF	$12,500	$18,000	$32,500

J-1484 and J-1485:
1876 $5

Trial piece struck from regular dies.

J-1484

Number	Metal	Edge	Rarity	Pop	T/A	Last Traded at Auction				60	63	65
						Firm	Date	Amount	Grade			
1484	C	RE	8	2	3	Superior	2/2003	$14,950	PCGSPF65RB	$6,000	$11,000	$20,000
1485	Alu	RE	–	1	0	N/A	N/A	N/A	N/A	Unconf	Unconf	Unconf

Patterns of 1876

J-1486 and J-1487: 1876 $10

Trial piece struck from regular dies.

J-1486

Number	Metal	Edge	Rarity	Pop	T/A	Last Traded at Auction				60	63	65
						Firm	Date	Amount	Grade			
1486	C	RE	H7	6	6	Bowers & Merena	3/2004	$7,303	NGCPF63	$6,000	$10,000	$18,500
1487	Alu	RE	U	0	0	N/A	N/A	N/A	N/A	N/A	N/A	N/A

J-1488 and J-1489: 1876 $20

Transitional pattern.[6]

Obverse: Regular double eagle die as adopted in 1877, with coronet tip midway between stars six and seven.
Reverse: Regular die of the 1866 to 1876 years with denomination as TWENTY D.

J-1489

Number	Metal	Edge	Rarity	Pop	T/A	Last Traded at Auction				60	63	65
						Firm	Date	Amount	Grade			
1488	Gold	RE	U	0	1	Sotheby's	2/1954	$292	PF	N/A	$400,000	$600,000
1489	C	RE	8	0	2	Bowers & Merena	5/1999	$14,950	PCGSPF66BN	$10,000	$17,500	$35,000

J-1490 to J-1492: 1876 $20

Obverse: Dies similar to the regular design, but slightly modified, with the letters in LIB-ERTY farther from the beads than on regular issues of this year; date 1876 lower on the die than on J-1488.
Reverse: In the words of John W. Haseltine: in the style of regular issue, but "entirely different from [J-1488]; the TW in TWENTY nearly touch the scroll or label inscribed E PLURIBUS, and there are other slight varia-tions. The whole heraldic eagle design is larger and TWENTY DOLLARS below; in fact, an entirely different die."[7]

J-1491

Number	Metal	Edge	Rarity	Pop	T/A	Last Traded at Auction				60	63	65
						Firm	Date	Amount	Grade			
1490	Gold	RE	U	1	1	Superior	7/1986	$99,000	GemPF	N/A	N/A	$450,000
1491	C	RE	H7	1	1	Superior	6/1977	$1,350	PF	$10,000	$17,500	$35,000
1492	C	PE	U	2	1	Heritage	1/2004	$36,225	PCGSPF64Gilt	N/A	$27,000	$45,000

J-1493 and J-1494: 1876 $20

Trial piece struck from regular dies.

J-1493

Number	Metal	Edge	Rarity	Pop	T/A	Last Traded at Auction				60	63	65
						Firm	Date	Amount	Grade			
1493	C	RE	H7	5	1	Heritage	8/2001	$11,500	NGCPF63BN	$10,000	$17,500	$35,000
1494	Alu	RE	–	0	0	N/A	N/A	N/A	N/A	Unconf	Unconf	Unconf

Patterns of 1877

History and Overview

The year 1877 is remarkable for the beauty and diversity of its patterns, especially those from the hand of George T. Morgan, a British die cutter who came to America in 1876.

In 1877 several engravers went to work creating new coin motifs in anticipation that Congress would soon order the production of a new silver dollar, the first since the Liberty Seated dollar had been terminated in 1873.

The half dollar denomination was selected for these efforts. The various heads of Liberty are interesting to contemplate today, some having great beauty. The reverse motifs for the half dollars are varied and elegant and in themselves form a rich study, displaying widely different treatments of the eagle, one of which (J-1512) reappears in numismatics later, on the reverse of the 1879 Schoolgirl dollar (J-1608), as well as the 1915-S Panama-Pacific Exposition commemorative $2.50.

Not only did Morgan contribute to the repertoire of pattern half dollars this year, but also William Barber added his own ideas, one of the more dramatic being a helmeted head of Liberty, on which an eagle is incorporated. J-1540 is popularly attributed to Anthony C. Paquet and is quite different from the others in style, enough so that this combination might prove fruitful for close study. Other half dollar dies are unknown as to the engraver and are probably by William Barber or his son Charles.

Half Dollar Obverse Dies of 1877

Obverse 1: "Barber's Coronet Head with pearls." William Barber's head of Liberty facing left, wearing a coronet inscribed LIBERTY, with pearl border above, hair tied back with a ribbon, IN GOD WE TRUST in small letters above, seven stars left, six stars right, date 1877 below. This is stylistically similar to a pattern dollar of 1876 (J-1464) and dime, quarter, and dollar obverses made by Barber in 1877 (J-1497 to J-1500, J-1542). • Used with J-1501 to J-1502.

Obverse 2: "Morgan's 'silver dollar style' Liberty Head." Liberty facing left, same style and arrangement of motto and stars as later used on the regular silver dollar. Coronet with LIBERTY incused, with heads of wheat, cotton, and bolls above, E PLURIBUS UNUM at top border, seven stars left, six stars right, date 1877 below. There are two obverse die varieties. The first is distinguished by having a wheat tip between R and I (in PLURIBUS) and having a curl mostly over the second 7 (in 1877). The second has the wheat tip touching the lower right of the R and has the curl centered over the left edge of the 7.[8] • Used with J-1503 to J-1509.

Obverse 3: "Morgan's Liberty Head, with motto to left and right." Portrait at the center as preceding but with a different border. E PLURIBUS to the left, seven stars above, UNUM to the right, and with date below, flanked with two stars to the left and four to the right, date 1877 below. • Used with J-1510 to J-1511.

Obverse 4: "Morgan's Liberty Head in beaded circle." Portrait at the center, same as preceding but smaller in size, within a beaded circle. Outside the circle and within the dentils E PLURIBUS UNUM above, date 1877 below, six stars left, seven stars right, date 1877 below. • Used with J-1512 to J-1523.

Obverse 5: "Barber's Liberty Head with broad band." William Barber's head of Liberty facing left, wearing a cap encircled by a broad band inscribed LIBERTY (incused). Cap is ornamented with heads of wheat, cotton, and bolls. Below the neck is B for Barber, date 1877 below. Two die varieties exist. • Used with J-1524 and J-1525.

Obverse 6: "Barber's Helmeted Liberty Head." William Barber's head of Liberty wearing a helmet on the side of which is a small defiant eagle holding an olive branch in the right talon and two arrows in the left. On the helmet visor is the incuse inscription, LIBERTY. Date 1877 below. • Used with J-1526 to J-1531.

Obverse 7: "Barber's Liberty Head with coronet and wheat and cotton." Barber's Liberty Head with coronet, wheat, and cotton. Liberty wearing coronet inscribed LIBERTY in raised letters. Behind the coronet is a wreath of heads of

Patterns of 1877

wheat, cotton leaves, and bolls. IN GOD WE TRUST in small letters above, seven stars left, six stars right, date 1877 below. • Used with J-1532 to J-1536.

Obverse 8: "Barber's Liberty head with Phrygian cap." Liberty wearing Phrygian cap bordered by a band inscribed LIBERTY. Beneath the cap is a laurel wreath encircling the hair. IN GOD WE TRUST is in small letters above; seven stars left, six right, date 1877 below. • Used with J-1537 to J-1539a.

Obverse 9: "Paquet's Liberty Head." Design attributed to Anthony C. Paquet, featuring head of Liberty facing left, wearing a ribbon, decorated at the front with one star, inscribed LIBERTY incused, hair tied in a knot at back of the neck, 13 stars around, date 1877 below. There are two obverse die varieties. The first is distinguished by having the 1 (in 1877) behind or to the right of the tip of the neck truncation. This die cracked at an early time. It was then replaced by a second die on which the 1 is below the neck tip, and the bottom left serif of the 1 is left of the tip.[9] • Used with J-1540 to J-1541.

Half Dollar Reverse Dies of 1877

Reverse A: "Barber's Small Heraldic Eagle." William Barber's stocky, small heraldic eagle with raised wings with shield on breast, holding an olive branch in right talon and eight arrows in left. E PLURIBUS UNUM in field between wings. Around border, UNITED STATES OF AMERICA / HALF DOLLAR. • Used with J-1501, J-1502, J-1528, J-1529, J-1535, J-1536.

Reverse B: "Morgan's shield design, with motto on ribbon above." Small eagle on spade-shaped shield holding olive branch in right talon and three overlapping arrows in left, laurel branch on either side. IN GOD WE TRUST on ribbon above shield. Around border, UNITED STATES OF AMERICA / HALF DOLLAR. • Used with J-1503, J-1518, J-1519.

Reverse C: "Morgan's shield design, with motto around shield." Small eagle on spade-shaped shield holding olive branch in right talon and three overlapping arrows in left. IN GOD WE TRUST in raised letters on band around shield, laurel wreath around band. Around border, UNITED STATES OF AMERICA / HALF DOLLAR. • Used with J-1504, J-1505, J-1520, J-1521.

Reverse D: "Morgan's indented shield design." Left and right sides of shield curved inward. IN GOD WE TRUST in incused letters on band around shield. Laurel wreath with large berries around band. Around border, UNITED STATES OF AMERICA / HALF DOLLAR. • Used with J-1506, J-1507, J-1522, J-1523.

Reverse E: "Morgan's 'silver dollar style' die." Reverse similar to that used on the adopted silver dollar of 1878. Eagle with raised wings holding an olive branch with three leaves in right talon and three arrows in left. IN GOD WE TRUST between wings in upper and lower case Gothic letters, partially surrounded by two laurel branches tied with ribbon. Eagle has seven tail feathers. Around border, UNITED STATES OF AMERICA / HALF DOLLAR. • Used with J-1508 to J-1511.

Reverse F: "Morgan's defiant eagle." Motif within a circle of beads. Defiant eagle standing on broad pedestal inscribed IN GOD / WE TRUST, with olive branch to left, three arrows to right. Between the beaded circle and the dentils is the inscription UNITED STATES OF AMERICA / HALF DOLLAR. • Used with J-1512 to J-1513.

Reverse G: "Morgan's spread eagle, small feathers." Motif within a circle of beads. Eagle with small feathers, smooth curved outline to left and right side of wings, perched on a pedestal inscribed IN GOD WE TRUST. Three arrows to left, olive branch to right. Between the beaded circle and the dentils is the inscription, UNITED STATES OF AMER-ICA / HALF DOLLAR. • Used with J-1514 to J-1515.

Reverse H: "Morgan's spread eagle, large feathers." Motif within a circle of beads. Eagle with large feathers interrupting the outline to left and right side of wings, perched on a pedestal inscribed IN GOD WE TRUST. Three arrows to left, olive branch to right. Between the beaded circle and the dentils is the inscription, UNITED STATES OF AMERICA / HALF DOLLAR. • Used with J-1516 to J-1517.

Reverse I: "Barber's eagle in front of shield." Small perched eagle in front of a shield. Around is a broad band ornamented with scrollwork and dots divided into four sections, IN GOD WE TRUST in top two, E PLURIBUS UNUM in bottom two sections. Mottos in upper and lower case Gothic letters. Around border, UNITED STATES OF AMER-ICA / HALF DOLLAR. • Used with J-1524 to J-1527.

Reverse J: "Barber's eagle on pedestal." Eagle perched on pedestal inscribed E PLURIBUS UNUM, holding three arrows in left talon, olive branch in right. Around border, UNITED STATES OF AMERICA / HALF DOLLAR. • Used with J-1530 to J-1533, J-1537 to J-1538.

Reverse K: "Barber's eagle holding shield on pedestal." Eagle holding a shield, perched on arrows and branch on a pedestal inscribed E PLURIBUS UNUM. Around border, UNITED STATES OF AMERICA / HALF DOLLAR. • Used with J-1534a, J-1534, J-1539a, J-1539.

Reverse L: "Paquet's Heraldic Eagle." Large eagle, wings widely spread, with shield on breast, olive branch in right talon, three arrows in left. Ribbon held in beak is inscribed E PLURIBUS UNUM. Around border, UNITED STATES OF AMERICA / HALF DOL. • Used with J-1540 to J-1541.

Several silver dollar patterns were produced by William Barber in 1877 and are also rare, while Morgan made none of this denomination. A pattern $10 piece by Morgan features a version of the same head used on the half dollar, and an eagle of similar style is employed.

Then come the large and impressive $50 patterns of the year. The inspiration for these came directly from the $50 gold "slugs" of California, produced in 1851 and 1852, as well as the round $50 coins of Wass, Molitor & Company and, separately, Kellogg & Company, in 1855.

In 1877, Dr. Linderman reactivated the idea, although the need at that time for a $50 coin is not recorded in any account seen by the editor. Most likely, it was a pet project. Not much can be added to Don Taxay's comment that these $50 coins "are believed to have been ordered by Director Linderman (an avid coin collector) for his own use."[10] Moreover, Mint correspondence suggests that such a large and heavy coin would be especially susceptible to sawing and filling with base metal, an ongoing concern of Mint officials.[11] The gold impressions of the two varieties (J-1546 and J-1548) are treasures in the National Numismatic Collection at the Smithsonian Institution. Interestingly, these are believed to have been part of the Mint Cabinet earlier, but had been traded away in the late 19th century, going to none other than John W. Haseltine, the Philadelphia dealer with close Mint connections.[12]

Collecting Perspective

Somewhat similar to the situation for 1876, the pattern coins of 1877, although extensive in variety, are exceedingly rare, as such pieces were made as numismatic delicacies, not for distribution to congressmen, numismatists, or other outsiders. Still, in the aggregate there are enough pieces in numismatic hands that with persistence a representative holding can be gathered. The most sought after items for this year are the half dollars, these being a special quest for several generations of numismatists.

Although no one has ever assembled a complete collection of 1877 halves, the possibility of obtaining impressions of most of the individual obverse and reverse dies is closer to reality, but even the well-financed numismatist must be set to spend a decade or two in the hunt.[13] Interestingly, in the period from the Fred Collection sale (1995) to the sale of certain parts of the Bass Collection (1999–2001), at least one specimen of each and every confirmed different variety of 1877 half dollar crossed the auction block.[14] Certain of the 1877 halves, particularly those of the Morgan designs, are apt to be flatly struck at the center of the obverse.

The pattern silver dollars of 1877 are likewise very rare and seldom encountered. Among those that are found, most have been cleaned at one time or another and are less than ideal, but one cannot be choosy in such matters! The dime and quarter by Barber (J-1497 to J-1500) are sufficiently rare that few people have ever seen them, let alone have had the opportunity to buy examples. The two large and impressive varieties of 1877 $50 pieces are each unique in gold. Copper impressions are seen occasionally, sometimes gold-plated, and are attractions when offered.

J-1495 and J-1496: 1877 Cent

Struck from regular dies. Not patterns, but mint errors struck on Venezuelan 1-centavo planchets. Often collected with patterns of this year.

J-1495

Number	Metal	Edge	Rarity	Pop	T/A	Last Traded at Auction				60	63	65
						Firm	Date	Amount	Grade			
1495	C-N	PE	8	0	0	N/A	N/A	N/A	0	$6,500	$13,000	$20,000
1496	Nick	PE	8	0	0	N/A	N/A	N/A	0	$6,500	$13,000	$20,000

J-1497 and J-1498: 1877 Dime

Not confirmed in modern times, but at least two silver-plated copper pieces have been studied.

Obverse: Barber's Liberty Head facing left, wearing coronet inscribed LIBERTY, with pearl border above, hair tied back with a ribbon. Stars around, 1877 below.
Reverse: Regular die of the year.

J-1498

Number	Metal	Edge	Rarity	Pop	T/A	Last Traded at Auction				60	63	65
						Firm	Date	Amount	Grade			
1497	Silv	RE	–	0	0	N/A	N/A	N/A	N/A	Unconf	Unconf	Unconf
1498	C	RE	L7	10	8	Bowers & Merena	1/2005	$6,325	PCGSPF64RD	$4,200	$7,500	$12,500

J-1499 and J-1500:
1877 Quarter Dollar

Not confirmed in modern times, but at least two silver-plated copper pieces have been studied.

Obverse: Barber's Liberty Head facing left, wearing coronet inscribed LIBERTY, with pearl border above, hair tied back with a ribbon. IN GOD WE TRUST above, stars to left and right, 1877 below.
Reverse: Regular dies.

J-1500

Number	Metal	Edge	Rarity	Pop	T/A	Last Traded at Auction				60	63	65
						Firm	Date	Amount	Grade			
1499	Silv	RE	U	1	0	N/A	N/A	N/A	N/A	N/A	$22,500	N/A
1500	C	RE	L7	1	1	Superior	1/1990	$2,860	PCGSPF60	$5,800	$11,000	$20,000

J-1501 and J-1502:
1877 Half Dollar
Dies 1-A

Obverse: Barber's Coronet Head with pearls.
Reverse: Barber's Small Heraldic Eagle.

J-1502

Number	Metal	Edge	Rarity	Pop	T/A	Last Traded at Auction				60	63	65
						Firm	Date	Amount	Grade			
1501	Silv	RE	8	1	1	Bowers & Merena	8/1998	$25,300	PF63	$22,500	$32,500	$52,000
1502	C	RE	L7	3	2	Superior	10/1991	$3,960	PF64BN	$15,000	$22,500	$32,000

J-1503:
1877 Half Dollar
Dies 2-B

Obverse: Morgan's "silver dollar style" Liberty Head. Die varieties exist.
Reverse: Morgan's shield design, with motto on ribbon above.

J-1503

Number	Metal	Edge	Rarity	Pop	T/A	Last Traded at Auction				60	63	65
						Firm	Date	Amount	Grade			
1503	Silv	RE	H7	5	3	Stack's	10/2003	$28,750	PF	$16,000	$30,000	$42,500

J-1504 and J-1505:
1877 Half Dollar
Dies 2-C

Obverse: Morgan's "silver dollar style" Liberty Head. Die varieties exist.
Reverse: Morgan's shield design, with motto around shield.

J-1504

Number	Metal	Edge	Rarity	Pop	T/A	Last Traded at Auction				60	63	65
						Firm	Date	Amount	Grade			
1504	Silv	RE	H7	7	2	Bowers & Merena	5/1999	$8,625	PCGSPF64	$12,500	$25,000	$39,000
1505	C	RE	8	2	1	Bowers & Merena	5/1999	$5,060	PCGSPF61RD	$16,000	$24,000	$39,000

J-1506 and J-1507:
1877 Half Dollar
Dies 2-D

Obverse: Morgan's "silver dollar style" Liberty Head.
Die varieties exist.
Reverse: Morgan's indented shield design.

J-1507

Number	Metal	Edge	Rarity	Pop	T/A	Last Traded at Auction				60	63	65
						Firm	Date	Amount	Grade			
1506	Silv	RE	H7	6	5	Superior	7/2003	$31,050	PCGSPF65	$13,000	$25,000	$39,000
1507	C	RE	8	1	1	Bowers & Merena	11/1995	$13,750	PCGSPF66RB	$17,000	$23,500	$37,500

J-1508 and J-1509:
1877 Half Dollar
Dies 2-E

This is, in effect, a half-dollar version of the later 1878
Morgan silver dollar.

Obverse: Morgan's "silver dollar style" Liberty Head.
Reverse: Morgan's "silver dollar style" die.

J-1509

Number	Metal	Edge	Rarity	Pop	T/A	Last Traded at Auction				60	63	65
						Firm	Date	Amount	Grade			
1508	Silv	RE	–	0	0	N/A	N/A	N/A	N/A	Unconf	Unconf	Unconf
1509	C	RE	L7	6	5	Heritage	2/2005	$16,100	NGCPF65BN	$9,600	$15,000	$23,000

J-1510 and J-1511:
1877 Half Dollar
Dies 3-E

Obverse: Morgan's Liberty Head, with motto to left
and right.
Reverse: Morgan's "silver dollar style" die.

J-1510

Number	Metal	Edge	Rarity	Pop	T/A	Last Traded at Auction				60	63	65
						Firm	Date	Amount	Grade			
1510	Silv	RE	H7	2	4	Superior	5/2004	$40,250	PCGSPF64	$17,500	$30,000	$55,000
1511	C	RE	H7	1	1	Bowers & Merena	8/1998	$13,800	PF65RB	$16,000	$22,500	$32,500

J-1512 and J-1513:
1877 Half Dollar
Dies 4-F

Obverse: Morgan's Liberty Head in beaded circle.
Reverse: Morgan's defiant eagle.

J-1512

Number	Metal	Edge	Rarity	Pop	T/A	Last Traded at Auction				60	63	65
						Firm	Date	Amount	Grade			
1512	Silv	RE	H7	5	4	Bowers & Merena	5/1999	$24,850	PCGSPF65	$13,000	$26,000	$38,500
1513	C	RE	L7	6	7	Heritage	5/2005	$29,900	PCGSPF65BN	$11,500	$18,000	$30,000

J-1514 and J-1515:
1877 Half Dollar
Dies 4-G
Obverse: Morgan's Liberty Head in beaded circle.
Reverse: Morgan's spread eagle, small feathers.

J-1514

Number	Metal	Edge	Rarity	Pop	T/A	Last Traded at Auction				60	63	65
						Firm	Date	Amount	Grade			
1514	Silv	RE	L7	9	5	ANR	12/2003	$32,200	NGCPF66	$12,000	$25,000	$37,500
1515	C	RE	H7	3	4	ANR	3/2005	$48,300	PCGSPF66RB	$15,000	$22,500	$40,000

J-1516 and J-1517:
1877 Half Dollar
Dies 4-H
Obverse: Morgan's Liberty Head in beaded circle.
Reverse: Morgan's spread eagle, large feathers.

J-1516

Number	Metal	Edge	Rarity	Pop	T/A	Last Traded at Auction				60	63	65
						Firm	Date	Amount	Grade			
1516	Silv	RE	H7	6	4	Superior	7/2003	$33,925	NGCPF66	$12,500	$25,000	$37,500
1517	C	RE	L7	4	6	Heritage	7/2003	$18,400	PCGSPF65RB	$9,500	$16,000	$26,000

J-1518 and J-1519:
1877 Half Dollar
Dies 4-B
Obverse: Morgan's Liberty Head in beaded circle.
Reverse: Morgan's shield design, with motto on ribbon above.

J-1519

Number	Metal	Edge	Rarity	Pop	T/A	Last Traded at Auction				60	63	65
						Firm	Date	Amount	Grade			
1518	Silv	RE	–	0	0	N/A	N/A	N/A	N/A	Unconf	Unconf	Unconf
1519	C	RE	H7	4	5	Bowers & Merena	12/2003	$17,250	NGCPF63S-P	$9,500	$18,000	$28,000

J-1520 and J-1521:
1877 Half Dollar
Dies 4-C
Obverse: Morgan's Liberty Head in beaded circle.
Reverse: Morgan's shield design, with motto around shield.

J-1520

Number	Metal	Edge	Rarity	Pop	T/A	Last Traded at Auction				60	63	65
						Firm	Date	Amount	Grade			
1520	Silv	RE	U	1	1	Superior	7/2003	$108,100	NGCPF66	N/A	$70,000	$110,000
1521	C	RE	H7	3	3	Bowers & Merena	5/1999	$12,650	PCGSPF66RB	$14,000	$20,000	$32,000

J-1522 and J-1523:
1877 Half Dollar
Dies 4-D
Obverse: Morgan's Liberty Head in beaded circle.
Reverse: Morgan's indented shield design.

J-1522

Number	Metal	Edge	Rarity	Pop	T/A	Last Traded at Auction				60	63	65
						Firm	Date	Amount	Grade			
1522	Silv	RE	8	2	2	Superior	7/2003	$57,500	NGCPF64	$24,000	$42,000	$70,000
1523	C	RE	H7	3	4	Bowers & Merena	8/1998	$16,100	PF65RB	$14,000	$20,000	$32,000

J-1524 and J-1525:
1877 Half Dollar
Dies 5-I
Obverse: Barber's Liberty Head with broad band.
Die varieties exist.
Reverse: Barber's eagle in front of shield.

J-1524

Number	Metal	Edge	Rarity	Pop	T/A	Last Traded at Auction				60	63	65
						Firm	Date	Amount	Grade			
1524	Silv	RE	L7	8	4	Stack's	3/2005	$8,625	PF	$11,500	$23,000	$35,000
1525	C	RE	L7	3	3	Heritage	1/2004	$10,925	PCGSPF63RB	$11,000	$17,000	$28,000

J-1526 and J-1527:
1877 Half Dollar
Dies 6-I
Obverse: Barber's Helmeted Liberty Head.
Reverse: Barber's eagle in front of shield.

J-1526

Number	Metal	Edge	Rarity	Pop	T/A	Last Traded at Auction				60	63	65
						Firm	Date	Amount	Grade			
1526	Silv	RE	H7	5	4	Heritage	1/2004	$24,150	PCGSPF62	$20,000	$35,000	$37,500
1527	C	RE	–	0	0	N/A	N/A	N/A	N/A	Unconf	Unconf	Unconf

J-1528 and J-1529:
1877 Half Dollar
Dies 6-A
Obverse: Barber's Helmeted Liberty Head.
Reverse: Barber's Small Heraldic Eagle.

J-1529

Number	Metal	Edge	Rarity	Pop	T/A	Last Traded at Auction				60	63	65
						Firm	Date	Amount	Grade			
1528	Silv	RE	H7	3	4	ANR	12/2003	$32,200	PCGSPF65CA	$16,000	$30,000	$42,500
1529	C	RE	8	1	1	Bowers & Ruddy	8/1981	$2,600	PF60	$18,200	$26,000	$37,500

Patterns of 1877

J-1530 and J-1531:
1877 Half Dollar
Dies 6-J
Obverse: Barber's Helmeted Liberty Head.
Reverse: Barber's eagle on pedestal.

J-1530

Number	Metal	Edge	Rarity	Pop	T/A	Last Traded at Auction				60	63	65
						Firm	Date	Amount	Grade			
1530	Silv	RE	H7	3	5	ANR	9/2003	$29,325	PCGSPF64	$16,000	$30,000	$42,500
1531	C	RE	H7	5	1	Bowers & Merena	5/1999	$17,250	PCGSPF66RB	$9,500	$15,500	$23,000

J-1532 and J-1533:
1877 Half Dollar
Dies 7-J
Obverse: Barber's Liberty Head with coronet and wheat and cotton.
Reverse: Barber's eagle on pedestal.

J-1533

Number	Metal	Edge	Rarity	Pop	T/A	Last Traded at Auction				60	63	65
						Firm	Date	Amount	Grade			
1532	Silv	RE	–	0	0	N/A	N/A	N/A	N/A	Unconf	Unconf	Unconf
1533	C	RE	8	2	2	Bowers & Merena	8/1998	$10,350	PF63BN	$15,000	$23,500	$36,000

J-1534a and J-1534:
1877 Half Dollar
Dies 7-K
Obverse: Barber's Liberty Head with coronet and wheat and cotton.
Reverse: Barber's eagle holding shield on pedestal.

J-1534a

Number	Metal	Edge	Rarity	Pop	T/A	Last Traded at Auction				60	63	65
						Firm	Date	Amount	Grade			
1534a	Silv	RE	U	2	1	Superior	7/2003	$79,350	NGCPF65	N/A	N/A	$100,000
1534	C	RE	8	2	1	Bowers & Merena	5/1999	$13,800	PCGSPF66RB	$17,500	$23,500	$33,800

J-1535 and J-1536:
1877 Half Dollar
Dies 7-A
Obverse: Barber's Liberty Head with coronet and wheat and cotton.
Reverse: Barber's Small Heraldic Eagle.

J-1535

Number	Metal	Edge	Rarity	Pop	T/A	Last Traded at Auction				60	63	65
						Firm	Date	Amount	Grade			
1535	Silv	RE	8	6	2	ANR	12/2003	$35,650	PCGSPF65	$16,000	$27,000	$45,000
1536	C	RE	H7	2	2	Bowers & Merena	5/1999	$12,650	PCGSPF66RB	$14,000	$20,500	$32,000

J-1537 and J-1538:
1877 Half Dollar
Dies 8-J

Obverse: Barber's Liberty Head with Phrygian cap.
Reverse: Barber's eagle on pedestal.

J-1538

Number	Metal	Edge	Rarity	Pop	T/A	Last Traded at Auction				60	63	65
						Firm	Date	Amount	Grade			
1537	Silv	RE	–	0	0	N/A	N/A	N/A	N/A	Unconf	Unconf	Unconf
1538	C	RE	H7	4	4	Superior	8/2002	$16,100	NGCPF64BN	$14,000	$20,000	$32,000

J-1539a and J-1539:
1877 Half Dollar
Dies 8-K

Obverse: Barber's Liberty Head with Phrygian cap.
Reverse: Barber's eagle holding shield on pedestal.

J-1539

Number	Metal	Edge	Rarity	Pop	T/A	Last Traded at Auction				60	63	65
						Firm	Date	Amount	Grade			
1539a	Silv	RE	8	3	3	Stack's	10/2003	$41,400	VChPF	$19,500	$36,000	$52,000
1539	C	RE	8	2	4	Heritage	11/2003	$32,200	NGCPF65RD	$16,000	$23,500	$36,000

J-1540 and J-1541:
1877 Half Dollar
Dies 9-L

This die pair shows some unusual features. Perhaps done outside of the Mint by Paquet, on a contract basis.

Obverse: Paquet's Liberty Head. Two die varieties exist.
Reverse: Paquet's Heraldic Eagle.

J-1540

Number	Metal	Edge	Rarity	Pop	T/A	Last Traded at Auction				60	63	65
						Firm	Date	Amount	Grade			
1540	Silv	RE	H7	5	12	Heritage	8/2004	$27,025	NGCPF65	$12,500	$25,000	$38,500
1541	C	RE	L7	3	4	ANR	3/2005	$34,500	PCGSPF65RD	$14,000	$20,000	$35,000

J-1542: 1877 Dollar

Obverse: William Barber's head of Liberty facing left, wearing coronet inscribed LIBERTY, with pearl border above, hair tied back with a ribbon, IN GOD WE TRUST in small letters above, seven stars left, six right, date 1877 below. A companion to the pattern dime, quarter dollar, and one variety of half dollar this year.
Reverse: Open agricultural wreath enclosing 1 DOLLAR. UNITED STATES OF AMERICA / E PLURIBUS UNUM and stars around border.

J-1542

Number	Metal	Edge	Rarity	Pop	T/A	Last Traded at Auction				60	63	65
						Firm	Date	Amount	Grade			
1542	C	RE	L7	9	5	Heritage	11/2003	$18,400	PCGSPF66RB	$6,400	$10,500	$19,000

J-1543: 1877 Dollar

Obverse: Head of Liberty by Barber, facing left, wearing coronet inscribed LIBERTY with beads above, hair brushed smoothly back, with ribbon extending downward from back of hair. IN GOD WE TRUST above in small letters, date 1877 below.
Reverse: Open agricultural wreath, as preceding.

J-1543

Number	Metal	Edge	Rarity	Pop	T/A	Last Traded at Auction				60	63	65
						Firm	Date	Amount	Grade			
1543	C	RE	8	2	2	Heritage	8/2001	$16,100	NGCPF65RB	N/A	$22,500	$39,000

J-1544: 1877 Dollar

Obverse: Similar to the preceding, except with plain (not beaded) border to the coronet.
Reverse: Open agricultural wreath, as preceding.

J-1544

Number	Metal	Edge	Rarity	Pop	T/A	Last Traded at Auction				60	63	65
						Firm	Date	Amount	Grade			
1544	C	RE	H7	3	3	Heritage	8/2001	$17,256	NGCPF65RB	$9,600	$16,000	$35,000

J-1545: 1877 $10

Obverse: Liberty Head by George T. Morgan, E PLURIBUS to the left, UNUM to the right, date 1877 below.
Reverse: Eagle with similarities to that used on the adopted silver dollar of 1878, with raised wings holding an olive branch with three leaves in right talon and three arrows in left. IN GOD WE TRUST between wings in upper and lower case Gothic letters. Eagle has seven tail feathers. Around border, UNITED STATES OF AMERICA / TEN DOL.

J-1545

Number	Metal	Edge	Rarity	Pop	T/A	Last Traded at Auction				60	63	65
						Firm	Date	Amount	Grade			
1545	C	RE	L7	5	3	Bowers & Merena	11/1998	$14,950	PCGSPF66RB	$6,000	$11,000	$25,000

J-1546 and J-1547: 1877 $50

The unique gold piece, J-1546, resides in the Smithsonian Institution.

Obverse: Liberty Head by William Barber, facing left, wearing coronet inscribed LIBERTY and with top border of coronet ornamented with beads. Hair wavy and thick, B below for Barber. Thirteen stars around border, date 1877 below.

Reverse: Similar in style to the contemporary double eagle but with different details: a heraldic eagle with ornaments to left and right, stars, IN GOD WE TRUST above, rays above stars. Around border, UNITED STATES OF AMERICA / FIFTY DOLLARS, and ornaments. Coronet tip between stars six and seven.

J-1547

Number	Metal	Edge	Rarity	Pop	T/A	Last Traded at Auction				60	63	65
						Firm	Date	Amount	Grade			
1546	Gold	RE	U	0	0	N/A	N/A	N/A	N/A	N/A	N/A	N/A
1547	C	RE	L7	4	2	Stack's/ANR	6/2004	$143,750	PCGSPF62Gilt	$100,000	$160,000	$250,000

J-1548 and J-1549: 1877 $50

The unique gold piece, J-1548, resides in the Smithsonian Institution.

Obverse: Similar to the preceding but with smaller head of Liberty, with the coronet ornamented at the top border, and also with decorations at the bottom border. The hair is somewhat smoother. Coronet tip close to star seven.

Reverse: Same die as preceding.

J-1549

Number	Metal	Edge	Rarity	Pop	T/A	Last Traded at Auction				60	63	65
						Firm	Date	Amount	Grade			
1548	Gold	RE	U	0	0	N/A	N/A	N/A	N/A	N/A	N/A	N/A
1549	C	RE	L7	4	1	Stack's	7/1987	$29,700	PF	$95,000	$140,000	$225,000

Patterns of 1878

History and Overview

In the early part of 1876, the Treasury Department had opened communication with the Royal Mint of England for the purpose of procuring the services of an expert designer and engraver, whom it was desired should come to this country and take a position in the Philadelphia Mint. As a result of these negotiations, a talented young man named George T. Morgan was hired.

While Morgan was engaged in his labors to produce something that would startle the country, Mr. Barber, the chief designer at the U.S. Mint, was hard at work upon the same subject. For weeks and months, Morgan toiled, failing to produce a design that he considered satisfactory. His attention at first was given to the reverse side, and eagles in various attitudes appeared, but at last, he designed a copy of the great American bird which pleased him. This was not the one that appears on the coin now, but was larger, and the wings longer. An afterthought occurred, when the wings were clipped, the bird reduced in size, and the one that holds a position on the reverse side of the "dollar of the daddies" was adopted as the proper design.[3]

While engaged in his labors, Morgan visited the Academy of Fine Arts for the purpose of studying American art. He first wanted the principal figure on the coin to be a representative head of an American female beauty. Then it was determined that the head should be the representation of some living American girl, who should sit while the artist sketched her features. But where to find such a lady was difficult. A newfound friend of Morgan's encouraged Anna W. Williams to sit as the model.

Numismatists generally associate the year 1878 with the introduction of the "Morgan" silver dollar, bearing on the obverse George T. Morgan's portrait of Liberty, and on the reverse an eagle with its wings spread. This motif, so famous today as hundreds of millions of regular-issue coins were struck with the design from 1878 to 1921, was borrowed from Morgan's illustrious series of 1877 pattern half dollars with the same images, most particularly J-1508.

The regular-issue Morgan dollar had its genesis under the Bland-Allison Act, passed by Congress on February 28, 1878, which provided for the resumption of coinage of silver dollars for circulation, this denomination not having been struck since 1873. Now, in 1878, the price of silver metal had fallen dramatically on world markets, and the reason that Liberty Seated dollars did not circulate from 1850 through 1873 was no longer relevant.[1] The bustling silver centers of the West, especially in and around Virginia City, Nevada, had fallen upon hard times. Silver had become more plentiful than anyone would have imagined a decade earlier, and added to the production of domestic mines were vast amounts of metal from melted-down coins from Europe. The new Morgan silver dollar contained 89¢ worth of silver bullion, as compared to, for example, $1.04 in a Liberty Seated silver dollar of 1853.

This legislation was a political boondoggle, a gift to Western mining interests who now found a vast market for silver, as the government itself was the purchaser, not individual companies or people who then had coins struck to order (as had been the case with the 1873 to 1878 trade dollar). The problem was that such coins were not needed in commerce, as in the East and Midwest the paper dollar had become familiar in circulation and was satisfactory.[2] Time would prove that certain Western areas, particularly from the Sierras to the Rocky Mountains, would use Morgan silver dollars in everyday transactions, but to the extent of only a tiny fraction of those minted. The rest piled up in vaults in the various mints (Philadelphia, Carson City, New Orleans, and San Francisco), overflowed to Post Offices, and then to other government storage facilities—until hundreds of millions of unwanted silver dollars were on hand.

In the meantime, early in 1878, there was a call for a new motif to use on the dollar, as it was proposed that silver purchases begin almost immediately. Mint Director Henry R. Linderman had done his homework, and the suite of 1877 pattern half dollar motifs beckoned as well as three varieties of silver dollar patterns, the last the work of Chief Engraver William Barber. A few new silver dollar patterns were made with Morgan and Barber motifs in early 1878 (J-1550 to J-1556a). Then in March, less than two weeks after the legislation passed, the first silver dollars left the high-speed coining presses, employing motifs by George T. Morgan.

Perhaps if coinage for circulation had not been so rushed, Morgan's design would have been finessed. As it was, during the next several months in particular, but also in 1879, a number of modifications were made to the regular design, including changing the number of tail feathers in the eagle from seven to eight, making the breast of the eagle more rounded, and a few other refinements, a discussion of which is beyond the purview of the present text.

In addition to the aforementioned Morgan and Barber suggestions for regular silver dollars, there was an illustrious pattern coinage of experimental dollars made of goloid, an alloy that had been patented by Dr. Wheeler W. Hubbell of Pennsylvania, on May 22, 1877. This was a mixture containing 90% gold and silver, each of these metals being of equal proportions from the value standpoint, to which coin 10% copper was added to strengthen the alloy. These pieces became known as goloid dollars or goloid metric dollars (sometimes with Goloid and Metric capitalized). Two such coins would contain a total $1 worth of gold and $1 worth of silver.

These pieces were in response to legislation that was introduced into Congress in 1877 to provide for goloid metal as a basic alloy for legal tender coins, and stating that the pieces be struck on the metric system of weights and measures. The dollar was to contain 258 grains (or 16.718 grams), the half dollar 129 grains (8.359 grams), the quarter dollar 64.5 grains (4.179 grams), and the dime 25.8 grains (1.671 grams). Gold coins of the denominations $5, $10, and $20 were to be produced as well, along with one-cent and five-cent pieces in nickel. The legislation stated that the weight and fineness of the metal and the proportion of the gold and silver be stated as part of the inscription.

Patterns of 1878

The Congressional Committee of Coinage, Weights, and Measures wrote to Mint Director Henry R. Linderman on December 29, 1877, to ask for examples of what the goloid dollars, half dollars, and quarter dollars would look like. The request included this:

> We want each dollar to contain 258 grains of the goloid metal, and the same proportions for the half and quarter dollars. That is, the half dollar to have in it 129 grains of goloid and the quarter 64-1/2 grams, etc.
>
> Let the coins, if you please, have stamped these words: on the dollar, GOLOID ONE DOLLAR. 1 G. 24S. .9 FINE. 258 GRAINS. On the half dollar, GOLOID HALF DOLLAR 1 G. 24S. .9 FINE. 129 GRS. On the quarter dollar, GOLOID QUARTER DOLLAR 1 G. 24S. .9 FINE. 64-1/2 GRS.
>
> The committee would like to have these specimens in sufficient numbers for the convenience of members of Congress by the 10th of January next or as soon as practicable.[4]

Accordingly, in early 1878, goloid metric dollars were made, and examples of the coins exist today (J-1557 and J-1563). Whether half dollars and quarter dollars were produced is not known, as none have been traced.

The basic fault of the goloid alloy proposal was one that had been discussed at the Mint many times earlier: there would be no way upon sight to determine the metallic content of such coins, the gold would not be visible, and counterfeits or copies could be made of silver and few would be the wiser. This had been the telling argument against fusible alloy (1792), billon (1836 and later), and other proposals.

Judd relates that when Mint Director Linderman came before the Congressional Committee of Coinage, Weights, and Measures on January 17, 1878, he brought a pattern dollar struck in goloid alloy and also one struck in standard silver (90% silver and 10% copper). "The only way they could be distinguished was that the letter 'o' in the 'of' on the reverse of the silver piece was blurred, while that of the goloid piece was perfect."

The goloid proposal did not achieve much interest anywhere—not in Congress, the Mint, or in the general press. However, it did leave a legacy of several interesting pattern varieties of the 1878 year, J-1557 through J-1564, and also set the stage for certain goloid issues of 1879 and 1880, the last mostly made as numismatic delicacies.

In 1878, Linderman reiterated a fear that had been discussed at the Mint for a long time when he noted that he had "long been impressed with the belief that the worst danger which threatens our gold coins, from counterfeiters, is the filling with an inferior metal or alloy." Further:

> By this art the piece presents genuine exteriors, but the inner part having been removed, a disk of platinum, pure or alloyed, is inserted in its place and closed with a ribbed rim of gold. It is, therefore partly genuine and partly counterfeit, and its value is reduced by several dollars, differing according to the denomination of the piece.
>
> The largest chance of spoliation of course occurs with the twenty-dollar piece, but the pieces of ten and five dollars have also been filled. So far the mischief has been very limited, as it evidently requires first-class workmen, and is slow work; but pieces of this sort are, of all false issues, the most difficult to detect.
>
> Some experiments were made at the Philadelphia Mint in 1860 to determine whether this fraud might not be prevented by materially lessening the thickness of the coin and consequently enlarging its diameter, at the same time giving the disks a slight concavity, so as to make the piece of a minimum thickness at the center. A pair of dies was engraved for the half-eagle, and a few specimens prepared on this basis.
>
> Nothing further was done, for in fact, the very next year gold disappeared from circulation and has so continued, until we are now on the eve of resuming its use. I have therefore thought it desirable, in order to give our gold coin greater security, to experiment still further in this line, and to this end experimental dies will be expanded to nearly the surface of the present eagle, and adjusted both to ordinary and metrical scales, viz., one inch or about twenty-six millimeters in diameter.
>
> The smaller piece will be of the diameter of the present three-dollar piece, about four-fifths of an inch, or twenty millimeters.
>
> These measures make the planchet so thin that sawing out the interior part would be a very critical, not to say impossible, feat, and not likely to pay for the labor. At the same time the coins would be thick enough at the raised border to be easily taken up by the fingers, and stiff enough to resist bending.
>
> The dimensions of our coins have never been a matter of legal enactment, and alteration could be made, if so desired, with the approval of the Secretary of the Treasury.

A panorama of patterns of various gold denominations, including the $2.50, $5, and $10, were made in 1878, combining motifs by Morgan and Barber, but no examples of such designs were ever made for circulation.

Collecting Perspective

Patterns for the Morgan silver dollar (J-1550 to J-1553) have always been in demand from collectors of regular silver dollars as a nice addition for a specialized cabinet. Similarly, Barber's contender for the silver dollar, J-1554 through J-1556a, has always played to a responsive audience. To the preceding can be added the curious mule of J-1565.

The goloid metric dollars, as they are usually called (although the word *metric* did not appear on two of the dies of 1878 but was used on a third, J-1563), have been popular as well. Variations are described in the text.

Certain of the gold denomination patterns were struck in that precious metal and are rarities today. More often encountered are copper impressions, but these are quite elusive.

J-1550a and J-1550b: 1878 Silver Dollar

Obverse: Morgan's design, Liberty Head facing left, E PLURIBUS UNUM above, seven stars left, six stars right, date 1878 below. Two obverse die varieties exist.

Reverse: Perched eagle holding arrows and olive branch, the branch with just three leaves, and thus different from the circulating design. IN GOD WE TRUST in Gothic letters above the eagle, wreath below and to the sides of the eagle. UNITED STATES OF AMERICA / ONE DOLLAR around border. The exact style as used on the J-1508 and J-1509 half dollars of 1877.

J-1550a

Number	Metal	Edge	Rarity	Pop	T/A	Firm	Date	Amount	Grade	60	63	65
						Last Traded at Auction						
1550a	Silv	RE	L6	19	17	Heritage	8/2004	$6,900	PCGSPF64	$3,850	$6,250	$12,500
1550b	C	RE	H6	0	1	Superior	2/1991	$5,610	PCGSPF64RD	$3,850	$6,250	$12,000

J-1550 and J-1551: 1878 Silver Dollar

Obverse: Morgan's design as preceding, but from two other dies.

Reverse: Motif as preceding, but with notch or indentation at bottom of each wing where it meets the eagle's body.

J-1550

Number	Metal	Edge	Rarity	Pop	T/A	Firm	Date	Amount	Grade	60	63	65
						Last Traded at Auction						
1550	Silv	RE	L6	20	16	ANR	8/2004	$4,485	NGCPF62	$5,000	$8,500	$14,000
1551	C	RE	H6	14	9	Heritage	11/2003	$6,900	PCGSPF64BN	$3,850	$6,250	$12,000

J-1552 and J-1553: 1878 Silver Dollar

Obverse: Generally similar to J-1550b, but with minor differences.

Reverse: Similar to the preceding, notch or indentation at the bottom of each wing, but with nine leaves and five berries in the olive branch, and with certain other differences. The initial M of the designer is not present.

J-1552

Number	Metal	Edge	Rarity	Pop	T/A	Firm	Date	Amount	Grade	60	63	65
						Last Traded at Auction						
1552	Silv	RE	8	2	2	Bowers & Merena	5/1999	$20,700	PCGSPF64	$8,500	$20,000	$36,000
1553	C	RE	U	0	0	Sotheby's	2/1954	N/A	N/A	N/A	N/A	N/A

J-1554a and J-1554b:
1878 Silver Dollar

Obverse: Barber Head, Liberty facing left, general style used on the $50 pieces of 1877. IN GOD WE TRUST above, seven stars left, six stars right, 1878 below.

Reverse: Perched eagle with drooped wings, holding olive branch and arrows. Motto E PLURIBUS UNUM in small Gothic letters curved above eagle. Around border, UNITED STATES OF AMERICA / ONE DOLLAR. No stars on reverse.

J-1554a

Number	Metal	Edge	Rarity	Pop	T/A	Last Traded at Auction				60	63	65
						Firm	Date	Amount	Grade			
1554a	Silv	RE	8	0	1	Bowers & Merena	5/1994	$1,430	EF	$10,000	$15,000	$22,500
1554b	C	RE	8	1	2	Bowers & Merena	11/2002	$6,038	PCGSPF65RB	$11,000	$16,000	$24,000

J-1554 to J-1556a:
1878 Silver Dollar

Obverse: Die as preceding.

Reverse: Perched eagle with drooped wings, holding olive branch and arrows. Motto E PLURIBUS UNUM in small Gothic letters curved above eagle. Around border, UNITED STATES OF AMERICA / ONE DOLLAR. Stars added in front of O (in ONE) and after R (in DOLLAR).

J-1554

Number	Metal	Edge	Rarity	Pop	T/A	Last Traded at Auction				60	63	65
						Firm	Date	Amount	Grade			
1554	Silv	RE	5	48	35	Heritage	1/2005	$4,428	PCGSPF62	$2,550	$4,800	$8,000
1555	C	RE	L7	10	9	Heritage	11/2003	$3,565	PCGSPF62BN	$3,000	$4,750	$8,000
1556	Alu	RE	U	0	N/A	NY Coin & Stamp	4/1891	$6	N/A	N/A	N/A	N/A
1556a	WM	RE	8	1	1	Heritage	5/2003	$8,625	NCSPF EnvDmg	$19,500	N/A	N/A

J-1557 to J-1559:
1878 Goloid Dollar

The differentiation of any goloid dollar of this year, silver vis-à-vis goloid alloy, can only be determined by elemental analysis.

Obverse: Head of Liberty by William Barber, style as used on a pattern half dollar of 1877 (J-1524). LIBERTY, incuse, on band, wheat and cotton behind. E PLURIBUS UNUM above, seven stars left, six stars right, date below.

Reverse: Circle of 38 stars enclosing inscription: GOLOID. / 1 G. / 24 S. / .9 FINE. / 258 GRS. Around border, UNITED STATES OF AMERICA / ONE DOLLAR.

J-1557

Number	Metal	Edge	Rarity	Pop	T/A	Last Traded at Auction				60	63	65
						Firm	Date	Amount	Grade			
1557	Golo	RE	L6	22	9	Heritage	3/2005	$2,530	PCGSPF63	$1,950	$3,200	$5,100
1558	Silv	RE	L7	3	2	Superior	1/1994	$2,860	PF63	$4,800	$9,000	$16,500
1559	C	RE	H7	4	4	ANR	7/2003	$10,925	PCGSPF64RB	$4,500	$8,250	$15,500

Patterns of 1878

J-1560 to J-1562: 1878 Goloid Dollar

Obverse: Barber's Liberty Head, as preceding.
Reverse: Inscription within continuous wreath of laurel: GOLOID. / 1 GOLD. / 24 SILVER. / .9 FINE. / 258 GRS. Around border, UNITED STATES OF AMERICA / ONE DOLLAR.

J-1562

Number	Metal	Edge	Rarity	Pop	T/A	Last Traded at Auction				60	63	65
						Firm	Date	Amount	Grade			
1560	Golo	RE	H7	3	3	Heritage	8/2004	$13,800	NGCPF65	$7,000	$12,000	$20,000
1561	Silv	RE	H7	0	1	Bowers & Ruddy	1/1975	$1,900	ChPF	$5,000	$10,000	$15,000
1562	C	RE	H6	13	9	ANR	8/2004	$11,500	NGCPF67RB	$2,300	$4,000	$7,500

J-1563 and J-1564: 1878 Goloid Metric Dollar

The only die of the year with METRIC as part of the inscription.

Obverse: Barber's Liberty Head, as preceding.
Reverse: Inscription within circle of 38 stars: GOLOID. / METRIC. / 1-G. / 16.1-S. / 1.9-C / GRAMS 14.25. Around border, UNITED STATES OF AMERICA / 100 CENTS.

J-1563

Number	Metal	Edge	Rarity	Pop	T/A	Last Traded at Auction				60	63	65
						Firm	Date	Amount	Grade			
1563	Golo	RE	L6	20	18	Bowers & Merena	3/2005	$3,335	PCGSPF64	$1,800	$2,800	$5,400
1564	Silv	RE	L7	8	6	Stack's	1/2005	$7,360	NGCPF65	$3,850	$7,000	$12,500

J-1565: 1878 Silver Dollar

A combination of the obverse used on J-1550 and the reverse used on J-1554.

Obverse: Morgan's regular silver dollar design.
Reverse: Barber's design, eagle with drooped wings.

J-1565

Number	Metal	Edge	Rarity	Pop	T/A	Last Traded at Auction				60	63	65
						Firm	Date	Amount	Grade			
1565	C	RE	H7	3	6	Bowers & Merena	5/1999	$13,800	PCGSPF65RD	$7,000	$12,500	$22,500

J-1566 and J-1567: 1878 $2.50

The first in a series of gold patterns this year. The head seems to be too large for the field, and the design is hardly finessed. The widely-spaced motto, typically a minor part of any coin design, is placed in a very prominent position here.

Obverse: Liberty Head by Morgan, with hair combed back and held by a ribbon; band extending back from forehead inscribed LIBERTY. Around border, E PLURIBUS UNUM / 1878 at border.
Reverse: Eagle with drooped wings, holding an olive branch (with seven leaves) and three arrows. Around border, UNITED STATES OF AMERICA / 2-1/2 DOLLARS around.

J-1567

Number	Metal	Edge	Rarity	Pop	T/A	Last Traded at Auction				60	63	65
						Firm	Date	Amount	Grade			
1566	Gold	RE	8	1	3	Auction '90	8/1990	$210,000	PCGSPF65	N/A	N/A	$275,000
1567	C	RE	L7	4	5	Ira & Larry Goldberg	5/2005	$9,200	NGCPF64	$5,000	$9,250	$15,000

J-1568: 1878 $5

Obverse: Morgan's Liberty Head, as preceding.
Reverse: Eagle with drooped wings, but larger. Around border, UNITED STATES OF AMERICA / FIVE DOLLARS, periods before and after denomination.

J-1568

Number	Metal	Edge	Rarity	Pop	T/A	Last Traded at Auction				60	63	65
						Firm	Date	Amount	Grade			
1568	C	RE	L7	4	4	Heritage	5/2003	$10,925	PCGSPF62BN	$5,000	$8,500	$16,000

J-1568a: 1878 $5

Larger diameter, apparently part of the nagging problem and continuing experiments to make gold coins thinner and wider to eliminate filling.

Obverse: Morgan's Liberty Head, as preceding, only larger.
Reverse: Eagle with drooped wings, but larger. Around border, UNITED STATES OF AMERICA / FIVE DOLLARS / 5. No periods in reverse border.

J-1568a

Number	Metal	Edge	Rarity	Pop	T/A	Last Traded at Auction				60	63	65
						Firm	Date	Amount	Grade			
1568a	C	RE	L7	1	8	ANR	1/2005	$19,550	PCGSPF66RB	$4,800	$9,000	$16,000

J-1569: 1878 $5

Larger-diameter issue.

Obverse: Morgan's Liberty Head, as preceding.
Reverse: Similar to preceding, but with slightly smaller eagle and with IN GOD WE TRUST in arc. Around border, UNITED STATES OF AMERICA / FIVE DOL.

J-1569

Number	Metal	Edge	Rarity	Pop	T/A	Last Traded at Auction				60	63	65
						Firm	Date	Amount	Grade			
1569	C	RE	L7	8	7	Heritage	11/2003	$7,763	PCGSPF64RB	$5,000	$7,500	$15,000

Patterns of 1878

J-1570 and J-1571: 1878 $5

Larger-diameter issue.

Obverse: Morgan's Liberty Head, as preceding, except with periods added between the words of the motto.
Reverse: Die as preceding.

J-1571

Number	Metal	Edge	Rarity	Pop	T/A	Firm	Date	Amount	Grade	60	63	65
							Last Traded at Auction					
1570	Gold	RE	U	2	1	Superior	8/2002	$189,750	PCGSPF65	N/A	N/A	$300,000
1571	C	RE	L7	5	9	Bowers & Merena	3/2002	$6,210	PCGSPF65BN	$5,000	$7,500	$15,000

J-1572 and J-1573: 1878 $5

Larger-diameter issue.

Obverse: Morgan's Liberty Head, as preceding.
Reverse: Same as J-1568 (without IN GOD WE TRUST, denomination as FIVE DOLLARS, periods to each side of denomination).

J-1573

Number	Metal	Edge	Rarity	Pop	T/A	Firm	Date	Amount	Grade	60	63	65
							Last Traded at Auction					
1572	Gold	RE	U	0	1	Sotheby's	2/1954	$200	PF	N/A	N/A	$300,000
1573	C	RE	L7	4	4	Bowers & Merena	3/2000	$5,290	PCGSPF64BN	$5,000	$7,500	$15,000

J-1573a: 1878 $5

Larger-diameter issue. Two specimens in the Smithsonian Institution; first identified by staff member Lynn Vosloh. A third is in private hands.

Obverse: Morgan's Liberty Head.
Reverse: Identical to J-1568a.

J-1573a

Number	Metal	Edge	Rarity	Pop	T/A	Firm	Date	Amount	Grade	60	63	65
							Last Traded at Auction					
1573a	C	RE	8	0	1	Superior	1/2003	$8,625	PCGSPF64BN	N/A	$15,000	N/A

J-1574 and J-1574a: 1878 $5

Larger-diameter issue.

Obverse: Head of Liberty with flowing hair, by William Barber. Around border, E PLURIBUS UNUM / 1878.
Reverse: Perched eagle holding an olive branch (with six leaves) and three arrows (which pass behind the wing).

J-1574a

Number	Metal	Edge	Rarity	Pop	T/A	Firm	Date	Amount	Grade	60	63	65
							Last Traded at Auction					
1574	C	RE	H6	8	13	Stack's	6/2005	$6,900	NGCPF65RB	$4,000	$6,500	$11,000
1574a	Brs	RE	U	0	1	Robert L. Hughes	7/1980	$4,000	PF65	N/A	N/A	N/A

J-1575 and J-1576: 1878 $5

Regular-diameter issue.

Obverse: Head of Liberty by William Barber. Liberty wears a Phrygian cap ornamented by two heads of wheat; LIBERTY incused. IN GOD WE TRUST above, seven stars left, six stars right, 1878 below.
Reverse: Perched eagle holding olive branch and arrows, each wing with a slightly different shape. E PLURIBUS / UNUM in two lines above. Around border, UNITED STATES OF AMERICA / FIVE DOLLARS.

J-1576

Number	Metal	Edge	Rarity	Pop	T/A	Firm	Date	Amount	Grade	60	63	65
						Last Traded at Auction						
1575	Gold	RE	8	1	1	Stack's	10/2003	$299,000	GemPF	N/A	$185,000	$375,000
1576	C	RE	L7	4	7	Ira & Larry Goldberg	5/2003	$16,675	NGCPF66RD	$6,000	$9,500	$17,500

J-1577 and J-1578: 1878 $5

Regular-diameter issue.

Obverse: Head of Liberty attributed to George T. Morgan, with Phrygian cap with LIBERTY incused on band. E PLURIBUS to left and UNUM to right, date below.
Reverse: Perched eagle holding olive branch (with three leaves) and arrows, somewhat similar to that used on the Morgan dollar except not as delicate. Around border, UNITED STATES OF AMERICA / FIVE DOL.

J-1578

Number	Metal	Edge	Rarity	Pop	T/A	Firm	Date	Amount	Grade	60	63	65
						Last Traded at Auction						
1577	Gold	RE	8	0	1	C.F. Libbie & Co.	10/1901	$44	PF	$100,000	$185,000	$325,000
1578	C	RE	L7	6	6	Bowers & Merena	5/1999	$6,613	PCGSPF65RB	$5,000	$8,000	$12,500

J-1579 and J-1580: 1878 $10

Obverse: Head of Liberty by William Barber. Liberty wears a Phrygian cap ornamented by two heads of wheat, LIBERTY incused, IN GOD WE TRUST above, seven stars left, six stars right, 1878 below.
Reverse: Perched eagle holding olive branch and arrows, each wing with a slightly different shape. E PLURIBUS UNUM above. Around border, UNITED STATES OF AMERICA / TEN DOLLARS.

J-1580

Number	Metal	Edge	Rarity	Pop	T/A	Firm	Date	Amount	Grade	60	63	65
						Last Traded at Auction						
1579	Gold	RE	8	1	1	Stack's	10/2003	$345,000	GemPF	N/A	N/A	$400,000
1580	C	RE	L7	6	8	Ira & Larry Goldberg	2/2000	$34,500	PCGSPF66RD	$6,000	$9,000	$16,000

J-1581 and J-1582: 1878 $10

Obverse: Head of Liberty attributed to George T. Morgan, with Phrygian cap with LIBERTY incused on band. E PLURIBUS to left and UNUM to right, date below.
Reverse: Perched eagle holding olive branch (with three leaves) and arrows, somewhat similar to that used on the Morgan dollar except not as delicate. Around border, UNITED STATES OF AMERICA / TEN DOL.

J-1581

Number	Metal	Edge	Rarity	Pop	T/A	Firm	Date	Amount	Grade	60	63	65
						Last Traded at Auction						
1581	Gold	RE	8	1	1	Auction '90	8/1990	$210,000	PCGSPF64	N/A	N/A	$425,000
1582	C	RE	8	1	1	Heritage	5/2001	$8,740	PCGSPF62RB	$7,500	$14,000	$29,000

Patterns of 1879

A panorama of patterns was produced in 1879, highlighted by the misnamed "Washlady" silver denominations, the elegant "Schoolgirl" silver dollar, and the $4 gold Stellas in two styles.

Assistant engraver Charles E. Barber's suite of silver patterns of the dime, quarter dollar, half dollar, and dollar denominations stands today as among his finest work. In the late 19th century, this depiction of Liberty was dubbed the "Washlady" design, a rather unfortunate designation, as the woman depicted is elegantly coiffed, and certainly not styled as a laundress might have been. The addition of the ten-cent or dime denomination to these patterns is quite unusual, as after the Standard Silver series, relatively few new pattern designs were made of this value.

Beyond the "Washlady" pieces, a further suite of patterns of the same denomination was made featuring George T. Morgan's famous Liberty Head, by now familiar on the regularly circulating silver dollar, but in combination with a large perched eagle on the reverse. As engravers are wont to do, Morgan swiped his eagle motif from an earlier work— essentially the same bird appears on certain gold patterns of 1878.

Further silver patterns in the series include another dollar portrait attributed to William Barber (J-1605), and perhaps the most commanding issue of the year: George T. Morgan's elegant "Schoolgirl" design. Generations of pattern enthusiasts have considered this to be one of the very finest pieces in the entire series. For the obverse, George T. Morgan pictured a schoolgirl with long flowing tresses, facing to the left, and wearing a string of pearls. The reverse represents a reappearance of one of Morgan's boldest concepts: a defiant eagle facing left, as first used on an 1877 pattern half dollar (J-1512), but deemed to be of sufficient interest that years later it would be utilized for the reverse of the 1915-S Panama-Pacific International Exposition commemorative quarter eagle.

Hubbell's goloid metric alloy furnished the theme for several dollar patterns in 1879, some of which may have actually been used as true patterns (for passing around among congressmen and the like), but the situation is not clear today. Of imposing beauty and simplicity, with a relatively small portrait surrounded by a large shimmering mirror Proof field, is the new motif traditionally attributed to George T. Morgan (although Charles Barber also worked on the die), with Liberty facing left, her hair braided in the back. This has been called the Coiled Hair style and also was used in modified form on the rarer type of the $4 of this year.

This brings us to the most famous of all gold patterns: the 1879 $4 "Stella," so called from the five-pointed star on the reverse of each. Such coins were the brainchild of the Honorable John A. Kasson, the United States envoy extraordinary and minister plenipotentiary to Austria-Hungary, who had earlier served as the chairman of the Committee of Coinage, Weights, and Measures in Congress. Once again the tired and rejected concept of an international coinage came to the fore. Then and now, the valuations of different world monetary units varied with each other, often over a short span of time. It was Kasson's thought that a United States $4 coin would be approximately the same value as the Austrian 8 florins, French 20 francs, Italian 20 lire, Spanish 20 pesetas, and Dutch 8 florins. The entire idea was absurd at the start, as approximate values would never satisfy the needs of commerce, and such pieces would eventually be valued on their gold content and would not come out in even units of foreign currency.

The current Committee of Coinage, Weights, and Measures, was in favor of the idea (congressmen then and now often have little acquaintance with the lessons of history, and act upon the idea of the day) and thought that a suitable name would be "One Stella," as a nickname that would go along with "one eagle," that being used for the $10 coin, with both the star (as on the Stella) and the eagle bird (as on the $10) being national emblems. Whether the star was actually an important American emblem is a matter of question, but it was important to the committee at the time.

It is thought that assistant engravers Charles E. Barber and George T. Morgan were each commissioned to devise an obverse design to be shared with a common reverse, the last featuring the aforementioned five-pointed star with the inscription ONE STELLA / 400 CENTS incuse, with the mottos E PLURIBUS UNUM and DEO EST GLORIA surrounding, and with UNITED STATES OF AMERICA / FOUR DOL. around the border. The DEO EST GLORIA motto must have been popular with someone at the Mint in this era, for it is also seen on certain goloid metric dollar patterns.

Barber's motif featured Liberty facing left, her hair in tresses behind, the Flowing Hair style as it became known. Morgan's motif featured Liberty with her hair in braids, Coiled Hair style. It was announced by someone, perhaps a Mint official, that 15 of the 1879 Flowing Hair $4 Stellas were struck, these as patterns, but there was a sufficient demand for them that a few hundred more were struck for congressmen, who are allowed to acquire them for $6.50 each. This was an era of great secrecy at the Mint, and virtually the entire pattern coinage of 1879, including the "Washlady" and Schoolgirl silver coins, were produced for the private profit of Mint officials. These were not given to congressmen or openly sold to collectors at the time, and, indeed, for many issues, their very existence was not disclosed. Collectors learned of them years later, and at that time were only able to piece together information as no facts are known to have been recorded. There was furor concerning the 1879 Flowing Hair Stella, and dealer S.K. Harzfeld, for one, sought to find out about it. His and other efforts led to certain pieces being available to the numismatic fraternity. The total number made is not known, but has been estimated to be 600 to 700, all but 15 of which are believed to have been struck in calendar year 1880 from the 1879-dated dies.

With regard to Morgan's Coiled Hair Stella, this was strictly a delicacy for Mint officials. None were shown to congressmen, and none were made available to the numismatic fraternity—the whole matter was hush-hush. How many were struck is not known, and estimates have ranged from about a dozen up to perhaps two or three dozen. Whatever the figure, it is but a tiny fraction of the 1879 Flowing Hair style. In 1880, small numbers of both Flowing Hair and

Coiled Hair styles were made for numismatic purposes and sold privately over a period of time. Remarkably, it was not until many years later, in *The Numismatist* in March 1911, that all four 1879 and 1880 dates and combinations were illustrated in one place, in "The Stellas of 1879 and 1880," by Edgar H. Adams.

As a further consequence of the Kasson proposal for international coinage, a metric $20 double eagle was proposed. Apparently this also was a numismatic delicacy, for the motif did not match that suggested by the Committee of Coinage, Weights, and Measures, and the pieces were made in very small numbers and privately sold. The obverse depicted Longacre's standard portrait similar to that used on the current double eagle, but from a different hub and also with surrounding inscriptions relating to the metric system. The reverse was an adaptation of the standard design except with the motto DEO EST GLORIA instead of IN GOD WE TRUST.

Chief Engraver William Barber died on August 31, 1879. In early 1880 his son, Charles E. Barber, designer of the Flowing Hair Stella, was named to the position. Charles was a man of modest talent at best, especially in comparison to his assistant engraver George T. Morgan (at the Mint since 1876, and capable of doing truly artistic work).[5]

Collecting Perspective

The 1879-dated pattern coin most readily available by far is the famous and much loved Flowing Hair Stella. Probably the best part of 500, or perhaps a few more, are in numismatic hands, ranging from grade EF to gem Proof. A popular story, first printed in the early 1880s, has it that some of the worn ones represent pieces that were acquired by congressmen, shown to madams in Washington bordellos (dwellers in the *demi-monde* per the popular term) and given to them as presents, and afterward were used as jewelry. In any event, more than just a few pieces show signs of light wear and signs of having been used as jewelry, perhaps with an untold pedigree if only the coins could speak! Fortunately for numismatists, most pieces are in higher grades, Proof-60 to Proof-63 being about the norm, although enough true gems exist that they can be found without much difficulty. These and other varieties of the $4 Stellas of 1879 and 1880 are listed in *A Guide Book of United States Coins*, although they are not regular issues. As such, they have been adopted by collectors of regular gold coins, vastly multiplying the demand for them. Indeed, ever since the 19th century, just about every gold specialist has hoped to own a Stella. The 1879 Coiled Hair Stella by Morgan is in great demand, and only two or three dozen exist. Fortunately, most of these are in the choice or gem category. The exceedingly rare 1879 metric double eagle in gold is not listed in the *Guide Book*, but over the years a number of numismatists have endeavored to locate an example as a natural go-with for a set of four 1879 and 1880 $4 Stellas. Most if not all strikings of gold 1879 patterns show some lightness of details in one area or another, typically on the portrait on the $4 and the stars on the $20.

Regarding patterns of the silver denominations: these were generally struck in silver and copper, typically in a limited quantity of a dozen or two, it would seem. Patience is required, but examples from the various dies can generally be obtained over a period of time. As is true of all patterns, the silver pieces often are found quite "nice" while the copper coins have often been cleaned, or even polished, sometimes later vividly retoned, and represent a much stronger challenge—the nemesis of the specialist. Fortunately, in recent times some good conservation methods have been used to bring back some polished, etc., pieces to numismatic respectability, many of these copper casualties tracing their pedigree to King Farouk of Egypt, who polished the copper and many of the silver pieces in his collection. The silver (and related copper) dimes of this year have always been in great demand, combining, as they do, two different obverse designs with three different reverses, motifs again by assistant engravers Barber and Morgan.

The 1879 Schoolgirl dollars (J-1608 to J-1610) exist to the extent of perhaps 20 or so impressions in silver, few enough that they are expensive and do not come to the market frequently, but still a sufficient number that a dedicated specialist with the means to buy one can usually do so. Among the goloid metric dollars, J-1618 and J-1627 were struck to the extent of many hundreds of pieces, perhaps to pass around among congressmen to reignite the Hubbell proposals of the year before. Whatever the situation, many acquired wear, and today the vast majority of such coins are in grades from Proof-50 to -60, with scarcely a gem in sight. A paradox is the fact that these two varieties were minted in silver, not in goloid alloy—and thus distributing them as true patterns would have been illogical.

J-1583: 1879 Cent

Struck from regular dies. This may be a mint error, a wrong-planchet strike.

J-1583

Number	Metal	Edge	Rarity	Pop	T/A	Last Traded at Auction				60	63	65
						Firm	Date	Amount	Grade			
1583	Nick	PE	8	0	1	Stack's	1/1987	$1,017	BU	N/A	N/A	N/A

Patterns of 1879

J-1584 and J-1585: 1879 Dime

A very popular pattern, as are others through J-1589, as specialists in regular issues ten-cent pieces have been drawn to them.

Obverse: Charles E. Barber's Society Lady (popularly called Washlady) design, UNITED STATES OF AMERICA around, date 1879 below.
Reverse: At the center a circle of beads or dots enclosing ONE DIME, around which is an open wreath of wheat and cotton, with E PLURIBUS UNUM in a cartouche above.

J-1584

Number	Metal	Edge	Rarity	Pop	T/A	Last Traded at Auction				60	63	65
						Firm	Date	Amount	Grade			
1584	Silv	RE	H6	17	19	ANR	3/2004	$13,800	NGCPF67CA	$5,100	$8,900	$15,000
1585	C	RE	H6	12	11	ANR	11/2004	$8,625	NGCPF64RD	$4,500	$8,900	$16,000

J-1586 and J-1587: 1879 Dime

Popularly called the "Morgan dime" by generations of collectors.

Obverse: Morgan's familiar Liberty Head as used on the contemporary silver dollar, UNITED STATES OF AMERICA surrounding, 1879 below.
Reverse: Larger (than on the preceding) circle of beads enclosing E PLURIBUS UNUM / ONE DIME and an arc of 13 stars. Around the border is a wreath of wheat, corn, cotton, and tobacco, not joined at the top.

J-1587

Number	Metal	Edge	Rarity	Pop	T/A	Last Traded at Auction				60	63	65
						Firm	Date	Amount	Grade			
1586	Silv	RE	H6	8	7	ANR	7/2003	$8,740	PCGSPF63CA	$4,500	$8,900	$16,000
1587	C	RE	H6	14	10	Heritage	9/2002	$7,188	PCGSPF65RB	$3,200	$5,100	$8,900

J-1588 and J-1589: 1879 Dime

Obverse: Morgan's Liberty Head die, as preceding.
Reverse: Different die, but with center similar to the preceding. The wreath around the border is differently styled, is continuous, and consists of six clusters with four laurel leaves each, with berries on twin (unusual style) branch or vine.

J-1589

Number	Metal	Edge	Rarity	Pop	T/A	Last Traded at Auction				60	63	65
						Firm	Date	Amount	Grade			
1588	Silv	RE	H6	11	2	Bowers & Merena	5/1999	$24,150	PCGSPF68	$4,450	$9,000	$16,000
1589	C	RE	L7	7	2	Heritage	7/2003	$8,050	PCGSPF64RD	$6,400	$10,500	$19,000

J-1590 to J-1592: 1879 Quarter Dollar

The reverse of this and the preceding are loosely styled after certain pattern eagles found on 1879 gold denominations.

Obverse: Charles E. Barber's Society Lady (popularly called Washlady) design. IN GOD WE TRUST above, seven stars left, six stars right, date 1879 below.
Reverse: Perched eagle holding olive branch (with seven leaves) and three arrows (passing behind the wing). E PLURIBUS UNUM in arc above. Around border, UNITED STATES OF AMERICA / QUAR DOLLAR.

J-1590

Number	Metal	Edge	Rarity	Pop	T/A	Last Traded at Auction				60	63	65
						Firm	Date	Amount	Grade			
1590	Silv	RE	H6	15	20	ANR	3/2004	$9,200	NGCPF63	$7,500	$12,500	$22,500
1591	C	RE	L7	7	4	MARCA	1/1990	$15,000	PCGSPF65BN	$5,150	$9,000	$15,500
1592	WM	PE	U	0	0	N/A	N/A	N/A	N/A	N/A	N/A	N/A

J-1593 to J-1594a: 1879 Quarter Dollar

Obverse: Morgan's familiar Liberty Head with different border, here with E PLURIBUS to the left, seven stars above, UNUM to the right, and date 1879 below (flanked by two stars to the left and four to the right).
Reverse: Large perched eagle holding an olive branch (with seven leaves) and three arrows, styled after Morgan's 1878 work on $5 patterns. IN GOD WE TRUST in arc around lower part of eagle. Around border, UNITED STATES OF AMERICA / QUARTER DOLLAR.

J-1593

Number	Metal	Edge	Rarity	Pop	T/A	Last Traded at Auction				60	63	65
						Firm	Date	Amount	Grade			
1593	Silv	RE	H6	10	3	Heritage	11/2004	$12,075	PCGSPF64	$4,500	$8,250	$15,500
1594	C	RE	H6	11	9	Heritage	1/2003	$14,375	PCGSPF66RD	$4,500	$8,000	$12,500
1594a	WM	PE	–	0	0	N/A	N/A	N/A	N/A	Unconf	Unconf	Unconf

J-1595: 1879 Quarter Dollar

Trial piece struck from regular dies.

J-1595

Number	Metal	Edge	Rarity	Pop	T/A	Last Traded at Auction				60	63	65
						Firm	Date	Amount	Grade			
1595	WM	PE	–	0	0	N/A	N/A	N/A	N/A	Unconf	Unconf	Unconf

J-1596: 1879 Quarter Dollar

Mule made as a numismatic delicacy.

Obverse: Barber's die used to coin J-1590.
Reverse: Regular reverse die of the year.

J-1596

Number	Metal	Edge	Rarity	Pop	T/A	Last Traded at Auction				60	63	65
						Firm	Date	Amount	Grade			
1596	WM	PE	U	1	1	NY Coin & Stamp	4/1892	$1	Unc	N/A	N/A	N/A

J-1597 to J-1598a: 1879 Half Dollar

Obverse: Charles E. Barber's Society Lady (popularly called Washlady) design. IN GOD WE TRUST above, seven stars left, six stars right, date 1879 below.
Reverse: Perched eagle holding olive branch (with seven leaves) and three arrows (passing behind the wing). E PLURIBUS UNUM in arc above. Around border, UNITED STATES OF AMERICA / HALF DOLLAR.

J-1598

Number	Metal	Edge	Rarity	Pop	T/A	Last Traded at Auction				60	63	65
						Firm	Date	Amount	Grade			
1597	Silv	RE	H6	9	10	Stack's	10/2003	$25,300	GemPF	$10,000	$18,000	$27,500
1598	C	RE	H6	12	19	ANR	11/2004	$16,428	NGCPF66RB	$7,000	$13,000	$20,000
1598a	WM	RE	U	0	2	Heritage	7/2003	$4,600	ANACSPF40 Dmg	N/A	N/A	N/A

Patterns of 1879

J-1599 and J-1600: 1879 Half Dollar

Obverse: Morgan's Liberty Head with different border. Portrait at the center, as preceding, but with E PLURIBUS to the left, seven stars above, UNUM to the right, and date below (flanked by two stars to the left and four to the right).

Reverse: Large perched eagle holding an olive branch (with seven leaves) and three arrows. IN GOD WE TRUST in arc around lower part of eagle. Around border, UNITED STATES OF AMERICA / HALF DOLLAR.

J-1599

Number	Metal	Edge	Rarity	Pop	T/A	Last Traded at Auction				60	63	65
						Firm	Date	Amount	Grade			
1599	Silv	RE	H6	10	6	ANR	1/2004	$24,725	NGCPF66	$10,000	$16,500	$28,500
1600	C	RE	L7	7	6	Superior	9/2003	$9,200	NGCPF64BN	$7,500	$12,500	$21,000

J-1601 and J-1602: 1879 Half Dollar

Obverse: Morgan's Liberty Head. Liberty facing left, same style as used on the regular silver dollar. Coronet with LIBERTY incused, with heads of wheat, cotton and bolls above. E PLURIBUS UNUM at top border, seven stars left, six stars right, date 1879 below.

Reverse: Die as preceding.

J-1601

Number	Metal	Edge	Rarity	Pop	T/A	Last Traded at Auction				60	63	65
						Firm	Date	Amount	Grade			
1601	Silv	RE	H6	10	4	Heritage	2/2005	$23,000	NGCPF67	$10,000	$16,500	$26,000
1602	C	RE	L7	8	10	Superior	5/2003	$12,650	PCGSPF65RB	$6,500	$11,000	$19,000

J-1603 to J-1604a: 1879 Silver Dollar

Obverse: Charles E. Barber's popular Washlady design. IN GOD WE TRUST above, seven stars left, six stars right, date 1879 below.

Reverse: Perched eagle holding olive branch (with seven leaves) and three arrows (passing behind the wing). E PLURIBUS UNUM in wide semicircular arc above. Around border, UNITED STATES OF AMERICA / ONE DOLLAR.

J-1603

Number	Metal	Edge	Rarity	Pop	T/A	Last Traded at Auction				60	63	65
						Firm	Date	Amount	Grade			
1603	Silv	RE	H6	5	6	Bowers & Merena	3/2000	$35,650	NGCPF65	$20,000	$35,000	$52,500
1604	C	RE	H6	7	7	ANR	8/2004	$21,850	PCGSPF65BN	$7,500	$12,500	$24,000
1604a	WM	RE	U	0	1	RARCOA	7/1979	$1,700	EF	N/A	N/A	N/A

J-1605 to J-1607:
1879 Silver Dollar

Obverse: William Barber's head of Liberty with hair gathered and held by a ribbon tied behind, wearing a band inscribed LIBERTY (incused) behind which are two heads of wheat with cotton leaves and bolls. IN GOD WE TRUST above, seven stars left, six stars right, date 1879 below.[6]

Reverse: Open wreath enclosing perched eagle, E PLURIBUS UNUM in field above. Around border, UNITED STATES OF AMERICA / ONE DOLLAR.

J-1605

Number	Metal	Edge	Rarity	Pop	T/A	Last Traded at Auction				60	63	65
						Firm	Date	Amount	Grade			
1605	Silv	RE	L7	8	10	Stack's/ANR	6/2004	$10,350	NGCPF62	$10,000	$16,000	$29,000
1606	C	RE	L7	9	7	Heritage	1/2004	$23,000	PCGSPF66CA	$5,150	$9,000	$16,000
1607	WM	RE	U	1	1	Heritage	5/2003	$9,775	PF	$15,000	N/A	N/A

J-1608 to J-1610:
1879 Silver Dollar

This is one of the most famous and most highly desired of all dollar patterns.

Obverse: Morgan's famous "Schoolgirl" dollar. Head of young girl facing left, wearing strand of pearls, hair falling down to her neck. E PLURIBUS to left, UNUM to right, spaced by stars, date below.

Reverse: Defiant eagle standing on pedestal inscribed IN GOD WE TRUST; olive branch to left, three arrows to right. Around border, UNITED STATES OF AMERICA / ONE DOLLAR.

J-1609

Number	Metal	Edge	Rarity	Pop	T/A	Last Traded at Auction				60	63	65
						Firm	Date	Amount	Grade			
1608	Silv	RE	H6	8	12	ANR	11/2004	$63,250	PCGSPF62	$40,000	$65,000	$175,000
1609	C	RE	L7	7	9	Bowers & Merena	7/2002	$39,100	PCGSPF64RB	$22,000	$42,500	$80,000
1610	Lead	RE	U	0	1	Superior	6/1977	$1,700	PF	$32,500	N/A	N/A

J-1611 and J-1612:
1879 Silver Dollar

Obverse: Regular die.

Reverse: Large perched eagle holding an olive branch (with seven leaves) and three arrows. Around border, UNITED STATES OF AMERICA / ONE DOLLAR.

J-1611

Number	Metal	Edge	Rarity	Pop	T/A	Last Traded at Auction				60	63	65
						Firm	Date	Amount	Grade			
1611	Silv	RE	L7	13	16	Heritage	1/2004	$12,650	PCGSPF65	$4,800	$9,500	$16,000
1612	C	RE	L7	11	10	ANR	10/2004	$4,313	NGCPF63BN	$4,200	$7,700	$14,000

Patterns of 1879

J-1613 and J-1614: 1879 Silver Dollar

Obverse: Regular die.
Reverse: Similar to preceding except eagle lower, letters smaller, and with IN GOD WE TRUST in field above the eagle, widely spaced.

J-1614

Number	Metal	Edge	Rarity	Pop	T/A	Last Traded at Auction				60	63	65
						Firm	Date	Amount	Grade			
1613	Silv	RE	L7	11	10	ANR	11/2004	$50,600	PCGSPF68	$7,000	$12,000	$20,000
1614	C	RE	L7	11	10	ANR	3/2005	$6,325	PCGSPF64BN	$4,200	$7,700	$14,000

J-1615 and J-1616: 1879 Silver Dollar

Obverse: Regular die.
Reverse: William Barber's Perched Eagle holding olive branch (with seven leaves) and three arrows (passing behind the wing). E PLURIBUS UNUM in small arc above. Around border, UNITED STATES OF AMERICA / ONE DOLLAR.

J-1616

Number	Metal	Edge	Rarity	Pop	T/A	Last Traded at Auction				60	63	65
						Firm	Date	Amount	Grade			
1615	Silv	RE	H6	21	15	ANR	11/2004	$46,000	PCGSPF68	$6,000	$10,000	$17,500
1616	C	RE	H6	12	18	ANR	3/2005	$6,670	PCGSPF64BN	$4,200	$7,500	$12,500

J-1617 to J-1621: 1879 Goloid Metric Dollar

Obverse: Head of Liberty by William Barber, somewhat similar to that used on the 1877 $50 (J-1546). E PLURIBUS UNUM above, seven stars left, six stars right, date below.
Reverse: Circle of dots at the center enclosing 895.8 S. / 4.2—G. / 100—C. / 25 GRAMS, this within open wreath of wheat and cotton. E PLURIBUS UNUM in a cartouche above. Around border, UNITED STATES OF AMER-ICA / ONE DOLLAR.

J-1617

Number	Metal	Edge	Rarity	Pop	T/A	Last Traded at Auction				60	63	65
						Firm	Date	Amount	Grade			
1617	Golo	RE	4	158	107	Stack's	6/2005	$3,680	PCGSPF64	$1,550	$3,000	$4,000
1618	Silv	RE	5	18	10	Heritage	3/2003	$2,243	NGCPF64	$1,900	$3,500	$6,750
1619	C	RE	L7	11	11	Heritage	2/2005	$7,475	NGCPF65RB	$2,250	$3,850	$7,500
1620	Alu	RE	H7	0	1	Paramount	3/1981	$4,400	PF	$13,000	$22,500	$36,000
1620a	WM	–	U	0	1	RARCOA	8/1978	$500	PF	N/A	N/A	N/A
1621	Lead	RE	U	0	1	Bowers & Merena	11/1985	$121	PFCorr	N/A	N/A	N/A

J-1622 to J-1625:
1879 Goloid Metric Dollar

Obverse: Liberty Head facing left, by Morgan, ribbon on hair inscribed LIBERTY in incuse letters, hair in bun at right. E PLURIBUS UNUM above, seven stars left, six stars right, date below.
Reverse: Die as preceding.

J-1623

Number	Metal	Edge	Rarity	Pop	T/A	Last Traded at Auction				60	63	65
						Firm	Date	Amount	Grade			
1622	Golo	RE	L7	15	9	Heritage	11/2003	$7,475	PCGSPF64CA	$3,200	$7,000	$12,500
1623	C	RE	L7	6	5	Bowers & Merena	11/2001	$9,775	PCGSPF67RB	$4,200	$7,000	$12,500
1624	Alu	RE	H7	1	1	Heritage	5/2003	$16,100	NGCPF63	$13,000	$22,500	$36,000
1625	WM	RE	U	1	1	Auction '90	8/1990	$6,500	PCGSPF62	N/A	$22,500	N/A

J-1626 to J-1630:
1879 Goloid Metric Dollar

Obverse: Liberty Head design by William Barber, as used on J-1563 of 1878. LIBERTY incused on band, wheat and cotton behind. E PLURIBUS UNUM above, seven stars left, six stars right, date below.
Reverse: Circle of 38 stars enclosing 15.3—G. / 236.7—S. / 28—C. / 14 GRAMS. with GOLOID METRIC DOLLAR. above, DEO EST GLORIA. below, and around the border, UNITED STATES OF AMERICA / 100 CENTS.

J-1628

Number	Metal	Edge	Rarity	Pop	T/A	Last Traded at Auction				60	63	65
						Firm	Date	Amount	Grade			
1626	Golo	RE	4	152	98	Ira & Larry Goldberg	5/2005	$1,438	PCGSPF60	$1,550	$2,500	$4,000
1627	Silv	RE	5	40	24	Heritage	5/2005	$2,530	PCGSPF62	$1,800	$3,150	$5,000
1628	C	RE	L7	10	9	ANR	12/2003	$13,800	NGCPF67RB	$4,200	$7,000	$12,500
1629	Alu	RE	H7	3	2	Bowers & Merena	11/2001	$8,050	NGCPF66	$5,500	$11,000	$20,000
1629a	WM	–	U	0	1	Bowers & Merena	1/1986	$523	EF	N/A	N/A	N/A
1630	Lead	RE	U	0	0	N/A	N/A	N/A	N/A	N/A	N/A	N/A

J-1631 to J-1634:
1879 Goloid Metric Dollar

Usually with a deep mirror Proof finish.

Obverse: Coiled Hair Head of Liberty by George T. Morgan. E PLURIBUS UNUM above seven stars left, six stars right, date below.
Reverse: Die as preceding.

J-1631

Number	Metal	Edge	Rarity	Pop	T/A	Last Traded at Auction				60	63	65
						Firm	Date	Amount	Grade			
1631	Golo	RE	L7	5	2	Bowers & Merena	11/2001	$5,290	PCGSPF64	$4,800	$9,000	$16,000
1632	C	RE	L7	10	10	Heritage	2/2005	$5,463	PCGSPF62BN	$3,200	$6,500	$11,000
1633	Alu	RE	H7	3	5	Heritage	5/2004	$2,300	NCSPFObvPIFI	$5,500	$11,000	$19,000
1633a	Alu	PE	U	0	0	N/A	N/A	N/A	N/A	N/A	N/A	N/A
1634	WM	RE	U	1	2	Southelp	11/2001	$31,050	NGCPF64	N/A	$25,000	$45,000

Patterns of 1879

J-1635 to J-1637a: 1879 $4 Stella

It is said that in 1879 the "originals" were made to the extent of 15 pieces, followed by an unknown number of restrikes, perhaps 700 or so, in 1880. All gold impressions seen have parallel planchet striations near the top of the hair.[8] This reverse die was used to strike all $4 Stellas of 1879 and 1880.

Obverse: Flowing Hair portrait by Charles E. Barber; LIBERTY on coronet. Inscription punctuated by stars: *6*G*.3*S*.7*G*R*A*M*S*, date 1879 below.
Reverse: At the center is a large five-pointed star with the incuse inscription ONE STELLA / 400 CENTS; around is E PLURIBUS UNUM. DEO EST GLORIA; at the border is UNITED STATES OF AMERICA / FOUR DOL.[7]

J-1635

Number	Metal	Edge	Rarity	Pop	T/A	Last Traded at Auction				60	63	65
						Firm	Date	Amount	Grade			
1635	Gold	RE	3	482	82	Ira & Larry Goldberg	9/2003	$201,250	PF66	$85,000	$125,000	$175,000
1636	C	RE	L7	6	9	Heritage	12/2004	$20,700	PCGSPF63Corr	$22,500	$35,000	$55,000
1637	Alu	RE	H7	5	4	Bowers & Merena	1/2002	$24,150	PCGSPF64	$25,000	$37,500	$57,500
1637a	WM	RE	U	1	1	Bowers & Merena	6/1991	$9,625	PF50	$30,000	N/A	N/A

J-1636a: 1879 $4 Stella

The Small Head variation is not widely differentiated in the literature and is often grouped with the varieties listed above.

Obverse: "Flowing Hair, Small Head." Style as preceding, but of reduced design. Head slightly smaller, tip of neck near 1 (1879).[9]
Reverse: Die as preceding.

J-1636a

Number	Metal	Edge	Rarity	Pop	T/A	Last Traded at Auction				60	63	65
						Firm	Date	Amount	Grade			
1636a	C	RE	U	0	1	Kagin's	3/1985	N/A	N/A	$30,000	$50,000	$75,000

J-1638 to J-1641: 1879 $4 Stella

Obverse: Coiled Hair design by George T. Morgan. Liberty with braided hair, band inscribed LIBERTY. Around the border the letters and numbers are punctuated by stars: *6*G*.3*S*.7*G*R*A*M*S* with date 1879 below.
Reverse: Die as preceding.

J-1638

Number	Metal	Edge	Rarity	Pop	T/A	Last Traded at Auction				60	63	65
						Firm	Date	Amount	Grade			
1638	Gold	RE	6	25	10	Sotheby's	10/2001	$345,000	GemPF	$225,000	$300,000	$500,000
1639	C	RE	L7	10	8	Ira & Larry Goldberg	2/2002	$28,750	NGCPF62	$30,000	$52,500	$75,000
1640	Alu	RE	H7	1	1	Superior	8/2004	$89,125	PCGSPF66	$30,000	$57,500	$80,000
1641	WM	RE	U	1	1	Sotheby's	10/2001	$43,125	ChPF	N/A	$125,000	N/A

J-1642: 1879 Metric $20

Obverse: Longacre's Liberty Head as used on regular $20 issues but with inscription surrounding, punctuated by stars: *30*G*1.5*S*35*C*35*G*R*A*M*S* and with date 1879 below.[10]
Reverse: Similar to the regular design except with the motto stated as DEO EST GLORIA instead of IN GOD WE TRUST.[11]

J-1642

Number	Metal	Edge	Rarity	Pop	T/A	Last Traded at Auction				60	63	65
						Firm	Date	Amount	Grade			
1642	C	RE	U	1	1	Sotheby's	10/2001	$32,200	ChPF	N/A	$75,000	N/A

J-1643 and J-1644: 1879 $20

Five pieces are known of J-1643.

Obverse: As preceding, except with decimal point inserted between 3 and 5 on the obverse legend, having it now as:
*30*G*1.5*S*3.5*C*35*G*R*A*M*S*.
Reverse: Die as preceding.

J-1644

Number	Metal	Edge	Rarity	Pop	T/A	Last Traded at Auction				60	63	65
						Firm	Date	Amount	Grade			
1643	Gold	RE	H7	10	1	Stack's	10/2000	$258,750	PCGSPF63	$200,000	$350,000	$550,000
1644	C	RE	L7	5	3	Heritage	1/2003	$46,000	PCGSPF65RB	$17,500	$30,000	$50,000

Patterns of 1880

History and Overview

Patterns of the year 1880 are similar to certain of the metric varieties issued in 1879, but with the date advanced. Included are the well known $4 Stellas of the Flowing Hair and Coiled Hair styles by Charles E. Barber and George T. Morgan respectively, mates to those issued the year before. The various patterns struck in 1880 are not known to have been distributed to members of Congress or anyone else except privately for the benefit of Mint officials. In 1879 and 1880, there were many pointed comments and accusations by collectors and dealers, printed in the pages of *Numisma* and the *American Journal of Numismatics*. It seems that the private pattern production quieted down as a result. The existence of certain 1880 patterns was not generally known until years later, by which time it was "safe" to reveal them.

Collecting Perspective

Similar to the patterns of 1879, those of 1880, though considerably fewer in number, are highly prized by numismatists today. Excepting the J-1645 and J-1651 metric dollars,[12] most are rare or extremely rare. In special demand are the 1880 Flowing Hair and Coiled Hair $4 Stellas. These coins are listed in the annual *Guide Book of United States Coins* and thus play to a very wide audience.

Most of the patterns in existence of this year are in higher grades, exceptions being certain copper pieces that have been cleaned or polished.

J-1645 to J-1647: 1880 Goloid Metric Dollar

Obverse: Liberty Head by William Barber (from Barber's $50 of 1877 and later related motifs, especially J-1617), facing left, wearing coronet inscribed LIBERTY and with top border of coronet ornamented with beads. Hair wavy and thick, 13 stars around border, date 1880 below.
Reverse: Circle of dots at the center enclosing 895.8 S. / 4.2—G. / 100—C. / 25 GRAMS, this within an open wreath of wheat and cotton. E PLURIBUS UNUM in a cartouche above. Around border, UNITED STATES OF AMERICA / ONE DOLLAR; as used on J-1617 of 1879.

J-1647

Number	Metal	Edge	Rarity	Pop	T/A	Last Traded at Auction				60	63	65
						Firm	Date	Amount	Grade			
1645	Gold	RE	H6	13	13	Heritage	8/2004	$3,450	NGCPF63	$3,200	$4,800	$8,900
1646	C	RE	L6	21	13	Heritage	5/2005	$4,370	PCGSPF64RD	$2,300	$3,850	$6,250
1647	Alu	RE	H7	3	2	Stack's	10/2003	$25,300	GemPF	$10,000	$17,000	$28,000

J-1648 to J-1650: 1880 Goloid Metric Dollar

Obverse: Liberty Head by Morgan, as used on J-1622 of 1879, ribbon on hair inscribed LIBERTY (incused letters) hair in bun at right. E PLURIBUS UNUM above, seven stars left, six stars right, date below.
Reverse: Die as preceding.

J-1650

| Number | Metal | Edge | Rarity | Pop | T/A | Last Traded at Auction | | | | 60 | 63 | 65 |
						Firm	Date	Amount	Grade			
1648	Golo	RE	L7	8	6	Heritage	4/2002	$3,680	PCGSPF63	$4,500	$8,350	$14,000
1649	C	RE	L7	5	9	Heritage	5/2005	$16,100	PCGSPF65RB	$4,500	$8,750	$17,500
1650	Alu	RE	L7	10	8	Bowers & Merena	8/2000	$7,475	PCGSPF65	$4,500	$8,350	$16,000

J-1651 to J-1653: 1880 Goloid Metric Dollar

Obverse: Design by William Barber, portrait as used on J-1563 of 1878. Head of Liberty attributed to George T. Morgan, with Phrygian cap with LIBERTY incused on band. E PLURIBUS to left and UNUM to right, date below.
Reverse: Circle of 38 stars enclosing 15.3—G. / 236.7—S. / 28—C. / 14 GRAMS. with GOLOID METRIC DOLLAR. above, DEO EST GLORIA. below, and around the border, UNITED STATES OF AMERICA / 100 CENTS. Die of J-1626 of 1879.

J-1651

| Number | Metal | Edge | Rarity | Pop | T/A | Last Traded at Auction | | | | 60 | 63 | 65 |
						Firm	Date	Amount	Grade			
1651	Golo	RE	H6	9	14	Stack's/ANR	6/2004	$8,913	PCGSPF63	$2,900	$5,150	$9,600
1652	C	RE	H6	17	9	Heritage	11/2003	$4,945	PCGSPF65RD	$2,500	$4,500	$8,750
1653	Alu	RE	H7	6	9	Heritage	8/2004	$8,625	PCGSPF64	$4,500	$7,700	$14,000

J-1654 to J-1656: 1880 Goloid Metric Dollar

Usually with a deep mirror Proof finish.

Obverse: Coiled Hair head of Liberty by George T. Morgan. E PLURIBUS UNUM above seven stars left, six stars right, date below. 1880 version of J-1631 of 1879.
Reverse: Die as preceding.

J-1655

| Number | Metal | Edge | Rarity | Pop | T/A | Last Traded at Auction | | | | 60 | 63 | 65 |
						Firm	Date	Amount	Grade			
1654	Golo	RE	L7	9	8	Bowers & Merena	5/1999	$8,625	PCGSPF65	$4,200	$7,500	$12,500
1655	C	RE	L7	9	6	ANR	9/2003	$9,200	NGCPF65BN	$4,200	$7,500	$12,500
1656	Alu	RE	H7	3	1	Superior	1/1990	$35,750	NGCPF67	$6,400	$11,500	$19,000

J-1657 to J-1659: 1880 $4 Stella

Reverse die used for all $4 issues of 1879 and 1880. Gold impressions (J-1657) are usually seen in high grades.

Obverse: Flowing Hair portrait by Charles E. Barber (as used on J-1635 of 1879), LIBERTY on coronet. Inscription punctuated by stars: *6*G*.3*S*.7*G*R*A*M*S*, date 1880 below.

Reverse: At the center is a large five-pointed star with the incuse inscription ONE STELLA / 400 CENTS. Around the star is E PLURIBUS UNUM / DEO EST GLORIA. Around border, UNITED STATES OF AMERICA / FOUR DOL.

J-1657

Number	Metal	Edge	Rarity	Pop	T/A	Last Traded at Auction				60	63	65
						Firm	Date	Amount	Grade			
1657	Gold	RE	H6	39	16	Sotheby's	10/2001	$241,500	GemPF	$115,000	$165,000	$300,000
1658	C	RE	L7	10	13	Heritage	5/2005	$37,375	NGCPF64	$24,000	$38,000	$60,000
1659	Alu	RE	H7	6	2	Stack's	9/2003	$32,200	VChPF	$25,000	$40,000	$65,000

J-1660 to J-1662: 1880 $4 Stella

Gold impressions (J-1660) are usually seen in high grades.

Obverse: Coiled Hair design by George T. Morgan (as used in 1879). Liberty with braided hair, band inscribed LIBERTY. Around the border the letters and numbers are punctuated by stars: *6*G*.3*S*.7*G*R*A*M*S*, with date 1880 below.

Reverse: Die as preceding.

J-1660

Number	Metal	Edge	Rarity	Pop	T/A	Last Traded at Auction				60	63	65
						Firm	Date	Amount	Grade			
1660	Gold	RE	L7	17	7	Sotheby's	10/2001	$77,750	AU	$350,000	$450,000	$750,000
1661	C	RE	L7	6	7	Heritage	12/2004	$31,625	NCSPF	$30,000	$60,000	$87,500
1662	Alu	RE	H7	3	5	Superior	8/2004	$86,250	PCGSPF65	$32,500	$62,500	$92,500

J-1663: 1880 $5

Trial piece struck from regular dies.

J-1663

Number	Metal	Edge	Rarity	Pop	T/A	Last Traded at Auction				60	63	65
						Firm	Date	Amount	Grade			
1663	C	RE	8	2	2	Heritage	8/2001	$5,980	PCGSPF61RB	$10,000	$15,000	$25,000

J-1663a: 1880 $20

Struck from regular dies. Reported in 1942; currently untraced.[13]

J-1663a

Number	Metal	Edge	Rarity	Pop	T/A	Last Traded at Auction				60	63	65
						Firm	Date	Amount	Grade			
1663a	C	RE	–	0	0	N/A	N/A	N/A	N/A	Unconf	Unconf	Unconf

Patterns of 1881

History and Overview

In 1881, the focus of pattern coins shifted from the large denominations that had prevailed for several years, to the one-cent, three-cent, and five-cent pieces. These issues all have in common the head of Liberty designed by Charles E. Barber, featuring a classical portrait, said by some to be of the goddess Diana. This motif became familiar in later years when it was used on the regular Liberty Head nickels beginning in 1883, and is generally highly regarded by numismatists.

The reverses of the patterns of 1881 follow a common theme of an open wreath enclosing a denomination expressed in Roman numerals. The concept is similar to that employed for certain patterns of 1869, reflecting a desire for the sameness of motifs across multiple denominations, such as the Liberty Seated motif used for silver coins from the dime to the half dollar and the Liberty Head on the $1 and $3 and, of different style, the Liberty Head on the $2.50, $5, and $10. The lack of variation of designs later inspired President Theodore Roosevelt (in 1905) to commission new motifs for all coins, cent to double eagle.

Collecting Perspective

Forming a trio of the Liberty Head cent, three-cent piece, and five-cent piece is possible, although some patience is required. In addition to the foregoing, one five-cent pattern (J-1764a) has a "rare reverse" not used elsewhere in 1881, but employed extensively in 1883.

J-1664: 1881 Cent

Struck from regular dies. Perhaps a mint error, not a pattern. At least one is on a nickel three-cent piece planchet.

J-1664

Number	Metal	Edge	Rarity	Pop	T/A	Last Traded at Auction				60	63	65
						Firm	Date	Amount	Grade			
1664	Nick	PE	8	0	1	Kagin's	11/1974	$810	Unc	N/A	N/A	N/A

J-1665 to J-1667: 1881 Cent

Obverse: Liberty Head by Charles E. Barber. Around border, UNITED STATES OF AMERICA / 1881.
Reverse: Open wreath of wheat and cotton enclosing Roman numeral I.

J-1665

Number	Metal	Edge	Rarity	Pop	T/A	Last Traded at Auction				60	63	65
						Firm	Date	Amount	Grade			
1665	Nick	PE	H6	18	11	Heritage	6/2005	$4,025	PCGSPF66CA	$1,300	$2,000	$3,500
1666	C	PE	H6	14	11	Heritage	6/2005	$3,278	PCGSPF64RB	$1,800	$2,800	$4,250
1667	Alu	PE	L7	8	4	Heritage	6/2005	$5,865	PCGSPF65CA	$2,000	$4,000	$6,750

J-1668 to J-1670: 1881 Three-Cent Piece

Obverse: Liberty Head by Charles E. Barber. Around border, UNITED STATES OF AMERICA / 1881.
Reverse: Open wreath of cotton and corn enclosing Roman numeral III.

J-1669

Number	Metal	Edge	Rarity	Pop	T/A	Last Traded at Auction				60	63	65
						Firm	Date	Amount	Grade			
1668	Nick	PE	H6	15	5	Stack's/ANR	6/2004	$3,450	PCGSPF65	$1,600	$2,550	$4,450
1669	C	PE	H6	16	9	Heritage	6/2005	$4,025	PCGSPF66BN	$2,000	$3,900	$7,500
1670	Alu	PE	L7	5	5	Heritage	6/2005	$7,475	NGCPF66	$2,750	$5,000	$9,500

Patterns of 1881

J-1671 to J-1673: 1881 Five-Cent Piece

Obverse: Liberty Head by Charles E. Barber. Around border, UNITED STATES OF AMERICA / 1881.
Reverse: Open wreath of wheat and cotton enclosing Roman numeral V.

J-1671

Number	Metal	Edge	Rarity	Pop	T/A	Last Traded at Auction				60	63	65
						Firm	Date	Amount	Grade			
1671	Nick	PE	H6	20	20	Heritage	3/2005	$5,750	PCGSPF65	$2,300	$4,150	$7,650
1672	C	PE	H6	11	10	Superior	2/2005	$3,795	NGCPF65RB	$2,300	$4,150	$7,650
1673	Alu	PE	L7	6	4	ANR	12/2003	$7,130	PCGSPF64	$2,250	$4,800	$9,000

J-1674a: 1881 Five-Cent Piece

Discovered in recent years by Smithsonian staffer Lynn Vosloh, correcting a modern error, although the variety was correctly listed in curator T.L. Comparette's records when the Mint Collection (as it was then designated) was in Philadelphia.[14]

Obverse: Die as preceding.
Reverse: Similar to the preceding but with IN GOD WE TRUST in small letters above the wreath.

J-1674a

Number	Metal	Edge	Rarity	Pop	T/A	Last Traded at Auction				60	63	65
						Firm	Date	Amount	Grade			
1674a	Nick	PE	U	0	0	N/A	N/A	N/A	N/A	N/A	N/A	N/A

Patterns of 1882

History and Overview

In 1882, the emphasis on patterns was on the nickel five-cent denomination, déjà vu 1866! Charles E. Barber's Liberty Head, introduced in 1881, found extensive use in 1882, but with various treatments of stars and inscriptions. Several reverse dies were used. A transitional pattern (J-1690) features the obverse and reverse styles as actually adopted in the following year, 1883.

A series of three silver denomination patterns with a new and elegant motif by assistant engraver George T. Morgan made its first and last appearance this year. This suite depicts Liberty wearing a shield-shaped ornament, thereby giving the designation "Shield Earring" to the set. The reverse illustrates a defiant eagle—perched, and facing left, one of the most powerful national emblems seen on any pattern—at once bold, set with ample surrounding field, and commanding to the eye. Shield Earring coins were struck in silver and copper. Never seriously intended as a replacement for Morgan's "regular" dollar then in production, these pieces were numismatic delicacies produced for the pleasure and profit of Mint insiders.

Collecting Perspective

The nickel five-cent pieces of 1882 are highly collectible today, and with perseverance examples of most dies can be acquired. Among the more curious issues are J-1683 and J-1697, each a so-called "blind man's nickel," with five equally spaced bars on the edge, not as much noticed by collectors today as it was years ago when this was a favorite variety for dealer Abe Kosoff (today if encapsulated in a holder the distinguishing feature cannot be seen).[15]

The Shield Earring series of silver coins is highly desired, but offerings of examples are few and far between. As is always the case, silver pieces are apt to be more attractive to the eye than are copper, the latter often having been cleaned, retoned, etc. This of course is the everlasting challenge for virtually all copper patterns, many of which invite careful numismatic restoration and conservation.

J-1675 and J-1676: 1882 Five-Cent Piece

Obverse: Liberty Head by Charles E. Barber. Around border, UNITED STATES OF AMERICA / 1882.
Reverse: Die used for J-1671 in 1881. Open wreath of wheat and cotton enclosing Roman numeral V.

J-1675

Number	Metal	Edge	Rarity	Pop	T/A	Last Traded at Auction				60	63	65
						Firm	Date	Amount	Grade			
1675	Nick	PE	8	0	1	Stack's	7/1984	$4,840	ChPF	$8,500	$16,500	$26,000
1676	C	PE	U	1	2	Bowers & Merena	3/2005	$46,000	PCGSPF64BN	$8,500	$20,000	$52,500

Patterns of 1882

J-1677 to J-1679: 1882 Five-Cent Piece

Obverse: Die as preceding.
Reverse: Similar to the preceding but with IN GOD WE TRUST added in tiny letters above the wreath. Die used for J-1674a in 1881.

J-1677

Number	Metal	Edge	Rarity	Pop	T/A	Last Traded at Auction				60	63	65
						Firm	Date	Amount	Grade			
1677	Nick	PE	L7	7	4	Bowers & Merena	5/1999	$3,680	PCGSPF65	$3,850	$5,500	$9,000
1678	C	PE	H7	2	1	Bowers & Merena	1/1991	$1,320	PF55	$3,550	$7,000	$13,000
1679	Alu	PE	L7	5	4	Bowers & Merena	1/2003	$7,130	NGCPF65	$2,250	$4,500	$10,000

J-1680 to J-1683: 1882 Five-Cent Piece

J-1683 has five equally spaced bars on the edge, one of two die combinations of the "blind man's nickel" (also see J-1697).

Obverse: Die as preceding.
Reverse: Die used to coin J-1674 in 1881, with E PLURIBUS UNUM added in small letters above the wreath.

J-1680

Number	Metal	Edge	Rarity	Pop	T/A	Last Traded at Auction				60	63	65
						Firm	Date	Amount	Grade			
1680	Nick	PE	L6	30	16	Heritage	6/2005	$3,450	PCGSPF65	$1,500	$2,400	$4,000
1681	C	PE	H7	5	2	Bowers & Merena	11/1999	$2,645	NGCPF65RB	$2,250	$3,500	$6,250
1682	Alu	PE	L7	7	2	Heritage	1/1998	$4,715	PCGSPF64	$2,600	$3,850	$7,700
1683	Nick	*	8	3	5	Heritage	8/2004	$16,100	PCGSPF64	$6,500	$15,000	$23,500

* J-1683: five equally spaced bars on edge

J-1684 to J-1686: 1882 Five-Cent Piece

Obverse: Die similar to preceding in configuration, but with smaller dentils (toothlike serrations around the inner border).
Reverse: Similar to the preceding, but with smaller dentils.

J-1684

Number	Metal	Edge	Rarity	Pop	T/A	Last Traded at Auction				60	63	65
						Firm	Date	Amount	Grade			
1684	Nick	PE	L6	33	24	Heritage	6/2005	$5,175	PCGSPF66	$2,200	$2,800	$4,800
1685	C	PE	8	2	1	Heritage	8/1996	$4,620	PCGSPF63BN	$4,250	$8,500	$16,500
1686	Alu	PE	H7	3	3	Bowers & Merena	1/2003	$10,925	PCGSPF65	$4,500	$8,350	$15,500

J-1687 to J-1689: 1882 Five-Cent Piece

The "Without CENTS" reverse die is the same used for regular issues in early 1883.

Obverse: Liberty Head by Charles E. Barber. IN GOD WE TRUST above, seven stars left, six stars right, date 1882 below.
Reverse: Open wreath of cotton and corn enclosing Roman numeral V. Around border, UNITED STATES OF AMERICA / E PLURIBUS UNUM.

J-1687

Number	Metal	Edge	Rarity	Pop	T/A	Last Traded at Auction				60	63	65
						Firm	Date	Amount	Grade			
1687	Nick	PE	L6	21	15	Heritage	6/2005	$2,990	PCGSPF63	$1,750	$3,000	$4,500
1688	C	PE	U	0	0	N/A	N/A	N/A	N/A	N/A	N/A	N/A
1689	Alu	PE	H7	2	2	ANR	11/2004	$10,695	NGCPF64	$3,500	$7,500	$13,500

J-1690 to J-1692: 1882 Five-Cent Piece

Transitional variety, with obverse and reverse of 1883.

Obverse: Liberty Head by Charles E. Barber, 13 stars surrounding, date below. Type adopted for regular use in 1883, but with slight differences in the position of the stars.
Reverse: Die as preceding; "Without CENTS" style adopted in 1883 (but used only for a short time).

J-1690

Number	Metal	Edge	Rarity	Pop	T/A	Last Traded at Auction				60	63	65
						Firm	Date	Amount	Grade			
1690	Nick	PE	5	54	40	Heritage	6/2005	$12,650	PCGSPF66	$4,250	$6,500	$11,500
1691	C	PE	H6	12	17	ANR	3/2005	$4,140	PCGSPF64BN	$2,550	$4,800	$9,750
1692	Alu	PE	L7	6	7	Superior	8/2002	$10,925	NGCPF65	$3,850	$7,500	$11,000

J-1693 to J-1696: 1882 Five-Cent Piece

J-1694 was struck on a small, thin planchet.

Obverse: Shield nickel design, modified, lacking the ball from the base of the shield.
Reverse: Regular die of the year.

J-1693

Number	Metal	Edge	Rarity	Pop	T/A	Last Traded at Auction				60	63	65
						Firm	Date	Amount	Grade			
1693	Nick	PE	L7	10	7	Heritage	8/2004	$4,600	PCGSPF64CA	$3,200	$5,800	$11,000
1694	C	PE	L7	5	4	Bowers & Merena	1/2003	$7,130	PCGSPF66	$2,600	$4,500	$8,250
1694a	C	PE	U	0	1	Superior	6/1977	$325	PF	$8,500	$16,000	$26,000
1695	Alu	PE	L7	6	6	ANR	7/2003	$12,075	PCGSPF65	$2,850	$7,000	$12,500
1696	WM	PE	U	0	1	Empire	4/1960	$55	No Grade	N/A	N/A	N/A

J-1697: 1882 Five-Cent Piece

Struck from regular dies. Edge with five equally spaced bars, the second die combination of the "blind man's nickel."

J-1697

Number	Metal	Edge	Rarity	Pop	T/A	Last Traded at Auction				60	63	65
						Firm	Date	Amount	Grade			
1697	Nick	*	H7	3	2	Stack's	10/2003	$21,850	GemPF	$8,000	$12,000	$23,000

* J-1697: five equally spaced bars on edge

J-1698 and J-1699: 1882 Quarter Dollar

Obverse: George T. Morgan's Shield Earring design. Liberty faces to the right and wears a band inscribed LIBERTY, compressing the back part of her hair. A shield-shaped ornament dangles from her earlobe, creating the nickname for this pattern. E PLURIBUS UNUM above, seven stars to the left, and six to the right, with the date 1882 below.
Reverse: A boldly defiant perched eagle, wings uplifted, facing to the right, and holding in its talons an olive branch and arrows. Around border, UNITED STATES OF AMERICA / QUARTER DOLLAR.

J-1698

Number	Metal	Edge	Rarity	Pop	T/A	Last Traded at Auction				60	63	65
						Firm	Date	Amount	Grade			
1698	Silv	RE	L7	5	6	Stack's	10/2003	$48,875	GemPF	$14,000	$22,500	$40,000
1699	C	RE	H7	2	2	Ira & Larry Goldberg	9/2003	$26,450	PCGSPF65RB	$9,600	$18,000	$28,000

Patterns of 1882

J-1700 and J-1701: 1882 Half Dollar

Obverse: George T. Morgan's Shield Earring design, as preceding.
Reverse: Die similar to preceding except with denomination as HALF DOLLAR.

J-1700

| Number | Metal | Edge | Rarity | Pop | T/A | Last Traded at Auction | | | | 60 | 63 | 65 |
						Firm	Date	Amount	Grade			
1700	Silv	RE	L7	6	6	Bowers & Merena	5/2004	$28,750	NGCPF66	$16,000	$24,000	$37,000
1701	C	RE	H7	4	5	Heritage	5/2003	$24,150	PCGSPF65BN	$11,500	$19,000	$31,000

J-1702 and J-1703: 1882 Silver Dollar

Obverse: George T. Morgan's Shield Earring design, as preceding.
Reverse: Die similar to preceding except with denomination as ONE DOLLAR.

J-1702

| Number | Metal | Edge | Rarity | Pop | T/A | Last Traded at Auction | | | | 60 | 63 | 65 |
						Firm	Date	Amount	Grade			
1702	Silv	RE	L7	7	4	Bowers & Merena	5/1996	$85,250	PF67	$30,000	$55,000	$95,000
1703	C	RE	H7	7	3	Superior	3/2001	$29,900	PCGSPF66RB	$20,000	$32,000	$47,500

J-1703a: 1882 Silver Dollar

Trial piece struck from regular dies.

J-1703a

| Number | Metal | Edge | Rarity | Pop | T/A | Last Traded at Auction | | | | 60 | 63 | 65 |
						Firm	Date	Amount	Grade			
1703a	C	RE	U	1	1	Heritage	8/1992	$9,625	PF63BN	N/A	$22,500	N/A

J-1703b: 1882 Trade Dollar

Trial piece struck from regular dies.

J-1703b

Number	Metal	Edge	Rarity	Pop	T/A	Last Traded at Auction				60	63	65
						Firm	Date	Amount	Grade			
1703b	C	RE	U	0	1	Paramount	8/1972	$900	PF	N/A	$22,500	N/A

Patterns of 1883

History and Overview

Continuing the wide variety of pattern nickel five-cent pieces made in 1882, in early 1883 several interesting die combinations were produced. All feature Charles E. Barber's head of Liberty facing left, as used on the regular issue, but some have variations with regard to the placement of the stars and inscriptions. Among the reverses, four boldly stated their metallic composition, rather ironic in terms of actuality, for today the elemental analysis of certain pieces has revealed that other metals were used—inscriptions notwithstanding. How curious it is that the dies for J-1704, proclaiming itself to be "PURE NICKEL," were also used to make specimens in aluminum! However, there were some struck in pure nickel, these being attracted to a magnet.

Collecting Perspective

Patterns of this year are highly collectible, and the various die combinations of the nickel five-cent pieces can be obtained with some patience. These have always been popular as add-ons for collectors of the regular series. Off-metal strikes from regular dies (or in the case of certain Liberty Head nickels, similar to but not identical to regular dies), are sufficiently rare as to be virtually unobtainable.

J-1704 to J-1706: 1883 Five-Cent Piece

Obverse: Liberty Head by Charles E. Barber. UNITED STATES OF AMERICA / 1883 around the border.
Reverse: Open wreath of wheat and cotton enclosing PURE NICKEL. Around border: FIVE above, CENTS below, seven stars left, and six stars right.

J-1704

Number	Metal	Edge	Rarity	Pop	T/A	Last Traded at Auction				60	63	65
						Firm	Date	Amount	Grade			
1704	*	PE	L6	25	20	Heritage	6/2005	$3,738	NGCPF66CA	$1,550	$3,000	$4,900
1705	Nick	PE	8	0	1	Bowers & Ruddy	9/1975	In Set	No Grade	N/A	N/A	N/A
1706	Alu	PE	H7	4	3	Heritage	11/2003	$11,500	PCGSPF64CA	$4,800	$9,000	$17,500

* J-1704: pure nickel

J-1706a: 1883 Five-Cent Piece

Obverse: Die as preceding.
Reverse: The regular "Without CENTS" die introduced this year. Open wreath of cotton and corn enclosing Roman numeral V. Around border, UNITED STATES OF AMERICA / E PLURIBUS UNUM.

J-1706a

Number	Metal	Edge	Rarity	Pop	T/A	Last Traded at Auction				60	63	65
						Firm	Date	Amount	Grade			
1706a	Nick	PE	U	0	0	Sotheby's	2/1954	N/A	N/A	N/A	N/A	N/A

J-1707 to J-1709: 1883 Five-Cent Piece

Obverse: Die as preceding.
Reverse: Open wreath of wheat and cotton enclosing 75 N. / 25 C. Around border: FIVE above, CENTS below, seven stars left, and six stars right.

J-1708

Number	Metal	Edge	Rarity	Pop	T/A	Last Traded at Auction				60	63	65
						Firm	Date	Amount	Grade			
1707	*	PE	L6	20	14	Heritage	6/2005	$3,738	NGCPF66CA	$1,600	$2,550	$4,750
1708	Nick	PE	H7	2	1	Ira & Larry Goldberg	2/2001	$7,187	PCGSPF66	$3,550	$7,000	$12,500
1709	Alu	PE	L7	8	5	Bowers & Merena	1/2003	$7,820	PCGSPF66	$2,600	$5,800	$11,000

* J-1707: pure nickel

J-1710 and J-1711: 1883 Five-Cent Piece

Obverse: Die as preceding.
Reverse: Open wreath of wheat and cotton enclosing 50 N. / 50 C. Around border: FIVE above, CENTS below, seven stars left, and six stars right.

J-1710

Number	Metal	Edge	Rarity	Pop	T/A	Last Traded at Auction				60	63	65
						Firm	Date	Amount	Grade			
1710	Nick	PE	5	35	24	Heritage	6/2005	$4,888	NGCPF67	$1,550	$2,100	$4,250
1711	Alu	PE	L7	5	3	Heritage	8/1996	$3,630	PCGSPF64	$2,600	$4,500	$10,000

J-1711a: 1883 Five-Cent Piece

Obverse: Regular Liberty Head die of the year.
Reverse: Open wreath of wheat and cotton enclosing 50 N. / 50 C. Around border: FIVE above, CENTS below, seven stars left, and six stars right (reverse of J-1710).[16]

J-1711a

Number	Metal	Edge	Rarity	Pop	T/A	Last Traded at Auction				60	63	65
						Firm	Date	Amount	Grade			
1711a	Nick	PE	U	0	0	Sotheby's	2/1954	N/A	N/A	N/A	N/A	N/A

J-1712 and J-1713: 1883 Five-Cent Piece

Obverse: Liberty Head by Charles E. Barber. UNITED STATES OF AMERICA / 1883 around the border; die as J-1704, etc.
Reverse: Open wreath of wheat and cotton enclosing 33 N. / 67 C. Around border: FIVE above, CENTS below, seven stars left, and six stars right.

J-1712

Number	Metal	Edge	Rarity	Pop	T/A	Last Traded at Auction				60	63	65
						Firm	Date	Amount	Grade			
1712	Nick	PE	L6	32	29	Heritage	6/2005	$3,450	PCGSPF64CA	$1,950	$2,550	$3,850
1713	Alu	PE	H7	3	3	Stack's	10/2003	$12,650	VChPF	$3,550	$7,250	$14,000

J-1714 to J-1716: 1883 Five-Cent Piece

Obverse: Charles E. Barber's head of Liberty wearing a necessarily plain coronet so as not to be redundant with the word LIBERTY appearing above the head and near the border. Six stars left and seven stars right, date 1883 below.
Reverse: Regular die of the year, without CENTS.

J-1714

Number	Metal	Edge	Rarity	Pop	T/A	Last Traded at Auction				60	63	65
						Firm	Date	Amount	Grade			
1714	Nick	PE	L6	23	24	Heritage	6/2005	$4,025	PCGSPF65CA	$1,550	$2,700	$4,350
1715	C	PE	H7	2	3	Ira & Larry Goldberg	2/2000	$4,600	PCGSPF66BN	$3,550	$7,000	$12,500
1716	Alu	PE	H7	4	2	Superior	1/1996	$2,200	PF60	$3,550	$7,000	$12,500

J-1717 to J-1719: 1883 Five-Cent Piece

This reverse must have been a very early proposal to correct the omission of the word CENTS on coins made for circulation, a situation which had led to certain people gold plating pieces and passing them as $5 gold coins.

Obverse: Regular Liberty Head die of the year.
Reverse: Similar to the regular issue, but with the word CENTS added on a curved ribbon across the V.

J-1719

Number	Metal	Edge	Rarity	Pop	T/A	Last Traded at Auction				60	63	65
						Firm	Date	Amount	Grade			
1717	Nick	PE	H6	13	14	Heritage	6/2005	$5,031	NGCPF66	$2,000	$3,000	$4,500
1718	C	PE	U	1	1	Heritage	8/1996	$10,890	PCGSPF65RD	N/A	N/A	$32,500
1719	Alu	PE	L7	5	6	Bowers & Merena	1/2003	$10,925	PCGSPF65	$4,200	$7,700	$15,000

J-1719a: 1883 Five-Cent Piece

Obverse: Regular Liberty Head die of the year, as preceding.
Reverse: Similar to regular With CENTS style, but from a different master die, with I (in PLURIBUS) below the upright of the E (in STATES), rather than under the main part of the E.

J-1719a

Number	Metal	Edge	Rarity	Pop	T/A	Last Traded at Auction				60	63	65
						Firm	Date	Amount	Grade			
1719a	C	PE	U	0	1	Stack's	8/1989	$2,310	ChBU	N/A	$10,000	N/A

J-1720: 1883 Five-Cent Piece

Obverse: Regular Liberty Head die of the year, as preceding.
Reverse: Similar to regular With CENTS style, but with differences including bent-back tassels in relation to the tops of the arms of V, and differences in the position of the I (PLURIBUS) to the upright of E (in STATES); a different die from that used for J-1719a.[17]

J-1720

Number	Metal	Edge	Rarity	Pop	T/A	Last Traded at Auction				60	63	65
						Firm	Date	Amount	Grade			
1720	Alu	PE	H7	4	4	Stack's	5/1998	$3,520	PCGSPF64	$3,500	$6,500	$11,000

J-1720a: 1883 Trade Dollar

Trial piece struck from regular dies.

J-1720a

Number	Metal	Edge	Rarity	Pop	T/A	Last Traded at Auction				60	63	65
						Firm	Date	Amount	Grade			
1720a	C	RE	8	2	1	Superior	1/1996	$6,600	PF63RB	N/A	$26,000	N/A

Patterns of 1884

History and Overview

The pattern scenario for this year features one-cent and five-cent pieces popularly known as the Eastman Johnson "holey designs," from the hole at the center. Eastman Johnson was an artist of the era, and these apparently followed certain of his suggestions made in May 1870.[18] The "holey" cents and nickels were struck on perforated planchets, which resulted in metal being squeezed inward during the minting process and creating holes of irregular outline.

It is doubtful if any serious effort was being made to issue coins with perforated centers for circulation, as decades earlier such had caused problems in planchet preparation and striking. Other patterns of the year include off-metal strikes in copper, some of which trace their pedigrees to a set of silver and gold denominations in copper once owned by Philadelphia dealer A.M. Smith. Within this set was a copper impression of the 1884 trade dollar. While silver examples of this date were not revealed to the numismatic community until 1907, their existence was suspected at an earlier time, although Mint officials forthrightly stated that none had been coined.[19]

Collecting Perspective

Both of the Eastman Johnson "holey" patterns are collectible, although rare. When encountered, they are usually attractive and in high grades. The copper strikings from regular Proof dies are exceedingly rare. It is likely that just one set was made.

J-1721 and J-1722: 1884 Cent

Eastman Johnson's "holey" design.

Obverse: UNITED STATES OF AMERICA above, 1884 below. Open field within, perforation at center.
Reverse: ONE CENT above, inverted shield and wreath stalks below, open field within, perforation at center.

J-1722

Number	Metal	Edge	Rarity	Pop	T/A	Last Traded at Auction				60	63	65
						Firm	Date	Amount	Grade			
1721	Nick	PE	5	40	36	Heritage	6/2005	$2,990	PCGSPF66CA	$1,400	$2,000	$3,000
1722	Alu	PE	L7	9	8	ANR	3/2005	$3,680	NGCPF66	$1,600	$2,750	$4,250

J-1723: 1884 Cent

Variation of Eastman Johnson's "holey" design.

Obverse: Motifs as preceding, but with raised rims bordering the central perforation (which upon striking still had an irregularly shaped opening).
Reverse: Similar to preceding.

J-1723

Number	Metal	Edge	Rarity	Pop	T/A	Last Traded at Auction				60	63	65
						Firm	Date	Amount	Grade			
1723	WM	PE	8	0	2	Bowers & Merena	11/2002	$5,290	PF63	N/A	$13,000	N/A

J-1723a: 1884 Cent

Struck from regular dies. Believed to be a mint error struck on a foreign planchet.

J-1723a

Number	Metal	Edge	Rarity	Pop	T/A	Last Traded at Auction				60	63	65
						Firm	Date	Amount	Grade			
1723a	Nick	PE	8	0	1	NERCG	3/1977	$875	PF	N/A	N/A	N/A

J-1724 to J-1726: 1884 Five-Cent Piece

Eastman Johnson's "holey" design.

Obverse: FIVE above, CENTS below, shield to each side. Open field at center with an irregular perforation.
Reverse: Around border, UNITED STATES OF AMERICA / 1884 enclosing circle of 13 stars. Open field at center enclosing irregular perforation.

J-1724

Number	Metal	Edge	Rarity	Pop	T/A	Last Traded at Auction				60	63	65
						Firm	Date	Amount	Grade			
1724	Nick	PE	L6	23	16	Bowers & Merena	1/2003	$3,565	PCGSPF65	$1,550	$2,200	$4,150
1725	Alu	PE	L7	10	5	Heritage	6/2005	$8,625	PCGSPF66	$2,000	$3,350	$6,500
1726	WM	PE	U	0	0	N/A	N/A	N/A	N/A	N/A	N/A	N/A

J-1727 and J-1728 (1884 pattern five-cent piece in aluminum and dime in copper) are no longer believed to exist.

J-1729: 1884 Quarter Dollar

Trial piece struck from regular dies. This pattern, and all of those that made up the unique 1884 copper set (from quarter dollar to double eagle, including the rare trade dollar), was presented to A.M. Smith, who authored the Mint's visitor's guides.

J-1729

Number	Metal	Edge	Rarity	Pop	T/A	Last Traded at Auction				60	63	65
						Firm	Date	Amount	Grade			
1729	C	RE	U	1	2	Superior	5/2003	$17,250	PCGSPF62RB	$17,000	$28,000	N/A

J-1730: 1884 Half Dollar

Trial piece struck from regular dies. This piece was sold by M.H. Bolender as Lot 27 in his 101st sale of the A.M. Smith collection (February 1936). It later appeared in the 1953 ANA sale, and has not been seen since.

J-1730

Number	Metal	Edge	Rarity	Pop	T/A	Last Traded at Auction				60	63	65
						Firm	Date	Amount	Grade			
1730	C	RE	U	1	1	Kosoff	8/1953	$40	BrPF	N/A	$35,000	N/A

J-1731: 1884 Silver Dollar

Trial piece struck from regular dies.

J-1731

Number	Metal	Edge	Rarity	Pop	T/A	Last Traded at Auction				60	63	65
						Firm	Date	Amount	Grade			
1731	C	RE	U	1	2	Superior	7/2003	$19,838	NGCPF62BN	$18,000	$30,000	N/A

Patterns of 1884

J-1731a: 1884-O Silver Dollar

Struck from regular dies. First announced in 1993.[20]

J-1731a

Number	Metal	Edge	Rarity	Pop	T/A	Last Traded at Auction				60	63	65
						Firm	Date	Amount	Grade			
1731a	C	RE	U	0	0	N/A	N/A	N/A	N/A	N/A	N/A	N/A

J-1732: 1884 Trade Dollar

Struck from regular dies. The two confirmed examples have been silver plated. These are of special interest, as the related silver strikings of the 1884 trade dollar are classic rarities (just 10 were struck) and are desired by a wide audience. One is in the Smithsonian Institution.

J-1732

Number	Metal	Edge	Rarity	Pop	T/A	Last Traded at Auction				60	63	65
						Firm	Date	Amount	Grade			
1732	C	RE	8	1	1	ANR	1/2004	$55,200	SEGSPF62	$27,500	$55,000	$90,000

J-1733: 1884 Gold Dollar

Struck from regular dies.

J-1733

Number	Metal	Edge	Rarity	Pop	T/A	Last Traded at Auction				60	63	65
						Firm	Date	Amount	Grade			
1733	C	RE	U	0	0	N/A	N/A	N/A	N/A	$8,500	$18,000	$26,000

J-1734: 1884 $2.50

Trial piece struck from regular dies.

J-1734

Number	Metal	Edge	Rarity	Pop	T/A	Last Traded at Auction				60	63	65
						Firm	Date	Amount	Grade			
1734	C	RE	U	1	1	Bowers & Ruddy	10/1977	$900	ChPF	N/A	$20,000	$32,500

J-1735: 1884 $3

Trial piece struck from regular dies.

J-1735

Number	Metal	Edge	Rarity	Pop	T/A	Last Traded at Auction				60	63	65
						Firm	Date	Amount	Grade			
1735	C	RE	U	1	3	Bowers & Merena	10/2000	$8,050	PCGSPF64RB	N/A	$18,000	$30,000

J-1736: 1884 $5

Trial piece struck from regular dies.

J-1736

Number	Metal	Edge	Rarity	Pop	T/A	Last Traded at Auction				60	63	65
						Firm	Date	Amount	Grade			
1736	C	RE	U	1	1	Stack's	4/1966	$105	PF	N/A	$15,000	$25,000

J-1737: 1884 $10

Trial piece struck from regular dies.

J-1737

Number	Metal	Edge	Rarity	Pop	T/A	Last Traded at Auction				60	63	65
						Firm	Date	Amount	Grade			
1737	C	RE	U	1	1	Stack's	4/1966	$105	PF	$10,000	$20,000	$35,000

J-1738: 1884 $20

Trial piece struck from regular dies.

J-1738

Number	Metal	Edge	Rarity	Pop	T/A	Last Traded at Auction				60	63	65
						Firm	Date	Amount	Grade			
1738	C	RE	U	1	1	Superior	10/1989	$11,550	PF60	$20,000	N/A	N/A

Patterns of 1885

History and Overview

The year 1885 continues Eastman Johnson's "holey" proposal, but with the perforations uniform and surrounded with interior rims containing dentils.

A pair of regular Proof dies for the Morgan silver dollar was used to strike J-1747 through J-1749, with an experimental edge displaying in raised letters the motto E PLURIBUS UNUM. The purpose for such a pattern is not known, as the same motto was included on the obverse die. Such issues were mainly distributed privately, not openly to collectors. This year also marks the last time that sets of coins from Proof dies were made in off-metals, in this case aluminum.

In July 1885, James P. Kimball became director of the Mint, and the numismatic shenanigans that began in the spring of 1859 under Director James Ross Snowden (and had continued uninterruptedly through several changes of officers since that time) came to an end. To be sure, there were a few numismatic delicacies made at a later date, particularly in 1907 as part of the Saint-Gaudens coinage, but the productions of thousands of patterns for profits to line pockets of Mint officials no longer took place.

Although the morality and legality of the 1859 through 1885 coining scenario falls apart even under the most casual scrutiny, numismatists are everlastingly grateful for the beautiful products made during this span, which would not have been created otherwise. Where would we be without enough 1856 Flying Eagle cents to satisfy everyone, or without more than a dozen varieties of pattern 1858 cents to choose from, or all those GOD OUR TRUST patterns of 1861 to 1863, or aluminum and copper Proof sets of silver and gold denominations, or Standard Silver oddities, or 1872 Amazonian coins, or 1877 pattern half dollars, or so many other things? As John Greenleaf Whittier wrote, one can only imagine "what might have been," but was not—if Mint officials had continued privately producing patterns for another 35 or more years, through the early 1920s. The present book might have to be double its size! Such things are fun to contemplate.

Collecting Perspective

Both varieties of the Eastman-inspired "holey" patterns are rare, but over a period of time, examples come to market. When found, they are usually in high grades. The 1885 lettered-edge Morgan dollar is a prime curiosity, and the demand for this is extended to include many collectors of the regular dollars, although when in a certified holder, the all-important edge feature cannot be seen. The off-metal pieces in aluminum are extremely rare.

J-1739: 1885 Cent

Trial piece struck from regular dies.

J-1739

Number	Metal	Edge	Rarity	Pop	T/A	Last Traded at Auction				60	63	65
						Firm	Date	Amount	Grade			
1739	Alu	PE	8	0	1	Doyle Galleries	12/1983	$1,700	PF65	N/A	N/A	N/A

J-1740 and J-1740a: 1885 Cent

Apparently the obverse date was erroneously cut as 1883, then corrected, yielding 1885/3. Possibly two die varieties exist, but this has not been confirmed. The striking of this silver piece confirms its status as a numismatic delicacy, for no regular cents were considered in this metal.

Obverse: UNITED STATES OF AMERICA above, 1885 below. Open field at center except for border of dentils surrounding perforation.
Reverse: ONE CENT above, shield flanked by branches below, open field at center except for border of dentils surrounding perforation.

J-1740

Number	Metal	Edge	Rarity	Pop	T/A	Last Traded at Auction				60	63	65
						Firm	Date	Amount	Grade			
1740	Silv	PE	H6	12	8	ANR	8/2004	$6,038	NGCPF66	$1,700	$2,750	$5,000
1740a*	Silv	PE	U	0	0	N/A	N/A	N/A	N/A	N/A	N/A	N/A

* J-1740a is not perforated.

J-1741: 1885 Three-Cent Piece

Trial piece struck from regular dies.

J-1741

Number	Metal	Edge	Rarity	Pop	T/A	Last Traded at Auction				60	63	65
						Firm	Date	Amount	Grade			
1741	Alu	PE	8	3	2	Heritage	6/2005	$9,200	PCGSPF66	$2,900	$5,150	$9,500

J-1742: 1885 Five-Cent Piece

Struck in silver, this piece is the very definition of a numismatic delicacy.

Obverse: Similar to reverse of J-1724 of 1884, but with date 1885. UNITED STATES OF AMERICA / 1885 around border, enclosing circle of 13 stars. Open field at center except for border of dentils surrounding perforation.
Reverse: FIVE CENTS above, shield flanked by branches below. Open field at center except for border of dentils surrounding perforation.

J-1742

Number	Metal	Edge	Rarity	Pop	T/A	Last Traded at Auction				60	63	65
						Firm	Date	Amount	Grade			
1742	Silv	PE	H6	13	10	Bowers & Merena	1/2003	$5,750	PCGSPF64	$2,100	$3,450	$7,000

J-1743: 1885 Five-Cent Piece

Trial piece struck from regular dies.

J-1743

Number	Metal	Edge	Rarity	Pop	T/A	Last Traded at Auction				60	63	65
						Firm	Date	Amount	Grade			
1743	Alu	PE	8	0	1	Paramount	8/1980	$4,000	GemPF	$8,500	$16,500	$26,000

J-1744: 1885 Dime

Trial piece struck from regular dies.

J-1744

Number	Metal	Edge	Rarity	Pop	T/A	Last Traded at Auction				60	63	65
						Firm	Date	Amount	Grade			
1744	Alu	RE	8	2	3	ANR	12/2003	$20,700	PCGSPF67CA	$7,000	$12,000	$20,000

J-1745: 1885 Quarter Dollar

Trial piece struck from regular dies.

J-1745

Number	Metal	Edge	Rarity	Pop	T/A	Last Traded at Auction				60	63	65
						Firm	Date	Amount	Grade			
1745	Alu	RE	8	1	1	Heritage	5/1989	$5,100	PCGSPF65	$7,800	$15,500	$23,500

J-1746: 1885 Half Dollar

Trial piece struck from regular dies.

J-1746

Number	Metal	Edge	Rarity	Pop	T/A	Last Traded at Auction				60	63	65
						Firm	Date	Amount	Grade			
1746	Alu	RE	8	1	2	Bowers & Merena	11/1992	$3,740	PCGSPF63	$8,500	$15,000	$26,000

Patterns of 1885

J-1747 to J-1749: 1885 Silver Dollar

Struck from regular dies, with experimental raised edge lettered E PLURIBUS UNUM.

J-1747

Number	Metal	Edge	Rarity	Pop	T/A	Last Traded at Auction				60	63	65
						Firm	Date	Amount	Grade			
1747	Silv	LE	L6	17	16	ANR	11/2004	$16,100	NGCPF66	$3,850	$7,500	$12,000
1748	C	LE	L7	6	7	ANR	3/2004	$7,820	NGCPF65RB	$3,200	$5,500	$11,000
1749	Alu	LE	L7	9	8	Ira & Larry Goldberg	9/2003	$13,225	PCGSPF66CA	$4,200	$8,000	$14,000

J-1750: 1885 Silver Dollar

Trial piece struck from regular dies.

J-1750

Number	Metal	Edge	Rarity	Pop	T/A	Last Traded at Auction				60	63	65
						Firm	Date	Amount	Grade			
1750	Alu	RE	8	3	4	ANR	3/2005	$17,250	NGCPF64	$5,500	$11,000	$20,000

J-1751: 1885 Gold Dollar

Trial piece struck from regular dies.

J-1751

Number	Metal	Edge	Rarity	Pop	T/A	Last Traded at Auction				60	63	65
						Firm	Date	Amount	Grade			
1751	Alu	RE	8	1	1	Superior	10/1989	$7,150	PCGSPF65	$6,500	$13,000	$22,500

J-1752: 1885 $2.50

Trial piece struck from regular dies.

J-1752

Number	Metal	Edge	Rarity	Pop	T/A	Last Traded at Auction				60	63	65
						Firm	Date	Amount	Grade			
1752	Alu	RE	8	1	1	Superior	10/1989	$7,975	PCGSPF65	$10,000	$16,500	$27,500

J-1753: 1885 $3

Trial piece struck from regular dies.

J-1753

Number	Metal	Edge	Rarity	Pop	T/A	Last Traded at Auction				60	63	65
						Firm	Date	Amount	Grade			
1753	Alu	RE	8	1	1	Ira & Larry Goldberg	2/2000	$4,600	PCGSPF63	$10,500	$17,500	$25,000

J-1754: 1885 $5

Trial piece struck from regular dies.

J-1754

Number	Metal	Edge	Rarity	Pop	T/A	Last Traded at Auction				60	63	65
						Firm	Date	Amount	Grade			
1754	Alu	RE	8	1	2	Heritage	6/2004	$17,250	PCGSPF64CA	$10,000	$15,000	$25,000

J-1755: 1885 $10

Trial piece struck from regular dies.

J-1755

Number	Metal	Edge	Rarity	Pop	T/A	Last Traded at Auction				60	63	65
						Firm	Date	Amount	Grade			
1755	Alu	RE	8	5	2	Superior	7/2003	$21,850	PCGSPF65CA	$8,000	$17,500	$27,500

J-1756: 1885 $20

Trial piece struck from regular dies.

J-1756

Number	Metal	Edge	Rarity	Pop	T/A	Last Traded at Auction				60	63	65
						Firm	Date	Amount	Grade			
1756	Alu	RE	8	2	1	Superior	5/1990	$38,500	PCGSPF66	$13,500	$22,500	$40,000

History and Overview

The single pattern issue of 1889 is the trial $3 piece, struck in copper from regular dies of the Indian Princess Head design. While traditionally listed as a trial piece, it actually might have been struck for sale to a collector.

J-1756a: 1889 $3

Trial piece struck from regular dies.

J-1756a

Number	Metal	Edge	Rarity	Pop	T/A	Last Traded at Auction				60	63	65
						Firm	Date	Amount	Grade			
1756a	C	RE	U	1	1	Superior	10/1990	–	PCGSPF63BN	N/A	$19,000	$34,000

Patterns of 1890

History and Overview

The patterns of 1890 comprise several off-metal strikings, J-1757 being discernable only upon elemental analysis. From time to time, Indian Head cents from the 1880s onward have been offered as "copper-nickel," but in reality are simply discolored bronze cents. Any transaction for off-metal pieces should be subjected to thorough analysis. From this era onward, most off-metal strikings of regular denominations fall into the class of mint errors, not patterns (and for that reason are not listed here). J-1758 are probably mint errors.

J-1757 to J-1759: 1890 Cent

Trial piece struck from regular dies.

J-1758

Number	Metal	Edge	Rarity	Pop	T/A	Last Traded at Auction				60	63	65
						Firm	Date	Amount	Grade			
1757	C	PE	8	1	0	N/A	N/A	N/A	N/A	$5,000	$10,000	$15,000
1758	C-N	PE	8	2	2	Heritage	1/1997	$4,600	PCGSMS64	$2,500	$4,000	$7,000
1759	Alu	PE	–	0	0	N/A	N/A	N/A	N/A	Unconf	Unconf	Unconf

Patterns of 1891

History and Overview

The Liberty Seated motif, so prized by numismatists today, became tiresome to certain influential people in the 19th century. In the mid-1850s, there was a call to redesign the coinage, but nothing materialized. In 1891, Mint Director James P. Kimball wrote to Secretary of the Treasury Charles Foster with regard to the "popular desire for an improvement of the coinage in respect to the present designs as prescribed by law."

Artists and engravers were invited to create sketches and ideas, and many were submitted, but all were either found to be impractical for coinage or failed to meet basic requirements of the competition. The result was that by default it fell to the current chief engraver, Charles E. Barber, to replace the Liberty Seated motif on the dime, quarter, and half dollar. The largest denomination, the dollar, had already been replaced by George T. Morgan in 1878.

It should be noted here that Chief Engraver Charles E. Barber was a very jealous man. Time and again he found the idea of talented outsiders poaching on his domain (coin design) offensive. Barber, possessed of modest inherent talent, bitterly complained about prominent artists and others who sought to have their elegant designs employed for circulating coins. (This situation would come to a head from 1905 to 1907, when President Theodore Roosevelt collaborated with Augustus Saint-Gaudens in the production of the MCMVII gold $20 and other issues.)

Barber's coins featured a standardized head of Liberty facing right, crowned with a laurel wreath and the word LIBERTY.[1] The reverse in its final form showed a heraldic eagle with stars, adapted from the Great Seal of the United States (and used on certain early coinage commencing with the 1796 $2.50).

Collecting Perspective

The only known examples of the Barber coinage of 1891 are in the Smithsonian Institution. All have been cleaned and polished several times (before the era of modern curatorship, which commenced in the mid-20th century), accounting for their appearance in illustrations. An example of J-1766 may be in private hands in addition to a pair in the Smithsonian, but it has not been traced in recent generations.

J-1760: 1891 Dime

Transitional issue, obverse and reverse of 1892. Two pieces are known, both in the Smithsonian Institution.

Obverse: Barber's head of Liberty facing right, UNITED STATES OF AMERICA surrounding, date below. This is the design adopted in 1892.
Reverse: Wreath of oak, corn, and wheat, open at top, enclosing ONE DIME (the regular issue, essentially the style adopted in 1860[2] and not changed in the meantime).

J-1760

Number	Metal	Edge	Rarity	Pop	T/A	Last Traded at Auction				60	63	65
						Firm	Date	Amount	Grade			
1760	Silv	RE	8	0	0	N/A	N/A	N/A	N/A	N/A	N/A	N/A

J-1761: 1891 Quarter Dollar

Two pieces are known, both in the Smithsonian Institution.

Obverse: Barber's head of Liberty facing right, IN GOD WE TRUST above, seven stars left, six stars right, date 1891 below. Similar to the design adopted in 1892.
Reverse: Heraldic eagle. Somewhat similar in general concept to the adopted issue, except for certain stars being below the ribbon and for a group of clouds above.

J-1761

Number	Metal	Edge	Rarity	Pop	T/A	Last Traded at Auction				60	63	65
						Firm	Date	Amount	Grade			
1761	Silv	RE	8	0	0	N/A	N/A	N/A	N/A	N/A	N/A	N/A

J-1762: 1891 Half Dollar

In the Smithsonian Institution.

Obverse: Barber's head of Liberty facing right, IN GOD WE TRUST above, seven stars left, six stars right, date 1891 below. Stars each have six points. Similar to the design adopted in 1892.
Reverse: Heraldic eagle. Somewhat similar in concept to the adopted design, except for certain stars being below the ribbon and for a group of clouds above.

J-1762

Number	Metal	Edge	Rarity	Pop	T/A	Last Traded at Auction				60	63	65
						Firm	Date	Amount	Grade			
1762	Silv	RE	U	0	0	N/A	N/A	N/A	N/A	N/A	N/A	N/A

J-1763: 1891 Half Dollar

Transitional issue, obverse and reverse of 1892. In the Smithsonian Institution.

Obverse: Barber's head of Liberty, as preceding.
Reverse: Heraldic eagle, with stars above; the design adopted in 1892.

J-1763

Number	Metal	Edge	Rarity	Pop	T/A	Last Traded at Auction				60	63	65
						Firm	Date	Amount	Grade			
1763	Silv	RE	U	0	0	N/A	N/A	N/A	N/A	N/A	N/A	N/A

J-1764: 1891 Half Dollar

Two pieces are known, both in the Smithsonian Institution.

Obverse: Barber's head of Liberty, as preceding.
Reverse: Variation on the heraldic eagle, but with differences in the olive branch, a shorter scroll, and with clouds above the stars.

J-1764

Number	Metal	Edge	Rarity	Pop	T/A	Last Traded at Auction				60	63	65
						Firm	Date	Amount	Grade			
1764	Silv	RE	8	0	0	N/A	N/A	N/A	N/A	N/A	N/A	N/A

Patterns of 1891

J-1765: 1891 Half Dollar

Two pieces are known, both in the Smithsonian Institution.

Obverse: Barber's head of Liberty, similar to the adopted issue, but with each star having five points rather than six.
Reverse: Variation on the heraldic eagle theme, with an oak wreath, open at the top, encircling the eagle, and with other differences.

J-1765

Number	Metal	Edge	Rarity	Pop	T/A	Last Traded at Auction				60	63	65
						Firm	Date	Amount	Grade			
1765	Silv	RE	8	0	0	N/A	N/A	N/A	N/A	N/A	N/A	N/A

J-1766: 1891 Half Dollar

Two pieces are known, both in the Smithsonian Institution. A third was owned by collector Stephen Nagy at one time, but is now not traced.

Obverse: Barber's design with goddess standing, variously known as Liberty or Columbia, her right hand holding a sword, her left a pole on which a liberty cap is mounted. Resplendent rays behind, among which is the lettering IN GOD WE TRUST. Around the top border is L I B E R T Y interspersed by stars, with other stars at lower left and right, date below. A perched eagle, facing right, is seen behind the goddess.
Reverse: Variation on that used on J-1765, but with significantly smaller eagle, rays above the clouds, and other differences.

J-1766

Number	Metal	Edge	Rarity	Pop	T/A	Last Traded at Auction				60	63	65
						Firm	Date	Amount	Grade			
1766	Silv	RE	8	0	0	N/A	N/A	N/A	N/A	N/A	N/A	N/A

Patterns of 1896

History and Overview

The patterns of 1896 comprise two different denominations, each with a single die design combination, but in die varieties among those designs, and also in a bewildering array of metal possibilities, more than a dozen all told. The dies were by Charles E. Barber. Each featured a shield design on the obverse and a wreath on the reverse, a motif not particularly attractive to the modern eye, and certainly not seriously considered for replacing the Liberty Head nickel (also by Barber, and generally considered to be among his better works) in use at the time.

According to an official report, 15 different metal combinations were used to strike these pieces, and 10 pieces were struck from each alloy.

A resolution passed by the House of Representatives June 9, 1896, requested the secretary of the Treasury to report "as to the comparative merits and advantages of pure nickel alloy, aluminum combined or alloyed with other metals, and of copper bronze as material for our minor coins, and authorized the string of such experimental minor coins, of the metals above mentioned, pure and in combination with other metals, as he may deem necessary and proper."

In compliance with the resolution, experimental five- and one-cent pieces were struck at the Mint from pure nickel, pure aluminum; an alloy of 66% copper, 18% nickel, and 16% zinc; and three different alloys of aluminum. The technical aspects of the alloys are given below:

(1) 98.78% aluminum; 0.40% iron; 0.45% silicon; 0.37% copper • (2) 96.94% aluminum; 0.65% iron; 0.38% silicon; 2.03% copper • (3) 96.74% aluminum; 0.45% iron; 0.31% silicon; 1.94% copper; 0.56% manganese.

In addition to these, the five-cent pieces were struck in the standard alloy of 75% copper and 25% nickel and in four alloys of German silver: (1) 60% copper; 15% zinc; 25% nickel • (2) 60% copper; 20% zinc; 20% nickel • (3) 63% copper; 19% zinc; 18% nickel • (4) 65% copper; 20% zinc; 15% nickel.

The cents were also struck in alloys of (1) 95% copper; 3% tin; 2% zinc • (2) 88.95% copper; 0.05% tin; 10.55% zinc • (3) 95% copper; 5% tin • (4) 83-1/3% copper; 16-2/3% zinc.

The cents were also struck in two alloys of phosphor bronze: (1) 95% copper 4.6% tin; 0.4% phosphorus • (2) 93% copper; 6.5% tin; 0.5% phosphorus.

These pieces, many of which must have appeared virtually identical to the eye, were given to the Honorable Charles W. Stone, Chairman of the Committee of Coinage, Weights, and Measures. The results of the project were synopsized in a committee report:[3]

> The conclusions from these experiments were that (1) pure nickel was "difficult to work and was hard on dies," (2) the alloy of copper 66%, nickel 18% and zinc 16% was "practically too hard to coin," and (3) aluminum and its alloys were too soft and produced a blurred edge before the design was brought up and was liable to clog the dies.
>
> While a number of the alloys submitted for test were found to work satisfactorily, it is not believed that any of them would be an improvement upon the alloys at present in use. It is, however, recommended that authority be granted to make further experiments with a view to finding an alloy that would be an improvement upon that used in the manufacture of the bronze one-cent pieces.

On February 12, 1897, other experimental five-cent coins were struck from aluminum alloys and pure nickel in the presence of the members of the annual Assay Commission, then in session at the Philadelphia Mint, without satisfactory results, the alloys of aluminum again proving too soft and the pure nickel too hard.

The Mint continued to experiment with pure nickel and discovered that the difficulty encountered in the two above-mentioned strikings was due to improper annealing of the blanks. It was discovered that properly annealed blanks were malleable and received the impression from dies without any pressure greater than that required to strike the regular-issue minor coins.

Collecting Perspective

An example in one metal or another of each of the two denominations can be readily collected today. The striking of the pieces was not particularly satisfactory at the time of issue, for reasons of the alloys involved and also from lack of die polishing. The appearance is no more pleasing today. Beyond that, certain pieces, particularly in aluminum, were poorly stored years later when they were in the possession of William H. Woodin and his estate. These and "several crates" of patterns or restrikes were acquired by Woodin in 1909, through Philadelphia dealer John W. Haseltine, who knew all along that "all the patterns were packed away in the dark corners of the Philadelphia Mint."[4] This treasure trove of long-unseen patterns was acquired in a swap whereby Woodin gave to the Mint Collection the two gold strikings of the 1877 $50 (J-1546 and J-1548). Though many were sold by Woodin himself (and furnished the raison d'etre for his 1913 book on patterns), many were retained in his estate after his death on May 4, 1934. The Woodin estate coins went to F.C.C. Boyd, Abe Kosoff, and, residually, to Robert K. Botsford, of Nescopeck, a community near Woodin's home town of Berwick, Pennsylvania. Hundreds of the 1896 patterns were sold in the 1940s and early 1950s, some of the later sales being to the present editor.

J-1767 to J-1769: 1896 Cent

Two obverse die varieties and two reverse die varieties are known for J-1768. The following listing is simplified; for specific alloys coined, see "History and Overview."

Obverse: Charles E. Barber's design. At the center is a shield, across which is a ribbon inscribed LIBERTY, incused. Crossed poles behind support a liberty cap and an eagle. E PLURIBUS UNUM above, 1896 below, seven stars left, six right, all within a circle of dots.
Reverse: Olive wreath enclosing 1 CENT. Around the border inside a circle of dots is UNITED STATES OF AMERICA.

J-1768a

Number	Metal	Edge	Rarity	Pop	T/A	Last Traded at Auction				60	63	65
						Firm	Date	Amount	Grade			
1767	Nick	PE	L7	7	5	Heritage	11/2004	$1,064	NCSImpPF	$1,600	$2,900	$5,150
1767a	*	PE	L7	7	3	ANR	3/2005	$4,715	NGCPF65	$2,050	$3,550	$6,500
1768	Brz	PE	5	18	24	Stack's	6/2005	$6,900	NGCPF66RB	$2,000	$3,800	$5,750
1768a	Brs	PE	8	6	2	ANR	8/2004	$4,255	NGCPF64	$2,000	$4,000	$6,000
1769	Alu	PE	H6	16	13	Heritage	11/2003	$1,208	PCGSPF60	$2,200	$3,350	$5,750

* J-1767a: pure nickel

Patterns of 1896

J-1770 to J-1772: 1896 Five-Cent Piece

The following listing is simplified; for specific alloys coined, see "History and Overview."[5]

Obverse: Charles E. Barber's design. At the center is a shield, across which is a ribbon inscribed LIBERTY, incused. Crossed poles behind support a liberty cap and an eagle. E PLURIBUS UNUM above, 1896 below, seven stars left, six right, all within circle of dots.
Reverse: Olive wreath enclosing 5 CENTS. Around the border inside a circle of dots is UNITED STATES OF AMERICA.

J-1770

Number	Metal	Edge	Rarity	Pop	T/A	Last Traded at Auction			60	63	65
						Firm	Date	Amount	Grade			
1770	Nick	PE	L6	35	26	ANR	10/2004	$2,070	PCGSPF64	$1,250	$2,200	$3,100
1771	*	PE	L6	23	18	Heritage	6/2005	$4,025	PCGSPF65	$1,300	$2,300	$4,150
1771a	Brz	PE	8	0	2	Bowers & Merena	1/2003	$12,650	PCGSPF64	$6,000	$10,000	$16,000
1772	Alu	PE	H6	25	16	Heritage	1/2005	$1,840	PCGSPF62	$1,300	$2,300	$4,150

* J-171: pure nickel

Patterns of 1906

In 1906, Chief Engraver Charles E. Barber created a pattern double eagle, the background of which has not been recorded in detail. However, it does not take much of a stretch of the imagination to envision the possibility that Barber, confronted with noted sculptor Augustus Saint-Gaudens working on coinage designs (see Patterns of 1907), felt threatened and endeavored to create his own version. At the time the double eagle, the subject of J-1773 under discussion here, was the denomination to which Saint-Gaudens gave prime focus.

Barber's pattern of 1906 featured Liberty facing left, a Phrygian cap atop her head, a laurel wreath, the inscription LIBERTY, and the ends of the cap below, following the back of the neck. The reverse copied the figure of Liberty or Columbia from a half dollar pattern he had designed in 1891 (J-1766). This piece was struck with a raised edge, featuring E PLURIBUS UNUM punctuated by stars as later used on some 1907 Saint-Gaudens patterns. How many were struck is not known, nor in what metals. Today one gold impression has been accounted for, in the Smithsonian Institution.

Although no one-cent pattern coins are known to have been made in 1906 or 1907, Augustus Saint-Gaudens worked on new designs, with the obverses featuring a flying eagle with rays and the word LIBERTY; a Liberty head with olive leaves; and an Indian head. Certain of these motifs were used on patterns and regular coinage of the following year. A plaster model of a 1907 Flying Eagle cent with wreath reverse is preserved by the Saint-Gaudens National Historic Site.

Pattern coins struck in the third Mint facility in Philadelphia, included the J-1773 of 1906 discussed here, the illustrious Saint-Gaudens coinage of 1907, and the new silver designs for the dime, quarter dollar, and half dollar of 1916, among many others. No longer were patterns made available on an open basis to numismatists, and for some issues, no copies were preserved for posterity. In 1923, the Mint Collection, as it was called by then, was transferred to the Smithsonian Institution.

The existing record of 20th-century patterns is an incomplete one—very incomplete, as in the 1970s, Mint Director Stella Hackel ordered the unfortunate destruction of many unique, uncopied Mint records and much correspondence, as storage space was at a premium. However, many models and galvanos of proposals and patterns were retained.

J-1773: 1906 $20

Obverse: Charles E. Barber's head of Liberty, facing left, seven stars to the left, six to the right, date 1906 below.
Reverse: Standing Liberty or Columbia motif, her right hand holding a sword, her left a pole on which a liberty cap is mounted. A perched eagle, facing right, is seen behind the figure. Resplendent rays behind, among which is the lettering IN GOD to the left of figure and WE TRUST to the right. UNITED STATES OF AMERICA above, TWENTY to left of figure and DOLLARS to the right. In raised letters on the edge is the inscription from a three-part collar, E * P * L * U * R / * I * B * U * S / * U * N * U * M *.

J-1773

Number	Metal	Edge	Rarity	Pop	T/A	Last Traded at Auction			60	63	65
						Firm	Date	Amount	Grade			
1773	Gold	LE	U	0	0	N/A	N/A	N/A	N/A	N/A	N/A	N/A

History and Overview

The story of President Theodore Roosevelt and his collaboration with artist and sculptor Augustus Saint-Gaudens is one of the most interesting and familiar in American numismatics. In September 1901, "Teddy" Roosevelt, then vice president of the United States, unexpectedly became chief executive following the assassination of William McKinley at the Pan-American Exposition in Buffalo, New York.

Roosevelt, an accomplished writer, outdoorsman, and lover of the fine life, fit easily into the White House scene, bringing with him the trappings of education, familiarity with both high society and rustic surroundings, and a sense of practicality. Recently he had achieved national acclaim in the Battle of San Juan Hill in the Spanish-American War of 1898, in command of his "Rough Riders."

Later, in November 1904, Roosevelt was elected president, continuing his tenure in a position he obviously enjoyed. Soon, his thoughts turned to the coins then in use in America, and upon contemplation, he thought they could be improved, perhaps approaching the beauty of ancient Greek coins he had admired at the Smithsonian Institution. On December 27, 1904, he wrote to Leslie Mortier Shaw, his secretary of the Treasury: "I think our coinage is artistically of atrocious hideousness. Would it be possible, without asking permission of Congress, to employ a man like Saint-Gaudens to give us a coinage that would have some beauty?"

He was told that the way was clear, and he contacted Augustus Saint-Gaudens, at the time America's best-known sculptor, and asked if he would be interested in redesigning the entire American coinage from the cent to the double eagle. Saint-Gaudens had designed the medal for Roosevelt's 1905 inauguration. The sculptor wrote back in the affirmative, and stated that by all considerations his all-time favorite American coin motif was the flying eagle on the obverse of the cent of 1857 and 1858. This proved to be a poignant observation, for his own version of a flying eagle would soon be incorporated on the new double eagle; but first, in 1906 the artist envisioned it as the obverse motif for a one-cent piece (never made in pattern form).

Sketches and models were prepared, some based on new concepts, others on sculptures that Saint-Gaudens had done earlier. In particular, the standing figure of Miss Liberty, called *Victory*, was appealing and had been used as part of the 1903 Sherman Victory monument erected in the Grand Army Plaza at the southeast corner of Central Park in New York City. In that sculpture group, the goddess Victory, modeled by Miss Hettie Anderson, strode forward, her right hand holding aloft a torch, and her left an olive branch. The double eagle, considered to be the first focus of the artist's commission, was to feature her as the central obverse motif, with additions including resplendent rays behind, and a small depiction of the United States Capitol building at the lower left.

The reverse of the new double eagle reinforced Saint-Gaudens's appreciation of an eagle in flight, his own version not at all like that on the 1857 and 1858 cents. At the bottom of the reverse, the outline of a sun was given as an arc, radiating rays upward. A nod to the classic influence was given by proposing that the coin be in high relief, almost sculptured in appearance, similar in this regard to the coins of ancient Greece that Roosevelt had admired earlier. Beyond that, the date of 1907 in Roman numerals, MCMVII, was at once artistic and unusual.

While various sketches of models for the double eagle were being prepared, the artist also drew up designs for the $10 eagle, featuring a woman wearing an Indian headdress, facing to the left, with a standing eagle on the reverse. Models were made for other denominations as well, but only the $10 and $20 were ever translated into coinage form. Today, the preparatory work of the artist still exists, and much is on display at the Saint-Gaudens National Historic Site, in Cornish, New Hampshire, while the Dartmouth College Library in nearby Hanover holds other items. The Cornish site displays much of Saint-Gaudens's other work, and from a numismatic viewpoint is worth a special visit.

Chief Engraver Charles E. Barber learned early of the "interference" of Saint-Gaudens in the coinage design proposal, and nearly from the outset complained about it. After the ideas were translated to models, Barber remonstrated that high-relief designs could not be struck properly on high-speed coinage presses and that the entire project was doomed to failure. Roosevelt squared off against Barber and the Mint, calling the redesign project his "pet crime." Regardless of what Barber thought, the design was going to be created!

Patterns of 1907

The preceding is but a brief sketch of the scenario. In spring 1907, dies were prepared for patterns of the double eagle (J-1907), these having the field and a few other details slightly different from the finished versions. The first five specimens were struck between February 7 and 15, 1907 (J-1907). Seven blows of the press, at 150 tons of pressure, were required to fully bring up the design. The dies broke after four lettered-edge coins and one plain-edge coin (J-1908)[1] were struck. Specimens of J-1907 have the edge lettered in the style of Barber's 1906 pattern $20, from a three-part collar divided as, E * P * L * U * R / * I * B * U * S * / U * N * U * M *. A second pair of dies was completed by May 3, and additional specimens were made (J-1909).[2] The second press run was made with a newer version of the edge, as *******E* / PLURIBUS * / UNUM***. Examples of J-1907 to J-1910 today are called Ultra High Relief by numismatists. The number struck is not known, but estimates have ranged up to nearly two dozen.[3] In addition, at least one impression was made of a $20 featuring a woman wearing an Indian war bonnet, with LIBERTY in large letters below, stars above, and with the reverse flying eagle related to that on the $20 piece. This particular coin (J-1905) was made on direct orders from President Roosevelt so that Saint-Gaudens could see the concept in coined form.[4] Today the piece is in private hands.

Augustus Saint-Gaudens was suffering from intestinal cancer which proved terminal; he died on August 3, 1907. His assistant, Henry Hering, finished the models, and worked with the Philadelphia Mint to create circulating coins. It proved to be true that regular high-speed production presses could not be used, and therefore slow-speed presses were employed, with each coin struck three separate times to properly bring up the relief. The coinage of the regular MCMVII issue included 11,250 by December 30; another 272 on December 31; 267 on January 2, 1908; 278 on January 3; and 300 on January 6, bringing the total to 12,367.[5]

Part way through the coinage of these 12,367 MCMVII High Relief double eagles produced as regular issues, Roosevelt was satisfied that his goal had been accomplished, and the rest of the project was turned over to Chief Engraver Barber. The original design of the artist was lowered to shallow relief, the Roman numerals were abolished in favor of 1907, and new dies were made, suitable for production of coins in quantity. Low-relief pieces with the date as 1907 were made in December of that year (released on December 13[6]), parallel with continuing production of MCMVII coins. At the time the double eagle was the gold coin of choice—the easiest way to convert a large amount of bullion into coin form. In its modified version, revised with the addition of the motto IN GOD WE TRUST in May 1908, the Saint-Gaudens double eagle was produced through 1933.

While the regular MCMVII High Relief double eagle and its pattern counterpart, the Ultra High Relief J-1907 and related issues, have captured most of the limelight, two varieties of $10 gold eagles are listed among patterns. These are more properly described as regular-issue coins. These feature the portrait of Liberty, facing left, said to have been modeled from Hettie Anderson, who posed for Saint-Gaudens for the Sherman Victory monument.[7]

The war bonnet, in real Indian culture used only by males, is fanciful in this application, similar to its use on the Indian Head cent. On the reverse is an eagle, facing left. The versions listed with patterns have periods or dots before and after the reverse inscriptions: UNITED STATES OF AMERICA and E PLURIBUS UNUM, as well as TEN DOLLARS. These are absent on the issues made in larger quantities for circulation.

The dies for the first type ("wire rim") of the $10 were made from Saint-Gaudens's models delivered to the Mint in June 1907. Coins struck from the dies had a wire or knife rim and periods ("pellets") before and after the lettering on the reverse. The edge stars were crowded and of different sizes near one of the collar segment junctions, as if extra stars were added without thought to correct size and spacing (three collar segments with stars 15-15-16, with the last two stars on the 16-star segment larger than the others). In late August or early September, 500 were struck. On December 14, these were ordered to be transferred to the Treasury Department in Washington. On December 30, a further six specimens were made, presumably of the same format.

The dies for the second type ("rolled rim") were made from the same models as the preceding, but with the addition of a border to provide a wide rim and to allow the coins to stack better. The edge with irregular stars is the same as on the first type. The quantity struck with irregular stars is unknown. For circulation 31,500 were made, with equally sized and evenly spaced stars on the edge, under the order of Acting Mint Director Robert E. Preston. Assistant Secretary of the Treasury John H. Edwards directed them to be released into commerce, but this was countermanded by Mint Director Frank A. Leach, who ordered them melted. At least 23 pieces are known to have escaped the destruction and entered in records as having been sold to collectors and others (the figure of 42 coins is widely quoted elsewhere).

Dies and hubs, including rim modification, for the first two types were prepared by Charles E. Barber.

Hubs and dies for the third or "regular" $10 type made in large quantities for circulation were made by Barber following models supplied by Homer Saint-Gaudens and Henry Hering, the artist's son and assistant, respectively, as to the minimum relief acceptable for the design. These differ in having a wide rim, equally sized and evenly spaced stars on the edge, and no periods or pellets on the reverse. Production was ordered on December 2.

Numismatic researcher Roger W. Burdette suggests that the Mint openly sold examples of all three $10 varieties as well as the regular MCMVII High Relief and the pattern MCMVII Ultra High Relief "to any collector who requested them and enclosed payment plus postage. These were also available at the Philadelphia Mint cash window, but no records were kept of cash purchasers. President Roosevelt approved sale of the experimental coins to collectors."

This open sale arrangement existed only for a brief time and was nowhere publicized in collectors' periodicals (such as *The Numismatist*). Soon, such sales became private, with no records known to exist today. Nearly all of the 500 1907 Wire Rim eagles transferred to the Treasury Department were quietly dispersed among privileged officials.[8]

Collecting Perspective

Three of the patterns of 1907 are available on the market with some regularity, these being the $10 issues designated as J-1901 and J-1903 and the $20 variety listed as J-1909. The first two, the "With Periods" eagles, are typically encountered with a matte-like "Uncirculated" or "Mint State" surfaces, although some have been designated as Proofs. Whether they were all Proofs or all Mint State can be debated and will probably never be determined to everyone's satisfaction. J-1901 is the most often encountered, with several hundred being in numismatic hands. Nearly all are in Mint State, typically MS-62 to MS-65 or so. These are known by their rim characteristics, designated as "Wire Rim" issues, and are listed in the *Guide Book of United States Coins* and other popular references. The related piece, J-1903, is similar in design and punctuation, but has a "Rolled Rim." Only a few dozen are in numismatic hands. Again, all examples of J-1903 are either Proof or Mint State, depending on your point of view.[9]

The third collectible pattern is the well-known J-1908 Ultra High Relief double eagle dated MCMVII. Scarcely a year or two will pass on the calendar without an example being offered at auction. However, the issue is so famous and in such great demand that pieces are often listed high among record sale realizations.

Note: Effective with the 8th edition, all patterns of 1907 and later were assigned new ranges of Judd numbers, to admit many additional listings and to clarify old ones without excessive use of a, b, c, d, e. The new series begins with J-1901, thus avoiding any overlap with the old Judd numbers from the year 1907 forward.

J-1901 to J-1903: 1907 $10

Regular or pattern? This point can be debated. All seem to be of the same format, struck from dies with raised minute swirls. • J-1901 (listed as J-1774 prior to the 8th edition) ("Wire Rim"; about 500 struck): raised stars on edge. • J-1902 (listed as J-1774a prior to the 8th edition) ("Wire Rim"): plain edge. • J-1903 (listed as J-1775 prior to the 8th edition) ("Rolled Rim"; 32,500 struck, but all but 42 melted): raised stars on edge are of irregular sizes and are crowded near one of the collar segments.

Obverse: Indian head facing left, LIBERTY on headband, arc of 13 stars above, date below.
Reverse: Eagle standing on arrows and branch, facing left. Behind the eagle is the motto E PLURIBUS UNUM. Around the border, UNITED STATES OF AMERICA / TEN DOLLARS. Special style with periods before and after reverse legends. Wire rim.

J-1901

Number	Metal	Edge	Rarity	Pop	T/A	Last Traded at Auction				60	63	65
						Firm	Date	Amount	Grade			
1901	Gold	*	3	499	73	Heritage	9/2003	$32,200	PCGSMS64	$20,000	$27,500	$50,000
1902	Gold	PE	U	1	1	Heritage	1/2003	$195,500	NGCMS62	N/A	$275,000	N/A
1903	Gold	*	5	78	18	Bowers & Merena	7/2003	$111,550	PCGSMS66	$50,000	$90,000	$150,000

* J-1901 and J-1903: stars on edge

Patterns of 1907

J-1905 and J-1906: MCMVII (1907) $20, Indian Head

One of the most famous of all patterns, this piece is in private hands. It origin is not known, but Judd lists the pedigree to Charles E. Barber, who may have created it (this variation is not known to have been under consideration by Saint-Gaudens). • The gold specimen is in private hands. An impression in lead is in the American Numismatic Society Collection. • J-1905 (listed as J-1776 prior to the 8th edition): edge with raised letters E PLURIBUS UNUM and stars. • J-1906 (listed as J-1777 prior to the 8th edition): edge with raised letters E PLURIBUS UNUM and stars.

Obverse: Indian head facing left, similar to the $10, but of the standard diameter of a double eagle. LIBERTY in straight line below neck, arc of 13 stars at top border.
Reverse: Eagle in flight, similar to the adopted issue, but with date MCMVII on sun at bottom. UNITED STATES OF AMERICA / TWENTY DOLLARS above eagle at top border.

J-1905

Number	Metal	Edge	Rarity	Pop	T/A	Last Traded at Auction				60	63	65
						Firm	Date	Amount	Grade			
1905	Gold	LE	U	1	1	Bowers & Merena	8/1984	$467,500	GemPF	N/A	N/A	$5,000,000
1906	Lead	LE	U	0	N/A	N/A	N/A	N/A	N/A	N/A	N/A	N/A

J-1907 to J-1910: MCMVII (1907) $20, Ultra High Relief

J-1907 and J-1908 are from the first Ultra High Relief coinage of February 1907 (see "History and Overview"). The reverse of the only known specimen of J-1908 was struck from a cracked die.[10] • All known specimens of J-1909 are with a satiny Proof finish of bright yellow gold; edge lettering occurs right-side up as well as inverted, in relation to the obverse. These were struck later than a different die pair than used for J-1907 and 1908. • J-1907 (listed as J-1778 prior to the 8th edition): edge has E PLURIBUS UNUM and stars between letters, style of J-1773 (1906), as E * P * L * U * R / * I * B * U * S * / U * N * U * M *. • J-1908 (listed as J-1778b prior to the 8th edition): plain edge. • J-1909 (listed as J-1778 prior to the 8th edition): edge style of 1907, E PLURIBUS UNUM with stars between words plus a group of adjacent stars, as *******E* / PLURIBUS / UNUM***. • J-1910 (listed as J-1778a prior to the 8th edition): edge style not recorded.

Obverse: Obverse with goddess Victory walking forward, carrying a torch aloft in her right hand, an olive branch in her left. Resplendent rays are behind her. The Capitol building is shown at lower left. In an arc at the top border is LIBERTY. At the lower right the date is expressed as MCMVII.
Reverse: Similar to the adopted issue with flying eagle above sun and rays, with UNITED STATES OF AMERICA / TWENTY DOLLARS in two arcs at the top border, but with different details in the field and relief.

J-1909

Number	Metal	Edge	Rarity	Pop	T/A	Last Traded at Auction				60	63	65
						Firm	Date	Amount	Grade			
1907	Gold	LE	8	1	1	Stack's	3/2005	$488,750	PFChXF	$550,000	N/A	N/A
1908	Gold	PE	U	0	N/A	N/A	N/A	N/A	N/A	N/A	N/A	N/A
1909	Gold	LE	H6	12	7	Ira & Larry Goldberg	5/1999	$1,210,000	PCGSPF67	N/A	N/A	$1,250,000
1910	Lead	LE	U	0	N/A	N/A	N/A	N/A	N/A	$50,000	N/A	N/A

J-1914 and J-1915: MCMVII (1907) $20, High Relief

J-1914 was listed as J-1778c prior to the 8th edition. J-1915 was listed as J-1778b prior to the 8th edition. Struck from regular dies. 12,367 were made for general circulation plus an unknown number of patterns.

Obverse: Regular MCMVII style made for circulation, High Relief.
Reverse: Regular die of the circulating issue, High Relief.

J-1915

Number	Metal	Edge	Rarity	Pop	T/A	Last Traded at Auction				60	63	65
						Firm	Date	Amount	Grade			
1914	Gold	PE	U	0	N/A	N/A	N/A	N/A	N/A	N/A	N/A	N/A
1915	Lead	PE	U	0	N/A	N/A	N/A	N/A	N/A	N/A	N/A	N/A

J-1917: MCMVII (1907) $20, High Relief, Small Diameter

Listed as J-1779 prior to the 8th edition. Diameter reduced to the size of a $10 piece, with weight made up by extra thickness. Roger W. Burdette: "The purpose was to determine if a high-relief design could be better struck on a planchet of smaller diameter compensated by greater thickness. In effect, the force of the press was concentrated on a smaller area. These pieces were not illegal (contrary to the statement of Mint Collection curator T. Louis Comparette), as the Mint has always had the authority to experiment with metals, designs, or weights, etc., not of legal standard. Director Frank A. Leach wanted them returned to the Mint and melted because he was being pestered for samples. However, he did not learn of them until nearly a year after they had been made. The model was the same one used for J-1907. At least 16 were struck before February 21, 1907."[11] • The edge is lettered E PLURIBUS UNUM in small letters (following the same layout as on Barber's pattern 1906 $20).

Obverse: Similar in design to J-1907 and related Ultra High Relief issues.
Reverse: Similar to J-1907 and related Ultra High Relief varieties.

J-1917

Number	Metal	Edge	Rarity	Pop	T/A	Last Traded at Auction				60	63	65
						Firm	Date	Amount	Grade			
1917	Gold	LE	8	0	N/A	N/A	N/A	N/A	N/A	N/A	N/A	N/A

J-1919: 1907 Arabic Date $20

Listed as J-1779a prior to the 8th edition. This is the circulating issue first released on December 13, 1907, at a time when MCMVII High Relief pieces were still being coined. Known examples are in brass and were rolled out at the Mint, but the design still can be seen in outline or shadow form. The edge is lettered E PLURIBUS UNUM.

Obverse: Regular modified die for quantity mintage on high-speed presses for circulation, with Arabic date as 1907, low relief.
Reverse: Regular low-relief die made for general circulation.

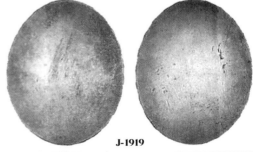

J-1919

Number	Metal	Edge	Rarity	Pop	T/A	Last Traded at Auction				60	63	65
						Firm	Date	Amount	Grade			
1919	Brs	LE	8	0	1	Heritage	8/1995	$605	PF	N/A	N/A	N/A

Patterns of 1908

History and Overview

Pattern strikings were made of the Indian Head half eagle before April 1, 1908, using Saint-Gaudens's design for the double eagle. The motif had been reworked slightly to permit IN GOD WE TRUST to be added to the reverse and E PLURIBUS UNUM to the obverse. Before coins could be struck for circulation, Dr. William Sturgis Bigelow, a close friend of President Roosevelt's, showed the president an Indian Head design prepared by Boston sculptor Bela Lyon Pratt. The idea of lettering and motifs to be incuse or sunken was Dr. Bigelow's, while Pratt contributed an Indian head that was close to life (male portrait with headdress, as compared to Saint-Gaudens's female on the 1907 $10).[12] Roosevelt was enthusiastic and approved the Pratt design.

On September 21, 1908, experimental strikes of the Indian Head quarter eagle and the half eagle were shipped from the Philadelphia Mint to Director Frank A. Leach in Washington, the package containing 10 pieces of each denomination. They were shown to Roosevelt on September 26 and approved.

Several of these patterns existed until at least September 1908. (None are known to exist today. They are listed here for reference only.) Leach then wrote to Philadelphia Mint Superintendent John H. Landis to advise that hubs could be made, leading to the production of coinage dies. Roosevelt kept one of the half eagles, and the remaining coins were sent back to Philadelphia to be melted.

Roger Burdette notes, "After examination of the September trial strikes, Director Leach, Superintendent Landis, and Chief Engraver Barber decided that changes had to be made to 'sharpen' the coins. Barber reworked the Indian Head design to remove the wide border and changed the modeling of the feathered headdress."[13]

Brass strikings of 1908 No Motto and With Motto double eagles are known. Each piece was struck in a normal fashion, then rolled out, becoming flattened and elliptical in shape. In addition, there is an undated brass piece in the Smithsonian Institution, without the obverse date, with the motto on the reverse.

J-1922: 1908 $2.50

Ten pieces are said to have been supplied to President Roosevelt, examined, then returned to the Mint for remelting. None are known today.

Obverse: Similar to the adopted design, but with details not as sharp.
Reverse: Similar to the adopted design, but with details not as sharp.

Number	Metal	Edge	Rarity	Pop	T/A	Last Traded at Auction				60	63	65
						Firm	Date	Amount	Grade			
1922	Gold	RE	U	0	N/A	N/A	N/A	N/A	N/A	N/A	N/A	N/A

J-1923: 1908 $5

Ten pieces are said to have been supplied to President Roosevelt, examined, then all but one returned to the Mint for remelting.

Obverse: Similar to the adopted design, but with details not as sharp.
Reverse: Similar to the adopted design, but with details not as sharp.

Number	Metal	Edge	Rarity	Pop	T/A	Last Traded at Auction				60	63	65
						Firm	Date	Amount	Grade			
1923	Gold	RE	U	0	N/A	N/A	N/A	N/A	N/A	N/A	N/A	N/A

J-1924: 1908 $20

Struck from regular dies of the Without Motto type. Flattened between rollers, distending its shape into an ellipse.

J-1924

Number	Metal	Edge	Rarity	Pop	T/A	Last Traded at Auction				60	63	65
						Firm	Date	Amount	Grade			
1924	Brs	LE	8	0	1	Heritage	8/1998	In Set	N/A	N/A	N/A	N/A

J-1925: 1908 $20

Struck from regular dies of the With Motto type. Flattened between rollers, distending its shape into an ellipse.

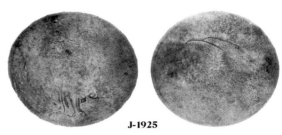

J-1925

Number	Metal	Edge	Rarity	Pop	T/A	Last Traded at Auction				60	63	65
						Firm	Date	Amount	Grade			
1925	Brs	LE	H7	0	1	Heritage	8/1998	In Set	No Grade	N/A	N/A	N/A

Patterns of 1909

History and Overview

In late 1908 and early 1909, President Theodore Roosevelt was in contact with sculptor (and numismatist) Victor David Brenner concerning the use of Brenner's image of Abraham Lincoln on a cent. In 1907, Brenner had created a plaque with Lincoln's portrait, and the president admired it highly. Patterns and die trials were produced, but little is known about them today. One rare pattern (or perhaps an off-metal mint error) is a copper-nickel impression from the regular Lincoln cent dies, made for purposes unknown (certainly, copper-nickel was not being considered as a coinage alternative in this year, and for testing purposes the alloy was harder than regular bronze). Likely, it is of the V.D.B. reverse type.

At the Mint, thought was given to revising the design of the five-cent piece, this seemingly under the new administration of President William Howard Taft, inaugurated in March 1909. The motifs for the five-cent piece suggest that these were concepts generated by Charles E. Barber within the Mint, as J-1939 employs many elements of the 1896 J-1770 pattern five-cent coin, and the uninspired treatment of George Washington on several other varieties does not suggest the work of an accomplished outside artist. During this period, Chief Engraver Barber resisted the thought of others encroaching upon the traditional prerogative of designing the nation's coinage, but already the Lincoln cent by outside artist Brenner and the $10 and $20 by the late sculptor Augustus Saint-Gaudens were realities.

The various patterns of 1909 were struck in very small numbers, and most are unique today, being represented in the Smithsonian. No Washington Head five-cent pieces were ever made for circulation. A few years later, the idea of changing the design of the denomination was heralded as a "new idea."

Collecting Perspective

While we can all admire the illustrations of the nickel five-cent patterns of 1909, obtaining one is a virtual impossibility, as the majority are in the Smithsonian Institution. An exception is J-1939, of which two are known, one in private hands. In addition, the rare J-1930 Lincoln cent in copper-nickel exists in a private collection.

J-1930: 1909 Cent, V.D.B. Reverse

Listed as J-1780 prior to the 8th edition. Struck from regular dies. Reverse type not known. Presumably with V.D.B. May be a mint error.

J-1930

Number	Metal	Edge	Rarity	Pop	T/A	Last Traded at Auction				60	63	65
						Firm	Date	Amount	Grade			
1930	C-N	PE	8	0	N/A	N/A	N/A	N/A	N/A	N/A	N/A	N/A

Patterns of 1909

J-1933: 1909 Five-Cent Piece

Listed as J-1781 prior to the 8th edition.

Obverse: Charles E. Barber's design. Shield in the center with a scroll across, inscribed LIBERTY (incused), crossed poles behind supporting a liberty cap on one and eagle on the other, 13 stars around, date 1909 below. **Reverse:** Olive wreath enclosing 5 CENTS, UNITED STATES OF AMERICA above at border, with E PLURIBUS UNUM at bottom border in very small letters. Stylistically similar to the reverse of J-1770 of 1896.

J-1933

Number	Metal	Edge	Rarity	Pop	T/A	Last Traded at Auction				60	63	65
						Firm	Date	Amount	Grade			
1933	Nick	PE	U	0	N/A	N/A	N/A	N/A	N/A	N/A	N/A	N/A

J-1934: 1909 Five-Cent Piece

Listed as J-1782 prior to the 8th edition.

Obverse: Bust of George Washington facing right, LIBERTY above in small letters, date 1909 below, seven stars left, six stars right. **Reverse:** Same die as preceding.

J-1934

Number	Metal	Edge	Rarity	Pop	T/A	Last Traded at Auction				60	63	65
						Firm	Date	Amount	Grade			
1934	Nick	PE	U	0	N/A	N/A	N/A	N/A	N/A	N/A	N/A	N/A

J-1935: 1909 Five-Cent Piece

Listed as J-1783 prior to the 8th edition.

Obverse: Similar to preceding, but with smaller date. **Reverse:** Same die as preceding.

J-1935

Number	Metal	Edge	Rarity	Pop	T/A	Last Traded at Auction				60	63	65
						Firm	Date	Amount	Grade			
1935	Nick	PE	U	0	N/A	N/A	N/A	N/A	N/A	N/A	N/A	N/A

J-1936: 1909 Five-Cent Piece

Listed as J-1784 prior to the 8th edition.

Obverse: Similar to preceding, but with LIBERTY to right at border in front of bust. **Reverse:** Same die as preceding.

J-1936

Number	Metal	Edge	Rarity	Pop	T/A	Last Traded at Auction				60	63	65
						Firm	Date	Amount	Grade			
1936	Nick	PE	U	0	N/A	N/A	N/A	N/A	N/A	N/A	N/A	N/A

J-1937: 1909 Five-Cent Piece

Listed as J-1785 prior to the 8th edition.

Obverse: Similar to preceding, but with L**I**B**E**R**T**Y* at border. **Reverse:** Same die as preceding.

J-1937

Number	Metal	Edge	Rarity	Pop	T/A	Last Traded at Auction				60	63	65
						Firm	Date	Amount	Grade			
1937	Nick	PE	U	0	N/A	N/A	N/A	N/A	N/A	N/A	N/A	N/A

J-1938: 1909 Five-Cent Piece

Listed as J-1786 prior to the 8th edition.

Obverse: Large bust of Washington facing left, 1909 in front of bust, LIBERTY behind at border.
Reverse: Same die as preceding.

J-1938

| Number | Metal | Edge | Rarity | Pop | T/A | Last Traded at Auction | | | | 60 | 63 | 65 |
						Firm	Date	Amount	Grade			
1938	Nick	PE	U	0	N/A	N/A	N/A	N/A	N/A	N/A	N/A	N/A

J-1939: 1909 Five-Cent Piece

Listed as J-1787 prior to the 8th edition.

Obverse: Similar to preceding, but with date in different style.
Reverse: Large outlined 5, crossed by the word CENTS, within two laurel branches. At top border is UNITED STATES OF AMERICA with E PLURIBUS UNUM beneath in smaller letters.

J-1939

| Number | Metal | Edge | Rarity | Pop | T/A | Last Traded at Auction | | | | 60 | 63 | 65 |
						Firm	Date	Amount	Grade			
1939	Nick	PE	8	0	N/A	N/A	N/A	N/A	N/A	N/A	N/A	N/A

History and Overview

In 1910, a pattern nickel five-cent piece was struck, being an adaptation of a style used in 1909 (J-1939), but with different placement of the date.

J-1942: 1910 Five-Cent Piece

Listed as J-1788 prior to the 8th edition.

Obverse: Large bust of Washington facing left, LIBERTY at border in front of bust, 1910 at border to right.
Reverse: Large outlined 5, crossed by the word CENTS, within two laurel branches. At border, UNITED STATES OF AMERICA with E PLURIBUS UNUM beneath in smaller letters. IN GOD WE TRUST in minute letters at bottom of border.

J-1942

| Number | Metal | Edge | Rarity | Pop | T/A | Last Traded at Auction | | | | 60 | 63 | 65 |
						Firm	Date	Amount	Grade			
1942	Nick	PE	8	0	N/A	N/A	N/A	N/A	N/A	N/A	N/A	N/A

Patterns of 1913

History and Overview

In 1911, Franklin MacVeagh held the post of secretary of the Treasury, the Cabinet position that oversaw and furnished general direction to changes in that department, including coinage designs.

James Earle Fraser, a well-known sculptor in the private sector, created motifs for five-cent coins depicting a Native American (Indian) on the obverse and a bison (popularly called "buffalo") on the reverse. The obverse was a composite of three different models, namely a Sioux Chief named Iron Tail, a Cheyenne Chief named Two Moons,[14] and a third whose name he did not remember. The bison on the reverse, imprecisely called a buffalo in popular parlance, was modeled from an actual animal.

Various models were made and electrotypes (not struck coins) taken from them. With regard to actual coinage germane to the present text, trial pieces were struck before the incuse initial F (for Fraser) was added. These exist in variations described below.

Early versions of the five-cent piece show the bison on a raised mound, this being called the Type I design. Later, it was found that the inscription FIVE CENTS, on the base of the mound, would be subject to excessive wear, and the motif was redesigned to position the buffalo on a flat or plain surface (Type II) with FIVE CENTS recessed.

Collecting Perspective

Although patterns of 1913 are practically unobtainable, certain are said to have been in the private sector.

J-1950: 1913 Five-Cent Piece

Listed as J-1789 prior to the 8th edition. Seventeen were struck on January 13, 1913.[15] Two are in the Smithsonian Institution, six were melted, the other nine are held privately.

Obverse: Head of Indian facing right, date 1913 (with flat-top 3) on shoulder. LIBERTY at border in front of face.
Reverse: Bison or "buffalo" standing on mound facing left. UNITED STATES OF AMERICA above at border, E PLURIBUS UNUM beneath in small letters. FIVE CENTS on mound below.

J-1950

Number	Metal	Edge	Rarity	Pop	T/A	Last Traded at Auction				60	63	65
						Firm	Date	Amount	Grade			
1950	Nick	PE	L7	0	1	Heritage	1/2003	$66,700	PCGSPF62	$38,500	$83,000	N/A

J-1951: 1913 Five-Cent Piece

Listed as J-1789a prior to the 8th edition. Four were struck on oversize planchets to see what the design would look like if moved farther in from the rim, as requested by the Hobbs Manufacturing Co., which was developing a coin-detecting device for use in vending machines. The large planchets allowed the use of regular dies, thus saving the expense of cutting new hubs and dies.[16] Two are in the Smithsonian Institution, one was melted, the fourth went to Secretary of the Treasury Franklin MacVeagh.

Obverse: Similar to preceding, but with rounded-top 3 and with raised rims distant from devices.
Reverse: Similar to preceding.

J-1951

Number	Metal	Edge	Rarity	Pop	T/A	Last Traded at Auction				60	63	65
						Firm	Date	Amount	Grade			
1951	Nick	PE	8	0	N/A	N/A	N/A	N/A	N/A	N/A	N/A	N/A

J-1954: 1913 Five-Cent Piece, Type II Reverse

Listed as J-1790 prior to the 8th edition. Struck from regular dies.

J-1954

Number	Metal	Edge	Rarity	Pop	T/A	Last Traded at Auction				60	63	65
						Firm	Date	Amount	Grade			
1954	Brz	PE	U	0	N/A	N/A	N/A	N/A	N/A	N/A	N/A	N/A

History and Overview

Patterns of 1915 emphasize certain commemoratives made in connection with the Panama-Pacific International Exposition held in San Francisco that year. A set of commemoratives for the event was produced; it contained the silver half dollar, gold dollar, gold quarter eagle, and two varieties of the gold $50 (octagonal and round). Known in pattern form are strikings of the half dollar and gold dollar. Walter Breen states that Farran Zerbe, who had the numismatic concession at the exposition, suggested that the commemoratives "may have been struck as trial pieces at the Philadelphia Mint by the instructions of the (then) Secretary of the Treasury, who was a coin collector."[1]

Whatever the reason, the majority of the pieces went into private hands, perhaps those of Zerbe himself (who sometimes had difficulty distinguishing fact from hyperbole) or of Secretary of the Treasury William G. McAdoo. Curiously, each of the two known gold impressions of the half dollars are made from planchets cut down from a double eagle, a rather unusual procedure if the pieces had been made openly, as it would have been simpler to have cut a blank from a gold planchet strip currently in use for making double eagles.

The gold dollars include various striking sequences, interestingly enough, offering one of relatively few instances in which die deterioration progressions can be studied through existing pattern coins. Most of these pattern pieces went to King Farouk of Egypt.

Collecting Perspectives

Examples of all 1915 patterns are rare, but occasionally an example comes on the market.

J-1960 to J-1962: 1915 Panama-Pacific Commemorative Half Dollar

J-1960 was listed as J-1793 prior to the 8th edition.
J-1961 was listed as J-1791 prior to the 8th edition.
J-1962 was listed as J-1792 prior to the 8th edition.
Struck from regular dies, but without S mintmark. Gold impressions are over cut-down double eagles.

J-1960

Number	Metal	Edge	Rarity	Pop	T/A	Last Traded at Auction				60	63	65
						Firm	Date	Amount	Grade			
1960	Gold	RE	8	1	1	Heritage	11/2003	$165,000	NGCPF64	N/A	$115,000	$210,000
1961	Silv	RE	8	1	1	Heritage	11/2003	$92,000	NGCPF64	$26,000	$70,000	$120,000
1962	C	RE	8	1	1	Heritage	11/2003	$63,250	NGCPF65RB	$24,000	$40,000	$65,000

J-1965 to J-1967: 1915 Panama-Pacific Commemorative Gold Dollar

J-1965 was listed as J-1793a-1, -2, and -5 to -9 varieties prior to the 8th edition.
J-1966 was listed as J-1793a-3 and -4 prior to the 8th edition.
J-1967 was listed as J-1793b-1 and -2 prior to the 8th edition.
Struck from regular dies, but without S mintmark. Coins differ in weight and strikings. J-1965 and J-1966 exist in various die states (see 7th edition Judd).

J-1965

Number	Metal	Edge	Rarity	Pop	T/A	Last Traded at Auction				60	63	65
						Firm	Date	Amount	Grade			
1965	Gold	RE	L7	3	1	Heritage	11/2003	$33,350	NGCPF62	$20,000	$35,000	$50,000
1966	Gold	PE	8	2	0	N/A	N/A	N/A	N/A	$15,000	$30,000	$45,000
1967	Silv	PE	8	1	1	Stack's	1/1994	$14,300	ChBU	$13,000	$20,000	$32,500

Patterns of 1915

J-1971: 1915 Panama-Pacific
Commemorative Gold $50, Octagonal
Struck from regular dies, but without S mintmark.

J-1971

Number	Metal	Edge	Rarity	Pop	T/A	Last Traded at Auction				60	63	65
						Firm	Date	Amount	Grade			
1971	Silv	RE	U	0	0	N/A	N/A	N/A	N/A	N/A	N/A	N/A

J-1973: 1915 Panama-Pacific
Commemorative Gold $50, Round
Struck from regular dies, but without S mintmark.

J-1973

Number	Metal	Edge	Rarity	Pop	T/A	Last Traded at Auction				60	63	65
						Firm	Date	Amount	Grade			
1973	Silv	RE	U	0	0	N/A	N/A	N/A	N/A	N/A	N/A	N/A

History and Overview

The year 1916 saw a sweeping redesign of the regular silver coinage then being minted, replacing the Barber dime, quarter dollar, and half dollar. Charles E. Barber's motifs, in circulation since 1892, had long been criticized for their sameness and lack of artistic appeal compared to motifs designed by outside artists, each coin having a different design. The silver dollar was not under consideration in 1916 as none had been minted since 1904. There were no plans to strike additional pieces, in view of hundreds of millions remaining in storage by the Treasury Department and banks.

Adolph A. Weinman designed the dime and half dollar. The dime depicted the winged head of Liberty; explained by Weinman, "the wings crowning her cap of Liberty are intended to symbolize liberty of thought."[2] More popularly, the motif became known as the "Mercury" dime from the messenger of mythology (with wings on his feet in most depictions, and possibly on his head as well)—never mind that Mercury was a male. On the reverse, Weinman depicted "the fasces and olive branch to symbolize the strength which lies in unity, while the battle-ax stands for preparedness to defend the union. The branch of olive is symbolic of our love of peace." The fasces, in a different depiction, had been used decades earlier by Anthony C. Paquet on the pattern half dollar and gold $20 of 1859.

The circumstances of creation of the Mercury dime have long been surrounded by mystery and conjecture, mainly because a significant number of patterns in existence today show ample wear. In his original 1959 text, Dr. Judd noted:

> In recent years some have expressed surprise that when a new specimen of a 1916 pattern is discovered it is usually worn, quite contrary to what one expects of a pattern. The fact is that these patterns so closely resembled the regular issue that they were put into circulation by one owner after another. It seems obvious that there are probably six or more different varieties with about a dozen specimens known overall.

Francis Robb, the daughter of Robert W. Woolley (director of the Mint in 1916), spoke with Rogers M. Fred, Jr. about her father's home being robbed in the 1920s. Fred wrote (as quoted in *Coin World*, October 9, 1974):

> Among the things taken was a box containing coins. … Her father had patterns of the 1916 coinage in that box. … The 1916 patterns are very similar in design to the regular issue, and it is reasonable to assume that the thieves thought that the coins were just regular issues and simply spent them. This would explain how the coins got out of the Mint in the first place, and how they got into worn condition in the second place.

Or, at least, this might explain how *some* of the coins reached circulation. However, Woolley was Mint director only until mid-July 1916, by which time only the first group of patterns had been produced. No others would be made until late August.

Hermon A. MacNeil created the motifs for the quarter dollar. Liberty is shown "stepping forward to the gateway of the country," while her shield is raised "in the attitude of protection." Further, "the right hand bears the olive branch of peace," as described by the Mint director.

Similar to Weinman, MacNeil was primarily known as a sculptor, although he had created a number of medals. Little information concerning his patterns of 1916 survives today, and what we know is mainly from examination of the coins themselves. Most survive in higher grades. In 1917, the MacNeil design was modified by clothing the partially nude Liberty in a coat of armor, and, on the reverse, adding three stars below the eagle, among other changes. Patterns were made in 1917 and shown to Secretary of the Treasury William G. McAdoo, Representative William A. Ashbrook (a well-known numismatist), and the new Mint director, Raymond T. Baker. None of these patterns are known to have survived.[3]

For the half dollar—the other 1916 denomination created by sculptor Adolph A. Weinman—the motif was described by the director of the Mint as depicting Liberty "progressing in full stride toward the dawn of a new day, carrying branches of laurel and oak, symbolical of the civil and military glory. The hand of the figure is outstretched in bestowal of the spirit of liberty." On the reverse, the eagle was said to be "fearless in spirit and conscious of his power," and "his size and proportions are in keeping with the greatness and power of the country." The branch of mountain pine springing from a rift in the rock was "symbolical of America."

Years later, a Mint official revealed that the pattern dies for the half dollar (and also the dimes?) were destroyed in January 1917:[4] "There is no record of the number of the experimental pieces from this design but in all probability they were very few.… The sculptor, Mr. Weinman, submitted three variations for the obverse of this half dollar and two for the reverse. Trial dies were made of only two of the obverse and two of the reverse." In actuality, all variations were used for patterns, and dies were made.

Collecting Perspective

The majority of 1916 pattern dimes, quarter dollars, and half dollars listed in the present text have one or more examples held in the private sector. Among dimes, many show extensive wear, this being somewhat true for the pattern half dollars as well, although occasional choice examples are encountered. The pattern quarters are usually seen in Mint State. The surfaces of all patterns range from lustrous to matte, not mirrorlike. "The first patterns from June 1916 exist in normal as well as polished versions from the same pairs of dies. The artists specifically objected to the polishing, and it was not done on the subsequent patterns made in late August and afterward."[5]

Under the best of circumstances, the pattern specialist is unlikely to encounter patterns of this date except when specialized collections are brought to market. Even then, only a few pieces are likely to be offered.

Patterns of 1916

J-1981: 1916 Dime

Listed as J-1794 prior to the 8th edition. Made from unpolished as well as polished dies; the last have thinner letters. Two examples are in the Smithsonian Institution.

Obverse: Neck truncation is larger, shaped slightly differently, and closer to the border than on the regular issue. Date is entirely below truncation. Above the head more of the E (in LIBERTY) is visible; the T is distant from back of the cap. No dots between words in motto.
Reverse: Details of branch are different from regular issue and border inscription is closer to the rim.

J-1981

Number	Metal	Edge	Rarity	Pop	T/A	Last Traded at Auction				60	63	65
						Firm	Date	Amount	Grade			
1981	Silv	RE	H7	1	3	Heritage	1/2005	$54,050	NGCPF62	$50,000	$90,000	N/A

J-1982: 1916 Dime

Listed as J-1794 prior to the 8th edition. Bold relief to motifs and lettering. Two examples are confirmed.

Obverse: Head is slightly enlarged, with top wing feather on the cap going past R (in LIBERTY). Less of E (in LIBERTY) is visible. Numeral 6 in date is more pointed than in regular issue.
Reverse: Die as preceding but strengthened.

J-1982

Number	Metal	Edge	Rarity	Pop	T/A	Last Traded at Auction				60	63	65
						Firm	Date	Amount	Grade			
1982	Silv	RE	8	2	0	N/A	N/A	N/A	N/A	N/A	N/A	N/A

J-1983: 1916 Dime

Listed as J-1794 prior to the 8th edition. Two examples are confirmed.

Obverse: No AW initials. Portrait slightly smaller than preceding.
Reverse: Die as preceding.

J-1983

Number	Metal	Edge	Rarity	Pop	T/A	Last Traded at Auction				60	63	65
						Firm	Date	Amount	Grade			
1983	Silv	RE	8	0	4	Heritage	1/2005	$11,385	NCSF12Scr	$17,500	N/A	N/A

J-1984: 1916 Dime

Listed as J-1794 prior to the 8th edition. Motifs and letters in higher relief than any other pattern dime.

Obverse: Similar to the adopted type, with 6 (in 1916) to right of neck truncation and with AW initials, but with slight differences in the neck truncation.
Reverse: Similar to the adopted issue, but the border letters touch the rim.

J-1984

Number	Metal	Edge	Rarity	Pop	T/A	Last Traded at Auction				60	63	65
						Firm	Date	Amount	Grade			
1984	Silv	RE	U	0	2	Superior	7/2003	$92,000	PCGSPF64	N/A	$90,000	$150,000

J-1988: 1916 Quarter Dollar

Listed as J-1796a prior to the 8th edition.

Obverse: Hermon MacNeil's full-length figure of Liberty, head turned to left (viewer's right), stepping through a gateway, her left arm upraised, bearing a shield from which the covering is being drawn, and with an olive branch in her right hand (slightly different from the regular-issue style). In an arc at the top border is LIBERTY. At the top of the wall, interrupted by the gateway, is IN GOD / WE TRUST. The date 1916 on step under Liberty's feet. On this pattern, unlike the regular issue, there is no M on the base of the right portal. Details in very shallow relief.
Reverse: Eagle in flight to right. Above the eagle is UNITED STATES OF AMERICA, beneath which is E PLURIBUS UNUM in smaller letters. Curved along the bottom border is QUARTER DOLLAR. Details in shallow relief. An olive branch is at the left border and another is at the right border. Eagle is higher in field than on regular issue.

J-1988

Number	Metal	Edge	Rarity	Pop	T/A	Last Traded at Auction				60	63	65
						Firm	Date	Amount	Grade			
1988	Silv	RE	8	0	1	Bowers & Merena	11/1985	$6,380	PF55	$163,000	N/A	N/A

J-1989: 1916 Quarter Dollar

Listed as J-1795 prior to the 8th edition. The Jimmy Hayes specimen is the only one seen in modern times.[6]

Obverse: Style as the regular-issue die, but with important differences, including a different treatment of the olive branch, no initial M, and certain other adjustments.

Reverse: Regular die. Eagle in flight to right. Above the eagle is UNITED STATES OF AMERICA, beneath which is E PLURIBUS UNUM in smaller letters. Curved along the bottom border is QUARTER DOLLAR. At the left border are seven stars and on the right are six stars.

J-1989

Number	Metal	Edge	Rarity	Pop	T/A	Last Traded at Auction				60	63	65
						Firm	Date	Amount	Grade			
1989	Silv	RE	U	1	1	Stack's	10/1985	$20,900	PF	N/A	N/A	$400,000

J-1991: 1916 Half Dollar

Listed as J-1798 prior to the 8th edition. Believed to have been struck between May 29 and June 21, 1916; accordingly given the first position in this list.[7] Struck from polished as well as unpolished dies.

Obverse: Full-length figure of Liberty striding toward the rising sun with rays, carrying branches of laurel and oak in her left hand, her right hand outstretched with palm forward. Behind her, a cape in the form of a flag with 13 stars. Arranged in a semicircle around the border is LIBERTY in widely spaced letters. Low to the right in the field is IN GOD WE TRUST in small, well-made letters. Lettering is thin and in low relief. The date 1916 is centered at the bottom border.

Reverse: Perched eagle as on regular issue, but with many differences. Eagle has more feathers than on the adopted version, but on the pattern they are mostly indistinctly defined. UNITED STATES OF AMERICA / HALF DOLLAR at top border in two concentric arcs. E PLURIBUS UNUM in tiny letters at bottom border. No AW monogram.

J-1991

Number	Metal	Edge	Rarity	Pop	T/A	Last Traded at Auction				60	63	65
						Firm	Date	Amount	Grade			
1991	Silv	RE	H7	3	3	Heritage	5/2005	$89,125	PCGSPF63	$52,000	$90,000	$140,000

J-1992: 1916 Half Dollar

Listed as J-1797 prior to the 8th edition. Believed to have been struck between July 27 and August 18, 1916.

Obverse: Adolph A. Weinman's full-length figure of Liberty striding toward the rising sun with 13 rays, carrying branches of laurel and oak in her left hand, her right hand outstretched with palm forward. Behind her, a cape in the form of a flag with 13 stars. The figure is tall, with head nearly touching the top border. In the right field is LIBERTY in large letters,[8] below which is IN GOD WE TRUST in thick medium-size letters. The date 1916 is centered at the bottom border.

Reverse: Same as preceding.

J-1992

Number	Metal	Edge	Rarity	Pop	T/A	Last Traded at Auction				60	63	65
						Firm	Date	Amount	Grade			
1992	Silv	RE	L7	6	3	Heritage	6/2005	$113,000	NGCPF65	$40,000	$71,500	$125,000

Patterns of 1916

J-1993: 1916 Half Dollar

Believed to have been struck after August 21 and before September 20, 1916.

Obverse: Same as preceding.
Reverse: Similar to the regular die, but with some slight differences due to the size reduction process and lack of details in cutting the hub. With AW monogram as approved by the secretary of the Treasury on August 10, 1916.

J-1993

Number	Metal	Edge	Rarity	Pop	T/A	Last Traded at Auction				60	63	65
						Firm	Date	Amount	Grade			
1993	Silv	RE	8	1	2	Heritage	8/2004	$52,900	NGCPF30	$65,000	$110,000	$175,000

J-1994: 1916 Half Dollar

Listed as J-1801 prior to the 8th edition. Believed to have been struck between September 25 and October 21, 1916.

Obverse: Somewhat similar to the adopted issue, but with date small and compact; letters in LIBERTY heavy.
Reverse: Similar to the preceding, but of slightly reduced scale. No AW. All known specimens have a die crack above R (in LIBERTY) and another downward from Y.

J-1994

Number	Metal	Edge	Rarity	Pop	T/A	Last Traded at Auction				60	63	65
						Firm	Date	Amount	Grade			
1994	Silv	RE	8	0	1	Stack's	10/1985	$13,750	PF	$65,000	$110,000	$175,000

J-1995: 1916 Half Dollar

Listed as J-1799 prior to the 8th edition. Believed to have been struck between October 1 and 21, 1916.

Obverse: Somewhat similar to the adopted design, but with differences. LIBERTY in thin letters. IN GOD WE TRUST in small, irregular letters. Date large with digits 9 and 6 open; second 1 leans left. Sun with ray 1 misshapen and connected to the sun. Foot at lower right with especially prominent slope in background.
Reverse: Similar to the preceding, but with slight reduction in size of design; letters farther from the rim. No AW.

J-1995

Number	Metal	Edge	Rarity	Pop	T/A	Last Traded at Auction				60	63	65
						Firm	Date	Amount	Grade			
1995	Silv	RE	8	1	1	Bowers & Merena	1/1996	$20,900	PCGSPF64	$52,000	$85,000	$140,000

J-1996: 1916 Half Dollar

Listed as J-1800 prior to the 8th edition. Believed to have been struck between October 21 and November 11, 1916.

Obverse: Similar to the preceding, but with date in larger numerals, E (in LIBERTY) differently positioned in relation to the top of Liberty's head, and a beaded border (instead of plain).

Reverse: Similar to the adopted design in general concept, but with smaller letters around the periphery and with a beaded border. "Considerable hand engraving on the hub/die."[9]

J-1996

Number	Metal	Edge	Rarity	Pop	T/A	Last Traded at Auction				60	63	65
						Firm	Date	Amount	Grade			
1996	Silv	RE	8	0	1	Christie's	12/1992	$4,620	PF	$60,000	$95,000	$160,000

J-2001: 1916 McKinley Gold Dollar

Listed as J-1802 prior to the 8th edition. Struck from regular dies.

J-2001

Number	Metal	Edge	Rarity	Pop	T/A	Last Traded at Auction				60	63	65
						Firm	Date	Amount	Grade			
2001	Nick	RE	U	0	1	Heritage	3/1999	$13,800	PCGSMS62	N/A	$28,000	N/A

History and Overview

Die trials are known of the 1918 Lincoln-Illinois Centennial commemorative half dollars. These seem to have been made to adjust the press prior to regular silver coinage.

J-2005 to J-2007: 1918 Lincoln-Illinois Commemorative Half Dollar

Struck from regular dies, without a collar. The various known pieces show incomplete details of the dies, as the dies were too widely spaced apart.

J-2005

Number	Metal	Edge	Rarity	Pop	T/A	Last Traded at Auction				60	63	65
						Firm	Date	Amount	Grade			
2005	C	PE	8	0	N/A	N/A	N/A	N/A	N/A	N/A	N/A	N/A
2006	Nick	PE	U	0	N/A	N/A	N/A	N/A	N/A	N/A	N/A	N/A
2007	WM	PE	U	0	N/A	N/A	N/A	N/A	N/A	N/A	N/A	N/A

According to Roger Burdette, the pieces erroneously listed as J-2015 in the 8th edition were in fact regular-issue 1921 Peace dollars.

Patterns of 1922

History and Overview

Early in 1922, patterns were made of a medium-relief version of the Peace silver dollar, as the high-relief style employed in 1921 had caused problems in fully striking up the detail at the centers.[11] Between January 5 and 23, coinage of 35,401 took place of the modified design—apparently a long run intended to test high-speed quantity production. Nearly all were melted. The only known specimen, authenticated by the Numismatic Guaranty Corporation of America (NGC) in 2001, is design-linked to the reverse of the 1922 Matte Proof high relief coins in the style of 1921 (in the Norweb Collection and others). The design modifications for the medium-relief patterns and the low-relief production coins were made by George T. Morgan with the knowledge of Mint Director Raymond T. Baker and independent artist James Earle Fraser, but the designer, Anthony deFrancisci, was not part of the change.

Trial production of low-relief issues for circulation began in late January. Those made for the first several weeks have slightly sharper obverse lettering than do the subsequent issues. The reverse also differs by the configuration of a gap between the olive branch and the eagle's talon. After these had been made, on February 14, 1922, Fraser approved the low-relief design and permitted the coins to be released into circulation. They were subsequently made at all three mints—Philadelphia, Denver, and San Francisco. These are regular issues and today are easily obtainable in all grades, although the variety is not widely known.

Trial strikings were made of the 1922 Grant Centennial commemorative gold dollar. It is not known if these are of the without-star or the with-star variety.

J-2020: 1922 Silver Dollar

One specimen is confirmed to exist.

Obverse: Design as used on the regular issues of 1921 (all in high relief), but now in medium relief. Some topological differences (including placement of the date relative to the rim and the shape of the base of the 1; distorted S in TRVST) in comparison to regular-issue or the rare High Relief 1922 dollars.
Reverse: Medium-relief version of the 1921 dollar, now with some differing design details, but almost identical, except for lower relief than that of the 1922 High Relief dollar.

J-2020

Number	Metal	Edge	Rarity	Pop	T/A	Last Traded at Auction				60	63	65
						Firm	Date	Amount	Grade			
2020	Silv	RE	U	0	N/A	N/A	N/A	N/A	N/A	N/A	N/A	N/A

J-2025 and J-2026: 1922 Grant Memorial Commemorative Gold Dollar

Trial piece struck from regular dies of the With Star variety.

J-2025

Number	Metal	Edge	Rarity	Pop	T/A	Last Traded at Auction				60	63	65
						Firm	Date	Amount	Grade			
2025	Brs	RE	U	0	N/A	N/A	N/A	N/A	N/A	N/A	N/A	N/A
2026	WM	RE	U	0	N/A	N/A	N/A	N/A	N/A	N/A	N/A	N/A

Patterns of 1923

History and Overview

Trial strikings were made of the 1923-S Monroe Doctrine Centennial commemorative half dollar. It is not known if these had the S mintmark punched into the working dies.

J-2030: 1923 Monroe Doctrine Centennial Commemorative Half Dollar

Struck from regular dies. Might be 1923-S if the mintmark were punched in the die.

J-2030

| Number | Metal | Edge | Rarity | Pop | T/A | Last Traded at Auction | | | | 60 | 63 | 65 |
						Firm	Date	Amount	Grade			
2030	C	RE	U	0	N/A	N/A	N/A	N/A	N/A	N/A	N/A	N/A

Patterns of 1925

History and Overview

Trial strikings were made of the 1925-S California Diamond Jubilee commemorative half dollar, from working dies before the S mintmark was added to the obverse.

J-2035: 1925 California Diamond Jubilee Commemorative Half Dollar

Struck from regular dies, except without the S mintmark.

J-2035

| Number | Metal | Edge | Rarity | Pop | T/A | Last Traded at Auction | | | | 60 | 63 | 65 |
						Firm	Date	Amount	Grade			
2035	Silv	RE	U	0	N/A	N/A	N/A	N/A	N/A	N/A	N/A	N/A

Patterns of 1935

History and Overview

Trial strikings were made of the second variety of the 1935 Boone Bicentennial commemorative half dollar, without a small "1934" added on the reverse.

J-2040: 1935 Boone Bicentennial Commemorative Half Dollar

Trial piece struck from regular dies.

J-2040

| Number | Metal | Edge | Rarity | Pop | T/A | Last Traded at Auction | | | | 60 | 63 | 65 |
						Firm	Date	Amount	Grade			
2040	C	RE	–	0	N/A	N/A	N/A	N/A	N/A	Unconf	Unconf	Unconf

Patterns of 1935

J-2041: 1935-S Boone Bicentennial Commemorative Half Dollar, Small "1934" on Reverse

Struck from regular dies. An unusual example of a branch mint die pair being used for a die trial. In the collection of the American Numismatic Society.

J-2041

| Number | Metal | Edge | Rarity | Pop | T/A | Last Traded at Auction | | | | 60 | 63 | 65 |
						Firm	Date	Amount	Grade			
2041	C	RE	U	0	N/A	N/A	N/A	N/A	N/A	N/A	N/A	N/A

Patterns of 1942

History and Overview

In the summer of 1941, America was the "arsenal of democracy," providing munitions, aircraft, ships, and other supplies to nations in Europe and Asia overrun by the Nazis and the Japanese. Copper and nickel, both strategic metals, were in tight supply, and the Treasury Department made plans to alter the alloys used in coinage, and use substitutes. Eventually, this translated into the silver-content "wartime" five-cent pieces made from 1942 to 1945 and the zinc-coated steel Lincoln cent made in 1943.

In 1942, by which time the United States was directly involved in World War II, several manufacturers were contacted and asked to perform experiments on substances that could be used in place of copper for the Lincoln cent.[12] Among the nearly 10 firms involved at the beginning were the Hooker Chemical Co. and Durez Plastics and Chemicals, Inc., both of North Tonawanda, New York; the Colt Patent Firearms Co. in Hartford, Connecticut; and Tennessee Eastman Corporation. Not wanting to release official coinage dies for testing, Chief Engraver John R. Sinnock created cent-sized dies with a female portrait on the obverse (as used on the Colombian two-centavo coin, but with the lettering LIBERTY / JUSTICE to the left and the right). The reverse motif was an open wreath enclosing UNITED STATES MINT.[13]

The companies were invited to explore various materials, including red fiber, plastic of various colors, hard rubber, Bakelite, tempered glass, zinc, aluminum, white metal, manganese, and thinner forms of bronze planchets. Many such pieces were made, but it seems that no precise record of them has ever been found.

In addition, regular 1942 Lincoln cent dies are said to have been used to strike coins in pure zinc, copper and zinc, zinc-coated steel, aluminum, copperweld, antimony, white metal, and lead, among other materials.

Collecting Perspective

In the 7th edition of this text, Dr. Judd noted, "The legal status of these experimental pieces remains in doubt. One piece was seized while another offering at auction was not disturbed. Perhaps one day a clear policy will be defined. As it is whenever any change in coinage is contemplated, a hazy situation develops surrounded by secrecy and misinformation."

The listings below represent materials known to have been used for these experimental pieces, or mentioned in numismatic or other literature. Not all may exist. The numbering is open-ended, reserved for future use if other materials are discovered.

J-2080 and J-2081: 1942 Cent

Trial piece struck from regular dies.

J-2080

| Number | Metal | Edge | Rarity | Pop | T/A | Last Traded at Auction | | | | 60 | 63 | 65 |
						Firm	Date	Amount	Grade			
2080	*	PE	–	0	N/A	N/A	N/A	N/A	N/A	Unconf	Unconf	Unconf
2081	WM	PE	H7	1	8	Ira and Larry Goldberg	5/2003	$46,000	PCGSMS64	N/A	$50,000	$85,000

* J-2080: zinc-coated steel

J-2051 to J-2069: 1942 Cent

Private issues struck from special Mint dies. The substances in the chart below are those known to have been considered for use. No doubt other materials were tried as well. Not all exist in coined form today.

Obverse: Female head facing right, from the Colombian two-centavo coin. LIBERTY to the left, JUSTICE to the right. Date 1942 at the bottom border.

Reverse: Open wreath enclosing UNITED STATES MINT.

J-2051

| Number | Metal | Edge | Rarity | Pop | T/A | Last Traded at Auction | | | | 60 | 63 | 65 |
						Firm	Date	Amount	Grade			
2051	Brz	PE	8	0	N/A	N/A	N/A	N/A	N/A	N/A	N/A	N/A
2052	Brs	PE	U	0	N/A	N/A	N/A	N/A	N/A	N/A	N/A	N/A
2053	Zinc	PE	U	0	N/A	N/A	N/A	N/A	N/A	N/A	N/A	N/A
2054	*	PE	H7	0	2	ANR	5/2005	$6,900	ANACSAU55	$7,500	$12,500	N/A
2055	*	PE	U	0	N/A	N/A	N/A	N/A	N/A	N/A	N/A	N/A
2056	WM	PE	U	1	N/A	N/A	N/A	N/A	N/A	N/A	N/A	N/A
2057	Alu	–	U	0	N/A	N/A	N/A	N/A	N/A	N/A	N/A	N/A
2058	Lead	PE	U	0	N/A	N/A	N/A	N/A	N/A	N/A	N/A	N/A
2059	*	PE	L7	0	N/A	N/A	N/A	N/A	N/A	$1,000	$1,500	$2,500
2060	*	PE	L7	0	N/A	N/A	N/A	N/A	N/A	$1,000	$1,500	$2,800
2061	*	PE	L7	0	N/A	N/A	N/A	N/A	N/A	$1,000	$1,500	$2,500
2062	*	PE	L7	0	1	Stack's	1/2005	$2,760	About as Made	$1,000	$1,500	$2,800
2063	*	PE	L7	0	N/A	N/A	N/A	N/A	N/A	N/A	N/A	N/A
2064	*	PE	L7	0	N/A	N/A	N/A	N/A	N/A	$1,000	$1,500	$2,500
2065	*	PE	L7	0	N/A	N/A	N/A	N/A	N/A	$1,500	$2,500	$4,000
2066	*	–	U	0	N/A	N/A	N/A	N/A	N/A	N/A	N/A	N/A
2067	*	PE	L7	0	N/A	N/A	N/A	N/A	N/A	$1,000	$1,500	$2,500
2068	*	PE	L7	0	N/A	N/A	N/A	N/A	N/A	$1,250	$2,000	$3,000
2069	*	PE	L7	0	N/A	N/A	N/A	N/A	N/A	$1,500	$2,500	$4,000

* Compositions as follows:
J-2054: zinc-coated steel
J-2055: manganese
J-2059: black plastic

J-2060: brown plastic
J-2061: gray plastic
J-2062: red plastic
J-2063: tan plastic

J-2064: light yellow plastic
J-2065: transparent amber plastic
J-2066: red fiber composition

J-2067: Bakelite
J-2068: hard rubber
J-2069: tempered glass

Patterns of 1965

History and Overview

An experiment by the Bureau of the Mint to determine suitable metals to replace the 90% silver coins resulted in trial strikes of dies for dimes, quarter dollars, and half dollars. The design was the same for each denomination, and the strikes conform in size to the regular coinage. Somewhat similar to the scenario of 1942, fantasy designs were prepared with no relation to current coinage motifs, in the present instance to avoid creating "rarities" by using regular dies. The dies bear neither denominations nor any inscriptions normal for circulating coins (UNITED STATES OF AMERICA, IN GOD WE TRUST, LIBERTY) and are, in effect, tokens or medals.

Edward P. Grove and Philip Fowler, both on the engraving staff at the Philadelphia Mint, designed the obverse and reverse, respectively. The pieces were supposedly struck in the following materials:[14]

75% copper, 25% nickel • Cupronickel-copper (multi-layer composite) • 50% silver, 50% copper • Coin silver-copper (multi-layer composite) • Columbium (Type I) • Columbium (Type II) • Zirconium • Monel (nickel-base alloy) • Nickel, 5% silicon, with magnetic core • Stainless steel (Type 301-Type I) • Stainless steel (Type 301-Type II) • Stainless steel (Type 302).

The Mint study also considered nickel and titanium but neither of these was actually tested. No records have been located on the quantities made, whether all were made inside the Mint, and what metal varieties might exist today.

Collecting Perspective

Two sets of coins were given to the Smithsonian Institution. No others were officially distributed, but over the years, a few have been shown in numismatic circles. Their legality has not been defined.

As it is not known which pieces might survive and in what metals, each of the three "denominations" below is assigned a Judd number based on the 12 metals in the above list. Also, the values are hypothetical, in view that for some alloys there has been no confirmation of existence.

Patterns of 1965

J-2100 to J-2111: 1965 (1759 Date on Obverse) Dime-Size Medal

Although various metals were used, only cupro-nickel clad is confirmed to exist.

Obverse: Martha Washington facing right, VIRGINIA above, fantasy date 1759 below. At lower right, MARTHA WASHINGTON.
Reverse: View of Washington's home off the back left corner, with MOUNT VERNON below. Around the border, HOME OF THE WASHINGTON FAMILY.

J-2101

Number	Metal	Edge	Rarity	Pop	T/A	Firm	Date	Amount	Grade	60	63	65
2100	*	RE	–	0	N/A	N/A	N/A	N/A	N/A	Unconf	Unconf	Unconf
2101	*	RE	L7	1	1	Bowers & Merena	7/2003	$51,750	NGCMS65	$18,000	$31,000	$52,000
2102	*	RE	–	0	N/A	N/A	N/A	N/A	N/A	Unconf	Unconf	Unconf
2103	*	RE	–	0	N/A	N/A	N/A	N/A	N/A	Unconf	Unconf	Unconf
2104	*	RE	–	0	N/A	N/A	N/A	N/A	N/A	Unconf	Unconf	Unconf
2105	*	RE	–	0	N/A	N/A	N/A	N/A	N/A	Unconf	Unconf	Unconf
2106	*	RE	–	0	N/A	N/A	N/A	N/A	N/A	Unconf	Unconf	Unconf
2107	*	RE	–	0	N/A	N/A	N/A	N/A	N/A	Unconf	Unconf	Unconf
2108	*	RE	–	0	N/A	N/A	N/A	N/A	N/A	Unconf	Unconf	Unconf
2109	*	RE	–	0	N/A	N/A	N/A	N/A	N/A	Unconf	Unconf	Unconf
2110	*	RE	–	0	N/A	N/A	N/A	N/A	N/A	Unconf	Unconf	Unconf
2111	*	RE	–	0	N/A	N/A	N/A	N/A	N/A	Unconf	Unconf	Unconf

* Compositions as follows (details under "History and Overview"):
J-2100: 75% copper, 25% nickel
J-2101: cupronickel-copper
J-2102: 50% silver, 50% copper

J-2103: coin silver-copper
J-2104: columbium (Type I)
J-2105: columbium (Type II)
J-2106: zirconium
J-2107: monel

J-2108: 95% nickel, 5% silicon
J-2109: stainless steel
J-2110: stainless steel
J-2111: stainless steel

J-2115 to J-2126: 1965 (1759 Date on Obverse) Quarter-Dollar-Size Medal

Designs as preceding, but larger diameter. Although various metals were used, only cupro-nickel clad is confirmed to exist.

J-2115

Number	Metal	Edge	Rarity	Pop	T/A	Firm	Date	Amount	Grade	60	63	65
2115	*	RE	–	0	N/A	N/A	N/A	N/A	N/A	Unconf	Unconf	Unconf
2116	*	RE	L7	1	1	Superior	11/2003	$17,250	NGCMS62	$12,500	$25,000	$37,500
2117	*	RE	–	0	N/A	N/A	N/A	N/A	N/A	Unconf	Unconf	Unconf
2118	*	RE	–	0	N/A	N/A	N/A	N/A	N/A	Unconf	Unconf	Unconf
2119	*	RE	–	0	N/A	N/A	N/A	N/A	N/A	Unconf	Unconf	Unconf
2120	*	RE	–	0	N/A	N/A	N/A	N/A	N/A	Unconf	Unconf	Unconf
2121	*	RE	–	0	N/A	N/A	N/A	N/A	N/A	Unconf	Unconf	Unconf
2122	*	RE	–	0	N/A	N/A	N/A	N/A	N/A	Unconf	Unconf	Unconf
2123	*	RE	–	0	N/A	N/A	N/A	N/A	N/A	Unconf	Unconf	Unconf
2124	*	RE	–	0	N/A	N/A	N/A	N/A	N/A	Unconf	Unconf	Unconf
2125	*	RE	–	0	N/A	N/A	N/A	N/A	N/A	Unconf	Unconf	Unconf
2126	*	RE	–	0	N/A	N/A	N/A	N/A	N/A	Unconf	Unconf	Unconf

* Compositions as follows (details under "History and Overview"):
J-2115: 75% copper, 25% nickel
J-2116: cupronickel-copper
J-2117: 50% silver, 50% copper

J-2118: coin silver-copper
J-2119: columbium (Type I)
J-2120: columbium (Type II)
J-2121: zirconium
J-2122: monel

J-2123: 95% nickel, 5% silicon
J-2124: stainless steel
J-2125: stainless steel
J-2126: stainless steel

J-2131 to J-2142: 1965 (1759 Date on Obverse) Half-Dollar-Size Medal

Designs as preceding, but larger diameter. Although various metals were used, only the silver-copper multi-layer composite is confirmed to exist, plus one struck on a quarter dollar planchet. Six examples of J-2134 are in the Smithsonian Institution.

J-2134

Number	Metal	Edge	Rarity	Pop	T/A	Last Traded at Auction				60	63	65
						Firm	Date	Amount	Grade			
2131	*	RE	–	0	N/A	N/A	N/A	N/A	N/A	Unconf	Unconf	Unconf
2132	*	RE	8	1	1	ANR	12/2003	$21,850	NGCMS63	$14,000	$24,000	$40,000
2133	*	RE	–	0	N/A	N/A	N/A	N/A	N/A	Unconf	Unconf	Unconf
2134	*	RE	H7	0	N/A	N/A	N/A	N/A	N/A	$15,000	$30,000	$42,500
2135	*	RE	–	0	N/A	N/A	N/A	N/A	N/A	Unconf	Unconf	Unconf
2136	*	RE	–	0	N/A	N/A	N/A	N/A	N/A	Unconf	Unconf	Unconf
2137	*	RE	–	0	N/A	N/A	N/A	N/A	N/A	Unconf	Unconf	Unconf
2138	*	RE	–	0	N/A	N/A	N/A	N/A	N/A	Unconf	Unconf	Unconf
2139	*	RE	–	0	N/A	N/A	N/A	N/A	N/A	Unconf	Unconf	Unconf
2140	*	RE	–	0	N/A	N/A	N/A	N/A	N/A	Unconf	Unconf	Unconf
2141	*	RE	–	0	N/A	N/A	N/A	N/A	N/A	Unconf	Unconf	Unconf
2142	*	RE	–	0	N/A	N/A	N/A	N/A	N/A	Unconf	Unconf	Unconf

* Compositions as follows (details under "History and Overview"):
J-2131: 75% copper, 25% nickel
J-2132: cupronickel-copper
J-2133: 50% silver, 50% copper

J-2134: coin silver-copper
J-2135: columbium (Type I)
J-2136: columbium (Type II)
J-2137: zirconium
J-2138: monel

J-2139: 95% nickel, 5% silicon
J-2140: stainless steel
J-2141: stainless steel
J-2142: stainless steel

History and Overview

In 1973, the Philadelphia Mint tested seven different alloys of aluminum for use in coining Lincoln cents, employing dies of the regular design but dated 1974. It was desired to perfect a composition of 96% aluminum plus other metal(s) for durability. At the time, the price of copper was rising on international markets, and the Treasury Department was fearful that bronze cents might become impractical to coin.

After this testing, 1,570,000 aluminum cents were made. Several dozen of these were distributed to members of the Senate Banking, Housing, and Urban Affairs Committee and the House Banking and Currency Committee. Other pieces were given out as curiosities and souvenirs to interested officials by Mint Director Mary Brooks. No request was made that the coins be returned. Soon afterward, news of their existence reached the numismatic press, and Brooks attempted to retrieve as many as possible. Only a few were found.

Collecting Perspective

Today, one confirmed specimen in private hands has been publicized (recently encapsulated by ICG with a grade of AU-58). Undoubtedly others are waiting in the wings to see if they are "legal" to hold, although logic suggests that there should be no question in this regard, as the pieces were distributed freely.

J-2151 and J-2152: 1974 Cent

Struck from regular dies. Seven different alloys of aluminum were tested.

J-2151

Number	Metal	Edge	Rarity	Pop	T/A	Last Traded at Auction				60	63	65
						Firm	Date	Amount	Grade			
2151	Alu	PE	H7	0	N/A	N/A	N/A	N/A	N/A	N/A	N/A	N/A
2152	*	PE	H7	0	N/A	N/A	N/A	N/A	N/A	N/A	N/A	N/A

* J-2152: bronze-clad steel

Patterns of 1975

History and Overview
At least 66 trial strikings of an aluminum cent were made from dies dated 1975.

J-2155: 1975 Cent
Trial piece struck from regular dies.

J-2155

Number	Metal	Edge	Rarity	Pop	T/A	Last Traded at Auction				60	63	65
						Firm	Date	Amount	Grade			
2155	Alu	PE	–	0	N/A	N/A	N/A	N/A	N/A	Unconf	Unconf	Unconf

Patterns of 1976

History and Overview
After designs were selected for the 1776–1976 Bicentennial quarter dollar, half dollar, and dollar, impressions were made from Proof dies that lacked the S mintmark used on regular Proofs. These pieces are all unconfirmed, with the exception of J-2164. It is said that at least three impressions of each were made. One set is known to have been destroyed.

J-2161: 1776–1976 Quarter Dollar
Struck from regular Proof dies, but lacking the S mintmark.

J-2161

Number	Metal	Edge	Rarity	Pop	T/A	Last Traded at Auction				60	63	65
						Firm	Date	Amount	Grade			
2161	*	RE	–	0	N/A	N/A	N/A	N/A	N/A	Unconf	Unconf	Unconf

    * J-2161: silver-clad metal

J-2162: 1776–1976 Half Dollar
Struck from regular Proof dies, but lacking the S mintmark.

J-2162

Number	Metal	Edge	Rarity	Pop	T/A	Last Traded at Auction				60	63	65
						Firm	Date	Amount	Grade			
2162	*	RE	–	0	N/A	N/A	N/A	N/A	N/A	Unconf	Unconf	Unconf

    * J-2162: silver-clad metal

J-2163: 1776–1976 Dollar, Type I Reverse

Struck from regular Proof dies, but lacking the S mintmark.

J-2163

Number	Metal	Edge	Rarity	Pop	T/A	Last Traded at Auction				60	63	65
						Firm	Date	Amount	Grade			
2163	*	RE	–	0	N/A	N/A	N/A	N/A	N/A	Unconf	Unconf	Unconf

* J-2163: silver-clad metal

J-2164: 1776–1976 Dollar, Type II Reverse

Struck from regular Proof dies, but lacking the S mintmark.

J-2164

Number	Metal	Edge	Rarity	Pop	T/A	Last Traded at Auction				60	63	65
						Firm	Date	Amount	Grade			
2164	*	RE	U	0	N/A	N/A	N/A	N/A	N/A	N/A	N/A	N/A

* J-2164: silver-clad metal

History and Overview

In 1977, Chief Engraver Frank Gasparro prepared a design for a new small-diameter metal dollar to replace the large (regular-diameter) Eisenhower dollar then in use. The obverse design was inspired by Joseph Wright's Liberty Cap design as used on the 1793 copper cent, and had been recently used by Gasparro for a medal made for the American Numismatic Association. The reverse, also by Gasparro, is perhaps the engraver's tribute to Augustus Saint-Gaudens. It depicts an eagle in flight over the sun with resplendent rays. Gasparro was a strong advocate of this design and shared his views widely, but Congress found the motif to be anachronistic. He was directed to use the image of Susan B. Anthony. It is believed that one or more trial strikings were made, but none are known to exist today.

J-2171: 1977 Dollar

Obverse: Head of Liberty facing left, cap on pole behind head. LIBERTY at top border, seven stars left, six right, date 1977 at bottom border. IN GOD WE TRUST in field at lower left. Inside border forming an 11-sided polygon.

Reverse: Eagle, wings uplifted, flying to the right, over sun with resplendent rays. Galaxy of 13 stars above and to right of eagle. UNITED STATES OF AMERICA / ONE DOLLAR around border. Inside border forming an 11-sided polygon.

J-2171

Number	Metal	Edge	Rarity	Pop	T/A	Last Traded at Auction				60	63	65
						Firm	Date	Amount	Grade			
2171	*	RE	–	0	N/A	N/A	N/A	N/A	N/A	Unconf	Unconf	Unconf

* J-2171: copper-nickel-clad copper

Patterns of 1979

History and Overview

In preparation for the Susan B. Anthony small-sized dollar coinage, thousands of clad-metal "tokens" were made at the Mint, the weight and diameter of an Anthony dollar, and with 11 sides to the inner rim. The central areas consisted simply of raised machine-turned areas. These were given to makers of coin-detection devices and vending machines to test their utility and application.

J-2175 and J-2176:
1979 Dollar-Size Medal

Varieties may exist with regard to the blank inner area.

J-2175

Number	Metal	Edge	Rarity	Pop	T/A	Last Traded at Auction				60	63	65
						Firm	Date	Amount	Grade			
2175	*	RE	H6	2	N/A	N/A	N/A	N/A	N/A	N/A	N/A	N/A
2176	Nick	RE	H6	0	0	N/A	N/A	N/A	N/A	N/A	N/A	N/A

* J-2175: copper-nickel-clad copper

Patterns of 1982

History and Overview

In 1982, the Martha Washington fantasy design used in 1965 was employed to test a new composition for the cent coinage before there was a change from bronze to copper-coated zinc. Seemingly, these dies were used within the Mint and also by private entities to test various concepts. These have been tentatively attributed to 1982 but may have been made at other times as well.

J-2180: 1982 (1759 Date on Obverse) Cent-Size Medal

Obverse: Martha Washington facing right, VIRGINIA above, fantasy date 1759 below. At lower right, MARTHA WASHINGTON.
Reverse: View of Washington's home off the back left corner, with MOUNT VERNON below. Around the border, HOME OF THE WASHINGTON FAMILY.

J-2180

Number	Metal	Edge	Rarity	Pop	T/A	Last Traded at Auction				60	63	65
						Firm	Date	Amount	Grade			
2180	*	PE	H7	0	N/A	N/A	N/A	N/A	N/A	N/A	N/A	N/A

* J-2180: copper-plated zinc

Patterns of 1985

J-2182: Circa 1985 (1759 Date on Obverse)
Five-Cent-Piece-Size Medal

Obverse: Martha Washington facing right, VIRGINIA above, fantasy date 1759 below. At lower right, MARTHA WASHINGTON.
Reverse: View of Washington's home off the back left corner, with MOUNT VERNON below. Around the border, HOME OF THE WASHINGTON FAMILY.

J-2182

Number	Metal	Edge	Rarity	Pop	T/A	Last Traded at Auction				60	63	65
						Firm	Date	Amount	Grade			
2182	Nick	PE	8	0	0	N/A	N/A	N/A	N/A	N/A	N/A	N/A

History and Overview

In 1999, dies with the 1759-dated fantasy designs of Martha Washington, the motif created in 1965 and found to have been useful since that time, were made to test concepts for what would become the Sacagawea "golden" dollar. These dies are believed to have been used by the Mint as well as by outside companies.

J-2184 and J-2185: 1999 (1759 Date on Obverse) Dollar-Size Medal

J-2184, in copper-nickel-clad composition, has an intermittently reeded edge.

Obverse: Martha Washington facing right, VIRGINIA above, fantasy date 1759 below. At lower right, MARTHA WASHINGTON.
Reverse: View of Washington's home off the back left corner, with MOUNT VERNON below. Around the border, HOME OF THE WASHINGTON FAMILY.

J-2185

Number	Metal	Edge	Rarity	Pop	T/A	Last Traded at Auction				60	63	65
						Firm	Date	Amount	Grade			
2184	*	RE	8	1	0	N/A	N/A	N/A	N/A	N/A	N/A	N/A
2185	**	PE	L7	4	2	ANR	10/2004	$11,500	NGCMS66	N/A	$6,000	$10,000

* J-2184: copper-nickel-clad copper
** J-2185: magnesium brass-coated copper-clad metal

History and Overview

In 2000, about a dozen 2000-W Sacagawea dollars were struck in gold for purposes unstated. Despite inquiries from the numismatic community, no announcements have been made as to their disposition.

J-2190: 2000-W Dollar

Trial piece struck from regular dies.

J-2190

Number	Metal	Edge	Rarity	Pop	T/A	Last Traded at Auction				60	63	65
						Firm	Date	Amount	Grade			
2190	Gold	PE	L7	0	0	N/A	N/A	N/A	N/A	N/A	N/A	N/A

Appendix A: Die and Hub Trials and Splashers

Appendix A, compiled primarily by Saul Teichman, includes pieces, mostly one-sided, struck from uncancelled Mint dies or hubs.

No rarity ratings are listed, as most are unique. Exceptions are noted. We have assigned Judd numbers to these pieces with the exception of certain items which modern scholarship suggests are not genuine Mint products (an example being the 1800 half dime). These are listed at the end of this appendix in a "Miscellaneous Items" section. In some instances, citations are taken from catalogs published generations ago, and these pieces have not been examined by modern scholars. For some of these, authenticity may be in doubt.

A die trial is an impression from a working die with incuse features, resulting in a trial piece with the features raised or in relief, as on a regular coin.

A hub trial is an impression from a hub, with lettering and design raised in the hub, resulting in the features being incuse or recessed on the trial. Some hubs have but a single element, such as the head of Miss Liberty. Others include lettering and numerals. Until circa 1907 to 1908, hubs and master dies did not include dates. These were punched in separately using four-digit logotypes, a practice which began at the Mint in the very late 1830s and was used on all denominations by 1840. Thus, an obverse hub or master die trial with a date reflects two separate impressions on the trial piece: the hub or master die and, separately, the date logotype. Relevant examples are furnished by J-A1867-8 and J-A1867-9, each an impression of the same hub, but with the date logotype in a slightly different position.

A master die trial is similar to a hub trial and is listed as a hub trial. A master die has features raised, and if made before about 1907 to 1908, includes all features of the working die except the date, which was punched in separately on the working die. Master die impressions are incuse or recessed on the trial.

A whimsy or practice piece is a metal blank on which various date punches or hubs were impressed, perhaps for practice, but not related to any known pattern issue. Sometimes multiple different date punches were used.

Paper-backed splashers, not specifically identified as such in the descriptions below, are impressions on very thin metal (often white metal or lead), backed with paper (plain or from a newspaper) to give a greater body to the metal and to permit a better die impression. Usually, only the layer adhering to the back of the metal remains.

While most trials were struck in metals such as copper, white metal, or lead, some are in other substances, including cardboard and red wax.

Not included in this compilation are various uniface impressions from canceled Mint dies, often bearing chisel marks, or an X, or some other mark of cancellation. These were made after the dies were retired and in many instances in private hands. Such impressions continue to be made into modern times.

The study of items in Appendix A is ongoing, as this specialty has not received the scrutiny accorded to regular (two-sided) patterns. Additional information and corrections are welcomed and will be considered for the next edition of this book.

Some photos are reduced in size.

1792

J-A1792-1: Quarter Dollar: Obverse of J-12, by Wright. White metal, high rims. Ex Charles I. Bushnell; Chapman brothers, 5/1883; Garrett Collection (The Johns Hopkins University, sold by Bowers & Ruddy Galleries), 3/1981; Bowers and Merena Galleries, 1/1999.

J-A1792-2: Quarter Dollar • Reverse of J-12. White metal, high rims as foregoing. Ex Charles I. Bushnell; Chapman brothers, 5/1883; Garrett Collection (The Johns Hopkins University, sold by Bowers & Ruddy Galleries), 3/1981; Bowers and Merena Galleries, 1/1999.

1797

J-A1797-1: $2.50 or $5 • Reverse of regular die with "$2.50" below on half-eagle-sized copper planchet. Ex Bache I sale (Woodward, Lot 2867), 3/1865; Crosby (Heseltine, Lot 1717), 6/1883. It was called a half eagle trial in the Crosby sale.[1]

J-A1797-2: $10 • Reverse of the Heraldic Eagle type, regular die. Lead. Ex George W. Woodside. Genuineness doubted.

1804

J-A1804-1: Cent • Obverse of J-28 (so-called restrike). White metal. 1803 cent die altered to read 1804. Struck outside the Mint from a discarded die. Ex George Parsons; Charles H. Shinkle.

J-A1804-2: **Dime** • Obverse of regular die. Copper. Struck outside the Mint from a discarded die. Two known, one of which was struck over a large cent.

1805

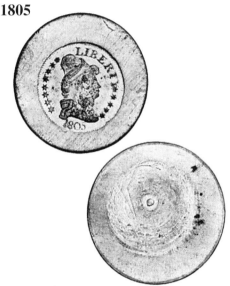

J-A1805-1: **$5** • Obverse of J-36 (rusted). White metal. Struck outside the Mint from a discarded die. Ex George Parsons; Virgil M. Brand; Abe Kosoff.

J-A1805-2: **$5** • Obverse from same die as above. Brass. Ex George Parsons.

1806

J-A1806-1: **Half Dollar** • Obverse regular die with pointed 6. White metal. Struck outside the Mint from a discarded die. Several are known, some of which have an impression of an embossing die for a 12¢ stamped envelope; bust of Henry Clay, Scott design U52. Die presently owned by the American Numismatic Society.

J-A1806-2: **$2.50** • Obverse of regular 1806/4 overdate die (rusted)[2]. White metal. Two struck outside the Mint from a discarded die. Ex King Farouk; Abe Kosoff, 5/1955; Edwin Hydeman; Bowers and Merena Galleries, 11/1985; Bowers and Merena Galleries, 6/1991.

1810

J-A1810-1: **Cent** • Obverse of Sheldon-285 (rusted). White metal. Struck outside the Mint from a discarded die. Ex Chapman brothers (sale of 7/1901, Lot 161).

J-A1810-2: **Half Dollar** • Reverse die, believed to be that used to coin J-42 (rusted). White metal. Struck outside the Mint from a discarded die. Ex George Parsons; Virgil M. Brand; New Netherlands Coin Co., 9/1953; ANA (1987 sale).

1811

J-A1811-1: **Half Dollar** • Obverse (die variety not known). White metal. Existence unconfirmed.

Appendix A: Die and Hub Trials and Splashers

1814

J-A1814-1: Dime • Reverse die of the John Reich-5 variety with STATES OF AMERICA as one word. Struck in England by John Pinches, Ltd., in the early 1960s, to the order of American entrepreneur Robert Bashlow, in combination with a new die reading GOD PRESERVE PHILADELPHIA AND THE LORD'S PROPRIETERS 1869. M. There were 536 impressions made in platinum, gold, silver, and bronze. The die and the coins were confiscated by the Treasury Department, and it is presumed that most if not all were destroyed (it would have been nice if the 1814 die had been given to the Smithsonian).[3]

1820

J-A1820-1: Cent • Reverse of Newcomb-12, as on J-28 and J-41 (rusted). White metal. Struck outside the Mint from a discarded die. One or two known. Last sold in Superior Galleries' sale of 9/1998.

1822

J-A1822-1: Half Dollar • Obverse of a regular die but not a variety listed in the Overton text. Copper. Struck outside the Mint from a discarded die. About six known. The die shows a large crack arcing from the left border, across the face to the right; perhaps a fatal crack that resulted in the die not being used for regular coinage.

1823

J-A1823-1: Quarter Dollar • Incomplete die trial reverse of the 1823/2 quarter dollar, with lower arrow tip missing. Lead. Ex Mason (Lot 916), 11/1878; Linderman (Lot 199), 2/1888 (possibly); American Numismatic Rarities, 8/2004.

1836

J-A1836-1: Half Dollar • Obverse of J-57 before LIBERTY was placed on headband. White metal. Ex R.E. Cox, Jr. Two known, one in the Smithsonian Institution.

J-A1836-2: Silver Dollar • Obverse with Liberty Seated motif, pointed index finger on hand holding pole, thick drapery over shield, short dentils, date below. White metal. Library Company of Philadelphia.

Appendix A: Die and Hub Trials and Splashers

J-A1836-3: Silver Dollar • Obverse similar to above, but with differences in drapery and Liberty's index finger now wrapped around pole. White metal. Library Company of Philadelphia.

J-A1836-4: Silver Dollar • Obverse similar to that on J-60, but with shorter neck and other minor differences. White metal. Two known.

J-A1836-5: Silver Dollar • Obverse of J-60, but without date. With name on base. White metal. Ex ANA (1976 sale); New England Rare Coin Auctions, 1/1981.

J-A1836-6: Silver Dollar • Obverse of J-60, but without date. With name on base. This impression has an extra fold of drapery over shield. White metal. Library Company of Philadelphia. It is unclear if this extra drapery was actually in the die or was cut by hand over a J-A1836-5.

J-A1836-7: Silver Dollar • Obverse of J-60 with date. Copper or white metal. Existence unconfirmed. The listing is from W. Elliot Woodward's 10/1863 Colburn sale, Lot 2789, metal not listed. This could also be a misdescription of another variety.

J-A1836-8: Silver Dollar • Reverse of J-60. Copper. Restrike made in 1859 or in the 1870s. Ex Steigerwalt (Lot 1989), 12/1884; Steigerwalt (Lot 990), 4/1885; George D. Woodside; William H. Woodin (exhibited at the ANS in 1914).

J-A1836-9: Silver Dollar • Reverse of J-60. White metal. Existence unconfirmed.

Appendix A: Die and Hub Trials and Splashers

1837

J-A1837-1: Half Dime • Obverse of Liberty Seated die, but without date. White metal. Library Company of Philadelphia.

J-A1837-2: Half Dollar • Obverse with Liberty Seated motif, date curved, no stars, LIBERTY not on shield ribbon. An exceptional trial as the Liberty Seated motif is not known to have been used on two-sided pattern coins until 1838, and then with stars, and not for regular coinage until 1839. Lead. Ex T.R. Peale estate (Stack's), 3/1986.

1838

J-A1838-1: Dime • Obverse of regular Liberty Seated die, but without date and with only one star placed between Liberty's head and the cap. White metal. Two known, one in the Library Company of Philadelphia.

J-A1838-2: Quarter Dollar • Obverse of regular Liberty Seated die, but without date. White metal. Unconfirmed.

J-A1838-3: Half Dollar • Reverse hub trial for either J-72 or J-73. Copper. Ex Joseph J. Mickley (Lot 2174); Charles S. Fellows. Untraced since.

J-A1838-4: Half Dollar • Reverse hub trial of central portion of J-80 with six arrows and an olive branch. Copper. Smithsonian Institution.

J-A1838-5: Silver Dollar • Reverse hub trial of J-104. Copper. Ex Major Lenox R. Lohr; ANA (1995 sale).

J-A1838-6: $5 • Reverse die of 1838 through 1840, with small letters. White metal.

1840

J-A1840-1: Half Dime • Obverse die, regular Liberty Seated motif, with drapery, but without stars or date. White metal. Library Company of Philadelphia.

J-A1840-2: Dime • Obverse die, regular Liberty Seated motif, without drapery. White metal.

J-A1840-3: Quarter Dollar • Obverse die, regular Liberty Seated motif, with drapery, stars around border, but without date. White metal. Library Company of Philadelphia.

J-A1840-4: Silver Dollar • Obverse hub or related trial,[4] with C. GOBRECHT. F. in field above date. White metal. Library Company of Philadelphia. This is perhaps Christian Gobrecht's response to Robert Ball Hughes's rendition on J-110.

J-A1840-5: Silver Dollar • Obverse hub trial with stars, but (as expected for a hub) without date. White metal. Library Company of Philadelphia.

J-A1840-6: Silver Dollar • Reverse die trial. White metal. Library Company of Philadelphia.

1849

J-A1849-1: Cent • Roman numeral I impressed (incuse) on planchet with raised rim. Billon. Two known, both offered in Lot 5707 in the Heritage, 1/1998 sale.

J-A1849-2: Three-Cent Piece • Small Roman numeral III, incused. Billon. Ex Joseph J. Mickley; Colonel Mendes I. Cohen; Virgil M. Brand; ANA (1976 sale).

J-A1849-3: Gold Dollar • Obverse and reverse (open wreath type), impressions side by side on single piece of thin cardboard. Two specimens in Library Company of Philadelphia.

J-A1849-4: $20 • Reverse die of regular design. White metal. Library Company of Philadelphia.

1850

J-A1850-1: $20 • Obverse with head of Liberty, but lacking date, stars, dentilation, and without LIBERTY on coronet. White metal. Library Company of Philadelphia.

Appendix A: Die and Hub Trials and Splashers

1851

J-A1851-1: Three-Cent Piece • Obverse and reverse die trial; impressions side by side on single piece of thin cardboard. Two known, one in Library Company of Philadelphia.

J-A1851-2: Three-Cent Piece • Obverse die trial. White metal. Listing is from W. Elliot Woodward's sale of 5/1863 (Lot 2206). Untraced since.[5]

1852

J-A1852-1: Three-Cent Piece • Obverse die trial. White metal. Existence unconfirmed. Possibly the same as J-A1851-2.

1854

J-A1854-1: Half Dollar • Obverse, regular die with date and arrows recut over an 1853 die. Copper. Library Company of Philadelphia.

J-A1854-2: $3 • Reverse hub trial of agricultural wreath, lacking dentilation, denomination, and date. White metal. Four in Library Company of Philadelphia.[6]

1856

J-A1856-1: Cent • Reverse with pattern agricultural wreath design, as used on reverse of the 1856 Flying Eagle cent, but lacking denomination in center. Copper-nickel. Struck on a square planchet. See Bache I, Lot 2940; G. Cogan (Lot 384), 4/1882. Untraced since.

J-A1856-2: Cent • Reverse as preceding, but with denomination in center. Brass or copper. Struck on a square planchet. Ex Joseph J. Mickley; Colonel Mendes I. Cohen; Charles Steigerwalt (Lot 1990), 12/1884; Charles Steigerwalt (Lot 991), 4/1885. Untraced since.

1857

J-A1857-1: Half Dime, Quarter Dollar, and Half Dollar Combined Inscriptions • Reverse inscriptions for the half dime, quarter dollar, and half dollar. A practice piece containing concentric inscriptions of UNITED STATES OF AMERICA and 1857. White metal. Ex ANA (1958 sale); Bowers and Merena Galleries, 3/1985.

J-A1857-2: Half Dollar • Reverse with heraldic eagle with drooping wings holding a plain scroll in its beak, grasping an olive branch in its right talon and three arrows in its left; 13 stars above; HALF DOLLAR below. White metal.[7] Ex ANA (1958 sale); Bowers and Merena Galleries, 11/1985; Superior Galleries, 10/1989.

J-A1857-3: $2.50 • Obverse of J-189, without date. White metal. Four known, of which two are in the Library Company of Philadelphia. Another is ex Empire Topics Mail Bid Auction No. 1 (Lot 101), 11/1958; Lester Merkin (Lot 923), 2/1971.

Appendix A: Die and Hub Trials and Splashers

J-A1857-4: $2.50 • Reverse of J-189. White metal. Library Company of Philadelphia.

J-A1857-5: $20 • Reverse hub trial showing heraldic eagle with a large ornamented shield on its breast; holding a plain scroll in its beak and grasping very large arrows and olive branch in its talon. Copper. Ex Hans M.F. Schulman; R.B. White; Bowers and Merena Galleries, 9/1989.

J-A1857-6: $20 • Reverse hub trial similar to above but with more detail. Lead. Ex Stephen K. Nagy; Dr. J. Hewitt Judd; Bowers and Merena Galleries, 11/1985.

J-A1857-7: $20 • Reverse trial featuring a heraldic eagle with drooping wings, holding a scroll inscribed E PLURIBUS UNUM in its beak, grasping olive branch in the right talon and 3 arrows in the left; UNITED STATES OF AMERICA, TWENTY DOLLARS in the margin (AW-321). White metal. Supposedly five known. Some are die struck while others are casts. At least one example made for Dr. J.T. Barclay by A.C. Paquet, July 6, 1857.

J-A1857-8: $20 • Reverse similar to last but with rays and a large five-pointed star added behind eagle; lacking borders, denomination, and legend. White metal. Ex Stephen K. Nagy; ANA (1958 sale); Bowers and Merena Galleries, 11/1985.

J-A1857-9: $20 • Reverse die. Completed design of above. Copper. Ex Edward D. Cogan, 9/1878: Charles P. Britton (George Cogan), 1/1883; Garrett Collection (The Johns Hopkins University, sold by Bowers & Ruddy Galleries), 3/1980.

1858

J-A1858-1: Cent • Reverse of J-208, with clusters of five leaves. White metal.

Appendix A: Die and Hub Trials and Splashers

J-A1858-2: Cent • Reverse of J-216, but lacking dentilation. Large center dot. White metal. Library Company of Philadelphia.

J-A1858-3: Cent • Obverse as used on J-202 to J-207. White metal. The genuineness of this piece has been questioned.

J-A1858-4: Half Dollar • Reverse similar to J-222, perfect ribbon variety, but a different die. This is lacking E PLURIBUS UNUM on the ribbon and lacks dentilation. White metal. Two known (Library Company of Philadelphia and Smithsonian Institution). Additional listings for this reverse on two-inch thick copper and leather are unconfirmed.

J-A1858-5: Half Dollar • Reverse lettering only as on J-222. White metal. Library Company of Philadelphia.

J-A1858-6: Gold Dollar • Obverse die trial of J-224. White metal. Library Company of Philadelphia. [8]

J-A1858-7: Gold Dollar • Reverse die trial of J-224, but lacking date. White metal. Library Company of Philadelphia.[9]

1859

J-A1859-1: Half Dime or Dime • Obverse die trial with Longacre's French Liberty Head design as on the half dollars of this year.[10] No date or legend. Copper. Ex New Netherlands Coin Co., 4/1951; ANA (1958 sale).

J-A1859-2: Half Dollar • Obverse Longacre design as on J-237 through J-246 without date, legend, or dentilation. White metal. Two or three known.

J-A1859-3: Half Dollar • Obverse as above, with legend and dentilation added, but date still lacking. White metal. Library Company of Philadelphia.

Appendix A: Die and Hub Trials and Splashers

J-A1859-4: Half Dollar • Obverse as above, now complete including date. Lead. Existence unconfirmed.

J-A1859-5: Half Dollar • Reverse of J-237. Copper. Existence unconfirmed.

J-A1859-6: Half Dollar • Reverse of J-239. Lead. Existence unconfirmed.

J-A1859-7: Silver Dollar • Obverse is Longacre's French Liberty Head, but without LIBERTY on ribbon. White metal. Three known.

J-A1859-8: $2.50 • Reverse style of 1859 to 1866 with short arrowheads. Gold. See Lester Merkin's sale of 10/1973 (Lot 469).

J-A1859-9: $20 • Obverse lacks dentilation and date, but has a date (1850?) or numbers scratched under truncation of neck. White metal. Library Company of Philadelphia.

J-A1859-10: $20 • Obverse as above, with dentilation added. White metal. Die varieties exist. Three known, two of which are in the Library Company of Philadelphia. The third is ex Empire Coin Mail Bid Sale #1; Stack's, 9/1988; Auction '89; Bowers and Merena, 9/1997.

J-A1859-11: $20 • Reverse of J-260. White metal. Library Company of Philadelphia.

1860[7]

J-A1860-1: Half Dime • Obverse hub trial of regular die, but lacking date. Copper. Ex Major Lenox R. Lohr; Robert Batchelder.

J-A1860-2: Dime • Obverse hub trial of regular die, but lacking date. Copper. Ex Major Lenox R. Lohr; Robert Batchelder.

J-A1860-3: $5 • Obverse die trial, as used on J-271. White metal. Ex Parmelee. Existence unconfirmed.

J-A1860-4: $5 • Reverse die trial of eagle holding olive branch and arrows, as later used on J-271 and J-661. White metal. Ex Major Lenox R. Lohr; Robert Batchelder; Bowers and Merena Galleries, 11/1987.

Appendix A: Die and Hub Trials and Splashers

J-A1860-5: $5 • Reverse hub trial of eagle holding olive branch and arrows with scroll in mouth, as later used on J-271. Lead. Ex Major Lenox R. Lohr; Robert Batchelder; Bowers and Merena Galleries, 11/1987; Superior Galleries, 6/1988.

J-A1860-6: $5 • Reverse hand-punched trial illustrating peripheral legends for J-271, but with different spacing. Copper. Ex Robert Coulton Davis; F.C.C. Boyd; Bowers and Merena Galleries, 11/1985; Stack's, 1/1989.

1863

J-A1863-1: Two-Cent Piece • Obverse style of J-312, but without date. White metal.

1864

J-A1864-1: Two-Cent Piece • Obverse similar to that of J-366, with small motto, but lacking date and dentilation. White metal. Library Company of Philadelphia.

1866

J-A1866-1: Five-Cent Piece • Obverse of J-461. Nickel. This may be an example of J-461 with the reverse planed off, as it is on a thin planchet weighing 62.7 grains, almost 14 grains less than a standard five-cent planchet. Ex Kagin's, 11/1974; ANA (1977 sale); Bowers and Merena Galleries, 3/1996; Bowers and Merena Galleries, 3/1999.

J-A1866-2: Five-Cent Piece • Obverse impressions on a silver bar of two dies: Washington die, UNITED STATES OF AMERICA, 1866, used to strike J-461; Washington die, UNITED STATES OF AMERICA, 1866, used to strike J-464.[13] Modern impressions struck in 1956 from die owned by the Boston Numismatic Society, donated in the late 19th century. One silver bar struck.

J-A1866-3: Five-Cent Piece • Obverse impressions as preceding, modern, but on an aluminum bar measuring about 1" x 3". Nine aluminum bars made. Apparently some were marketed through dealer Melvin Came; others may have been seized.

J-A1866-4: Five-Cent Piece • Obverse of J-464, but without inscription. White metal. Existence unconfirmed.

J-A1866-5: Five-Cent Piece • Obverse of J-489, but lacking date and dentilation. White metal. Library Company of Philadelphia.

J-A1866-6: Five-Cent Piece • Obverse of J-489 as above, with dentilation added, but still lacking date. White metal. Library Company of Philadelphia.

J-A1866-7: $10 • Reverse hub trial of regular die, motto IN GOD WE TRUST. Copper. Ex Major Lenox R. Lohr; Empire Review, 1/1963.

J-A1866-8: Five-Cent Piece • Obverse similar to that of J-416, but lacking date and dentilation. White metal. Library Company of Philadelphia.

J-A1866-9: Five-Cent Piece • Reverse similar to that of J-416. White metal. Two known, one on oversized planchet as illustrated. [12]

1867

J-A1867-1: Cent • Reverse hub trial with Roman numeral I within thick wreath of oak and olive branches, connected at the top by scrolls and a six pointed star with a pellet beneath. Copper. Ex Stephen K. Nagy; Bowers and Merena Galleries, 11/1985; Superior Galleries 10/1989.

J-A1867-2: Cent • Reverse hub trial, as above. Lead. Ex Major Lenox R. Lohr.

J-A1867-3: Cent • Reverse die trial, similar to above, with I incuse. Lead. Ex Major Lenox R. Lohr; Bowers and Merena Galleries, 6/1996.

J-A1867-4: Cent • Reverse die trial as above, but with I raised. Lead. Ex ANA (1958 sale); Major Lenox R. Lohr; Bowers and Merena Galleries, 6/1996.

J-A1867-5: Cent • Obverse trial of experimental master die(?), but with date[14], as normally used only on a working die (dates were not added to master dies of Indian Head cents until toward the end of the first decade of the 20th century). A very curious item. Copper. Ex Coin Galleries, 2/1991; Stack's, 2/2001.

J-A1867-6: Three-Cent Piece • Reverse die trial with Roman numeral III[15] in same wreath as on the cents above (J-A1867-1 and others). Copper. Ex C.E. Bullowa; Abe Kosoff; Bowers and Merena Galleries, 11/1985; Stack's, 9/1994.

J-A1867-7: Three-Cent Piece • Reverse die trial as above. Lead. Ex Thomas L. Elder's 37th sale; P.C. Clark (M.H. Bolender, 11/1932). In the Smithsonian Institution.

J-A1867-8: Five-Cent Piece • Obverse hand-made trial, similar to that used on J-561[16], but with irregularly spaced C and A (in AMERICA). Copper. Ex Louis S. Werner; Stack's; Auction '89.

Appendix A: Die and Hub Trials and Splashers

J-A1867-9: Five-Cent Piece • Obverse hand-made trial[17] of J-561, lacking dentilation and without LONGACRE F. below truncation. Copper. Ex Major Lenox R. Lohr; Bowers and Merena Galleries, 6/1991.

J-A1867-10: Five-Cent Piece • Obverse die trial of J-561, as above, lacking dentilation and without LONGACRE F. below truncation. Lead. Two known.

J-A1867-11: Five-Cent Piece • Reverse die trial of J-561, lacking dentilation. Lead. Ex Judd; Abe Kosoff; Bowers and Merena Galleries, 11/1985.

J-A1867-12: Five-Cent Piece • Reverse die trial of J-565 lacking dentilation, with lines through star and guide marks outlining the border. Lead. Ex Major Lenox R. Lohr; Robert Batchelder; Auction '89.

J-A1867-13: Five-Cent Piece • Reverse die trial of J-565, similar to above, still lacking dentilation, but with border; the center of the six pointed star is smooth. Copper. Ex Major Lenox R. Lohr; Robert Batchelder; Auction '89.

J-A1867-14: Five-Cent Piece • Obverse hand-made trial[18] of die similar to J-566, but with point of Liberty's coronet pointing to the second T (in STATES). Nickel. Ex Major Lenox R. Lohr; Robert Batchelder; Bowers and Merena Galleries, 11/1987.

J-A1867-15: Five-Cent Piece • Obverse hand-made trial[19] of J-566, lacking dentilation. Some reverse detail is visible. Copper. Ex Major Lenox R. Lohr; Robert Batchelder; R.B. White; Bowers and Merena Galleries, 9/1989.

J-A1867-16: Five-Cent Piece • Obverse die trial of J-566, lacking dentilation. White metal. Library Company of Philadelphia.

J-A1867-17: Five-Cent Piece • Obverse die trial of J-570, lacking dentilation and date. White metal. Library Company of Philadelphia.

J-A1867-18: Five-Cent Piece • Obverse die trial of J-570, lacking date. Lead. Ex Auction '89.

J-A1867-19: Five-Cent Piece • Regular reverse, lacking dentilation. White metal. Two confirmed: Major Lenox R. Lohr, and Library Company of Philadelphia. The example in the Connecticut State Library appears to be a die cap mint error.

1868

J-A1868-1: Cent • Reverse of J-608, lacking dentilation. Lead. Ex Major Lenox R. Lohr; Bowers and Merena Galleries, 6/1996.

J-A1868-2: Five-Cent Piece • Reverse of J-633, lacking dentilation, and before the Maltese cross was added above the scroll. White metal. Ex Major Lenox R. Lohr; Robert Batchelder; Bowers and Merena Galleries, 11/1987.

J-A1868-3: Five-Cent Piece • Reverse of J-633, as preceding, but with the Maltese cross added. White metal. Ex Lorin G. Parmelee. Existence unconfirmed; possibly a misdescription of J-A1868-2.

J-A1868-4: $10 • Obverse die trial of J-661. Copper. Ex J. Carson Brevoort (Lot 791); Lorin G. Parmelee. Existence unconfirmed.

J-A1868-5: $10 • Reverse die trial of J-661. Copper. Ex J. Carson Brevoort (Lot 791); Lorin G. Parmelee. Existence unconfirmed.

1869

J-A1869-1: Cent • Obverse die trial of J-666. Copper. Ex King Farouk. Untraced since.

J-A1869-2: Dime • Obverse hub trial of Liberty, as on J-702. Copper. Ex Major Lenox R. Lohr; Bowers and Merena Galleries, 11/1987; Superior Galleries, 6/1988.

J-A1869-3: Dime • Obverse hand-made trial of J-702, with point of Liberty's coronet pointing to the F (in OF) and lacking dentilation. Ex Major Lenox R. Lohr; Bowers and Merena Galleries, 11/1987; Superior Galleries, 6/1988.

J-A1869-4: Dime • Obverse hand-made trial of J-702, with point of Liberty's coronet pointing to the O (in OF). Reverse hub shows partial design; both sides lack dentilation. Copper. Ex Major Lenox R. Lohr; Robert Batchelder; R.B. White; Bowers and Merena Galleries, 9/1989.

J-A1869-5: Quarter Dollar • Obverse hub trial of Liberty, as on J-727. Copper. Two or three known.

J-A1869-6: Quarter Dollar • Obverse die trial of J-727, lacking dentilation. Lead. Ex Bowers and Merena Galleries, 11/1993; Heritage, 10/1994.

Appendix A: Die and Hub Trials and Splashers

J-A1869-7: Half Dollar • Obverse hub trial of Liberty head, as on J-748. Copper. At least two known.

J-A1869-8: Half Dollar • Obverse hub trial of J-748. White metal. Ex-Major Lenox R. Lohr; Empire Review, 1/1963; Bowers and Merena Galleries (Lot 1207), 6/1996; Heritage (Lot 6200), 9/1997.

J-A1869-9: Half Dollar • Obverse hand-made trial[20] similar to that of J-754, but LIBERTY is not inscribed on the headband, the date (very unusual feature on a Standard Silver die) is below Miss Liberty instead of the scroll, and the star on Liberty's headband points to the S (in STATES) instead of the O (in OF). Copper. Ex Stephen K. Nagy; R.E. Cox, Jr.

J-A1869-10: Half Dollar • Obverse hand-made trial[21] similar to that of J-754, but LIBERTY is not inscribed on the headband, and the date (not usual for patterns of this style) is below Miss Liberty instead of the scroll. Unlike J-A1869-9, the star on Liberty's headband points correctly to the O (in OF) instead of the S (in STATES). Copper. Ex Stephen K. Nagy; R.E. Cox, Jr.

J-A1869-11: Half Dollar • Reverse hub trial, lacking date and dentilation. White metal. In the Smithsonian Institution.

1870

J-A1870-1: Half Dollar • Reverse die trial of J-939, without circumscription. White metal. Ex Stephen K. Nagy; American Numismatic Rarities, 12/2003.

J-A1870-2: Half Dollar • Reverse of J-963 through J-992. White metal. Broken into two pieces. Ex Stack's, 3/1993; American Numismatic Rarities, 7/2005.

1872

J-A1872-1: Silver Dollar • Obverse of J-1208 (A-W 1241). White metal. Existence unconfirmed.

1875

J-A1875-1: Twenty-Cent Piece • Reverse (?) die trial showing UNITED STATES OF NORTH AMERICA and date, with no central device. White metal. Two known.

J-A1875-2: Twenty-Cent Piece • Reverse die trial of J-1398. Lead or white metal. Ex William H. Woodin (shown at the 1914 American Numismatic Society exhibit); Waldo C. Newcomer; Major Lenox R. Lohr; Robert Batchelder.

1876

J-A1876-1: Silver Dollar • Obverse die trial of J-1462. Cardboard. Ex Clarence S. Bement (Lot 163).

J-A1876-2: Silver Dollar • Obverse die trial of J-1462. Red wax. Ex Clarence S. Bement (Lot 163).

J-A1876-3: Trade Dollar • Reverse hub trial of J-1320/ J-1475a. Copper. Two known. Ex Virgil M. Brand; Bowers and Merena Galleries, 3/1990.

J-A1876-4: Whimsy • Practice piece showing dates 1873, 1874, and 1876, and the word DOLLARS. White metal. Ex Stephen K. Nagy. Existence unconfirmed; possibly the same as J-A1884-1.

1877

J-A1877-1: Dime • Obverse of just the portrait, as used on J-1498. Copper. Ex ANA (1958 sale).

J-A1877-2: Half Dollar • Obverse of just the portrait, as used on J-1501. Red wax. Ex Clarence S. Bement; B. Max Mehl, 11/1954; Major Lenox R. Lohr; Robert Batchelder; R.E. Cox, Jr.

J-A1877-3: Half Dollar • Reverse of J-1502. Lead. One or two known. One is struck on a square planchet. Ex Wayte Raymond, 1/1943; Numismatic Gallery, 7/1951. The other, illustrated, is in the Smithsonian Institution.

J-A1877-4: Half Dollar • Obverse hub trial of just the portrait, as used on J-1503 to J-1507 (first die). White metal. Ex ANA (1958 sale): R.E. Cox, Jr.; R.B. White; Bowers and Merena Galleries, 11/1989.

J-A1877-5: Half Dollar • Reverse of J-1530. Lead. Two known. One (illustrated) in American Numismatic Society. The other, on square planchet, is ex Wayte Raymond (Lot 16), 1/1943; Abe Kosoff (Numismatic Gallery Monthly), 7/1951.

J-A1877-6: Half Dollar • Obverse hub trial of just the portrait, as used on J-1538, without LIBERTY on ribbon. Copper. Ex ANA (1958 sale).

J-A1877-7: Half Dollar • Obverse die trial of J-1540, lacking date, Paquet's die. Lead. Two known, including the illustrated example (in the Smithsonian Institution). A second reportedly is on a square planchet.

Appendix A: Die and Hub Trials and Splashers

J-A1877-8: Half Dollar • Reverse die trial of J-1540, lacking E PLURIBUS UNUM on the scroll in the eagle's beak. Paquet's die. Lead. Two known, including the illustrated example (in the Smithsonian Institution). A second reportedly is on a square planchet.

J-A1877-10: $50 • Obverse hub trial of just the portrait of J-1546, but lacking LIBERTY on coronet. Lead. In the Smithsonian Institution.

J-A1877-11: $50 • Reverse hub trial of the central portion of J-1546. Lead. Ex Stephen K. Nagy; ANA (1958 sale); Kagin, 11/1964; Bowers & Ruddy Galleries, 5/1973; ANA (1993 sale).

1878

J-A1877-9: Silver Dollar • Obverse hub trial, similar to that used on J-1459 or J-1542, but with 13 stars around and drapery at neck. Reverse apparently used as a test piece for various legends; 1877 appears at least twice. Copper. Ex Chase Manhattan Bank collection, now in the Smithsonian Institution,

J-A1878-1: Silver Dollar • Obverse hub or related trial[22] of regular die. Copper. Ex Frossard, 5/1882; William H. Woodin (shown at the 1914 American Numismatic Society exhibit); King Farouk; Edwin Hydeman; Bowers and Merena Galleries, 11/1985; Superior Galleries, 10/1989; Bowers and Merena Galleries, 5/1994; Bowers and Merena Galleries, 1/1995.

J-A1878-2: Silver Dollar • Reverse hub trial of regular die with eight tail feathers. Copper. Ex Frossard 5/1882; William H. Woodin (shown at the 1914 American Numismatic Society exhibit); King Farouk; Edwin Hydeman; Bowers and Merena Galleries, 11/1985; Superior Galleries, 10/1989; Bowers and Merena Galleries, 5/1994; Bowers and Merena Galleries, 1/1995.

J-A1878-3: $5 • Reverse of J-1568. Struck on a planchet with a hub layout of a similar design. Unique. Copper. Ex David U. Proskey; F.C.C. Boyd; ANA (1976 sale).

J-A1878-4 $5 • Obverse of J-1570. Copper. Struck on a planchet previously used as a layout for half dollar legends. Only one known example. Ex David U. Proskey; F.C.C. Boyd; ANA (1976 sale).

J-A1878-5 $10 • Reverse hub trial, similar to that used on J-1581. Lead. Ex Stephen K. Nagy; ANA (1958 sale).

1879

J-A1879-1: Dime • Obverse hub trial of just the portrait, similar to that used on J-1586 and J-1588, but with only four leaves above the coronet instead of five; with LIBERTY very lightly impressed on coronet. White metal. In the Smithsonian Institution.

J-A1879-2: Silver Dollar • Obverse of J-1605. White metal. Existence unconfirmed.

J-A1879-3: Silver Dollar • Reverse of J-1605. White metal. Ex William H. Woodin (shown at the 1914 American Numismatic Society exhibit).

J-A1879-4: Silver Dollar • Obverse of J-1608. Lead. Ex ANA (1958 sale); Bowers and Merena Galleries, 11/1985.

J-A1879-5: Silver Dollar • Reverse of J-1615. White metal. Ex King Farouk; Abner Kreisberg-Hans M.F. Schulman, 2/1960.

J-A1879-6: Silver Dollar • Obverse of just the portrait, as used on J-1631. White metal. New Netherlands Coin Co., 4/1951.

1882

J-A1882-1: Silver Dollar • Obverse of just the portrait, as used on J-1702. Copper. Ex Stephen K. Nagy; ANA (1958 sale).

1884

J-A1884-1: Whimsy • Practice piece showing various dates in different sizes, including 1873, 1875, 1876, and 1884, and the words ONE CENT and DOLLARS. White metal. In the Smithsonian Institution.

1885

J-A1885-1: Silver Dollar • Edge trial showing E PLURIBUS UNUM as on J-1747. Copper. Ex R. Coulton Davis (Lot 1135).

1891

J-A1891-1: Dime • Obverse of the regular Liberty Seated design.[23] White metal. Ex William F. Dunham (Lot 1817).

J-A1891-2: Dime • Reverse die trial of the regular design. White metal. Ex William F. Dunham (Lot 1817). A second piece, listed in previous editions under 1899 (ex H.O. Granberg; G.F.E. Wilharm) is of questionable authenticity.

1893

J-A1893-1: Isabella Quarter Dollar • Obverse impression of the Isabella quarter dollar for the World's Columbian Exposition. Cardboard. Collection of the

American Numismatic Society. Reverse citation notes that it is the first striking from the die and was received from Superintendent Bosbyshell of the Philadelphia Mint.

J-A1893-2 Isabella Quarter Dollar • Reverse impression of the Isabella quarter dollar. Cardboard. Collection of the American Numismatic Society. Reverse citation notes that it is the first striking from the die and was received from Superintendent Bosbyshell of the Philadelphia Mint.

1899

J-A1899-1: Dime • Obverse of the regular Barber design. White metal. Ex H.O. Granberg; G.F.E. Wilharm. Of questionable authenticity.

1903

J-A1903-1: Louisiana Purchase Exposition Gold Dollars • Obverse and reverse of commemorative gold dollars struck on cardboard. The example in the Smithsonian has eight strikings—both Jefferson and McKinley obverses and six reverses, including the adopted design which is upside down relative to the others. A second example, ex Bowers and Merena Galleries, 11/1997, from the Pennsylvania Collection, has both obverses and one pattern reverse on it.

1904

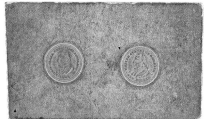

J-A1904-1: Lewis and Clark Exposition Gold Dollar • Obverse and reverse of the commemorative gold dollar on cardboard. In the Smithsonian Institution.

1906

J-A1906-1: $20 • Obverse of J-1773, by Charles E. Barber. Gilt copper. In the Smithsonian Institution.[24]

1908

J-A1908-1: $20 • Obverse and reverse trial of Saint-Gaudens With motto type, lacking date. Brass. Ex Stephen K. Nagy; Stack's. Now in the Smithsonian Institution.

1909

J-A1909-1: Cent • Obverse of the original Lincoln design with taller figure, lacking IN GOD WE TRUST and with different placement of the date and LIBERTY. Lead. Ex Dr. J. Hewitt Judd; Loye Lauder.

1915

J-A1915-1: Panama-Pacific Gold Dollar • Obverse of the Panama-Pacific International Exposition commemorative gold dollar, without S mintmark. White metal, bronzed. Ex ANA (1952 sale); Bowers & Ruddy Galleries, 11/1974.

J-A1915-2: Panama-Pacific Gold Dollar • Reverse of the Panama-Pacific International Exposition commemorative gold dollar. White metal, bronzed. Ex ANA (1952 sale); Bowers & Ruddy Galleries, 11/1974.

J-A1915-3: Panama-Pacific $50 • Obverse and reverse hub trial of the Panama-Pacific International Exposition commemorative octagonal $50. Copper. Ex Abner Kreisberg-Hans M.F. Schulman, 3/1994.

Appendix A: Die and Hub Trials and Splashers

1916

J-A1916-1: McKinley Gold Dollar • Obverse of McKinley Memorial commemorative gold dollar. Nickel. Ex James W. Curtis; Major Lenox R. Lohr; Robert Batchelder; Auction '80.

1920

J-A1920-1: Pilgrim Tercentenary Half Dollar • Reverse as above. Lead. Ex George T. Morgan estate; C.A. Whitford, 5/2002.

1922

J-A1922-1: Grant Memorial Half Dollar • Obverse hub trial of Grant Memorial commemorative half dollar, variety with star in field. Copper. Ex R.E. Cox, Jr.

J-A1922-2: Grant Memorial Half Dollar • Obverse of Grant Memorial commemorative half dollar, variety with star in field. Silver or silver-plated copper. American Numismatic Society Collection.

J-A1922-3: Grant Memorial Half Dollar • Obverse as above. Copper. Existence unconfirmed.

J-A1922-4: Grant Memorial Half Dollar • Obverse as above. Brass. Ex ANA (1958 sale); R.E. Cox, Jr.

J-A1922-5: Grant Memorial Half Dollar • Obverse as above. Nickel. Ex James Earle Fraser; Bowers & Ruddy Galleries, 5/1973; ANA (1996 sale).

J-A1922-6: Grant Memorial Half Dollar • Reverse of Grant Memorial commemorative half dollar. Silver or silver-plated copper. In American Numismatic Society Collection.

J-A1922-7: Grant Memorial Half Dollar • Reverse as above. Nickel. Ex James Earle Fraser; Bowers & Ruddy Galleries, 5/1973; ANA (1996 sale).

J-A1922-8: Grant Memorial Half Dollar • Reverse as above. White metal. Existence unconfirmed.

J-A1922-9: Grant Memorial Gold Dollar • Obverse and reverse. Obverse: Grant Memorial commemorative, with star, in relief. Reverse: hub trial with incuse, reversed features. Possibly first struck as a hub trial (or as an obverse die trial), then later struck with the other die or hub. A most unusual item. Brass. Ex ANA (1958 sale); Major Lenox R. Lohr; Heritage, 6/1995; Bowers and Merena Galleries, 7/2002.

J-A1922-10: Grant Memorial Gold Dollar • Obverse of Grant Memorial commemorative gold dollar with star. Copper. Ex Farran Zerbe; F.C.C. Boyd; ANA (1976 sale).

J-A1922-11: Grant Memorial Gold Dollar • Obverse as above. White metal. Ex James Earle Fraser; Jerome Cohen.

J-A1922-12: Grant Memorial Gold Dollar • Reverse of Grant Memorial commemorative gold dollar. Copper. Ex Farran Zerbe; F.C.C. Boyd; ANA (1976 sale). See below for image of a similar trial.

J-A1922-13: Grant Memorial Gold Dollar • Reverse as above. White metal. Ex James Earle Fraser; Jerome Cohen; Bowers and Merena Galleries, 7/2002.

Appendix A: Die and Hub Trials and Splashers

1923

J-A1923-1: Monroe Doctrine Centennial Half Dollar • Reverse of Monroe Doctrine Centennial commemorative half dollar. Copper. Ex R.E. Cox, Jr.

1924

J-A1924-1: Huguenot-Walloon Tercentenary Half Dollar • Reverse of Huguenot-Walloon Tercentenary commemorative half dollar. Brass. Ex Stephen K. Nagy; Stack's; Smithsonian Institution.

1925

J-A1925-1: California Diamond Jubilee Half Dollar • Obverse of California Diamond Jubilee commemorative half dollar. Lead. Ex ANA (1958 sale); R.E. Cox, Jr.

1926

J-A1926-1: Sesquicentennial Half Dollar • Obverse of Sesquicentennial of American Independence commemorative half dollar. Copper. Ex R.E. Cox, Jr.

J-A1926-2: Sesquicentennial Half Dollar • Reverse of Sesquicentennial of American Independence commemorative half dollar. Copper. Ex R.E. Cox, Jr.

J-A1926-3: Sesquicentennial $2.50 • Obverse of Sesquicentennial of American Independence commemorative $2.50 piece[25]. Copper. Ex ANA (1958 sale).

J-A1926-4 Sesquicentennial $2.50 • Obverse as above. Brass[26]. Ex ANA (1958 sale).

1932

J-A1932-1: Quarter Dollar • Reverse hub trial of the regular design. Copper. Two are in the American Numismatic Society Collection.

1935

J-A1935-1: Arkansas Centennial Half Dollar • Reverse of Arkansas Centennial commemorative half dollar with incuse S mintmark. Copper. Ex Empire Coin Co.; R.E. Cox, Jr.

J-A1935-2: Hudson Sesquicentennial Half Dollar • Obverse hub trial of Hudson, New York, commemorative half dollar. Copper. Three in R.E. Cox, Jr. sale.

J-A1935-3: San Diego Half Dollar • Reverse of San Diego, California Pacific Exposition commemorative half dollar. Copper. Ex R.E. Cox, Jr.

Appendix A: Die and Hub Trials and Splashers

1939

J-A1939-1: Half Dollar • Obverse of regular die. Copper. Ex R.E. Cox, Jr.

1942

J-A1942-1: Cent • Obverse die, with head of Columbia, as made in the Mint. Dies were distributed to outside manufacturers for use in testing various materials for cent coinage (see J-2051, et al., in regular listings). LIBERTY to left, JUSTICE to right. Uniface obverse trials reported in various metals and plastic. Existence unconfirmed; some examples may have been trial strikes with their reverses planed off.

1948

J-A1948-1: Half Dollar • Obverse of new Franklin type, but with XXXX in place of date. White metal. Existence unconfirmed.

J-A1948-2: Half Dollar • Obverse of new Franklin type, but with two sets of designer's initials, JRS, on Franklin's bust. White metal. Ex Herbert I. Melnick, 11/1982.

1964

J-A1964-1: Half Dollar • Obverse and reverse showing Kennedy portrait. The portraits are different. This is most noticeable at the bottom of the ear and the tip of the truncation. Aluminum. Now in the Smithsonian Institution.

J-A1964-2: Half Dollar • Reverse hub trial of regular type, but with two D mintmarks, one in the normal position to the right of the olive branch and a second to the right of the eagle's tail. Copper. Ex R.B. White; Bowers and Merena Galleries, 9/1989; Bowers and Merena Galleries, 11/1999.

1982

J-A1982-1: Cent • Obverse showing Martha Washington design first used in 1965 during testing for clad coinage. Struck on a copper-plated zinc planchet. Possibly struck outside the Mint by one of the firms engaged to test planchets. Ex Ira & Larry Goldberg's 10/2000 sale; Bowers and Merena Galleries, 1/2003.

Appendix A: Die and Hub Trials and Splashers

Miscellaneous Items

The following items are believed to have been made outside the Mint and are no longer considered part of this series. They are listed here for informational purposes, as many appeared in earlier editions.

1) Half dime • Obverse with Liberty bust facing right, similar to regular issue but in high relief; LIBERTY above, 1800 below (A-W 20). Copper. About 6 known. Not a Mint product. They have been around since the 1860s.

2) Half dollar • Reverse trial showing two eagles. Copper. Overstruck on an 1832 large cent. Ex ANA (1976 sale).

3) Two-cent piece • Eagle believed copied from J-52 (Pollock-3255). Copper. Ex Bowers and Merena, 3/1992.

4) Quarter dollar reverse hub trial and half eagle reverse hub trial • Brass. At least two known. One from Early American History Auctions (Lot 1292), 4/2003.

5) Medal • Reverse die trial of an eagle with lightning bolts in talons. White metal. This was probably made for use on a medal. In Library Company of Philadelphia.

6) Cent • 1856 Flying Eagle cent trials. Leather. Believed to be squeezings of a coin impressed into pieces of leather, and not true trials. Early American History Auction (Lot 1134), 8/2000.

7) Unknown (either 4-cent piece or $4 piece) • Design with numeral 4 and shield engraved on the reverse of a two-cent piece. Ex ANA (1958 sale); Loye Lauder.

8) Medal • Large eagle originally described as being a reverse for J-1546 and J-1548, but more likely for a medal. Ex ANA (1958 sale); Bowers & Ruddy, 11/1973; Bowers & Merena, 1/2001.

Notes

1. Actual date/era of reverse die not known; there are no known patterns or regular issues with the value stated as "2.50." Was this a notation scratched on the planchet? • Bache sale description: "Reverse of United States quarter eagle?" • Crosby sale description: "Reverse of an early half eagle, '2.50' below. Brass. Fine."
2. This was listed in error under 1796 in earlier editions.
3. Don Taxay, *Counterfeit, Mis-Struck, and Unofficial U.S. Coins*, 1963, p. 122. • George J. Fuld, "A Group of Restruck Patterns," *The Numismatist*, May 1998. • The modern "PROPRIETERS," etc., inscription was inspired by a 17th-century Elephant token struck in England. "M" was Bashlow's tribute to Joseph Mickley, apparently thought to be the source of the ex-Mint die.
4. Regular hubs of this era do not include the date.
5. Woodward was perhaps the most knowledgeable American auction cataloger of the 1860s.
6. These were listed as cent trials under 1856 in earlier editions of this book; cents of 1856–1858 employ the same wreath style, but of a smaller size.
7. Earlier editions lists one in copper; its existence is unconfirmed.
8. Listed under 1856 in earlier editions.
9. Listed under 1816 in earlier editions.
10. The listings of a dime and half dime in earlier editions both represent this piece.
11. The 1860 cent reverses listed in earlier editions have proven to be counterfeits. Additional Information can be found in "The Mystery of Lot #2091—The 1863 Pattern Cent," Richard Snow, *Longacre's Ledger*, March 2002.
12. The oversized piece may be a later restrike struck outside the Mint.
13. Struck by a Mr. Pollock (no kin to the pattern researcher), curator of the Society's collection, who also added his initial P in a separate punch. Details in "A Group of Restruck Patterns," George J. Fuld, *The Numismatist*, May 1998. The dies and some bars were seized and all destroyed, despite a request for the dies from Stuart Mosher, curator of the Smithsonian Institution.
14. Regular hubs of this era do not include the date.
15. Per conventional numismatic wisdom, this design was either used or copied on three-dollar pieces said by some to have been struck by Boston medalist and diesinker Joseph Merriam.
16. Regular hubs of this era do not include the date.
17. Regular hubs of this era do not include the date.
18. Regular hubs of this era do not include the date.
19. Regular hubs of this era do not include the date.
20. Regular hubs of this era do not include the date.
21. Regular hubs of this era do not include the date.
22. Regular hubs of this era do not include the date.
23. This was misdescribed as being the obverse of J-1734 in earlier editions.
24. Various electrotype (not struck) shells for the 1907 Saint-Gaudens gold coinage exist, with designs mostly similar to the adopted styles, and are in the collection of the American Numismatic Society. As they were not struck from dies, they are not listed here (illustrated in the seventh edition of this book, pp. 246–248). Certain later electrotypes of the Fraser designs of 1911 to 1913, 1915 Panama-Pacific commemoratives, etc., are listed as the designs differ markedly from those actually used.
25. This piece was listed under 1915 as a Panama-Pacific International Exhibition $2.50 in previous editions, in error.
26. This piece was listed under 1915 as a Panama-Pacific International Exhibition $2.50 in previous editions, in error.

Appendix B: Mint Errors

Mint errors include pieces struck on incorrect planchets during the regular coining process. As examples, an Indian Head cent struck on a planchet intended for a nickel three-cent piece is a mint error. While some mint errors may have been made intentionally to create curiosities, most were probably produced inadvertently. The present listing is a sketch or overview of certain early mint errors as well as general categories of later ones.

Over a long period of time the Philadelphia Mint and other mints have struck coins under contract for foreign countries, often using planchet sizes, weights, etc., different from those used for domestic coins. Occasionally such foreign planchets would be fed into presses making domestic coins, creating wrong-metal or wrong-weight mint errors.

Today there are many mint errors in numismatic hands, most made from the 1940s onward, when production often amounted to the hundreds of millions of regular coins. In the high-speed coinage of such pieces, many incorrect planchets were fed into the presses. No account of such errors can ever be complete, and an attempt at such is beyond the purview of the present text. Readers are recommended to contact specialists in mint errors.

The present listing includes certain pieces, especially those of early dates, which were sometimes sold as patterns in the past, but which are now considered to be mint errors.

As a general rule, mint errors, if not worn, are with lustrous (Mint State) surfaces and are not Proofs.

Some mint errors are listed in the main section of this work, especially among wrong-metal strikings of minor coins, and are identified as such. These listings are from numismatic tradition (no new mint error descriptions have been inserted).

Classic Mint Error Specimens

1795 Half Dollar: Reverse only (Overton's "H"); ex Haines (Bangs, Merwin and Co. [Lot 783]), 1/1863; Woodward (Lot 2182), 5/1863; Appleton; MHS-Stack's, 3/1973; Bowers & Ruddy, 2/1974; Crouch-Superior, 6/1977.

1795 Silver Dollar: Struck on a cent planchet (Adams-Woodin 18, Pollock-34) ex W. Elliott Woodward, 4/1863; Lorin G. Parmelee; George W. Woodside; William H. Woodin (1914 ANS exhibition); Waldo C. Newcomer; F.C.C. Boyd; Abe Kosoff, 7/1951; Numismatic Gallery Monthly; Kosoff, 5/1955; J. Hewitt Judd; Edwin Hydeman; Stack's, 5/1975. A very memorable mint error due to its early era and illustrious pedigree.

1795 $10: Struck on a small, thin copper planchet. Head defaced by seven dents. Ex Chapman, 1916; Kosoff Numismatic Gallery Monthly, 7/1951; Kosoff (Lot 594), 5/1955.

1818 Half Dollar: Struck over a struck cent. Copper. Two known.

1823 Half Dollar: Struck on a large cent planchet. Copper.

1831 $2.50: Struck on a dime planchet. Silver. Unique. See J-31.

1832 Half Dollar: Struck over a struck cent. Copper. Two known.

1832 Half Dollar: Struck on a foreign copper coin— Brazilian 80-reis (P-51). This and related half dollar overstrikes on Brazilian copper coins are counterfeits.

1851 $20: Struck on a cent planchet. Copper. Ex William H. Woodin (1914 ANS exhibit); Waldo C. Newcomer.

1858 Cent: Flying eagle with small letters struck uniface on a half dime planchet (A-W 249). Ex-J.W. Scott (Lot 474), 7/1880; George D. Woodside; William H. Woodin; Judson Brenner (1914 ANS exhibit); Virgil Brand; Charles Ruby-Superior, 2/1974; Herbert I. Melnick, 11/1982.

1859 Cent: Indian Head cent struck over a previously struck half dime (A-W 310 and A-W 319, P-3188). Ex George F. Seavey; Lorin G. Parmelee; Charles Ruby-Superior, 2/1974; Bowers and Merena, 4/1986.

1860 Quarter Dollar: Struck on a copper-nickel planchet. See J-268.

1861 $2.50: Struck on a dime planchet. Silver. See J-281.

1864 $3: Struck on a copper-nickel cent planchet. Possible the same as J-401 and J-402.

General Categories of Mint Errors

Indian Head Cents: Struck on nickel three-cent planchets. These may include some examples of J-404 and J-406, J-669 and J-670, J-1180 and J-1182, J-1583 and J-1664.

Indian Head Cents: Struck on foreign nickel-alloy planchets. These include examples of J-1347a, J-1451, J-1495, J-1496, J-1723a, J-1758 and probably others. Over the years, the Philadelphia Mint produced coins for several countries, including Venezuela, the Dominican Republic, Columbia, Nicaragua, Haiti, and Costa Rica.

Indian Head Cents: Struck on silver dime planchets. These include A-W 825.

Indian Head Cents: Struck on gold quarter eagle planchets. These include P-1990. Other dates are known. Some of these may have been made as souvenirs or curiosities.

Two-Cent Pieces: Struck on Shield nickel planchets. These may include some examples of J-792.

Three-Cent Pieces: Nickel three-cent pieces struck on silver half dime planchets. Examples are known dated 1868 and 1869.

Shield Nickels: Struck on cent planchets. These may include examples of J-510 and J-511, J-572, J-573, J-635 and J-1264.

Shield Nickels: Struck on three-cent nickel planchets.

Lincoln Cents: Struck on foreign nickel planchets. These include J-1930 (J-1780 in earlier editions) and P-2028. At least two are known of the 1915 date. Examples of dates of the 1940s onward are plentiful in the context of mint errors.

Lincoln Cents: Struck on gold quarter eagle planchets. This includes P-2027 and other dates. Presumably, some or all were made as curiosities or souvenirs.

Buffalo Nickels: Struck on full size copper-alloy planchets. These possibly include J-1954 (J-1790 in earlier editions) which is listed as 95% copper, 5% nickel and zinc; and the 1920 which supposedly is 89% copper, 8% zinc, and 3% tin.

Some photos are reduced in size.

1792

rounded by retooling. At least three known, in the Smithsonian Institution and the Massachusetts Historical Society.

1794

J-C1792-1 through -4: Cent. Obverse designs include eagle on a half shield (Obverse A); and eagle on a full shield (Obverse B). A reverse die with legend TRIAL PIECE DESIGNED FOR UNITED STATES CENT 1792 was combined with each. Uniface examples exist.

These are fabrications by Dr. M. W. Dickeson, struck outside the Mint using non-Mint dies, but often collected with the pattern series. Sometime in the 1850s, Dickeson found the obverse dies that had been used, or had been intended for use, in embossing the stamp on revenue paper of 1816.[1] He got the idea that these dies had been meant to be part of the 1792 pattern cent series, apparently because of the resemblance to the reverse device of the Mint pattern of 1792 known as the Eagle Cent (J-12). In his *Coin Manual*, Dickeson illustrated these side by side as Nos. 12 and 13 on plate XII.[2] He therefore had the reverse die cut, and struck the pieces described. Some of the copper pieces have been bronzed, and the white-metal impressions sometimes are found silver plated.

J-C1792-1: Cent. Obverse A. Copper.
J-C1792-2: Cent. Obverse A. White metal.
J-C1792-3: Cent. Obverse B. Copper.
J-C1792-4: Cent. Obverse B. White metal.

There are two mule varieties that use the obverse of the half eagle of 1805 (see next page).

1793

J-C1793-1: Washington Half Cent. Obverse bust of George Washington facing right; above, LIBERTY; below, 1793. Reverse of the regular half cent die. Baker-27. Copper. This is a fabrication made by brazing an electrotype shell of a Washington bust to a genuine 1793 half cent with the Liberty head ground off. The 3 in the date was slightly

J-C1794-1: Washington Dollar. Obverse of a bust of George Washington. Reverse of a crude copy of the regular die. Baker-28. This is a fabrication made around 1863 or 1864. The unique silver specimen is in the Appleton collection (now in the Massachusetts Historical Society); two copper pieces are in private hands.

1803

J-C1803-1 through -3: Kettle Tokens. Gaming counters by Kettle & Sons of Birmingham, England. These use the same devices as on regular U.S. coins. The quarter eagle and half eagle in brass are sometimes gilt. The quarter eagle in silver (or silver-plated brass) is the so-called Kettle dime. On some of these the name KETTLE, to the right of the date, has been removed.

J-C1803-1: Quarter Eagle. Brass; often gilt.
J-C1803-2: Quarter Eagle. Silver or silver-plated brass.
J-C1803-3: Half Eagle. Brass; often gilt.

1804

J-C1804-1: Washington Half Cent. Obverse bust of George Washington. Reverse of the regular half cent die. Baker-27f. Copper. This is a fabrication made by joining a cast of the Washington bust to a genuine half cent with the head of Liberty ground off. At least two pieces known (one using an 1804 coin as a base, per Judd; the other an 1806, per Fuld). One is in the Massachusetts Historical Society.

1805

J-C1805-1: Quarter Dollar. P-6105. Obverse of regular quarter dollar die of 1805 (Browning-2). Reverse of eagle on a half shield. Copper. Ex Haseltine, 4/1882; Metzger; Brand; Norweb; New Netherlands, 9/1953; Kagin, 9/1965; Bowers and Merena, 1/1994; Bowers and Merena 5/1995; Heritage, 9/1997.

J-C1805-2: Half Eagle. P-6125. Obverse of rusted regular $5 die of 1805. Reverse of eagle on a half shield. Copper. Old listings for these include Frossard's (5/1882) and Mehl's (2/1944, Roach).

J-C1805-3: Half Eagle. P-6130. Obverse of rusted regular $5 die of 1805. Reverse of eagle on a full shield. Copper. Frossard's 5/1882 and 9/1890 sales and the Brand journal lists one under #68340. The last modern listing noted is Lot 596 in Kosoff's 5/1955 sale.

1818

J-C1818-1: Cent. Obverse of a small bust of Liberty within a raised double circle, surrounded by two bands of engine-turned designs; date in cartouche below. Reverse of a central disk surrounded by two rings, each of a different type of engine-turned work; in the outer ring, UNITED STATES OF AMERICA / ONE CENT. The copper piece (A-W 33) has a plain edge, as does the silver-plated version (A-W 32). Three or four electrotypes are also known. All apparently were made by Jacob Perkins of Newburyport, who engraved some of the dies for the Massachusetts copper coins.

J-C1818-2: Undated Dollar. Obverse of bust of Washington facing left, surrounded by rings of engine-turned design. By Jacob Perkins. The bust is from the same hub as that used on Perkins's well-known Funeral medals. Two pieces are known, both in silver. One is solid (ex Boyd; Ford; Stack's, 5/2004); the other a shell (ex Stickney; Granberg; ANA [1947 sale]).

1819

J-C1819-1: Dollar. Obverse of head of Liberty facing left, with flowing hair, within rings of engine-turned design; in cartouche above, thirteen stars; below, 1819. Uniface design by Jacob Perkins. The unique example, in silver, is in the collection of the American Numismatic Society (ex Boyd).

J-C1837-1: Cent. Obverse legend of ONE CENT within an olive wreath, surrounded by a circle of dots. Reverse of similar design, from different die. German silver or Feuchtwanger's composition. Plain edge. A-W 150 and A-W 151. Four or five are known.

1849

J-C1849-1: $10. Obverse (designed by Bouvet) of head of Liberty facing left, wearing plain coronet inscribed LIBERTY; around, 13 eight-pointed stars; below, 1849. Signed BOUVET F. below bust. Reverse of eagle standing with wings spread, shield on breast; olive branch in right talon and three arrows in left; small wreath in field above eagle's head. Copper. Plain edge. Thick and thin planchets. Later restrikes were struck after 1885. Two known. One is ex Guttag, 10/1927; Colonel Green; King Farouk; Baldenhofer; Bolt. The other (illustrated) is ex Colonel Green; Farouk; Empire Coin Mail Bid Sale #1, 11/1958; Stack's, 9/1988; Novoselsky; Kagin's; Teletrade, 10/2002.

Bouvet, the engraver for the Paris Mint, was apparently contacted by the director of the U.S. Mint (as were C.C. Wright and other top engravers) after Longacre, though a fine engraver, was found to be incompetent as a die-cutter.

1855

J-C1855-1: $5 Gaming Token. Obverse of a bust in a circle of stars, with date below. Reverse of an eagle on a globe with OUR COUNTRY below. Brass.

1866

J-C1866-1 through -5: $3. Obverse (by Merriam) of a bearded bust of Lincoln facing right; GOD AND OUR COUNTRY 1866. Reverse of a die made in the Mint for a pattern three-cent piece of 1867.

J-C1866-1: $3. Gold. Reeded edge. 76 grains. Three or four known.
J-C1866-2: $3. Gold. Plain edge. 100 grains. Unique.
J-C1866-3: $3. Silver. Reeded edge.
J-C1866-4: $3. Silver. Plain edge.
J-C1866-5: $3. Copper. Plain edge.

1868

J-C1868-1 through -4: $3. Obverse of bust of Lincoln, as on J-C1866-1, but with no motto. Reverse as J-C1866-1.

J-C1868-1: $3. Gold. Reeded edge. 70 grains.
J-C1868-2: $3. Nickel. Reeded edge.
J-C1868-3: $3. Nickel. Plain edge.
J-C1868-4: $3. Lead. Plain edge.

1911

J-C1911-1: Cent. Obverse of Indian head as on the nickel five-cent piece of 1913. Copper-plated white metal electrotype by James Earle Fraser.

J-C1911-2: Five-Cent Piece. Obverse of Abraham Lincoln with textured letters in LIBERTY. White metal electrotype by Fraser.

Appendix C: Pieces Not of Mint Origin

J-C1911-3: Five-Cent Piece. Obverse of Lincoln with smooth letters in LIBERTY. White metal electrotype by Fraser.

1912

J-C1912-1: Five-Cent Piece. Obverse of Indian head design similar to that used in regular coinage the following year. White metal electrotype by Fraser. Four known.

J-C1912-2: Five-Cent Piece. Reverse of bison similar to the Type 1 design used the following year. White metal electrotype by Fraser. Two known.

J-C1912-3: Quarter Dollar. Obverse of head of Liberty, 13 stars around, date below; loosely adopted from the contemporary Liberty Head nickel. White metal electrotype by Fraser.

1915

J-C1915-1: Panama-Pacific Quarter Dollar. Obverse proposal for the Panama Pacific International Exposition commemorative quarter dollar, showing a man working a field with a scythe; above, IN GOD WE TRUST; 1915 in left field. White metal electrotype by Fraser.

J-C1915-2: Panama-Pacific Quarter Dollar. Reverse proposal for the Panama Pacific International Exposition commemorative quarter dollar, showing a tree with the Pacific Ocean and rising sun; UNITED STATES OF AMERICA QUARTER DOLLAR around. White metal electrotype by Fraser.

1938

J-C1938-1: Five-Cent Piece. Reverse proposal for the Jefferson nickel, showing Monticello centered low in the design with sun rays rising from behind; above, UNITED STATES OF AMERICA / E PLURIBUS UNUM; below, FIVE CENTS. Copper plated over a silver base metal; electrotype by Anthony DeFrancisci.

Notes:

[1] Ford, John J. Jr. "Odds and Ends in the U.S. Series." *The Numismatist*, Vol. 62, p. 501, August 1949.

[2] Breen, Walter. "Trial Piece Designed for U. S. Cent 1792." *The Numismatist*, Vol. 64, pp. 1310–1313.

Appendix D: Pattern Coinage Metals

The following listing gives the main metals and alloys used to strike United States pattern coins:

Aluminum: Elemental metal. Aluminum was a precious metal in the 1850s, but by the 1860s it came into limited use to strike patterns as well as delicacies for collectors. Aluminum tended to oxidize quickly. This formed a protective gray coating, which then stabilized and endured in many instances to the present day. In 1973, the Mint contemplated using aluminum for regular coinage of cents, as on the commercial market copper was rising sharply in price. About a million and a half aluminum Lincoln cents were struck with the date 1974. Some were given out as samples, but the metal was never used for regular coinage.

Billon: This is an alloy of copper and silver, with copper dominant, sometimes silver-washed or -plated to enhance the silver appearance. Billon was used for certain circulating coinage by foreign countries, such as France, but never by the United States. Although compositions were apt to vary, the billon alloy used to strike certain 1836 pattern two-cent pieces (J-52 and J-53) was found to be 55% copper and 45% silver,[1] and specified to be 90% copper and 10% silver, respectively. Coins struck of billon became dull and unattractive after slight handling. Moreover, the silver content was not verifiable to the casual observer, as elemental analysis was needed.

Bimetallic coins: A coin can be struck on a planchet utilizing two different metals not alloyed with each other, and still visible separately. In 1865, pattern two-cent pieces were struck by compressing a light strip of silver into a strip of bronze, giving a true bimetallic coin (J-407 and others, including later dates). The purpose for making these unusual coins is not known. A 1792 silver-center cent (J-1) is also bimetallic.

Brass: Brass is an alloy of copper, generally about 85% copper and 15% zinc. Selected patterns were made in brass, probably for the numismatic trade, as this alloy was never seriously considered for regular United States coinage. Outside of the federal series, brass was widely used for tokens and political campaign badges.

Bronze: Beginning in 1863 (with patterns) and in the spring of 1864 (with regular issues), an alloy of 95% copper and 5% tin and zinc—generally called bronze, sometimes called French bronze—was used to make Indian Head cents and two-cent pieces. Mint correspondence reveals that a 95% copper, 3% tin, and 2% zinc mixture was used to make pattern cents in 1863 (J-299). Bronze became a popular metal for pattern use. Although some patterns were made in pure copper, in general, pieces listed as "copper" and dated in the 1860s or later are actually in bronze. Elemental analysis is required to tell the difference. French bronze was sometimes defined as 95% copper, 4% tin, and 1% zinc. Later bronze pieces had a mixture of zinc and copper.

Copper: Elemental metal. Copper was the metal in which half cents and cents were regularly struck from 1793 to 1857. Copper was obtained from various commercial and other sources and varied in its purity, but no specific alloy was added. Quality and purity of the copper varied over a period of time, as did its hardness. The term *copper* is often used today to designate not only pure or nearly pure copper, as for the 1792 to 1857 half cent and cent coinage, but also to indicate bronze and other alloys that resemble copper. Thus, a pattern 1877 half dollar struck in "copper," per traditional listings, is most likely in bronze. Many other alloys of copper were used over the years and are discussed in the text (such as for 60% copper and 40% nickel used to strike the J-170 1855 pattern cent); these mixtures were not given specific names. In 1863, a pattern 10-cent piece (J-326a) was made of an alloy of 75% copper and 25% silver; this alloy might be called billon, but no special designation was made at the time. Most collectors are not concerned with the exact nature of the alloy. However, they are concerned with the color of the alloy; therefore, collectors rarely differentiate between copper and bronze (as they are very close in color), but they will differentiate between copper and copper-nickel (which are quite different in color). Nevertheless, among late-19th-century patterns, there are a few patterns and die trials in pure copper, distinguishable only by elemental analysis.

Copper-nickel: In 1856, a new coinage alloy was developed for the one-cent piece. It was called copper-nickel, actually mostly copper, consisting of 88% copper and 12% nickel. This metal, light yellow-gold in color, was used to strike Flying Eagle and Indian Head cents for circulation from 1857 through the spring of 1864. Cupro-nickel is an alternative term for the same alloy. Copper-nickel is a very hard alloy, and difficulty was encountered in striking cents from the composition, as it accelerated die wear and breakage.

Fusible alloy: This is the popular numismatic designation for an alloy used to coin certain 1792 pattern cents (J-2) consisting of (by value, not weight), 1/4¢ worth of silver and 3/4¢ of copper. The designation *billon* might be more correct. This is an alloy with a fairly low melting point, such as solder and various compositions containing tin or lead, sometimes used to create die trials and splashers.[2]

German silver: No one has ever been able to define "German silver," although the term is widely used in numismatics. Variations have been called argentan, packfong, Feuchtwanger's composition, and American silver. This alloy found its main use in providing a cheap substitute for silver in tableware, ornamental articles, and several proposals for coinage. Generally, German silver contained large proportions of nickel and copper, but also sometimes zinc, lead, and/or tin. Elemental analysis of certain "German silver" tokens has revealed that some actually contained a small amount of silver. There were no standards.

Gold: Elemental metal. Gold coins were first minted for circulation in 1795 and last struck for circulation in 1933. From the start, copper was added for strength, with the alloy standardized by the Act of January 18, 1837, as 90% gold and 10% copper. The copper added a warm, rosy orange hue to the gold. Sometimes, silver was present as an "impurity," particularly for metal brought from California after the Gold Rush. Pieces with silver generally have a

Appendix D: Pattern Coinage Metals

lighter color. The 10% specified for copper allowed amounts of other metals as well, so long as the gold remained at 90%. In 1834, at the Mint, six different gold alloys were devised to strike patterns, but none are known to exist today. These alloys were not given specific names.

Goloid: This was an alloy patented by Dr. Wheeler W. Hubbell on May 22, 1877, consisting of a mixture of gold and silver, by value, with 16 parts' value of gold and 1 part's value of silver, to which 10% copper was added for strength. The inscription on certain patterns indicated that by weight such pieces included 1 part gold and 24 parts silver. The intent was to create a coin that would be pleasing to both advocates of silver metal and advocates of gold, these being two combative political factions of the era. Goloid was rejected for coinage, as the gold content could not be determined other than by elemental analysis, and counterfeits could be made by only using silver. An extensive series of Goloid and Goloid Metric pattern coins were made from 1878 to 1880.

Lead: Elemental metal Many splashers (*chichés* in French), or one-sided strikings on (usually) thin planchets, were made of lead, a soft metal that was easy to use for testing dies in progress or finished dies. A few pattern coins were made in lead, an example being the 1907 $20 piece (J-1777). Lead oxidized rapidly, and such pieces soon became dull and porous.

Nickel: The term *nickel* (often used indiscriminately in numismatic literature) generally refers to an alloy consisting of 75% copper and 25% nickel, first introduced for regular coinage for use on the three-cent piece of 1865, then the five-cent piece of 1866. Regarding pure nickel, a few patterns were struck of this metal (such as the 1883 five-cent piece [J-1704]) and are specifically noted as such in the text.

Oroide: Oroide was a cheap alloy made in the 1860s and other times to produce jewelry, watch cases, ornaments, and the like, with a color approximating that of gold. The term was derived from the Spanish *oro*, meaning gold. In 1864, an alloy of 19 parts copper and 1 part aluminum resulted in a golden coin called oroide, and other variations occurred.

Pewter: See *white metal.*

Platinum: Elemental metal. Platinum was used to strike pattern half dollars of 1814 (J-44).

Ruolz's alloy: In 1869, at the Philadelphia Mint, pattern strikings were made in an alloy compounded by a Frenchman, Monchal Ruolz,[3] said to consist of 26% silver, 33% nickel, and 41% copper. The alloy did not strike well, and the idea was abandoned. This was one of many "pet" metals proposed by private interests (goloid being another).

Silver: Elemental metal. Silver was used to strike coins for circulation from 1792 through the 1960s. Alloys varied over a period of years, but copper was always added to lend strength. Beginning with the Act of January 18, 1837, coin silver was standardized at 90% silver and 10% copper. The regular-issue silver three-cent piece (or *trime*) of 1851 to 1853 was made in a special alloy of 75% silver and 25% copper. Other variations of silver alloys are noted in the text.

Steel: An alloy of iron. Dies were made of steel, but few pattern coins were struck in this metal, due to its hardness. One such pattern is an impression of the regular Proof dies used to strike 1866 Shield nickels (J-512). Another steel patterns (J-1058) was struck from regular 1871 Shield nickel dies. Pieces historically described as "steel" in some instances may be other metals such as pure nickel, iron, or even cobalt.[4]

Tin: Elemental metal. Numismatic texts use *tin* to describe coins of a soft silver-colored alloy, better called *white metal*. In this text, such are listed as white metal. Pure or nearly pure tin oxidizes at cold temperatures, producing unsightly black "tinpest."

White metal: A pewter-like metal, of no fixed specifications, employing lead, tin, antimony, and other elements to create a metal silver in appearance but fairly soft. The popular term *pewter* is sometimes used in the field of antiques and artifacts to describe such items; the term is not widely used for pattern coins. White metal was used to strike many different patterns in the 19th century. In general, white metal was not chemically stable, and sometimes pieces oxidized or blistered. Sometimes white metal strikings have been described as tin.

Zinc: Elemental metal. Bluish-white and lustrous, zinc is brittle at room temperature but becomes malleable when hot. It was used as a component in many pattern alloys (mixed with copper, nickel, and other metals).

Notes:

1. Elemental analysis by Alan Meghrig.

2. Andrew W. Pollock III, communication to the editor, April 24, 2003.

3. Earlier referred to in numismatic references as "Koulz" (sometimes "Kouly"), and given a German nationality. The error was corrected by David Cassel following four years of investigation.

4. Per Saul Teichman.

Appendix E: Rarities and Curiosities

While many different patterns can be enjoyed by *collecting* them, many are so rare that they seldom if ever come on the market. These rarities can also be enjoyed, although vicariously: by reading about them and studying their images—not much different from enjoying, for example, paintings by Rembrandt or Toulouse-Lautrec. Here we focus on several interesting sets and groups of patterns rarely seen in the marketplace. We also look at some illogical oddities and curiosities from over the years.

Patterns of 1792

Following the Mint Act of April 2, 1792, the federal government of the United States, then with its capital in Philadelphia, set about erecting facilities for coinage. A few months later, on July 31, the cornerstone was laid for what became the first Philadelphia Mint, succeeded in time by the second Mint (occupied in 1833), the third Mint (1901), and the present-day fourth Mint (1967).

Coin designs needed to be created, and patterns struck as proposals for new motifs. Records are scarce as to what happened, and in what order. Among the first coins made were the 1792-dated silver half dismes (J-7). These are among the more fascinating early federal issues, mainly because facts concerning them are scarce and legends and rumors abound. It has been said that Martha Washington posed for the portrait, but if this is true, her image on the coin is not even remotely similar to illustrations from life. President Washington is said to have taken his own silverware to the Mint, where it was melted down and converted into these small coins, which were then given to him.

Although a related copper striking of the half disme, J-8, can be called a pattern, the record shows that the silver versions were paid out in circulation, becoming the first coins struck in quantity after the Mint Act. As the minting facility was not yet ready, and would not be until that autumn, the half dismes were coined at a nearby shop conducted by mechanic John Harper.

Today, we know of 13 different varieties of 1792-dated patterns, if the silver half disme is included in this category. Among them are the so-called Birch cents, impressive in size, with portraits similar to that used on the 1792 half disme. The first name of Mr. Birch is not known with certainty. This sets the scene for many later mysteries and unsolved questions of history in the pattern series—providing a fertile hunting ground for numismatic researchers. Recently, Dr. Joel Orosz and Carl Herkowitz created a monograph on the 1792 silver half disme, published by the American Numismatic Society. The series is rounded out by a disme (about 20 known, in both copper and silver varieties) and a quarter dollar (in copper and white metal).

J-1

J-4

J-7

J-10

J-12

Appendix E: Rarities and Curiosities

Gobrecht's Silver Dollars

Of the illustrious individuals who have served as chief engraver at the Mint, Christian Gobrecht is among the most highly acclaimed by numismatists today. Born in 1785, he began his career as an engraver of bank notes, portraits, and book illustrations while in his twenties. Soon, he created dies for medals, including some on commission for the Mint. His talents were impressive. Gobrecht invented a medal-ruling machine by which the design of a medal could be translated mechanically onto a plate for engraving pictures; he invented a talking doll (the details of which are not known today); and he devised improvements for the reed organ.

In September 1835, Gobrecht was hired as the *second engraver* at the Mint, to work with Chief Engraver William Kneass. The latter had been incapacitated by a stroke, and it fell to Gobrecht to create a suite of designs to revise American coinage. Later, after the passing of Kneass, Gobrecht became chief engraver, a post he occupied from 1840 to 1844.

As his first important commission at the Mint, Gobrecht created what we know as the Liberty Seated design, first used on the silver dollar of 1836, from a sketch by Thomas Sully, a local artist of renown. The reverse depicts an eagle in flight, from a sketch by Titian Peale, modeled after "Peter," an eagle kept at the Mint as a mascot.

Following the creation of pattern dollars with Gobrecht's name positioned above the date and below the base seating Miss Liberty, the motif was slightly revised. The engraver's name was removed to an inconspicuous place on the base of Liberty. One thousand coins were struck, most of which were placed into circulation at face value. An additional 600 coins were made in early 1837 from the same 1836-dated dies. In 1838, pattern dollars of a revised design were made, with stars added to the obverse, and in 1839 more were struck. Dollars of these three years have been popular for a long time, not only with pattern enthusiasts, but with those who collect regular series as well. Listings can be found in the annual *Guide Book of United States Coins*, the popular hobby guide known as the Red Book.

J-59 (name below base) **J-60** (name on base)

Reverse of J-84
(Showing die alignment used in 1838 and 1839)

A Mixture of Mottoes

On November 13, 1861, The Reverend M.R. Watkinson of Ridleyville, Pennsylvania, sent a letter to Secretary of the Treasury Salmon P. Chase, suggesting that coins should bear a reference to God, to whom many citizens looked for help in that uncertain time. The Civil War had been underway since April, and what had been envisioned as an easy win for the North had turned into a bloody conflict with no clear victor in sight.

Director of the Mint James Pollock had Chief Engraver James B. Longacre prepare patterns mentioning the Deity, suggesting the motto OUR TRUST IS IN GOD. Today, no patterns are known with this inscription, and it is presumed that it was shortened to GOD OUR TRUST, used on certain patterns made in December 1861. In 1863, other mottoes were considered, including GOD AND OUR COUNTRY and IN GOD WE TRUST (on two-cent pieces of 1863). In 1864, the last was decided upon as the standard, and IN GOD WE TRUST first appeared on a circulating coin, the new bronze two-cent denomination. In time, it was added to the designs of many other coins, including certain silver and gold designs in 1866. It was not until 1957 that it was used on federal paper money.

Shown here are patterns with the mottoes of the early 1860s as well as some other mottoes used on later patterns, but never adopted on circulating coinage. These include UNION & LIBERTY on Longacre's pattern five-cent piece of 1867 (J-561 to J-565) and DEO EST GLORIA on the Goloid Metric dollar of 1879 (J-1631 and others).

J-295: GOD OUR TRUST
(used on various patterns dated 1861, 1862, and 1863; in a plain field, and on a scroll)

J-306: GOD AND OUR COUNTRY
(first used on the 1863 two-cent piece, the earliest Mint pattern depicting George Washington)

J-387: IN GOD WE TRUST
(well known from modern coinage; introduced during the American Civil War)

J-564: UNION & LIBERTY
(an unusual motto treatment by James B. Longacre, incorporated into the Indian princess's headress)

J-1631: DEO EST GLORIA
("God is Glorious"; a Latin motto that also appeared on the $4 Stella of the same era)

Appendix E: Rarities and Curiosities

The Amazonian "Panorama" of 1872

In 1872, an incredible suite of pattern coins was created by Chief Engraver William Barber. Today these are called the "Amazonian" issues, the name being derived from the obverse of the quarter dollar, half dollar, and silver dollar. The design shows a goddess of Amazonian appearance, caressing the head of a quiescent eagle, while her left arm rests on a shield. The reverse depicts a bold standing eagle holding a shield inscribed IN GOD WE TRUST.

The same reverse, in combination with a distinctive head of Miss Liberty, was used to make a full run of gold patterns, including the $1, $2.50, $3, $5, $10, and $20 pieces—the first and last time such a suite of new-design patterns had been so extensive.

There is no record of the quantities struck. It is presumed that no more than two dozen each were made of the three silver denominations, and just one set of the gold issues. The gold set stands today as one of the great highlights of American coinage.

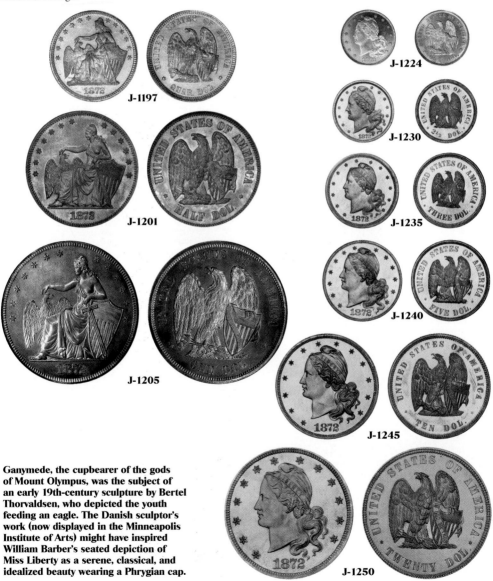

J-1197

J-1201

J-1205

J-1224

J-1230

J-1235

J-1240

J-1245

J-1250

Ganymede, the cupbearer of the gods of Mount Olympus, was the subject of an early 19th-century sculpture by Bertel Thorvaldsen, who depicted the youth feeding an eagle. The Danish sculptor's work (now displayed in the Minneapolis Institute of Arts) might have inspired William Barber's seated depiction of Miss Liberty as a serene, classical, and idealized beauty wearing a Phrygian cap.

Appendix E: Rarities and Curiosities

The Gold Stellas of 1879 and 1880

Among the most famous of all pattern coins are the gold $4 Stellas of 1879 and 1880, made as a proposal for international coinage. Although details are not known, the Flowing Hair motif is attributed to Charles E. Barber, assistant engraver at the time and son of Chief Engraver William E. Barber. The Coiled Hair version is said to be the work of assistant engraver George T. Morgan. The reverse, shared by both coins, was done by Charles Barber. However, archival records state that Barber worked on "both sides" of the Coiled Hair coin, meaning the obverse as well. Whether this included the portrait is not known.

An estimated 600 to 700 of the 1879 Flowing Hair Stellas were coined, creating a classic that is widely desired today. Examples come on the market with frequency and always attract attention. In the *great rarity* class are the other three gold versions: the 1879 and 1880 Coiled Hair and the 1880 Flowing Hair. Over a long period of years, several advanced collectors have assembled complete sets of four—a daunting task.

The Stella was the brainchild of the Honorable John A. Kasson, who by 1879 had served as chairman of the Committee of Coinage, Weights, and Measures in Congress and as U.S. envoy extraordinary and minister plenipotentiary to Austria-Hungary. He thought that such $4 coins could be spent in Europe and elsewhere, as they approximated the weight of other European gold coins. However, the regular $5 gold half eagle would have served just as well, and as no utility was found for a $4 coin, it never went beyond pattern form.

The field of pattern coins has other entries with the same concept. An 1868 $5 gold coin (J-656) noted in its inscription that it was also worth 25 FRANCS. Best known is Dana Bickford's 1874 international $10 coin (the coin pictured on the cover of the 8th edition of this book), with an inscription giving precise exchange rates in terms of America dollars, British sterling pounds, German marks, Swedish kronen, Dutch gulden, and French francs. The fatal flaw for these patterns was that exchange rates fluctuated rapidly, and such coins would be useless within a short time.

Stellas of 1879

J-1635

J-1638

Stellas of 1880

J-1657

J-1660

Flowing Hair design
(enlarged 2x)

Coiled Hair design
(enlarged 2x)

Appendix E: Rarities and Curiosities

Illogical Patterns and Curiosities

Now and again in the annals of pattern coins, two dies would be combined to create an illogical coin—lacking any identification of the country of origin, or with the same motto given on each side. A gallery of such curiosities includes the following:

J-113

The "Ugly Duckling" is the name sometimes given to this pattern. Its combination of dies simply depict a numeral on each side. Without a reference book, a numismatist shown such a coin would have no idea what it was or when it was made—it might be a merchant's trade token, an apothecary's weight, or a gaming counter. This pattern was made in 1849, simply to show what a coin of this diameter, struck in silver, might look like. The design for what later became known as the trime, ultimately issued in 1851, had not yet been created.

J-362

Two heads are better than one, it has been said, and numismatists contemplating this curious pattern cent would certainly agree. For good measure it also features two different dates, 1858 and 1864. This was one of many different die combinations made to attract the wallets of collectors and to privately profit Mint officials.

J-996

This 1871 pattern Standard Dollar is beautiful, given James B. Longacre's Indian Princess design on the obverse and a luxuriant wreath on the reverse. However, on close examination no clue can be found as to the country of origin: UNITED STATES OF AMERICA is nowhere to be found. Across the spectrum of patterns there are quite a few "stateless" coins, as they are called. Of additional interest is the fact that Longacre died on January 1, 1869, and this particular motif was not struck until after his passing.

J-579

UNITED STATES OF AMERICA is a great country, and on coins it is, or should be, an essential part of the inscription. While quite a few patterns forgot to mention it, this five-cent-sized mule has it twice—using an illogical combination of two obverse dies, one dated 1866 and the other 1867. The denomination of the coin is not mentioned.

J-1050

Whoever made the reverse die for this 1871 pattern nickel—whether Chief Engraver William Barber or one of his assistants—used an incorrect V punch to represent the denomination. The heavier weight is given to the right side of the numeral when it should be on the left.

J-1423

William Barber must not have been familiar with travel on the high seas, for on the obverse of this pattern Commercial dollar, he shows a ship with sails billowing to the right, before the wind, while, in defiance of the laws of physics, smoke from the auxiliary engine goes against the wind, trailing off to the left. This same error can be seen on several other Barber patterns of the era.

J-525

The United States Mint sought to honor the Father of Our Country on several patterns, including two-cent pieces in 1863 and nickel five-cent pieces in 1866. Collectors of Washingtoniana get a double treat with J-525, which shows him twice. In this instance it seems that someone spirited a pair of dies out of the Mint, both of the same design (but with minor differences), and made his own rarities.

J-531

IN GOD WE TRUST is a fine, honorable motto, welcomed by Americans newly emerged from the turmoil of the Civil War in 1866. Most people appreciate having the motto on our coins today. This pattern nickel of 1866 serves it up twice—once on each side—but the designer forgot to include UNITED STATES OF AMERICA, leaving the WE (in IN GOD WE TRUST) unidentified.

Endnotes for Introduction

1. Taxay, *The U.S. Mint and Coinage*, 1966, title of Chapter 14.
2. James Ross Snowden, *The Medallic Memorials of Washington in the Mint of the United States*, Philadelphia: B. Lippincott, 1861.
3. These likely including items listed today in A Guide Book of United States Coins, such as the 1791 Washington "Large Eagle" and "Small Eagle" cents, among others.
4. Sold in New York City by Bangs & Brother, via *Catalogue of a Valuable Collection of American and Foreign Coins and Medals in Gold, Silver, Copper and Bronze*.
5. The editor regards a scenario of "Midnight Minters" involving workmen producing rarities at the Mint at night in 1858 to be pure fiction. There is, for example, no evidence that secret restriking of Gobrecht dollars occurred before spring 1859.
6. In a few instances, edge reeding was applied ("broaching") after the coins were struck with plain edges, as J-55b (see Alan Meghrig). Post-strike reeding was also employed in other areas of coinage, such as for certain Civil War tokens.
7. See discussion under Patterns of 1836 of alignment types I, II, III, and IV.
8. See Andrew Lustig.
9. Saul Teichman has tracked a number of instances in which coins earlier sold as cleaned and polished Proofs are now certified, with no mention of this improvement, as Proof-64 or finer.
10. In 2003, an article in Coin World estimated that 12 to 15 commercial grading services were active, some highly respected, and others simply being used for telemarketing or promotional purposes, and assigning grades far higher than experienced old-time numismatists would suggest.
11. See Andrew Lustig.
12. Believed to be marks from the drawing-bench process in planchet preparation (see John Dannreuther).
13. Judd, seventh edition, page 180. • The year 1982 was a generally low period in coin market prices for many different series, not only patterns.

Endnotes for 1795–1806

1. Parmelee began collecting coins in the 1850s, and thus was not on the scene in 1799. The various curators of the Mint Cabinet did sell or trade away specimens from time to time, and perhaps this particular piece was deaccessioned in this manner, but, if so, at an early time, for it appeared in the 1870 sale of the William Fewsmith Collection by E.B. Mason, Jr. The story will remain unknown.
2. Occasionally, brass tokens resembling $2.50 and $5 gold pieces of 1803 are encountered. These were made as game counters by Kettle, a British firm, are from crude dies, and have no connection with the pattern series, although years ago many of them were offered as such. See Appendix C.
3. Walter Breen, *Encyclopedia of Early United States Cents 1793–1814*, ed. Mark Borckardt (Wolfeboro, NH: Bowers and Merena, 2000), pp. 747–750. The earliest auction appearance traced in that text is in an Edward D. Cogan sale of 1868.
4. These dies survived until the late 1950s, when they were acquired by an Eastern rare coin firm as part of a large transaction and were subsequently discarded by throwing them off a bridge crossing the Susquehanna River.
5. Andrew Pollock, *United States Patterns and Related Issues* (Wolfeboro, NH: Bowers and Merena, 1994), p. 458. Here Pollock cites Taxay's *Comprehensive Catalogue*.
6. See Judd's seventh edition.
7. Breen, *Encyclopedia of Early United States Cents 1793–1814*, p. 762, describes the die in detail, further noting, "Overstruck on a cent of an unknown date between 1808 and 1839."

Endnotes for 1808–1827

1. See description in the Russell Logan Collection catalog (Wolfeboro, NH: Bowers and Merena Galleries, 2002). Example of 1814 platinum half dollar cataloged by Mark Borckardt.
2. Karl Moulton has discovered that this is a triple overdated die, first made as 1822, then used for coinage in over-date form as 1823/2, and later relapped and used to strike 1827/3 quarter dollars (confirmed only in Proof format).
3. Said by Breen to have been a Mint restrike, struck at the Mint from dies known to exist there in 1860 and later. The earliest auction appearance located by Saul Teichman is J.W. Haseltine's sale of February 1877, Lot 556.

Endnotes for 1831–1849

1. A cluster of these, more than a dozen in all, was obtained by the editor in the early 1950s from Sol Kaplan. They were from the Woodin estate.
2. Certain data courtesy of Alan Meghrig.
3. No example seen by Alan Meghrig in years of studying this denomination.
4. "Broached" edge, per Alan Meghrig. The Eliasberg specimen is an example.
5. R.W. Julian notes that these half dollars were struck under the provisions of the Act of 1792 and thus were of standard weight in use at the time. There is no way they can be considered to be patterns.
6. Pieces earlier listed as J-86 and J-90 are believed to be misdescriptions of J-87 and J-89, respectively (per Saul Teichman).
7. Pollock, p. 36.
8. A second example attributed to the Mickley Collection has been discredited (per Saul Teichman).
9. Breen, "Some Unpublished Gobrecht Rarities," *The Numismatist* (May 1957): Here Breen noted the discovery of this overstrike. Bought by A.M. ("Art") Kagin from Louis S. Werner and "shown around" to various dealers and collectors who were suitably impressed.
10. Strikings from perfect reverse die as well as cracked die.
11. Perfect reverse die (Smithsonian Institution). An example, certainly an original, was in the Roper Sale in 1851.
12. Cracked reverse die.
13. Cracked reverse die.
14. Per Saul Teichman.
15. Clusters and groups of the 1838 and 1839 pattern half dollars remained from the William H. Woodin estate and were handled by Sol Kaplan in the early 1950s, dozens of such pieces going to the editor of the present text, including three further examples of a variety earlier thought to be unique. These coins were pristine and had never been dipped or cleaned. Most were lightly toned from age, but not with halo-like toning from albums, as the pieces had been stored differently.
16. A variety earlier listed as J-100a is a regular issue (per Saul Teichman).
17. Perfect reverse die.
18. Cracked reverse die.
19. See Appendix A.
20. Cataloged by company partner John J. Ford, Jr., who had joined the firm in 1950.
21. Possibly all are in an alloy of gold with a generous mixture of silver (per Andy Lustig).
22. It is this coin for which J.P. Morgan reportedly offered $35,000 in the early 20th century (Akers, p. 9). His offer was not taken (although some years earlier in the late 19th century the curator of the Mint Cabinet did sell or trade away certain pieces, such as the famous 1877 $50 gold pattern pair).
23. Don Taxay, *Counterfeit, Mis-Struck, and Unofficial U.S. Coins* (New York: Arco, 1963), p. 105.
24. Judd, p. 36. Believed to have been struck no earlier than the 1870s (per Saul Teichman). • Robert Coulton Davis was a Philadelphia druggist and numismatist with close connections to the Mint. In the July 1885 issue of *The Coin Collector's Journal*, p. 97 his serial article began, titled "Pattern and Experimental Issues of the United States Mint," the first serious study of the subject. The scenario devised by Walter Breen that Davis furnished laudanum (an opiate) to Mint officials in exchange for rare patterns and restrikes has no basis in either logic or fact, as opium derivatives were commonly available over the counter at the time to anyone (a situation that would remain in effect until the implementation on January 1, 1907, of the Pure Food and Drug Act of 1906).

Endnotes for 1850–1858

1. This aspect gave the incentive for the Mint to coin copper cents in particular for a long period of time, in eras in which deposits of silver and gold by customers were sporadic. That the Mint had its own profit motive in making a more economical cent has not been mentioned in earlier literature on patterns.
2. Suggestion of Andrew W. Pollock III.
3. In the philatelic world, stamps without perforations are called imperforate. In the numismatic world, coins of varieties intended to made with perforations, but lacking perforations, are called unperforated.
4. Pollock-144.
5. Formerly in Judd Appendix A. Pollock-145 and Pollock-146. Specific metal alloys not determined.
6. Die also used to coin J-124e, listed under 1850.
7. This same die was used to strike J-124a, listed with the 1850 coinage, but the 1850 coin is possibly a later restrike.
8. Snowden, p. 120.
9. Certain of these were listed in Appendix A of the seventh edition of this text, but are now listed under the pattern issues of the year.
10. Cf. Pollock, there further designated as oroide. The composition given here is of the Norweb Collection specimen; R. Tettenhorst described the analysis in two articles in *Penny-Wise*. • One was in the F.W. Doughty Collection sale in 1891 and at one time was owned by S.S. Crosby (per Saul Teichman).

Endnotes for 1850–1858

11. Snowden, p. 120. As is the case with many alloyed copper and nickel patterns in the present text, it is likely that elemental analysis may reveal compositions different from those in standard numismatic texts and reports.
12. Ibid., p. 120.
13. Snow, *Flying Eagle and Indian Cent Attribution Guide, Vol. 1, 1856–1858*. The High Leaves style (high leaves at the base of C and T of CENT) is "found on most 1856 Flying Eagle cents, all 1857s, and less than half of the 1858 Large Letters cents, plus a few 1858 Small Letters coins; this is a rare die among 1858 pattern cents." The Low Leaves is "a lower relief design believed to have been first put in service in early 1858." However, it is seen on some 1856-dated restrike cents made after that time.
14. Snowden, p. 120.
15. Snow, *Flying Eagle and Indian Cent Attribution Guide, Vol. 2, 1859–1869*. 2nd. ed. (Tucson, AZ: Eagle Eye Rare Coins, 2003).
16. Style with broad bust point (per Richard E. Snow).
17. Reverse D of the style with five leaves per cluster (per Richard E. Snow).
18. For an early study of varieties, see Judd, seventh ed., p. 49.
19. Snow, *Flying Eagle and Indian Cent Attribution Guide, Vol. 2, 1859–1869*.

Endnotes for 1859–1867

1. However, circulated examples are conspicuously absent from catalog listings. • Moreover, Director Snowden noted: "Near the close of the year another pattern cent was struck. This is the same as the cent of the year 1860." James Ross Snowden, *A Description of Ancient and Modern Coins in the Cabinet of the Mint of the United States* (Philadelphia: J.B. Lippincott, 1860), p. 121.
2. Described by Mint Director Snowden as a "cereal wreath"; see below.
3. Stateless pattern varieties were endemic in 1870, to which year refer.
4. Snowden, p. 121.
5. Listed as a regular issue in the 18th (last) edition of the *Standard Catalogue*, 1958. In the 1950s, small groups and hoards were sometimes seen, a dozen or two at a time, probably remnants from the Woodin holdings. In the early 1960s, John J. Ford, Jr., who considered this piece to possibly be a regular issue, owned 17 examples. • Mint State pieces are from a different die pair than are Proof pieces; Richard E. Snow estimates that no more than 20 Proofs were originally struck.
6. An example was in the William Gable Collection sale conducted by S.H. Chapman in 1914, and was purchased by Edgar H. Adams. See Don Taxay, *Scott's Comprehensive Catalogue and Encyclopedia of U.S. Coins* (New York and Omaha, Scott Publishing, 1971) and Saul Teichman. This or a similar specimen was found and publicized in June 2000, later illustrated on the cover of *Longacre's Ledger* (December 2000), accompanied by an article by Chris Pilliod, "Can a Two-Headed Cent Really Exist??? Yes, But Only in 1859." The case is made for an obverse die being fitted in error in the chuck for a reverse die.
7. Snow, *Flying Eagle and Indian Cent Attribution Guide 1859–1869*.
8. Judd states: "The genuineness of all pieces from these dies has been doubted as the style is far inferior to that of J-224" (seventh ed.). Pollock delisted it from the regular patterns and moved it to "Uncertain Issues," there described as P-7010, in part: "Both the obverse and reverse are much like those of the 1858 pattern gold dollar…but somewhat cruder in appearance, a caricature of the 1858 issue. This has led to the conclusion by some writers that [these] are non Mint products. Many specimens have Proof surfaces and are not gilt. If they are indeed spurious, it seems certain they were made for collectors' cabinets rather than for circulation." In favor of J-256 being a Mint product is the related crudeness of the seated figure on Paquet's unquestioned J-257 and J-257a. Moreover, an example appeared on the market as early as the March 1865 Bache Collection sale by W.E. Woodward, giving Woodward's imprimatur to the variety.
9. Per Saul Teichman.
10. Saul Teichman has examined all three specimens.
11. Per Saul Teichman.
12. See definition of "bronzed" in the glossary.
13. Throughout the present text, many other illogical examples will be encountered.
14. The portrait of this and the vast majority of other coins, tokens, and medals made with Washington's image over a period of years is taken from the bust by Jean Antoine Houdon, modeled by Washington at Mount Vernon in October 1785.
15. George J. Eckfeldt's notes.
16. Research by David Cassel indicates that these 1868-dated pieces were actually struck early in May 1863, through comparison of the die-crack progression with other Postage Currency coins known to have been struck in 1863.
17. Taxay, *Scott's*, p. 213. Here he states that the reverse die used to coin the 1863 and 1864 with-motto silver dollars was also regularly used in 1868 to strike regular Proofs.
18. Snow, *Flying Eagle and Indian Cent Attribution Guide, Vol. 2, 1859–1869*.

Endnotes for 1859–1867

19. Per Richard E. Snow, who assigns 1869 as the year that the 1863 With L cents were first made. Also see William E. Hidden, "1863 Cent with Letter 'L,'" *The Numismatist* (December 1903), p. 375. He had obtained a specimen from New York City dealer William P. Brown.
20. Pollock, pp. 115–116. He discusses varying weights.
21. Present listing arrangement by Judd numbers per Saul Teichman, in view of confusing alloys, earlier published. Appreciation is expressed to David Cassel for his help with all Postage Currency listings.
22. Erroneously listed in all earlier editions of Judd as having a dateless Liberty Seated obverse die; the present listing is correct (per Saul Teichman).
23. Pollock, pp. 123–124. He discusses these alloys in detail.
24. Per Saul Teichman.
25. As late as the 1950s, Stephen K. Nagy had a cache of nearly two dozen copper impressions of the transitional $5, $10, and $20 pieces (correspondence of Nagy to the editor). Nearly all of these were of a warm orange-brown color, pristine in quality, having never been dipped or cleaned. Presumably, these were leftovers or out-takes from the cache of patterns that in the first decade of the 20th century went to William H. Woodin.
26. Coins listed as "five-cent pieces" from here onward are of the format related to the nickel five-cent coins; silver five-cent pieces continue to be listed as "half dimes."
27. Pollock, p. 159. He distinguishes two die varieties of our Reverse F: Pollock's Reverse A was used to coin 1866 pattern Shield nickels. Stars point to the left foot of the first T and upright of E (in STATES), and slightly to the left of C, to the left serif of the N, and the left edge of S (in CENTS). Pollock's Reverse B was used to coin regular Proof 1867 Shield nickels. Stars point to the left foot of A and the right edge of E (in STATES) and to the center of E and the center of T (in STATES). • J-476 to J-479, J-516 to J-520, and J-532 use Pollock's Reverse B; J-507 to J-509a use Pollock's Reverse A.
28. Edgar H. Adams, *The Numismatist* (February 1909), p. 41.
29. Per Saul Teichman.
30. Reverse die used to coin regular Proof 1867 Shield nickels. Stars point to the left foot of A and the right edge of E (in STATES) and to the center of E and the center of T (in STATES), per Pollock, p. 159.
31. Die used to coin 1866 pattern Shield nickels; stars point to the left foot of the first T and upright of E (in STATES), and slightly to the left of C, to the left serif of the N, and the left edge of S (in CENTS), per Pollock, p. 159.
32. None of these varieties, J-513 to J-515, have been confirmed in modern times (per Saul Teichman).
33. Illustrated in Russ Rulau and George Fuld, *Medallic Portraits of Washington*, 2nd ed. (Iola, WI: Krause, 1999), p. 51. Ex B. Max Mehl's sale of the Belden Roach Collection, 1944, Lot 2903.
34. Two different dies of the without-rays type were used to coin these issues; this is Pollock's Reverse B. It is believed that in perfect state it was used to strike all the pieces listed here, except J-520, for which the die was cracked (per Saul Teichman).
35. Per Saul Teichman.
36. Two different reverse dies of the same type, differing in minor particulars. One die was cracked.
37. Saul Teichman dates the striking of this and the related half dollar and dollar as the 1870s.
38. This reverse die was also combined with later dated dies (J-601 [1867] and J-778 [1869]). These were struck outside of the Mint.
39. As to the various pieces attributed as private (outside of the Mint) strikings, there is no documentation on these, but most are crudely struck, sometimes without collars, and have been designated as private productions by such numismatists as Dr. George J. Fuld, Andrew Lustig, and Saul Teichman, among others.
40. See figures 255 and 256 in Pollock, p. 157.
41. Ibid., p. 159. Pollock notes that two die varieties of this reverse were employed, one used to coin 1866 patterns. On one reverse, in STATES stars point to the left foot of the first T and the upright of the E; and in CENTS slightly to the left of C, to the left serif of the N, and the left edge of the S. On the other, used regularly to coin Proof 1867 Shield nickels, in STATES stars point to the left foot of A and to the right edge of E, and in CENTS to the center of the E and the center of the T. These are Pollock's Reverses A and B.
42. Per Saul Teichman, noting the possibility that the Farouk piece may have had Reverse C of 1866 instead of the "Dutch 5" die reverse.

Endnotes for 1868–1871

1. Research by David Cassel has revealed that through examination of die state progressions these "1868" coins were actually struck in early May 1863, despite the later date on them.
2. A gold specimen was reported in 2002, but questions arose concerning it, and it is now under study.
3. Andrew Lustig adds: "If not THE greatest!"
4. One of the reverse dies also used to make restrikes of regular Proof 1864 With L cents (per Richard E. Snow); this die is not known to have been used to strike regular issue 1868 Proof cents, but was widely used from 1869 to 1871 (per Snow). This, plus the use of two die pairs, would seem to indicate that aluminum cents were struck on at least two different occasions.

Endnotes for 1868–1871

5. J-640 has been classified as unconfirmed based on the research of David Cassel.
6. J-643 has been classified as unconfirmed based on the research of David Cassel.
7. The Liberty Head with cap and three stars is a notable exception, having been used in 1860 for the J-271 $5 and in 1861 for the J-283 $5.
8. Per Richard E. Snow.
9. Pollock-767.
10. The illustration in Judd, seventh edition, may be a composite from two regular coins, as the Indian Head cent die, being smaller in diameter, would necessitate an extra plain planchet around the border.
11. Per tests made by David Cassel.
12. Of the four coins David Cassel tested of the J-716 and J-717a varieties, only one came close to Ruolz's alloy, this coin having 30.4% silver, 42.1% nickel, and 24.% copper.
13. Here a posthumous die, but motif employed earlier in Longacre's lifetime as J-661, etc., of 1868.
14. The Indian Princess motif had its roots in circa 1852 sketches by Longacre (per Cory Gillilland, "U.S. Gold Bullion Coins: A Nineteenth Century Proposal," *America's Gold Coinage* (New York: American Numismatic Society, 1990). Longacre wrote to Mint Director George Eckert noting in part that the sketch was intended to "express a representation of America, by a female figure, in aboriginal costume, seated contemplating one of the usual emblems of liberty, elevated on a spear, which she holds in her right hand; her left hand resting on a globe, presenting the Western Hemisphere." In numismatics the liberty cap ("one of the usual emblems of liberty") is usually referred to as on a pole, not a spear.
15. Pollock-880. "Mostly copper with streaks of silver."
16. Pollock, pp. 211–213. For those with a technical turn of mind, an appropriate description for J-939 of a given variety might be: "Judd-939, obverse die 3a."
17. It seems rather curious that new reverse dies were made for J-1050 to J-1055, when the much-combined dies from the various issues of 1866–1867 could have been employed.
18. Since the seventh edition of Judd, numerous other varieties have been published (Pollock, p. 237). This die combination has been renumbered.
19. The use of the motto GOD OUR TRUST is particularly interesting, as no information has been learned to the effect that the usual motto, IN GOD WE TRUST, needed modification, and GOD OUR TRUST had been rejected years earlier.

Endnotes for 1872–1877

1. In the late 20th century, some copy dies were made of the Bickford $10. Authentication is recommended for any items offered.
2. Twenty-cent pieces for circulation were minted at Philadelphia, Carson City, and San Francisco in 1875 and Philadelphia and Carson City in 1876. The Philadelphia coins could not have circulated at par in the East until April 20, 1876, or later, this being the date that the Treasury placed large amounts of various silver coins in circulation, thus ending the market premium on them.
3. Although this is a trade dollar obverse, it is specifically denominated in the manner of a silver dollar and is thus listed as a silver dollar pattern. Judd notes that the reverse die was that used to coin regular Proofs of 1857–1859, this based on minute characteristics. It would be interesting to compare the minute characteristics of this die with certain Proof restrikes in the regular Liberty Seated dollar series (a project beyond the purview of the present study).
4. Pollock-1601 (copper) and Pollock-1602 (nickel). A copper piece was shown by F.C.C. Boyd at the Bronx Coin Club in 1937; most of the Boyd patterns were sold to King Farouk by Numismatic Gallery (Abe Kosoff and Abner Kreisberg) in the mid-1940s; Palace Collection, Lot 1967; possibly the same as that in Lester Merkin's sale of September 1967, Lot 534. Pollock traces several auction appearances of one or more nickel strikings. Today, two are confirmed in copper, one in nickel (per Saul Teichman).
5. This particular reverse die is one of the several "smoking gun" pieces of evidence that old dies at the Mint, which officials said had been destroyed, were still on hand by 1876! The statements concerning pattern coins made by Mint officials have no credibility with numismatists today.
6. John W. Haseltine, "Two Unique Double Eagle Varieties," *The Numismatist* (June 1909), pp. 173–174.
7. Ibid. Excerpt from letter written to Farran Zerbe. Haseltine had just sold two gold impressions, J-1488 and J-1490, to William H. Woodin.
8. Both varieties are described in Pollock, pp. 292–294. The discovery of two dies was made by Harry W. Bass, Jr.
9. Both varieties are illustrated in Pollock, p. 302. The discovery of two dies was made by Harry W. Bass, Jr.
10. Taxay, Scott's, p. 190.
11. Pollock, p. 291. He quotes relevant correspondence.
12. Alternatively from Davis in The Coin Collector's Journal: "Of these extraordinary patterns one specimen only of each variety was struck in gold for the cabinet of the U.S. Mint, but owing to the lack of appropriation they were rejected and melted up by the superintendent and coiner." See David Akers, *United States Gold Patterns*

Endnotes for 1872–1877

(Englewood, OH: Paramount International Coin Corporation, 1975), p. 41. Stephen K. Nagy stated that these were held by the curator of the Mint Collection, if not in the cabinet itself, and were traded or sold to Haseltine in the early 1890s. This would square with a 1909 account in *The Numismatist*, "The piece [singular] in the Mint was originally represented by a gold specimen, but some 10 or more years ago, the one in charge of the cabinet at the time considered $50 too much to be confined in one specimen, when he could have the type duplicated in copper. The Mint specimen is said to have been sold to the bullion department and melted up, and the proceeds of it used to purchase a lot of very ordinary Spanish and Mexican dollars." This account would seem to have several flaws, including that in the 1890s the curator of the Mint Collection could have a copper restrike made up at will, and that at least one coin, owned by the Mint Collection, was "sold" and the Mint Collection curator bought a "lot of very ordinary Spanish and Mexican dollars," certainly a strange thing to do. The truth went to the grave with Haseltine. Also see Akers, pp. 41–43.

13. Certain listings in the seventh edition of Judd represent errors and are not listed in the present study, these being J-1509a, J-1509b, J-1509c, J-1523a, J-1523b, J-1541a, and J-1541b (per Saul Teichman).

14. Logically excluding those for which no specimens have been confirmed by modern scholars (i.e., J-1508, J-1518, J-1527, J-1532, and J-1537), such confirmation is important as more than just a few patterns of this era listed as "silver" in the past have proved to be silver-plated copper (per Saul Teichman).

Endnotes for 1878–1884

1. It would be recalled that the Coinage Act of February 21, 1853, which reduced the authorized weight of the half dime, dime, quarter dollar, and half dollar, did not affect the silver dollar. The dollar remained at the old standard, and thenceforth was coined only upon request from depositors, who had to furnish more than $1 in bullion silver to obtain one. Such pieces were nearly all used in the export trade, where they were valued on their silver weight, not their face value. The Liberty Seated dollar was discontinued by the Coinage Act of 1873, and the trade dollar, a highly successful denomination, took its place and was minted from 1873 through 1878. The trade dollar was also struck specifically on the demand of depositors, not on speculation by the Treasury Department.

2. Legal Tender Notes, as they were called, of $1 and other denominations, first appeared in circulation in 1862 and had been in use since that time, later joined by Original Series and Series of 1875 National Bank notes, which also included the $1 denomination. These were widely accepted in their time and were valued at discounts in terms of silver and gold coins. After April 20, 1876, such bills traded at par with silver coins (and after mid-December 1878 on par with gold coins as well).

3. In popular parlance at the time, older silver dollars, which had not been seen in circulation since about 1850, were called the "dollars of our daddies."

4. Cited by Edgar H. Adams and William H. Woodin, *United States Pattern, Trial and Experimental Pieces* (New York: American Numismatic Society, 1913), p. 154.

5. The chief engravership was a political appointment, and artistic ability above a minimum was not a requirement. Over a long period of years the true artistic talent of chief engravers ranged from such gifted artists as Christian Gobrecht (joined the Mint staff in 1835 and served as chief engraver 1840–1844) and Elizabeth Jones (1981–1991), down to a large group of people in the class of Barber and his son.

6. Pollock-1801. He observes that the facial features are essentially the same as on the "Washlady" dollar.

7. This reverse die was made in haste, and the spacing and alignment of the inscriptions around the center star are irregular.

8. Per Akers, p. 52. He suggests that the 15 originals lack these marks.

9. Described by Edgar H. Adams, "The Stellas of 1879 and 1880," *The Numismatist* (March 1911), p. 103. J-1636a is Pollock-1837.

10. Die notes: The portrait is from a different hub than that used on regular double eagles of this date. On the pattern the word LIBERTY in the coronet is in shorter letters, the leftmost beads at the top of the coronet are much smaller, and the neck truncation at lower left is closer to the dentils. On the pattern star 10 is sharply repunched, star 11 slightly so. The 1879 logotype is identical to that used on regular-issue double eagles.

11. Die notes: D (in DEO) is missing its lower left serif. Stars 2, 5, and 8 above the eagle, counting clockwise from the leftmost star, are repunched.

12. Perhaps part of "150 Goloid Metric sets" at the Mint in late 1880, scheduled to be sent to the Committee of Coinage, Weights, and Measures in Congress, a "set" sometimes being Mint terminology for a single coin (per S.K. Harzfeld under his description of Lot 1081a, sale of January 24–25, 1881).

13. Pollock-1864, noting that Joseph Stack exhibited one in 1942.

14. Pollock-1876. • J-1674 does not exist; previous listings were misdescriptions of J-1674a (per Saul Teichman). • The Mint Collection was moved to the Smithsonian Institution in spring 1923. The era of enlightened curatorship began in the late 1950s when Dr. Vladimir Clain-Stefanelli was appointed curator, assisted by his wife Elvira (who later, upon his passing, became curator). In the early 21st century Dr. Richard Doty, well-known author and researcher earlier connected with the American Numismatic Society, is curator.

Endnotes for 1878–1884

15. Examples, although not openly made available to numismatists, were early on the market, as in John W. Haseltine's sale of March 1, 1883, in which he stated these were "made for the use of the blind," and that the "bold ridges" were "placed on the edge so that the blind could determine by the touch its denomination."
16. Pollock-1925. • Morgenthau, September 1935, Lot 443; Abe Kosoff, March 1942, Lot 337; Farouk Collection, 1954, Lot 2011; currently unlocated.
17. Per Saul Teichman.
18. Pollock, p. 353. Here Pollock cites "The Eastman Johnson 'Holey Design' Patterns," Numismatic Scrapbook Magazine, June 1963.
19. On the factual side of matters, researcher R.W. Julian examined Mint records and found that a pair of 1884 trade dollar dies was furnished to the chief coiner on January 3, 1884; however, there are no records that the dies were used. Falsely, the die destruction list prepared on January 2, 1885, for the previous year's dies noted that for the trade dollar, none were struck.
20. Study by Richard E. Snow, article by Paul Gilkes, *Coin World*, March 1, 1993. Described in detail under Pollock-355.

Endnotes for 1885–1896

1. The Judd text relates: "In making the dies the Mint adopted an entirely new process. A large cameo model of the design was made out of wax and a resinous gum. It was given a hard copper surface by electrotyping and placed in a pantograph or transfer lathe by which the design was transferred and engraved on a hub die of the desired size in perfect proportion to the original." Actually, the process was hardly "entirely new," but may have had some new elements. The pantographic reproduction of coin models had taken place for decades, since the 1830s, in fact.
2. From Harold P. Newlin's "cereal wreath" used on certain pattern half dollars of 1859.
3. Comments by Lee F. Hewitt, quoted material from original report, "The Experimental Coins of 1896," *The Numismatic Scrapbook Magazine* (January 1950), pp. 9–14.
4. *Abe Kosoff Remembers*, Chapter 211 (June 25, 1980), quoting recollections of F.C.C. Boyd; Kosoff said that Boyd had Woodin's private records and showed them to him.
5. To these can be added an unlisted variation, Pollock-1988, of nickel-copper-iron alloy: 74.5% copper, 12.6% nickel, and 12.9% iron. Plain edge. This was discovered by Devonshire Coin Galleries, authenticated by Rick Montgomery, and publicized in *Coin World* (January 4, 1993).

Endnotes for 1906–1913

1. The attribution of J-1908 to the coinage of February 1907, instead of the May or later coinage, is conjectural.
2. Burdette, communication to the editor, further noting that recollections given by Henry Hering in an 1935 article are "not fully reliable as to details."
3. Records exist of the following Ultra High Relief pieces being sold or transferred by the Treasury Department: February 15, 1907 (2 pieces) to George Roberts for the government; September (?) 1907 (2) to Margaret Valentine Kelly; January 1, 1908 (1) to George Kunz for the ANS; June 30, 1908 (1) to Augusta Saint-Gaudens, widow of the sculptor; January 1, 1908 (4) to Mint Director Leach, including one for himself and others for Cortelyou, the Saint-Gaudens family, and Theodore Roosevelt; January 1, 1908 (1) to Assistant Secretary of the Treasury Edwards; January 9, 1908 (2) to the Mint Collection (per Burdette, *Renaissance of American Coinage, 1905–1908*; National Archives records). • In addition, others were sold at the Mint itself, and certain others were privately sold by George T. Morgan (per Farran Zerbe account to Louis S. Werner to the editor).
4. Burdette, *Renaissance of American Coinage, 1905–1908*, manuscript copy.
5. The figure of 11,250 used in nearly all numismatic publications is not correct. See Burdette, *Renaissance of American Coinage, 1905–1908*.
6. Per letter from Superintendent Landis to Director Leach.
7. Per William Hagans in *American Art*, Summer 2002.
8. See correspondence between Henry Chapman and Robert Garrett in Q. David Bowers, *The History of United States Coinage as Illustrated by the Garrett Collection*, (Wolfeboro, NH: Bowers, 1979) and various auction descriptions by the same author in the early 2000s.
9. Burdette, who has studied the 1907 coinage carefully, notes: "I believe there were no 'Proofs' made as the term is commonly used. The surface is simply that produced by fresh dies which have not been polished."
10. The editor would be receptive to receiving information from anyone concerning minute die differences and characteristics, other than the edge lettering, for J-1908 to J-1915.
11. Burdette, *Renaissance of American Coinage, 1905–1908*.
12. However, the use of incuse motifs and inscriptions on coinage was hardly new, and certain ancient coins were made this way.
13. Burdette, *Renaissance of American Coinage, 1905–1908*.

Endnotes for 1906–1913

14. A different chief from Two Moons (per Burdette, *Renaissance of American Coinage, 1908–1913*), the incorrect usage being popular in numismatic texts.
15. Disposition included one for the cornerstone of the All Souls' Church in Washington, DC; one to Fraser; three to the secretary of the Treasury; one to Charles E. Barber; one to Norris; among others.
16. Burdette, *Renaissance of American Coinage, 1908–1913*.

Endnotes for 1915–2000

1. Walter Breen, "Research in the Archives," *The Coin Collector's Journal*, March–April, 1951, p. 33. • McAdoo's numismatic interests, whatever they might have been, were not widely chronicled at the time. Roger W. Burdette, who carefully examined McAdoo's personal and official papers, could find no evidence that he ever collected coins.
3. Although no such claim was ever made by Weinman, the suggestion was made by Wayte Raymond in *The Numismatist*, December 1916, that the sculptor had been inspired by the denarii of ancient Rome. Frank Duffield, editor, obligingly inserted photographs of Roman denarii as if to prove the case.
3. Burdette, *Renaissance of American Coinage, 1916–1921*.
4. See The Numismatist, (Feb. 1938), p. 118, quoted at length by Pollock, p. 385. This official, whose name was not given, must have had access to certain documents. Decades later many Mint documents were destroyed by Mint Director Stella Hackel, thus making further research impossible.
5. Burdette, *Renaissance of American Coinage, 1916–1921*.
6. Other variations may exist, unrecognized, in collections. MacNeil reported that "many" variations were shown to him at the Mint in January 1917 (per Burdette, *Renaissance of American Coinage, 1916–1921*).
7. Listing order per Burdette, *Renaissance of American Coinage, 1916–1921*. His illustrations have been used for general descriptions.
8. With T larger and with top overlapping adjacent letters, seemingly a direct inspiration from the large T in the well-known WurliTzer company logotype of the era.
9. Roger W. Burdette, *Renaissance of American Coinage, 1916–1921*, manuscript copy.
10. Roger W. Burdette, *Renaissance of American Coinage, 1916–1921*, manuscript copy.
11. Roger W. Burdette, *Renaissance of American Coinage, 1916–1921*, manuscript copy.
12. Also see William G. Anderson, "The United States Experimental Cents of 1942," *The Numismatist*, December 1975.
13. Taken from a popular 19th-century Washington medalet by Anthony C. Paquet (Baker No. 155), now with BORN / 1732 / DIED / 1799, replaced by the new inscription. The Colombia two-centavo original had the inscription REPUBLICA DE COLOMBIA, with LIBERTAD on the headband of the portrait figure.
14. Judd, seventh edition, p. 224, with credit to David L. Ganz and *Coin World*.

Glossary

In the marketplace (auction catalogs, pricelists, etc.), most pattern coins are listed simply by Judd attribution number, basic design, metal, edge, grade, and price. Pattern specialists often use certain terms, usually encountered in narrative descriptions or historical studies of a given piece. The following are among those frequently encountered.

bronzed—Description of a special surface used at the Mint for many medals and for some pattern coins, especially copper strikings of circa 1861 to 1863.

bullion—Precious metal such as gold or silver brought to the Mint for coinage, often in the form of ingots or other unwrought shapes. Deposits of these metals brought to the Mint in the form of foreign or other coins were generally referred to as *specie*, and old tableware was referred to as *plate*. Such terms are occasionally encountered in early Mint correspondence.

design—Same as *motif*. The (usually) central feature of a die, such as the head of Miss Liberty, a heraldic eagle, a shield, or other object. The design or motif was usually the work of the chief engraver or an assistant. Stars, numerals, and letters were added separately by punches.

die—See *working die* and *master hub*.

die state—A reference to the condition of a particular die. During the coinage process, dies often developed light cracks or breaks. In time, many dies acquired rust pits if they were stored in damp surroundings. Sometimes a die was refurbished by grinding down or relapping to remove rust and imperfections from the surface; in the process, some details were removed. The study of the die state is important to research, for in all instances a coin exhibiting a perfect die, or one with just a few evidences of wear, was struck at an earlier time than one from the same die exhibiting rust or large cracks.

die striae—Tiny raised lines on a coin, often but not always parallel and oriented in the same direction, resulting from filing or dressing a working die. These differ from recessed hairlines, which were created by cleaning a coin after it was struck, such as while in the custody of a collector. Die striae are very common on pattern coins and have no effect on their value. Mirrorlike coin surfaces indicate the striae were carefully polished off the dies (such as on Proof dies).

electrotype—Reproduction or copy of a coin made by a specific process. Metal is electrodeposited on an incuse or reverse impression of one side of a coin (obverse or reverse) to create a one-sided copper piece. Two such pieces are then dressed to remove roughness and are attached to each other to represent a finished "coin" (with a telltale seam on the edge that betrays its true nature). The majority of electrotypes have little or no numismatic value. At one time, most were made as "fillers" for collectors who were not able to obtain the authentic coins. This was a widespread practice in the 19th century; the American Numismatic Society and the British Museum were among the institutions making electrotypes or loaning coins for this purpose. All prominent coin dealers routinely offered electrotypes, described as such, in auction or other catalogs.

frosted die surface—The matte surface quality imparted by dies made for medals and patterns in the 1850s and 1860s.

gilt—Gold-plated; not referring to any specific metal or alloy. Many patterns struck in lesser metals, such as the 1879 and 1880 $4 denominations in bronze, were gold plated outside of the Mint to given them the appearance of gold—not as a deception, but for cabinet purposes or to illustrate their appearance. A few patterns may have been gilt at the Mint, including some on planchets plated before striking (such coins having deep mirror fields and frosted devices and inscriptions).

hub, hub punch—A steel punch or die with a motif raised (in relief), such as the head of Miss Liberty. In some instances this is used, technically imprecisely, as a synonym for a master die with lettering. Per Andrew W. Pollock III: "A hub die, of hardened steel, was used to create a master die, which in turn created a working die. Beginning in the late 1830s, master hubs were produced directly from galvanos (electrotype copies of enlarged models) or artists' models. These master hubs would be used to sink master dies which would have recessed design elements similar to working dies. Master dies were used to raise working hubs. Working hubs were then used to sink working dies" (from communication to the editor, April 24, 2003).

master hub—Steel cylinder with the features of a coin raised (in relief), often complete except for the date (which was punched separately with a four-digit logotype). Master hubs, sometimes called master dies, were widely used after the advent of steam-powered coinage (1836).

Mint—When capitalized, the Philadelphia Mint, where nearly all federal pattern and related pieces were made.

mint restrike—A coin restruck within the Philadelphia Mint (as opposed to a private restrike, made from Mint dies but struck outside of the Mint).

motif—Same as *design*.

motto—Patriotic, religious, or other inscription added to the design of a coin. Familiar on American coinage are E PLURIBUS UNUM and IN GOD WE TRUST. Many others were employed on patterns.

mule, muling—Two dies, not originally intended for use with each other, combined to strike a pattern coin, such as an 1866 pattern nickel five-cent die muled with the reverse of a $5 gold piece (J-547); or two 1858 pattern cent obverse dies combined (J-220). Such pieces are nonsensical from a utility viewpoint and were made as curiosities or for the numismatic trade. Most are great rarities.

novodel—A term used in world numismatics, such as for the coinage of Russia, and recently adopted by many students of the American series, referring to a coin struck at a later date, from new or old dies bearing an earlier date, but not a die pair actually used in that earlier date.

numismatic delicacy—A *pièce de caprice* (see definition): a coin created from regular or pattern dies, in an unusual combination or metal or edge style, to provide a rarity for numismatists.

pièce de caprice—A term, from the French, popularized by Don Taxay and Walter Breen. According to Dr. Judd, it is "An authorized piece struck for some reason other than as a pattern, experimental, or trial piece. They apparently were struck solely to satisfy the whim of some collector or to perhaps create a rarity that would bring a good price…." (from the seventh edition of this book). *Numismatic delicacy* is a more easily pronounced synonym.

private pattern—A pattern coin made outside of the Mint, such as an 1849 $10 piece made on speculation by French engraver Bouvet; or several cent-size patterns produced in 1942 by various American companies to test the idea of using substances other than bronze for cent coinage.

private restrike—A restrike made outside of the Mint from dies that left the Mint in one way or another. In the 1850s, and perhaps at other times, many old dies were sold as "scrap iron," and were later acquired by numismatists and others. The private or out-of-mint origin of such pieces is generally omitted from descriptions of coins for sale, as knowledge is implicit among informed collectors and dealers. In the present listings they are designated as private restrikes. (See discussion of *restrike*, below.)

production die—See *working die*.

punch—A small rod of hardened steel, at the tip of which are one or more letters, numerals, or design elements, in relief (raised). A punch was used by an engraver to enter stars or letters into a working die.

pure metal—Pure copper, pure silver, pure nickel, etc.; a metal element without alloy.

regular issue, regular-issue dies—Dies of the type used in a given year to produce coins for circulation or regular-design Proofs for collectors. Often, a regular-issue obverse or reverse die was combined with a pattern die to test a design concept or to create a numismatic delicacy.

relapping—The grinding down or filing of the face of an already-used or prepared die to remove signs of wear, rust pits, etc. The relapping process often removes design elements that are in low relief, such as ribbon ends. Many novodels and restrikes are from relapped dies, but are not usually described as such, as the subject is primarily of interest to scholars, not to casual collectors.

restrike—This term has many applications. In its strictest definition, a restrike is a coin made at a later date from earlier-dated dies actually used in the earlier year. As an example: in 1859, Mint Director Snowden, seeking to create items for sale or trade to collectors, took from storage old dies by Christian Gobrecht, mostly dated 1836 to 1839, and struck new impressions from them. These can be properly described as restrikes. However, the term is also used to refer to what might best be called *novodels*, or entirely new creations, combining two old dies that were never used together at the time of the date on the obverse. The imagination of the coiners ran wild with old dies dated 1836, 1838, and

Glossary

1839. While *restrike* can be said to have unfavorable connotations, the fact is that the Mint has engaged in restriking coins for a long time, including in recent years. Certain 1982 Washington commemorative half dollars were struck after 1982, and thus were restruck. However, most numismatists apply the term *restrike* to the use of dies that were long retired, then used again. For certain varieties of patterns, originals and restrikes can be differentiated, sometimes by weight, such as 1839-dated half dollars struck in 1839, with a weight of 206 grains, being the coinage standard of the time, and those restruck in 1859 or later, with the later weight of 192 grains (the standard adopted in 1853). The Mint officials restriking the coins simply used planchets on hand, never dreaming that later generations of numismatists, such as present readers, would make technical studies! Generally, restrikes in the pattern series are of two categories: Mint restrikes (made at the Philadelphia Mint), and private restrikes (made outside of the Mint).

simulated series coins—Rarities made at the Mint, of regular-issue designs, but of dates privately minted and unofficially sold. Some of these have been listed among patterns in the past, but most have not.

splasher—An impression from a single die, often on an oversized planchet or metal blank, with no impression on the other side. Some were made on very thin pieces of metal, sometimes backed with newsprint or other papers; these are similar to what are called *chichés* by French numismatists. Often, a molten white metal was poured onto a surface, and when the metal had cooled somewhat (but was still soft), a die was pressed into it.

Standard Silver—A series of pattern coins mostly made in 1869 and 1870, bearing the inscription STANDARD SILVER. These are different from regular-issue or standard silver (not capitalized) coins. Beginning in 1862 all regular-issue silver coins disappeared from circulation in the East and Midwest. Citizens, uncertain as to the outcome of the Civil War, hoarded "hard money"—at first gold, then silver, and for a short time (commencing in July 1862), even copper-nickel cents. After the Civil War ended, the value of silver coins in terms of paper money remained high, and they did not circulate. The Standard Silver series of patterns was intended to create silver coins of lighter weight, so that if they were made for circulation they would not be attractive to hoarders and speculators. As it developed, these pieces never went further than the pattern stage. Finally, beginning significantly on April 20, 1876, silver coins of the old series were returned to circulation along with pieces long stored by the Treasury Department.

striae—See *die striae*.

working die, production die—Steel cylinder with a flat end upon which are the incuse or recessed features of the obverse or reverse of a coin, including the motif and lettering. Working dies were fitted into presses and used for coinage production. In the early days, working dies were made by hand, with the motif, stars, letters, and numerals added separately by an engraver. After the advent of steam coinage, master hubs, sometimes loosely referred to as master dies, were generally used to create working hubs, which in turn were used to make working dies. From about 1840 to circa 1907 to 1908, dates were added to the working die by the use of a four-digit logotype punch. After the early 20th century, dates were included in the hub dies and transferred to the working dies.

Bibliography and Suggested Reading

Adams, Edgar H. 1909. *The Numismatist* (February): 41.

Adams, Edgar H. 1911. "The Stellas of 1879 and 1880." *The Numismatist* (March): 103–103.

Adams, Edgar H. and William H. Woodin. 1913. *United States Pattern, Trial and Experimental Pieces.* New York: American Numismatic Society.

Adams, John W. 1982. *United States Numismatic Literature. Volume 1. Nineteenth Century Auction Catalogs.* Mission Viejo, CA: George Frederick Kolbe. (A major source for early biographical information.)

Adams, John W. 1990. *United States Numismatic Literature: Volume 2. Twentieth Century Auction Catalogs.* Crestline, CA: George Frederick Kolbe. (Second volume of Adams' planned trilogy.)

Akers, David W. 1975. *United States Gold Patterns.* Englewood, OH: Paramount International Coin Corporation. (A photographic appreciation of patterns with emphasis on the Dr. John E. Wilkison Collection.)

American Journal of Numismatics. Various issues of the late 19th century (as cited). New York and Boston.

American Numismatic Society. Various issues of the late 19th century (as cited). *Exhibition of U.S. and Colonial Coins.* New York: American Numismatic Society.

Anderson, William G. 1975. "The United States Experimental Cents of 1942." *The Numismatist* (December): 2643–2648.

The Asylum. Various issues: 1980s onward. Published by the Numismatic Bibliomania Society.

Attinelli, Emmanuel J. 1876. *Numisgraphics, or A List of Catalogues, Which Have Been Sold by Auction in the United States.* New York: Emmanuel J. Attinelli.

Boosel, Harry X. 1960. *1873–1873.* Chicago: Hewitt Brothers. (Summary of articles Boosel created for *The Numismatic Scrapbook Magazine.*)

Borckardt, Mark. 1951. "Research in the Archives." *The Coin Collector's Journal* (March–April): 33.

Borckardt, Mark. 1996. "Restriking the Issues: The Large Cent Restrikes of 1804, 1810, and 1823." American Numismatic Society Coinage of the Americas Conference. Nov. 9.

Borckardt, Mark. 1997. "Restriking the Issues: The Large Cent Restrikes of 1804, 1810, and 1823." New York: American Numismatic Society.

Borckardt, Mark. 1957. "Some Unpublished Gobrecht Rarities." *The Numismatist* (May): 531–532.

Borckardt, Mark. 2000. "A History and Appreciation of the $4 Gold Stella." *Rarities Sale Catalogue.* Wolfeboro, NH: Bowers and Merena.

Bosbyshell, O.C. 1891. *An Index to the Coins and Medals of the Cabinet of the Mint of the United States at Philadelphia.* Philadelphia: Avil Printing and Lithograph Company.

Bowers, Q. David. 1979. *The History of United States Coinage.* Los Angeles: Bowers and Ruddy Galleries. (Also see later printings by Bowers and Merena Galleries, Wolfeboro, NH.)

Bowers, Q. David. 1982. *United States Gold Coins: An Illustrated History.* Los Angeles: Bowers and Ruddy Galleries. (Also see later printings by Bowers and Merena Galleries, Wolfeboro, NH.)

Bowers, Q. David. 1985. *Abe Kosoff: Dean of Numismatics.* Wolfeboro, New Hampshire: Bowers and Merena Galleries. (Includes much information about the King Farouk sale, 1954.)

Bibliography and Suggested Reading

Bowers, Q. David. 1991. *American Numismatic Association Centennial History, 1891–1991.* Wolfeboro, NH: Bowers and Merena Galleries.

Bowers, Q. David. 1989. "Collecting United States Gold Coins: A Numismatic History." *America's Gold Coinage.* The Coinage of the Americas Conference, American Numismatic Society (Nov. 4–5). New York: ANS.

Bowers, Q. David. 1993. *Silver Dollars and Trade Dollars of the United States.* (2 vols.). Wolfeboro, NH: Bowers and Merena Galleries. (Includes much information on the 1804 dollar, including contributions by R.W. Julian.)

Bowers, Q. David. 1997. *Woodward's Sale of the John F. McCoy Collection, 1864.* Wolfeboro, NH: Bowers and Merena Galleries. (Part of the "Little Editions" monograph series. Much information from this monograph was employed re: Woodward in the present text. John W. Adams was of great assistance in 1997 when the monograph was prepared.)

Bowers, Q. David. 1998. *The History of American Numismatics Before the Civil War, 1760–1860.* Wolfeboro, NH: Bowers and Merena Galleries.

Breen, Walter H. 1954. "Secret History of the Gobrecht Coinages." *The Coin Collector's Journal*: 157–158.

Breen, Walter H. 1977. *Walter Breen's Encyclopedia of U.S. and Colonial Proof Coins, 1792–1977.* Albertson, New York: FCI.

Breen, Walter H. 1988. *Walter Breen's Complete Encyclopedia of U.S. and Colonial Coins.* Garden City, NY: Doubleday.

Breen, Walter H. 2000. *Walter Breen's Encyclopedia of Early United States Cents 1793–1814.* Ed. Mark Borckardt. Wolfeboro, NH: Bowers and Merena Galleries. (Posthumous publication, edited and with additions, of one of Breen's exhaustive studies.)

Bressett, Kenneth E., comp. and ed. 2005. *A Guide Book of United States Coins.* (59th ed.) Atlanta, GA: Whitman. (Also see earlier editions.)

Bressett, Kenneth E. and A. Kosoff. 1991. *The Official American Numismatic Association Grading Standards for United States Coins.* (4th ed.) Colorado Springs, CO: American Numismatic Association.

Burdette, Roger W. *Renaissance of American Coinage, 1905–1908.* (Manuscript) (Detailed examination of the origin, design, and original production of the 1907 Saint-Gaudens and 1908 Pratt coinage.)

Burdette, Roger W. *Renaissance of American Coinage, 1908–1913.* (Manuscript) (Detailed examination of the origin, design, and original production of the 1909 Lincoln cent by Brenner and the 1913 nickel by Fraser.)

Burdette, Roger W. *Renaissance of American Coinage, 1916–1921.* (Manuscript) (Detailed examination of the origin, design, and initial production of the regular silver denominations of 1916, the quarter of 1917, and the Peace dollar of 1921–1922, by artists Weinman, MacNeil, and deFrancisci.)

Burdette, Roger W. 2002. *Examination of 1916 Pattern Quarters in the Smithsonian National Numismatic Collection.* www.uspatterns.com

Carlson, Carl W.A. 1982. "Birch and the Patterns of '92: An Historical and Critical Reanalysis." *The Numismatist* (March): 628–645.

Carothers, Neil. 1930. *Fractional Money.* New York: John Wiley & Sons.

Cassel, David. 2000. *United States Pattern Postage Currency Coins.* Miami: David Cassel. (Detailed study of the 1863 issues, as well as those erroneously dated 1868, but struck in 1863).

Catalogue of Coins, Tokens, and Medals in the Numismatic Collection of United States at Philadelphia, Pa. 1914. Washington, D.C.: Government Printing Office.

Bibliography and Suggested Reading

Clain-Stefanelli, Elvira Eliza. 1990. "From the Drawing Board of a Coin Engraver." *The American Numismatic Association Centennial Anthology.* Colorado Spring, CO: ANA.

Clain-Stefanelli, Elvira Eliza. 1991. "Old Friends—Common Goals: The Evolution of Numismatics in the United States." *The American Numismatic Association Centennial Anthology.* Wolfeboro, NH: Bowers and Merena Galleries.

Clain-Stefanelli, Vladimir. 1970. "History of the National Numismatic Collections." *Smithsonian Institution, Bulletin 229.*

Coin World. 1960 to date. Sidney, OH: Amos Press.

Coin World Almanac. 1976 and later editions. Sidney, OH: Coin World.

Coinage Laws of the United States 1792–1894. 1991. Modern foreword to reprint by David L. Ganz. Wolfeboro, NH: Bowers and Merena Galleries.

Comparette, T.L. 1912. *Catalogue of Coins, Tokens, and Medals in the Numismatic Collection of the Mint of the United States at Philadelphia, Pennsylvania.* Washington, DC. (Government Printing Office, 1914)

Davis, Charles E. 1992. *American Numismatic Literature: An Annotated Survey of Auction Sales 1980–1991.* Lincoln, MA: Quarterman.

Davis, Robert Coulton. 1885. "Pattern and Experimental Issues of the United States Mint." *The Coin Collector's Journal* (July): 97–101.

Dickeson, Montroville Wilson. *The American Numismatical Manual.* Philadelphia: J.B. Lippincott. (1859. 1860 and 1865 editions were slightly retitled as *The American Numismatic Manual.*)

Dubois, William E. 1851. *Pledges of History: A Brief Account of the Collection of Coins Belonging to the Mint of the United States, More Particularly of the Antique Specimens.* (2nd ed.) New York: George P. Putnam. (Original published 1846)

Eckfeldt, George J. 1840s–1860s. Untitled manuscript. (Personal notebook discussing die records, formulae, and miscellaneous items, compiled from the 1840s to the 1860s. Includes information on gold coins, patterns, and medals.)

Eckfeldt, Jacob Reese and William Ewing Dubois. 1842. *A Manual of Gold and Silver Coins of All Nations, Struck Within the Past Century.* Philadelphia: Assay Office of the Mint.

Eckfeldt, Jacob Reese and William Ewing Dubois. 1850 and 1851. *New Varieties of Gold and Silver Coins, Counterfeit Coins, Bullion with Mint Values.* New York: George P. Putnam.

Evans, George G. 1890. *Illustrated History of the United States Mint.* Philadelphia: George G. Evans.

"The Experimental Coins of 1896." 1950. *The Numismatic Scrapbook Magazine* (Jan.): 9–14.

Forrer, Leonard S. *Biographical Dictionary of Medallists.* (8 vols.). London: Spink & Son, 1923.

Fuld, George J. 1998. "A Group of Restruck Patterns." *The Numismatist* (May): 512–518, 568–574. (Study of five-cent dies of the 1866–1867 era.)

Gilkes, Paul. 1993. *Coin World.* (Mar. 1).

Gilliland, Cory. 1990. "U.S. Gold Bullion Coins: A Nineteenth-Century Proposal." *America's Gold Coinage.* New York: American Numismatic Society.

The Gobrecht Journal. Various issues: 1974 to date. (Publication of the Liberty Seated Collectors Club, ed. Dr. John W. McCloskey)

Bibliography and Suggested Reading

Haseltine, John W. 1909. "Two Unique Double Eagle Varieties." *The Numismatist* (June): 173–174.

Hidden, William E. 1903. "1863 Cent with 'L' Letter to the Editor." *The Numismatist*: 375.

Hodder, Michael. 1987. "The Mystery of the Stella Solved." *Rare Coin Review* 65: 57–59. (Inquiry into the minting of the Stella and planchet preparation.)

Hodder, Michael. 1987. "Mystery of the Stella Revisited." *Rare Coin Review* 66: 63–64. (International Monetary Conference Held in Paris, in August 1878. Report, no author stated. Senate Executive Document No. 48, Forty-fifth Congress, Third Session. Washington, DC: Government Printing Office, 1879.)

Judd, J. Hewitt, M.D. 1982. *United States Pattern, Experimental and Trial Pieces.* 7th ed. Racine, WI: Western. (An update on the Adams-Woodin 1913 work on patterns. Research by Walter Breen, coordinated by Dr. Judd and by Abe Kosoff. Foundation of the present text and the Judd numbering system.)

Julian, R.W. 1977. *Medals of the United States Mint. The First Century 1792–1892.* El Cajon, CA: Token and Medal Society, 1977.

Julian, R.W. 1877. "The Stella: Its History and Mystery." *The Numismatist*: 2304–2312.

Linderman, Henry Richard. 1877. *Money and Legal Tender in the United States.* New York: G.P. Putnam's Sons.

Mason's Monthly Illustrated Coin Collector's Magazine. Various issues: 1860s onward. Philadelphia and Boston: Ebenezer Locke Mason.

Newman, Eric P., and Kenneth E. Bressett. 1962. *The Fantastic 1804 Dollar.* Racine, WI: Whitman.

Numismatic Guaranty Corporation of America Census Report. Orlando, FL: Numismatic Guaranty Corporation of America.

Numismatic News. Various issues: 1960s to date. Iola, WI: Krause Publications.

The Numismatist. Various issues: 1888 onward (as cited). Journal of the American Numismatic Association.

Orosz, Joel J. 1985. "Robert Gilmor, Jr. and the Cradle Age of American Numismatics." *Rare Coin Review* 58: 18–21.

Orosz, Joel J. 1990. "Robert Gilmor, Jr. and the Cradle Age of American Numismatics." *The Numismatist* (May): 704–712, 819–822, 829–830. (Expansion of 1985 article in the *Rare Coin Review.*)

Parish, Daniel, Jr. 1866. "List of Catalogues of Coin Sales, Held in the United States from 1828 to the Present Time." Serial article in the *American Journal of Numismatics*, 1866. 1.4 (1866): 29–30; 1.5 (1866): 35–36.

PCGS Population Report. Professional Coin Grading Service. Newport Beach, CA.

Peale, Franklin. 1837. "Description of the New Coining Presses Lately Introduced into the U.S. Mint, Philadelphia." *Journal of the Franklin Institute* 18: 307–310.

Pollock, Andrew W., III. 1994. *United States Patterns and Related Issues.* Wolfeboro, NH: Bowers and Merena Galleries.

Rulau, Russ, and George Fuld. 1999. *Medallic Portraits of Washington, 2nd ed.* Iola, WI: Krause.

Smith, A.M. 1885. *Coins and Coinage: The United States Mint, Philadelphia, History, Biography, Statistics, Work, Machinery, Products, Officials.* (Also issued as *Visitor's Guide and History.*) Philadelphia, PA: A.M. Smith.

Smith, Pete. 1997. "The 1804 Dollar and the Midnight Minter." *The Numismatist* (September): 1007–1009, 1049–1050.

Snow, Richard E. 2001. *Flying Eagle and Indian Cent Attribution Guide, Vol. 1, 1856–1858* (2nd ed.). Tucson, AZ: Eagle Eye Rare Coins.

Snow, Richard E. 2003. *Flying Eagle and Indian Cent Attribution Guide, Vol. 2, 1859–1869.* (2nd ed.) Tucson, AZ: Eagle Eye Rare Coins, 2003.

Snowden, James Ross. 1860. *A Description of Ancient and Modern Coins in the Cabinet of the Mint of the United States.* Philadelphia: J.B. Lippincott. (Mostly researched and written by George Bull, then curator of the Mint Cabinet, and William E. Dubois.)

Snowden, James Ross. 1861. *The Medallic Memorials of Washington in the Mint of the United States.* Philadelphia: J.B. Lippincott.

Stewart, Frank H. 1974 Lawrence, MA. *History of the First United States Mint, Its People and Its Operations.* (Original published Philadelphia: Frank H. Stewart Electric, 1924); Lawrence, MA: Quarterman, 1974.

Swift, Michael. 1998. *Historical Maps of the United States.* London: PRC Publishing.

Taxay, Don. 1963. *Counterfeit, Mis-Struck, and Unofficial U.S. Coins.* New York, NY: Arco.

Taxay, Don. 1975. *The Comprehensive Catalogue and Encyclopedia of United States Coins.* New York: Scott.

Taxay, Don. 1966. *U.S. Mint and Coinage.* New York: Arco.

Taxay, Don. 1971. *Scott's Comprehensive Catalogue and Encyclopedia of U.S. Coins.* New York and Omaha: Scott Publishing.

Treasury Department, United States Mint, et al. *Annual Report of the Director of the Mint.* Philadelphia (later, Washington). 1795 onward; 19th century issues. (Early reports were published in a variety of ways: in presidential messages, in newspaper accounts, and in separate pamphlets.)

United States Mint, Bureau of the Mint, et al. 1790s onward. *Annual Report of the Director of the Mint.* Philadelphia (later, Washington). (Reports were on a calendar year basis through 1856, then in 1857 they went to a fiscal year (July 1 through June 30 of the following year) basis. The 1857 report is transitional and covers only January 1 through June 30, 1857, a period of six months.)

Vermeule, Cornelius. 1971. *Numismatic Art in America: Aesthetics of United States Coinage.* Cambridge, MA: Belknap Press of Harvard University Press.